D1407463

WA 1188427 4

PLEASE CHECK
BACK OF BOOK
FOR CD

John Zukowski's Definitive Guide to Swing for Java 2

**UNIVERSITY OF GLAMORGAN
LEARNING RESOURCES CENTRE**

Pontypridd, Mid Glamorgan, CF37 1DL
Telephone: Pontypridd (01443) 482626

Books are to be returned on or before the last date below

3 0 JAN 2001	1 5 MAY 2008
2 9 MAR 2001	
1 0 JAN 2003	
0 3 MAR 2003	
2 5 APR 2003	
1 ? JUN 2003	
- 7 DEC 2004	
2 2 FEB 2005	
1 5 FEB 2006	

Apress™

John Zukowski's Definitive Guide to Swing for Java 2
Copyright ©1999 by John Zukowski

All rights reserved. No part of this work may be reproduced or transmitted in any form or by any means, electronic or mechanical, including photocopying, recording, or by any information storage or retrieval system, without the prior written permission of the copyright owner and the publisher.

Library of Congress Cataloging-in-Publication Data
        Zukowski, John.
            [Definitive Swing Guide]
            John Zukowski's Definitive Swing Guide / John Zukowski.
                p.   cm.
            1. Java (Computer program language)   2. Swing (Computer file)
        I. Title.
        QA76.73.J38Z8493   1999   99-34562
        005.13'3—dc21   CIP

ISBN (pbk): 1-893115-02-X

Printed and bound in the United States of America
1 2 3 4 5 6 7 8 9 10

Learning Resources
Centre

Trademarked names may appear in this book. Rather than use a trademark symbol with every occurrence of a trademarked name, we use the names only in an editorial fashion and to the benefit of the trademark owner, with no intention of infringement of the trademark.

Project Manager: Nancy DelFavero
Project Editor: Carol Lombardi
Technical Reviewers: Gary Cornell,
    Randy Kahle, Blake Ragsdell, Tim Rohaly,
    and Laurence Vanhelsuwé
Copyeditor: Mark Woodworth

Proofreaders: Valerie Cover and
    Christine Sabooni
Production Assistance: Lori Ash
Indexer: Nancy Humphreys
Cover and Interior Design: Derek Yee Design

Distributed to the book trade worldwide by Springer-Verlag New York, Inc.
175 Fifth Avenue, New York, NY 10010
In the United States, phone 1-800-SPRINGER; orders@springer-ny.com;
http://www.springer-ny.com

For information on translations, please contact APress directly:
APress, 6400 Hollis Street, Suite 9, Emeryville, CA 94608
Phone: 510/595-3110; Fax: 510/595-3122; info@apress.com; www.apress.com

The information in this book is distributed on an "As Is" basis, without warranty. Although every precaution has been taken in the preparation of this work, neither the author nor APress shall have any liability to any person or entity with respect to any loss or damage caused or alleged to be caused directly or indirectly by the information contained in this work.

Author's Acknowledgments

WORKING WITH APRESS ON THIS BOOK has been fun. I would like to personally thank everyone who helped along the way, both in the formation of a new technical publisher and for the help in converting my rough manuscript into the material you have in your hands today.

At APress, I would first like to thank Gary Cornell, Bill Pollock, and Dan Appleman for allowing me to work with them at such an early stage of company development. Now that we have Dan Appleman's book and my book, we can work at filling some spaces between the A's and Z's. I would especially like to thank Nancy DelFavero and Carole Lombardi for their help in shaping what you're reading. Special thanks to the technical editors, Laurence Vanhelsuwé, Blake Ragsdell, Gary Cornell, Tim Rohaly, and Randy Kahle, who helped to ensure the technical accuracy of the content. Any remaining technical inaccuracies are my fault alone. On the graphics side, thanks to Derek Yee Design for helping to convert my rough sketches, mostly in Visio, to the quality illustrations you see in this book.

For some of the images used in the example programs, I would like to thank Dean Jones for the JavaLobby Foundation Applications — Icon Collection (http://webart.javalobby.org/jlicons/) and Deb Felts at the Image Addict's Attic (http://members.xoom.com/imageaddict/). (There is a reason why I am not a graphic artist.) They retain the copyrights on their respective images, and the images are used with permission.

For their ideas and assistance during development, I would like to thank Joe Sam Shirah, Wong Kok Wai, Tomoko Iwama, Carlos Lucasius and the Licensee Support team in Ontario, the Swing! Team, and everyone at MageLang Institute. This book is that much better because of them.

As always, I am grateful to my wife, Lisa, for her never-ending patience during the development of this book and our playful pup, Jaeger, who helps keep me sane (sometimes). Thanks to Mom and Dad, too, even though they don't remember getting me that Vic 20.

About the Author

JOHN ZUKOWSKI IS A WELL-KNOWN FIGURE in the Java community. He is a popular columnist for *JavaWorld* magazine and a member of the *JavaWorld* Senior Advisory Board. Zukowski provides significant content for Sun's *Java Developer Connection* and is the guide for Java at About.com. In addition, he is a faculty member of the MageLang Institute, an instructor-led training firm that is the leading provider of advanced Java training to the computer industry. He is also the author of *Java AWT Reference* (O'Reilly), *Mastering Java 2* (Sybex), and *Borland's JBuilder: No Experience Required* (Sybex).

Contents

Chapter 3 The Model-View-Controller Architecture

Chapter 4 Core Swing Components

Chapter 16 Sculpting Trees...........619

Introduction

HAVE YOU EVER TAKEN LOOK AT the Swing libraries and been so overwhelmed at where to start that you simply gave up? It isn't an uncommon feeling: Just by themselves, the Swing libraries are much larger than the *entire* Java 1.0 platform. According to the *The Java Developers Almanac 1999* (Addison-Wesley), what started out as a collection of 212 classes with 2,125 member fields and methods in 8 packages for all of Java 1.0 is now 752 classes with 9,589 members in 16 packages for the Swing libraries alone—and that doesn't include the `com.sun.java.swing` packages!

An earlier book of mine, *Java AWT Reference* (O'Reilly), on the older and now obsolete AWT package (at least as far as the components that are used for graphical user interface development go), consisted of two parts: a tutorial-like section in the front and an API reference in the back. By and large, it was the same material presented in two different ways describing the five `java.awt` packages.

In this book, I provide the same level of coverage for the Java Swing libraries, but I stick with a mostly how-to, tutorial-like treatment. If all you want is a reference book on API, this probably isn't the one for you. However, if you are hoping to learn how to use the essential parts of Swing, you've come to the right place.

Although I believe the AWT component set is obsolete for graphical user interface development, Swing does use the AWT structural parts, such as the delegation-based event model and layout managers. In the following chapters, you'll find a general review of the delegation-based event model and an explanation of the new layout managers provided with the Swing components.

I won't describe the process of installing the JDK, compiling a Java program, or running a program. Those topics are covered in other Java books, including one of my own, *Mastering Java 2* (Sybex). Besides, I assume that you're capable of setting up your own development environment.

So, is this book for you? If you are brand new to Java, you should probably get the basics down first before jumping onto the Swing bandwagon. On the other hand, if you've been developing with Java for a while and have decided that it's a good time to start using the Swing component set or the Java 2 platform instead of the AWT, you'll find this book extremely useful. With this book, you won't have to drudge through the countless Swing classes for a way to accomplish a task that was impossible with AWT, and you'll find out how to become more productive and make the most of the many reusable components and techniques in Swing.

This book covers the key capabilities of the Swing components. If you've played with the early versions of Swing components and found them to be immature, you'll be pleased to know that the latest version of Swing is much improved. Feel free to use this book to try out the more-mature Swing components that I cover in the following chapters.

Development Versions

Although this book was written with the Java 2 platform developer in mind, the majority of the examples will also run under JDK 1.1. However, a handful will not, and they are flagged accordingly. Because Swing is written with 100% Pure Java source code, any JDK 1.1 or Java 2 platform environment will suffice to get you started.

All of the examples in the book rely on either the Java 2 platform or JFC 1.1 with Swing 1.1. They will *not* work with JFC 1.1 with Swing 1.0.3. Although the Swing 1.0.3 version is an officially supported version from Sun, none of the existing bugs in it will ever be fixed and all of the Swing packages are in another package hierarchy. While some examples may work if you simply change the import lines, I encourage you to upgrade to the latest Swing version.

Even though I tried to gear all the examples to the Swing 1.1 release (either as part of JFC 1.1 or as part of the Java 2 platform), Sun changed some non-API-related capabilities with the Swing 1.1.1 release. I've made a special note of these capabilities when appropriate, and warn you to use them with care because not all your users may be able to support them.

I didn't attempt to point out all the bugs in the Swing libraries, of which there are many. Most of the bugs have already been fixed; they just haven't been publicly released. If you are trying to determine if a problem you're having is due to a bug, be sure to stop by the Bug Parade at Sun's Java Developer Connection at http://developer.java.sun.com/developer/bugParade/. You'll find a searchable list of Java bugs there. If you have uncovered an unreported bug, submit a bug report to http://java.sun.com/cgi-bin/bugreport.cgi.

How This Book Is Structured

This book can be read from cover to cover if you wish, but it doesn't have to be used that way. It's true that later sections of the book assume you've absorbed knowledge from the earlier sections. However, if you need to find something on a topic covered in a later chapter, you don't have to read all the chapters that precede it first. If you come across something that's unfamiliar to you, you can always go back to an earlier chapter or search the Index to get the information you need.

The chapters of the book are grouped into three general sections: Chapters 1 through 4, Chapters 5 through 14, and Chapters 15 through 19 (plus an appendix on Swing component properties and an appendix on this book's companion CD-ROM).

- Chapters 1 through 4 provide some general knowledge that will prove to be useful as you read through the remainder of the book. In Chapter 1, you'll find an overview of the Swing component set. It points out what's new and different, as well as what has stayed the same. Chapter 2 details event handling with the Swing component set. It describes both the delegation-based event model and the many new ways to handle events with the Swing components. In Chapter 3, you'll learn about the Model-View-Controller (MVC) architecture. You can avoid using the MVC if you wish, but to take full advantage of everything the Swing components have to offer, it helps to have a good grasp of MVC concepts. In Chapter 4, I begin into covering the specific Swing components. All Swing components share many of the same attributes, and in Chapter 4 you'll learn about those common behaviors.

- In Chapters 5 through 14, you'll discover the many aspects of reusable Swing components. You'll find out about menus, borders, high-level containers, popup dialogs, Swing layout managers, advanced Swing containers, bounded range components, list model components, and text components, and components that toggle. Most of what you'll want to accomplish with the Swing libraries is discussed in these chapters.

- In Chapters 15 through 19, some of the more advanced Swing topics are covered. These tend to be the areas that even experienced developers find the most confusing. In Chapter 15, I move beyond the basic text component material covered in Chapter 14 and describe the more advanced aspects of working with the powerful Swing text components. Chapters 16 and 17 deal with using the Swing tree and table components. These components allow you to display hierarchical data or tabular data. In Chapter 18, you'll find out how to customize the appearance of your application. Because the Swing libraries are completely Java-based, if you don't like the way something is done or how it appears, you can change it. Finally, in Chapter 19 you will find a description of the undo framework, which offers undo/redo support for your applications.

- Appendix A contains a list of the more than 500 settable properties the user interface manager employs to configure the appearance of the Swing components for the current look and feel. The Swing components manage various defaults, such as colors and borders applied to components, so you don't need to subclass a component in order to customize its appearance. Appendix A combines all the property settings listed throughout the chapters into one list for easy reference. In Appendix B, you'll find out how to navigate the CD-ROM that comes with this book. The sample code from all the chapters can be found on the CD, and Appendix B describes how to use this code.

Reading the UML Diagrams

In order to provide a standard diagramming format to help you visualize associations and roles among classes, I've used the Unified Modeling Language (UML) and its various notations and diagrams. If you're already familiar with the UML, you should have no problem understanding the diagrams in this book. For those of you not familiar with the UML, what follows is a brief primer on the diagramming format I used. (I recommend *The Unified Modeling Language User Guide* [Addison-Wesley] for a more complete tutorial on the subject.)

An arrowhead at the end of a solid line denotes a subclass relationship. In Figure I-1, for example, the Shape class is the superclass and the Circle class is the subclass. If the class name is in *italics* (the box with *Shape*, for example) the class is abstract.

A circle at the end of a solid line denotes an interface implementation relationship. In Figure I-2, the Circle class implements the Drawable interface. Interfaces will have the «Interface» stereotype above their names and will be shown in italics because they are abstract.

An arrowhead at the end of a dashed line signifies a dependency relationship. In Figure I-3, the Circle class is dependent on the Border class. A change to

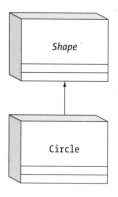

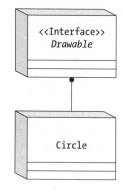

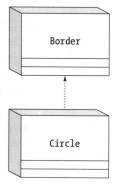

Figure I-1: A class Circle subclass of class Shape

Figure I-2: A class Circle implementation of the Drawable interface

Figure I-3: A class Circle dependent on class Border

the Border class will therefore affect the Circle class. Occasionally, dependency relationships are labeled with something like a «Uses» stereotype.

A diamond at the end of a solid line indicates an aggregation relationship. In Figure I-4, the Polygon class is made up of a collection of Point objects. The diamond signifies which side of the relationship is the whole. The side without the diamond is the parts. Occasionally, some relationships will show cardinality. For example, Figure I-4 basically says that a Polygon can have anywhere from 0 to n Point objects associated to it, where n is boundless.

In addition to UML relationship diagrams, you'll find several sequence diagrams. These diagrams show a sequenced pattern of interactions among objects over time (see Figure I-5 for example). Although sequence diagrams may take a bit of work to read, they serve to illustrate the time ordering of messages. The boxes at the top of the sequence diagrams represent the objects involved in the process, which progresses from top to bottom. The boxes beneath the "objects" represent a specific focus of control, in which an object is performing some action. The action being performed is based upon the messages being sent (those messages are shown adjacent to the arrows).

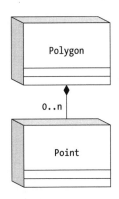

Figure I-4: A class Polygon aggregation of multiple class Point objects

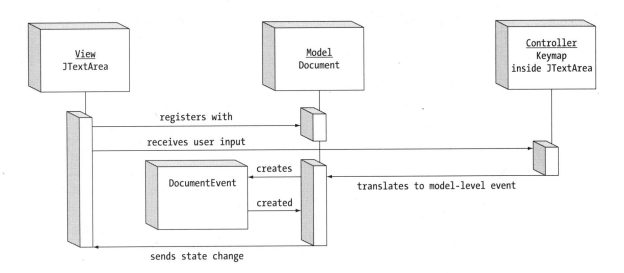

Figure I-5: Sample sequence diagram

Support

You can head to many places online to get technical support for Swing and answers to general questions on Java. I've provided a list of some of the most useful sites around:

- The Swing Connection at http://www.theswingconnection.com — An online magazine coming directly from Sun and the Swing development team

- The Java Developer Connection at http://java.sun.com/jdc — A free Java support center sponsored by Sun

- Swing Mailing List at http://www.egroups.com/list/swing/ — A mailing list for Swing-related questions

- Focus on Java at http://java.about.com — A Java resource list that I personally maintain

- JavaWorld at http://www.javaworld.com — An online Java-centric magazine

CHAPTER 1

Swing Overview

ONCE UPON A TIME, A TIME not so very long ago, Java was born. With its birth came a creature called the Abstract Window Toolkit, or AWT. In turn, with AWT came native widgets, and with native widgets came . . . trouble.

As Java technologies became popular in recent years, users realized AWT was extremely slow and that in any case you couldn't really do much with the components that it provided. Very few of them were available, and you couldn't use them in a visual programming environment. So technologies were introduced, such as Just-in-Time compilers to improve performance and JavaBeans for component-based development.

With these new technologies came more and more widget sets, for the AWT component set itself was very basic. So applet download times grew and grew, because these new widget sets weren't part of the core Java platform, and Java archive (JAR) files were introduced to improve delivery time. Eventually, each of the major browser vendors added its favorite component library to its virtual machine — AFC, IFC, and WFC, to name just a few. Yet all the libraries used different design models, and there were no true cross-browser standards. Eventually, Sun Microsystems teamed up with Netscape Communication and other partners to create yet another library called the Java Foundation Classes, or JFC. And part of JFC is a piece called the Swing component set. This Swing component set is what this book is all about.

NOTE *A later technology introduced to help people use the Swing components within a browser is the Java Plug-in code named Activator. Although not strictly intended to help users employ the Swing components, the Java Plug-in helps keep the Java Virtual Machine (JVM) in the browser current and includes the Swing component extensions.*

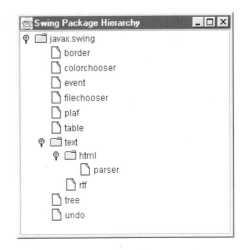

Figure 1-1: The Swing package hierarchy

The book will serve as a guide to forms-based development using the Swing component set. Over the course of its pages, we'll look at every package in the javax.swing package hierarchy, as shown in Figure 1-1.

NOTE *The javax.swing.plaf package contains several subpackages and related packages, some of which are located outside the javax.swing package hierarchy. "Plaf" stands for pluggable look and feel — a Swing concept that will be described more fully in Chapter 18.*

This chapter will familiarize you with the various Swing pieces. We'll first take a quick look at the replacement components for the AWT component set. We'll then look at the added components in the Swing component set. Next, we'll peek at the world of event handling and layout management in the land of Swing. Afterward, we'll explore the new undo/redo framework available within the Swing architecture. Then, we'll look at how to use the Swing components with Java Development Kit (JDK) 1.1 and discuss the SwingSet demonstration provided with the JDK so that you can see some of the new capabilities. Lastly, I'll point out where in the book all the components are discussed.

AWT Component Replacements

The Swing component set was created because the basic Abstract Window Toolkit (AWT) components were insufficient for real-world, forms-based applications. All the basic components were there, but the existing set was too small and far too restrictive. To alleviate this situation, the newer Swing component set now offers replacements for each of the AWT components. The new components support all the capabilities of the original set and offer a whole lot more besides.

NOTE *Although the Swing components replace the AWT components, you'll still need to understand several basic AWT concepts, such as layout managers, event handling, and drawing support. In addition, you'll need to grasp the concept that all of Swing is built on top of the core AWT libraries.*

When transitioning Java programs from AWT to Swing, for a quick port you need to only add import lines for the Swing packages and a "J" before the component class name. For instance, AWT's `Button` component is now Swing's `JButton`. However, the `Choice` component was replaced by the `JComboBox`, not `JChoice`. At the application programming interface (API) level, the Swing components are almost equivalent to the features the AWT components support. While they support additional capabilities, the basic AWT capabilities are there for everything but the `List` component, whose `JList` replacement is completely unlike the API for the List component. Table 1-1 maps the original AWT components to their replacement Swing components.

AWT COMPONENT	NEAREST SWING REPLACEMENT
Button	JButton
Canvas	JPanel
Checkbox	JCheckBox
Checkbox in CheckboxGroup	JRadioButton in ButtonGroup
Choice	JComboBox
Component	JComponent
Container	JPanel
Label	JLabel
List	JList
Menu	JMenu
MenuBar	JMenuBar
MenuItem	JMenuItem
Panel	JPanel
PopupMenu	JPopupMenu
Scrollbar	JScrollBar
ScrollPane	JScrollPane
TextArea	JTextArea
TextField	JTextField

Table 1-1: AWT/Swing component mapping

To help you understand how to use these components in both new and familiar ways, we'll examine each of the components later in the book. For instance, Chapter 4 looks at how the JButton component can be used like the Button, with just a single line of text as its label. In addition, using image icons on buttons is also explored there, as are multiple lines of text, just some of the new capabilities of the JButton component. To find out where each component is discussed throughout the book, see the "JComponent to Chapter Mapping" section later in this chapter, or look in the Table of Contents or index.

In addition to replacing each of the basic components, the Swing component set has a replacement for each of the higher-level window objects. While most of these also just add a "J" in front of the AWT component class name, you'll discover in Chapter 8 how the high-level container objects are *much* different in the Swing world. Swing's replacement to the old FileDialog differs even more and is discussed in Chapter 9. Table 1-2 maps the high-level window objects from the AWT component world to the Swing universe.

AWT WINDOW	NEAREST SWING REPLACEMENT
Applet	JApplet
Dialog	JDialog
FileDialog	JFileChooser
Frame	JFrame
Window	JWindow

Table 1-2: AWT/Swing Window mapping

Whereas the AWT components rely on the user's operating system to provide the actual component to a Java program, Swing components are all controlled from within the Java runtime. The AWT approach is called either the "heavyweight" or the "peered" approach; most Swing components are "lightweight" or "peerless." We'll explore the basics of this approach in Chapter 4 with the JComponent. Additional features of customizing the look and feel are discussed in Chapter 18.

New Components

In addition to offering replacements for all the basic AWT components, the Swing component set includes twice as many new components. For instance, as Table 1-1 shows, there are two components replacing the single Checkbox component of AWT. A Checkbox in a CheckboxGroup in AWT is now a JRadioButton in a ButtonGroup. Whereas the AWT component had two different appearances depending on whether it was in a group, with the Swing components there are two independent appearances. While you might think of this as merely a cosmetic difference, the use of the component is in fact different, depending on whether it's in a group.

The new set of components can be thought of in various ways. Some members of the new set enhance the capabilities of the original AWT components. Others are completely new and different, and others are merely containers offering specialized capabilities. Here's a brief look at each of the new components.

- JPasswordField (Figure 1-2) — This specialized text field is for the entering of passwords. Unlike the AWT TextField, you can't clear the mask character to make the contents visible nor use cut/copy operations.

- JEditorPane and JTextPane (Figure 1-3) — These two components provide support for displaying as well as editing multi-attributed content, such as an HTML viewer.

- JToggleButton (Figure 1-4) — This component offers a button that stays depressed when selected.

- JSlider (Figure 1-5)—This component is like the Scrollbar component of AWT. However, its purpose in Swing is for user input. It offers various clues to help the user choose a value.

- JProgressBar (Figure 1-6)—This component allows the user to visually see the progress of an activity.

- JTable (Figure 1-7)—This new component provides for the display of two-dimensional row/column information, such as for stock quotes.

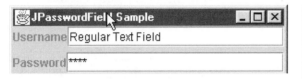

Figure 1-2: The Swing JPasswordField

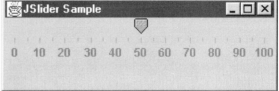

Figure 1-5: The Swing JSlider

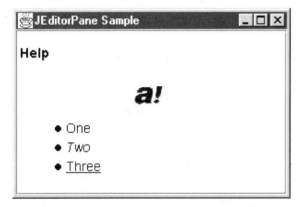

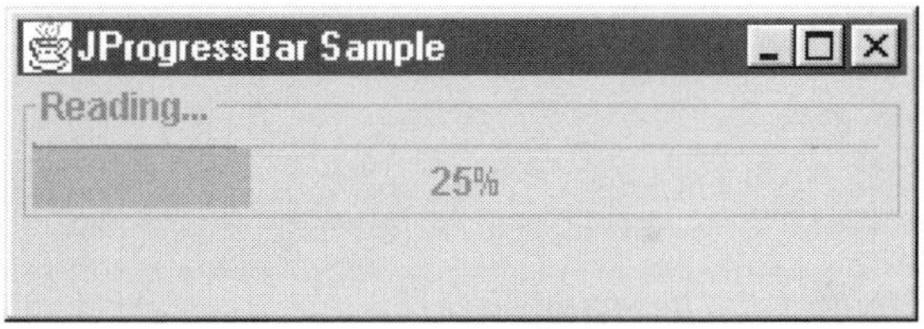

Figure 1-3: The Swing JEditorPane

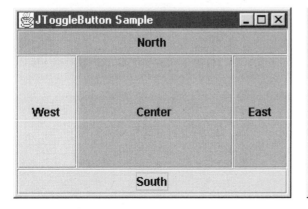

Figure 1-6: The Swing JProgressBar

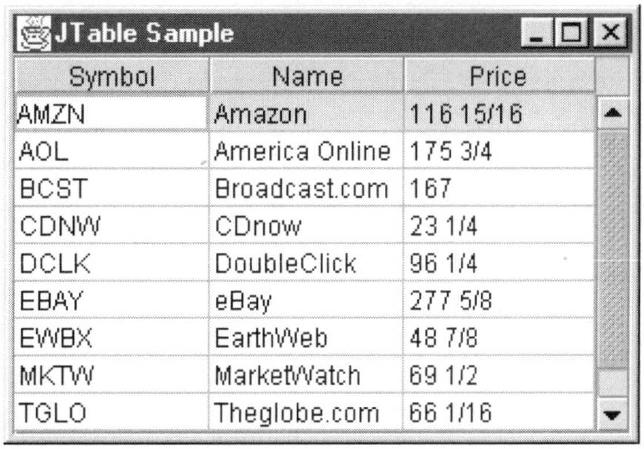

Figure 1-4: The Swing JToggleButton

Figure 1-7: The Swing JTable

- JTree (Figure 1-8) — This component supports the display of hierarchical data.

- JToolTip (Figure 1-9) — Through this component, all Swing components support pop-up text for offering useful tips.

- JToolBar (Figure 1-10) — This container offers a draggable toolbar to be included within any program window.

- JRadioButtonMenuItem (Figure 1-11) — An addition to the set of menu components, with it you can have radio buttons on a menu of mutually exclusive choices.

Figure 1-8: The Swing JTree

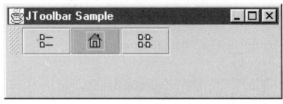

Figure 1-10: The Swing JToolBar

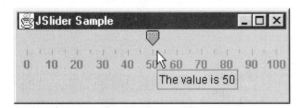

Figure 1-9: The Swing JToolTip in action

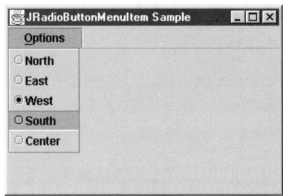

Figure 1-11: The Swing JRadioButtonMenuItem

- JSeparator (Figure 1-12) — The menu's separator bar is now its own component and can be used outside of menus, too.

- JDesktopPane and JInternalFrame (Figure 1-13) — This pair of components allows you to develop applications using the familiar Windows multi-document interface (MDI).

- JOptionPane (Figure 1-14) — This component allows you to easily create pop-up windows with varied content.

- JColorChooser (Figure 1-15) — This component is for choosing a color, with different views available to select the color.

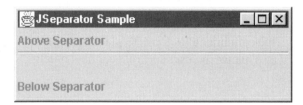

Figure 1-12: The Swing JSeparator

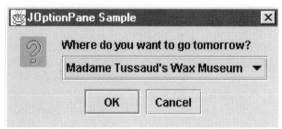

Figure 1-14: The Swing JOptionPane

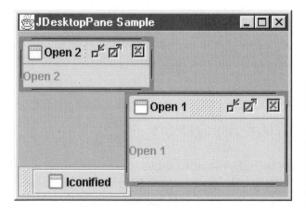

Figure 1-13: The Swing JDesktopPane and JInternaFrame

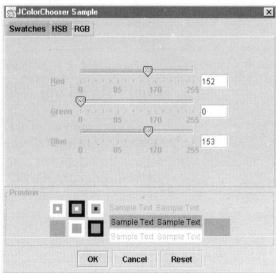

Figure 1-15: The Swing JColorChooser

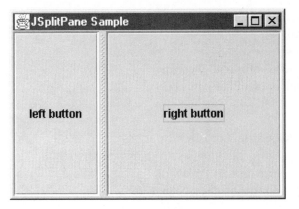

Figure 1-16: The Swing JSplitPane

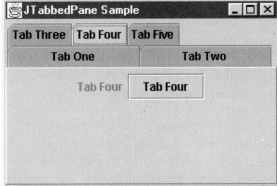

Figure 1-17: The Swing JTabbedPane

- JSplitPane (Figure 1-16) — This container allows you to place multiple components in a window. It also allows the user control over how much of each component is visible.

- JTabbedPane (Figure 1-17) — This component is like a container whose layout manager is CardLayout, with labeled tabs automatically provided to allow the user swap cards. This provides you with the familiar property-sheet motif.

In addition to the set of new components shown in these figures, a great many other classes support the new Swing components. You'll learn about *all* of them in this book.

Event Handling and Layout Management

To use the Swing components successfully, you must understand numerous parts of the original AWT component set. For instance, the Swing components all support the delegation-based event model, which was introduced with JDK 1.1 and is supported by the AWT 1.1 component set. In addition, screen layout is still controlled by layout managers.

NOTE *The Swing components don't support the original JDK 1.0 event model. They no longer utilize the public boolean* handleEvent(Event) *method and all its helper methods. If you need to convert an AWT program that uses the JDK 1.0 event model to one that uses the Swing components, you'll need to convert the program to use the delegation-based event model in addition to changing the component set.*

Although directly porting old Java AWT programs (or programmers!) to Swing programs is done most easily by continuing to use the delegation-based event model, this solution isn't always the best one. Besides supporting the delegation-based event model, the Swing components in fact provide other, more efficient ways of dealing with events for components. In Chapter 2, we review the delegation-based event model and look at the new ways of managing event handling. In addition to new event-handling capabilities, the Swing components utilize the Model-View-Controller (MVC) design to separate their user interfaces from their underlying data models. Using the MVC architecture provides yet another way of event handling with a component. While MVC might be new to most developers, the basic constructs utilize the delegation-based event model. For a look at the MVC architecture, consult Chapter 3.

Besides all the support for extended event handling with the Swing classes, these classes share the need to use a layout manager for positioning components on the screen. In addition to using the layout managers that come with AWT, you can use other layout managers that come with the Swing classes. In Chapter 10, we explore these new layout managers.

Undo Framework

Situated within the javax.swing class hierarchy are the javax.swing.undo classes. These classes offer a framework for supporting undo and redo capabilities within Java programs. Instead of creating the basic framework yourself, the framework is provided as part of the Swing classes. Although the undo classes don't use anything directly outside their package, the Swing text components utilize the undo function. Chapter 19 provides a detailed explanation of undo.

Using Swing Classes with JDK 1.1

The Swing classes are considered a standard part of the Java 2 platform, frequently referred to as JDK 1.2 by developers. To try out anything in this book, all you need is the latest Java Development Kit (JDK). However, if you want to use anything in this book with JDK 1.1 or within a browser, you must obtain the Swing classes separately.

From the developer's side, you only need to acquire the latest JFC release, install it, and modify your CLASSPATH. Getting the latest release involves going to Sun Microsystem's Web site, http://java.sun.com/products/jfc/, and downloading the latest JFC 1.1 with Swing 1.1 release. This release maps to the latest one available with the Java 2 platform. There's also a JFC 1.1 with Swing 1.0.3 release available, which is supported by Sun. However, many improvements have been made since then, and those classes don't map to the latest JDK release.

The most recent JFC 1.1 with Swing 1.1 release is available from Sun either as a compressed library file (ZIP or compressed TAR) or as an installable executable file for Windows, Solaris, or MacOS. You then must manually add the location of the swingall.jar file from the JFC installation to your CLASSPATH.

> **WARNING** *The JFC 1.1 release that's available separately isn't meant for use with the Java 2 platform. Instead, you must use the Swing release with the Java 2 JDK, because it internally uses the new Java security capabilities as well as other Java 2–specific features. The external APIs are the same, though.*

Once you've created a product utilizing the Swing classes, you can deliver it to your users with a Java Runtime Environment that includes the Swing classes. If the runtime environment is meant to be a browser, your users will need to install the Java Plug-in available from Sun's Web site at http://java.sun.com/products/plugin. If the Java Plug-in isn't installed, the swingall.jar file that comes with the JFC release will need to be either downloaded every time the applet is run or manually installed for each user.

> **NOTE** *The plug-in comes in two varieties, one ensuring the latest JDK 1.1.x release and one for the Java 2 platform. The one supporting JDK 1.1.x also includes the Swing classes, so which one you decide to use depends on your own requirements.*

As a developer, you don't need to get and install the Java Plug-in. Be aware, however, that use of the plug-in requires modifications to the HTML file that loads an applet. That's something you'll need to do yourself. To help you update the HTML files, Sun provides a tool called the HTML Converter, available from http://java.sun.com/prodcuts/plugin/1.2/features.html.

> **NOTE** *The Java Plug-in is required only if your users are employing a browser that doesn't have the Swing classes installed with it. As of the writing of this book, that is all of them. Once Netscape Communicator 5.0 comes out with its OpenJava API architecture, it may be possible that its current Java virtual machine will support the Java 2 platform. Unless you're sure that everyone needing to use your program has this already, your best bet is to use the Java Plug-in with any applets requiring Swing.*

SwingSet Demonstration

As part of the demo/jfc directory with the Java 2 platform (or part of the examples directory with the separate JFC distribution), you have available a Swing demonstration program called SwingSet. This program provides a quick preview of the majority of the Swing capabilities. All the source code is included, so if you see something you like and are interested in learning how it was done, just dig through the code to find the appropriate lines.

With the Java 2 platform, you'd start this up from the SwingSet directory with the java SwingSet command. With JDK 1.1, there's a command/batch file appropriate to your platform for starting: either runnit (for UNIX) or runnit.bat (Windows). If you used the installer, shortcuts might exist for starting the demos. After starting the SwingSet demonstration, you'd see the opening screen, as shown in Figure 1-18.

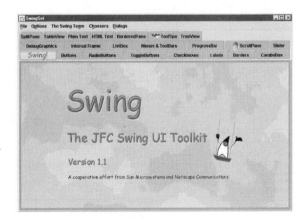

Figure 1-18: SwingSet startup screen

> **TIP** *If you're running the SwingSet program with JDK 1.1, be sure to set the SWING_HOME environment variable to the directory where you installed the Swing release.*

Choose the different tabs to see many of the features supported by the Swing components.

JComponent to Chapter Mapping

The Swing packages contain many classes and components. To help you find where all the different components are discussed, Table 1-3 provides a handy reference.

SWING COMPONENT	CHAPTER
JApplet	8
JButton	4
JCheckBox	5
JCheckBoxMenuItem	6
JColorChooser	9
JComboBox	13
JComponent	4
JDesktopPane	8
JDialog	8
JEditorPane	14
JFileChooser	9
JFrame	8
JInternalFrame	8
JLabel	4
JLayeredPane	8
JList	13
JMenu	6
JMenuBar	6
JMenuItem	6
JOptionPane	9
JPanel	4
JPasswordField	14
JPopupMenu	6
JProgressBar	12
JRadioButton	5
JRadioButtonMenuItem	6
JRootPane	8
JScrollBar	12
JScrollPane	11
JSeparator	6
JSlider	12

(continued)

Table 1-3 (continued)

SWING COMPONENT	CHAPTER
JSplitPane	11
JTabbedPane	11
JTable	17
JTextArea	14
JTextField	14
JTextPane	14
JToggleButton	5
JToolBar	6
JToolTip	4
JTree	16
JViewport	11
JWindow	8

Table 1-3: Mapping of Swing components to chapters in this book

Summary

In this chapter, I provided a brief overview of what will be covered in this book, such as the many essential (and complicated) parts of the Swing component set that you need to understand in order to use Swing components. The combined set of javax.swing packages is larger than the entire first Java Development Kit.

The following chapters feature diagrams that utilize the Unified Modeling Language (UML). Each diagram serves to illustrate the various interrelationships of a particular component. In addition, you'll find a table for each component that lists the JavaBeans properties defined by the component. Each table notes whether a property has a setter — set PropertyName(newValue) — or a getter — get PropertyName() or isPropertyName() — method defined by the class, and whether a property is bound and you can listen for a PropertyChangeEvent.

Inherited properties aren't listed, so even though a property for a component is listed as write-only, a getter method might still be provided by the parent class. Besides the diagrams and tables, you'll find information about important aspects of each component and the techniques for using them. (*Note:* This book is not intended to be an API reference, nor does it cover everything about each component. For the lesser-used aspects of a component, see the online "javadoc" documentation.)

In Chapter 2, we'll explore how to deal with event handling using the Swing components. In addition to reviewing the delegation-based event model, we'll look at the new and different ways you can deal with events by using Swing components.

Event Handling with the Swing Component Set

IN CHAPTER 1, YOU WERE PROVIDED with a brief overview of everything that's covered in this book. In this chapter, we start to look at the details of one specific part of that "everything": event handling. When working with the Swing component set, you have the option of continuing to use the delegation-based event-handling mechanism introduced with JDK 1.1 and JavaBeans. In addition, the Swing component set offers several additional ways to respond to user-initiated actions (as well as to programmatic events). In this chapter, we'll explore all these event-handling response mechanisms.

> **NOTE** *To explain the event-handling capabilities used by the Swing component set, we'll need to look at some actual Swing components. In this chapter, we'll be using the components in the simplest manner possible. Feel free to first read up on the components covered in later chapters of this book, and then come back to this chapter for a general discussion of event handling. The later chapters of this book also contain specific details on event handling for each component.*

Delegation-Based Event Handling

Sun Microsystems introduced the delegation-based event-handling mechanism into the Java libraries with the release of JDK 1.1 and JavaBeans. Although the Java 1.0 libraries included the Observer–Observable pair of objects that followed the Observer behavioral design pattern, this wasn't an adequate long-term solution for user-interface programming (The Java 1.0 containment event-handling mechanism was even worse).

The delegation-based event-handling mechanism of JDK 1.1 and higher versions is a specialized form of the Observer design pattern. The Observer pattern is used when an observer wants to know when a watched object's state changes and what that state change is. In the case of the delegation-based event-handling mechanism, instead of the observer's listening for a state change, the observer listens for events to happen.

Figure 2-1 shows the structure of the modified Observer pattern as it relates to the specific classes within the Java libraries for event handling. The generic Subject participant in the pattern manages a list, or lists, of generic Observer objects for each event that the subject can generate. The Observer objects in the list must provide a specific interface through which the Subject participant can notify them. When an event that the Observer objects are interested in happens within the Subject participant, all the registered Observer objects are notified. In the Java world, the specific interface for the Observer objects to implement must extend the java.util.EventListener interface. The specific event the Subject participant must create needs to extend the java.util.EventObject class.

To make this a little clearer, let's take a second look at the delegation-based event-handling mechanism without all the design pattern terms. GUI components (and JavaBeans) manage lists of listeners with a pair of methods for each listener type: add*XXX*Listener() and remove*XXX*Listener(). When an event happens within the subject component, the component notifies all registered listeners of the event. Any observer class interested in such an event needs to register with the component an implementer of the appropriate interface. Then each implementation is notified when the event happens. Figure 2-2 illustrates sequence.

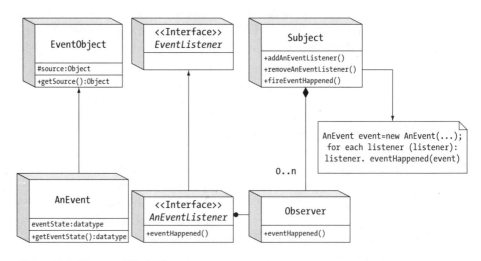

Figure 2-1: The modified Observer pattern

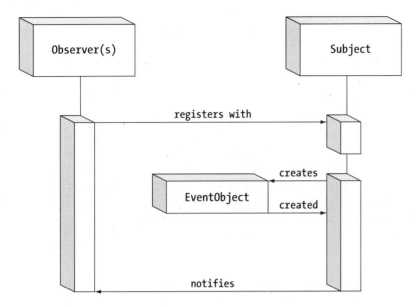

Figure 2-2: Event delegation sequence diagram

NOTE *Some users like to call the event delegation model a "publish-subscribe" model, in which components publish a set of available listeners for subscription, and others can subscribe to them.*

Using Event Listeners as Observers

To demonstrate the delegation-based event-handling model for Swing (and AWT) components, we'll create a button that responds to selection. When the button is selected, a message is printed.

Using event listeners to handle an event is a three-step process. First, you must define a class that implements the appropriate listener interface (this includes providing implementations for all the methods of the interface). Second, you must create an instance of this listener. Third, you must register this listener to the component whose events you're interested in. Let's look at the three steps separately.

1. Define the listener.

In this example, we're going to create an `ActionListener`, because the `JButton` generates `ActionEvent` objects when selected.

```
class AnActionListener implements ActionListener {
  public void actionPerformed(ActionEvent actionEvent) {
    System.out.println("I was selected.");
  }
}
```

NOTE *Part of the problem of creating responsive user interfaces is figuring out which event listener to associate with a component to get the appropriate response for the event you're interested in. For the most part, this process becomes more natural with practice. Until then, you can examine the different component APIs for a pair of add/remove listener methods, or reference the appropriate component material in this book.*

2. Create an instance of the listener.

This simply involves creating an instance of the listener just defined.

```
ActionListener actionListener = new AnActionListener();
```

If you use anonymous inner classes for event listeners, you can combine steps 1 and 2:

```
ActionListener actionListener = new ActionListener() {
  public void actionPerformed(ActionEvent actionEvent) {
    System.out.println("I was selected.");
  }
};
```

3. Register the listener with a component.

Once you've created the listener, you can associate it with the appropriate component. Assuming the JButton has already been created with a reference stored in the variable button, this would merely entail calling the button's addActionListener() method:

```
button.addActionListener(actionListener);
```

If the class that you're currently defining is the class that implements the event listener interface, then you don't need to create a separate instance of the listener.

You just need to associate your class as the listener for the component. The following source demonstrates this:

```
public class YourClass implements ActionListener {
  ... // other code for your class
  public void actionPerformed(ActionEvent actionEvent) {
    System.out.println("I was selected.");
  }
  // code within some method
  JButton button = new JButton(...);
  button.addActionListener(this);
}
```

> **TIP** *Personally, I don't like this approach because it doesn't scale well when the situation gets more complicated. For instance, as soon as you add another button onto the screen and want the same event listener to handle its selection, the* actionPerformed() *method must figure out which button triggered the event before it can respond. Although creating a separate event listener for each component adds another class to the set of deliverables, creating separate listeners is more maintainable than sharing a listener across multiple components. In addition, most Integrated Development Environment (IDE) tools such as Inprise's JBuilder automatically create the listener objects as separate classes.*

Using event handlers such as creating a listener and associating it to a component, was really the only predefined way to respond to events with JDK 1.1. Working with the Swing components in this same manner is really no different. Whereas there are additional ways of responding to events, the basic event listener approach continues to work for all components.

> **TIP** *The Swing event package (*javax.swing.event*) adds the* MouseInputListener *interface, which is a combination of the* MouseListener *and* MouseMotionListener *of AWT 1.1. The package also provides a* MouseInputAdapter *class with stubbed-out implementations of all the older mouse interface methods.*

A Quick Look at the JFrame Class

Before examining the complete source for the button selection example, we need to take a quick look at the JFrame class. The JFrame class serves as the Swing replacement to the AWT Frame class for a top-level window with appropriate window decorations for the operating system (such as a title bar with Minimize, Maximize, and Close buttons).

Whereas the JFrame class is a subclass of the Frame class, several differences exist between the two objects. The first difference is the default close operation triggered when the Close button on the title bar is selected. By default, the Frame does nothing when this button is selected. Instead, the JFrame class is hidden by default. If you don't like the default behavior, you can change it.

The Close button of a frame is shown in Figure 2-3. The appearance of this button will differ depending on the operating system.

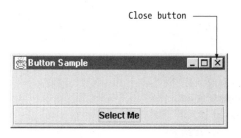

Figure 2-3: The Close button for a Windows NT frame

The other major difference has to do with how you add components to the frame, as well as how you change its layout manager. With a Frame, you add components directly or modify the layout manager. By comparison, the JFrame relies on a third party for support of capabilities that Frame doesn't support. This third party keeps track of how to layer items such as pop-up menus and tooltip text and adds support for Swing-specific menu bars. Now, with JFrame, instead of adding components directly to the frame object, you can add or modify its content pane, which is called a Container. To get the content pane, just ask for it with public Container getContentPane(). If you don't use the content pane and try to directly add components to the frame or set its layout manager, an Error will be thrown at runtime.

Your top-level frame source code changes from

```
Frame frame = new Frame(...);
frame.add(...);
frame.setLayout(...);
```

to the following:

```
JFrame frame = new JFrame(...);
Container contentPane = frame.getContentPane();
contentPane.add(...);
contentPane.setLayout(...);
```

When first transitioning to Swing from AWT, you will probably find this to be one of the most annoying adjustments because if you forget to use the content pane the program will still compile, but it won't run. At least the default layout manager of this content pane remained BorderLayout.

NOTE *The* JFrame *class will be fully discussed in Chapter 8.*

Creating an ExitableJFrame Class

One last thing I'm going to do before showing you the source for the button selection example is to create a frame that exits the Java runtime when the Close button of the frame is selected. This class will be used by all the examples in this book. Once this class is created, you won't need to associate a WindowListener to every JFrame you create in order to shut down the runtime environment.

The class being created is called ExitableJFrame. When the frame is closed by a user, by default the frame causes the runtime to exit. It can return a value that's settable if you don't like the default return code of zero. The source code for this class follows:

```
import javax.swing.*;
import java.awt.event.*;
public class ExitableJFrame extends JFrame {
  public static final int EXIT_ON_CLOSE = -1;
  private int returnCode = 0;

  public ExitableJFrame () {
    init();
  }
  public ExitableJFrame (String title) {
    super(title);
    init();
  }

  private void init() {
    setDefaultCloseOperation(EXIT_ON_CLOSE);
  }

  public void setReturnCode(int newValue) {
    returnCode = newValue;
  }

  protected void processWindowEvent(WindowEvent windowEvent) {
```

```
      super.processWindowEvent(windowEvent);
      int defaultCloseOperation = getDefaultCloseOperation();
      if ((windowEvent.getID() == WindowEvent.WINDOW_CLOSING) &&
          (defaultCloseOperation == EXIT_ON_CLOSE)) {
        System.exit(returnCode);
      }
    }

  protected String paramString() {
      String returnValue = "";
      int defaultCloseOperation = getDefaultCloseOperation();
      if (defaultCloseOperation == EXIT_ON_CLOSE) {
        returnValue = ",EXIT_ON_CLOSE";
      }
      return super.paramString() + returnValue;
    }
}
```

Now that we have that class out of the way for all our examples, we can list the source code for the first example: the button selection demonstration with an event listener. When it runs, you'll see Figure 2-3 as the created frame. The program creates the frame and button. Then the program creates the action listener, which is associated with the button. The button is placed in the frame's content pane and the frame is shown. You'll find yourself creating listeners frequently when working with the user interface components.

```
import javax.swing.*;
import java.awt.*;
import java.awt.event.*;

public class ButtonSample {
  public static void main(String args[]) {
    JFrame frame = new ExitableJFrame("Button Sample");
    JButton button = new JButton("Select Me");

    // Define ActionListener
    ActionListener actionListener = new ActionListener() {
      public void actionPerformed(ActionEvent actionEvent) {
        System.out.println("I was selected.");
      }
    };

    // Attach Listeners
```

```
button.addActionListener(actionListener);

Container contentPane = frame.getContentPane();
contentPane.add(button, BorderLayout.SOUTH);
frame.setSize(300, 100);
frame.setVisible(true);
  }
}
```

Using SwingUtilities for Mouse Button Identification

The Swing component set includes a utility class called SwingUtilities that provides a collection of generic helper methods. We'll look at this class periodically in this book when a particular set of methods for this class seems useful. In the following example, the methods we're interested in are related to determining which mouse button has been selected.

The MouseInputListener interface consists of seven methods: mouseClicked (MouseEvent), mouseEntered(MouseEvent), mouseExited(MouseEvent), mousePressed (MouseEvent), mouseReleased(MouseEvent) from MouseListener, and mouseDragged (MouseEvent) and mouseMoved(MouseEvent) from MouseMotionListener. If you need to determine which buttons on the mouse were selected (or released) when the event happened, check the modifiers property of MouseEvent and compare it to various mask-setting constants of the InputEvent class.

For instance, to check if a middle mouse button was pressed for a mouse press event, you'd have the following code in your mouse listener's mousePressed() method:

```
public void mousePressed(MouseEvent mouseEvent) {
  int modifiers = mouseEvent.getModifiers();
  if ((modifiers & InputEvent.BUTTON2_MASK) == InputEvent.BUTTON2_MASK) {
    System.out.println("Middle button pressed.");
  }
}
```

Although this works fine and dandy, the SwingUtilities class adds three methods to make this process much simpler.

```
SwingUtilities.isLeftMouseButton(MouseEvent mouseEvent);
SwingUtilities.isMiddleMouseButton(MouseEvent mouseEvent);
SwingUtilities.isRightMouseButton(MouseEvent mouseEvent);
```

Now, instead of having to manually get the modifiers and compare them against the mask, you can simply ask the SwingUtilities, as follows. This makes your code much more readable, and more easily maintainable.

```
if (SwingUtilities.isMiddleMouseButton(mouseEvent)) {
  System.out.println("Middle button released.");
}
```

Using Property Change Listeners as Observers

Besides the basic event-delegation mechanism introduced with JDK 1.1 and JavaBeans, JavaBeans introduced yet another incarnation of the Observer design pattern, this time through the property change listener. The PropertyChangeListener implementation is a truer representation of the Observer pattern. Each Observer watches for changes to an attribute of the Subject. The Observer is then notified of the new state when changed in the Subject. Figure 2-4 shows the structure of this Observer pattern, as it relates to the specific classes within the JavaBeans libraries for property change handling.

In this particular case, the observable Subject has a set of add/remove property change listener methods and a property (or properties) whose state is being watched. With a PropertyChangeListener, the registered set of listeners is managed within the PropertyChangeSupport class. When the watched property value changes, this support class notifies any registered listeners of the new and old property state values.

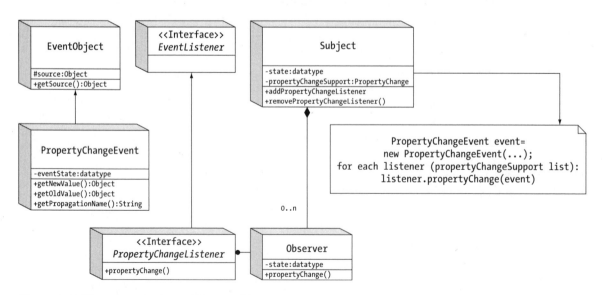

Figure 2-4: The property change listener Observer pattern

TIP *Although* `PropertyChangeListener` *observers are registered at the class level, not all properties of the class might be* bound. *A property is bound when a change to the property causes the registered listeners to be notified. In addition, although JavaBeans introduced the concept of property change listeners in JDK 1.1, none of the properties of the AWT components were bound. The Swing components have many of their properties bound. To find out which ones are bound, see the property tables for each Swing component that appear in later chapters of this book.*

By registering `PropertyChangeListener` objects with the various components that support this type of listener, you can reduce the amount of source code you must generate after the initial listening setup. For instance, the background color of a Swing component is bound, meaning someone can register a `PropertyChangeListener` to a component to be notified when the background setting changes. When the value of the background property for that component changes, anyone listening is notified, allowing an observer to change its background color to the new setting. Therefore, if you want all the components of your program to have the same background color, you can register them all with one component. Then, when that single component changes its background color, all the other components would be notified of the change and would modify their backgrounds to the new setting.

NOTE *Although you can use a* `PropertyChangeListener` *to "share" a common property setting among components, you can also map the property of a subject to a different property of the observer.*

To demonstrate a `PropertyChangeListener`, the following program contains two buttons. When either button is selected, the background of the selected button is changed to some random color. The second button is listening for property changes within the first button. When the background color changes for the first button, the background color of the second button is changed to that new value. The first button isn't listening for property changes for the second button. Therefore, when the second button is selected, changing its background color, this change doesn't propagate back to the first button.

```
import javax.swing.*;
import java.awt.*;
import java.awt.event.*;
import java.beans.*;
```

```java
public class BoundSample {
  public static void main(String args[]) {
    JFrame frame = new ExitableJFrame("Button Sample");
    final JButton button1 = new JButton("Select Me");
    final JButton button2 = new JButton("No Select Me");

    // Define ActionListener
    ActionListener actionListener = new ActionListener() {
      public void actionPerformed(ActionEvent actionEvent) {
        JButton button = (JButton)actionEvent.getSource();
        int red = (int)(Math.random()*255);
        int green = (int)(Math.random()*255);
        int blue = (int)(Math.random()*255);
        button.setBackground(new Color(red, green, blue));
      }
    };

    // Define PropertyChangeListener
    PropertyChangeListener propertyChangeListener = new PropertyChangeListener()
{
      public void propertyChange(PropertyChangeEvent propertyChangeEvent) {
        String property = propertyChangeEvent.getPropertyName();
        if ("background".equals(property)) {
          button2.setBackground((Color)propertyChangeEvent.getNewValue());
        }
      }
    };

    // Attach Listeners
    button1.addActionListener(actionListener);
    button1.addPropertyChangeListener(propertyChangeListener);
    button2.addActionListener(actionListener);

    Container contentPane = frame.getContentPane();
    contentPane.add(button1, BorderLayout.NORTH);
    contentPane.add(button2, BorderLayout.SOUTH);
    frame.setSize(300, 100);
    frame.setVisible(true);
  }
}
```

> **NOTE** *Although the previous example only causes a color change from button selection, imagine if the background color of the first button could be changed from a couple of hundred different places other than buttons! Without a property change listener, each of those places would be required to also change the background color of the second button. With the property change listener, it's only necessary to modify the background color of the primary object — the first button, in this case. The change would then automatically propagate to the other components.*

The Swing library also uses the `ChangeEvent` / `ChangeListener` pair to signify state changes. Although similar to the `PropertyChangeEvent` / `PropertyChangeListener` pair, the `ChangeEvent` doesn't carry with it the new and old data value settings. You can think of it as a lighter-weight version of a property change listener. Nevertheless, the `ChangeEvent` is useful when more than one property value changes, because `ChangeEvent` doesn't need to package up the changes.

> **TIP** *The Swing components use the `SwingPropertyChangeSupport` class, instead of the `PropertyChangeSupport` class, to manage and notify their `PropertyChangeListener` list. The Swing version, `SwingPropertyChangeSupport`, isn't thread-safe, but it is faster and takes up less memory. For more about Swing component thread safety, see the "Multithreaded Swing Event Handling" section later in this chapter.*

Managing Listener Lists

If you're creating your own components and want those components to fire off events, you need to maintain a list of listeners to be notified. If the listener list is for AWT 1.1 events, you can use the `AWTEventMulticaster` class for help with list management. Prior to the Swing libraries, if the event wasn't a predefined AWT event type you had to manage this list of listeners yourself. Now, with the help of the `EventListenerList` class in the `javax.swing.event` package, you no longer have to manually manage the listener list and worry about thread safety.

Class `AWTEventMulticaster`

Whether you realize it or not, the `AWTEventMulticaster` class is used by each and every AWT component to manage event listener lists. The class implements all the AWT 1.1 event listeners (ActionListener, AdjustmentListener, ComponentListener, ContainerListener, FocusListener, ItemListener, KeyListener, MouseListener, MouseMotionListener, TextListener, and WindowListener) and in Java 2 adds support for the new AWT event listener InputMethodListener. Whenever you call an add- or remove-listener method of a component, the AWTEventMulticaster is used for support.

If you want to create your own component and manage a list of listeners for one of the AWT event/listener pairs, you can use the AWTEventMulticaster. To demonstrate, we'll create a generic component that generates ActionEvent objects whenever a key is pressed within the component. The component uses the public static String getKeyText(int keyCode) method of KeyEvent to convert the key code to its appropriate text string and passes this string back as the action command for the ActionEvent.

Because the component is meant to serve as the source for ActionListener observers, it needs a pair of add/remove methods to handle the registration of listeners. This is where the AWTEventMulticaster comes in because it will do the adding and removing of listeners from your listener list variable:

```java
private ActionListener actionListenerList = null;
public void addActionListener(ActionListener actionListener) {
  actionListenerList = AWTEventMulticaster.add(actionListenerList,
actionListener);
}
public void removeActionListener(ActionListener actionListener) {
  actionListenerList = AWTEventMulticaster.remove(actionListenerList,
actionListener);
}
```

The remainder of the class definition describes how to handle the internal events. An internal KeyListener needs to be registered in order to send keystrokes to an ActionListener. In addition, the component must be able to get the input focus, otherwise all keystrokes will go to other components. The complete class definition follows. The line of source code for notification of the listener list is in **boldface**. That one line notifies all the listeners.

```java
import java.awt.*;
import java.awt.event.*;

public class KeyTextComponent extends Canvas {
  private ActionListener actionListenerList = null;

  public KeyTextComponent() {
    setBackground(Color.cyan);
```

```
  KeyListener internalKeyListener = new KeyAdapter() {
    public void keyPressed(KeyEvent keyEvent) {
      if (actionListenerList != null) {
        int keyCode = keyEvent.getKeyCode();
        String keyText = KeyEvent.getKeyText(keyCode);
        ActionEvent actionEvent = new ActionEvent(
          this,
          ActionEvent.ACTION_PERFORMED,
          keyText);
        actionListenerList.actionPerformed(actionEvent);
      }
    }
  };

  MouseListener internalMouseListener = new MouseAdapter() {
    public void mousePressed(MouseEvent mouseEvent) {
      requestFocus();
    }
  };

  addKeyListener(internalKeyListener);
  addMouseListener(internalMouseListener);
}

public void addActionListener(ActionListener actionListener) {
  actionListenerList = AWTEventMulticaster.add(actionListenerList,
actionListener);
}
public void removeActionListener(ActionListener actionListener) {
  actionListenerList = AWTEventMulticaster.remove(actionListenerList,
actionListener);
}

public boolean isFocusTraversable() {
  return true;
}
}
```

Figure 2-5 shows the component in use. The top portion of the figure is the component, and the bottom is a text field. An ActionListener is registered with the KeyTextComponent that updates the text field in order to display the text string for the key pressed. The source code for the example follows the figure.

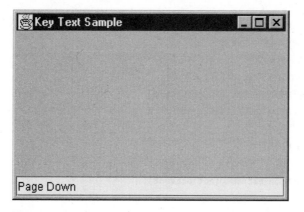

Figure 2-5: Demonstrating the KeyTextComponent

```java
import java.awt.*;
import java.awt.event.*;
import javax.swing.*;

public class KeyTextTester  {
  public static void main(String args[]) {
    JFrame frame = new ExitableJFrame("Key Text Sample");
    KeyTextComponent keyTextComponent = new KeyTextComponent();
    final JTextField textField = new JTextField();

    ActionListener actionListener = new ActionListener() {
      public void actionPerformed(ActionEvent actionEvent) {
        String keyText = actionEvent.getActionCommand();
        textField.setText(keyText);
      }
    };
    keyTextComponent.addActionListener(actionListener);

    Container contentPane = frame.getContentPane();
    contentPane.add(keyTextComponent, BorderLayout.CENTER);
    contentPane.add(textField, BorderLayout.SOUTH);
    frame.setSize(300, 200);
    frame.setVisible(true);
  }
}
```

Class `EventListenerList`

Although the `AWTEventMulticaster` class is easy to use, it doesn't work for managing lists of custom event listeners. You can either create a custom extension of the class for each type of event listener list you need to manage (not practical), or you could just store the list in a data structure such as a `Vector`. Although using a `Vector` works satisfactorily, with it you'd have to worry about synchronization issues. If you don't program the list management properly, the listener notification may happen with the wrong set of listeners.

To help simplify this situation, the Swing component library includes a special event-listener support class, `EventListenerList`. One instance of the class can manage all the different types of event listeners for a component. To demonstrate the class usage, I've rewritten the previous example to use `EventListenerList`, instead of `AWTEventMulticaster`.

> **NOTE** *In this particular example, using the `AWTEventMulticaster` class is the simpler solution. However, imagine a similar situation in which the event listener isn't one of the predefined AWT event listeners.*

The adding and removing of listeners is similar to the technique you used with the `AWTEventMulticaster` in the previous section of this chapter. You need to create a variable of the appropriate type—this time `EventListenerList`—as well as define add- and remove-listener methods. One key difference between the two approaches is that the initial `EventListenerList` is non-null, whereas the other starts off being null. A reference to an empty `EventListenerList` must be created to start. This removes the need for several checks for a `null` list variable later. The adding and removing of listeners is also slightly different. Because an `EventListenerList` can manage a list of listeners of any type, when you add or remove the listener, you must provide the class type for the listener being acted upon.

```
EventListenerList actionListenerList = new EventListenerList();
public void addActionListener(ActionListener actionListener) {
  actionListenerList.add(ActionListener.class, actionListener);
}
public void removeActionListener(ActionListener actionListener) {
  actionListenerList.remove(ActionListener.class, actionListener);
}
```

This leaves only the notification of the listeners to be done. No generic method exists in the class to notify all the listeners of a particular type that an event has happened, so you must create the code yourself. A call to the following code (fireActionPerformed(actionEvent)) will replace the one line of boldfaced source code (actionListenerList.actionPerformed(actionEvent)) from the example a few pages back. The code gets a copy of all the listeners from the list as an array (in a thread-safe manner). You then need to loop through the list and notify the appropriate listeners. Each listener in the array has a pair of entries: the listener interface class object and the actual implementation. Just having the listeners in the list isn't sufficient, however, because a listener can implement multiple event-listener interfaces but have only one registered.

```
protected void fireActionPerformed(ActionEvent actionEvent) {
  Object listenerList[] = actionListenerList.getListenerList();
  for (int i=listenerList.length-2; i>=0; i-=2) {
    if (listenerList[i] == ActionListener.class) {
      ((ActionListener)listenerList[i+1]).actionPerformed(actionEvent);
    }
  }
}
```

The complete source for the new and improved class follows. When using the EventListenerList class, don't forget that the class is in the javax.swing.event package. Other than the class name, the testing program doesn't change.

```
import java.awt.*;
import java.awt.event.*;
import javax.swing.event.*;
import java.util.EventListener;

public class KeyTextComponent2 extends Canvas {
  private EventListenerList actionListenerList = new EventListenerList();

  public KeyTextComponent2() {
    setBackground(Color.cyan);
    KeyListener internalKeyListener = new KeyAdapter() {
      public void keyPressed(KeyEvent keyEvent) {
        if (actionListenerList != null) {
          int keyCode = keyEvent.getKeyCode();
          String keyText = KeyEvent.getKeyText(keyCode);
          ActionEvent actionEvent = new ActionEvent(
            this,
            ActionEvent.ACTION_PERFORMED,
            keyText);
          fireActionPerformed(actionEvent);
        }
```

```
    }
  };

  MouseListener internalMouseListener = new MouseAdapter() {
    public void mousePressed(MouseEvent mouseEvent) {
      requestFocus();
    }
  };

  addKeyListener(internalKeyListener);
  addMouseListener(internalMouseListener);
}

public void addActionListener(ActionListener actionListener) {
  actionListenerList.add(ActionListener.class, actionListener);
}
public void removeActionListener(ActionListener actionListener) {
  actionListenerList.remove(ActionListener.class, actionListener);
}

protected void fireActionPerformed(ActionEvent actionEvent) {
  Object listenerList[] = actionListenerList.getListenerList();
  for (int i=listenerList.length-2; i>=0; i-=2) {
    if (listenerList[i] == ActionListener.class) {
      ((ActionListener)listenerList[i+1]).actionPerformed(actionEvent);
    }
  }
}

public boolean isFocusTraversable() {
  return true;
}
}
```

Swing-Specific Event Handling

Besides using all the familiar event-handling mechanisms from JDK 1.1, the Swing component library adds several improved capabilities to make event handling much easier. The capabilities improve on several of AWT's core event-handling features, from basic action listening to focus management.

To simplify event handling, the Swing library extends the original ActionListener interface with the Action interface to store visual attributes with the event handler. This allows the creation of event handlers independent of visual components. Then, when the Action is later associated with a component, the component automatically gets information (such as a button label) directly from the event handler. This includes notification of updates for the label when the Action is modified. The AbstractAction and TextAction classes are implementations of this concept.

The Swing library also adds a KeyStroke class that allows you to more easily respond to key events. Instead of watching all key events for a specific key, you can tell a component that when a specific key stroke sequence is pressed it must respond with a particular action. The Swing text components rely on a Keymap to store the mapping of keystrokes to actions. The Keymap interface and the TextAction support class will be described in more detail in Chapter 15, along with the remainder of the text event-handling capabilities.

If you found the focus management capabilities of AWT lacking, you'll be happy to learn about Swing's enhancements through the abstract FocusManager class and DefaultFocusManager implementation. But because Swing is built *on top of* AWT, you'll never be able to completely rid yourself of AWT's focusing capabilities.

When working with Swing components pay particular attention to thread safety. Accessing visible Swing components must be done from the event dispatch thread. You can use two methods from the SwingUtilities class to ensure that this accessing is properly done by creating Runnable objects to be run in the event dispatch thread. In addition, the Timer class allows you to create periodic events that also run within the event dispatch thread.

Figure 2-6 shows a class hierarchy diagram of these classes and interfaces.

Interface Action

The Action interface is an extension to the ActionListener interface that's very flexible for defining shared event handlers independent of the components that act as the triggering agents. As the following interface definition may (or may not) immediately reveal, the interface implements ActionListener and defines a lookup table data structure whose keys act as bound properties. Then, when an Action is associated with a component, these display properties are automatically carried over to it.

```
public interface Action implements ActionListener {
  // Constants
  public final static String DEFAULT;
  public final static String LONG_DESCRIPTION;
```

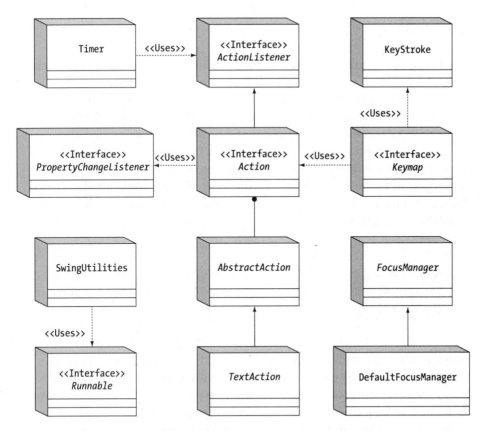

Figure 2-6: Swing-specific, event-related class hierarchy

```
    public final static String NAME;
    public final static String SHORT_DESCRIPTION;
    public final static String SMALL_ICON;
    // Listeners
    public void addPropertyChangeListener(PropertyChangeListener listener);
    public void removePropertyChangeListener(PropertyChangeListener listener);
    // Properties
    public boolean isEnabled();
    public void setEnabled(boolean newValue);
    // Other Methods
    public Object getValue(String key);
    public void putValue(String key, Object value);
}
```

Because Action is merely an interface, the Swing libraries offer a class to implement the interface. That class is AbstractAction.

Class AbstractAction

The AbstractAction class provides a default implementation of the Action interface. This is where the bound property behavior is implemented.

Once you define an AbstractAction by subclassing and providing a public void actionPerformed(ActionEvent actionEvent) method, you can then pass it along to some special Swing components. The JMenu, JPopupMenu, and JToolBar directly support the adding of Action objects, whereas the Swing text components have their own built-in support for Action objects through their Keymap. When you add an action with add(Action newAction) to a JMenu or JPopupMenu, a JMenuItem is created and placed within the menu container. For a JToolBar, the add(Action newAction) method creates a JButton component.

> **NOTE** *The add(Action newAction) methods of* JMenu, JPopupMenu, *and* JToolBar *all return the object created: a* JMenuItem, JMenuItem, *or* JButton, *respectively.*

When the Action is added to the respective Swing container, selection of the component created by the container triggers the calling of the method of the Action, actionPerformed(ActionEvent actionEvent). The display of the component is defined by the property elements added to the internal data structure. I'll demonstrate by presenting an Action with a "Print" label and an image icon. When this is activated, a "Hello World" message is printed.

```
import java.awt.event.*;
import javax.swing.*;

public class PrintHelloAction extends AbstractAction {
  private static final Icon printIcon = new ImageIcon("Print.gif");
  PrintHelloAction() {
    super("Print", printIcon);
    putValue(Action.SHORT_DESCRIPTION, "Hello World");
  }
  public void actionPerformed(ActionEvent actionEvent) {
    System.out.println("Hello World");
  }
}
```

Once the Action has been defined, you can create Action and associate it with as many other components as you want.

```
Action printAction = new PrintHelloAction();
menu.add(printAction);
toolbar.add(printAction);
```

After the Action has been associated with the various objects, if you find that you
need to modify the label, icon, or state of the Action, you only have to change the
setting in one place. Because the properties are all bound, they propagate to
anyone who uses the Action. For instance, disabling the
Action (printAction.setEnabled(false)) will disable the
JMenuItem and JButton created on the JMenu and JToolBar,
respectively. In contrast, changing the name of the Action
with printAction.putValue(Action.NAME, "Hello World")
changes the text label of the associated components.

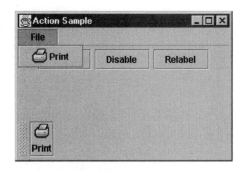

Figure 2-7 shows what the PrintHelloAction might look
like on a JToolBar and a JMenu. Selectable buttons are provided to enable or disable the Action as well as change its
name.

The complete source code for this example follows.
Don't worry just yet about the specifics of creating toolbars
or menu bars. They'll be discussed in more detail later.

Figure 2-7: The PrintHelloAction in use

```
import java.awt.*;
import java.awt.event.*;
import javax.swing.*;

public class ActionTester {

  public static void main(String args[]) {
    JFrame frame = new ExitableJFrame("Action Sample");
    final Action printAction = new PrintHelloAction();

    JMenuBar menuBar = new JMenuBar();
    JMenu menu = new JMenu("File");
    menuBar.add(menu);
    menu.add(printAction);

    JToolBar toolbar = new JToolBar();
    toolbar.add(printAction);

    JButton enableButton = new JButton("Enable");
    ActionListener enableActionListener = new ActionListener() {
      public void actionPerformed(ActionEvent actionEvent) {
        printAction.setEnabled(true);
      }
```

```
  };
  enableButton.addActionListener(enableActionListener);

  JButton disableButton = new JButton("Disable");
  ActionListener disableActionListener = new ActionListener() {
    public void actionPerformed(ActionEvent actionEvent) {
      printAction.setEnabled(false);
    }
  };
  disableButton.addActionListener(disableActionListener);

  JButton relabelButton = new JButton("Relabel");
  ActionListener relabelActionListener = new ActionListener() {
    public void actionPerformed(ActionEvent actionEvent) {
      printAction.putValue(Action.NAME, "Hello World");
    }
  };
  relabelButton.addActionListener(relabelActionListener);

  JPanel buttonPanel = new JPanel();
  buttonPanel.add(enableButton);
  buttonPanel.add(disableButton);
  buttonPanel.add(relabelButton);

  frame.setJMenuBar(menuBar);

  Container contentPane = frame.getContentPane();
  contentPane.add(toolbar, BorderLayout.SOUTH);
  contentPane.add(buttonPanel, BorderLayout.NORTH);
  frame.setSize(300, 200);
  frame.setVisible(true);
  }
}
```

AbstractAction Properties

As Table 2-1 shows, the AbstractAction class has only a single bound property available from setter/getter methods.

PROPERTY NAME	DATA TYPE	ACCESS
enabled	boolean	read-write bound

Table 2-1: AbstractAction properties

The remainder of the bound properties are placed in the lookup table with `putValue(String key, Object value)`. Table 2-2 describes the predefined set of `Action` constants that can be used as the key. You're not limited to using only this set, though.

CONSTANT	DESCRIPTION
NAME	Action name, used as button label
SMALL_ICON	Icon for action, used as button label
SHORT_DESCRIPTION	Short description of action; could be used as tooltip text, but not by default
LONG_DESCRIPTION	Long description of action; could be used by accessibility
DEFAULT	Unused constant that could be used for your own property

Table 2-2: AbstractAction Lookup property keys

Once a property has been placed in the lookup table, you can get it with `public Object getValue(String key)`. It works similarly to the `java.util.Hashtable` class, with one distinction: If you try to put a key-value pair into the table with a `null` value, the table removes the key, if it's present.

> **NOTE** *There are many public subclasses of this class. Although you might never need to worry about any of them, this list is provided for those present in Swing 1.1:*
>
> *BasicInternalFrameTitlePane.CloseAction*
> *BasicInternalFrameTitlePane.IconifyAction*
> *BasicInternalFrameTitlePane.MaximizeAction*
> *BasicInternalFrameTitlePane.MoveAction*
> *BasicInternalFrameTitlePane.RestoreAction*
> *BasicInternalFrameTitlePane.SizeAction*
> *BasicSliderUI.ActionScroller*
> *BasicTreeUI.TreeCancelEditingAction*
> *BasicTreeUI.TreeHomeAction*
> *BasicTreeUI.TreeIncrementAction*
> *BasicTreeUI.TreePageAction*
> *BasicTreeUI.TreeToggleAction*
> *BasicTreeUI.TreeTraverseAction*
> *TextAction*
>
> *In some cases, you might find it useful to associate the preexisting Action with your own event trigger.*

Creating an Action JButton

To let you see what happens behind the scenes when using an Action with a
JMenuBar or a JToolBar, we'll create a JButton that accepts an Action for configuration. Surprisingly, this isn't available by default. To make this example even more
helpful, we'll provide built-in support for tooltip text—something that's not provided with the built-in Action support for JMenu, JPopupMenu, or JToolBar.

When extending a component to support an Action, you need to provide a
constructor that accepts the Action as its sole argument. The constructor then
maps all the Action attributes to the appropriate property of the component.
We'll add a helper method to do the mapping, making the Action a full-fledged
property for the button that can be changed later.

For a JButton, the Action.NAME and Action.SMALL_ICON are included for the
label, and they get mapped to the text and icon properties. The initial state of
the JButton must also match the state of the Action, so you need to ask for the
enabled property value of the Action. The tooltip text will be provided by the
Action.SHORT_DESCRIPTION. Lastly, you'll need to associate the Action as the
ActionListener for the JButton.

To ensure that the button property values change when the Action changes,
we need to add our own PropertyChangeListener to the Action. In addition, if you
associate a new Action with the button, you need to remember to remove the old
one. The source for the constructor and setAction(Action) method follow.

```
private Action action;
PropertyChangeListener propertyChangeListener;

public ActionButton(Action action) {
  setAction(action);
}
public void setAction(Action newValue) {

  // Disconnect current action;
  if ((action != null) && (propertyChangeListener != null)) {
    action.removePropertyChangeListener(propertyChangeListener);
    removeActionListener(action);
  }

  action = newValue;

  if (action == null) {
    setText("");
    setIcon(null);
  } else {
    setText((String)action.getValue(Action.NAME));
```

```
    setIcon((Icon)action.getValue(Action.SMALL_ICON));
    setEnabled(action.isEnabled());
    String toolTipText = (String)action.getValue(Action.SHORT_DESCRIPTION);
    if (toolTipText != null) {
      setToolTipText(toolTipText);
    }
    addActionListener(action);
    if (propertyChangeListener == null) {
      propertyChangeListener = new OurPropertyChangeListener();
    }
    action.addPropertyChangeListener(propertyChangeListener);
  }
}
```

The real workhorse here is the PropertyChangeListener. It directs specific Action property changes in order to modify the appropriate property setting of the JButton. The source for the listener follows.

```
class OurPropertyChangeListener implements PropertyChangeListener {
  public void propertyChange(PropertyChangeEvent propertyChangeEvent) {
    String propertyName = propertyChangeEvent.getPropertyName();
    if (propertyName.equals(Action.NAME)) {
      String text = (String)propertyChangeEvent.getNewValue();
      setText(text);
    } else if (propertyName.equals(Action.SMALL_ICON)) {
      Icon icon = (Icon)propertyChangeEvent.getNewValue();
      setIcon(icon);
    } else if (propertyName.equals(Action.SHORT_DESCRIPTION)) {
      String text = (String)propertyChangeEvent.getNewValue();
      setToolTipText(text);
    } else if (propertyName.equals("enabled")) {
      Boolean enabledState = (Boolean)propertyChangeEvent.getNewValue();
      setEnabled(enabledState.booleanValue());
    }
  }
}
```

By adding the following line of code to the ActionTester example shown in the section "Class AbstractAction", the three components in the example share the same Action. Figure 2-8 shows the updated display with the new component.

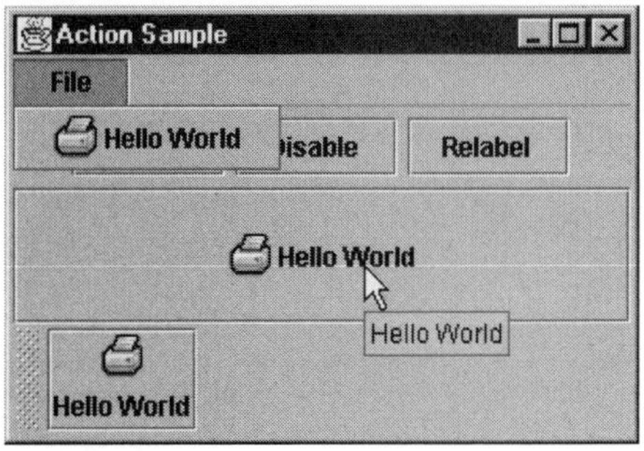

Figure 2-8: The ActionButton in use

```
contentPane.add(new ActionButton(printAction), BorderLayout.CENTER);
```

The complete source for the `ActionButton` follows.

```
import java.awt.*;
import java.awt.event.*;
import javax.swing.*;
import java.beans.*;

public class ActionButton extends JButton {

  class OurPropertyChangeListener implements PropertyChangeListener {
    public void propertyChange(PropertyChangeEvent propertyChangeEvent) {
      String propertyName = propertyChangeEvent.getPropertyName();
      if (propertyName.equals(Action.NAME)) {
        String text = (String)propertyChangeEvent.getNewValue();
        setText(text);
      } else if (propertyName.equals(Action.SMALL_ICON)) {
        Icon icon = (Icon)propertyChangeEvent.getNewValue();
        setIcon(icon);
      } else if (propertyName.equals(Action.SHORT_DESCRIPTION)) {
        String text = (String)propertyChangeEvent.getNewValue();
        setToolTipText(text);
      } else if (propertyName.equals("enabled")) {
        Boolean enabledState = (Boolean)propertyChangeEvent.getNewValue();
        setEnabled(enabledState.booleanValue());
      }
    }
  }

  private Action action;
  PropertyChangeListener propertyChangeListener;

  public ActionButton() {
  }

  public ActionButton(Action action) {
    setAction(action);
  }

  public void setAction(Action newValue) {

    // Disconnect current action;
```

```
if ((action != null) && (propertyChangeListener != null)) {
  action.removePropertyChangeListener(propertyChangeListener);
  removeActionListener(action);
}

action = newValue;

if (action == null) {
  setText("");
  setIcon(null);
} else {
  setText((String)action.getValue(Action.NAME));
  setIcon((Icon)action.getValue(Action.SMALL_ICON));
  setEnabled(action.isEnabled());
  String toolTipText = (String)action.getValue(Action.SHORT_DESCRIPTION);
  if (toolTipText != null) {
    setToolTipText(toolTipText);
  }
  addActionListener(action);
  if (propertyChangeListener == null) {
    propertyChangeListener = new OurPropertyChangeListener();
  }
  action.addPropertyChangeListener(propertyChangeListener);
}
}
}
```

> **NOTE** *Notice that the* PropertyChangeListener *is attached to the* Action, *and not to the* JButton.

Class KeyStroke

The KeyStroke class and the public void registerKeyboardAction(ActionListener actionListener, KeyStroke keyStroke, int condition) method of JComponent provide a simple replacement for registering KeyListener objects to components and watching for specific keys to be pressed. The KeyStroke class allows you to define a single combination of key strokes, such as SHIFT-CTRL-P or F4. You can then activate the keystroke by registering it with a component and telling the keystroke what to do when the component recognizes it, causing the ActionListener to be notified.

Before finding out how to create keystrokes, let's look at the different conditions that can be activated. Three conditions can activate a registered keystroke, and there are four constants in JComponent to help. The fourth is for an undefined state. If you want the keystroke to activate when the actual component has the input focus, you would use the JComponent.WHEN_FOCUSED constant. If you want the keystroke to activate when the *window* that the component is in has the input focus, you would use JComponent.WHEN_IN_FOCUSED_WINDOW. The remaining constant, JComponent.WHEN_ANCESTOR_OF_FOCUSED_COMPONENT, is used when the keystroke is pressed in the component or a container of the component. The four available constants are listed in Table 2-3.

CONSTANTS

WHEN_FOCUSED
WHEN_IN_FOCUSED_WINDOW
WHEN_ANCESTOR_OF_FOCUSED_COMPONENT
UNDEFINED_CONDITION

Table 2-3: Keystroke registration conditions

Creating a KeyStroke

The KeyStroke class has no public constructor. You create a keystroke by using one of the static getKeyStroke() methods plus the one getKeyStrokeForEvent() method, which follow:

```
public static KeyStroke getKeyStroke(char keyChar)
public static KeyStroke getKeyStroke(String representation)
public static KeyStroke getKeyStroke(int keyCode, int modifiers)
public static KeyStroke getKeyStroke(int keyCode, int modifiers, boolean
onKeyRelease)
public static KeyStroke getKeyStrokeForEvent(KeyEvent keyEvent)
```

The first version in this list, `public static KeyStroke getKeyStroke(char keyChar)`, allows you to create a keystroke from a char variable, such as 'Z'.

```
KeyStroke space = KeyStroke.getKeyStroke('Z');
```

> **NOTE** *I prefer to avoid the first method because as you don't know whether to specify an uppercase or lowercase letter. There is also an outdated, or deprecated, version of this constructor that adds a* boolean onKeyRelease *argument. This, too, should be avoided.*

The `public static KeyStroke getKeyStroke(String representation)` version is the most interesting of the lot. It allows you to specify a keystroke as a text string, such as "control F4". The set of modifiers to the string are "shift | control | meta | alt | button1 | button2 | button3", and multiple modifiers can be specified. The remainder of the string comes from one of the many `VK_*` constants of the `KeyEvent` class.

```
KeyStroke controlAlt7 = KeyStroke.getKeyStroke("control alt 7");
```

> **NOTE** *The method I just listed didn't work prior to Swing 1.1.1.*

The `public static KeyStroke getKeyStroke(int keyCode, int modifiers)` and `public static KeyStroke getKeyStroke(int keyCode, int modifiers, boolean onKeyRelease)` methods are the most clear-cut. They allow you to directly specify the `VK_*` key constant and the `InputEvent` masks for the modifiers (or zero for no modifiers). When not specified, `onKeyRelease` is `false`.

```
KeyStroke enter = KeyStroke.getKeyStroke(KeyEvent.VK_ENTER, 0, true);
KeyStroke shiftF4 = KeyStroke.getKeyStroke(KeyEvent.VK_F4,
InputEvent.SHIFT_MASK);
```

The last version listed, `public static KeyStroke getKeyStrokeForEvent(KeyEvent keyEvent)`, maps a specific `KeyEvent` directly to a `KeyStroke`. This is useful when you want to allow a user to supply the keystroke to activate an event. You ask the user to press a key for the event and then register the `KeyEvent` so that the next time it happens the event is activated.

```
KeyStroke fromKeyEvent = KeyStroke.getKeyStrokeForEvent(keyEvent);
```

Registering a KeyStroke

After you've created the keystroke, you need to register it with a component. When you register a keystroke with a component, you provide an `ActionListener` to call when pressed. The following example creates four buttons, each with a different keystroke registered to it and a possibly different focus activation condition, as listed in Table 2-3. The button label signifies the keystroke activation conditions. The `ActionListener` simply prints out a message.

```
import javax.swing.*;
import java.awt.*;
```

```java
import java.awt.event.*;

public class KeyStrokeSample {
  public static void main(String args[]) {
    JFrame frame = new ExitableJFrame("KeyStroke Sample");
    JButton buttonA = new JButton("<html><center>FOCUSED<br>control alt 7");
    JButton buttonB = new JButton("<html><center>FOCUS/RELEASE<br>VK_ENTER");
    JButton buttonC = new JButton("<html><center>ANCESTOR<br>VK_F4+SHIFT_MASK");
    JButton buttonD = new JButton("<html><center>WINDOW<br>' '");

    // Define ActionListener
    ActionListener actionListener = new ActionListener() {
      public void actionPerformed(ActionEvent actionEvent) {
        System.out.println("Activated");
      }
    };

    KeyStroke controlAlt7 = KeyStroke.getKeyStroke("control alt 7");
    buttonA.registerKeyboardAction(actionListener, controlAlt7,
JComponent.WHEN_FOCUSED);

    KeyStroke enter = KeyStroke.getKeyStroke(KeyEvent.VK_ENTER, 0, true);
    buttonB.registerKeyboardAction(actionListener, enter,
JComponent.WHEN_FOCUSED);

    KeyStroke shiftF4 = KeyStroke.getKeyStroke(KeyEvent.VK_F4,
InputEvent.SHIFT_MASK);
    buttonC.registerKeyboardAction(actionListener, shiftF4,
JComponent.WHEN_ANCESTOR_OF_FOCUSED_COMPONENT);

    KeyStroke space = KeyStroke.getKeyStroke(' ');
    buttonD.registerKeyboardAction(actionListener, space,
JComponent.WHEN_IN_FOCUSED_WINDOW);

    Container contentPane = frame.getContentPane();
    contentPane.setLayout(new GridLayout(2,2));
    contentPane.add(buttonA);
    contentPane.add(buttonB);
    contentPane.add(buttonC);
    contentPane.add(buttonD);
    frame.setSize(400, 200);
    frame.setVisible(true);
  }
}
```

> **NOTE** *If you try to run the previous program with JFC/Swing release 1.1, a* `NullPointerException` *will be generated.*

Using Mnemonics and Accelerators

Besides your creating `KeyStroke` objects yourself, the Swing libraries use `KeyStroke` objects for several internal functions. Two such instances of this are component mnemonics and accelerators. In a component mnemonic, one character in a label appears underlined. When that character is pressed using a platform-specific hot-key combination, the component is activated. For instance, pressing ALT-A in Figure 2-9 would select the About button on a Windows 98 platform.

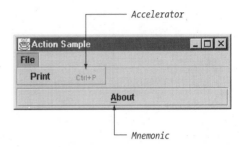

Menu accelerators activate menu items when they're not visible. For instance, pressing CTRL-P would select the Print menu item in Figure 2-9 when the File menu isn't visible. You'll learn more about mnemonics and accelerators in later chapters of this book.

Figure 2-9: Mnemonics and menu shortcuts

Swing Focus Management

The term *focus* refers to when a component acquires the *input focus*. When a component has the input focus, it serves as the source for all key events, such as text input. In addition, certain components have some visual markings to indicate that they have the input focus, as shown in Figure 2-10. When certain components have the input focus, you can trigger selection with a keyboard key (usually the spacebar or ENTER key), in addition to selection with a mouse. For instance, with a button, pressing the spacebar activates it.

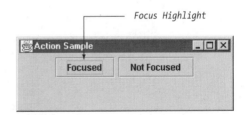

Figure 2-10: A `JButton` showing it has input focus

You can find out when the Swing component gets the input focus by registering a `FocusListener`, just as you'd do with all AWT 1.1 components. Although this doesn't change when you move from the AWT component set to the Swing component set, what does differ is the set of methods used programatically to move the focus around.

With AWT components, you can explicitly set the focus to a component with the `public void requestFocus()` method. In addition, you can transfer focus to the next component with the `public void transferFocus()` method. In the AWT world, the next component is defined by the order in which components are added to a container, as shown in Figure 2-11. By default, this focus traversal starts at the top left of the figure and goes across each row and down to the bottom right. When all the components are in the same container, this traversal order is called a *focus cycle* and can be limited to remain within the container.

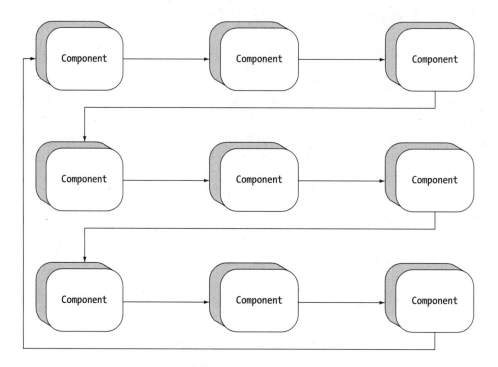

Figure 2-11: Default focus ordering

> **NOTE** *Besides your programmatically using* transferFocus() *to move the input focus, a user can press T*AB *or S*HIFT-T*AB to move forward or backward around the components in a container.*

To demonstrate the use of the two methods I mentioned earlier in this section, we'll create a MouseListener that moves the input focus to a component when the mouse enters its space and an ActionListener that transfers the input focus to the next component. The MouseListener merely needs to call requestFocus() when the mouse enters the component.

```java
import java.awt.*;
import java.awt.event.*;
public class MouseEnterFocusMover extends MouseAdapter {
  public void mouseEntered(MouseEvent mouseEvent) {
    Component component = mouseEvent.getComponent();
    if (!component.hasFocus()) {
      component.requestFocus();
    }
  }
}
```

For the `ActionListener`, you need to call the `transferFocus()` method for the event source.

```java
import java.awt.*;
import java.awt.event.*;
public class ActionFocusMover implements ActionListener {
  public void actionPerformed(ActionEvent actionEvent) {
    Object source = actionEvent.getSource();
    if (source instanceof Component) {
      Component component = (Component)source;
      component.transferFocus();
    }
  }
}
```

Because Swing components are built *on top of* AWT, these event handlers would work for Swing components, too. However, there's one difference with `requestFocus()` in Swing components: It can be turned off. Swing's `JComponent` has a `public void setRequestFocusEnabled(boolean newValue)` method that allows you to give components the power to accept focus requests. This differs from the read-only `focusTraversable` property of `Component`, which removes a component from the TAB focus cycle. When you set the `requestFocusEnabled` property to `false` for a Swing component and someone then calls `requestFocus()` on the component, it won't accept the input focus. If you really want a component to get the input focus, Swing provides a `grabFocus()` method that can't be disabled.

We'll now use the two event handlers with some components that deny requesting a focus. For example, we'll create a 3-by-3 grid of buttons in which each button has an attached mouse listener and a focus listener. The even-numbered components permit requesting focus, whereas the odd-numbered ones don't. Because the odd buttons don't permit requesting focus, pressing an even button doesn't move the focus to the next component, nor does moving the mouse over an odd button. The only way an odd button can get the input focus is if the user presses the TAB/SHIFT-TAB keys as part of the focus cycle. Figure 2-12 shows the main window of the program.

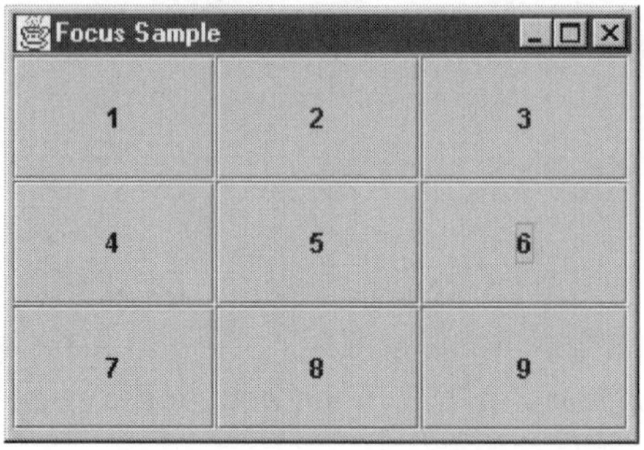

Figure 2-12: Focus management example

The source code follows:

```
import javax.swing.*;
import java.awt.*;
import java.awt.event.*;

public class FocusSample {
  public static void main(String args[]) {
    JFrame frame = new ExitableJFrame("Focus Sample");

    ActionListener actionListener = new ActionFocusMover();
    MouseListener  mouseListener  = new MouseEnterFocusMover();

    Container contentPane = frame.getContentPane();
    contentPane.setLayout(new GridLayout(3,3));
    for (int i=1; i<10; i++) {
      JButton button = new JButton("" + i);
      button.addActionListener(actionListener);
      button.addMouseListener(mouseListener);
      if ((i%2) != 0) { // odd - enabled by default
        button.setRequestFocusEnabled(false);
      }
      contentPane.add(button);
    }

    frame.setSize(300, 200);
```

```
    frame.setVisible(true);
  }
}
```

In addition to the requestFocusEnabled property of JComponent and focusTraversable property of Component that were just discussed, three additional focus-oriented properties of the JComponent class exist. All five are listed in Table 2-4. A description on the usage of each property is included in the following sections of this chapter.

PROPERTY	DESCRIPTION	DATATYPE	ACCESS
focusCycleRoot	By default false for a Swing component; when true, the input focus cycle stays within the container.	boolean	read-only
focusTraversable	Default value is component specific; when false, the component isn't focus traversable. Comes from Component.	boolean	read-only
managingFocus	By default false; when true, allows Swing components to monitor keyboard input for focus-oriented keystrokes.	boolean	read-only
nextFocusableComponent	By default null, honoring natural focus cycle. When set, allows you to explicitly set the next component to receive the input focus.	component	read-write
requestFocusEnabled	By default true; when false, doesn't honor requestFocus() calls to programmatically change input focus.	boolean	read-write

Table 2-4: JComponent focus-oriented properties

> **NOTE** *To change any of the read-only properties in Table 2-4, you must subclass the specific component you want to customize.*

Examining Focus Cycles

One customization option available at the Swing container level is the focus cycle. Remember that the focus cycle for a container is a map of the focus traversal order for the closed set of components. You can limit the focus cycle to stay within the bounds of a container by overriding the `public boolean isFocusCycleRoot()` method to return `true`, thus restricting the focus traversal from going beyond an inner container. Then, when a TAB key is pressed within the last component of the container, the focus cycle will wrap back to the first component in the container, instead of moving the input focus to the first component outside the container. When SHIFT-TAB is pressed in the first component, it wraps to the last component of the container, instead of to the prior component in the outer container. Figure 2-13 illustrates how it would look if you placed the middle three buttons from Figure 2-11 within a container restricted in this way. Notice that there is no way of getting to the first component on the third row by just pressing the TAB key to move forward.

> **WARNING** *There seems to be a bug in the Swing 1.1 release with SHIFT-TAB in a focus-cycle–constrained container. Sometimes, it lets you out of the inner container.*

Instead of having to recreate a focus-cycle–restricted container every time you need one, the following class definition is one you can keep handy for that use. Feel free to shorten the name.

```java
import javax.swing.*;
public class FocusCycleConstrainedJPanel extends JPanel {
  public boolean isFocusCycleRoot() {
    return true;
  }
}
```

Using the new `FocusCycleConstrainedJPanel` class, the following program demonstrates the behavior illustrated in Figure 2-13. The on-screen program will look just like Figure 2-12; it just behaves differently.

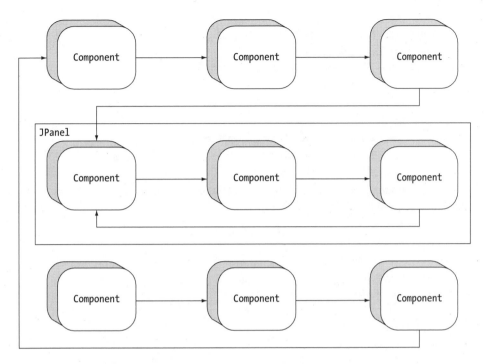

Figure 2-13: Restrictive focus cycle

```
import javax.swing.*;
import java.awt.*;
import java.awt.event.*;

public class FocusCycleSample {
  public static void main(String args[]) {
    JFrame frame = new ExitableJFrame("Focus Cycle Sample");

    Container contentPane = frame.getContentPane();
    contentPane.setLayout(new GridBagLayout());
    GridBagConstraints constraints = new GridBagConstraints();
    constraints.weightx    = 1.0;
    constraints.weighty    = 1.0;
    constraints.gridwidth  = 1;
    constraints.gridheight = 1;
    constraints.fill       = GridBagConstraints.BOTH;

    // Row One
    constraints.gridy=0;
    for (int i=0; i<3; i++) {
```

```
        JButton button = new JButton("" + i);
        constraints.gridx=i;
        contentPane.add(button, constraints);
    }

    // Row Two
    JPanel panel = new FocusCycleConstrainedJPanel();
    panel.setLayout(new GridLayout(1,3));
    for (int i=0; i<3; i++) {
      JButton button = new JButton("" + (i+3));
      panel.add(button);
    }
    constraints.gridx=0;
    constraints.gridy=1;
    constraints.gridwidth=3;
    contentPane.add(panel, constraints);

    // Row Three
    constraints.gridy=2;
    constraints.gridwidth=1;
    for (int i=0; i<3; i++) {
      JButton button = new JButton("" + (i+6));
      constraints.gridx=i;
      contentPane.add(button, constraints);
    }

    frame.setSize(300, 200);
    frame.setVisible(true);
  }
}
```

Customizing Component-Level Focus Management

One other thing you can do at the component level is to subclass a Swing component and override the `public boolean isManagingFocus()` method to return true. This allows you to manage focus traversal yourself by listening for TAB key presses in a `KeyListener`. Then when the TAB key is pressed, you can `consume()` the `KeyEvent` if you don't want the input focus to move on, for example, because of an invalid data state. When consumed, the `FocusManager` would check the consumption status of the `KeyEvent` and not transfer the input focus if already consumed. The `FocusManager` class is described later in this chapter.

> **TIP** *Because the* managingFocus *property of* JComponent *is read-only, you must subclass a Swing component to internally manage focus.*

The following source demonstrates how you would abort the transferal of the input focus in the keyPressed() method of a KeyEvent.

```
public void keyPressed(KeyEvent keyEvent) {
  if ((keyEvent.getKeyCode == KeyEvent.VK_TAB) || (keyEvent.getKeyChar() ==
'\t')) {
    if (!(data is valid)) { // Define validation condition here
      keyEvent.consume();
    }
  }
}
```

Setting the Next Focusable Component

The JComponent class allows you to programmatically reorder the forward focus-traversal order by setting the nextFocusableComponent property. Any AWT component — and not just Swing components — can be the next focusable component. When this property is set for a component, it defines where the input focus moves when the TAB key is pressed. No way exists to explicitly set the response for SHIFT-TAB. The response is determined by the system's finding the *first* component that has the current component as its *next* component.

To demonstrate, the following program reverses the functionality of TAB and SHIFT-TAB. The screen for the program is shown in Figure 2-12, with the 3-by-3 set of buttons.

```
import javax.swing.*;
import java.awt.*;
import java.awt.event.*;

public class NextComponentSample {
  public static void main(String args[]) {
    JFrame frame = new ExitableJFrame("Next Component Sample");

    Container contentPane = frame.getContentPane();
    contentPane.setLayout(new GridLayout(3,3));

    int COUNT = 9;
    JButton components[] = new JButton[COUNT];
```

```
    for (int i=0; i<COUNT; i++) {
      JButton button = new JButton("" + (i+1));
      components[i] = button;
      contentPane.add(button);
    }

    // Reverse tab order
    for (int i=0; i<COUNT; i++) {
      System.out.println(components[i].getText() + ":" + components[(i+COUNT-1) %
COUNT].getText());
      components[i].setNextFocusableComponent(components[(i+COUNT-1) % COUNT]);
    }

    frame.setSize(300, 200);
    frame.setVisible(true);
  }
}
```

Class FocusManager and DefaultFocusManager

The abstract FocusManager class in the Swing library serves as the control mechanism framework for input focus behavior of Swing components. The Swing FocusManager is the basic control mechanism, but because Swing components live within the AWT world, the AWT focus manager has overall control. The abstract class defines a series of static methods and three abstract methods for the concrete focus manager to implement.

```
public abstract class FocusManager {
  // Constructors
  public FocusManager();
  // Constants
  public final static String FOCUS_MANAGER_CLASS_PROPERTY;
  // Class Methods
  public static void disableSwingFocusManager();
  public static FocusManager getCurrentManager();
  public static boolean isFocusManagerEnabled();
  public static void setCurrentManager(FocusManager focusManager);
  // Other Methods
  public abstract void focusNextComponent(Component component);
  public abstract void focusPreviousComponent(Component component);
  public abstract void processKeyEvent(Component focusedComponent, KeyEvent
keyEvent);
}
```

NOTE   *Although the class definition may imply that at most one FocusManager is working at a time, in reality each ThreadGroup manages its own FocusManager.*

You can disable the Swing focus manager for an application by calling the public static void disableSwingFocusManager() method of FocusManager. This gives the AWT focus manager complete control. To enable it again, call the public static void setCurrentManager(FocusManager newValue) method with a new manager as the argument. To get the default manager for the look and feel, ask the UIManager the following:

```
FocusManager focusManager = (FocusManager)UIManager.get(FocusManager.FOCUS_MAN-
AGER_CLASS_PROPERTY)
```

NOTE   *It is necessary to disable the focus manager when mixing Swing and AWT components within the same window.*

The FocusManager doesn't remember what has the input focus when it's asked to find the next component to get the input focus. When asked to adjust the input focus, all three of the abstract methods take the last component, with the input focus as an argument.

The default implementation of the FocusManager interface is the DefaultFocusManager class, which provides the predefined behavior for the five properties listed back in Table 2-4.

```
public class DefaultFocusManager extends FocusManager {
  // Constructors
  public DefaultFocusManager();
  // Other Methods
  public boolean compareTabOrder(Component a, Component b);
  public Component getComponentAfter(Container aContainer, Component component);
  public Component getComponentBefore(Container aContainer, Component component);
  public Component getFirstComponent(Container container);
  public Component getLastComponent(Container container);
  public void focusNextComponent(Component component);
  public void focusPreviousComponent(Component component);
  public void processKeyEvent(Component focusedComponent, KeyEvent keyEvent);
}
```

TIP *If you don't like the default left-to-right, top-to-bottom tab ordering, simply subclass DefaultFocusManager and override compareTabOrder().*

Writing Your Own Focus Manager

Although the behavior of the DefaultFocusManager might suffice for most needs, it won't for all. There might come a time when you need to customize the focus behavior. Before wandering down this path, be sure the behavior you desire can't first be accomplished by using the properties listed in Table 2-4.

After you define your custom focus manager, you need to install it. Once installed, it takes over the duties originally performed by the DefaultFocusManager.

```
FocusManager focusManager = new MyFocusManager();
FocusManager.setCurrentManager(focusManager);
```

Multithreaded Swing Event Handling

To increase their efficiency and decrease the complexity, all Swing components were designed *not* to be thread-safe. Although this might sound scary, it simply means that all access to displayed, or *realized*, Swing components needs to be done from a single thread — the event-dispatch thread. If you are unsure that you're in a particular thread, you can ask SwingUtilities with its public static boolean isEventDispatchThread() method.

Whenever you need to get or set a property value of a Swing component, it must be done from the event-dispatch thread. Again, not to worry; it isn't that difficult a task. Once you've created a program's screen — probably in an init() method of an applet or a main() method of an application — you show it. The components on the screen are then responsive to user input. When a component is activated, the component might look at another component for its state and pass the state data along to something else. All this happens in the event-dispatch thread by default while the event handler for the activated component executes in the event-dispatch thread. Even the paint() method executes in the event-dispatch thread in response to paint events (java.awt.PaintEvent).

NOTE *The addition and removal of event listeners can be done from any thread.*

If an event-handling task is going to take too much time, the handler needs to get the appropriate information from the Swing components first, then create another Thread to do the task. If a secondary thread isn't created, the user interface becomes nonresponsive.

If a nonevent-handling task needs to access a Swing component, it must create a task to be run on the event-dispatch thread and then process the results when done.

Using SwingUtilities for Thread Safety

The Swing libraries provide two ways of creating tasks to be run on the event-dispatch thread. If you need to execute a task on the event-dispatch thread, but you don't need any results and don't care exactly when the task finishes, you can use the public static void invokeLater(Runnable runnable) method of SwingUtilities. If, on the other hand, you can't continue with what you're doing until the task completes and returns you a value, you can use the public static void invokeAndWait(Runnable runnable) method of SwingUtilities. The code to get the value is left up to *you* and not the return value to the invokeAndWait() method.

> **WARNING** *The invokeAndWait(Runnable) method can throw an InterrutpedException or an InvocationTargetException.*

To demonstrate, let's first look at invokeLater(). The method requires a Runnable object as its argument, so you only need to create a Runnable object and pass it along to the invokeLater() method. Some time after the current event dispatching is done, this runnable object will execute.

```
Runnable runnable = new Runnable() {
  public void run() {
    // do work to be done
  }
}
SwingUtilities.invokeLater(runnable);
```

Similarly, the invokeAndWait() method also accepts a Runnable object. However, the line after the call to invokeAndWait() isn't executed until the Runnable object finishes.

```
try {
  Runnable runnable = new Runnable() {
    public void run() {
```

```
      // do work to be done
      // save/return results
    }
  }
  SwingUtilities.invokeAndWait(runnable);
} catch (InterruptedException interruptedException) {
  // Do something special
} catch (InvocationTargetException invocationTargetException) {
  // Do something special
}
```

Here are some tips about using the two methods I just described and Swing component thread safety:

- Both invokeLater() and invokeAndWait() wait until all pending AWT events finish before they execute.

- Don't call invokeAndWait() from the event-dispatch thread within an AWT event handler, because the event processing will never finish in order for invokeAndWait() to execute.

- When using invokeAndWait(), be sure the object being blocked doesn't retain any system locks, otherwise the method may never return because of a deadlock situation.

- Calls to repaint(), revalidate(), and invalidate() don't have to be done from the event-dispatch thread.

> **NOTE** *In the Java 2 SDK, AWT's EventQueue class has its own pair of invokeAndWait() and invokeLater() methods. They function in the same way as the SwingUtilities methods; however, their usage should be limited to interactions with AWT components.*

Class Timer

In addition to the invokeAndWait() and invokeLater() methods of SwingUtilities, you can use the Timer class to create actions to be executed on the event-dispatch thread. A Timer provides a way of notifying an ActionListener after a predefined number of milliseconds. The timer can repeatedly notify the listeners, or just call them once.

Creating Timer Objects

Following is the single constructor for creating a Timer that specifies the millisecond delay time between calls to the ActionListener:

```
public Timer(int delay, ActionListener actionListener);
// 1 second interval
Timer timer = new Timer(1000, anActionListener);
```

Using Timer Objects

After a Timer object has been created, you need to start() it. Once the Timer is started, the ActionListener will be notified after the given number of milliseconds. If the system is busy, the delay could be longer but it won't be shorter.

If there comes a time when you want to stop a Timer, call its stop() method. The Timer also has a restart() method, which calls stop() and start(), restarting the delay period.

To demonstrate, the following defines an ActionListener that simply prints a message. You then create Timer to call this listener every half-second. After creating the timer, you need to start it.

```
import javax.swing.*;
import java.awt.event.*;

public class TimerSample {
  public static void main(String args[]) {
    new ExitableJFrame().setVisible(true); // To create dummy screen
    ActionListener actionListener = new ActionListener() {
      public void actionPerformed(ActionEvent actionEvent) {
        System.out.println("Hello World Timer");
      }
    };
    Timer timer = new Timer(500, actionListener);
    timer.start();
  }
}
```

TIP *A Timer doesn't start up the AWT event-dispatch thread. If the event-dispatch thread isn't running, your program might end relatively quickly. That's why the previous program creates and displays a dummy frame.*

Timer Properties

Table 2-5 lists the five properties of Timer. Four allow you to customize the behavior of the timer, and the fifth (running) tells you if a timer has been started but not stopped. The delay property is the same as the constructor argument. If you change the delay of a running timer, the new delay won't be used until the existing delay runs out.

The initialDelay property allows you to have another startup delay besides the periodic delay after the first execution. For instance, if you don't want to do a task for an hour, but then want to do it every 15 minutes thereafter, you need to change the initialDelay setting before you start the timer. By default, the initialDelay and delay properties are set to the same setting in the constructor.

The repeats property is true by default, which results in a repeating timer. When false, the timer notifies action listeners only once. You then need to restart() the timer to trigger the listener again. Nonrepeating timers are good for one-time notifications that need to happen after a triggering event.

The coalesce property allows for a busy system to throw away notifications that haven't happened yet when a new event needs to be fired to the registered ActionListener objects. By default, the coalesce value is true. This means if a timer runs every 500 milliseconds, but its system is bogged down and doesn't respond for a whole 2 seconds, the timer only needs to send one message without all the missing ones, too. If the setting were false, four messages would still need to be sent.

PROPERTY NAME	DATA TYPE	ACCESS
coalesce	boolean	read-write
delay	int	read-write
initialDelay	int	read-write
repeats	boolean	read-write
running	boolean	read-only

Table 2-5: Timer properties

In addition to the properties just listed, you can turn on log messages with the following line of source. Log messages are good for actions that lack a visual element, allowing you to see when something happens.

```
Timer.setLogTimers(true);
```

Summary

In this chapter, we looked at the many ways of dealing with event handling when using Swing components. Because the components are built *on top of* AWT components, you can continue to use the delegation-based event mechanism first introduced into the Java class libraries with JDK 1.1. We also explored how the Swing components use the JavaBeans `PropertyChangeListener` approach for notification of bound property changes. With the description of some enhancements, such as simplified mouse button identification, we learned how the transition to the Swing component set from the AWT component set can be relatively painless.

Besides exploring the similarities between the Swing components and AWT components, we also looked at several of the new features the Swing library offers. We explored the `Action` interface and how it can simplify complex user-interface development by completely separating the event-handling task from the visual component. We looked at the technique for registering `KeyStroke` objects to components to simplify listening for key events. We explored Swing's focus management capabilities and how to customize the focus cycle with and without the `FocusManager`. Lastly, we looked at the multithreading limitations of the Swing components and how to get around them with the `invokeAndWait()` and `invokeLater()` methods of `SwingUtilities`.

In Chapter 3, we'll cover the Model-View-Controller (MVC) architecture of the Swing component set. You'll learn how MVC can make your user interface development efforts much easier to maintain.

CHAPTER 3

The Model-View-Controller Architecture

CHAPTER 2 EXPLORED HOW TO deal with event producers and consumers with regard to Swing components. We looked at how event handling with Swing components goes beyond the event-handling capabilities of the original AWT components. Now, in this chapter, I take the Swing component design one step further to examine the model-view-controller (MVC) architecture.

The MVC architecture was first introduced in Smalltalk in the late 1980s. The MVC is a special form of the Observer pattern described in Chapter 2. The model part of the MVC holds the state of a component and serves as the Subject. The view part of the MVC serves as the Observer of the Subject to display the model's state. The view creates the controller, which defines how the user interface reacts to user input.

MVC Communications

Figure 3-1 shows how the MVC elements communicate—in this case, with Swing's multi-line text component, the JTextArea. In MVC terms, the JTextArea

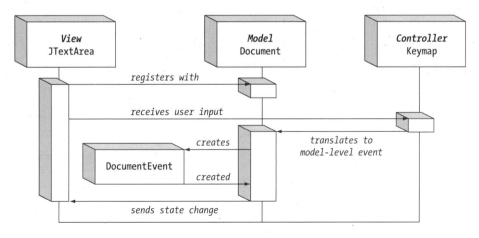

Figure 3-1: MVC communication mechanism

serves as the view part within the MVC architecture. Displayed within the component is a Document, which is the model for the JTextArea. The Document stores the state information for the JTextArea, such as the text contents. Within the JTextArea is the controller, in the form of a Keymap. It maps keyboard input to TextAction objects, which can modify the Document. When the modification happens, the Document creates a DocumentEvent and sends it back to the JTextArea.

This example demonstrates an important aspect of the MVC architecture within the Swing world. Complex interactions need to happen between the view and the controller. The Swing design combines these two elements into a *delegate* object to simplify the overall design. This results in each Swing component having

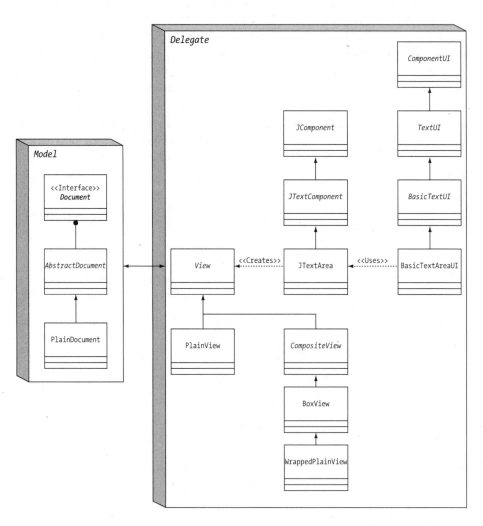

Figure 3-2: The JTextArea MVC architecture

a UI delegate that's in charge of rendering the current state of the component and dealing with user input events. Sometimes, the user events result in changes to the view that don't affect the model. For instance, the cursor position is an attribute of the view. The model doesn't care about the position of the cursor, only the text contents. User input that affects the cursor position isn't passed along to the model. At other times, user input that affects the contents of the Document (for example, pressing the BACKSPACE key) *is* passed along. Pressing the BACKSPACE key results in a character being removed from the model. Because of this tight coupling, each Swing component has a UI delegate.

To demonstrate, Figure 3-2 shows the makeup of the JTextArea, with respect to the model and UI delegate. The UI delegate for the JTextArea starts with the TextUI interface, with its basic implementation in the BasicTextUI class. In turn, this is specialized with the BasicTextAreaUI for the JTextArea. The BasicTextAreaUI in turn creates a View that's either a PlainView or a WrappedPlainView. On the model side, things are much simpler. The Document interface is implemented by the AbstractDocument class, which is further specialized by the PlainDocument.

> **NOTE** *The text components will be explained more fully in Chapters 14 and 15. As the diagram in Figure 3-2 demonstrates, much is involved in working with the text components. In most cases, you don't need to deal with the specifics to the degree shown in this figure. However, all of these classes are working behind the scenes.*

Sharing Data Models

Because data models store only the state information, you can share a model across multiple components. Then, each component view can be used to modify the model. In the case of Figure 3-3, three different text area components are used to modify one document model. If a user modifies the contents of one text area, the model is changed, causing the other text areas to automatically reflect the updated document state. It isn't necessary for any document view to manually notify others sharing the model.

Sharing of a data model can be done in either one of two ways. You can create the data model apart from any component and tell each component to use the data model, or you can create one component first, get the model from the first component, and then share it with the other components. The following program demonstrates how to do the latter.

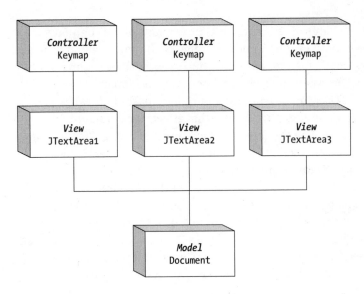

Figure 3-3: Sharing MVC data models

```java
import java.awt.*;
import javax.swing.*;
import javax.swing.text.*;

public class ShareModel {
  public static void main (String args[]) {
    JFrame f = new ExitableJFrame("Sharing Sample");
    Container content = f.getContentPane();
    JTextArea textarea1 = new JTextArea();
    Document document = textarea1.getDocument();
    JTextArea textarea2 = new JTextArea(document);
    JTextArea textarea3 = new JTextArea(document);
    content.setLayout(new BoxLayout(content, BoxLayout.Y_AXIS));
    content.add(new JScrollPane(textarea1));
    content.add(new JScrollPane(textarea2));
    content.add(new JScrollPane(textarea3));
    f.setSize (300, 400);
    f.setVisible (true);
  }
}
```

Figure 3-4 shows how this program might look after editing the shared document. Notice that the three text areas are capable of viewing (or modifying) different areas of the document. They aren't limited to an add only at the end, for instance.

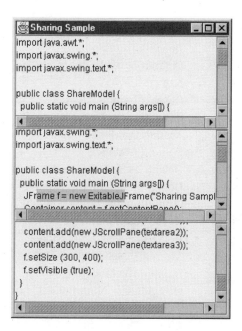

```
Sharing Sample                    _ □ ✕
import java.awt.*;
import javax.swing.*;
import javax.swing.text.*;

public class ShareModel {
  public static void main (String args[]) {
◀                                        ▶
import javax.swing.*;
import javax.swing.text.*;

public class ShareModel {
  public static void main (String args[]) {
    JFrame f = new ExitableJFrame("Sharing Sampl
    Container content = f.getContentPane();
◀                                        ▶
    content.add(new JScrollPane(textarea2));
    content.add(new JScrollPane(textarea3));
    f.setSize (300, 400);
    f.setVisible (true);
  }
}
◀                                        ▶
```

Figure 3-4: Sharing a Document between JTextArea components

Understanding the Predefined Data Models

When working with Swing components it's helpful to understand the data models behind each of them because the data models store the state of the components. Understanding the data model for each component helps you to separate the parts of the component that are *visual* (and thus part of the view) from those that are *logical* (and thus part of the data model). For example, by understanding this separation, you can see why the cursor position within a JTextArea isn't part of the data model, but rather is part of the view.

Table 3-1 provides a complete listing of the Swing components, the interface that describes the data model for each component, as well as the specific implementations. If a component isn't listed, that component inherits its data model from its parent class, most likely AbstractButton. In addition, in some cases, multiple interfaces are used to describe a component, because the data is stored in one model and the selection of the data in a second model. In the case of the JComboBox, the MutableComboBoxModel interface extends from ComboBoxModel. No predefined class implements the ComboBoxModel interface without also implementing the MutableComboBoxModel interface.

COMPONENT	DATA MODEL INTERFACE	IMPLEMENTATIONS
AbstractButton	ButtonModel	DefaultButtonModel
JColorChooser	ColorSelectionModel	DefaultColorSelectionModel
JComboBox	ComboBoxModel	N/A
	MutableComboBoxModel	DefaultComboBoxModel
JFileChooser	ListModel	BasicDirectoryModel
JList	ListModel	AbstractListModel
		DefaultListModel
	ListSelectionModel	DefaultListSelectionModel
JProgressBar	BoundedRangeModel	DefaultBoundedRangeModel
JScrollBar	BoundedRangeModel	DefaultBoundedRangeModel
JSlider	BoundedRangeModel	DefaultBoundedRangeModel
JTabbedPane	SingleSelectionModel	DefaultSingleSelectionModel
JTable	TableModel	AbstractTableModel
		DefaultTableModel
	TableColumnModel	DefaultTableColumnModel
	ListSelectionModel	DefaultListSelectionModel
JTextComponent	Document	AbstractDocument
		PlainDocument
		StyledDocument
		DefaultStyleDocument
		HTMLDocument
JToggleButton	ButtonModel	JToggleButton. ToggleButtonModel
JTree	TreeModel	DefaultTreeModel
	TreeSelectionModel	DefaultTreeSelectionModel, JTree.EmptySelectionModel

Table 3-1: Swing component models

When directly accessing the model of a Swing component, if you change the model, all registered views are automatically notified. This in turn causes the views to revalidate themselves to ensure that the components display their proper current states. This automatic propagation of state changes is one reason why MVC is becoming so popular. In addition, using the MVC architecture helps programs become more maintainable as they change over time and their complexity grows. No longer will you need to worry about losing state information if you change visual component libraries!

NOTE *The UI-delegate part of the MVC architecture will be discussed further in Chapter 18 where we explore how to customize delegates.*

Summary

In this chapter, we took a look at how the Swing components use a modified MVC architecture. We explored what makes up this modified architecture and how one particular component, the JTextArea, maps into this architecture. In addition, I discussed the sharing of data models between components, and listed all the data models for the different Swing components.

In Chapter 4, we start to look at the individual components that make up the Swing component library. In addition, we'll explore the Swing component class hierarchy as we examine the JComponent base component from the Swing component library.

CHAPTER 4

Core Swing Components

IN CHAPTER 3, WE EXPLORED THE Model-View-Controller pattern used by the components of the JFC/Swing project. In this chapter, we'll begin to explore how to use the key parts of the many available components.

All Swing components start with the JComponent class. Although some parts of the Swing libraries aren't rooted with the JComponent class, all the components share JComponent as the common parent class at some level of their ancestry. It's with this JComponent class that common behavior and properties are defined. In this chapter, we look at common functionality such as component painting, customization, tooltips, and sizing.

As far as specific JComponent descendent classes are concerned, we'll look at the JLabel, JButton, and JPanel, three of the more commonly used Swing component classes. They require understanding of the Icon interface for displaying images within components, as well as of the ImageIcon class for when using predefined images and GrayFilter class for support. In addition, we'll look at the AbstractButton class, which serves as the parent class to the JButton. The data model shared by all AbstractButton subclasses is the ButtonModel interface; we'll look at that and the specific implementation class, the DefaultButtonModel.

Class JComponent

The JComponent class serves as the abstract root class from which all Swing components descend. The JComponent class has 39 descendent subclasses, each of which inherits much of the JComponent functionality. Figure 4-1 shows this hierarchy.

Although the JComponent class serves as the common root class for all Swing components, many classes in the libraries for the Swing project descend from JComponent. Those include all the high-level container objects such as

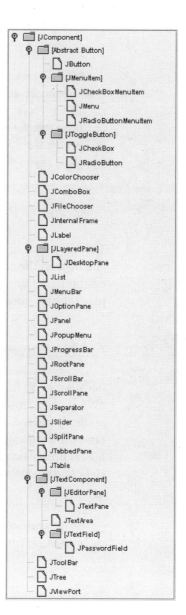

Figure 4-1: JComponent class hierarchy diagram

JFrame, JApplet, and JInternalFrame, as well as Box, all the Model-View-Controller (MVC)-related classes, event-handling–related interfaces and classes, and much more. All of these will be discussed in later chapters.

Although all Swing components extend JComponent, the JComponent class extends the AWT Container class, which in turn extends from the AWT Component class. This means that many aspects of the JComponent are shared with both the AWT Component and Container classes.

> **NOTE** *JComponent extends from the Container class, but most of the JComponent subclasses aren't themselves containers of other components. To see if a particular Swing component is truly a container, check the bean info for the class to see if the isContainer property is set to true. To get the BeanInfo for a class, ask the Introspector.*

Component Pieces

The JComponent class defines many aspects of AWT components that go above and beyond the capabilities of the original AWT component set. This includes customized painting behavior and the several different ways to customize display settings, such as colors, fonts, and any other client-side settings.

Painting JComponent Objects

Because the Swing JComponent class extends from the Container class, the basic AWT painting model is followed: All painting is done through the paint() method, and the repaint() method is used to trigger updates. However, many tasks are done differently. The JComponent class optimizes many aspects of painting for improved performance and extensibility. In addition, the RepaintManager class is available to customize painting behavior even further.

> **NOTE** *The public void update(Graphics g) method, inherited from Component, is never invoked on Swing components.*

To improve painting performance and extensibility, the JComponent splits the painting operation into three tasks. The public void paint(Graphics g) method is subdivided into three separate (protected) method calls. In the order called, they are paintComponent(g), paintBorder(g), paintChildren(g), with Graphics argument passed through from the original paint() call. The component itself is first painted through paintComponent(g). If you want to customize the painting of a Swing component, you override paintComponent() instead of paint(). Unless you want to completely replace all the painting, you would call super.paintComponent() first, as shown here, to get the default paintComponent() behavior.

```
public class MyComponent extends JPanel {
  protected void paintComponent(Graphics g) {
    super.paintComponent(g);
    // customize after calling super.paintComponent(g)
  }
  ...
}
```

> **NOTE** *When running a program that uses Swing components within the Java 2 platform, the Graphics argument passed to the paint() method and on to paintComponent() is technically a Graphics2D argument. Therefore, after casting the Graphics argument to a Graphics2D object, you could use the Java2D capabilities of the Java 2 platform, as you would when defining a drawing Stroke, Shape, or AffineTransform.*

The paintBorder() and paintChildren() methods tend not to be overridden. The paintBorder() method draws a border around the component, a concept described more fully in Chapter 7. The paintChildren() method draws the components within the Swing container object, if any are present.

To optimize painting, the JComponent class provides three painting properties: opacity, optimization, and double buffering.

The opacity setting for a JComponent defines whether a component is transparent. When transparent, the container of the JComponent must paint the background behind the component. To improve performance, you can leave the JComponent opaque and let the JComponent draw its own background, instead of relying on the container to draw the covered background.

The optimization setting determines whether immediate children can overlap or not. If children can't overlap, the repaint time is reduced considerably. By default, optimized drawing is enabled for most Swing components, except for JDesktopPane, JLayeredPane, and JViewport.

By default, all Swing components double buffer their drawing operations into a buffer shared by the complete container hierarchy, that is, all the components within a window (or subclass). This greatly improves painting performance, because when double buffering is enabled there is only a single screen update drawn.

> **NOTE** *For synchronous painting, you can call one of the* `public void`
> `paintImmediately()` *methods. (Arguments are either a* `Rectangle` *or its*
> *parts — position and dimensions.) However, you'll rarely need to call this*
> *directly unless your program has real-time painting requirements.*

The public void `revalidate()` method of `JComponent` also offers painting support. When called, the high-level container of the component validates itself. This is unlike the AWT approach requiring a direct call to the `revalidate()` method of that high-level component.

The last aspect of the Swing component painting enhancements is the `RepaintManager`.

Class RepaintManager

The `RepaintManager` is responsible for ensuring the efficiency of repaint requests on the currently displayed Swing components, making sure the smallest "dirty" region of the screen is updated when a region becomes invalid.

Although rarely customized, the `RepaintManager` class is public and provides a static installation routine to use a custom manager: `public static void` `setCurrentManager(RepaintManager manager)`.

Table 4-1 shows the two properties of `RepaintManager`. They allow you to disable double buffering for all drawing operations of a component (hierarchy) and to set the maximum double buffer size, which defaults to the end user's screen size.

PROPERTY NAME	DATA TYPE	ACCESS
doubleBufferingEnabled	boolean	read-write
doubleBufferMaximumSize	Dimension	read-write

Table 4-1: RepaintManager properties

> **TIP** *To globally disable double-buffered drawing, call the following:*
> `RepaintManager.currentManager(aComponent).`
> `setDoubleBufferingEnabled(false).`

Although it's rarely done, providing your own `RepaintManager` subclass does allow you to customize the mechanism of painting dirty regions of the screen, or at least track when they're done. The mechanisms can be customized by overriding any of the following four methods:

```
public synchronized void addDirtyRegion(JComponent component, int x, int y, int
width, int height)
public Rectangle getDirtyRegion(JComponent component)
public void markCompletelyClean(JComponent component)
public void markCompletelyDirty(JComponent component)
```

Class UIDefaults

The UIDefaults represents a lookup table containing the display settings installed for the current look and feel, such as which font to use within a JList, as well as what color or icon should be displayed within a JTree node. The use of UIDefaults will be completely described in Chapter 18 with the coverage of Java's pluggable look and feel architecture. Nevertheless, a short description of its usage is needed here.

Whenever you create a component, the component automatically asks the UIManager to look in the UIDefaults settings for the current settings for that component. Most color- and font-related component settings, as well as some others not related to colors and fonts, are configurable. If you don't like a particular setting, you can simply change it.

> **NOTE** *All predefined resource settings in the* UIDefaults *table implement the* UIResource *interface, which allows the components to monitor which settings have been customized just by looking for those settings that don't implement the interface.*

You can find the listed settings in either one of two places in this book. Appendix A contains a complete alphabetical listing of all known settings for the predefined look-and-feels. In addition, included with the description of each component is a table containing the UIResource-related property elements. (To find the specific component section in the book, consult the Index.)

Once you know the name of a setting, you can store a new setting with the public static void put(Object key, Object value) method of UIManager, where key is the string key. For instance, the following code will change the default background color of a new button to black and the foreground color to red:

```
UIManager.put("Button.background", Color.black);
UIManager.put("Button.foreground", Color.red);
```

If you're creating your own components or just need to find out the current value setting, you need only ask the `UIManager`. Although the `public static Object get(Object key)` method is the most generic, it requires you to cast the return value to the appropriate class type. Alternately, you could use one of the more specific get*XXX*() methods, which does the casting for you, to return the appropriate type. Those methods are listed in Table 4-2.

UIMANAGER GETTER METHODS

public static Border getBorder(Object key)

public static Color getColor(Object key)

public static Dimension getDimension(Object key)

public static Font getFont(Object key)

public static Icon getIcon(Object key)

public static Insets getInsets(Object key)

public static int getInt(Object key)

public static String getString(Object key)

public static ComponentUI getUI(JComponent target)

Table 4-2: UIManager methods for getting UIResource properties

> **NOTE** *You can also work with the* `UIDefaults` *directly, by calling the public static* `UIDefaults getDefaults()` *method of* `UIManager`.

Client Properties

In addition to the `UIManager` maintaining a table of key-value pair settings, each instance of every component can manage its own set of key-value pairs. This is useful for maintaining aspects of a component that may be specific to a particular look and feel, or for maintaining data associated with a component without requiring the definition of new classes to store such data.

```
public final void putClientProperty(Object key, Object value)
public final Object getClientProperty(Object key)
```

> **NOTE** *Calling* `putClientProperty()` *with a value of* `null` *causes the key to be removed from the client property table.*

For instance, the `JTree` class has a property with the Metal look and feel for configuring the line style for connecting or displaying nodes within a `JTree`. Because the setting is specific to one look and feel, it doesn't make sense to add something to the tree API. Instead, the property can be set by calling the following on a particular tree instance:

```
tree.putClientProperty("JTree.lineStyle", "Angled")
```

Then, when the look and feel is the default Metal, lines will connect the nodes of the tree. If another look and feel is installed, the client property will be ignored.

Figure 4-2 shows a tree with and without lines.

> **NOTE**   *The list of client properties is probably one of the least documented aspects of Swing. Chapter 18 lists the available properties I was able to determine.*

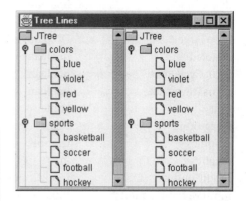

Figure 4-2: A JTree, with and without angled lines

JComponent Properties

You've seen some of the pieces shared by the different `JComponent` subclasses. Now it's time to look at the JavaBeans properties. Table 4-3 shows the complete list of properties defined by `JComponent`, including those inherited through the AWT `Container` and `Component` classes.

PROPERTY NAME	DATA TYPE	JCOMPONENT ACCESS	CONTAINER ACCESS	COMPONENT ACCESS
accessibleContext	AccessibleContext	read-only	N/A	N/A
alignmentX	float	read-write	read-only	read-only
alignmentY	float	read-write	read-only	read-only
autoscrolls	boolean	read-write	N/A	N/A
background	Color	write-only bound	N/A	read-write
border	Border	read-write bound	N/A	N/A
bounds	Rectangle	N/A	N/A	read-write
colorModel	ColorModel	N/A	N/A	read-only
componentCount	int	N/A	read-only	N/A
componentOrientation*	ComponentOrientation	N/A	N/A	read-write
components	Component[ ]	N/A	read-only	N/A
cursor	Cursor	N/A	N/A	read-write

(continued)

Table 4-3 (continued)

PROPERTY NAME	DATA TYPE	JCOMPONENT ACCESS	CONTAINER ACCESS	COMPONENT ACCESS
debugGraphicsOption	int	read-write	N/A	N/A
displayable*	boolean	N/A	N/A	read-only
doubleBuffered*	boolean	read-write	N/A	read-only
dropTarget*	DropTarget	N/A	N/A	read-write
enabled	boolean	write-only bound	N/A	read-write
focusCycleRoot	boolean	read-only	N/A	N/A
focusTraversable	boolean	read-only	N/A	read-only
font	Font	write-only bound	write-only	read-write
foreground	Color	write-only bound	N/A	read-write
graphics	Graphics	read-only	N/A	read-only
height*	int	read-only	N/A	read-only
inputContext*	InputContext	N/A	N/A	read-only
inputMethodRequests*	InputMethodRequests	N/A	N/A	read-only
insets	Insets	read-only	read-only	N/A
layout	LayoutManager	N/A	read-write	N/A
lightweight*	boolean	N/A	N/A	read-only
locale	Locale	N/A	N/A	read-write
location	Point	N/A	N/A	read-write
locationOnScreen	Point	N/A	N/A	read-only
managingFocus	boolean	read-only	N/A	N/A
maximumSize	Dimension	read-write bound	read-only	read-only
minimumSize	Dimension	read-write bound	read-only	read-only
name	String	N/A	N/A	read-write
nextFocusableComponent	Component	read-write	N/A	N/A
opaque*	boolean	read-write bound	N/A	read-only
optimizedDrawingEnabled	boolean	read-only	N/A	N/A
paintingTile	boolean	read-only	N/A	N/A
parent	Container	N/A	N/A	read-only
preferredSize	Dimension	read-write bound	read-only	read-only
registeredKeyStrokes	KeyStroke[ ]	read-only	N/A	N/A
requestFocusEnabled	boolean	read-write	N/A	N/A
rootPane	JRootPane	read-only	N/A	N/A
showing	boolean	N/A	N/A	read-only
size	Dimension	N/A	N/A	read-write
toolkit	Toolkit	N/A	N/A	read-only
toolTipText	String	read-write	N/A	N/A
topLevelAncestor	Container	read-only	N/A	N/A
treeLock	Object	N/A	N/A	read-only

(continued)

Table 4-3 (continued)

PROPERTY NAME	DATA TYPE	JCOMPONENT ACCESS	CONTAINER ACCESS	COMPONENT ACCESS
UIClassID	String	read-only	N/A	N/A
valid	boolean	N/A	N/A	read-only
validateRoot	boolean	read-only	N/A	N/A
visible	boolean	write-only	N/A	read-write
visibleRect	Rectangle	read-only	N/A	N/A
width*	int	read-only	N/A	read-only
x*	int	read-only	N/A	read-only
y*	int	read-only	N/A	read-only

Table 4-3: JComponent properties

* = Component property in Java 2 platform only, N/A = Not applicable

> **NOTE**   *Additionally, there's a read-only* class *property defined at the* Object *level, the parent of the* Component *class.*

Including the properties from the parent hierarchy, approximately 60 properties of JComponent exist. As that number indicates, the JComponent class is extremely well oriented for visual development. There are roughly eight categories of JComponent properties, which are summarized as follows:

- Position-oriented properties — The x and y properties define the location of the component relative to its parent. The locationOnScreen is just another location for component, this time relative to the screen's origin (upper-left corner). The width and height properties define the size of the component. The visibleRect describes the part of the component visible within the topLevelAncestor, whereas the bounds property defines the component's area, whether visible or not.

- Component-set oriented properties — The components and componentCount properties enable you to find out what the children components are of the particular JComponent. For each component in the components property array, the current component would be its parent. In addition to determining a component's parent, you can find out its rootPane or topLevelAncestor.

- Focus-oriented properties — The managingFocus, focusCycleRoot, focusTraversable, nextFocusableComponent, and requestFocusEnabled properties define the set of focus-oriented properties. These properties control the focus behavior of JComponent and are discussed in greater depth in Chapter 2.

- Layout-oriented properties — alignmentX, alignmentY, componentOrientation, layout, maximumSize, minimumSize, and preferredSize are used to help with layout management.

- Painting support properties — The background/foreground properties describe the current drawing colors and font describes the text style to draw. The insets and border properties are intermixed to describe the drawing of a border around a component. The graphics property permits real-time drawing, although the paintImmediately() method might now suffice. To improve performance, there are the opaque (false is transparent), doubleBuffered, and optimizedDrawingEnabled properties. For debugGraphicsOption, this allows you to slow down the drawing of your component if you can't figure out why it's not painted properly. The remaining two, colorModel and paintingTile, store intermediate drawing information.

  The debugGraphicsOption property is set to one or more of the settings in Table 4-4. Multiple settings would be combined with the bitwise OR ("|") operator.

```
JComponent component = new ...();
component.setDebugGraphicsOptions(DebugGraphics.BUFFERED_OPTION |
DebugGraphics.FLASH_OPTION | DebugGraphics.LOG_OPTION);
```

DEBUGGRAPHICS SETTINGS	DESCRIPTION
DebugGraphics.BUFFERED_OPTION	Causes window to pop up, displaying the drawing of the double-buffered image
DebugGraphics.FLASH_OPTION	Causes the drawing to be done more slowly, flashing between steps
DebugGraphics.LOG_OPTION	Causes a message to be printed to the screen as each step is done
DebugGraphics.NONE_OPTION	Disables all options

Table 4-4: DebugGraphics settings

- Internationalization support — The inputContext, inputMethodRequests, and locale properties help when creating multilingual operations. The first two are limited to Java 2 environments.

- State support—To get state information about a component, all you have to do is ask; there's much you can discover. The autoscrolls property lets you place a component within a JViewport and it automatically scrolls when dragged. The validateRoot property is used when revalidate() has been called and returns true when the current component is at the point it should stop. The remaining seven properties are self-explanatory: displayable, dropTarget, enabled, lightweight, showing, valid, and visible.

- The rest—The remaining properties don't seem to have any kind of logical grouping. The accessibleContext property is for support with the javax.accessibility package. The registeredKeyStrokes property allows you to register keystroke responses with an application. The cursor property lets you change the cursor to one of the available cursors. The toolTipText property is set to display pop-up support text over a component. The toolkit property encapsulates platform-specific behaviors for accessing system resources. The name property gives you the means to recognize a particular instance of a class. The treelock property is the component tree-synchronization locking resource. The UIClassID property is new; it allows subclasses to return the appropriate class ID for their specific instance.

Handling JComponent Events

Three event-handling capabilities are shared by all JComponent subclasses. We'll look at these shared capabilities as well as review the ones inherited from Component.

Listening to JComponent Events with a PropertyChangeListener

The JComponent class makes several previously defined component properties bound. By binding a PropertyChangeListener to the component, you can listen for particular JComponent property changes and then respond accordingly.

```
public interface PropertyChangeListener extends EventListener {
  public void propertyChange(PropertyChangeEvent propertyChangeEvent);
}
```

To demonstrate, the following PropertyChangeListener was pulled from the Action class definition. The property that changes determines which if-block gets executed.

```
public class ActionChangedListener implements PropertyChangeListener {

  public void propertyChange(PropertyChangeEvent e) {
    String propertyName = e.getPropertyName();
    if (e.getPropertyName().equals(Action.NAME)) {
      String text = (String) e.getNewValue();
      button.setText(text);
      button.repaint();
    } else if (propertyName.equals("enabled")) {
      Boolean enabledState = (Boolean) e.getNewValue();
      button.setEnabled(enabledState.booleanValue());
      button.repaint();
    } else if (e.getPropertyName().equals(Action.SMALL_ICON)) {
      Icon icon = (Icon) e.getNewValue();
      button.setIcon(icon);
      button.invalidate();
      button.repaint();
    }
  }
}
```

For property change support with the JComponent class, no class constants exist for the property names. (An instance of a constant existing Action.SMALL_ICON in the Action class example just listed.) Instead, the class uses hard-coded String constants. These strings are listed in Table 4-5.

PROPERTY CHANGE SETTING

ancestor
background
border
enabled
font
foreground
maximumSize
minimumSize
opaque
preferredSize
UI

Table 4-5: JComponent PropertyChangeListener support constants

> **NOTE** *With the Java 2 platform, some bound properties of* JComponent *aren't notified by* JComponent *directly. Instead,* JComponent *relies on its superclass* Component *to do the notification because some properties of* Component, *such as foreground color, aren't bound with JDK 1.1 but are bound with the Java 2 SDK.*

The bound UI property is a protected property overridden by each of the JComponent subclasses.

The ancestor property name is used when the parent of the component is updated whenever the addNotify() / removeNotify() methods are called.

Listening to JComponent Events with a VetoableChangeListener

The VetoableChangeListener is another JavaBeans listener that Swing components use. It works with constrained properties, whereas the PropertyChangeListener works with only bound properties. A key difference between the two is that the public void vetoableChange(PropertyChangeEvent propertyChangeEvent) method can throw a PropertyVetoException if the listener doesn't like the requested change.

```
public interface VetoableChangeListener extends EventListener {
  public void vetoableChange(PropertyChangeEvent propertyChangeEvent) throws
PropertyVetoException;
}
```

> **NOTE** *Only one class,* JInternalFrame, *has constrained properties. The listener is meant primarily for programmers to use with their own newly created components.*

Listening to JComponent Events with an AncestorListener

You can use an AncestorListener to find out when a component moves, is made visible, or is made invisible. It's useful if you permit your users to customize their screens by moving components around and possibly removing them from the screens. The AncestorListener definition is shown below.

```
public interface AncestorListener extends EventListener {
  public void ancestorAdded(AncestorEvent ancestorEvent);
  public void ancestorMoved(AncestorEvent ancestorEvent);
  public void ancestorRemoved(AncestorEvent ancestorEvent);
}
```

To demonstrate, the following program associates an AncestorListener with the root pane of a JFrame. You'll see the messages "Removed," "Added," and "Moved" when the program first starts up. In addition, you'll see "Moved" messages when you drag the frame around.

```
import java.awt.*;
import javax.swing.*;
import javax.swing.event.*;

public class AncestorSampler {
  public static void main (String args[]) {
    JFrame f = new ExitableJFrame("Ancestor Sampler");
    AncestorListener ancestorListener = new AncestorListener() {
      public void ancestorAdded(AncestorEvent ancestorEvent) {
        System.out.println ("Added");
      }
      public void ancestorMoved(AncestorEvent ancestorEvent) {
        System.out.println ("Moved");
      }
      public void ancestorRemoved(AncestorEvent ancestorEvent) {
        System.out.println ("Removed");
      }
    };
    f.getRootPane().addAncestorListener(ancestorListener);
    f.getRootPane().setVisible(false);
    f.getRootPane().setVisible(true);
    f.setSize (300, 200);
    f.setVisible (true);
  }
}
```

Listening to Inherited Events of a JComponent

In addition to the ability to listen for an instance of an AncestorEvent or PropertyChangeEvent with a JComponent, the JComponent inherits the ability to listen to many other events from its Container and Component superclasses.

Table 4-6 lists eight event listeners. You may find yourself using the new listener interfaces quite a bit, but nothing prevents the older ones from working.

CLASS	EVENT LISTENER	EVENT OBJECT
Component	ComponentListener	componentHidden(ComponentEvent)
		componentMoved(ComponentEvent)
		componentResized(ComponentEvent)
		componentShown(ComponentEvent)
Component	FocusListener	focusGained(FocusEvent)
		focusLost(FocusEvent)
Component	InputMethodListener*	caretPositionChanged (InputMethodEvent)
		inputMethodTextChanged (InputMethodEvent)
Component	KeyListener	keyPressed(KeyEvent)
		keyReleased(KeyEvent)
		keyTyped(KeyEvent)
Component	MouseListener	mouseClicked(MouseEvent)
		mouseEntered(MouseEvent)
		mouseExited(MouseEvent)
		mousePressed(MouseEvent)
		mouseReleased(MouseEvent)
Component	MouseMotionListener	mouseDragged(MouseEvent)
		mouseMoved(MouseEvent)
Component	PropertyChangeListener*	propertyChange(PropertyChangeEvent)
Container	ContainerListener	componentAdded(ContainerEvent)
		componentRemoved(ContainerEvent)

Table 4-6: JComponent inherited event listeners

* = Java 2 platform only

Class JToolTip

The Swing components support the ability to display brief pop-up messages when the cursor rests over them. The class used to display pop-up messages is JToolTip.

Creating a JToolTip

Calling the public void setToolTipText(String text) method of JComponent automatically causes the creation of a JToolTip instance when the mouse rests over a component with the installed pop-up message. You don't normally call the `JToolTip` constructor directly. There's only one constructor, and it's of the no-argument variety.

Tooltip text is normally one line long. However, if the text string begins with <html> then the contents can be any HTML 3.2 formatted text. (**Note:** <html> must be entered as lowercase text.) For instance, the following line causes the pop-up message shown in Figure 4-3.

```
component.setToolTipText("<html>Tooltip<br>Message");
```

> **NOTE**   *The <html> tag support was introduced with the JFC/Swing 1.1.1 release. It works with all Swing components that have text labels. If you (or your users) are still using JFC/Swing 1.1 (or the Java 2 Runtime Environment, v. 1.2 or v 1.2.1), these capabilities aren't supported and raw HTML will be seen instead.*

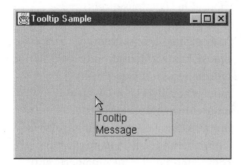

Figure 4-3: HTML-based tooltip text

Creating Customized JToolTip Objects

You can easily customize the display characteristics for all pop-up messages by setting `JToolTip` `UIResource` elements, as shown in "Customizing JToolTip Look and Feel" later in this chapter. The `JComponent` class defines an easy way for you to customize the display characteristics of the tooltip when it's placed over a specific component. Simply subclass the component you want to customize and override its inherited `public JToolTip createToolTip()` method. The `createToolTip()` method is called when the `ToolTipManager` has determined that its time to display the pop-up message.

To customize the pop-up tooltip appearance, just override the method and customize the `JToolTip` returned from the inherited method. For instance, the

following source demonstrates the setting of a custom coloration for the tooltip
for a JButton, as shown in Figure 4-4.

```
JButton b = new JButton("Hello World") {
  public JToolTip createToolTip() {
    JToolTip tip = super.createToolTip();
    tip.setBackground(Color.yellow);
    tip.setForeground(Color.green);
    return tip;
  }
};
```

Figure 4-4: Tooltip text displayed with custom colors

After the JToolTip has been created, you can configure the inherited JComponent
properties or any of the properties specific to JToolTip as shown in Table 4-7.

PROPERTY NAME	DATA TYPE	ACCESS
accessibleContext	AccessibleContext	read-only
component	JComponent	read-write
tipText	String	read-write
UI	ToolTipUI	read-only
UIClassID	String	read-only

Table 4-7: JToolTip properties

Displaying Positional ToolTip Text

Swing components can even support the display of different tooltip text, depending
on where the mouse pointer is located. This requires overriding the public boolean
contains(int x, int y) method, which originates from the Component class.

For instance, after enhancing the customized JButton created in the previous
section of this chapter, the tooltip text will differ, depending on whether or not
the mouse pointer is within 50 pixels from the left edge of the component.

```
JButton button = new JButton("Hello World") {
  public JToolTip createToolTip() {
    JToolTip tip = super.createToolTip();
    tip.setBackground(Color.yellow);
    tip.setForeground(Color.green);
    return tip;
  }
  public boolean contains(int x, int y) {
    if (x < 50) {
      setToolTipText("Got Green Eggs?");
    } else {
      setToolTipText("Got Ham?");
    }
    return super.contains(x, y);
  }
};
```

Customizing a JToolTip Look and Feel

Each installable Swing look and feel provides a different JToolTip appearance and a set of default UIResource value settings. Figure 4-5 shows the appearance of the JToolTip component for the preinstalled set of look and feels: Motif, Windows, Metal, and Macintosh.

The available set of UIResource-related properties for a JToolTip is shown in Table 4-8. For the JToolTip component, there are five different properties.

PROPERTY STRING	OBJECT TYPE
ToolTip.background	Color
ToolTip.border	Border
ToolTip.font	Font
ToolTip.foreground	Color
ToolTipUI	String

Table 4-8: JToolTip UIResource elements

As noted earlier in this chapter, the JToolTip class supports the display of arbitrary HTML content with JFC/Swing version 1.2.1. This permits the display of multi-column/row input. With the original JFC/Swing 1.2 release, this HTML and multi-line tip support wasn't available. It was necessary to create and install a new ToolTipUI delegate, a concept described more fully in Chapter 18.

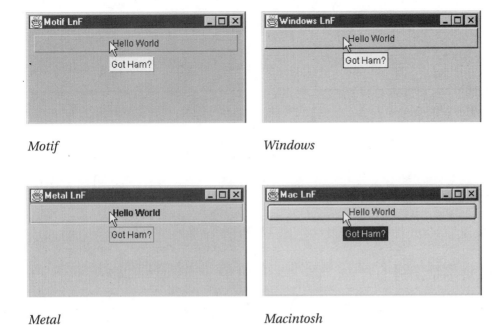

Motif

Windows

Metal

Macintosh

Figure 4-5: JToolTip under different look and feels

Class ToolTipManager

Although the JToolTip is something of a passive object, in the sense that the JComponent creates and shows the JToolTip on its own, there are many more configurable aspects of its usage. However, these configurable aspects are the responsibility of the class that manages tooltips, and not the JToolTip itself. The class that manages tooltip usage is aptly named ToolTipManager. With the Singleton design pattern, no constructor for ToolTipManager exists. Instead, you have access to the current manager through the static sharedInstance() method of ToolTipManager.

ToolTipManager Properties

Once you have accessed the shared instance of ToolTipManager, you can customize when and if tooltip text appears. As Table 4-9 shows, there are five configurable properties.

PROPERTY NAME	DATA TYPE	ACCESS
dismissDelay	int	read-write
enabled	boolean	read-write
initialDelay	int	read-write
lightWeightPopupEnabled	boolean	read-write
reshowDelay	int	read-only

Table 4-9: ToolTipManager properties

> **NOTE** *The `lightWeightPopupEnabled` property has a deprecated setter method and the javadoc comments tell you to instead use `setToolTipWindowUsePolicy(int newPolicy)`. Unfortunately, this method doesn't exist. For the time being, I suspect that using the deprecated method is okay.*

Initially, tooltips are enabled, but you can disable them with `ToolTipManager.sharedInstance().setEnabled(false)`. This allows you always to associate tooltips with components, while letting the end user enable/disable them when desired.

There are three timing-oriented properties: `initialDelay`, `dismissDelay`, and `reshowDelay`. They all measure time in milliseconds. The `initialDelay` property is the number of milliseconds the user must rest the mouse inside the component before the appropriate tooltip text appears. The `dismissDelay` specifies the length of time the text appears while the mouse remains motionless; if the user moves the mouse, it also causes the text to disappear. The `reshowDelay` determines how long a user must remain outside a component before reentry would cause the pop-up text to reappear.

The remaining property `lightWeightPopupEnabled` is used to determine the pop-up window type to hold the tooltip text. If the property is `true` and the pop-up text fits entirely within the bounds of the top-level window, the text appears within a Swing `JPanel`. If this property is `false` and the pop-up text fits entirely within the bounds of the top-level window, the text appears within an AWT `Panel`. If part of the text wouldn't appear within the top-level window no matter what the property setting is, the pop-up text would appear within a `Window`.

Although not properties of `ToolTipManager`, there are two other methods of `ToolTipManager` worth mentioning:

```
public void registerComponent(JComponent component)
public void unregisterComponent(JComponent component)
```

When you call the setToolTipText() method of JComponent, this causes the component to register itself with the ToolTipManager. There are times, however, when you need to register a component directly. This is necessary when the display of part of a component is left to another renderer (see Chapter 16). With JTree, for instance, each node of the tree is displayed by a TreeCellRenderer. When the renderer displays the tooltip text, you "register" the JTree and tell the renderer what text to display.

```
JTree tree = new JTree(...);
ToolTipManager.sharedInstance().registerComponent(tree);
TreeCellRenderer renderer = new ATreeCellRenderer(...);
tree.setCellRenderer(renderer);
...
public class ATreeCellRenderer implements TreeCellRenderer {
...
  public Component getTreeCellRendererComponent(JTree tree, Object value, boolean
selected, boolean expanded, boolean leaf, int row, boolean hasFocus) {
  ...
    renderer.setToolTipText("Some Tip");
    return renderer;
  }
}
```

NOTE *If this sounds confusing, not to worry. We'll revisit the JTree in Chapter 16.*

Class JLabel

The first Swing component we'll examine closely is the simplest, the JLabel. The JLabel serves as the replacement component for the AWT Label but it can do *much* more. Whereas the AWT Label is limited to a single line of text, the Swing JLabel can have text, or images, or both. The text can be a single line of text or HTML. In addition JLabel can support different enabled and disabled images. Figure 4-6 shows some sample JLabel components.

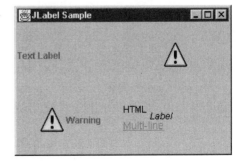

Figure 4-6: Sample JLabel components

> **NOTE** *A JLabel subclass is used as the default renderer for each of the JList, JComboBox, JTable, and JTree components.*

Creating a JLabel

With the six constructors for JLabel, you can customize any of three properties of the JLabel: its text, icon, or horizontalAlignment. By default, the text and icon properties are empty, whereas the initial horizontal alignment depends on the constructor arguments. These settings can be either JLabel.LEFT, JLabel.CENTER, or JLabel.RIGHT. In most cases, not specifying the horizontal alignment setting results in a left-aligned label. However, if only the initial icon is specified, then the default alignment is centered.

1. ```
   public JLabel()
   JLabel label = new JLabel();
   ```

2. ```
   public JLabel(Icon image)
   Icon icon = new ImageIcon("dog.jpg");
   JLabel label = new JLabel(icon);
   ```

3. ```
   public JLabel(Icon image, int horizontalAlignment)
   JLabel label = new JLabel(icon, JLabel.RIGHT);
   ```

4. ```
   public JLabel(String text)
   JLabel label = new JLabel("Dog");
   ```

5. ```
   public JLabel(String text, int horizontalAlignment)
   JLabel label = new JLabel("Dog", JLabel.RIGHT);
   ```

6. ```
   public JLabel(String text, Icon icon, int horizontalAlignment)
   JLabel label = new JLabel("Dog", icon, JLabel.RIGHT);
   ```

JLabel Properties

Table 4-10 shows the 13 properties of JLabel. They allow you to customize the content, position, and (in a limited sense) the behavior of the JLabel.

PROPERTY NAME	DATA TYPE	ACCESS
accessibleContext	AccessibleContext	read-only
disabledIcon	Icon	read-write bound
displayedMnemonic	char	read-write bound
horizontalAlignment	int	read-write bound
horizontalTextPosition	int	read-write bound
icon	Icon	read-write bound
iconTextGap	int	read-write bound
labelFor	Component	read-write bound
text	String	read-write bound
UI	LabelUI	read-write
UIClassID	String	read-only
verticalAlignment	int	read-write bound
verticalTextPosition	int	read-write bound

Table 4-10: JLabel properties

The content of the JLabel is the text and its associated image. Displaying an image within a JLabel will be discussed in the section "Interface Icon" later in this chapter. However, different icons can be displayed, depending on whether the JLabel is enabled or disabled. By default, the icon is a grayscaled version of the enabled icon, if the enabled icon comes from an Image object (ImageIcon to be described later in the chapter). If the enabled icon doesn't come from an Image, there's no icon when JLabel is disabled, unless manually specified.

The position of the contents of the JLabel is described by four different properties: horizontalAlignment, horizontalTextPosition, verticalAlignment, and verticalTextPosition. The horizontalAlignment and verticalAlignment properties describe the position of the entire contents of the JLabel.

> **TIP** *Alignments have an effect only if there's extra space for the layout manager to position the component. If you're using a layout manager such as FlowLayout, which sizes components to their preferred size, these settings will effectively be ignored.*

The horizontal position can be any of the JLabel constants LEFT, RIGHT, or CENTER. The vertical position can be TOP, BOTTOM, or CENTER. Figure 4-7 shows various alignment settings, with the label reflecting the alignments.

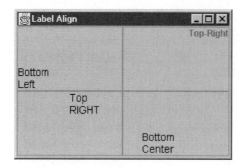

Figure 4-7: Various JLabel alignments

WARNING *As this Figure 4-7 demonstrates, you should be careful when using HTML in rendered output. The runtime tends to think the content is wider than it really is, affecting right/center alignment positions.*

The text position properties reflect where the text is positioned relative to the icon when both are present. The properties can be set to the same constants as the alignment constants. Figure 4-8 shows various text position settings, with each label reflecting the setting.

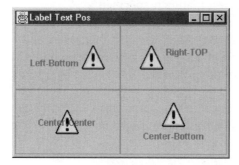

Figure 4-8: Various JLabel text positions

NOTE *The constants for the different positions come from the* SwingConstants *interface that the* JLabel *class implements.*

Handling JLabel Events

No event-handling capabilities are specific to the JLabel. Besides the event-handling capabilities inherited through JComponent, the closest thing there is for event handling with the JLabel is the combined usage of the displayedMnemonic and labelFor properties.

When the displayedMnemonic and labelFor properties are set, pressing the keystroke specified by the mnemonic, along with the platform-specific hotkey (usually ALT), causes the input focus to shift to the component associated with the labelFor property. This can be helpful when a component doesn't have its own manner of displaying a mnemonic setting, such as with all the text input components, as shown in Figure 4-9.

```
JLabel label = new JLabel("Username");
JTextField textField = new JTextField();
label.setDisplayedMnemonic(KeyEvent.VK_U);
label.setLabelFor(textField);
```

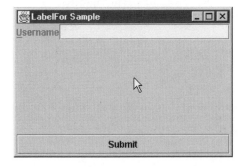

Figure 4-9: Using a JLabel to display the mnemonic for another component

> **NOTE** *The component setting of the* labelFor *property is stored as a client property of the* JLabel *with the* LABELED_BY_PROPERTY *key constant. The setting is used for accessibility purposes.*

Customizing JLabel Look and Feel

Each installable Swing look and feel provides a different JLabel appearance and set of default UIResource value settings. Although appearances differ based on the current look and feel, the differences are minimal within the preinstalled set of look and feels. For the available set of `UIResource`-related properties for a `JLabel`, see Table 4-11. There are six different properties for the `JLabel` component.

PROPERTY STRING	OBJECT TYPE
Label.background	Color
Label.disabledForeground	Color
Label.disabledShadow	Color
Label.font	Font
Label.foreground	Color
LabelUI	LabelUI

Table 4-11: JLabel UIResource elements

Interface Icon

The `Icon` interface is used to associate glyphs with various components. These *glyphs* (like a symbol on a highway sign that conveys information nonverbally, such as "winding road ahead!") can be simple drawings or GIF images loaded from disk with the `ImageIcon` class. The interface contains two properties describing the size and a method to paint the glyph.

```
public interface Icon {
  // Properties
  public int getIconHeight();
  public int getIconWidth();
  // Other Methods
  public void paintIcon(Component c, Graphics g, int x, int y);
}
```

Creating an Icon

Creating an `Icon` is as simple as implementing the interface. All you have to do is specify the size of the icon and what to draw. The following is one such `Icon` implementation. It will be used throughout the rest of the book. The icon is a diamond-shaped glyph in which the size, color, and filled-status are all configurable.

One tip in implementing the `paintIcon()` method of the `Icon` interface: Translate the drawing coordinates of the graphics context based on the x and y position passed in, and then translate them back when the drawing is done. This greatly simplifies the different drawing operations.

```java
import javax.swing.*;
import java.awt.*;
public class DiamondIcon implements Icon {
  private Color color;
  private boolean selected;
  private int width;
  private int height;
  private Polygon poly;
  private static final int DEFAULT_WIDTH = 10;
  private static final int DEFAULT_HEIGHT = 10;

  public DiamondIcon(Color color) {
    this (color, true, DEFAULT_WIDTH, DEFAULT_HEIGHT);
  }

  public DiamondIcon(Color color, boolean selected) {
    this (color, selected, DEFAULT_WIDTH, DEFAULT_HEIGHT);
  }

  public DiamondIcon (Color color, boolean selected, int width, int height) {
    this.color = color;
    this.selected = selected;
    this.width = width;
    this.height = height;
    initPolygon();
  }

  private void initPolygon() {
    poly = new Polygon();
    int halfWidth = width/2;
    int halfHeight = height/2;
    poly.addPoint (0, halfHeight);
    poly.addPoint (halfWidth, 0);
    poly.addPoint (width, halfHeight);
    poly.addPoint (halfWidth, height);
  }

  public int getIconHeight() {
    return height;
  }

  public int getIconWidth() {
    return width;
```

```
    }

  public void paintIcon(Component c, Graphics g, int x, int y) {
    g.setColor (color);
    poly.translate (x, y);
    if (selected) {
      g.fillPolygon (poly);
    } else {
      g.drawPolygon (poly);
    }
    poly.translate (-x, -y);
  }
}
```

Using an Icon

Once you have your Icon implementation, using the Icon is as simple as finding a
component with an appropriate property. We've already discussed JLabel, so
we'll use the icon with a JLabel.

```
Icon icon = new DiamondIcon(Color.red, true, 25, 25);
JLabel label = new JLabel(icon);
```

Figure 4-10 shows what such a label might look like.

Figure 4-10: Using an Icon in a JLabel

Class ImageIcon

The ImageIcon class presents an implementation of the Icon interface for creating
glyphs from AWT Image objects, whether from memory (a byte[ ]), off a disk (a
file name), or over the network (a URL). Unlike regular Image objects, the loading
of an ImageIcon is immediately started when the ImageIcon is created, though it

might not be fully loaded when used. In addition, ImageIcon objects are serializable so that they can be easily used by JavaBean components, unlike Image objects.

Creating an ImageIcon

There are nine constructors for an ImageIcon. The no-argument version creates an uninitialized version (empty). The remaining eight offer the ability to create an ImageIcon from an Image, byte array, file name String, or URL, with or without a description.

1.  ```
    public ImageIcon()
    Icon icon = new ImageIcon();
    icon.setImage(anImage);
    ```

2.  ```
    public ImageIcon(Image image)
    Icon icon = new ImageIcon(anImage);
    ```

3.  ```
    public ImageIcon(String filename)
    Icon icon = new ImageIcon(filename);
    ```

4.  ```
    public ImageIcon(URL location)
    Icon icon = new ImageIcon(url);
    ```

5.  ```
    public ImageIcon(byte imageData[])
    Icon icon = new ImageIcon(aByteArray);
    ```

6.  ```
    public ImageIcon(Image image, String description)
    Icon icon = new ImageIcon(anImage, "Duke");
    ```

7.  ```
    public ImageIcon(String filename, String description)
    Icon icon = new ImageIcon(filename, filename);
    ```

8.  ```
    public ImageIcon(URL location, String description)
    Icon icon = new ImageIcon(url, location.getFile());
    ```

9.  ```
    public ImageIcon(byte imageData[], String description)
    Icon icon = new ImageIcon(aByteArray, "Duke");
    ```
    ```

Using an ImageIcon

Using an ImageIcon is as simple as using an Icon: just create the ImageIcon and associate it with a component.

```
Icon icon = new ImageIcon("Warn.gif");
JLabel label3 = new JLabel("Warning", icon, JLabel.CENTER)
```

ImageIcon Properties

Table 4-12 shows the six properties of ImageIcon. The height and width of the ImageIcon are the height and width of the actual Image object. The imageLoadStatus property represents the results of the loading of the ImageIcon from the hidden MediaTracker, either MediaTracker.ABORTED, MediaTracker.ERRORED, or MediaTracker.COMPLETE.

PROPERTY NAME	DATA TYPE	ACCESS
description	String	read-write
iconHeight	int	read-only
iconWidth	int	read-only
image	Image	read-write
imageLoadStatus	int	read-only
imageObserver	ImageObserver	read-write

Table 4-12: ImageIcon properties

Sometimes it's useful to use an ImageIcon to load an Image and then just ask for the Image object from the Icon.

```
ImageIcon imageIcon = new ImageIcon(...);
Image image = imageIcon.getImage();
```

There is one major problem with using ImageIcon objects: They don't work when the image and class file using the icon are loaded in a JAR (Java archive) file. You can't specify the file name as a String and let the ImageIcon find the file. You must manually get the image data first and then pass the data along to the ImageIcon constructor.

    The following ImageLoader class provides a public static Image getImage (Class relativeClass, String filename) method. You specify both the base class where the image file relative is found and the file name for the image file. Then, you just need to pass the Image object returned to the constructor of ImageIcon.

```java
import java.awt.*;
import java.io.*;

public final class ImageLoader {

  private ImageLoader() {
  }

  public static Image getImage(Class relativeClass, String filename) {
    Image returnValue = null;
    InputStream is = relativeClass.getResourceAsStream(filename);
    if (is != null) {
      BufferedInputStream bis = new BufferedInputStream(is);
      ByteArrayOutputStream baos = new ByteArrayOutputStream();
      try {
        int ch;
        while ((ch = bis.read()) != -1) {
          baos.write(ch);
        }
        returnValue =
Toolkit.getDefaultToolkit().createImage(baos.toByteArray());
      } catch (IOException exception) {
        System.err.println("Error loading: " + filename);
      }
    }
    return returnValue;
  }
}
```

Here's how you use the helper class:

```java
Image warnImage = ImageLoader.getImage(LabelJarSample.class, "Warn.gif");
Icon warnIcon = new ImageIcon(warnImage);
JLabel label2 = new JLabel(warnIcon);
```

> **TIP** *Keep in mind that Java supports GIF89A animated images.*

Class GrayFilter

One additional class worth mentioning here is the GrayFilter class. Many of the Swing component classes rely on this class to create a disabled version of an Image to be used as an Icon. The components use the class automatically, but there might be times when you need an AWT ImageFilter that does grayscales. You can convert an Image from normal to grayed out with a call to the one useful method of the class: public static Image createDisabledImage(Image image).

```
Image normalImage = ImageLoader.getImage(LabelJarSample.class, "Warn.gif");
Image grayImage = GrayFilter.createDisabledImage(normalImage)
```

You can now use the grayed-out image as the Icon on a component:

```
Icon warningIcon = new ImageIcon(grayImage);
JLabel warningLabel = new JLabel(warningIcon);
```

Class AbstractButton

The AbstractButton class is an important Swing class that works behind the scenes as the parent class of all the Swing button components, as shown in Figure 4-11. The JButton, described in the section "Class Button" later in this chapter, is the simplest of the subclasses. The remaining subclasses are described in later chapters.

Each of the AbstractButton subclasses uses the ButtonModel interface to store their data model. The DefaultButtonModel class is the default implementation used. In addition, you can group any set of AbstractButton objects into a ButtonGroup. Although this grouping is most natural with the JRadioButton and JRadioButtonMenuItem components, any of the AbstractButton subclasses will work. Figure 4-12 shows these UML relationships.

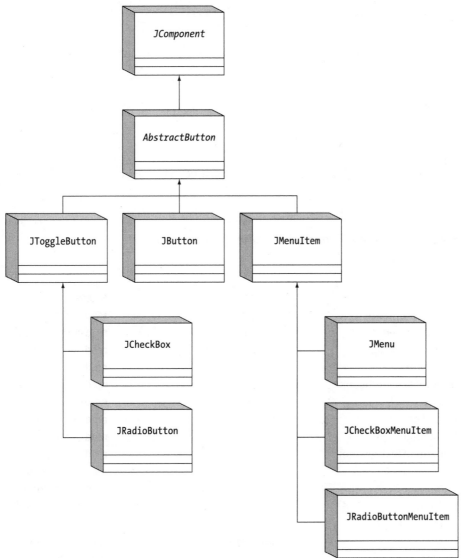

Figure 4-11: AbstractButton class hierarchy

AbstractButton Properties

Table 4-13 lists the 24 properties (with mnemonic listed twice) of AbstractButton shared by all its subclasses. They allow you to customize the appearance of all the buttons.

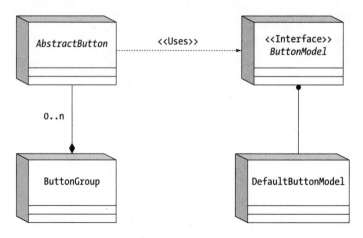

Figure 4-12: AbstractButton UML relationship diagram

PROPERTY NAME	DATA TYPE	ACCESS
actionCommand	String	read-write
borderPainted	boolean	read-write bound
contentAreaFilled	boolean	read-write bound
disabledIcon	Icon	read-write bound
disabledSelectedIcon	Icon	read-write
enabled	boolean	write-only
focusPainted	boolean	read-write bound
horizontalAlignment	int	read-write bound
horizontalTextPosition	int	read-write bound
icon	Icon	read-write bound
margin	Insets	read-write bound
mnemonic	char	read-write bound
mnemonic	int	write-only
model	ButtonModel	read-write bound
pressedIcon	Icon	read-write bound
rolloverEnabled	boolean	read-write bound
rolloverIcon	Icon	read-write bound
rolloverSelectedIcon	Icon	read-write bound
selected	boolean	read-write
selectedIcon	Icon	read-write bound
selectedObjects	Object[ ]	read-only
text	String	read-write bound
UI	ButtonUI	read-write
verticalAlignment	int	read-write bound
verticalTextPosition	int	read-write bound

Table 4-13: AbstractButton properties

> **NOTE** *AbstractButton has a deprecated* label *property. You should use the equivalent* text *property instead.*

> **TIP** *Keep in mind that all* AbstractButton *children can use HTML with its* text *property to display HTML content within the label. Just prefix the property setting with the string* <html>.

Interface ButtonModel/Class DefaultButtonModel

The ButtonModel interface is used to describe the current state of the AbstractButton component. In addition, it describes the set of event listeners objects that are supported by all the different AbstractButton children. Its definition follows:

```
public interface ButtonModel extends ItemSelectable {
  // Properties
  public String getActionCommand();
  public void setActionCommand(String newValue);
  public boolean isArmed();
  public void setArmed(boolean newValue);
  public boolean isEnabled();
  public void setEnabled(boolean newValue);
  public void setGroup(ButtonGroup newValue);
  public int getMnemonic();
  public void setMnemonic(int newValue);
  public boolean isPressed();
  public void setPressed(boolean newValue);
  public boolean isRollover();
  public void setRollover(boolean newValue);
  public boolean isSelected();
  public void setSelected(boolean newValue);
  // Listeners
  public void addActionListener(ActionListener listener);
  public void removeActionListener(ActionListener listener);
  public void addChangeListener(ChangeListener listener);
  public void removeChangeListener(ChangeListener listener);
  public void addItemListener(ItemListener listener);
  public void removeItemListener(ItemListener listener);
}
```

The specific implementation of ButtonModel you'll use, unless you create your own, is the DefaultButtonModel class. The DefaultButtonModel class defines all the event registration methods for the different event listeners and manages the button state and grouping within a ButtonGroup. Its set of nine properties is shown in Table 4-14. They all come from the ButtonGroup interface, except selectedObjects, which is new to the DefaultButtonModel class, but more useful to the JToggleButton.ToggleButtonModel, which is discussed in Chapter 5.

PROPERTY NAME	DATA TYPE	ACCESS
actionCommand	String	read-write
armed	boolean	read-write
enabled	boolean	read-write
group	ButtonGroup	write-only
mnemonic	int	read-write
pressed	boolean	read-write
rollover	boolean	read-write
selected	boolean	read-write
selectedObjects	Object[ ]	read-only

Table 4-14: DefaultButtonModel properties

Most of the time, you don't access the button model directly. Instead, the components that use the ButtonModel wrap their property calls to update the button model properties.

Understanding AbstractButton Mnemonics

A mnemonic is a special keyboard accelerator that when pressed causes a particular action to happen. In the case of the JLabel discussed earlier in the section "Class JLabel," pressing the displayed mnemonic causes the associated component to get the input focus. In the case of an AbstractButton, pressing the mnemonic for a button causes its selection.

The actual pressing of the mnemonic requires the pressing of a look-and-feel–specific hotkey (the key tends to be the ALT key). So, if the mnemonic for a button was the "B" key, you'd need to press ALT-B to activate the button with the B-key mnemonic. When the button is activated, registered listeners will be notified of appropriate state changes. For instance, with the JButton all ActionListener objects would be notified.

If the mnemonic key is part of the text label for the button, you'll see the character underlined. This does depend on the current look and feel and could be displayed differently. In addition, if the mnemonic isn't part of the text label, there'll be no visual indicator for selecting the particular mnemonic key.

Figure 4-13 shows two buttons: one with a "W" mnemonic and the other with an "H" mnemonic. The left button has a label with W in its contents, so it shows the first W underlined. The second component doesn't benefit from this behavior.

To assign a mnemonic to an abstract button, you can use either one of the setMnemonic() methods. One accepts a char argument and the other an int. Personally, I prefer the int variety, in which the value is one of the many VK_* constants from the KeyEvent class.

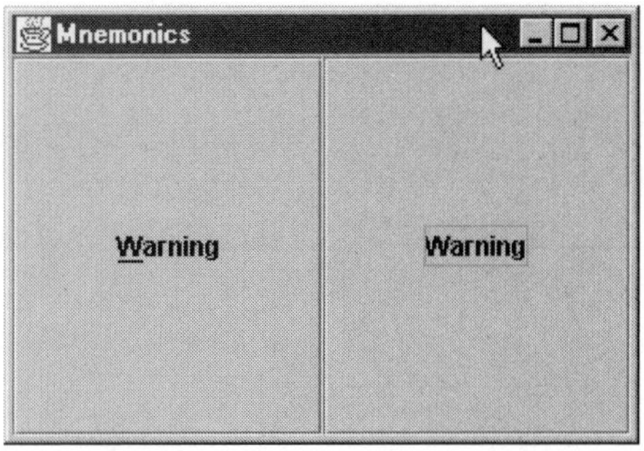

Figure 4-13: AbstractButton mnemonics

```
AbstractButton button1 = new JButton("Warning");
button1.setMnemonic(KeyEvent.VK_W);
content.add(button1);
```

Understanding AbstractButton Icons

AbstractButton has seven specific icon properties. The natural or default icon is the icon property. It is used for all cases unless a different icon is specified or there's a default behavior provided by the component. The selectedIcon property is the icon used when the button is selected. The pressedIcon is used when the button is pressed. Which of these two icons is used depends on the component, because a JButton is pressed but not selected, whereas a JCheckBox is selected but not pressed.

The disabledIcon and disabledSelectedIcon properties are used when the button has been disabled [setEnabled(false)]. By default, if the icon is an ImageIcon, a grayscaled version of the icon will be used.

The remaining two icon properties, rolloverIcon and rolloverSelectedIcon, allow you to display different icons when the mouse moves over the button (and rolloverEnabled is true).

Understanding Internal AbstractButton Positioning

The horizontalAlignment, horizontalTextPosition, verticalAlignment, and verticalTextPosition properties share the same settings and behavior as the JLabel class. They're listed in Table 4-15.

POSITION PROPERTY	AVAILABLE SETTINGS
horizontalAlignment	LEFT, CENTER, RIGHT
horizontalTextPosition	LEFT, CENTER, RIGHT
verticalAlignment	TOP, CENTER, BOTTOM
verticalTextPosition	TOP, CENTER, BOTTOM

Table 4-15: AbstractButton position constants

Handling AbstractButton Events

Although you do *not* create AbstractButton instances directly, you *do* create subclasses. All of them share a common set of event-handling capabilities. You can register PropertyChangeListener, ActionListener, ItemListener, and ChangeListener objects with abstract buttons. The PropertyChangeListener object will be discussed next, and the remaining objects I just listed will be discussed in later chapters of this book, with the appropriate components.

Listening to AbstractButton Events with a PropertyChangeListener

Like the JComponent class, the AbstractButton component supports the registering of PropertyChangeListener objects to detect when bound properties of an instance of the class change.

Unlike the JComponent class, the AbstractButton component provides a set of class constants to signify the different property changes. These constants are listed in Table 4-16.

PROPERTY CHANGE CONSTANT
BORDER_PAINTED_CHANGED_PROPERTY
CONTENT_AREA_FILLED_CHANGED_PROPERTY
DISABLED_ICON_CHANGED_PROPERTY
DISABLED_SELECTED_ICON_CHANGED_PROPERTY
FOCUS_PAINTED_CHANGED_PROPERTY
HORIZONTAL_ALIGNMENT_CHANGED_PROPERTY
HORIZONTAL_TEXT_POSITION_CHANGED_PROPERTY
ICON_CHANGED_PROPERTY
MARGIN_CHANGED_PROPERTY
MNEMONIC_CHANGED_PROPERTY
MODEL_CHANGED_PROPERTY

(continued)

Table 4-16 (continued)

....

PROPERTY CHANGE CONSTANT

PRESSED_ICON_CHANGED_PROPERTY
ROLLOVER_ENABLED_CHANGED_PROPERTY
ROLLOVER_ICON_CHANGED_PROPERTY
ROLLOVER_SELECTED_ICON_CHANGED_PROPERTY
SELECTED_ICON_CHANGED_PROPERTY
TEXT_CHANGED_PROPERTY
VERTICAL_ALIGNMENT_CHANGED_PROPERTY
VERTICAL_TEXT_POSITION_CHANGED_PROPERTY

....

Table 4-16: AbstractButton PropertyChangeListener support constants

Therefore, instead of hard-coding specific text strings, you can create a
PropertyChangeListener that uses these constants.

```
public class AbstractButtonPropertyChangeListener implements
PropertyChangeListener {

  public void propertyChange(PropertyChangeEvent e) {
    String propertyName = e.getPropertyName();
    if (e.getPropertyName().equals(AbstractButton.TEXT_CHANGED_PROPERTY)) {
      String newText = (String) e.getNewValue();
      String oldText = (String) e.getOldValue();
      System.out.println(oldText + " changed to " + newText);
    } else if (e.getPropertyName().equals(AbstractButton.ICON_CHANGED_PROPERTY))
{
      Icon icon = (Icon) e.getNewValue();
      if (icon instanceof ImageIcon) {
        System.out.println("New icon is an image");
      }
    }
  }
}
```

Class Button

The JButton component is your basic AbstractButton component that can be
selected. It replaces the AWT Button class. Whereas the AWT Button is restricted
to a single line of text, the JButton supports text, images, and HTML-based
labels, as shown in Figure 4-14.

Figure 4-14: Example JButton components

Creating a JButton

The JButton class has four constructors. You can create a button with or without a text label or icon. The icon represents the default or selected icon property from AbstractButton.

1. `public JButton()`
   `JButton button = new JButton();`

2. `public JButton(Icon image)`
   `JButton button = new JButton();`

3. `public JButton(String text)`
   `JButton button = new JButton();`

4. `public JButton(String text, Icon icon)`
   `JButton button = new JButton();`

JButton Properties

The JButton component doesn't add much to the AbstractButton. As Table 4-17 shows, of the four properties of JButton, the only *new* behavior added is enabling the button to be the default.

PROPERTY NAME	DATA TYPE	ACCESS
accessibleContext	AccessibleContext	read-only
defaultButton	boolean	read-only
defaultCapable	boolean	read-write bound
UIClassID	String	read-only

Table 4-17: JButton properties

The default button tends to be drawn with a different and darker border than the remaining buttons. When a button is the default, pressing the ENTER key while in the top-level window causes the button to be selected. This only works as long as the component with the input focus, such as a text component or another button, doesn't consume the ENTER key. Because the `defaultButton` property is read-only, how (you might be asking) do you set a button as the default? All top-level Swing windows contain a `JRootPane`, to be described in Chapter 8. You tell this `JRootPane` which button is the default by setting its `defaultButton` property. Only buttons whose `defaultCapable` property is `true` can be configured to be the default. Figure 4-15 shows the top-right button set as the default.

Figure 4-15: Setting a default button

The following source code demonstrates the setting of the default button component, as well as the basic `JButton` usage. If the default button appearance doesn't seem that obvious in Figure 4-15, wait until the `JOptionPane` is described in Chapter 9, where the difference in appearance will be more obvious.

```java
import javax.swing.*;
import java.awt.*;
import java.awt.event.*;

public class DefaultButton {

  public static void main(String args[]) {
    JFrame frame = new ExitableJFrame("DefaultButton");

    Container content = frame.getContentPane();
    content.setLayout(new GridLayout(2, 2));

    JButton button1 = new JButton("Text Button");
    button1.setMnemonic(KeyEvent.VK_B);
    content.add(button1);

    Icon warnIcon = new ImageIcon("Warn.gif");
    JButton button2 = new JButton(warnIcon);
    content.add(button2);

    JButton button3 = new JButton("Warning", warnIcon);
    content.add(button3);

    String htmlButton = "<html><sup>HTML</sup> <sub><em>Button</em></sub><br>" +
```

```
        "<font color=\"#FF0080\"><u>Multi-line</u></font>";
      JButton button4 = new JButton(htmlButton);
      content.add(button4);

      JRootPane rootPane = frame.getRootPane();
      rootPane.setDefaultButton(button2);

      frame.setSize(300, 200);
      frame.setVisible(true);
    }
  }
```

Handling JButton Events

The JButton component itself has no specific event-handling capabilities. They're all inherited from AbstractButton. Although you can listen for change events, item events, and property change events, the most helpful listener with the JButton is the ActionListener.

Listening to JButton Events with an ActionListener

When the JButton component is selected, all registered ActionListener objects are notified. This behavior is identical to the AWT Button component and makes transitioning from the AWT Button to the Swing JButton that much easier.

When the button is selected, an ActionEvent is passed to each listener. This event passes along the actionCommand property of the button to help identify which button was selected when a shared listener is used across multiple components. If the actionCommand property hasn't been explicitly set, the current text property is passed along instead.

Figure 4-15 shows the sample program screen. The following source code adds the event-handling capabilities to the default button example in the previous section of this chapter. Notice that the default button status is ignored, because all the components consume the ENTER key. Another component such as a JList or JComboBox, is necessary to get the input focus for the ENTER key to work properly.

```
import javax.swing.*;
import java.awt.*;
import java.awt.event.*;

public class ActionButtonSample {
```

```
public static void main(String args[]) {
  JFrame frame = new ExitableJFrame("DefaultButton");

  ActionListener actionListener = new ActionListener() {
    public void actionPerformed(ActionEvent actionEvent) {
      String command = actionEvent.getActionCommand();
      System.out.println ("Selected: " + command);
    }
  };

  Container content = frame.getContentPane();
  content.setLayout(new GridLayout(2, 2));

  JButton button1 = new JButton("Text Button");
  button1.setMnemonic(KeyEvent.VK_B);
  button1.setActionCommand("First");
  button1.addActionListener(actionListener);
  content.add(button1);

  Icon warnIcon = new ImageIcon("Warn.gif");
  JButton button2 = new JButton(warnIcon);
  button2.setActionCommand("Second");
  button2.addActionListener(actionListener);
  content.add(button2);

  JButton button3 = new JButton("Warning", warnIcon);
  button3.setActionCommand("Third");
  button3.addActionListener(actionListener);
  content.add(button3);

  String htmlButton = "<html><sup>HTML</sup> <sub><em>Button</em></sub><br>" +
    "<font color=\"#FF0080\"><u>Multi-line</u></font>";
  JButton button4 = new JButton(htmlButton);
  button4.setActionCommand("Fourth");
  button4.addActionListener(actionListener);
  content.add(button4);

  JRootPane rootPane = frame.getRootPane();
  rootPane.setDefaultButton(button2);

  frame.setSize(300, 200);
  frame.setVisible(true);
  }
}
```

Customizing a JButton Look and Feel

Each installable Swing look and feel provides a different JButton appearance and set of default UIResource value settings. Figure 4-16 shows the appearance of the JButton component for the preinstalled set of look and feels: Motif, Windows, Metal, and Macintosh.

The available set of UIResource-related properties for a JButton is shown in Table 4-18. For the JButton component, there are 16 different properties.

PROPERTY STRING	OBJECT TYPE
Button.background	Color
Button.border	Border
Button.dashedRectGapHeight	Integer
Button.dashedRectGapWidth	Integer
Button.dashedRectGapX	Integer
Button.dashedRectGapY	Integer
Button.disabledText	Color
Button.focus	Color
Button.font	Font
Button.foreground	Color
Button.margin	Insets
Button.select	Color
Button.selectText	Color
Button.textIconGap	Integer
Button.textShiftOffset	Integer
ButtonUI	ButtonUI

Table 4-18: JButton UIResource elements

Class JPanel

The last of the basic Swing components is the JPanel component. The JPanel component serves as a replacement for two of the AWT components. It's both a general-purpose container object, replacing the Panel container, and a replacement for the Canvas component, for those times when you need a drawable Swing component area.

Motif

Windows

Metal

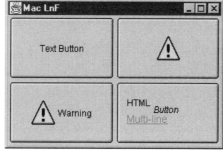

Macintosh

Figure 4-16: JButton under different look and feels

Creating a JPanel

There are four constructors for JPanel. With the constructors, you can either change the default layout manager from FlowLayout or change the default double buffering that's performed from true to false.

1.  ```
    public JPanel()
    JPanel label = new JPanel();
    ```

2.  ```
    public JPanel(boolean isDoubleBuffered)
    JPanel label = new JPanel(false);
    ```

3.  ```
    public JPanel(LayoutManager manager)
    JPanel label = new JPanel(new GridLayout(2,2));
    ```

4.  ```
    public JPanel(LayoutManager manager, boolean isDoubleBuffered)
    JPanel label = new JPanel(new GridLayout(2,2), false);
    ```

Using a JPanel

You can use JPanel as your general-purpose container or as a base class for a new component. For the general purpose container, the procedure is simple: Just create the panel, set its layout manager if necessary, and add components using the add() method.

```
JPanel panel = new JPanel();
JButton okButton = new JButton("OK");
panel.add(okButton);
JButton cancelButton = new JButton("Cancel");
panel.add(CancelButton);
```

When you want to create a new component, subclass JPanel and override the public void paintComponent(Graphics g) method. Although you can subclass JComponent directly, it seems more appropriate to subclass JPanel. The following demonstrates a simple component that draws an oval to fit the size of the component; it also includes a test driver. Figure 4-17 shows the test driver program results.

```
import java.awt.*;
import javax.swing.*;

public class OvalPanel extends JPanel {

  Color color;

  public OvalPanel() {
    this(Color.black);
  }
  public OvalPanel(Color color) {
    this.color = color;
  }
```

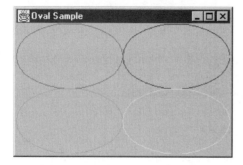

Figure 4-17: Our new OvalPanel component

```
public void paintComponent(Graphics g) {
  int width = getWidth();
  int height = getHeight();
  g.setColor(color);
  g.drawOval(0, 0, width, height);
}

public static void main(String args[]) {
  JFrame frame = new ExitableJFrame("Oval Sample");

  Container content = frame.getContentPane();
  content.setLayout(new GridLayout(2, 2));

  Color colors[] = {Color.red, Color.blue, Color.green, Color.yellow};
  for (int i=0; i<4; i++) {
    OvalPanel panel = new OvalPanel(colors[i]);
    content.add(panel);
  }

  frame.setSize(300, 200);
  frame.setVisible(true);
  }
}
```

NOTE   *One feature worth noting about the JPanel: By default, JPanel components are opaque. This differs from JComponent, whose opaque setting by default is false.*

Customizing a JPanel Look and Feel

The available set of UIResource-related properties for a JPanel is shown in Table 4-19. For the JPanel component, there are four different properties. These settings may have an effect on the components within the panel.

PROPERTY STRING	OBJECT TYPE
Panel.background	Color
Panel.font	Font
Panel.foreground	Color
PanelUI	PanelUI

Table 4-19: JPanel UIResource elements

Summary

In this chapter, we explored the root of all Swing components: the JComponent class. From there, we looked at some of the common elements of all components, such as tooltips, as well as specific components such as JLabel. I also discussed how to put glyphs (nonverbal images) on components with the help of the Icon interface and the ImageIcon class, and the GrayFilter image filter for disabled icons.

We also dealt with the AbstractButton component, which serves as the root component for all Swing button objects. We looked at its data model interface, ButtonModel, and the default implementation of this interface, DefaultButtonModel. Next, we looked at the JButton class, which is the simplest of the AbstractButton implementations. And lastly, we looked at the JPanel as the basic Swing container object.

In the Chapter 5, we'll start to dig into some of the more complex AbstractButton implementations: the toggle buttons.

CHAPTER 5
Toggle Buttons

NOW THAT YOU'VE SEEN THE CAPABILITIES of the relatively simple Swing components JLabel and JButton, it's time to take a look at more-active components, specifically those that can be toggled. These so-called toggleable components—JToggleButton, JCheckBox, and JRadioButton—provide the means for your users to select from among a set of options. These options are either on or off, or enabled or disabled. When presented in a ButtonGroup, only one of the options in the group can be selected at a time. To deal with this selection state, the components share a common data model with ToggleButtonModel. Let's take a look at the data model, the components' grouping mechanism with ButtonGroup, and the individual components.

Class ToggleButtonModel

The JToggleButton.ToggleButtonModel class is a public inner class of JToggleButton. The class customizes the behavior of the DefaultButtonModel class, which in turn is an implementation of the ButtonModel interface. Figure 5-1 shows the inheritance to help visualize this relationship.

The customization affects the data models of all AbstractButton components in the same ButtonGroup—a class we'll explore next. In short, a ButtonGroup is a logical grouping of AbstractButton components. At any one time, only one of the AbstractButton components in the ButtonGroup can have the selected property of its data model set to true. The remaining ones must be false. This does not mean that only one selected component in the group can exist at a time. If multiple components in a ButtonGroup share a ButtonModel, multiple selected components in the group can exist. If no components share a model, at most the user can select one component in the group. Once the user has selected that one component, the user can't interactively deselect the selection. However, programmatically you can deselect *all* group elements.

The definition of JToggleButton.ToggleButtonModel follows.

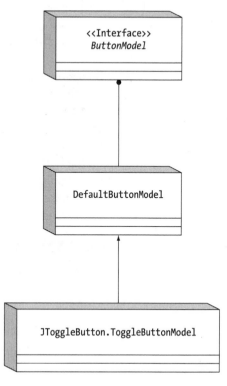

Figure 5-1: Class hierarchy of JToggleButton.ToggleButtonModel

```
public class ToggleButtonModel extends DefaultButtonModel {
  // Constructors
  public ToggleButtonModel();
  // Properties
  public boolean isSelected();
  public void setPressed(boolean newValue);
  public void setSelected(boolean newvalue);
}
```

The ToggleButtonModel class defines the default data model for both the JToggleButton and its subclasses JCheckBox and JRadioButton, described in this chapter, as well as the JCheckBoxMenuItem and JRadioButtonMenuItem classes described in Chapter 6, "Swing Menus and Tool Bars."

> **NOTE** *Internally, Swing's HTML viewer component uses the ToggleButtonModel for its check box and radio button input form elements.*

Class ButtonGroup

Before describing the ButtonGroup class, I'll demonstrate its usage. The following program creates ToggleButtonModel objects and places them into a single group. As the program demonstrates, in addition to adding the components into the screen's container, you must add each component to the same ButtonGroup. This results in a pair of add() method calls for each component. Further, the container for the button group tends to place components in a single column and to label the grouping for the user with a titled border, though neither of these treatments are required. Figure 5-2 shows the output of the program; its source follows:

Figure 5-2: ButtonGroup/ToggleButtonModel example

```java
import javax.swing.*;
import javax.swing.border.*;
import java.awt.*;

public class AButtonGroup {
  public static void main(String args[]) {
    JFrame frame = new ExitableJFrame("Button Group");
    JPanel panel = new JPanel(new GridLayout(0, 1));
    Border border = BorderFactory.createTitledBorder("Examples");
    panel.setBorder(border);
    ButtonGroup group = new ButtonGroup();
    AbstractButton abstract1 = new JToggleButton("Toggle Button");
    panel.add(abstract1);
    group.add(abstract1);
    AbstractButton abstract2 = new JRadioButton("Radio Button");
    panel.add(abstract2);
    group.add(abstract2);
    AbstractButton abstract3 = new JCheckBox("Check Box");
    panel.add(abstract3);
    group.add(abstract3);
    AbstractButton abstract4 = new JRadioButtonMenuItem("Radio Button Menu Item");
    panel.add(abstract4);
    group.add(abstract4);
    AbstractButton abstract5 = new JCheckBoxMenuItem("Check Box Menu Item");
    panel.add(abstract5);
    group.add(abstract5);
    Container contentPane = frame.getContentPane();
    contentPane.add(panel, BorderLayout.CENTER);
    frame.setSize(300, 200);
    frame.setVisible(true);
  }
}
```

As previously stated, the ButtonGroup class represents a logical grouping of AbstractButton components. The ButtonGroup is not a visual component, therefore there's nothing visual on screen when a ButtonGroup is used. Any AbstractButton component can be added to the grouping with public void add(AbstractButton abstractButton). Although any AbstractButton component can belong to a ButtonGroup, only when the data model for the component is ToggleButtonModel will the grouping have any effect. The result of having a component with a data model of ToggleButtonModel in a ButtonGroup is that after the component is selected, the ButtonGroup deselects any currently selected component in the group.

> **NOTE** *Technically speaking, the model doesn't have to be `ToggleButtonModel` as long as the custom model exhibits the same behavior of limiting the number of selected component models to one.*

Although the `add()` method is probably the only `ButtonGroup` method you'll ever need, the following class definition shows that it's not the only method of `ButtonGroup` in existence:

```
public class ButtonGroup implements Serializable {
  // Constructor
  public ButtonGroup();
  // Properties
  public Enumeration getElements();
  public ButtonModel getSelection();
  // Other Methods
  public void add(AbstractButton aButton);
  public boolean isSelected(ButtonModel theModel) ;
  public void remove(AbstractButton aButton);
  public void setSelected(ButtonModel theModel, boolean newValue);
}
```

One interesting thing the class definition shows is that given a `ButtonGroup` you can't directly find out the selected `AbstractButton`. You can only directly ask which `ButtonModel` is selected. However, `getElements()` returns an `Enumeration` of all the `AbstractButton` elements in the group. You can then loop through all the buttons to find the selected one (or ones) by using code similar to the following:

```
Enumeration elements = group.getElements();
while (elements.hasMoreElements()) {
  AbstractButton button = (AbstractButton)elements.nextElement();
  if (button.isSelected()) {
    System.out.println("The winner is: " + button.getText());
    break; // Don't break if sharing models - could show multiple buttons
selected
  }
}
```

The other interesting method of `ButtonGroup` is `setSelected()`. The two arguments of the method are a `ButtonModel` and a `boolean`. If the `boolean` value is `false`, the selection request is ignored. If the `ButtonModel` isn't the model for a button in the `ButtonGroup`, then the `ButtonGroup` deselects the currently selected model, causing no buttons in the group to be selected. The proper usage of the method is to call the method with a model of a component in the group and a new state of true. For example, if aButton is an AbstractButton and aGroup is the ButtonGroup, then the method call would look like aGroup.setSelected(aButton.getModel(), true).

> **NOTE** *If you add a selected button to a* ButtonGroup *that already has a previously selected button, the previous button retains its state and the newly added button loses its selection.*

Now, let's look at the various components whose data model is ToggleButtonModel.

Class JToggleButton

The JToggleButton is the first of the toggleable components. It's discussed first because it's the parent class of the two other non-menu–oriented components, JCheckBox and JRadioButton. The JToggleButton is like a JButton that stays depressed when selected, instead of bouncing back to an unselected state. To deselect the selected component, you must reselect it. JToggleButton isn't a commonly used component, but you might find it useful on a toolbar, such as in Microsoft Word (for paragraph alignment, among other instances) or on a file dialog box, as shown in the upper-right corner of Figure 5-3.

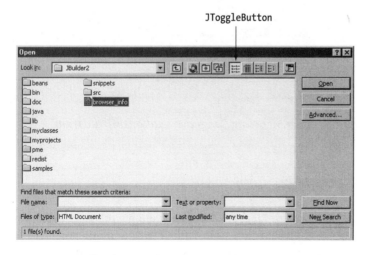

Figure 5-3: Sample JToggleButton components from file chooser

Defining the `JToggleButton` structure are two objects that customize the `AbstractButton` parent class: `ToggleButtonModel` and `ToggleButtonUI`. The `ToggleButtonModel` class represents a customized `ButtonModel` data model for the component, whereas `ToggleButtonUI` is the user interface delegate. Figure 5-4 shows the relationships of these objects to the `JToggleButton`.

Now that you've seen the different pieces of a `JToggleButton`, let's find out how to use them.

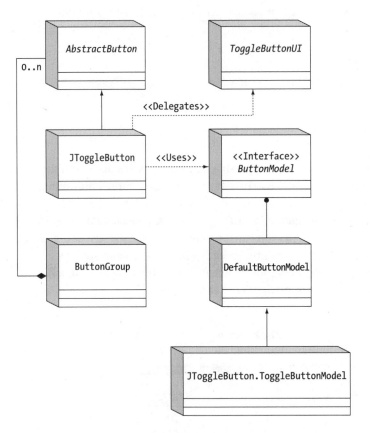

Figure 5-4: JToggleButton Unified Modeling Language relationship diagram

Creating JToggleButton Components

Seven constructors are available for `JToggleButton`. Each allows you to customize one or more label, icon, or initial selection state. Unless specified otherwise, the label is empty with no text or icon and the button initially is not selected.

1. public JToggleButton()
   JToggleButton aToggleButton = new **JToggleButton**();

2. public JToggleButton(Icon icon)
   JToggleButton aToggleButton = new **JToggleButton**(new
   DiamondIcon(Color.brown));

3. public JToggleButton(Icon icon, boolean selected)
   JToggleButton aToggleButton = new **JToggleButton**(new
   DiamondIcon(Color.brown), true);

4. public JToggleButton(String text)
   JToggleButton aToggleButton = new **JToggleButton**("Sicilian");

5. public JToggleButton(String text, boolean selected)
   JToggleButton aToggleButton = new **JToggleButton**("Thin Crust", true);

6. public JToggleButton(String text, Icon icon)
   JToggleButton aToggleButton = new **JToggleButton**("Thick Crust", new
   DiamondIcon(Color.brown));

7. public JToggleButton(String text, Icon icon, boolean selected)
   JToggleButton aToggleButton = new **JToggleButton**("Stuffed Crust", new
   DiamondIcon(Color.brown), true);

> **NOTE** *Surprisingly, Swing lacks a constructor that accepts only an initial state or a boolean setting. Lacking this constructor, you need to create a JToggleButton with the no-argument constructor variety and then call setSelected(boolean newValue) directly.*

JToggleButton Properties

After creating a JToggleButton, you can modify each of its many properties. Although there are about 100 inherited properties, Table 5-1 shows only the two introduced with JToggleButton. The remaining properties come from AbstractButton, JComponent, Container, and Component.

PROPERTY NAME	DATA TYPE	ACCESS
accessibleContext	AccessibleContext	read-only
UIClassID	String	read-only

Table 5-1: JToggleButton properties

You can change one or more of the text, icon, or selected properties set in the constructor, as well as any of the other AbstractButton properties described in Chapter 4. You configure the primary three properties with the appropriate getter and setter methods: get/setText(), get/setIcon(), and is/setSelected(). The other properties have corresponding getter and setter methods.

The more visual configurable options of JToggleButton (and its subclasses) include the various icons for the different states of the button. Besides the standard icon, you can display a different icon when the button is selected, among other state changes. However, if you're changing icons based on the currently selected state, then JToggleButton probably isn't the most appropriate component to use. You should use one of its subclasses, JCheckBox or JRadioButton, explored later in this chapter.

> **NOTE** *Keep in mind that the JButton component ignores the selectedIcon property.*

Handling JToggleButton Selection Events

After configuring a JToggleButton, you can handle selection events in one of three ways: with an ActionListener, an ItemListener, or a ChangeListener.

Listening to JToggleButton Events with an ActionListener

If you're only interested in what happens when a user selects or deselects the JToggleButton, you can attach an ActionListener to the component. After the user selects the button, the component notifies any registered ActionListener objects. Unfortunately, this isn't the desired behavior, because you must then actively determine the state of the button so that you can respond appropriately for selecting or deselecting. To find out the selected state, you must get the model for the event source and then ask for its selection state, as the following sample ActionListener source shows:

```
ActionListener actionListener = new ActionListener() {
  public void actionPerformed(ActionEvent actionEvent) {
    AbstractButton abstractButton = (AbstractButton)actionEvent.getSource();
    boolean selected = abstractButton.getModel().isSelected();
    System.out.println("Action - selected=" + selected + "\n");
  }
};
```

Listening to JToggleButton Events with an ItemListener

The better listener to attach to a JToggleButton is the ItemListener. The ItemEvent passed to the itemStateChanged() method of ItemListener includes the current selection state of the button. This allows you to respond appropriately, without having to go out in search of the current button state.

To demonstrate, the following ItemListener reports the state of a selected ItemEvent-generating component:

```
ItemListener itemListener = new ItemListener() {
  public void itemStateChanged(ItemEvent itemEvent) {
    int state = itemEvent.getStateChange();
    if (state == ItemEvent.SELECTED) {
      System.out.println("Selected");
    } else {
      System.out.println("Deselected");
    }
  }
};
```

Listening to JToggleButton Events with a ChangeListener

Attaching a ChangeListener to a JToggleButton provides even more flexibility. Any attached listener will be notified of the data model changes for the button, corresponding to changes in its armed, pressed, and selected properties. Listening for notification from the three listeners—ActionListener, ItemListener, and ChangeListener—allows you to react seven different times. Figure 5-5 shows the sequencing of the ButtonModel property changes, and when the model notifies each of the listeners.

To demonstrate the ChangeListener notifications, the following code fragment defines a ChangeListener that reports the state changes to the three properties of the button model:

```
ChangeListener changeListener = new ChangeListener() {
  public void stateChanged(ChangeEvent changeEvent) {
    AbstractButton abstractButton = (AbstractButton)changeEvent.getSource();
    ButtonModel buttonModel = abstractButton.getModel();
    boolean armed = buttonModel.isArmed();
    boolean pressed = buttonModel.isPressed();
    boolean selected = buttonModel.isSelected();
    System.out.println("Changed: " + armed + "/" + pressed + "/" + selected);
  }
};
```

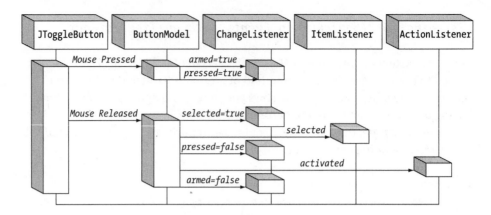

Figure 5-5: JToggleButton notification sequencing diagram

After you attach the ChangeListener to a JToggleButton and select the component by pressing and releasing the mouse over the component, the following output results:

```
Changed: true/false/false
Changed: true/true/false
Changed: true/true/true
Changed: true/false/true
Changed: false/false/true
```

Had I attached all three listeners to the same button, notification of registered ItemListener objects would happen after the selected property changes — in other words, between lines 3 and 4. In fact, the following program demonstrates all three listeners attached to the same JToggleButton. With regard to the registered ActionListener objects, notification happens after releasing the button, but before the armed state changes to false, falling between lines 4 and 5

```
import javax.swing.*;
import javax.swing.event.*;
import java.awt.*;
import java.awt.event.*;

public class SelectingToggle {
  public static void main(String args[]) {
    JFrame frame = new ExitableJFrame("Selecting Toggle");
    JToggleButton toggleButton = new JToggleButton("Toggle Button");
    // Define ActionListener
    ActionListener actionListener = new ActionListener() {
```

```
      public void actionPerformed(ActionEvent actionEvent) {
        AbstractButton abstractButton = (AbstractButton)actionEvent.getSource();
        boolean selected = abstractButton.getModel().isSelected();
        System.out.println("Action - selected=" + selected + "\n");
      }
    };
    // Define ChangeListener
    ChangeListener changeListener = new ChangeListener() {
      public void stateChanged(ChangeEvent changeEvent) {
        AbstractButton abstractButton = (AbstractButton)changeEvent.getSource();
        ButtonModel buttonModel = abstractButton.getModel();
        boolean armed = buttonModel.isArmed();
        boolean pressed = buttonModel.isPressed();
        boolean selected = buttonModel.isSelected();
        System.out.println("Changed: " + armed + "/" + pressed + "/" + selected);
      }
    };
    // Define ItemListener
    ItemListener itemListener = new ItemListener() {
      public void itemStateChanged(ItemEvent itemEvent) {
        int state = itemEvent.getStateChange();
        if (state == ItemEvent.SELECTED) {
          System.out.println("Selected");
        } else {
          System.out.println("Deselected");
        }
      }
    };
    // Attach Listeners
    toggleButton.addActionListener(actionListener);
    toggleButton.addChangeListener(changeListener);
    toggleButton.addItemListener(itemListener);
    Container contentPane = frame.getContentPane();
    contentPane.add(toggleButton, BorderLayout.NORTH);
    frame.setSize(300, 100);
    frame.setVisible(true);
  }
}
```

Customizing a JToggleButton Look and Feel

Each installable Swing look and feel provides a different JToggleButton appearance and set of default UIResource values. Figure 5-6 shows the appearance of the JToggleButton component for the preinstalled set of look and feels: Motif, Windows, Metal, and Macintosh. As the button labels might indicate, the first button is selected, the second has the input focus (and isn't selected), and the third button isn't selected.

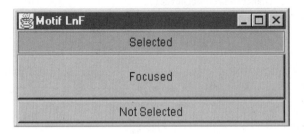

Motif

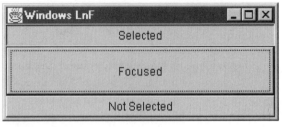

Windows

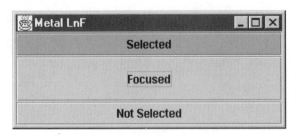

Metal

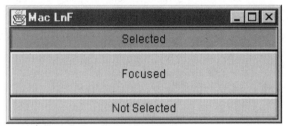

Macintosh

Figure 5-6: JToggleButton under different look and feels

The available set of UIResource-related properties for a JToggleButton is shown in Table 5-2. The JToggleButton component has 15 different properties.

PROPERTY STRING	OBJECT TYPE
ToggleButton.background	Color
ToggleButton.border	Border
ToggleButton.disabledBackground	Color
ToggleButton.disabledSelectedBackground	Color
ToggleButton.disabledSelectedText	Color

(continued)

Table 5-2 (continued)

PROPERTY STRING	OBJECT TYPE
ToggleButton.disabledText	Color
ToggleButton.focus	Color
ToggleButton.font	Font
ToggleButton.foreground	Color
ToggleButton.margin	Insets
ToggleButton.select	Color
ToggleButton.text	Color
ToggleButton.textIconGap	Integer
ToggleButton.textShiftOffset	Integer
ToggleButtonUI	ButtonUI

Table 5-2: JToggleButton UIResource elements

Class JCheckBox

The JCheckBox class represents the toggle component that, by default, displays a check box icon next to the text label for a two-state option. The check box icon uses an optional check mark to show the current state of the object, instead of keeping the button depressed, as with the JToggleButton. With the JCheckBox, the icon shows the state of the object, whereas with the JToggleButton the icon is part of the label and isn't usually used to show state information. With the exception of the UI-related differences between JCheckBox and JToggleButton, the two components are identical. Figure 5-7 demonstrates how check box components might appear in a pizza-ordering application.

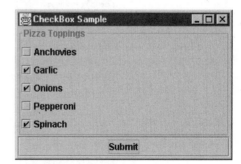

Figure 5-7: Sample JCheckBox components

The JCheckBox is made up of several pieces. Like JToggleButton, the JCheckBox uses a ToggleButtonModel to represent its data model. The user interface delegate is CheckBoxUI. Figure 5-8 shows the relationships of these objects for the JCheckBox. Although the ButtonGroup is available to group together check boxes, it isn't normally appropriate. When multiple JCheckBox components are within a ButtonGroup, they behave like JRadioButton components but look like JCheckBox components. Because of this visual irregularity, you shouldn't put JCheckBox components into a ButtonGroup.

Now that you've seen the different pieces of a JCheckBox, let's find out how to use them.

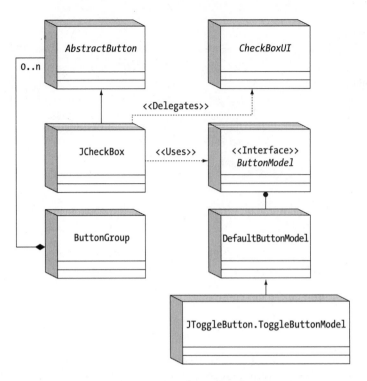

Figure 5-8: JCheckBox UML relationship diagram

Creating JCheckBox Components

Seven constructors exist for JCheckBox. Each allows you to customize either none
or up to three properties for the label, icon, or initial selection state. Unless specified otherwise, there's no text in the label and the default selected/unselected
icon for the check box appears unselected.

If you do initialize the icon in the constructor, it's the icon for the unselected
state of the check box, with the same icon displayed when the check box is
selected. You must also either initialize the selected icon with the
setSelectedIcon(Icon newValue) method, described later, or make sure the icon is
state aware and updates itself. If you don't configure the selected icon and don't
use a state-aware icon, then the same icon will appear for both the selected and
unselected state. Normally, an icon that doesn't change its visual appearance
between selected and unselected states isn't desirable for a JCheckBox. The seven
constructors are as follows:

> **NOTE** *A state-aware icon is one that asks the associated component for
> the value of the selected property.*

```
1.  public JCheckBox()
    JCheckBox aCheckBox = new JCheckBox();

2.  public JCheckBox(Icon icon)
    JCheckBox aCheckBox = new JCheckBox(new DiamondIcon(Color.red, false));
    aCheckBox.setSelectedIcon (new DiamondIcon(Color.pink, true));

3.  public JCheckBox(Icon icon, boolean selected)
    JCheckBox aCheckBox = new JCheckBox(new DiamondIcon(Color.red, false),
    true);
    aCheckBox.setSelectedIcon (new DiamondIcon(Color.pink, true));

4.  public JCheckBox(String text)
    JCheckBox aCheckBox = new JCheckBox("Spinach");

5.  public JCheckBox(String text, boolean selected)
    JCheckBox aCheckBox = new JCheckBox("Onions", true);

6.  public JCheckBox(String text, Icon icon)
    JCheckBox aCheckBox = new JCheckBox("Garlic", new DiamondIcon(Color.red,
    false));
    aCheckBox.setSelectedIcon (new DiamondIcon(Color.pink, true));

7.  public JCheckBox(String text, Icon icon, boolean selected)
    JCheckBox aCheckBox = new JCheckBox("Anchovies", new
    DiamondIcon(Color.red, false), true);
    aCheckBox.setSelectedIcon (new DiamondIcon(Color.pink, true));
```

JCheckBox Properties

After creating a JCheckBox you can modify each of its many properties. The two properties specific to JCheckBox (shown in Table 5-3) override the behavior of its parent JToggleButton. All the remaining properties are inherited through parents of JToggleButton.

PROPERTY NAME	DATA TYPE	ACCESS
accessibleContext	AccessibleContext	read-only
UIClassID	String	read-only

Table 5-3: JCheckBox properties

As the constructor listing demonstrated, if you choose to set an icon with a constructor, the constructor only sets one icon for the unselected state. If you want the check box icon to show the correct state visually, you must also use a state-

aware icon or associate a different icon for the selected state with
`setSelectedIcon()`. Having two different visual state representations is what most
users expect from a JCheckBox, so unless you have a good
reason to do otherwise, it's best to follow the design convention for normal user interfaces.

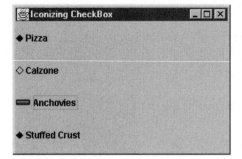

Figure 5-9: A JCheckBox with various icons

The fourth button at the bottom of the screen shown in
Figure 5-9 demonstrates confusing icon usage within a
JCheckBox. The check box always appears selected. The figure displays what the screen looks like with Pizza selected,
Calzone unselected, Anchovies unselected, and Stuffed
Crust unselected (though the last one *appears* selected).

The following source code demonstrates three valid
means of creating JCheckBox components with different
icons, one using a state-aware icon.

```java
import javax.swing.*;
import java.awt.*;
import java.awt.event.*;

public class IconCheckBoxSample {
  private static class CheckBoxIcon implements Icon {
    private ImageIcon checkedIcon = new ImageIcon("Plus.gif");
    private ImageIcon uncheckedIcon = new ImageIcon("Minus.gif");

    public void paintIcon(Component component, Graphics g, int x, int y) {
      AbstractButton abstractButton = (AbstractButton)component;
      ButtonModel buttonModel = abstractButton.getModel();
      g.translate(x,y);
      ImageIcon imageIcon = buttonModel.isSelected() ?
        checkedIcon : uncheckedIcon;
      Image image = imageIcon.getImage();
      g.drawImage(image, 0, 0, component);
      g.translate(-x,-y);
    }
    public int getIconWidth() {
      return 20;
    }
    public int getIconHeight() {
      return 20;
    }
  }
  public static void main(String args[]) {
    JFrame frame = new ExitableJFrame("Iconizing CheckBox");
    Icon checked = new DiamondIcon (Color.black, true);
```

```
Icon unchecked = new DiamondIcon (Color.black, false);
JCheckBox aCheckBox1 = new JCheckBox("Pizza", unchecked);
aCheckBox1.setSelectedIcon(checked);
JCheckBox aCheckBox2 = new JCheckBox("Calzone");
aCheckBox2.setIcon(unchecked);
aCheckBox2.setSelectedIcon(checked);
Icon checkBoxIcon = new CheckBoxIcon();
JCheckBox aCheckBox3 = new JCheckBox("Anchovies", checkBoxIcon);
JCheckBox aCheckBox4 = new JCheckBox("Stuffed Crust", checked);
Container contentPane = frame.getContentPane();
contentPane.setLayout(new GridLayout(0,1));
contentPane.add(aCheckBox1);
contentPane.add(aCheckBox2);
contentPane.add(aCheckBox3);
contentPane.add(aCheckBox4);
frame.setSize(300, 200);
frame.setVisible(true);
  }
}
```

Handling JCheckBox Selection Events

As with the JToggleButton, you can handle JCheckBox events in any one of three ways: with an ActionListener, an ItemListener, or a ChangeListener.

Listening to JCheckBox Events with an ActionListener

Subscribing to ActionEvent generation with an ActionListener allows you to find out when the user toggles the state of the JCheckBox. As with JToggleButton, the subscribed listener is told of the selection, but not the new state. To find out the selected state, you must get the model for the event source and ask, as the following sample ActionListener source shows. This listener modifies the check box label to reflect the selection state.

```
ActionListener actionListener = new ActionListener() {
  public void actionPerformed(ActionEvent actionEvent) {
    AbstractButton abstractButton = (AbstractButton)actionEvent.getSource();
    boolean selected = abstractButton.getModel().isSelected();
    String newLabel = (selected ? SELECTED_LABEL : DESELECTED_LABEL);
    abstractButton.setText(newLabel);
  }
};
```

Listening to JCheckBox Events with an ItemListener

For JCheckBox, as with JToggleButton, the better listener to subscribe to is an ItemListener. The ItemEvent passed to the itemStateChanged() method of ItemListener includes the current state of the check box. This allows you to respond appropriately, without having to go in search of the current button state.

To demonstrate, the following ItemListener swaps the foreground and background colors based on the state of a selected component.

```
ItemListener itemListener = new ItemListener() {
  public void itemStateChanged(ItemEvent itemEvent) {
    AbstractButton abstractButton = (AbstractButton)itemEvent.getSource();
    Color foreground = abstractButton.getForeground();
    Color background = abstractButton.getBackground();
    int state = itemEvent.getStateChange();
    if (state == ItemEvent.SELECTED) {
      abstractButton.setForeground(background);
      abstractButton.setBackground(foreground);
    }
  }
};
```

NOTE *In this* ItemListener, *the foreground and background colors are swapped* only *when the state is selected.*

Listening to JCheckBox Events with a ChangeListener

The ChangeListener responds to the JCheckBox just as with the JToggleButton. A subscribed ChangeListener would be notified when the button is armed, pressed, selected, or released. In addition, the ChangeListener is also notified of changes to the ButtonModel, such as for the keyboard mnemonic (KeyEvent.VK_S) of the check box. Because there's no ChangeListener differences to demonstrate between a JToggleButton and a JCheckBox, you could just attach the same listener from JToggleButton to the JCheckBox and you'll get the same selection responses.

The following sample program demonstrates all the listeners subscribed to the events of a single JCheckBox. To demonstrate that the ChangeListener is notified of changes to other button model properties, a keyboard mnemonic is associated with the component. Given that the ChangeListener is registered before the mnemonic property is changed, the ChangeListener is notified of the property change. Because foreground and background colors as well as the text label aren't button model properties, the ChangeListener isn't told of these changes made by the other listeners.

> **NOTE** *If you did want to listen for changes to the foreground or background color properties, you'd need to attach a PropertyChangeListener to the JCheckBox.*

```
import javax.swing.*;
import javax.swing.event.*;
import java.awt.*;
import java.awt.event.*;

public class SelectingCheckBox {
  private static String DESELECTED_LABEL = "Deselected";
  private static String SELECTED_LABEL = "Selected";
  public static void main(String args[]) {
    JFrame frame = new ExitableJFrame("Selecting CheckBox");
    JCheckBox checkBox = new JCheckBox(DESELECTED_LABEL);
    // Define ActionListener
    ActionListener actionListener = new ActionListener() {
      public void actionPerformed(ActionEvent actionEvent) {
        AbstractButton abstractButton = (AbstractButton)actionEvent.getSource();
        boolean selected = abstractButton.getModel().isSelected();
        String newLabel = (selected ? SELECTED_LABEL : DESELECTED_LABEL);
        abstractButton.setText(newLabel);
      }
    };
    // Define ChangeListener
    ChangeListener changeListener = new ChangeListener() {
      public void stateChanged(ChangeEvent changeEvent) {
        AbstractButton abstractButton = (AbstractButton)changeEvent.getSource();
        ButtonModel buttonModel = abstractButton.getModel();
        boolean armed = buttonModel.isArmed();
        boolean pressed = buttonModel.isPressed();
        boolean selected = buttonModel.isSelected();
        System.out.println("Changed: " + armed + "/" + pressed + "/" + selected);
      }
    };
    // Define ItemListener
```

```
    ItemListener itemListener = new ItemListener() {
      public void itemStateChanged(ItemEvent itemEvent) {
        AbstractButton abstractButton = (AbstractButton)itemEvent.getSource();
        Color foreground = abstractButton.getForeground();
        Color background = abstractButton.getBackground();
        int state = itemEvent.getStateChange();
        if (state == ItemEvent.SELECTED) {
          abstractButton.setForeground(background);
          abstractButton.setBackground(foreground);
        }
      }
    };
    // Attach Listeners
    checkBox.addActionListener(actionListener);
    checkBox.addChangeListener(changeListener);
    checkBox.addItemListener(itemListener);
    checkBox.setMnemonic(KeyEvent.VK_S);
    Container contentPane = frame.getContentPane();
    contentPane.add(checkBox, BorderLayout.NORTH);
    frame.setSize(300, 100);
    frame.setVisible(true);
  }
}
```

Customizing a JCheckBox Look and Feel

Each installable Swing look and feel provides a different JCheckBox appearance and set of default UIResource values. Figure 5-10 shows the appearance of the JCheckBox component for the preinstalled set of look and feels: Motif, Windows, Metal, and Macintosh. The first, third, and fifth check boxes are selected; the third has the input focus.

Table 5-4 shows the set of available UIResource-related properties for a JCheckBox. The JCheckBox component has 12 different properties.

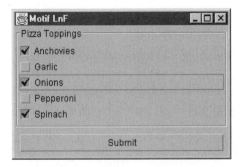

Motif

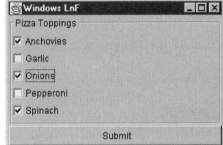

Windows

Metal

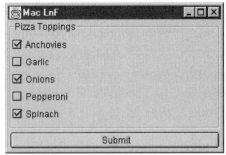

Macintosh

Figure 5-10: JCheckBox under different look and feels

PROPERTY STRING	OBJECT TYPE
CheckBox.background	Color
CheckBox.border	Border
CheckBox.disabledText	Color
CheckBox.focus	Color
CheckBox.font	Font
CheckBox.foreground	Color
CheckBox.icon	Icon
CheckBox.margin	Insets
Checkbox.select*	Color
CheckBox.textIconGap	Integer
CheckBox.textShiftOffset	Integer
CheckBoxUI	ButtonUI

Table 5-4: JCheckBox UIResource Elements

* Lowercase "b" is correct.

Class `JRadioButton`

`JRadioButton` is used when you want to use a mutually exclusive group of `JCheckBox` components. Although, technically speaking, you could place a group of `JCheckBox` components into a `ButtonGroup` and only one would be selectable at a

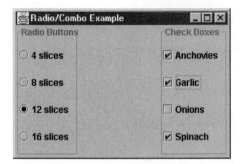

Figure 5-11: Comparing JRadioButton appearance to JCheckBox

time, they wouldn't look quite right. At least with the predefined look and feels, the two components appear different to an end user, as Figure 5-11 shows. This difference in appearance tells the end user to expect specific behavior from the components.

The `JRadioButton` is made up of several pieces. Like `JToggleButton` and `JCheckBox`, the `JRadioButton` uses a `ToggleButtonModel` to represent its data model. It uses a `ButtonGroup` through `AbstractButton` to provide the mutually exclusive grouping, and the user interface delegate is the `RadioButtonUI`. Figure 5-12 shows the relationships of these components for the `JRadioButton`.

Let's now explore how to use the different pieces of a `JRadioButton`.

Creating `JRadioButton` Components

As with `JCheckBox` and `JToggleButton`, there are seven constructors for `JRadioButton`. Each allows you to customize one or more label, icon, or initial selection state. Unless specified otherwise, there's no text in the label, and the default selected/unselected icon for the check box appears unselected. After creating a group of radio button components, you need to place each into a single `ButtonGroup` so that they work as expected, with only one button in the group selectable at a time. If you do initialize the icon in the constructor, it's the icon for the unselected state of the check box, with the same icon displayed when the check box is selected. You must also either initialize the selected icon with the `setSelectedIcon(Icon newValue)` method, described with `JCheckBox`, or make sure the icon is state-aware and updates itself. The seven contructors follow:

1.  ```
    public JRadioButton()
    JRadioButton aRadioButton = new JRadioButton();
    ```

2.  ```
    public JRadioButton(Icon icon)
    JRadioButton aRadioButton = new JRadioButton(new DiamondIcon(Color.cyan,
    false));
    aRadioButton.setSelectedIcon (new DiamondIcon(Color.blue, true));
    ```

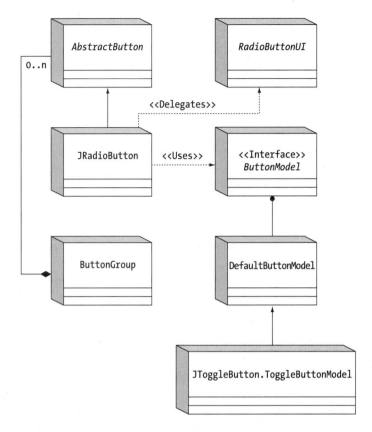

Figure 5-12: JRadioButton UML relationship diagram

3. `public JRadioButton(Icon icon, boolean selected)`
   ```
   JRadioButton aRadioButton = new JRadioButton(new DiamondIcon(Color.cyan,
   false), true);
   aRadioButton.setSelectedIcon (new DiamondIcon(Color.blue, true));
   ```

4. `public JRadioButton(String text)`
   ```
   JRadioButton aRadioButton = new JRadioButton("4 slices");
   ```

5. `public JRadioButton(String text, boolean selected)`
   ```
   JRadioButton aRadioButton = new JRadioButton("8 slices", true);
   ```

6. `public JRadioButton(String text, Icon icon)`
   ```
   JRadioButton aRadioButton = new JRadioButton("12 slices", new
   DiamondIcon(Color.cyan, false));
   aRadioButton.setSelectedIcon (new DiamondIcon(Color.blue, true));
   ```

```
7.  public JRadioButton(String text, Icon icon, boolean selected)
    JRadioButton aRadioButton = new JRadioButton("16 slices", new
    DiamondIcon(Color.cyan, false), true);
    aRadioButton.setSelectedIcon (new DiamondIcon(Color.blue, true));
```

JRadioButton Properties

As with JCheckBox, JRadioButton has two properties that override the behavior of its parent JToggleButton. Table 5-5 shows them.

PROPERTY NAME	DATA TYPE	ACCESS
accessibleContext	AccessibleContext	read-only
UIClassID	String	read-only

Table 5-5: JRadioButton properties

Grouping JRadioButton Components in a ButtonGroup

The JRadioButton is the only JToggleButton subclass that should be placed in a ButtonGroup in order to work properly. Merely creating a bunch of radio buttons and placing them on the screen isn't enough to make them behave appropriately. In addition to adding each radio button to a container, you need to create a ButtonGroup and add each radio button to the same ButtonGroup. Once all the JRadioButton items are in a group, whenever an unselected radio button is selected, the ButtonGroup causes the currently selected radio button to be deselected.

Placing a set of JRadioButton components within a ButtonGroup on the screen breaks down into a four-step process:

1. Create a container for the group.
    ```
    JPanel aPanel = new JPanel(new GridLayout(0, 1));
    ```

> **NOTE** *The Box class described in Chapter 11 serves as a good container for a group of JRadioButton components.*

2. Place a border around the container, to label the grouping.
    ```
    Border border = BorderFactory.createTitledBorder("Slice Count");
    aPanel.setBorder(border);
    ```

Note: Step 2 is an optional step. However, you'll find yourself doing this almost all the time to label the group for the user.

3. Create a `ButtonGroup`.
    ```
    ButtonGroup aGroup = new ButtonGroup();
    ```

4. For each selectable option
    a. Create `JRadioButton`.
        ```
        JRadioButton aRadioButton = new JRadioButton(...);
        ```
    b. Add to container.
        ```
        aPanel.add(aRadioButton);
        ```
    c. Add to group.
        ```
        aGroup.add(aRadioButton);
        ```

You might find the whole process, especially the fourth step, a bit tedious after a while, especially when you add another step for handling selection events. The following helper class, with its static `createRadioButtonGrouping(String elements[], String title)` method, could prove time-saving. It takes a `String` array for the radio button labels as well as the border title, and then it creates a set of `JRadioButton` objects with a common `ButtonGroup` in a `JPanel` with a titled border.

```java
import javax.swing.*;
import javax.swing.border.*;
import java.awt.*;

public class RadioButtonUtils {
  private RadioButtonUtils() {
    // private constructor so you can't create instances
  }
  public static Container createRadioButtonGrouping (String elements[], String
title) {
    JPanel panel = new JPanel(new GridLayout(0, 1));
// If title set, create titled border
    if (title != null) {
      Border border = BorderFactory.createTitledBorder(title);
      panel.setBorder(border);
    }
// Create group
    ButtonGroup group = new ButtonGroup();
    JRadioButton aRadioButton;
// For each String passed in:
// Create button, add to panel, and add to group
    for (int i=0, n=elements.length; i<n; i++) {
```

```
        aRadioButton = new JRadioButton (elements[i]);
        panel.add(aRadioButton);
        group.add(aRadioButton);
      }
      return panel;
    }
}
```

Now, you can create the grouping much more easily, as with the following example program:

```
import javax.swing.*;
import java.awt.*;

public class GroupRadio {
  private static final String sliceOptions[] =
    {"4 slices", "8 slices", "12 slices", "16 slices"};
  private static final String crustOptions[] =
    {"Sicilian", "Thin Crust", "Thick Crust", "Stuffed Crust"};
  public static void main(String args[]) {
    JFrame frame = new ExitableJFrame("Grouping Example");
    Container sliceContainer =
      RadioButtonUtils.createRadioButtonGrouping(sliceOptions, "Slice Count");
    Container crustContainer =
      RadioButtonUtils.createRadioButtonGrouping(crustOptions, "Crust Type");
    Container contentPane = frame.getContentPane();
    contentPane.add(sliceContainer, BorderLayout.WEST);
    contentPane.add(crustContainer, BorderLayout.EAST);
    frame.setSize(300, 200);
    frame.setVisible(true);
  }
}
```

When you run this example, the screen shown in Figure 5-13 is generated.

> **NOTE** *If you're familiar with the standard AWT library, the* JRadioButton /
> ButtonGroup *combination works exactly like the* Checkbox / CheckboxGroup *pair.*

Handling JRadioButton Selection Events

Although the JRadioButton supports the registration of an ActionListener, an ItemListener, and a ChangeListener, just like JToggleButton and JCheckBox, their usage with JRadioButton is somewhat different.

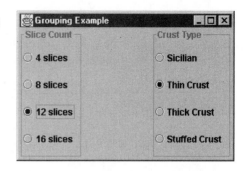

Listening to JRadioButton Events with an ActionListener

Figure 5-13: Grouping JRadioButton components with the RadioButtonUtils helper class

With a JRadioButton, it's common to attach the same ActionListener to all the radio buttons in a ButtonGroup. That way, when one of the radio buttions is selected, the subscribed ActionListener will be notified. By overloading the earlier createRadioButtonGrouping() method, the method can accept an ActionListener argument and attach the listener object to each of the buttons as they're created.

```
public static Container createRadioButtonGrouping (String elements[], String
title, ActionListener actionListener) {
  JPanel panel = new JPanel(new GridLayout(0, 1));
// If title set, create titled border
  if (title != null) {
    Border border = BorderFactory.createTitledBorder(title);
    panel.setBorder(border);
  }
// Create group
  ButtonGroup group = new ButtonGroup();
  JRadioButton aRadioButton;
// For each String passed in:
//   Create button, add to panel, and add to group
  for (int i=0, n=elements.length; i<n; i++) {
    aRadioButton = new JRadioButton (elements[i]);
    panel.add(aRadioButton);
    group.add(aRadioButton);
    if (listener != null) {
      aRadioButton.addActionListener(actionListener);
    }
  }
  return panel;
}
```

Now, if a group is created with the following source, the same `ActionListener` will be notified for each of the `JRadioButton` components created. Here, the listener prints out only the currently selected value. How you choose to respond may vary.

```
ActionListener sliceActionListener = new ActionListener() {
  public void actionPerformed(ActionEvent actionEvent) {
    AbstractButton aButton = (AbstractButton)actionEvent.getSource();
    System.out.println("Selected: " + aButton.getText());
  }
};
Container sliceContainer =
  RadioButtonUtils.createRadioButtonGrouping(sliceOptions, "Slice Count",
sliceActionListener);
```

Two problems with the above approach should be noted. First, if a `JRadioButton` is already selected and then selected again, any attached `ActionListener` objects will still be notified once more. Although you can't stop the double notification of subscribed `ActionListener` objects, with a little work you *can* handle it properly. You need to retain a reference to the last selected item and check for reselection. The following modified `ActionListener` checks for this:

```
ActionListener crustActionListener = new ActionListener() {
  String lastSelected;
  public void actionPerformed(ActionEvent actionEvent) {
    AbstractButton aButton = (AbstractButton)actionEvent.getSource();
    String label = aButton.getText();
    String msgStart;
    if (label.equals(lastSelected)) {
      msgStart = "Reselected: ";
    } else {
      msgStart = "Selected: ";
    }
    lastSelected = label;
    System.out.println(msgStart + label);
  }
};
```

The second problem has to do with determining which `JRadioButton` is selected at any given time. With the overloaded `RadioButtonUtils.createRadioButtonGrouping()` helper methods, neither the `ButtonGroup` nor the individual `JRadioButton` components are visible outside the method. As a result, there's no direct route to find out which `JRadioButton` object (or objects) is selected within the `ButtonGroup` of the returned container. This may be necessary if there's an "Order Pizza" button on the screen and if after selecting the order button you wanted to find out which pizza-order options were selected. The following helper method, public Enumeration getSelectedElements(Container container), when added to the previously created RadioButtonUtils class, will provide the necessary answer. The method will only work only if the container passed into the method is full of AbstractButton objects. This is true for those containers created with the previously described createRadioButtonGrouping() methods, although the helper method is usable separate from the first method.

```
public static Enumeration getSelectedElements(Container container) {
  Vector selections = new Vector();
  Component components[] = container.getComponents();
  for (int i=0, n=components.length; i<n; i++) {
    if (components[i] instanceof AbstractButton) {
      AbstractButton button = (AbstractButton)components[i];
      if (button.isSelected()) {
        selections.addElement(button.getText());
      }
    }
  }
  return selections.elements();
}
```

To use the getSelectedElements() method, you'd just need to pass the container returned from createRadioButtonGrouping() to the getSelectedElements() method to get an Enumeration of the selected items. The following example demonstrates this.

```
final Container crustContainer =
    RadioButtonUtils.createRadioButtonGrouping(crustOptions, "Crust Type");

ActionListener buttonActionListener = new ActionListener() {
  public void actionPerformed(ActionEvent actionEvent) {
    Enumeration selected = RadioButtonUtils.getSelectedElements(crustContainer);
    while (selected.hasMoreElements()) {
      System.out.println ("Selected -> " + selected.nextElement());
    }
  }
};
JButton button = new JButton ("Order Pizza");
button.addActionListener(buttonActionListener);
```

It may be necessary for getSelectedElements() to return more than one value, because if the same ButtonModel is shared by multiple buttons in the container, multiple components of the ButtonGroup will be selected. Sharing a ButtonModel between components isn't the norm. If you're sure this can't happen, then you may want to provide a similar method that returns only a String.

Listening to JRadioButton Events with an ItemListener

Depending on what you're trying to do, using an ItemListener with a JRadioButton is usually not the desired event listening approach. When an ItemListener is registered, a new JRadioButton selection notifies the listener twice: once for deselecting the old value, and once for selecting the new value. For reselections (selecting the same choice again), the listener is only notified once.

To demonstrate, the following listener will detect reselections, like the ActionListener did earlier, and will report the selected (or deselected) element.

```
ItemListener itemListener = new ItemListener() {
  String lastSelected;
  public void itemStateChanged(ItemEvent itemEvent) {
    AbstractButton aButton = (AbstractButton)itemEvent.getSource();
    int state = itemEvent.getStateChange();
    String label = aButton.getText();
    String msgStart;
    if (state == ItemEvent.SELECTED) {
      if (label.equals(lastSelected)) {
        msgStart = "Reselected -> ";
      } else {
        msgStart = "Selected -> ";
      }
      lastSelected = label;
    } else {
      msgStart = "Deselected -> ";
    }
    System.out.println(msgStart + label);
  }
};
```

To work properly, some new methods will be needed for RadioButtonUtils to enable you to attach the ItemListener to each JRadioButton in the ButtonGroup. They're listed in the following section with the complete example source.

Listening to JRadioButton Events with a ChangeListener

The ChangeListener responds to the JRadioButton just as it does with the JToggleButton and JCheckBox. A subscribed listener is notified when the selected radio button is armed, pressed, selected, or released, and for various other properties of the button model. The only difference with JRadioButton is that the ChangeListener is also notified of the state changes of the radio button being deselected. The ChangeListener from the earlier examples could be attached to the JRadioButton as well. It will just be notified more frequently.

Figure 5-14: The GroupActionRadio program sample screen

The following sample program demonstrates all the listeners registered to the events of two different JRadioButton objects. In addition, a JButton reports on the selected elements of one of the radio buttons. Figure 5-14 shows the main window of the program.

```
import javax.swing.*;
import javax.swing.event.*;
import java.awt.*;
import java.awt.event.*;
import java.util.Enumeration;

public class GroupActionRadio {
  private static final String sliceOptions[] =
    {"4 slices", "8 slices", "12 slices", "16 slices"};
  private static final String crustOptions[] =
    {"Sicilian", "Thin Crust", "Thick Crust", "Stuffed Crust"};
  public static void main(String args[]) {

    JFrame frame = new ExitableJFrame("Grouping Example");

    // Slice Parts
    ActionListener sliceActionListener = new ActionListener() {
      public void actionPerformed(ActionEvent actionEvent) {
        AbstractButton aButton = (AbstractButton)actionEvent.getSource();
        System.out.println("Selected: " + aButton.getText());
      }
    };
    Container sliceContainer =
      RadioButtonUtils.createRadioButtonGrouping(sliceOptions, "Slice Count",
```

```
        sliceActionListener);

          // Crust Parts
          ActionListener crustActionListener = new ActionListener() {
            String lastSelected;
            public void actionPerformed(ActionEvent actionEvent) {
              AbstractButton aButton = (AbstractButton)actionEvent.getSource();
              String label = aButton.getText();
              String msgStart;
              if (label.equals(lastSelected)) {
                msgStart = "Reselected: ";
              } else {
                msgStart = "Selected: ";
              }
              lastSelected = label;
              System.out.println(msgStart + label);
            }
          };
          ItemListener itemListener = new ItemListener() {
            String lastSelected;
            public void itemStateChanged(ItemEvent itemEvent) {
              AbstractButton aButton = (AbstractButton)itemEvent.getSource();
              int state = itemEvent.getStateChange();
              String label = aButton.getText();
              String msgStart;
              if (state == ItemEvent.SELECTED) {
              · if (label.equals(lastSelected)) {
                  msgStart = "Reselected -> ";
                } else {
                  msgStart = "Selected -> ";
                }
                lastSelected = label;
              } else {
                msgStart = "Deselected -> ";
              }
              System.out.println(msgStart + label);
            }
          };
          ChangeListener changeListener = new ChangeListener() {
            public void stateChanged(ChangeEvent changEvent) {
              AbstractButton aButton = (AbstractButton)changEvent.getSource();
              ButtonModel aModel = aButton.getModel();
              boolean armed = aModel.isArmed();
```

```
        boolean pressed = aModel.isPressed();
        boolean selected = aModel.isSelected();
        System.out.println("Changed: " + armed + "/" + pressed + "/" + selected);
      }
    };
    final Container crustContainer =
        RadioButtonUtils.createRadioButtonGrouping(crustOptions, "Crust Type",
crustActionListener, itemListener,

changeListener);

    // Button Parts
    ActionListener buttonActionListener = new ActionListener() {
      public void actionPerformed(ActionEvent actionEvent) {
        Enumeration selected =
RadioButtonUtils.getSelectedElements(crustContainer);
        while (selected.hasMoreElements()) {
          System.out.println ("Selected -> " + selected.nextElement());
        }
      }
    };
    JButton button = new JButton ("Order Pizza");
    button.addActionListener(buttonActionListener);

    Container contentPane = frame.getContentPane();
    contentPane.add(sliceContainer, BorderLayout.WEST);
    contentPane.add(crustContainer, BorderLayout.EAST);
    contentPane.add(button, BorderLayout.SOUTH);
    frame.setSize(300, 200);
    frame.setVisible(true);
  }
}
```

A few more changes were made to the RadioButtonUtils class to deal with registering ChangeListener objects to all the radio buttons in a ButtonGroup. The complete and final class definition follows.

```
import javax.swing.*;
import javax.swing.event.*;
import javax.swing.border.*;
import java.awt.*;
import java.awt.event.*;
import java.util.Enumeration;
```

```java
import java.util.Vector;

public class RadioButtonUtils {
  private RadioButtonUtils() {
    // private constructor so you can't create instances
  }

  public static Enumeration getSelectedElements(Container container) {
    Vector selections = new Vector();
    Component components[] = container.getComponents();
    for (int i=0, n=components.length; i<n; i++) {
      if (components[i] instanceof AbstractButton) {
        AbstractButton button = (AbstractButton)components[i];
        if (button.isSelected()) {
          selections.addElement(button.getText());
        }
      }
    }
    return selections.elements();
  }

  public static Container createRadioButtonGrouping (String elements[]) {
    return createRadioButtonGrouping(elements, null, null, null, null);
  }

  public static Container createRadioButtonGrouping (String elements[], String
title) {
    return createRadioButtonGrouping(elements, title, null, null, null);
  }

  public static Container createRadioButtonGrouping(String elements[], String
title, ItemListener itemListener) {
    return createRadioButtonGrouping(elements, title, null, itemListener, null);
  }

  public static Container createRadioButtonGrouping(String elements[], String
title, ActionListener actionListener) {
    return createRadioButtonGrouping(elements, title, actionListener, null,
null);
  }
```

```
   public static Container createRadioButtonGrouping(String elements[], String
title, ActionListener actionListener, ItemListener itemListener) {
     return createRadioButtonGrouping(elements, title, actionListener,
itemListener, null);
     }


  public static Container createRadioButtonGrouping(String elements[], String
title, ActionListener actionListener, ItemListener itemListener, ChangeListener
changeListener) {
     JPanel panel = new JPanel(new GridLayout(0, 1));
// If title set, create titled border
     if (title != null) {
       Border border = BorderFactory.createTitledBorder(title);
       panel.setBorder(border);
     }
// Create group
     ButtonGroup group = new ButtonGroup();
     JRadioButton aRadioButton;
// For each String passed in:
// Create button, add to panel, and add to group
     for (int i=0, n=elements.length; i<n; i++) {
       aRadioButton = new JRadioButton (elements[i]);
       panel.add(aRadioButton);
       group.add(aRadioButton);
       if (actionListener != null) {
         aRadioButton.addActionListener(actionListener);
       }
       if (itemListener != null) {
         aRadioButton.addItemListener(itemListener);
       }
       if (changeListener != null) {
         aRadioButton.addChangeListener(changeListener);
       }
     }
     return panel;
  }
}
```

Customizing a JRadioButton Look and Feel

Each installable Swing look and feel provides a different JRadioButton appearance and set of default UIResource values. Figure 5-15 shows the appearance of the JRadioButton component for the preinstalled set of look and feels: Motif, Windows, Metal, and Macintosh. All four screens show "4 slices" of "Thin Crust" pizza as the order. In addition, the "Thick Crust" option has the input focus. Table 5-6 shows the set of available UIResource-related properties for a JRadioButton. The JRadioButton component has 18 different properties available.

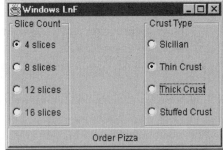

Motif

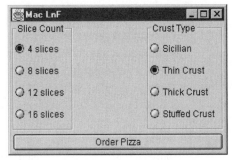

Windows

Metal

Macintosh

Figure 5-15: JRadioButton under different look and feels

PROPERTY STRING	OBJECT TYPE
RadioButton.background	Color
RadioButton.border	Border
RadioButton.disabledOff	Icon
RadioButton.disabledOn	Icon
RadioButton.disabledText	Color
RadioButton.focus	Color
RadioButton.font	Font
RadioButton.foreground	Color
RadioButton.icon	Icon
RadioButton.margin	Insets
RadioButton.off	Icon
RadioButton.on	Icon
RadioButton.pressedOff	Icon
RadioButton.pressedOn	Icon
RadioButton.select	Color
RadioButton.textIconGap	Integer
RadioButton.textShiftOffset	Integer
RadioButtonUI	ButtonUI

Table 5-6: JRadioButton UIResource elements

Summary

This chapter described the components that can be toggled: `JToggleButton`, `JCheckBox`, and `JRadioButton`. You've seen how each component uses the `JToggleButton.ToggleButtonModel` class for its data model and how you can group the components into a `ButtonGroup`. In addition, you also saw how to handle selection events for each of the components.

Chapter 6 looks into working with the various menu-oriented components available from Swing.

CHAPTER 6

Swing Menus and Toolbars

MANY OF THE LOW-LEVEL SWING COMPONENTS were covered in the previous two chapters of this book. This chapter will delve into Swing's menu-related components. Menus and toolbars help make your applications more user-friendly by providing visual command options. Users can avoid the somewhat archaic multi-key command sequences that are holdovers from programs such as the early word processor Word Star and the more current emacs programmer's editor. Although Swing menus still support multi-key command sequences, the menus (and toolbars) are designed primarily for on-screen graphical selection with a mouse, instead of a keyboard.

The menu components discussed in this chapter are used as follows:

- For each cascading menu, you create a JMenu component and add it to the JMenuBar.

- For the selections available from the JMenu, you create JMenuItem components and add them to the JMenu.

- To create submenus, you add a new JMenu to a JMenu and place JMenuItem options on the new menu.

- Then, when a JMenu is selected, the system displays its current set of components within a JPopupMenu.

In addition to the basic JMenuItem elements, this chapter covers other menu items, such as JCheckBoxMenuItem and JRadioButtonMenuItem, that you can place on a JMenu. I also discuss the JSeparator class, which serves to divide menu items into logical groups. You'll find out how to use the JPopupMenu class for general support of pop-up menus that appear after a JMenu is selected. As with abstract buttons (the AbstractButton class was introduced in Chapter 4), each menu element can have a mnemonic associated with it for keyboard selection. I also tell you about the Class JToolBar support for keyboard accelerators so you can avoid having to go through all the menuing levels for selection. To see these various components in action, take a look at Figure 6-1.

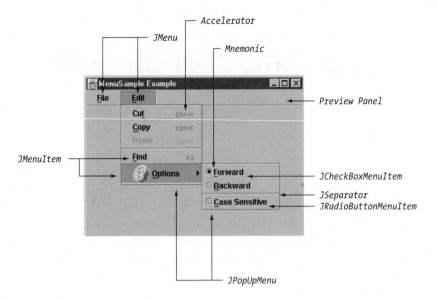

Figure 6-1: Menu component examples

Besides the individual menu-related components, in this chapter we'll look at the JMenuBar selection model and event-related classes specific to menus. The selection model interface we'll examine is the SingleSelectionModel interface; we'll also look at its default implementation DefaultSingleSelectionModel. I also discuss the menu-specific listeners and events MenuListener/MenuEvent, MenuKeyListener/ MenuKeyEvent, and MenuDragMouseListener/MenuDragMouseEvent. In addition, we'll also examine creating and using toolbars with the JToolBar class.

Working with Menus

With menus, it's easier to first explain how everything fits together and then look at the individual pieces. After each example, I delve into the individual menuing components.

Getting Started

We'll start by creating a frame with a menu bar, as shown in Figure 6-1. On the menu bar will be two ubiquitous menus, one called "File" and the other called "Edit." Under the File menu, the familiar options of "New," "Open," "Close," and "Exit" will appear (although they aren't shown in the figure), while under the Edit menu are options for "Cut," "Copy," "Paste," and "Find," and a submenu of Find options. The Options submenu will contain choices for search direction — forward or backward — and a toggle for case sensitivity. None of the menu choices will do anything other than print which menu choice was selected; for now, we're just creating the menu choices.

> **NOTE** *Selecting an option displays something like the following:*
> *Selected: Copy*
> *Selected: Forward*
> *Selected: Case Sensitive*

In various places within the different menus, menu separators will be added to divide the options into more-logical sets. To better visualize the menu system just described, look again at Figure 6-1.

Each of the menu options has a *mnemonic* associated with it to help with keyboard navigation and selection. The mnemonic allows users to make menu selections via the keyboard, for instance, by pressing ALT-F on a Windows platform to open the File menu. In addition to the keyboard mnemonic, a keystroke associated with several options acts as a keyboard *accelerator*. Unlike the mnemonic, the accelerator can directly activate a menu option, even when the menu option isn't visible.

In addition to its keyboard navigation support, the Options submenu has an icon associated with it. Although only one icon is shown in Figure 6-1, all menu components can have an icon, except for the JSeparator and JpopupMenu components.

```java
import java.awt.*;
import java.awt.event.*;
import javax.swing.*;

public class MenuSample {
  static class MenuActionListener implements ActionListener {
    public void actionPerformed (ActionEvent actionEvent) {
      System.out.println ("Selected: " + actionEvent.getActionCommand());
    }
  }
  public static void main(String args[]) {
    ActionListener menuListener = new MenuActionListener();
    JFrame frame = new ExitableJFrame("MenuSample Example");
    JMenuBar menuBar = new JMenuBar();

    // File Menu, F - Mnemonic
    JMenu fileMenu = new JMenu("File");
```

```
fileMenu.setMnemonic(KeyEvent.VK_F);
menuBar.add(fileMenu);

// File->New, N - Mnemonic
JMenuItem newMenuItem = new JMenuItem("New", KeyEvent.VK_N);
newMenuItem.addActionListener(menuListener);
fileMenu.add(newMenuItem);

// File->Open, O - Mnemonic
JMenuItem openMenuItem = new JMenuItem("Open", KeyEvent.VK_O);
openMenuItem.addActionListener(menuListener);
fileMenu.add(openMenuItem);

// File->Close, C - Mnemonic
JMenuItem closeMenuItem = new JMenuItem("Close", KeyEvent.VK_C);
closeMenuItem.addActionListener(menuListener);
fileMenu.add(closeMenuItem);

// Separator
fileMenu.addSeparator();

// File->Save, S - Mnemonic
JMenuItem saveMenuItem = new JMenuItem("Save", KeyEvent.VK_S);
saveMenuItem.addActionListener(menuListener);
fileMenu.add(saveMenuItem);

// Separator
fileMenu.addSeparator();

// File->Exit, X - Mnemonic
JMenuItem exitMenuItem = new JMenuItem("Exit", KeyEvent.VK_X);
exitMenuItem.addActionListener(menuListener);
fileMenu.add(exitMenuItem);

// Edit Menu, E - Mnemonic
JMenu editMenu = new JMenu("Edit");
editMenu.setMnemonic(KeyEvent.VK_E);
menuBar.add(editMenu);

// Edit->Cut, T - Mnemonic, CTRL-X - Accelerator
JMenuItem cutMenuItem = new JMenuItem("Cut", KeyEvent.VK_T);
cutMenuItem.addActionListener(menuListener);
KeyStroke ctrlXKeyStroke = KeyStroke.getKeyStroke(KeyEvent.VK_X,
```

```
Event.CTRL_MASK);
    cutMenuItem.setAccelerator(ctrlXKeyStroke);
    editMenu.add(cutMenuItem);


    // Edit->Copy, C - Mnemonic, CTRL-C - Accelerator
    JMenuItem copyMenuItem = new JMenuItem("Copy", KeyEvent.VK_C);
    copyMenuItem.addActionListener(menuListener);
    KeyStroke ctrlCKeyStroke = KeyStroke.getKeyStroke(KeyEvent.VK_C,
Event.CTRL_MASK);
    copyMenuItem.setAccelerator(ctrlCKeyStroke);
    editMenu.add(copyMenuItem);


    // Edit->Paste, P - Mnemonic, CTRL-V - Accelerator, Disabled
    JMenuItem pasteMenuItem = new JMenuItem("Paste", KeyEvent.VK_P);
    pasteMenuItem.addActionListener(menuListener);
    KeyStroke ctrlVKeyStroke = KeyStroke.getKeyStroke(KeyEvent.VK_V,
Event.CTRL_MASK);
    pasteMenuItem.setAccelerator(ctrlVKeyStroke);
    pasteMenuItem.setEnabled(false);
    editMenu.add(pasteMenuItem);


    // Separator
    editMenu.addSeparator();


    // Edit->Find, F - Mnemonic, F3 - Accelerator
    JMenuItem findMenuItem = new JMenuItem("Find", KeyEvent.VK_F);
    findMenuItem.addActionListener(menuListener);
    KeyStroke f3KeyStroke = KeyStroke.getKeyStroke(KeyEvent.VK_F3, 0);
    findMenuItem.setAccelerator(f3KeyStroke);
    editMenu.add(findMenuItem);


    // Edit->Options Submenu, O - Mnemonic, at.gif - Icon Image File
    JMenu findOptionsMenu = new JMenu("Options");
    Icon atIcon = new ImageIcon ("at.gif");
    findOptionsMenu.setIcon(atIcon);
    findOptionsMenu.setMnemonic(KeyEvent.VK_O);


    // ButtonGroup for radio buttons
    ButtonGroup directionGroup = new ButtonGroup();


    // Edit->Options->Forward, F - Mnemonic, in group
    JRadioButtonMenuItem forwardMenuItem = new JRadioButtonMenuItem("Forward",
true);
```

```
forwardMenuItem.addActionListener(menuListener);
forwardMenuItem.setMnemonic(KeyEvent.VK_F);
findOptionsMenu.add(forwardMenuItem);
directionGroup.add(forwardMenuItem);

// Edit->Options->Backward, B - Mnemonic, in group
JRadioButtonMenuItem backwardMenuItem = new JRadioButtonMenuItem("Backward");
backwardMenuItem.addActionListener(menuListener);
backwardMenuItem.setMnemonic(KeyEvent.VK_B);
findOptionsMenu.add(backwardMenuItem);
directionGroup.add(backwardMenuItem);

// Separator
findOptionsMenu.addSeparator();

// Edit->Options->Case Sensitive, C - Mnemonic
JCheckBoxMenuItem caseMenuItem = new JCheckBoxMenuItem("Case Sensitive");
caseMenuItem.addActionListener(menuListener);
caseMenuItem.setMnemonic(KeyEvent.VK_C);
findOptionsMenu.add(caseMenuItem);
editMenu.add(findOptionsMenu);

frame.setJMenuBar(menuBar);
frame.setSize(350, 250);
frame.setVisible(true);
  }
}
```

Menu Class Hierarchy

Now that you've seen an example of how to create the cascading menus for an application, you should be somewhat familiar with everything involved in using the Swing menu components. To help clarify, let's look at the class hierarchy diagram in Figure 6-2 to see how all the Swing menu components are interrelated.

The most important concept illustrated in the figure is that all the Swing menu elements, as subclasses of JComponent, are AWT components *in their own right*. You can place JMenuItem, JMenu, and JMenuBar components anywhere that AWT components can go, and not just on a frame. In addition, because JMenuItem inherits from AbstractButton, JMenuItem and its subclasses inherit support for various icons and for HTML text labels, as described in Chapter 5.

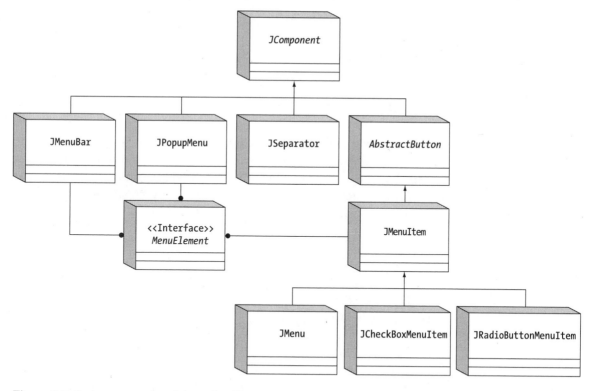

Figure 6-2: Swing menu class hierarchy diagram

> **TIP** *Although technically possible, placing menus in locations where users wouldn't expect them to be is poor user interface design.*

In addition to being part of the basic class hierarchy, each of the selectable menu components implements the MenuElement interface. The interface describes the menu behavior necessary to support keyboard and mouse navigation. The pre-defined menu components already implement this behavior so you don't have to. But if you're interested in how this interface works, the "Creating Custom MenuElement Components" section later in this chapter describes the process.

Now take a look at the different Swing menu components.

Class *JMenuBar*

Swing's menu bar component is the JMenuBar. Its operation requires you to fill the menu bar with JMenu elements that are full of JMenuItem elements. Then you add the menu bar to a JFrame or some other user interface component requiring a menu bar. The menu bar then relies on the assistance of a SingleSelectionModel to determine which JMenu to display or post after it's selected. Figure 6-3 shows these interconnections.

Creating JMenuBar Components

JMenuBar has a single constructor: the required no-argument Java Beans constructor [public JMenuBar()]. Once you create the menu bar, you can add it to a window either with the setJMenuBar() method of JApplet, JDialog, JFrame, JInternalFrame, or JRootPane, or with the add() method of a Container. Yes, even applets can have menu bars. This is certainly an improvement over the capabilities of AWT.

```
JMenuBar menuBar = new JMenuBar();
// add items to it
...
JFrame frame = new ExitableJFrame("MenuSample Example");
frame.setJMenuBar(menuBar);
```

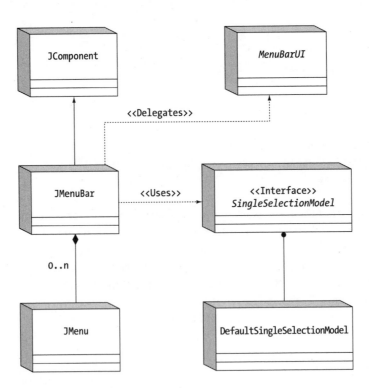

Figure 6-3: JMenuBar UML relationship diagram

With the system-provided look and feels, the menu bar would go to the top of the window, below any window title (if present), with setJMenuBar(). Other look and feels could place the menu bar elsewhere. When added with the add() method, a JMenuBar would be arranged by the layout manager of the Container.

After you have a JMenuBar, the remaining menu classes all work together to fill up the menu bar.

Adding to and Removing Menus from Menu Bars

You need to add JMenu objects to a JMenuBar. Otherwise, the only thing displayed is the border with nothing in it. There's a single method for adding menus to a JMenuBar:

```
public JMenu add(JMenu menu)
```

By default, consecutively added menus are displayed from left to right. This makes the first menu added the leftmost menu, and the last menu added the rightmost menu. Menus added in between are displayed in the order in which they're added. For instance, in the sample program from Figure 6-1, the menus were added as follows:

```
JMenu fileMenu = new JMenu("File");
menuBar.add(fileMenu);
JMenu editMenu = new JMenu("Edit");
menuBar.add(editMenu);
```

> **NOTE:** *Placing a JMenuBar in the EAST or WEST area of a BorderLayout does not make the menus appear vertically, stacked one on top of another. You have to customize the menu bar if you wanted them to appear this way. See Figure 6-5 for one implementation of a top-down menu bar.*

In addition to the add() method from JMenuBar, several overloaded varieties of the add() method inherited from Container offer more control over menu positioning. The only one of interest is the Component add(Component component, int index) method, which allows you to specify the position in which the new JMenu is to appear. Using this second variety of add() allows you to place the File and Edit JMenu components in a JMenuBar in a different order, but with the same results:

```
menuBar.add(editMenu);
menuBar.add(fileMenu, 0);
```

If you've added a `JMenu` component to a `JMenuBar`, you can remove it with either the `void remove(Component component)` or the `void remove(int index)` method inherited from `Container`:

```
bar.remove(edit);
bar.remove(0);
```

> **TIP** *Adding or removing menus from a menu bar is likely to confuse users. However, sometimes it's necessary to do so—especially if you want to have an expert mode that enables a certain functionality that a nonexpert mode hides. A better approach is to disable/enable individual menu items or entire menus.*

JMenuBar Properties

Table 6-1 shows the 12 properties of `JMenuBar`. Half the properties are read-only, only allowing you to query the current state of the menu bar. The remaining properties allow you to alter the appearance of the menu bar by deciding whether the border of the menu bar is painted and selecting the size of the margin between menu elements. The `selected` property and selection model control which menu on the menu bar, if any, is currently selected. When the selected component is set to a menu on the menu bar, the menu components appear in a pop-up menu within a window.

> **WARNING** *The `helpMenu` property, although available with a set-and-get method, is unsupported in Swing release 1.1. Calling either accessor method will throw an `Error`. With some future release of Swing, the `helpMenu` property will likely make a specific `JMenu` the designated help menu. Exactly what happens when a menu is flagged as the help menu is specific to the installed look and feel. What tends to happen is that the menu becomes the last, or rightmost, menu.*

> **WARNING** *The `selected` property of `JMenuBar` is nonstandard. The getter method returns a `boolean` to indicate if a menu component is selected on the menu bar, while the setter method accepts a `Component` argument to select a component on the menu bar.*

PROPERTY NAME	DATA TYPE	ACCESS
accessibleContext	AccessibleContext	read-only
borderPainted	boolean	read-write
component	Component	read-only
helpMenu	JMenu	read-write
managingFocus	boolean	read-only
margin	Insets	read-write
menuCount	int	read-only
selected	boolean/Component	read-write
selectionModel	SingleSelectionModel	read-write
subElements	MenuElement[ ]	read-only
UI	MenuBarUI	read-write
UIClassID	String	read-only

Table 6-1: JMenuBar properties

Customizing a JMenuBar Look and Feel

Each predefined Swing look and feel provides a different appearance and set of default UIResource values for the JMenuBar and each of the menu components. Figure 6-4 shows the appearance of all these menu components for the preinstalled set of look and feels: Motif, Windows, Metal, and Macintosh.

In regard to the specific appearance of the JMenuBar, the available set of UIResource-related properties is shown in Table 6-2. There are five different properties for the JMenuBar component.

PROPERTY STRING	OBJECT TYPE
MenuBar.background	Color
MenuBar.border	Border
MenuBar.font	Font
MenuBar.foreground	Color
MenuBarUI	MenuBarUI

Table 6-2: JMenuBar UIResource elements

If you want a vertical menu bar, instead of a horizontal one, simply change the LayoutManager of the menu bar component (see the following code listing). A setup such as a 0 row by 1 column GridLayout does the job because the number of rows will grow indefinitely for each JMenu added.

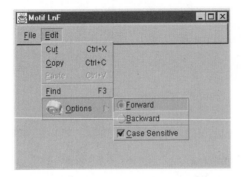

Motif

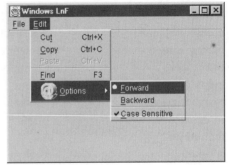

Windows

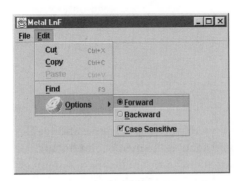

Metal

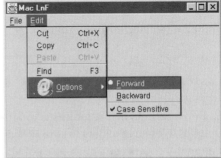

Macintosh

Figure 6-4: Menu components under different look and feels

```java
import java.awt.*;
import javax.swing.*;

public class VerticalMenuBar extends JMenuBar {
  private static final LayoutManager grid = new GridLayout(0,1);
  public VerticalMenuBar() {
    setLayout(grid);
  }
}
```

If you were to move the menu bar shown in Figure 6-1 to the east side of a
BorderLayout and make it a VerticalMenuBar instead of a JMenuBar, you'd get a
more workable setup, as shown in Figure 6-5. Although it may look a little
unconventional here, it's more desirable to have menu items appearing vertically, rather than horizontally, on the right side of a window. You may, however,
want to change the MenuBar.border property to a more appropriate border.

Figure 6-5: Using the VerticalMenuBar

> **NOTE** *Changing the layout manager of the* JMenuBar *has one negative side effect. Because top-level menus are pull-down menus, open menus on a vertical bar will obscure the menu bar. If you want to correct this pop-up placement behavior, you must extend the* JMenu *class and override its public void* setPopupMenuVisible(boolean visible) *method in order to make the pop-up menu span out, rather than drop down.*

SingleSelectionModel Interface

The SingleSelectionModel interface describes an index into an integer-indexed data structure where an element can be selected. The data structure behind the interface facade is most likely an array or vector in which repeatedly accessing the same position is guaranteed to return the same object. The SingleSelectionModel interface is the selection model for a JMenuBar as well as a JPopupMenu. In the case of a JMenuBar, the interface describes the currently selected JMenu that needs to be painted. In the case of a JPopupMenu, the interface describes the currently selected JMenuItem.

> **NOTE** *SingleSelectionModel also serves as the selection model for JTabbedPane, a class described in Chapter 10.*

The interface definition for SingleSelectionModel follows.

```
public interface SingleSelectionModel {
  // Listeners
  public void addChangeListener(ChangeListener listener);
  public void removeChangeListener(ChangeListener listener);
  // Properties
  public int getSelectedIndex();
```

```
        public void setSelectedIndex(int index);
        public boolean isSelected();
        // Other Methods
        public void clearSelection();
}
```

As you can see, in addition to the selection index, the interface requires the maintaining of a ChangeListener list to be notified when the selection index changes.

The default Swing-provided implementation of SingleSelectionModel is the DefaultSingleSelectionModel class. For both JMenuBar as well as JPopupMenu, it's very unlikely that you will change their selection model from this default implementation.

The DefaultSingleSelectionModel implementation manages the list of ChangeListener objects. In addition, the model uses a value of –1 to signify that nothing is currently selected.

When the selected index is –1, isSelected() returns false; otherwise the method returns true.

When the selected index changes, any registered ChangeListener objects will be notified.

Class *JMenuItem*

The JMenuItem component is the predefined component that a user selects on a menu bar. As a subclass of AbstractButton, JMenuItem acts as a specialized button component that behaves similarly to a JButton. Besides being a subclass of AbstractButton, the JMenuItem class shares the data model of JButton (ButtonModel interface and DefaultButtonModel implementation). Figure 6-6 shows these interrelationships.

Creating *JMenuItem* Components

Five constructors for JMenuItem follow. They allow you to initialize the menu item's string or icon label and the mnemonic of the menu item. There's no explicit constructor permitting you to set all three options at creation time.

1. ```
   public JMenuItem()
   JMenuItem jMenuItem = new JMenuItem();
   ```

2. ```
   public JMenuItem(Icon icon)
   Icon atIcon = new ImageIcon("at.gif");
   JMenuItem jMenuItem = new JMenuItem(atIcon);
   ```

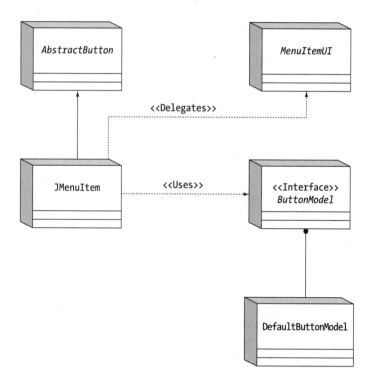

Figure 6-6: JMenuItem UML relationship diagram

3. ```
   public JMenuItem(String text)
   JMenuItem jMenuItem = new JMenuItem("Cut");
   ```

4. ```
   public JMenuItem(String text, Icon icon)
   Icon atIcon = new ImageIcon("at.gif");
   JMenuItem jMenuItem = new JMenuItem("Options", atIcon);
   ```

5. ```
   public JMenuItem(String text, int mnemonic)
   JMenuItem jMenuItem = new JMenuItem("Cut", KeyEvent.VK_T);
   ```

The mnemonic allows you to select the menu through keyboard navigation. For instance, you can simply select ALT-T on a Windows platform to select the Cut menu item if the item is part of an Edit menu that was already open. The mnemonic for a menu item usually appears underlined within the text label for the menu. However, if the letter doesn't appear within the text label or if there *is* no text label, the user will have no visual clue as to its setting. Letters are specified by the different key constants within the java.awt.event.KeyEvent class.
   ```

Other platforms might offer other meta-keys for selecting mnemonics. On UNIX, the meta key is also an ALT key; on a Macintosh, it's the Command key.

NOTE *Adding a `JMenuItem` with a label of "-" doesn't create a menu separator as it did with AWT's `MenuItem`.*

JMenuItem Properties

The `JMenuItem` class has many properties. Roughly 100 properties are inherited through its various superclasses. The eight properties specific to `JMenuItem` are shown in Table 6-3.

PROPERTY NAME	DATA TYPE	ACCESS
accelerator	KeyStroke	read-write bound
accessibleContext	AccessibleContext	read-only
armed	boolean	read-write
component	Component	read-only
enabled	boolean	write-only bound
subElements	MenuElement[ ]	read-only
UI	MenuElementUI	write-only bound
UIClassID	String	read-only

Table 6-3: JMenuItem properties

One truly interesting property is the accelerator. Recall the `KeyStroke` class from Chapter 2, a factory class that lets you create instances based on key and modifier combinations. For instance, the following statements, from the example in the section "Getting Started" earlier in this chapter, associate CTRL-X as the accelerator for one particular menu item.

```
KeyStroke ctrlXKeyStroke = KeyStroke.getKeyStroke(KeyEvent.VK_X,
Event.CTRL_MASK);
cutMenuItem.setAccelerator(ctrlXKeyStroke);
```

The first argument to `getKeyStroke()` is one of the many `VK_*` key constants from the `java.awt.event.KeyEvent` class. The second argument is one or a combination of modifier masks from the `java.awt.Event` class (`SHIFT_MASK`, `CTRL_MASK`, `META_MASK`, and `ALT_MASK`). For example, the following code would create a `KeyStroke` for ALT-CTRL-F3. You'd then associate the keystroke with a menu item as shown.

```
KeyStroke keyStroke =
  KeyStroke.getKeyStroke(KeyEvent.VK_F3, Event.CTRL_MASK | Event.ALT_MASK));
aJMenuItem.setAccelerator(keyStroke);
```

> **TIP** *If you don't want to have a keystroke mask, use zero (0) as the last getKeyStroke() argument.*

The read-only component and subElements properties are part of the MenuElement interface, which JMenuItem implements. The component property is the menu item renderer (the JMenuItem itself), and the subElements property is empty (that is, an empty array, not null), because a JMenuItem has no children.

> **NOTE** *Swing menus don't use AWT's MenuShortcut class.*

Handling JMenuItem Events

You can handle events within a JMenuItem in at least four different ways. The component inherits the ability to allow you to listen for the firing of ChangeEvent and ActionEvent through the ChangeListener and ActionListener registration methods of AbstractButton. In addition, the JMenuItem component supports registering MenuKeyListener and MenuDragMouseListener objects when MenuKeyEvent and MenuDragMouseEvent events happen.

Listening to JMenuItem Events with a ChangeListener

Normally, you wouldn't register a ChangeListener with a JMenuItem. However, demonstrating one hypothetical case helps to clarify the data model changes of the JMenuItem with respect to its ButtonModel. The changes with regard to arming, pressing, and selecting are the same as with a JButton. However, their naming might be a little confusing because the selected property of the model is never set.

A JMenuItem is armed when the mouse passes over the menu choice and it becomes selected. A JMenuItem is pressed when the user releases the mouse button over it. Immediately after being pressed, the menu item becomes unpressed and unarmed. Between the menu item being pressed and unpressed, the AbstractButton is notified of the model changes, causing any registered ActionListener objects of the menu item to be notified. The button model for a plain JMenuItem never reports being selected. If you move the mouse to another menu item without selecting, the first menu item automatically becomes

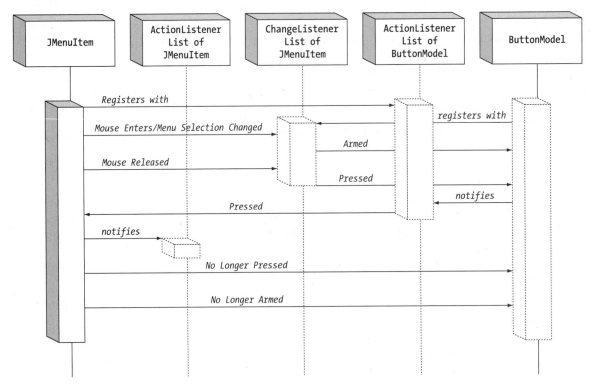

Figure 6-7: JMenuItem selection sequence diagram

unarmed. To help you better visualize the different changes, see Figure 6-7 for a sequence diagram.

> **NOTE** *Subclasses of* JMenuItem *can have their button model* selected *property set, like a toggle button—but your predefined* JMenuItem *can't.*

Listening to JMenuItem Events with an ActionListener

The better listener to attach to a JMenuItem is the ActionListener. It allows you to find out when a menu item is selected. Any registered ActionListener objects would be notified when a user releases the mouse button over a JMenuItem that's part of an open menu. Registered listeners are also notified if the user employs the keyboard (whether with arrow keys or mnemonics) or presses the menu item's keyboard accelerator to make a selection.

You must add an ActionListener to every JMenuItem on which you want an action to happen when selected. There's no automatic shortcut allowing you to register an `ActionListener` with a `JMenu` or `JMenuBar` and have all their contained `JMenuItem` objects notify a single `ActionListener`.

The earlier example program associates the same `ActionListener` with every `JMenuItem`. The source for the listener follows. What you'd more frequently do, though, is associate a different action with each item so that each menu item can do something different.

```
class MenuActionListener implements ActionListener {
  public void actionPerformed(ActionEvent e) {
    System.out.println("Selected: " + e.getActionCommand());
  }
}
```

Listening to JMenuItem Events with a MenuKeyListener

The `MenuKeyEvent` is a special kind of `KeyEvent` used internally by the user interface classes for a `JMenu` and `JMenuItem`, allowing the components to listen for when their keyboard mnemonic is pressed. To listen for this keyboard input, each menu component registers a `MenuKeyListener` to pay attention to the appropriate input. If the keyboard mnemonic is pressed, the event is consumed and not passed to any registered listeners. If the keyboard mnemonic is not pressed, any registered key listeners (instead of menu key listeners) are notified.

The `MenuKeyListener` interface definition follows.

```
public interface MenuKeyListener extends EventListener {
  public void menuKeyPressed(MenuKeyEvent e);
  public void menuKeyReleased(MenuKeyEvent e);
  public void menuKeyTyped(MenuKeyEvent e);
}
```

Normally, you wouldn't register objects as this type of listener yourself, although you could if you wanted to. If you do, and if a `MenuKeyEvent` happens (that is, a key is pressed/released), every `JMenu` on the `JMenuBar` will be notified, as will every `JMenuItem` (or subclass) on an open menu with a registered `MenuKeyListener`. That includes disabled menu items so that they can consume a pressed mnemonic. The definition of the `MenuKeyEvent` class follows.

```
public class MenuKeyEvent extends KeyEvent {
  public MenuKeyEvent(Component source, int id, long when, int modifiers, int
keyCode, char keyChar, MenuElement path[], MenuSelectionManager mgr);
  public MenuSelectionManager getMenuSelectionManager();
  public MenuElement[] getPath();
}
```

It's the job of the MenuSelectionManager to determine the current selection path. The selection path is the set of menu elements from the top-level JMenu on the JMenuBar to the selected components. For the most part, the manager lives behind the scenes just doing its thing, and you never have to worry about it.

Listening to JMenuItem Events with a MenuDragMouseListener

Like MenuKeyEvent, the MenuDragMouseEvent is another special kind of event used internally by the user interface classes for JMenu and JMenuItem. As its name implies, the MenuDragMouseEvent is a special kind of MouseEvent. By monitoring when a mouse is moved within an open menu, the user interface classes use the listener to maintain the selection path, thus determining the currently selected menu item. Its definition follows.

```
public interface MenuDragMouseListener extends EventListener {
  public void menuDragMouseDragged(MenuDragMouseEvent e);
  public void menuDragMouseEntered(MenuDragMouseEvent e);
  public void menuDragMouseExited(MenuDragMouseEvent e);
  public void menuDragMouseReleased(MenuDragMouseEvent e);
}
```

As with the MenuKeyListener, normally you don't listen for this event yourself. If you're interested in when a menu or submenu is about to be displayed, the better listener to register is the MenuListener, which can be registered with the JMenu, but not with an individual JMenuItem. We'll look at this in the next section, in our description of JMenu. The definition of the MenuDragMouseEvent class, the argument to each of the MenuDragMouseListener methods, is shown below:

```
public class MenuDragMouseEvent extends MouseEvent {
  public MenuDragMouseEvent(Component source, int id, long when, int modifiers,
int x, int y, int clickCount, boolean popupTrigger, MenuElement path[],
MenuSelectionManager mgr);
  public MenuSelectionManager getMenuSelectionManager();
  public MenuElement[] getPath();
}
```

Customizing a JMenuItem Look and Feel

As with the JMenuBar, the predefined look and feel classes each provide a different JMenuItem appearance and set of default UIResource values. Figure 6-4 showed the appearance of the JMenuItem component for the preinstalled set of look and feels: Motif, Windows, Metal, and Macintosh.

The available set of UIResource-related properties for a JMenuItem are shown in Table 6-4. The JMenuItem component offers 16 different properties.

PROPERTY STRING	OBJECT TYPE
MenuItem.acceleratorDelimiter	String
MenuItem.acceleratorFont	Font
MenuItem.acceleratorForeground	Color
MenuItem.acceleratorSelectionForeground	Color
MenuItem.arrowIcon	Icon
MenuItem.background	Color
MenuItem.border	Border
MenuItem.borderPainted	Boolean
MenuItem.checkIcon	Icon
MenuItem.disabledForeground	Color
MenuItem.font	Font
MenuItem.foreground	Color
MenuItem.margin	Insets
MenuItem.selectionBackground	Color
MenuItem.selectionForeground	Color
MenuItemUI	MenuItemUI

Table 6-4: JMenuItem UIResource elements

Class JMenu

The JMenu component is the basic menu item container that's placed on a JMenuBar. When a JMenu is selected, the menu displays the contained menu items within a JPopupMenu. As with JMenuItem, the data model for the JMenu is an implementation of ButtonModel, or more specifically DefaultButtonModel. Figure 6-8 will help you visualize these relationships.

Creating JMenu Components

Three constructors for JMenu allow you to initialize the string label of the menu if desired. One constructor offers tear-off menu support. However, tear-off menus aren't currently supported by Swing 1.1; therefore, the argument is ignored.

> **NOTE**   *Tear-off menus are menus that appear in a window and remain open after selection, instead of automatically closing.*

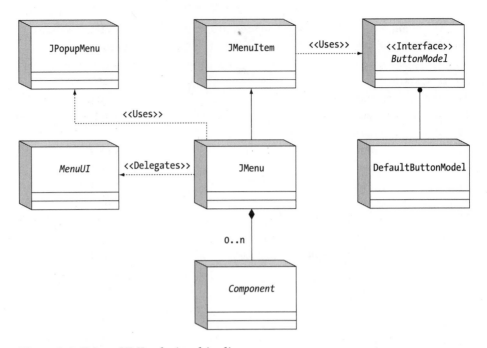

Figure 6-8: JMenu UML relationship diagram

The three constructors are:

1. `public JMenu()`
    `JMenu jMenu = new JMenu();`

2. `public JMenu(String label)`
    `JMenu jMenu = new JMenu("File");`

3. `public JMenu(String label, boolean useTearOffs)`

Adding Menu Items to a JMenu

Once you have a JMenu, you need to add JMenuItem objects to it; otherwise, the menu will display no choices. There are four methods for adding menu items defined within JMenu and one for adding a separator:

```
public JMenuItem add(JMenuItem menuItem);
public JMenuItem add(String label);
public Component add(Component component);
public JMenuItem add(Action action);
public void addSeparator();
```

In the example program in the section "Getting Started" earlier in this chapter, all the JMenuItem components were added to JMenu components with the first add() method. As a shortcut, you can pass the text label for a JMenuItem to the add() method of JMenu. This will create the menu item, set its label, and pass back the new menu item component. You can then bind a menu item event handler to this newly obtained menu item. The third add() method shows that you can place any Component on a JMenu, and not solely a JMenuItem. The last add() variety, with the Action argument, will be discussed in the next section of this chapter.

Adding separator bars to menus is done with the addSeparator() method of JMenu, instead of the AWT hack of adding a MenuItem with a label consisting of a dash ("-"). For instance, in the earlier example the File menu was created with code similar to the following:

```
JMenu fileMenu = new JMenu("File");
JMenuItem newMenuItem = new JMenuItem("New");
fileMenu.add(newMenuItem);
JMenuItem openMenuItem = new JMenuItem("Open");
fileMenu.add(openMenuItem);
JMenuItem closeMenuItem = new JMenuItem("Close");
fileMenu.add(closeMenuItem);
fileMenu.addSeparator();
JMenuItem saveMenuItem = new JMenuItem("Save");
fileMenu.add(saveMenuItem);
fileMenu.addSeparator();
JMenuItem exitMenuItem = new JMenuItem("Exit");
fileMenu.add(exitMenuItem);
```

In addition to adding menu items at the end of a menu, you can insert them at specific positions or insert a separator at a specific position, as follows:

```
public JMenuItem insert(JMenuItem menuItem, int pos);
public JMenuItem insert(Action a, int pos);
public void insertSeparator(int pos);
```

> **WARNING** *Unlike JMenuBar, you shouldn't try to use the inherited add() method from a Container that accepts an index argument. If you do use add(Component component, int index) to a menu component, it won't appear in the pop-up menu. With the Swing 1.1 release, there's a bug logged against this. In a future release, it should be corrected. You can still remove() menu items with the inherited methods.*

When a menu item is added to a JMenu, it's added to an internal JPopupMenu. By default, this pop-up menu uses a vertical BoxLayout to arrange the menu items so that the items are added from the top down. If you don't like this arrangement, you can change the layout manager of the JPopupMenu. Figure 6-9 shows a File menu in the window from Figure 6-1 in a 3-by-3 GridLayout.

> **NOTE** *See Chapter 10 for more information on BoxLayout.*

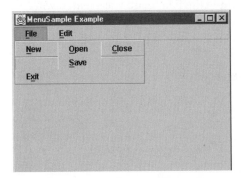

Figure 6-9: Menu items in a grid layout

Using Action Objects with Menus

The Action interface and its associated classes are described in Chapter 2. An Action is an extension of the ActionListener interface and contains some special properties for customizing components associated with its implementations. With the help of the AbstractAction implementation, you can easily define text labels, icons, and an ActionListener apart from a component. Then, you would create a component with an associated Action and not have to give the component a text label, icon, or ActionListener because those attributes would come from the Action. For a more complete description, refer to Chapter 2 .

To demonstrate, let's create a specific implementation of AbstractAction and add it to a JMenu multiple times. Once the Action is added to a JMenu, selecting the JMenuItem will display a pop-up dialog box with the help of the JOptionPane class, a topic covered in Chapter 9.

```java
public class ShowAction extends AbstractAction {
  Component parentComponent;
  public ShowAction(Component parentComponent) {
    super("About");
```

```
      this.parentComponent = parentComponent;
  }
  public void actionPerformed(ActionEvent actionEvent) {
    Runnable runnable = new Runnable() {
      public void run() {
        JOptionPane.showMessageDialog(
          parentComponent, "About Life",
          "About Box V1.0", JOptionPane.INFORMATION_MESSAGE);
      }
    };
    SwingUtilities.invokeLater(runnable);
  }
}
```

Because the JMenu component supports adding Action objects, you can create a
JMenuItem from the ShowAction. The menu item will then have a text label with the
word "About" and will perform the defined actionPerformed() method as its
ActionListener. In fact, you can create the Action once and then associate it
with as many menus as necessary (or other components that support adding
Action objects).

```
Action showAction = new ShowAction(aJFrame);
fileMenu.add(showAction);
editMenu.add(showAction);
```

One complexity-busting side effect when using AbstractAction is that it lets you
disable the Action with setEnabled(false), which in turn will disable all components created from it.

JMenu Properties

Besides the 100-plus inherited properties of JMenu, 15 properties are available
from JMenu-specific methods, as shown in Table 6-5. Several of the properties
override the behavior of the inherited properties. For instance, the setter
method for the accelerator property throws an Error if you try to assign such a
property. In other words, accelerators aren't supported within JMenu objects. The
remaining properties describe the current state of the JMenu object and its contained menu components.

PROPERTY NAME	DATA TYPE	ACCESS
accelerator	KeyStroke	write-only
accessibleContext	AccessibleContext	read-only
component	Component	read-only
delay	int	read-write
itemCount	int	read-only
menuComponentCount	int	read-only
menuComponents	Component[ ]	read-only
model	ButtonModel	write-only bound
popupMenu	JPopupMenu	read-only
popupMenuVisible	boolean	read-write
selected	boolean	read-write
subElements	MenuElement	read-only
tearOff	boolean	read-only
topLevelMenu	boolean	read-only
UIClassID	String	read-only

Table 6-5: JMenu properties

> **TIP** *Keep in mind that many property methods are inherited and that the parent class might offer a getter method where the current class only defines a new setter method, or vice versa.*

The delay property represents the value for the time that elapses between selection of a JMenu and posting of the JPopupMenu. By default, this value is zero, meaning that the submenu will appear immediately. Trying to set the value to a negative setting will throw an IllegalArgumentException.

> **WARNING** *As previously mentioned, the Swing 1.1 release doesn't support tear-off menus. If you try to access the tearOff property, an Error will be thrown.*

Selecting Menu Components

Normally, you don't need to listen for the selection of JMenu components. You only listen for selection of individual JMenuItem components. Nevertheless, you may be interested in the different ways that ChangeEvent works with a JMenu as compared with a JMenuItem. In addition, a MenuEvent can notify you whenever a menu is posted or canceled.

Listening to JMenu Events with a ChangeListener

As with a JMenuItem, you can register a ChangeListener with a JMenu if you're interested in making changes to the underlying ButtonModel. Surprisingly, the only possible state change to the ButtonModel with a JMenu is with the selected property. When selected, the JMenu displays its menu items. When not selected, the pop-up goes away.

Listening to JMenu Events with a MenuListener

The better way to listen for when a pop-up is displayed or hidden is by registering MenuListener objects with your JMenu objects. Its definition follows.

```
public interface MenuListener extends EventListener {
  public void menuCanceled(MenuEvent e);
  public void menuDeselected(MenuEvent e);
  public void menuSelected(MenuEvent e);
}
```

With a registered MenuListener, you're notified when a JMenu is selected before the pop-up menu is opened with the menu's choices. This allows you to customize its menu choices "on-the-fly" at runtime, with some potential interaction performance penalties. Besides being told when the associated pop-up menu is to be posted, you're also notified when the menu has been deselected when the menu has been canceled. As the following MenuEvent class definition shows, the only piece of information that comes with the event is the source (the menu):

```
public class MenuEvent extends EventObject {
  public MenuEvent(Object source);
}
```

Customizing a JMenu Look and Feel

As with the JMenuBar and JMenuItem, the predefined look and feel classes provide a different JMenu appearance and set of default UIResource values. Figure 6-4 shows the appearance of the JMenu object for the preinstalled set of look and feels.

The available set of UIResource-related properties for a JMenu is shown in Table 6-6. For the JMenu component, there are 18 different properties.

PROPERTY STRING	OBJECT TYPE
menu	Color
Menu.acceleratorFont	Font
Menu.acceleratorForeground	Color
Menu.acceleratorSelectionForeground	Color
Menu.arrowIcon	Icon
Menu.background	Color
Menu.border	Border
Menu.borderPainted	Boolean
Menu.checkIcon	Icon
Menu.consumesTabs	Boolean
Menu.disabledForeground	Color
Menu.font	Font
Menu.foreground	Color
Menu.margin	Insets
Menu.selectionBackground	Color
Menu.selectionForeground	Color
menuText	Color
MenuUI	MenuItemUI

Table 6-6: JMenu UIResource elements

Class JSeparator

The JSeparator class is a special component that acts as a separator on a JMenu. The JPopupMenu and JToolBar also support separators, but each one uses its own subclass of JSeparator. In addition to being placed on a menu, the JSeparator can be used anywhere you want to use a horizontal or vertical line to separate different areas of a screen.

The JSeparator is strictly a visual component; therefore, it has no data model.

Creating JSeparator Components

To create a separator for a JMenu, you don't directly create a JSeparator, although you can. Instead, you call JMenu.addSeparator(), whereupon the menu will create the separator and add it as the next item. The fact that it's a JSeparator (which isn't a JMenuItem subclass) is hidden. There's also an insertSeparator(int index) method of JMenu that allows you to add a separator at a specific position on the menu.

If you plan to use a JSeparator away from a menu (for example, to visually separate two panels in a layout), you'd use one of the two constructors for JSeparator.

They allow you to create a horizontal or vertical separator. If an orientation isn't specified, the orientation is horizontal. If you want to specify an orientation, you'd use either of the JSeparator constants of HORIZONTAL and VERTICAL.

1.  ```
    public JSeparator()
    JSeparator jSeparator = new JSeparator();
    ```

2.  ```
    public JSeparator(int orientation)
    JSeparator jSeparator = new JSeparator(JSeparator.VERTICAL);
    ```

JSeparator Properties

After you have a JSeparator, you add it to the screen like any other component. The initial dimensions of the component are empty (zero width and height), so if the layout manager of the screen asks the component what size it would like to be, the separator will reply that it needs no space. On the other hand, if the layout manager offers a certain amount of space, the separator will use the space if the orientation is appropriate. For instance, adding a horizontal JSeparator to the north side of a BorderLayout panel works fine and draws a separator line across the screen. However, adding a horizontal JSeparator to the east side of the same panel would result in nothing being drawn. For a vertical JSeparator, the behavior is reversed: The north side would be empty and a vertical line would appear on the east side.

The five properties of JSeparator are listed in Table 6-7.

PROPERTY NAME	DATA TYPE	ACCESS
accessibleContext	AccessibleContext	read-only
focusTraversable	boolean	read-only
orientation	int	read-write bound
UI	SeparatorUI	read-write bound
UIClassID	String	read-only

Table 6-7: JSeparator properties

> **WARNING** *If the orientation property isn't set to either JSeparator.HORIZON-TAL or JSeparator.VERTICAL, an IllegalArgumentException is thrown.*

Customizing a JSeparator Look and Feel

The appearance of the JSeparator under the preinstalled set of look and feels is shown with the other menu components in Figure 6-4.

The available set of UIResource-related properties for a JSeparator is shown in Table 6-8. For the JSeparator component, five different properties are available.

PROPERTY STRING	OBJECT TYPE
Separator.background	Color
Separator.foreground	Color
Separator.highlight	Color
Separator.shadow	Color
SeparatorUI	SeparatorUI

Table 6-8: JSeparator UIResource elements

Class JPopupMenu

The JPopupMenu component is the container for pop-up menu components, displayable anywhere and used for support by JMenu. When a programmer-defined triggering event happens, you display the JPopupMenu, and the menu displays the contained menu components. Like JMenuBar, the JPopupMenu uses the SingleSelectionModel to manage the currently selected element. Figure 6-10 shows these interconnections.

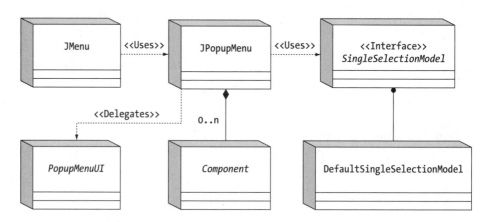

Figure 6-10: JPopupMenu UML relationship diagram

Creating JPopupMenu Components

There are two constructors for JPopupMenu. Only one allows you to initialize the string title of the menu if desired.

1. ```
   public JPopupMenu()
   JPopupMenu jPopupMenu = new JPopupMenu();
   ```

2. ```
   public JPopupMenu(String title)
   JPopupMenu jPopupMenu = new JPopupMenu("Welcome");
   ```

> **NOTE** *What happens with the title is dependent on the installed look and feel. The currently installed look and feel may ignore the title.*

Adding Menu Items to a JPopupMenu

As with a JMenu, once you have a JPopupMenu, you need to add menu item objects to it; otherwise, the menu will be empty. There are three JPopupMenu methods for adding menu items and one for adding a separator:

```
public JMenuItem add(JMenuItem menuItem);
public JMenuItem add(String label);
public JMenuItem add(Action action);
public void addSeparator();
```

In addition, an add() method is inherited from Container for adding regular AWT components:

```
public Component add(Component component);
```

> **WARNING** *It generally isn't wise to mix lightweight Swing components with heavyweight AWT components. However, because pop-up menus are always on top, it's less of an issue in this case.*

The natural way of adding menu items is with the first add() method. You create the menu item independently of the pop-up menu, including defining its behavior, then you attach it to the menu. With the second variety of add(), you must attach an event handler to the menu item returned from the method, otherwise the menu choice won't respond when selected. The following source demonstrates the two approaches. Which you use depends entirely on your preference. A visual programming environment like JBuilder will use the first. Because the first approach is inherently less complex, most if not all programmers should also use the first approach.

```
JPopupMenu popupenu = new JPopupMenu();
ActionListener anActionListener = ...;
JMenuItem firstItem = new JMenuItem("Hello");
firstItem.addActionListener(anActionListener);
popupMenu.add(firstItem);
JMenuItem secondItem = popupMenu.add("World");
secondItem.addActionListener(anActionListener);
```

Using an Action to create a menu item works the same with JPopupMenu as it does with JMenu. Plus, you can add a menu separator with addSeparator().

As well as adding menu items at the end of a menu, you can insert them at specific positions or insert a separator at a specific position:

```
public JMenuItem insert(Component component, int position);
public JMenuItem insert(Action action, int position);
```

There's no insertSeparator() method as there is with JMenu. But you can use the add(Component component, int position) method inherited from Container. If you want to remove components, use the remove(Component component) method specific to JPopupMenu.

> **WARNING** *Don't call the remove(int position) method inherited from Container because this doesn't remove the JMenuItem from the internal data structure of the JPopupMenu. In addition, if you try to insert() an Action, an Error will be thrown because the functionality hasn't yet been implemented in Swing 1.1.*

> **TIP** *Accelerators on attached JMenuItem objects are ignored. Mnemonics might also be ignored depending on the currently installed look and feel.*

Displaying the JPopupMenu

Unlike the JMenu, simply populating the pop-up menu isn't sufficient to use it. You need to add event-handling code to trigger the display of the pop-up menu.

How to display the pop-up menu hasn't changed between AWT and Swing. A MouseEvent can still tell you if a specific mouse event is the platform-specific event to trigger the display of a pop-up menu. The key JPopupMenu method to call is the public void show(Component invoker, int x, int y) method, which displays the menu at position x, y within the coordinate space of the invoker, with an origin in the invoker's upper-left corner.

With regard to listening for the pop-up–triggering mouse event, the source code to accomplish this can be easily wrapped up in its own class and reused regularly. The source for such a class follows.

```java
import java.awt.*;
import java.awt.event.*;
import javax.swing.*;

public class JPopupMenuShower extends MouseAdapter {

  private JPopupMenu popup;

  public JPopupMenuShower(JPopupMenu popup) {
    this.popup = popup;
  }

  private void showIfPopupTrigger(MouseEvent mouseEvent) {
    if (mouseEvent.isPopupTrigger()) {
      popup.show(mouseEvent.getComponent(), mouseEvent.getX(),
mouseEvent.getY());
    }
  }

  public void mousePressed(MouseEvent mouseEvent) {
    showIfPopupTrigger(mouseEvent);
  }
  public void mouseReleased(MouseEvent mouseEvent) {
    showIfPopupTrigger(mouseEvent);
  }
}
```

After you have this class, you simply need to create an instance and attach it to any component you want to have display the pop-up menu:

```java
MouseListener mouseListener = new JPopupMenuShower(popupMenu);
frame.addMouseListener(mouseListener);
```

JPopupMenu Properties

The 14 properties of JPopupMenu are listed in Table 6-9. Many properties are also inherited through JComponent, Container, and Component.

PROPERTY NAME	DATA TYPE	ACCESS
accessibleContext	AccessibleContext	read-only
borderPainted	boolean	read-write
component	Component	read-only
invoker	Component	read-only
label	String	read-write bound
lightWeightPopupEnabled	boolean	read-write
margin	Insets	read-only
popupSize	Dimension	write-only
selected	Component	write-only
selectionModel	SingleSelectionModel	read-write
subElements	MenuElement[ ]	read-only
UI	PopupMenuUI	read-write bound
UIClassID	String	read-only
visible	boolean	read-write

Table 6-9: JPopupMenu properties

The most interesting property of JPopupMenu is property lightWeightPopupEnabled. Normally, the JPopupMenu tries to avoid creating new heavyweight components for displaying its menu items. Instead, the pop-up menu uses a JPanel when the JPopupMenu can be displayed completely within the outermost window boundaries; if the menu items don't fit, the JPopupMenu uses a JWindow. If, however, you're mixing lightweight and heavyweight components on different window layers, displaying the pop-up within a JPanel might not work because a heavyweight component displayed in the layer of the menu will appear in front of the JPanel. To correct this behavior, the pop-up menu can use a Panel for displaying the menu choices. By default, the JPopupMenu never uses a Panel.

> **NOTE** *When the JPopupMenu is displayed in either a JPanel or a Panel, the outermost window relies on the layering effect of the JRootPane to ensure that the pop-up panel is displayed at the appropriate position in front of the other components. Chapter 8 describes the JRootPane class in more detail.*

If you need to enable the display of a Panel, you can configure it at the individual JPopupMenu level or for your entire applet or application. At the individual pop-up level, just set the `lightWeightPopupEnabled` property to `false`. At the system level, this is done through a call to the `public static void setDefaultLightWeightPopupEnabled(boolean newValue)` method of `JPopupMenu` (with an argument setting of `false`). The method must be called before creating the pop-up menu. `JPopupMenu` objects created before the change will have the original value (default is `true`):

```
// from now on, all JPopupMenus will be heavyweight
JPopupMenu.setDefaultLightWeightPopupEnabled(false);
```

Watching for Pop-up Menu Visibility

Like the `JMenu`, the `JPopupMenu` has a special event/listener combination to watch for when the pop-up menu is about to become visible, invisible, or canceled. The event is `PopupMenuEvent` and the listener is `PopupMenuListener`. The event class simply describes the source pop-up menu of the event.

```
public class PopupMenuEvent extends EventObject {
  public PopupMenuEvent(Object source);
}
```

When a `JPopupMenu` fires the event, any registered `PopupMenuListener` objects are notified through one of its three interface methods. This lets you customize the current menu items based on the system state or who/what the pop-up menu invoker happens to be. The `PopupMenuListener` interface definition follows:

```
public interface PopupMenuListener extends EventListener {
  public void popupMenuCanceled(PopupMenuEvent e);
  public void popupMenuWillBecomeInvisible(PopupMenuEvent e);
  public void popupMenuWillBecomeVisible(PopupMenuEvent e);
}
```

Customizing a JPopupMenu Look and Feel

Each installable Swing look and feel provides a different `JPopupMenu` appearance and set of default `UIResource` values. Figure 6-11 shows the appearance of the `JPopupMenu` component for the preinstalled set of look and feels: Motif, Windows, Metal, and Macintosh. Notice that none of the predefined look and feel classes utilize the title property of the `JPopupMenu`.

The available set of `UIResource`-related properties for a `JPopupMenu` is shown in Table 6-10. For the `JPopupMenu` component, there are five different properties.

PROPERTY STRING	OBJECT TYPE
PopupMenu.background	Color
PopupMenu.border	Border
PopupMenu.font	Font
PopupMenu.foreground	Color
PopupMenuUI	PopupMenuUI

Table 6-10: JPopupMenu UIResource elements

Motif

Windows

Metal

Macintosh

Figure 6-11: JPopupMenu under different look and feels

Class *JPopupMenu.Separator*

The JPopupMenu class maintains its own separator to permit a custom look and feel for the separator when on a JPopupMenu. This custom separator is an inner class to the JPopupMenu.

When you call JPopupMenu.addSeparator(), an instance of this class is automatically created and added to the pop-up menu. In addition, you can create this separator by calling its no-argument constructor:

```
JSeparator popupSeparator = new JPopupMenu.Separator();
```

Both methods create a horizontal separator. If you want to change the orientation of the separator, you must call the setOrientation() method inherited from JSeparator with an argument of JPopupMenu.Separator.VERTICAL. However, having a vertical separator on a pop-up menu isn't appropriate.

A Complete Pop-up Menu Usage Example

The following program puts together all the pieces of using a JPopupMenu, including listening for selection of all the items on the menu, as well as listening for when it's displayed. The program reuses our JPopupMenuShower class, defined earlier in the section "Displaying the JPopupMenu." The output for the program is shown in Figure 6-12, with the pop-up visible.

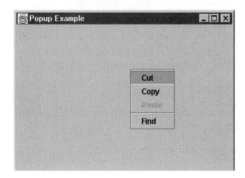

Figure 6-12: JPopupMenu usage example output

```
import java.awt.*;
import java.awt.event.*;
import javax.swing.*;
import javax.swing.event.*;
```

```java
public class PopupSample {

  public static void main(String args[]) {
    // Define ActionListener
    ActionListener actionListener = new ActionListener() {
      public void actionPerformed(ActionEvent actionEvent) {
        System.out.println("Selected: " + actionEvent.getActionCommand());
      }
    };

    // Define PopupMenuListener
    PopupMenuListener popupMenuListener = new PopupMenuListener() {
      public void popupMenuCanceled(PopupMenuEvent popupMenuEvent) {
        System.out.println("Canceled");
      }
      public void popupMenuWillBecomeInvisible(PopupMenuEvent popupMenuEvent) {
        System.out.println("Becoming Invisible");
      }
      public void popupMenuWillBecomeVisible(PopupMenuEvent popupMenuEvent) {
        System.out.println("Becoming Visible");
      }
    };

    // Create frame
    JFrame frame = new ExitableJFrame("Popup Example");

    // Create popup menu, attach popup menu listener
    JPopupMenu popupMenu = new JPopupMenu();
    popupMenu.addPopupMenuListener(popupMenuListener);

    // Cut
    JMenuItem cutMenuItem = new JMenuItem("Cut");
    cutMenuItem.addActionListener(actionListener);
    popupMenu.add(cutMenuItem);

    // Copy
    JMenuItem copyMenuItem = new JMenuItem("Copy");
    copyMenuItem.addActionListener(actionListener);
    popupMenu.add(copyMenuItem);

    // Paste
    JMenuItem pasteMenuItem = new JMenuItem("Paste");
    pasteMenuItem.addActionListener(actionListener);
```

```
    pasteMenuItem.setEnabled(false);
    popupMenu.add(pasteMenuItem);

    // Separator
    popupMenu.addSeparator();

    // Find
    JMenuItem findMenuItem = new JMenuItem("Find");
    findMenuItem.addActionListener(actionListener);
    popupMenu.add(findMenuItem);

    // Enable showing by binding popup to frame
    MouseListener mouseListener = new JPopupMenuShower(popupMenu);
    frame.addMouseListener (mouseListener);

    frame.setSize(350, 250);
    frame.setVisible(true);
  }
}
```

Class `JCheckBoxMenuItem`

Swing's `JCheckBoxMenuItem` component behaves as if you have a `JCheckBox` on a menu as a `JMenuItem`. The data model for the menu item is the `ToggleButtonModel`, described in Chapter 5. It allows the menu item to have a selected or unselected state, while showing an appropriate icon for the state. Because the data model is the `ToggleButtonModel`, when `JCheckBoxMenuItem` is placed in a `ButtonGroup` only one component in the group is ever selected. However, this isn't the natural way to use a `JCheckBoxMenuItem` and is likely to confuse users. If you need this behavior, see the next component, `JRadioButtonMenuItem`. Figure 6-13 shows the interrelationships of the `JCheckBoxMenuItem` class.

Creating `JCheckBoxMenuItem` Components

There are six constructors for `JCheckBoxMenuItem`. They allow you to initialize the text label, icon, and initial state. Unlike the `JCheckBox`, the icon is part of the label and *not* a separate device to indicate whether something is checked. If either the text label or the icon isn't passed to the constructor, that part of the item label will be set to its default value, empty. By default, a `JCheckBoxMenuItem` is unselected.

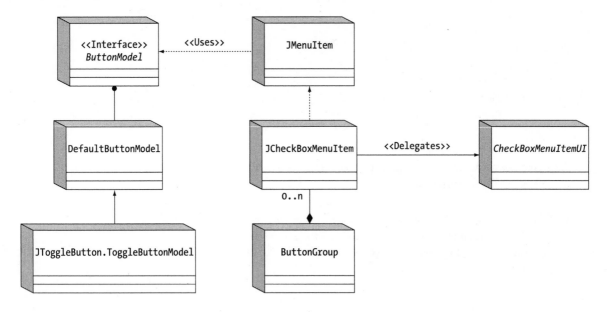

Figure 6-13: JCheckBoxMenuItem UML relationship diagram

1. `public JCheckBoxMenuItem()`
   `JCheckBoxMenuItem jCheckBoxMenuItem = new JCheckBoxMenuItem();`

2. `public JCheckBoxMenuItem(String text)`
   `JCheckBoxMenuItem jCheckBoxMenuItem = new JCheckBoxMenuItem("Boy");`

3. `public JCheckBoxMenuItem(Icon icon)`
   `Icon boyIcon = new ImageIcon("boy-r.jpg");`
   `JCheckBoxMenuItem jCheckBoxMenuItem = new JCheckBoxMenuItem(boyIcon);`

4. `public JCheckBoxMenuItem(String text, Icon icon)`
   `JCheckBoxMenuItem jCheckBoxMenuItem = new JCheckBoxMenuItem("Boy",`
   `boyIcon);`

5. `public JCheckBoxMenuItem(String text, boolean state)`
   `JCheckBoxMenuItem jCheckBoxMenuItem = new JCheckBoxMenuItem("Girl",`
   `true);`

6. `public JCheckBoxMenuItem(String text, Icon icon, boolean state)`
   `Icon girlIcon = new ImageIcon("girl-r.jpg");`
   `JCheckBoxMenuItem jCheckBoxMenuItem = new JCheckBoxMenuItem("Girl",`
   `girlIcon, true);`

> **NOTE** *Creating a* JCheckBoxMenuItem *with an icon has no effect on the appearance of the check box next to the menu item. It's strictly part of the label for the* JCheckBoxMenuItem.

JCheckBoxMenuItem Properties

Most of the JCheckBoxMenuItem properties are inherited from the many super-classes of JCheckBoxMenuItem. Table 6-11 lists the four properties defined by JCheckBoxMenuItem.

PROPERTY NAME	DATA TYPE	ACCESS
accessibleContext	AccessibleContext	read-only
selectedObjects	Object[ ]	read-only
state	boolean	read-write
UIClassID	String	read-only

Table 6-11: JCheckBoxMenuItem properties

Handling JCheckBoxMenuItem Selection Events

With a JCheckBoxMenuItem, you can attach many different listeners for a great variety of events:

- MenuDragMouseListener and MenuKeyListener from JMenuItem

- ActionListener, ChangeListener, and ItemListener from AbstractButton

- AncestorListener, PropertyChangeListener, and VetoableChangeListener from JComponent

- ContainerListener from Container

- ComponentListener, FocusListener, InputMethodListener, KeyListener, MouseListener, MouseMotionListener, and PropertyChangeListener (again) from Component

Although you can listen for 15 different types of events, the most interesting are the ActionEvent and the ItemEvent, described next.

Listening to JCheckBoxMenuItem Events with an ActionListener

Attaching an ActionListener to a JCheckBoxMenuItem allows you to find out when the menu item is selected. The listener is told of the selection, but not of the new state. To find out the selected state, you must get the model for the event source and query the selection state, as the following sample ActionListener source shows. This listener modifies both the check box text and the icon label, based on the current selection state.

```
ActionListener aListener = new ActionListener() {
  public void actionPerformed(ActionEvent event) {
    AbstractButton aButton = (AbstractButton)event.getSource();
    boolean selected = aButton.getModel().isSelected();
    String newLabel;
    Icon newIcon;
    if (selected) {
      newLabel = "Girl";
      newIcon = girlIcon;
    } else {
      newLabel = "Boy";
      newIcon = boyIcon;
    }
    aButton.setText(newLabel);
    aButton.setIcon(newIcon);
  }
};
```

Listening to JCheckBoxMenuItem with an ItemListener

If you listen for JCheckBoxMenuitem selection with an ItemListener, you don't have to query the event source for the selection state — the event already carries that information. Based on this state, you'd respond accordingly. Re-creating the ActionListener behavior with an ItemListener requires just a few minor changes to the previously listed source:

```
ItemListener iListener = new ItemListener() {
  public void itemStateChanged(ItemEvent event) {
    AbstractButton aButton = (AbstractButton)event.getSource();
    int state = event.getStateChange();
    String newLabel;
    Icon newIcon;
    if (state == ItemEvent.SELECTED) {
      newLabel = "Girl";
```

```
      newIcon = girlIcon;
    } else {
      newLabel = "Boy";
      newIcon = boyIcon;
    }
    aButton.setText(newLabel);
    aButton.setIcon(newIcon);
  }
};
```

Customizing a JCheckBoxMenuItem Look and Feel

The appearance of the JCheckBoxMenuItem under the preinstalled set of look and feels is shown with the other menu components in Figure 6-4.

The available set of UIResource-related properties for a JCheckBoxMenuItem is shown in Table 6-12. The JCheckBoxMenuItem component has 15 different properties.

PROPERTY STRING	OBJECT TYPE
CheckBoxMenuItem.acceleratorFont	Font
CheckBoxMenuItem.acceleratorForeground	Color
CheckBoxMenuItem.acceleratorSelectionForeground	Color
CheckBoxMenuItem.arrowIcon	Icon
CheckBoxMenuItem.background	Color
CheckBoxMenuItem.border	Border
CheckBoxMenuItem.borderPainted	Boolean
CheckBoxMenuItem.checkIcon	Icon
CheckBoxMenuItem.disabledForeground	Color
CheckBoxMenuItem.font	Font
CheckBoxMenuItem.foreground	Color
CheckBoxMenuItem.margin	Insets
CheckBoxMenuItem.selectionBackground	Color
CheckBoxMenuItem.selectionForeground	Color
CheckBoxMenuItemUI	MenuItemUI

Table 6-12: JCheckBoxMenuItem UIResource elements

The Icon associated with the CheckBoxMenuItem.checkIcon property key is the one displayed on the JCheckBoxMenuItem. If you don't like the default icon, you can change it with the following line of source, assuming the new icon has already been defined and created:

```
UIManager.put("CheckBoxMenuItem.checkIcon", someIcon);
```

For this new icon to display an appropriate selected image, the Icon implementation must check the state of the associated menu component within its paintIcon() method. The DiamondIcon created in Chapter 4 wouldn't work for this icon because it doesn't ask the component for its state. Instead, the state is fixed at constructor time. The following class represents one icon that could be used.

```java
import java.awt.*;
import javax.swing.*;

public class DiamondAbstractButtonStateIcon implements Icon {
  private final int width = 10;
  private final int height = 10;
  private Color color;
  private Polygon polygon;
  public DiamondAbstractButtonStateIcon(Color color) {
    this.color = color;
    initPolygon();
  }
  private void initPolygon() {
    polygon = new Polygon();
    int halfWidth = width/2;
    int halfHeight = height/2;
    polygon.addPoint (0, halfHeight);
    polygon.addPoint (halfWidth, 0);
    polygon.addPoint (width, halfHeight);
    polygon.addPoint (halfWidth, height);
  }
  public int getIconHeight() {
    return width;
  }
  public int getIconWidth() {
    return height;
  }
  public void paintIcon(Component component, Graphics g, int x, int y) {
    boolean selected = false;
    g.setColor (color);
    g.translate (x, y);
    if (component instanceof AbstractButton) {
      AbstractButton abstractButton = (AbstractButton)component;
      selected = abstractButton.isSelected();
    }
```

```
  if (selected) {
    g.fillPolygon (polygon);
  } else {
    g.drawPolygon (polygon);
  }
  g.translate (-x, -y);
  }
}
```

> **NOTE** *If the DiamondAbstractButtonStateIcon icon were used with a com-*
> *ponent that isn't an AbstractButton type, the icon would always be*
> *deselected because the selection state is a property of AbstractButton.*

Class JRadioButtonMenuItem

The JRadioButtonMenuItem component has the longest name of all the Swing components. It works like a JRadioButton, but lives on a menu. When placed with
other JRadioButtonMenuItem components within a ButtonGroup, only one component will be selected at a time. As with the JRadioButton, the button model for the
JRadioButtonMenuItem is the JToggleButton.ToggleButtonModel. Figure 6-14 shows
the interrelationships within the JRadioButtonMenuItem.

Creating JRadioButtonMenuItem Components

The JRadioButtonMenuItem has seven constructors. They allow you to initialize the
text label, icon, and initial state. Similar to the JCheckBoxMenuItem component, the
icon for the JRadioButtonMenuItem is part of the label. This is unlike the JRadioButton
in which the icon indicates whether the radio button is selected. If either the text
label or icon isn't part of the constructor, that part of the item label will be empty.
By default, a JRadioButtonMenuItem is unselected. If you create a JRadioButtonMenuItem
that is selected and then add it to a ButtonGroup, the button group will deselect
the menu item if the group already has a selected item in the group.

1. `public JRadioButtonMenuItem()`
   `JRadioButtonMenuItem jRadioButtonMenuItem = new JRadioButtonMenuItem();`

2. `public JRadioButtonMenuItem(String text)`
   `JRadioButtonMenuItem jRadioButtonMenuItem = new`
   `JRadioButtonMenuItem("Partridge");`

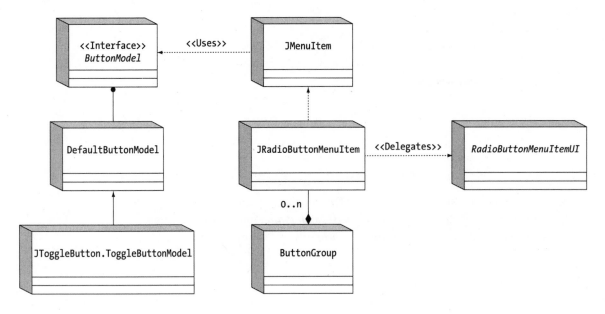

Figure 6-14: JRadioButtonMenuItem UML relationship diagram

3. public JRadioButtonMenuItem(String text, boolean state)
   JRadioButtonMenuItem jRadioButtonMenuItem = new
   JRadioButtonMenuItem("Turtle Doves", true);

4. public JRadioButtonMenuItem(String text, Icon icon)
   JRadioButtonMenuItem jRadioButtonMenuItem = new
   JRadioButtonMenuItem("French Hens", threeIcon);

5. public JRadioButtonMenuItem(String text, Icon icon, boolean state)
   Icon girlIcon = new ImageIcon("girl-r.jpg");
   JCheckBoxMenuItem jCheckBoxMenuItem = new JCheckBoxMenuItem("Girl",
   girlIcon, true);

6. public JRadioButtonMenuItem(Icon icon)
   Icon fiveIcon = new ImageIcon("5.gif");
   JRadioButtonMenuItem jRadioButtonMenuItem = new
   JRadioButtonMenuItem(fiveIcon);

7. public JRadioButtonMenuItem(Icon icon, boolean state)
   Icon girlIcon = new ImageIcon("girl-r.jpg");
   JRadioButtonMenuItem jRadioButtonMenuItem = new
   JRadioButtonMenuItem(sixIcon, true);

> **TIP** *After creating* JRadioButtonMenuItem *instances, remember to add them to a* ButtonGroup *so they will work as a mutually exclusive group.*

Handling JRadioButtonMenuItem Selection Events

The JRadioButtonMenuItem shares the same 15 different event/listener pairs with JCheckBoxMenuItem. To listen for selection, attaching an ActionListener is the normal approach. In addition, you might want to attach the same listener to all the JRadioButtonMenuItem objects in a ButtonGroup—after all, they're in a group for a reason. If you use the same listener, that listener can employ the current selection to perform some common operation. In other cases, such as that in Figure 6-1, selection of any JRadioButtonMenuItem option does nothing. Only when someone selects the "Find" menu element would the current selection of the ButtonGroup for the set of JRadioButtonMenuItem components have any meaning.

Configuring JRadioButtonMenuItem Properties

As with JCheckBoxMenuItem, most of the JRadioButtonMenuItem properties are inherited. The two shown in Table 6-13 merely override the behavior from the superclass.

PROPERTY NAME	DATA TYPE	ACCESS
accessibleContext	AccessibleContext	read-only
UIClassID	String	read-only

Table 6-13: JRadioButtonMenuItem properties

Customizing a JRadioButtonMenuItem Look and Feel

The appearance of the JRadioButtonMenuItem under the preinstalled set of look and feels is shown with the other menu components in Figure 6-4.

The available set of UIResource-related properties for a JRadioButtonMenuItem is shown in Table 6-14. For the JRadioButtonMenuItem component, there are 15 different properties.

PROPERTY STRING	OBJECT TYPE
RadioButtonMenuItem.acceleratorFont	Font
RadioButtonMenuItem.acceleratorForeground	Color
RadioButtonMenuItem.acceleratorSelectionForeground	Color
RadioButtonMenuItem.arrowIcon	Icon
RadioButtonMenuItem.background	Color
RadioButtonMenuItem.border	Border
RadioButtonMenuItem.borderPainted	Boolean
RadioButtonMenuItem.checkIcon	Icon
RadioButtonMenuItem.disabledForeground	Color
RadioButtonMenuItem.font	Font
RadioButtonMenuItem.foreground	Color
RadioButtonMenuItem.margin	Insets
RadioButtonMenuItem.selectionBackground	Color
RadioButtonMenuItem.selectionForeground	Color
RadioButtonMenuItemUI	MenuItemUI

Table 6-14: JRadioButtonMenuItem UIResource elements

A Complete JRadioButtonMenuItem Usage Example

To help you understand the JRadioButtonMenuItem usage, the following program demonstrates how to put everything together, including listening for selection of all the items on the menu, from either an ActionListener or an ItemListener.

```
import javax.swing.*;
import java.awt.*;
import java.awt.event.*;

public class RadioButtonSample {
  static Icon threeIcon = new ImageIcon("3.gif");
  static Icon fourIcon = new ImageIcon("4.gif");
  static Icon fiveIcon = new ImageIcon("5.gif");
  static Icon sixIcon = new ImageIcon("6.gif");

  public static void main(String args[]) {

    ActionListener actionListener = new ActionListener() {
      public void actionPerformed (ActionEvent actionEvent) {
        AbstractButton aButton = (AbstractButton)actionEvent.getSource();
        boolean selected = aButton.getModel().isSelected();
        System.out.println (actionEvent.getActionCommand() + " - selected? " +
```

```
selected);
      }
    };

    ItemListener itemListener = new ItemListener() {
      public void itemStateChanged(ItemEvent itemEvent) {
        AbstractButton aButton = (AbstractButton)itemEvent.getSource();
        int state = itemEvent.getStateChange();
        String selected = ((state == ItemEvent.SELECTED) ? "selected" : "not
selected");
        System.out.println (aButton.getText() + " - selected? " + selected);
      }
    };

    JFrame frame = new ExitableJFrame("Radio Menu Example");
    JMenuBar menuBar = new JMenuBar();
    JMenu menu = new JMenu("Menu");
    ButtonGroup buttonGroup = new ButtonGroup();
    menu.setMnemonic(KeyEvent.VK_M);

    JRadioButtonMenuItem emptyMenuItem = new JRadioButtonMenuItem();
    emptyMenuItem.setActionCommand("Empty");
    emptyMenuItem.addActionListener(actionListener);
    buttonGroup.add(emptyMenuItem);
    menu.add(emptyMenuItem);

    JRadioButtonMenuItem oneMenuItem = new JRadioButtonMenuItem("Partridge");
    oneMenuItem.addActionListener(actionListener);
    buttonGroup.add(oneMenuItem);
    menu.add(oneMenuItem);

    JRadioButtonMenuItem twoMenuItem = new JRadioButtonMenuItem("Turtle Doves",
true);
    twoMenuItem.addActionListener(actionListener);
    buttonGroup.add(twoMenuItem);
    menu.add(twoMenuItem);

    JRadioButtonMenuItem threeMenuItem = new JRadioButtonMenuItem("French Hens",
threeIcon);
    threeMenuItem.addItemListener(itemListener);
    buttonGroup.add(threeMenuItem);
    menu.add(threeMenuItem);
```

```
        JRadioButtonMenuItem fourMenuItem = new JRadioButtonMenuItem("Calling Birds",
fourIcon,

true);
    fourMenuItem.addActionListener(actionListener);
    buttonGroup.add(fourMenuItem);
    menu.add(fourMenuItem);

    JRadioButtonMenuItem fiveMenuItem = new JRadioButtonMenuItem(fiveIcon);
    fiveMenuItem.addActionListener(actionListener);
    fiveMenuItem.setActionCommand("Rings");
    buttonGroup.add(fiveMenuItem);
    menu.add(fiveMenuItem);

    JRadioButtonMenuItem sixMenuItem = new JRadioButtonMenuItem(sixIcon, true);
    sixMenuItem.addActionListener(actionListener);
    sixMenuItem.setActionCommand("Geese");
    buttonGroup.add(sixMenuItem);
    menu.add(sixMenuItem);

    menuBar.add(menu);
    frame.setJMenuBar(menuBar);
    frame.setSize(350, 250);
    frame.setVisible(true);
  }
}
```

> **NOTE** *Notice that the actionCommand property is set for those menu items lacking text labels. This allows registered ActionListener objects to determine what object was selected. This is only necessary when listeners are shared across components.*

Creating Custom MenuElement Components

One thing all the selectable menu components have in common is that they implement the MenuElement interface. The JSeparator doesn't implement the interface, but that's okay because it isn't selectable. The purpose of the MenuElement interface is to allow the MenuSelectionManager to notify the different menu elements as a user moves around a program's menu structure.

Interface MenuElement

As the following interface definition shows, the MenuElement interface is made up of five methods.

```
public interface MenuElement {
  public Component getComponent();
  public MenuElement[] getSubElements();
  public void menuSelectionChanged(boolean isInclude);
  public void processKeyEvent(KeyEvent event, MenuElement path[],
MenuSelectionManager mgr);
  public void processMouseEvent(MouseEvent event, MenuElement path[],
MenuSelectionManager mgr);
}
```

The getComponent() method returns the menu's rendering component. This is usually the menu component itself, although that isn't a requirement. The getSubElements() method returns an array of any menu elements contained within this element. If this menu element isn't the top of a submenu, the method should return a zero-length array of MenuElement objects, and not null.

The menuSelectionChanged() method is called whenever the menu item is placed in or taken out of the selection path for the menu selection manager.

The two processKeyEvent() and processMouseEvent() methods are for processing a key event or mouse event that's generated over a menu. How your menu item processes events depends on what the component supports. For instance, unless you support accelerators, you probably want to respond to key events only when your menu item is in the current selection path.

> **NOTE** *If, for example, your new menu element was something like a JComboBoxMenuItem, where the MenuElement acted like a JComboBox, the processKeyEvent() might pass along the key character to the KeySelectionManager. See Chapter 13 for more on the KeySelectionManager.*

Implementing the MenuElement Interface

To demonstrate the MenuElement interface, we'll create a new menu component called a JToggleButtonMenuItem. This component will look and act like a JToggleButton, though it can live on a menu. It's important to ensure that the menu goes away once the item is selected and that the component is displayed differently when in the current selection path.

> **NOTE** *Although you can add any component to a menu, if the component doesn't implement the* MenuElement *interface, it won't act properly when a mouse moves over the component or when the component is selected.*

```java
import java.awt.*;
import java.awt.event.*;
import javax.swing.*;
import javax.swing.event.*;

public class JToggleButtonMenuItem extends JToggleButton implements MenuElement {
  Color savedForeground = null;
  private static MenuElement NO_SUB_ELEMENTS[] = new MenuElement[0];
  public JToggleButtonMenuItem() {
    init();
  }
  public JToggleButtonMenuItem(String label) {
    super(label);
    init();
  }
  public JToggleButtonMenuItem(String label, Icon icon) {
    super(label, icon);
    init();
  }
  private void init() {
    updateUI();
    setRequestFocusEnabled(false);
    // Borrows heavily from BasicMenuUI
    MouseInputListener mouseInputListener = new MouseInputListener() {
      // If mouse released over this menu item, activate it
      public void mouseReleased(MouseEvent mouseEvent) {
        MenuSelectionManager menuSelectionManager =
MenuSelectionManager.defaultManager();
        Point point = mouseEvent.getPoint();
        if ((point.x >= 0) &&
            (point.x < getWidth()) &&
            (point.y >= 0) &&
            (point.y < getHeight())) {
          menuSelectionManager.clearSelectedPath();
          // component automatically handles "selection" at this point
          // doClick(0); // not necessary
        } else {
```

```
      menuSelectionManager.processMouseEvent(mouseEvent);
    }
  }
  // If mouse moves over menu item, add to selection path, so it becomes armed
  public void mouseEntered(MouseEvent mouseEvent) {
    MenuSelectionManager menuSelectionManager =
MenuSelectionManager.defaultManager();
    menuSelectionManager.setSelectedPath(getPath());
  }
  // When mouse moves away from menu item, disarm it and select something else
  public void mouseExited(MouseEvent mouseEvent) {
    MenuSelectionManager menuSelectionManager =
MenuSelectionManager.defaultManager();
    MenuElement path[] = menuSelectionManager.getSelectedPath();
    if (path.length > 1) {
      MenuElement newPath[] = new MenuElement[path.length-1];
      for(int i=0, c=path.length-1; i<c; i++) {
        newPath[i] = path[i];
      }
      menuSelectionManager.setSelectedPath(newPath);
    }
  }
  // Pass along drag events
  public void mouseDragged(MouseEvent mouseEvent) {
    MenuSelectionManager.defaultManager().processMouseEvent(mouseEvent);
  }
  public void mouseClicked(MouseEvent mouseEvent) {
  }
  public void mousePressed(MouseEvent mouseEvent) {
  }
  public void mouseMoved(MouseEvent mouseEvent) {
  }
};
addMouseListener(mouseInputListener);
addMouseMotionListener(mouseInputListener);
}

// MenuElement methods
public Component getComponent() {
  return this;
}

public MenuElement[] getSubElements() {
```

```
      // no subelements
      return NO_SUB_ELEMENTS;
    }

    public void menuSelectionChanged(boolean isIncluded) {
      ButtonModel model = getModel();
      // only change armed state if different
      if(model.isArmed() != isIncluded) {
        model.setArmed(isIncluded);
      }

      if (isIncluded) {
        savedForeground = getForeground();
        if (!savedForeground.equals(Color.blue)) {
          setForeground(Color.blue);
        } else {
          // In case foreground blue, use something different
          setForeground(Color.red);
        }
      } else {
        setForeground(savedForeground);
        // if null, get foreground from installed look and feel
        if (savedForeground == null) {
          updateUI();
        }
      }
    }

    public void processKeyEvent(KeyEvent keyEvent, MenuElement path[],
  MenuSelectionManager manager) {
      // If user presses space while menu item armed, select it
      if (getModel().isArmed()) {
        int keyChar = keyEvent.getKeyChar();
        if (keyChar == KeyEvent.VK_SPACE) {
          manager.clearSelectedPath();
          doClick(0); // inherited from AbstractButton
        }
      }
    }
```

```
    public void processMouseEvent(MouseEvent mouseEvent, MenuElement path[],
MenuSelectionManager manager) {
      // For when mouse dragged over menu and button released
      if (mouseEvent.getID() == MouseEvent.MOUSE_RELEASED) {
        manager.clearSelectedPath();
        doClick(0); // inherited from AbstractButton
      }
    }


    // Borrows heavily from BasicMenuItemUI.getPath()
    private MenuElement[] getPath() {
      MenuSelectionManager menuSelectionManager =
MenuSelectionManager.defaultManager();
      MenuElement oldPath[] = menuSelectionManager.getSelectedPath();
      MenuElement newPath[];
      int oldPathLength = oldPath.length;
      if (oldPathLength == 0)
        return new MenuElement[0];
      Component parent = getParent();
      if (oldPath[oldPathLength-1].getComponent() == parent) {
        // Going deeper under the parent menu
        newPath = new MenuElement[oldPathLength+1];
        System.arraycopy(oldPath, 0, newPath, 0, oldPathLength);
        newPath[oldPathLength] = this;
      } else {
        // Sibling/child menu item currently selected
        int newPathPosition;
        for (newPathPosition = oldPath.length-1; newPathPosition >= 0;
newPathPosition--) {
          if (oldPath[newPathPosition].getComponent() == parent) {
            break;
          }
        }
        newPath = new MenuElement[newPathPosition+2];
        System.arraycopy(oldPath, 0, newPath, 0, newPathPosition+1);
        newPath[newPathPosition+1] = this;
      }
      return newPath;
    }
}
```

> **NOTE** *The* MouseInputListener *defined in the* init() *method and the* getPath() *method borrow heavily from the* BasicMenuUI *class. Normally, the user interface delegate deals with what happens when the mouse moves over a menu component. Because the* JToggleButton *isn't a predefined menu component, its UI class doesn't deal with it. For better modularity, these two methods could be moved into an extended* ToggleButtonUI.

Once you've created this JToggleButtonMenuItem class, you can use it like any other menu item:

```
JToggleButtonMenuItem toggleItem = new JToggleButtonMenuItem("Balloon Help");
edit.add(toggleItem);
```

Working with Toolbars: Class JToolBar

Toolbars are an integral part of the main application windows in a modern user interface. Toolbars provide users with easy access to the more commonly used commands, which are usually buried within a hierarchical menuing structure. The Swing component that supports this capability is the JToolBar.

The JToolBar is a specialized Swing container for holding components. This container can then be used as a toolbar within your Java applet or application, with the potential for it to be floating, or draggable, outside of the main window of the program. As Figure 6-15 shows, JToolBar is a very simple component to use and understand.

Creating JToolBar Components

There are two constructors for creating JToolBar components. By default, a toolbar is created in a horizontal direction. However, you can explicitly set the orientation by using either of the JToolBar constants of HORIZONTAL and VERTICAL. By default, toolbars are floatable. Therefore, if you create the toolbar with one orientation, the user could change its orientation while dragging the toolbar around outside the window.

1.  ```
    public JToolBar()
    JToolBar jToolBar = new JToolBar();
    ```
    ```

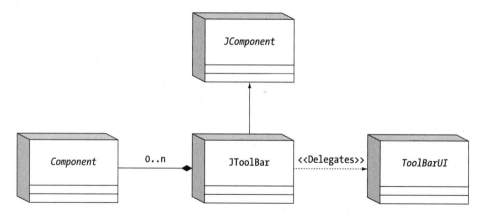

Figure 6-15: JToolBar UML relationship diagram

2.  ```
    public JToolBar(int orientation)
    JToolBar jToolBar = new JToolBar(JToolBar.VERTICAL);
    ```

Adding Components to a JToolBar

Once you have a JToolBar, you need to add components to it. Any Component can be added to the toolbar. When dealing with horizontal toolbars, for aesthetic reasons it's best if the toolbar components are all roughly the same height. For a vertical toolbar, it's best if they're roughly the same width. There's only one method defined by the JToolBar class for adding toolbar items; the remaining methods, such as add(Component), are inherited from Container. In addition, you can add a separator to a toolbar.

```
public JButton add(Action action);
public void addSeparator();
public void addSeparator(Dimension size);
```

When using the add(Action) method of JToolBar, the added Action is encapsulated within a JButton object. This is different from adding actions to JMenu or JPopupMenu components, in which JMenuItem objects are added instead. If you don't specify the separator size, the installed look and feel forces a default size setting.
```

> **NOTE** *For more information on dealing with the* Action *interface, see Chapter 2 or the section "Using Action Objects with Menus" earlier in this chapter.*

Removal of components from a toolbar is done with the `public void remove(Component component)` method.

JToolBar Properties

The `JToolBar` class defines seven properties, which are listed in Table 6-15.

PROPERTY NAME	DATA TYPE	ACCESS
accessibleContext	AccessibleContext	read-only
borderPainted	boolean	read-write bound
floatable	boolean	read-write bound
margin	Insets	read-write bound
orientation	int	read-write bound
UI	ToolBarUI	read-only
UIClassID	String	read-only

Table 6-15: JToolBar properties

By default, the border of a `JToolBar` is painted. If you don't want the border painted, you can set the `borderPainted` property to `false`. Without using the `borderPainted` property, you'd have to change the setting of the `border` property (inherited from the superclass `JComponent`).

The `orientation` property can be set to only one of the `HORIZONTAL` or `VERTICAL` constants of `JToolBar`. If another non-equivalent value is used, an `IllegalArgumentException` is thrown. Changing the orientation changes the layout manager of the toolbar. If you directly change the layout manager with `setLayout()`, changing the orientation will undo your layout change. Consequently, it's best not to manually change the layout manager of a `JToolBar`.

As previously mentioned, by default a toolbar is floatable. This means that a user can drag the toolbar from where you place it and move it elsewhere. Selecting an empty part of the toolbar allows you to drag the toolbar elsewhere. The toolbar can than be left outside the original program window, floating above the main window in its own window, or dropped onto another area of the original program window. If the layout manager of the original window is `BorderLayout`, the droppable areas are the edges of the layout manager without any components. (You can't drop the toolbar in the center of the window.) Otherwise, the toolbar would be dropped into the last spot of the container.

Handling JToolBar Events

There are no events specific to the JToolBar. You need to attach listeners to each item on the JToolBar that you want to respond to user interaction.

Customizing a JToolBar Look and Feel

Each installable Swing look and feel provides its own JToolBar appearance and set of default UIResource values. Most of this appearance is controlled by the components actually within the toolbar. Figure 6-16 shows the appearance of the JToolBar component for the preinstalled set of look and feels: Motif, Windows, Metal, and Macintosh. Each toolbar has five JButton components, with a separator between the fourth and fifth.

The available set of UIResource-related properties for a JToolBar is shown in Table 6-16. For the JToolBar component, there are ten different properties.

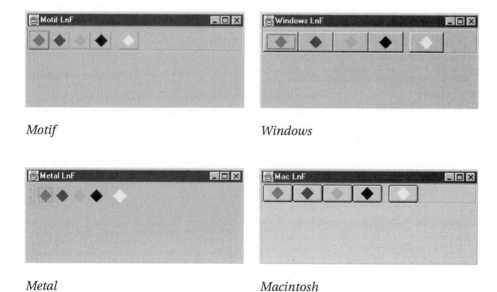

Motif

Windows

Metal

Macintosh

Figure 6-16: JToolBar under different look and feels

PROPERTY STRING	OBJECT TYPE
ToolBar.background	Color
ToolBar.border	Border
ToolBar.dockingBackground	Color
ToolBar.dockingForeground	Color
ToolBar.floatingBackground	Color
ToolBar.floatingForeground	Color
ToolBar.font	Font
ToolBar.foreground	Color
ToolBar.separatorSize	Dimension
ToolBarUI	ToolBarUI

Table 6-16: JToolBar UIResource elements

In addition, the Metal look and feel defines one client property for the JToolBar: JToolBar.isRollover. By default, this value is Boolean.FALSE. If you set it to Boolean.TRUE, a special border will be drawn for the component on the toolbar your mouse is moving over. As your mouse moves off the component, the border is reset to its original border.

```
aJToolBar.putClientProperty("JToolBar.isRollover", Boolean.TRUE);
```

A Complete JToolBar Usage Example

The following program demonstrates a complete JToolBar example that results in a toolbar with a series of diamonds on the buttons. The program also resuses the ShowAction defined for the menuing example described earlier in this chapter in the section "Using Action Objects with Menus."

The client-side JToolBar.isRollover property is enabled to show you how to set the property and how the border changes when you run the program. See Figure 6-17 for the output.

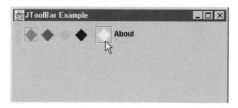

Figure 6-17: JToolBar example with isRollover enabled

```
import java.awt.*;
import java.awt.event.*;
import javax.swing.*;

public class ToolBarSample extends JPanel {

  private static final int COLOR_POSITION = 0;
  private static final int STRING_POSITION = 1;
  static Object buttonColors[][] = {
    {Color.red, "red"},
    {Color.blue, "blue"},
    {Color.green, "green"},
    {Color.black, "black"},
    null, // separator
    {Color.cyan, "cyan"}
  };

  public static void main (String args[]) {

    ActionListener actionListener = new ActionListener() {
      public void actionPerformed (ActionEvent actionEvent) {
        System.out.println(actionEvent.getActionCommand());
      }
    };

    JFrame frame = new ExitableJFrame("JToolBar Example");

    JToolBar toolbar = new JToolBar();
    toolbar.putClientProperty("JToolBar.isRollover", Boolean.TRUE);

    for (int i=0, n=buttonColors.length; i<n; i++) {
      Object color[] = buttonColors[i];
      if (color == null) {
        toolbar.addSeparator();
      } else {
        Icon icon = new DiamondIcon((Color)color[COLOR_POSITION], true, 20, 20);
        JButton button = new JButton(icon);
        button.setActionCommand((String)color[STRING_POSITION]);
        button.addActionListener(actionListener);
        toolbar.add(button);
      }
    }
```

```
    Action action = new ActionMenuSample.ShowAction(frame);
    toolbar.add(action);

    Container contentPane = frame.getContentPane();
    contentPane.add(toolbar, BorderLayout.NORTH);
    frame.setSize(350, 150);
    frame.setVisible(true);
  }
}
```

JToolBar.Separator

The JToolBar class maintains its own separator to permit a custom look and feel for the separator when on a JToolBar.

This separator is automatically created when you call the addSeparator() method of JToolBar. In addition, there are two constructors for creating a JToolBar.Separator if you want to manually create the component. Both constructors create a horizontal separator. What is configurable is the size. If the size isn't specified, the look and feel decides on it.

1. public JToolBar.Separator()
    JSeparator toolBarSeparator = new JToolBar.Separator();

2. public JToolBar.Separator(Dimension size)
    Dimension dimension = new Dimension(10, 10);
    JSeparator toolBarSeparator = new JToolBar.Separator(dimension);

As with JPopupMenu.Separator, if you want to change the orientation of the separator, you must call the setOrientation() method inherited from JSeparator, this time with an argument of JToolBar.Separator.VERTICAL.

Summary

This chapter introduced the many Swing menu-related classes and their interrelationships, and Swing's toolbar class. First, I introduced the JMenuBar and its selection model, and described how both could be used within applets as well as applications.

Next, I described the JMenuItem, which is the menu element the user selects, along with two new event/listener pairs the system uses for dealing with events, MenuKeyEvent/MenuKeyListener and MenuDragMouseEvent/MenuDragMouseListener. Then, I moved on to describe the element JMenu, upon which JMenuItem instances are placed, along with its new event/listener pair, MenuEvent/MenuListener, which is used to determine when a menu is about to be posted.

I discussed the JSeparator component and how you can use it as a menu separator or as a visual display separator outside of menus. I covered the JPopupMenu, which JMenu uses to display its set of JMenuItem components. For the JPopupMenu, I also described the pop-up menu's own event/listener pair, PopupMenuEvent/PopupMenuListener. Then, I described the selectable menu elements in JCheckBoxMenuItem and JRadioButtonMenuItem, explored the MenuElement interface, and created a menu component. Finally, I covered the JToolBar class, a close cousin of Swing's menu classes.

In Chapter 7, we'll look at the different classes Swing provides for customizing the border around a Swing component.

CHAPTER 7

Borders

SWING COMPONENTS OFFER THE OPTION OF customizing the border area surrounding a component. With great ease, you can use any one of the eight predefined borders (including one compound border that's a combination of any of the other seven), or you can create your own individualized borders. In this chapter, you'll learn how to best utilize each of the existing borders and how to fashion your own.

Some Basics on Working with Borders

A border is a JComponent property with the standard setBorder() and getBorder() property methods. Therefore, every Swing component that is a subclass of JComponent can have a border. By default, a component doesn't have a custom border associated with it (JComponent.getBorder() returns null). Instead, the default border displayed for a component is the border appropriate for its state, based on the current look and feel. For instance, with a JButton, the border could appear pressed, unpressed, or disabled, with different borders for each look and feel.

Although the initial border property setting for every component is null, you can change the border of a component with JComponent.setBorder(Border newValue). Once set, the changed value overrides the border for the current look and feel, and it draws the border in the area of the component's insets. If at a later time you want to reset the border back to a border that's appropriate for the state as well as the look and feel, change the border property to null [setBorder(null)] and call updateUI() for the component. The updateUI() call notifies the look and feel to reset the border. If you don't call updateUI(), the component will have no border.

> **NOTE** *Those Swing components that aren't subclasses of JComponent, such as JApplet and JFrame, lack a setBorder() method to change their border. If you want them to have a border, you must add a JPanel to the container and then change the border of the panel.*

Examine Figure 7-1 to see a sampling of the various border configurations around a JLabel, with a text label designating the border type. How to create the different

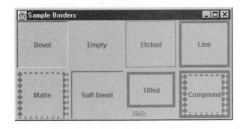

Figure 7-1: Border examples, using a 4-by-2 GridLayout with 5-pixel horizontal/vertical gaps

borders will be discussed in the following sections of this chapter.

The Border interface can be found in the javax.swing. border package. This interface forms the basis of all the border classes. As Figure 7-2 shows, the interface is directly implemented by the AbstractBorder class, which is the parent class of all the predefined Swing border classes: BevelBorder, CompoundBorder, EmptyBorder, EtchedBorder, LineBorder, MatteBorder, SoftBevelBorder, and TitledBorder. Also shown in the figure is the BorderFactory class, found in the javax.swing package. This class uses the Factory design pattern to create borders without your having to know the actual class names.

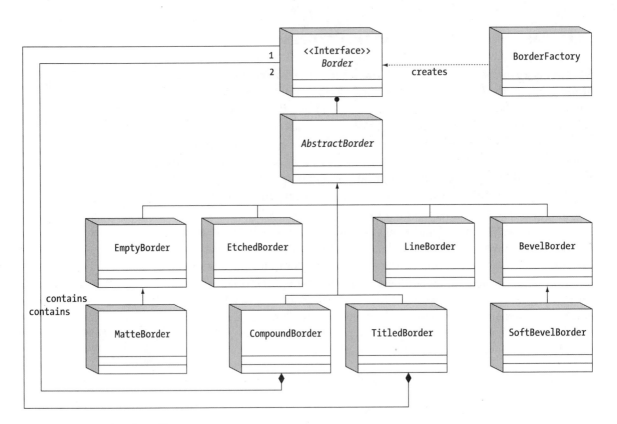

Figure 7-2: Border class diagram

Exploring the Border Interface

The Border interface shown here consists of three methods, which follow:

```
public interface Border {
  public void paintBorder(Component c, Graphics g, int x, int y, int width, int
height);
  public Insets getBorderInsets(Component c);
  public boolean isBorderOpaque();
}
```

1. `public void paintBorder(Component c, Graphics g, int x, int y, int width, int height)`

The paintBorder() method is the key method of the Border interface. In this method, the actual drawing of the border is done. Frequently, the Border implementation will ask for the Insets dimensions first and then draw the border in the four rectangular outer regions, shown in Figure 7-3. If a border is opaque, the paintBorder() implementation must fill the entire insets area. If a border is opaque and doesn't fill the area, then it's a bug and needs to be corrected.

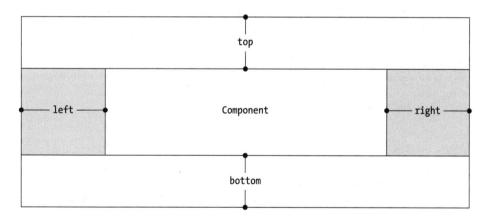

Figure 7-3: Areas of border insets

The following source shows a sample `paintBorder()` implementation.

```
public void paintBorder(Component c, Graphics g, int x, int y, int width, int
height) {
  Insets insets = getBorderInsets(c);
  Color color = c.getForeground();
  Color brighterColor = color.brighter();

// Translate coordinate space
  g.translate(x, y);

// top
  g.setColor(color);
  g.fillRect(0, 0, width, insets.top);

// left
  g.setColor(brighterColor);
  g.fillRect(0, insets.top, insets.left, height-insets.top-insets.bottom);

// bottom
  g.setColor(color);
  g.fillRect(0, height-insets.bottom, width, insets.bottom);

// right
  g.setColor(brighterColor);
  g.fillRect(width-insets.right, insets.top, insets.right,
    height-insets.top-insets.bottom);
}
```

When creating your own borders, you'll frequently find yourself filling in the same nonoverlapping rectangular regions. The use of the `translate()` method of `Graphics` simplifies the specification of the drawing coordinates. Without translating the coordinates, you'd need to offset the drawing by the origin (x, y).

> **WARNING** *You can't take a shortcut by inserting* `g.fillRect(x, y, width, height)` *because this would fill in the entire component area.*

2. `public Insets getBorderInsets(Component c)`

The `getBorderInsets()` method returns the space necessary to draw a border around the given component `c` as an `Insets` object. These inset areas, shown in Figure 7-3, define the only legal area in which a border can be drawn. The component argument allows you to use some of its properties to determine the size of the insets area.

> **WARNING**   *You can ask the component argument for font sizing information to determine the insets size, but if you ask about the size of the component, a `StackOverflowError` occurs.*

3. `public boolean isBorderOpaque()`

Borders can be opaque or transparent. When the method in step 3 returns `true`, the border needs to be opaque, filling its entire insets area. When it returns `false`, any area not drawn will retain the background of the component in which the border is installed.

Introducing BorderFactory

Now that you have a basic understanding of how the `Border` interface works, let's take a quick look at the `BorderFactory` class as a means to create borders swiftly and easily. What the `BorderFactory` offers is a series of static methods for creating predefined borders. Instead of laboriously calling the specific constructors for different borders, you can create almost all the borders through this factory class. The factory class also caches the creation of some borders to avoid re-creating the same border multiple times. The class definition follows.

```
public class BorderFactory {
  public static Border createBevelBorder(int type);
  public static Border createBevelBorder(int type, Color highlight, Color
shadow);
  public static Border createBevelBorder(int type, Color highlightOuter,
    Color highlightInner, Color shadowOuter, Color shadowInner);

  public static CompoundBorder createCompoundBorder();
  public static CompoundBorder createCompoundBorder(Border outside, Border
inside);
```

```
    public static Border createEmptyBorder();
    public static Border createEmptyBorder(int top, int left, int bottom, int
right);

    public static Border createEtchedBorder();
    public static Border createEtchedBorder(Color highlight, Color shadow);

    public static Border createLineBorder(Color color);
    public static Border createLineBorder(Color color, int thickness);

    public static Border createLoweredBevelBorder();

    public static MatteBorder createMatteBorder(int top, int left, int bottom, int
right, Color color);
    public static MatteBorder createMatteBorder(int top, int left, int bottom, int
right, Icon icon);

    public static Border createRaisedBevelBorder();

    public static TitledBorder createTitledBorder(Border border);
    public static TitledBorder createTitledBorder(Border border, String title);
    public static TitledBorder createTitledBorder(Border border, String title,
        int justification, int position);
    public static TitledBorder createTitledBorder(Border border, String title,
        int justification, int position, Font font);
    public static TitledBorder createTitledBorder(Border border, String title,
        int justification, int position, Font font, Color color);
    public static TitledBorder createTitledBorder(String title);
}
```

I'll describe the different methods of this class during the process of describing
the various borders they create. For instance, to create a border with a red line,
you can use the following statement, and then attach the border to a component.

```
Border lineBorder = BorderFactory.createLineBorder(Color.red);
```

> **NOTE** *Interestingly enough, no factory method exists for creating a soft
> beveled border.*

Starting with AbstractBorder

Before looking at the concrete borders available within the `javax.swing.border` package, one system border deserves special attention: `AbstractBorder`. As shown in Figure 7-2, the `AbstractBorder` class is the parent border of all the other predefined borders. When creating your own borders, you can just create a subclass of `AbstractBorder` and override just the necessary methods.

Creating Abstract Borders

There's one constructor for `AbstractBorder`, which follows. Because `AbstractBorder` is the parent class of all the other standard borders, this constructor is automatically called for all of them because it's a no-argument constructor.

```
public AbstractBorder()
```

> **NOTE** *Borders aren't JavaBeans. Some border classes will lack a no-argument ("no-arg" for short) constructor. Nevertheless, those border classes still call this constructor.*

Examining AbstractBorder Methods

The `AbstractBorder` class provides implementations for the three methods of the `Border` interface.

1. `public Insets getBorderInsets(Component c)`

The insets of an `AbstractBorder` are zero all around. Each of the predefined subclasses overrides this method.

2. `public boolean isBorderOpaque()`

The default `opaque` property setting of an abstract border is `false`. This means that if you were to draw something like dashed lines, the component background would show through. Most predefined subclasses override this method.

3. `public void paintBorder(Component c, Graphics g, int x, int y,`
   `int width, int height)`

The painted border for an AbstractBorder is empty. All subclasses should override this behavior to actually draw a border, except perhaps EmptyBorder.

Supporting Capabilities

In addition to providing default implementations of the Border methods, AbstractBorder adds two other capabilities that you can take advantage of, or just let the system use. First, there's an additional version of getBorderInsets() available that takes two arguments: Component and Insets: public Insets getBorderInsets(Component c, Insets insets). In this version of the method, instead of creating and returning a new Insets object, the insets object passed in is first modified and then returned. Use of this method avoids the creation and later destruction of an additional Insets object.

The second new method available is getInteriorRectangle(), which has both a static and a nonstatic version. Given the Component, Border, and four integer parameters (for x, y, width, and height), the method will return the inner Rectangle such that a component can paint itself only in the area within the border insets. (See the piece labeled "Component" in Figure 7-3.)

> **NOTE** *Currently, this capability isn't used anywhere in Sun's Swing source.*

Examining the Predefined Borders

Now that the basics have been described, let's look at the specifics of each of the predefined border classes, in order of complexity.

EmptyBorder Class

The empty border, logically enough, is a border with nothing drawn in it. You can use EmptyBorder where you might have otherwise overridden insets() or getInsets() with a regular AWT container. It allows you to "reserve" extra space around a component to spread your screen components out a little or to alter centering or justification somewhat. Figure 7-4 shows both an empty border and a nonempty one.

EmptyBorder has two constructors and two factory methods of BorderFactory shown in the following list. Each allows you to customize the border insets in its own manner. The no-argument version creates a truly empty border with zero

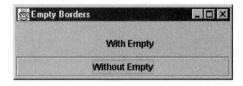

*Figure 7-4: EmptyBorder sample, with insets of 20 for top and left,
0 for right and bottom*

insets all around; otherwise, you can specify the insets as either an AWT Insets
instance or as the inset pieces. The EmptyBorder is transparent by default.

1. `public static Border createEmptyBorder()`

```
Border emptyBorder = BorderFactory.createEmptyBorder();
```

2. `public static Border createEmptyBorder(int top, int left, int
    bottom, int right)`

```
Border emptyBorder = BorderFactory.createEmptyBorder(5, 10, 5, 10);
```

3. `public EmptyBorder(Insets insets)`

```
Insets insets = new Insets(5, 10, 5, 10);
Border EmptyBorder = new EmptyBorder(insets);
```

4. `public EmptyBorder(int top, int left, int bottom, int right)`

```
Border EmptyBorder = new EmptyBorder(5, 10, 5, 10);
```

> **NOTE**   *In most cases, you should use the factory methods to create borders,
> avoiding the direct constructors.*

LineBorder *Class*

The line border is a single-color line of a user-defined thickness that surrounds a
component. If you want to alter the thickness on different sides, you'll need to
use MatteBorder, described in the section "Matte Border Class" later in this chapter. Figure 7-5 shows a sampling of using LineBorder, with 1- and 12-pixel line
thicknesses.

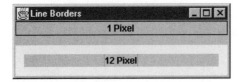

Figure 7-5: LineBorder sample

Creating Line Borders

LineBorder has two constructors, two factory methods within it, and two factory methods of BorderFactory. Each allows you to customize the border color and line thickness. If a thickness isn't specified, a default value of 1 is used. The two factory methods of LineBorder are for the commonly used colors of black and gray. Because the border fills in the given insets, the LineBorder is created to be opaque.

    1.   `public LineBorder(Color color)`

```
Border lineBorder = new LineBorder (Color.red);
```

    2.   `public LineBorder(Color color, int thickness)`

```
Border lineBorder = new LineBorder (Color.red, 5);
```

    3.   `public static Border createBlackLineBorder()`

```
Border blackLine = LineBorder.createBlackLineBorder();
```

    4.   `public static Border createGrayLineBorder()`

```
Border greyLine = LineBorder.createGrayLineBorder();
```

> **NOTE** *The LineBorder factory methods work as follows: If you create the same border twice, the same LineBorder object will be returned. However, as with all object comparisons, you should always use the equals() method for checking object equality.*

    5.   `public static Border createLineBorder(Color color)`

```
Border lineBorder = BorderFactory.createLineBorder(Color.red);
```

6. `public static Border createLineBorder(Color color, int`
    `thickness)`

```
Border lineBorder = BorderFactory.createLineBorder(Color.red, 5);
```

Configuring Properties

Table 7-1 lists the inherited `borderOpaque` property from `AbstractBorder` and the initialization settings for the immutable properties of `LineBorder`.

PROPERTY NAME	DATA TYPE	ACCESS
borderOpaque	boolean	read-only
lineColor	Color	read-only
thickness	int	read-only

Table 7-1: LineBorder properties

If you don't mind creating a subclass of `LineBorder`, you can gain access to a capability that's available only to sub-classes. There's built-in support for a `LineBorder` drawing rounded corners, although this capability isn't available to plain client classes. Subclassing `LineBorder` exposes the protected `roundedCorners` variable, which you can then simply set in the constructor. Figure 7-6 shows some results from the exposed property.

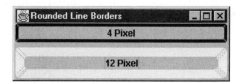

Figure 7-6: RoundedLineBorder sample

Here's some source code for the `RoundedLineBorder` class, which uses the exposed `roundedCorners` setting.

```
public class RoundedLineBorder extends LineBorder {
  public RoundedLineBorder(Color color, int thickness) {
    super(color, thickness);
    roundedCorners=true;
  }
}
```

BevelBorder Class

A bevel border draws a "three-dimensional" border than can appear to be raised or lowered. When the border is raised, a shadow effect appears along the bottom and right side of the border. When lowered, the position of the shading is reversed. Figure 7-7 shows raised and lowered bevel borders with default and custom colors.

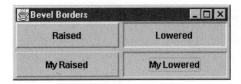

Figure 7-7: Raised/lowered BevelBorder sample

The simulated three-dimensional appearance is produced by drawing two different pairs of one-pixel-wide lines around a component. The border sides that aren't shaded are drawn with what's called a "highlight" color, whereas the other two sides are drawn with a "shadow" color. The highlight color and shadow color are each drawn in two different shades for the outer and inner edges of the bevel. As such, a drawn bevel border uses four different colors in all. Figure 7-8 shows how these four colors fit together.

There are three constructors for BevelBorder and five factory methods by which BorderFactory obtains BevelBorder objects. Each allows you to customize both the bevel type and the coloration of the highlighting and shadowing within the border. The bevel type is specified by one of two values: BevelBorder.RAISED or BevelBorder.LOWERED. If highlight and shadow colors aren't specified, the appropriate colors are generated by examining the background of the component for the border. If they *are* specified, remember that the highlight color should be brighter. A BevelBorder is opaque, by default.

1. `public BevelBorder(int bevelType)`

```
Border bevelBorder = new BevelBorder(BevelBorder.RAISED);
```

2. `public static Border createBevelBorder(int bevelType)`

```
Border bevelBorder = BorderFactory.createBevelBorder(BevelBorder.RAISED);
```

3. `public static Border createLoweredBevelBorder()`

```
Border bevelBorder = BorderFactory.createLoweredBevelBorder();
```

4. `public static Border createRaisedBevelBorder()`

```
Border bevelBorder = BorderFactory.createRaisedBevelBorder();
```

5. `public BevelBorder(int bevelType, Color highlight, Color shadow)`

```
Border bevelBorder = new BevelBorder(BevelBorder.RAISED, Color.pink, Color.red);
```

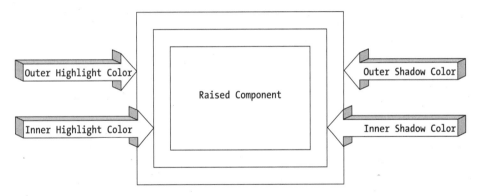

Figure 7-8: Bevel color analysis

6. `public static Border createBevelBorder(int bevelType, Color highlight, Color shadow))`

```
Border bevelBorder = BorderFactory.createBevelBorder(BevelBorder.RAISED,
Color.pink, Color.red);
```

7. `public BevelBorder(int bevelType, Color highlightOuter, Color highlightInner, Color shadowOuter, Color shadowInner)`

```
Border bevelBorder = new BevelBorder(BevelBorder.RAISED, Color.pink,
Color.pink.brighter(), Color.red, Color.red.darker());
```

8. `public static Border createBevelBorder(int bevelType, Color highlightOuter, Color highlightInner, Color shadowOuter, Color shadowInner)`

```
Border bevelBorder = BorderFactory.createBevelBorder(BevelBorder.RAISED,
Color.pink, Color.pink.brighter(), Color.red, Color.red.darker());
```

SoftBevelBorder Class

The soft bevel border is a close cousin of the bevel border. It rounds out the corners so that their edges aren't as sharp, and it draws only one line, using the appropriate outer color for the bottom and right sides. As Figure 7-9 shows, the basic appearance of the raised and lowered SoftBevelBorder is roughly the same as that of the BevelBorder.

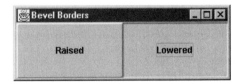

Figure 7-9: Raised/lowered SoftBevelBorder sample

SoftBevelBorder has three constructors. Each allows you to customize both the bevel type and the coloration of the highlighting and shadowing within the border. The bevel type is specified by one of two values: SoftBevelBorder.RAISED or SoftBevelBorder.LOWERED. As with BevelBorder, the default coloration is derived from the background color. A soft bevel border doesn't completely fill in the given insets area, so a SoftBevelBorder is created to be transparent (not opaque).

There are no static BorderFactory methods to create these borders.

1. public SoftBevelBorder(int bevelType)

```
Border softBevelBorder = new SoftBevelBorder(SoftBevelBorder.RAISED);
```

2. public SoftBevelBorder(int bevelType, Color highlight, Color shadow)

```
Border softBevelBorder = new SoftBevelBorder(SoftBevelBorder.RAISED, Color.red,
Color.pink);
```

3. public SoftBevelBorder(int bevelType, Color highlightOuter, Color highlightInner, Color shadowOuter, Color shadowInner)

```
Border softBevelBorder = new SoftBevelBorder(SoftBevelBorder.RAISED, Color.red,
Color.red.darker(), Color.pink, Color.pink.brighter());
```

EtchedBorder Class

An EtchedBorder is a special case of a BevelBorder, but it's not a subclass. When the outer highlight color of a BevelBorder is the same color, as the inner shadow color and the outer shadow color is the same color as the inner highlight color, as depicted in Figure 7-8, you have an EtchedBorder. Figure 7-10 shows what a raised and lowered etched border might look like.

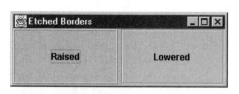

Figure 7-10: EtchedBorder samples

There are four constructors for EtchedBorder as well as two factory methods of BorderFactory for creating EtchedBorder objects. Each allows you to customize both the etching type and the coloration of the highlighting and shadowing within the border. If no etching type is specified, the border is lowered. As with BevelBorder and SoftBevelBorder, you can specify the etching type through one of two constants: EtchedBorder.RAISED or EtchedBorder.LOWERED. Again, if no colors are specified, they're derived from the background color of the component passed into paintBorder(). By default, all EtchedBorder objects are created to be opaque.

1. public EtchedBorder()

```
Border etchedBorder = new EtchedBorder();
```

2. public EtchedBorder(int etchType)

```
Border etchedBorder = new EtchedBorder(EtchedBorder.RAISED);
```

3. public EtchedBorder(Color highlight, Color shadow)

```
Border etchedBorder = new EtchedBorder(Color.red, Color.pink);
```

4. public EtchedBorder(int etchType, Color highlight, Color shadow)

```
Border etchedBorder = new EtchedBorder(EtchedBorder.RAISED, Color.red,
Color.pink);
```

5. public static Border createEtchedBorder()

```
Border etchedBorder = BorderFactory.createEtchedBorder();
```

6. public static Border createEtchedBorder(Color highlight, Color shadow)

```
Border etchedBorder = BorderFactory.createEtchedBorder(Color.red, Color.pink);
```

MatteBorder *Class*

MatteBorder is one of the more versatile borders available. It comes in two varieties. The first is demonstrated in Figure 7-11 and shows a MatteBorder used like a LineBorder to fill the border with a specific color, but with a different thickness on each side (something a plain LineBorder can't handle).

The second variety is an Icon tiled throughout the border area. This Icon could be an ImageIcon, if created from an Image object, or it could be one you create yourself by implementing the Icon interface. Figure 7-12 demonstrates both implementations.

Figure 7-11: MatteBorder color sample

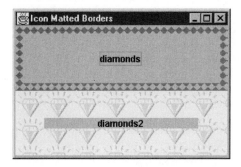

Figure 7-12: MatteBorder icon samples

> **TIP**   *When tiling an icon, note that the right and bottom areas may not look very attractive if the border size, component size, and icon size fail to mesh well.*

There are three constructors and two factory methods of `BorderFactory` for creating `MatteBorder` objects. Each allows you to customize what will be matted within the border area. When tiling an `Icon`, if you don't specify the border insets size, the actual icon dimensions will be used.

1. `public MatteBorder(int top, int left, int bottom, int right, Color color)`

```
Border matteBorder = new MatteBorder(5, 10, 5, 10, Color.green);
```

2. `public MatteBorder(int top, int left, int bottom, int right, Icon icon)`

```
Icon diamondIcon = new DiamondIcon(Color.red);
Border matteBorder = new MatteBorder(5, 10, 5, 10, diamondIcon);
```

3. `public MatteBorder(Icon icon)`

```
Icon diamondIcon = new DiamondIcon(Color.red);
Border matteBorder = new MatteBorder(diamondIcon);
```

4. `public static MatteBorder createMatteBorder(int top, int left, int bottom, int right, Color color)`

```
Border matteBorder = BorderFactory.createMatteBorder(5, 10, 5, 10, Color.green);
```

5. public static MatteBorder createMatteBorder(int top, int left, int bottom, int right, Icon icon)

```
Icon diamondIcon = new DiamondIcon(Color.red);
Border matteBorder = BorderFactory.createMatteBorder(5, 10, 5, 10, diamondIcon);
```

CompoundBorder *Class*

The CompoundBorder is probably one of the simplest predefined borders to use. It takes two existing borders and combines them, using the Composite design pattern, into a single border. A Swing component can have only one border associated with it, Therefore, the CompoundBorder allows you to combine borders *before* associating them to a component. Figure 7-13 shows two examples of CompoundBorder in action. The border on the left is a beveled line border. The one on the right is a six-line border, with several borders combined together.

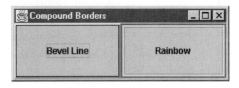

Figure 7-13: CompoundBorder sample

There are two constructors for CompoundBorder and two factory methods that BorderFactory offers for creating CompoundBorder objects. The no-argument constructor and factory methods are completely useless here because there are no set methods to later change the borders.

> **TIP** *CompoundBorder is itself a Border, so you can combine multiple borders into one border many levels deep.*

The opacity of a compound border depends on the opacity of the contained borders. If both contained borders are opaque, so too is the compound border. Otherwise, a compound border is considered transparent.

Because the first two constructors are useless, no source examples are shown.

1. public CompoundBorder()

2. public static CompoundBorder createCompoundBorder()

3 public CompoundBorder(Border outside, Border inside)

```
Border compoundBorder = new CompoundBorder(lineBorder, matteBorder);
```

4. `public static CompoundBorder createCompoundBorder(Border outside, Border inside)`

```
Border compoundBorder = BorderFactory.createCompoundBorder(lineBorder,
matteBorder);
```

TitledBorder Class

Probably the most useful border, `TitledBorder` can also be the most complicated to use. The titled border allows you to place a title string around a component. In addition to surrounding a single component, you can place a titled border around a group of components, like `JRadioButton` objects, as long as they're placed within a container such as a `JPanel`. The `TitledBorder` can be difficult to use, but several ways exist to simplify its usage. Figure 7-14 shows both a simple titled border and one that's a little more complex.

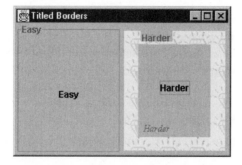

Figure 7-14: TitledBorder samples

Creating Titled Borders

Six constructors and six `BorderFactory` factory methods exist for creating `TitledBorder` objects. Each allows you to customize the text, position, and appearance of a title within a specified border. When unspecified, the current look and feel controls the border, title color, and title font. The default location for the title is the upper-left corner, while the default title is the empty string. A titled border is always at least partially transparent because the area beneath the title text shows through. Therefore, `isBorderOpaque()` reports `false`.

If you look at each of the following methods shown in pairs, this will be easier to understand. First shown is the constructor method; next shown is the equivalent `BorderFactory` method.

1a. `public TitledBorder(Border border)`

```
Border titledBorder = new TitledBorder(lineBorder);
```

1b. `public static TitledBorder createTitledBorder(Border border)`

```
Border titledBorder = BorderFactory.createTitledBorder(lineBorder);
```

2a. `public TitledBorder(String title)`

```
Border titledBorder = new TitledBorder("Hello");
```

2b. `public static TitledBorder createTitledBorder(String title)`

```
Border titledBorder = BorderFactory.createTitledBorder("Hello");
```

3a. `public TitledBorder(Border border, String title)`

```
Border titledBorder = new TitledBorder(lineBorder, "Hello");
```

3b. `public static TitledBorder createTitledBorder(Border border, String title)`

```
Border titledBorder = BorderFactory.createTitledBorder(lineBorder, "Hello");
```

4a. `public TitledBorder(Border border, String title, int justification, int position)`

```
Border titledBorder = new TitledBorder(lineBorder, "Hello", TitledBorder.LEFT,
TitledBorder.BELOW_BOTTOM);
```

4b. `public static TitledBorder createTitledBorder(Border border, String title, int justification, int position)`

```
Border titledBorder = BorderFactory.createTitledBorder(lineBorder, "Hello",
TitledBorder.LEFT, TitledBorder.BELOW_BOTTOM);
```

5a. `public TitledBorder(Border border, String title, int justification, int position, Font font)`

```
Font font = new Font("Serif", Font.ITALIC, 12);
Border titledBorder = new TitledBorder(lineBorder, "Hello", TitledBorder.LEFT,
TitledBorder.BELOW_BOTTOM, font);
```

5b. `public static TitledBorder createTitledBorder(Border border, String`
`      title, int justification, int position, Font font)`

```
Font font = new Font("Serif", Font.ITALIC, 12);
Border titledBorder = BorderFactory.createTitledBorder(lineBorder, "Hello",
TitledBorder.LEFT, TitledBorder.BELOW_BOTTOM, font);
```

6a. `public TitledBorder(Border border, String title, int justification, int`
`      position, Font font, Color color)`

```
Font font = new Font("Serif", Font.ITALIC, 12);
Border titledBorder = new TitledBorder(lineBorder, "Hello", TitledBorder.LEFT,
TitledBorder.BELOW_BOTTOM, font, Color.red);
```

6b. `public static TitledBorder createTitledBorder(Border border, String`
`      title, int justification, int position, Font font, Color color)`

```
Font font = new Font("Serif", Font.ITALIC, 12);
Border titledBorder = BorderFactory.createTitledBorder(lineBorder, "Hello",
TitledBorder.LEFT, TitledBorder.BELOW_BOTTOM, font, Color.red);
```

Configuring Properties

Unlike all the other predefined borders, titled borders have seven setter methods to modify their attributes *after* border creation. You can modify a titled border's underlying border, title, drawing color, font, text justification, and text position (see Table 7-2).

PROPERTY NAME	DATA TYPE	ACCESS
border	Border	read-write
borderOpaque	boolean	read-only
title	String	read-write
titleColor	Color	read-write
titleFont	Font	read-write
titleJustification	int	read-write
titlePosition	int	read-write

Table 7-2: TitledBorder properties

> **TIP** *To reduce screen redraws, it's better to modify the properties of a titled border prior to placing the border around a component.*

Text justification of the title string within a TitledBorder is specified by one of four class constants:

1. CENTER — Place title in center.
2. DEFAULT_JUSTIFICATION — Use the default setting to position the text. The value is equivalent to LEFT.
3. LEFT — Place title on left edge.
4. RIGHT — Place title on right edge.

Figure 7-15 shows the same TitledBorder with three different justifications.

You can position title strings in any one of six different locations, as specified by one of seven class constants:

1. ABOVE_BOTTOM — Place title above bottom line.
2. ABOVE_TOP — Place title above top line.
3. BELOW_BOTTOM — Place title below bottom line.
4. BELOW_TOP — Place title below top line.
5. BOTTOM — Place title on bottom line.
6. DEFAULT_POSTION — Use the default setting to place the text. This value is equivalent to TOP.
7. TOP — Place title on top line.

Figure 7-16 shows the six different positions available for the title on a TitledBorder.

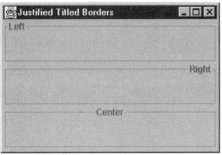

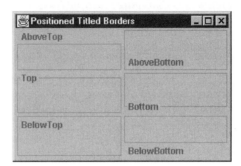

Figure 7-15: Title justifications *Figure 7-16: Title positioning*

Because a `TitledBorder` contains another `Border`, you can combine more than one border to place multiple titles along a single border. For example, Figure 7-17 shows a title along the top *and* bottom of the border.

The program used to generate Figure 7-17 follows.

```java
import javax.swing.*;
import javax.swing.border.*;
import java.awt.*;

public class DoubleTitle {
  public static void main(String args[]) {
    JFrame frame = new ExitableJFrame("Double Title");
    TitledBorder topBorder = BorderFactory.createTitledBorder("Top");
    topBorder.setTitlePosition(TitledBorder.TOP);
    TitledBorder doubleBorder = new TitledBorder (topBorder, "Bottom",
      TitledBorder.RIGHT, TitledBorder.BOTTOM);
    JButton doubleButton = new JButton();
    doubleButton.setBorder(doubleBorder);
    Container contentPane = frame.getContentPane();
    contentPane.add(doubleButton, BorderLayout.CENTER);
    frame.setSize(300, 100);
    frame.setVisible(true);
  }
}
```

Figure 7-17: Showing multiple titles on a TitledBorder

Customizing `TitledBorder` Look and Feel

The available set of `UIResource`-related properties for a `TitledBorder` is shown in Table 7-3. It has three different properties.

PROPERTY STRING	OBJECT TYPE
TitledBorder.font	Font
TitledBorder.titleColor	Color
TitledBorder.border	Border

Table 7-3: TitledBorder UIResource elements

Creating Your Own Borders

When you want to create your own distinctive border, you can either create a new class that implements the Border interface directly, or you can extend the AbstractBorder class. Extending the AbstractBorder is the better way to go becuase optimizations are built into certain Swing classes to take advantage of some of the AbstractBorder methods.

> **NOTE** *For instance, if a border is an* AbstractBorder, JComponent *will reuse an insets object when getting the* Insets *of a border. Thus, one fewer object will need to be created and destroyed.*

In addition to thinking about subclassing AbstractBorder versus implementing the Border interface yourself, you need to think about whether or not you want a static border. If you attach a border to a button, you want that button to be able to signal selection. You must examine the component passed into the paintBorder() method and react accordingly. In addition, you should also draw a disabled border to indicate when the component isn't selectable. Although setEnabled(false) disables the selection of the component, if the component has a border associated with it, then the border still has to be drawn, even when disabled. Figure 7-18 shows one border in action that looks at all these options for the component passed into the border's paintBorder() method.

Figure 7-18: Active custom border examples

The source for the custom border and the sample program follow.

```
import javax.swing.*;
import javax.swing.border.*;
import java.awt.*;

public class RedGreenBorder extends AbstractBorder {
  public boolean isBorderOpaque() {
```

```
        return true;
      }
    public Insets getBorderInsets(Component c) {
      return new Insets (3, 3, 3, 3);
    }
    public void paintBorder(Component c, Graphics g, int x, int y, int width, int
height) {
      Insets insets = getBorderInsets(c);
      Color horizontalColor;
      Color verticalColor;
      if (c.isEnabled()) {
        boolean pressed = false;
        if (c instanceof AbstractButton) {
          ButtonModel model = ((AbstractButton)c).getModel();
          pressed = model.isPressed();
        }
        if (pressed) {
          horizontalColor = Color.red;
          verticalColor = Color.green;
        } else {
          horizontalColor = Color.green;
          verticalColor = Color.red;
        }
      } else {
        horizontalColor = Color.lightGray;
        verticalColor = Color.lightGray;
      }
      g.setColor(horizontalColor);

      g.translate(x, y);

      // top
      g.fillRect(0, 0, width, insets.top);
       // bottom
      g.fillRect(0, height-insets.bottom, width, insets.bottom);

      g.setColor(verticalColor);
      // left
      g.fillRect(0, insets.top, insets.left, height-insets.top-insets.bottom);
       // right
      g.fillRect(width-insets.right, insets.top, insets.right, height-insets.top-
insets.bottom);
    }
```

```
public static void main(String args[]) {
  JFrame frame = new ExitableJFrame("My Border");
  Border border = new RedGreenBorder();
  JButton helloButton = new JButton ("Hello");
  helloButton.setBorder(border);
  JButton braveButton = new JButton ("Brave New");
  braveButton.setBorder(border);
  braveButton.setEnabled(false);
  JButton worldButton = new JButton ("World");
  worldButton.setBorder(border);
  Container contentPane = frame.getContentPane();
  contentPane.add(helloButton, BorderLayout.NORTH);
  contentPane.add(braveButton, BorderLayout.CENTER);
  contentPane.add(worldButton, BorderLayout.SOUTH);
  frame.setSize(300, 100);
  frame.setVisible(true);
  }
}
```

Summary

In this chapter, you learned about the usage of the Border interface and its many predefined implementations. You also learned how to create borders using the Factory design pattern provided by the BorderFactory class.

In Chapter 8, you'll move beyond low-level components and examine the window-like container objects available in Swing.

CHAPTER 8

Root Pane Containers

IN CHAPTER 7, WE LOOKED AT WORKING with borders around Swing components. In this chapter, we'll explore the high-level Swing containers and discover how they differ from their AWT counterparts.

Working with top-level containers in Swing is a bit different than working with top-level AWT containers. With the AWT containers of Frame, Window, Dialog, and Applet, you added components directly to the container, and there was only one place you could add them. In the Swing world, the top-level containers of JFrame, JWindow, JDialog, and JApplet, plus the new JInternalFrame container, rely on something called a JRootPane. Instead of adding components directly to the container, you add them to a part of the root pane. The root pane then manages them all internally.

Why was this indirect layer added? Believe it or not, it was done to simplify things. The root pane manages its components in layers so that elements such as tooltip text will always appear *above* components, and you won't have to worry about dragging some components around behind others.

The newest of the top-level containers, JInternalFrame, also provides some additional capabilities when placed within a desktop (within a JDesktopPane to be specific). The JInternalFrame class can be used as the basis for creating a multi-document interface (MDI) application architecture within a Swing program. You can manage a series of internal frames within your program, and they'll never go beyond the bounds of your main program window.

Let's begin by exploring the new JRootPane class, which manages the internals of all the top-level containers.

Class JRootPane

The JRootPane class acts as a container delegate for the top-level Swing containers. Because the container holds only a JRootPane when you add or remove components from a top-level container, instead of directly altering the components in the container, you would indirectly add or remove components from its JRootPane instance. In effect, the top-level containers are acting as proxies, with the JRootPane doing all the work.

The JRootPane container relies on its inner class RootLayout for layout management and takes up all the space of the top-level container that holds it. The basic contained pane is a JLayeredPane that consists of two other components:

an optional JMenuBar as well as a Container for holding the primary components of the container within a content pane. In front of the JLayeredPane is a single Component within a transparent glass pane. The glass pane ensures that tooltip text, for instance, appears in front of any other Swing components.

Figure 8-1 illustrates these relationships for the JRootPane.

Although the relationship diagram doesn't adequately describe the layering of components within the JRootPane, Figure 8-2 should help you visualize how the components are laid out by the RootLayout. There are only two components within a JRootPane: a JLayeredPane and a glass pane. The glass pane is in front, can be any component, and tends to be invisible. In the back is the JLayeredPane, which contains an optional JMenuBar on top and a content pane below it in another layer. It is within the content pane that you would normally place components in the JRootPane.

> **NOTE** *A JLayeredPane is just another Swing container (it's described later in this chapter). It can contain any components and has a special layering characteristic. The default JLayeredPane used within the JRootPane pane contains only a JMenuBar and a Container as its content pane. The content pane has its own layout manager, which is BorderLayout by default.*

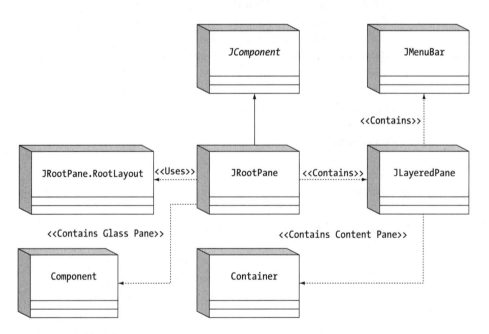

Figure 8-1: JRootPane UML relationship diagram

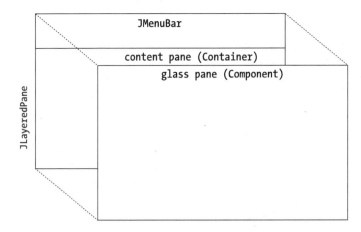

Figure 8-2: JRootPane containment diagram

Creating a JRootPane

Although the JRootPane has a public no-argument constructor, a JRootPane isn't something you would normally create yourself. Instead, a class that implements the RootPaneContainer interface creates the JRootPane. Then, you can get the root pane from that component, through the RootPaneContainer interface, described shortly.

```
public JRootPane()
JRootPane rootPane = new JRootPane();
```

JRootPane Properties

As Table 8-1 shows, there are only eight properties of JRootPane. Normally, when you get or set one of these properties for the top-level container, the container simply passes along the request to its JRootPane.

PROPERTY NAME	DATA TYPE	ACCESS
accessibleContext	AccessibleContext	read-only
contentPane	Container	read-write
defaultButton	JButton	read-write
focusCycleRoot	boolean	read-only
glassPane	Component	read-write
jMenuBar	JMenuBar	read-write
layeredPane	JLayeredPane	read-write
validateRoot	boolean	read-only

Table 8-1: JRootPane properties

NOTE *A ninth property also exists. It is a read-write menuBar property that's deprecated in favor of the jMenuBar property. The menuBar and jMenuBar properties control the same setting.*

For a JRootPane, the focusCycleRoot property setting is initially true. This is important for focus management, as discussed in Chapter 2. In addition, the validateRoot property is also true by default. If revalidate() is called on a component within the JRootPane, the contents of the root pane will be validated (redisplayed).

The glass pane for a JRootPane must not be opaque. Because the glass pane takes up the entire area in front of the JLayeredPane, an opaque glass pane would render the menu bar and content pane invisible.

Interface *RootPaneContainer*

The RootPaneContainer interface defines the setter/getter methods for accessing the different panes within the JRootPane, as well as accessing the JRootPane itself.

```
public interface RootPaneContainer {
  // Properties
  public Container getContentPane();
  public void setContentPane(Container contentPane);
  public Component getGlassPane();
  public void setGlassPane(Component glassPane);
  public JLayeredPane getLayeredPane();
  public void setLayeredPane(JLayeredPane layeredPane);
  public JRootPane getRootPane();
}
```

Among the predefined Swing components, the JFrame, JWindow, JDialog, JApplet, and JInternalFrame classes implement the RootPaneContainer interface. For the most part, these implementations simply pass along the request to a JRootPane implementation for the high-level container. The following source code is one such implementation for the glass pane of a RootPaneContainer implementer:

```
public Component getGlassPane() {
  return getRootPane().getGlassPane();
}
public void setGlassPane(Component glassPane) {
  getRootPane().setGlassPane(glassPane);
}
```

Class *JLayeredPane*

The JLayeredPane serves as the main component container of a JRootPane. The JLayeredPane manages the z-order, or layering, of components within itself. This ensures that the correct component is drawn on top of other components for tasks such as creating tooltip text, pop-up menus, and dragging for drag and drop. Several system-defined layers exist, or you can create your own.

Although initially a JLayeredPane container has no layout manager, there's nothing to stop you from setting the layout property of the container, defeating the layering aspect of the container.

Creating a *JLayeredPane*

As with the JRootPane, you'll almost never create an instance of the class yourself. When the default JRootPane is created for one of the predefined classes that implement RootPaneContainer, the JRootPane in turn creates a JLayeredPane for its main component area, adding an initial content pane.

```
public JLayeredPane()
JLayeredPane layeredPane = new JLayeredPane();
```

Adding Components in Layers

The z-order of components within a JLayeredPane is managed by an associated layer setting for each added component. The higher the layer setting, the closer to the top the component will be drawn. You can set the layer with the layout manager constraints when you add a component to a JLayeredPane:

```
Integer layer = new Integer(20);
aLayeredPane.add(aComponent, layer);
```

You can also call one of the public void setLayer(Component comp, int layer) or public void setLayer(Component comp, int layer, int position) methods *before* adding the component to the JLayeredPane.

```
aLayeredPane.setLayer(aComponent, 10);
aLayeredPane.add(aComponent);
```

The JLayeredPane class predefines six constants for special values. In addition, you can find out the topmost current layer with public void highestLayer() and the bottom layer with `public void lowestLayer()`. Table 8-2 lists the six predefined layer constants.

CONSTANT	DESCRIPTION
FRAME_CONTENT_LAYER	Level –30,000 for holding the menu bar and content pane; not normally used by developers
DEFAULT_LAYER	Level 0 for the normal component level
PALETTE_LAYER	Level 100 for holding floating toolbars and the like
MODAL_LAYER	Level 200 for holding pop-up dialog boxes that appear on top of components on the default layer, on top of palettes, and below pop-ups
POPUP_LAYER	Level 300 for holding pop-up menus and tooltips
DRAG_LAYER	Level 400 for ensuring that dragged objects remain on top

Table 8-2: JLayeredPane properties

Although you can use your own constants for layers, use them with care — because the system will use the predefined constants for *its* needs. If your constants don't fit in properly, the components may not work properly.

To visualize how the different layers fit in, see Figure 8-3.

Working with Component Layers and Positions

Components in a `JLayeredPane` have both a layer and a position. When a single component is on a layer, it's at position 0. When multiple components are on the same layer, components added later have higher position numbers. The lower the position setting, the closer to the top the component will appear. (This is the reverse of the layering behavior.) Figure 8-4 shows the positions for four components on the same layer.

To rearrange components on a single layer, you can use either the `public void moveToBack(Component component)` or `public void moveToFront(Component component)` method. When you move a component to the front, it goes to position 0 for the layer. When you move a component to the back, it goes to the highest position number for the layer. You can also manually set the position with `public void setPosition(Component component, int position)`. A position of –1 is automatically the bottom layer with the highest position. (See Figure 8-4.)

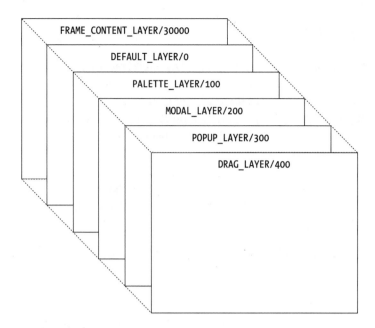

Figure 8-3: JLayeredPane layers

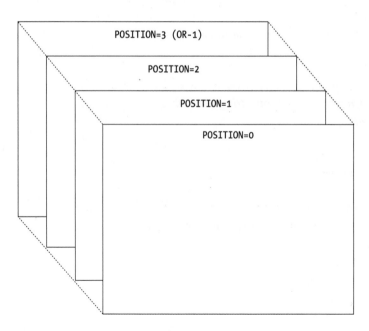

Figure 8-4: JLayeredPane positions

JLayeredPane Properties

Table 8-3 shows the two properties of JLayeredPane. The optimizedDrawingEnabled property determines whether components within the JLayeredPane can overlap. By default, this setting is true because in the standard usage with JRootPane the JMenuBar and content pane can't overlap. However, the JLayeredPane automatically validates the property setting to reflect the current state of the contents of the pane.

PROPERTY NAME	DATA TYPE	ACCESS
accessibleContext	AccessibleContext	read-only
optimizedDrawingEnabled	boolean	read-only

Table 8-3: JLayeredPane properties

Class JFrame

The JFrame class is the Swing equivalent of the Frame class of AWT. JFrame is a high-level container that uses a JRootPane and implements the RootPaneContainer interface. In addition, it uses the WindowConstants interface to help manage closing operations. Figure 8-5 shows these relationships for the JFrame class.

> **TIP** *Notice that JFrame subclasses Frame, not JComponent. This means that JFrame is a heavyweight component using the look and feel of the user's operating system.*

Creating a JFrame

Like the Frame class, the JFrame class provides two constructors: one for creating a frame without a title and one for creating a frame with a title.

1.  ```
    public JFrame()
    JFrame frame = new JFrame();
    ```

2.  ```
    public JFrame(String title)
    JFrame frame = new JFrame("Title Bar");
    ```

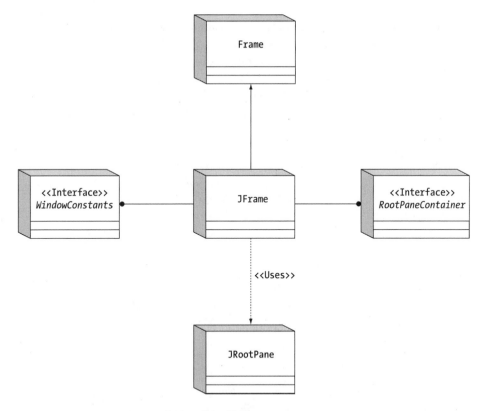

Figure 8-5: JFrame UML relationship diagram

JFrame Properties

Table 8-4 shows the eight properties of JFrame.

PROPERTY NAME	DATA TYPE	ACCESS
accessibleContext	AccessibleContext	read-only
contentPane	Container	read-write
defaultCloseOperation	int	read-write
glassPane	Component	read-write
jMenuBar	JMenuBar	read-write
layeredPane	JLayeredPane	read-write
layout	LayoutManager	write-only
rootPane	JRootPane	read-only

Table 8-4: JFrame properties

Although most properties are the result of implementing the RootPaneContainer interface, two properties are special: defaultCloseOperation and layout. (We first looked at defaultCloseOperation property in Chapter 2.) By default, a JFrame hides itself. This is unlike the default behavior of an AWT Frame, which is doing nothing. To change the setting, you can use one of the WindowConstants listed in Table 8-5 as arguments when setting the default close operation.

```
aFrame.setDefaultCloseOperation(JFrame.DISPOSE_ON_CLOSE);
```

CONSTANT	DESCRIPTION
3	Call System.exit(0)*
DISPOSE_ON_CLOSE	Call dispose( ) on the frame
DO_NOTHING_ON_CLOSE	Ignore the request
HIDE_ON_CLOSE	Call setVisible(false) on the frame [Default]

Table 8-5: Close operation constants

* Note: With Swing 1.1.1, the JFrame class has a close operation option of 3, which effectively is EXIT_ON_CLOSE without the class constant.

> **NOTE**   *Keep in mind that* JFrame *doesn't have an* EXIT_ON_CLOSE *option, but the* ExitableJFrame *class created in Chapter 2 does.*

The layout property protects the layout manager of the JFrame from changing. If you try to change the layout manager for a JFrame, an Error is thrown. If you want to change the layout manager for the components within the frame, you must change the layout manager for the content pane within the frame, and not the JFrame itself.

> **WARNING**   *If you use the* state *property (inherited from* Frame*) to say whether the* JFrame *is currently iconified, your program will be limited to the Java 2 platform. If you* do *use the property, be sure to use one of the additional* Frame *constants of* NORMAL *or* ICONIFIED *to set its state.*

Adding Components to a JFrame

Because JFrame implements the RootPaneContainer interface and uses a JRootPane, you don't add components directly to the JFrame. Instead, you add them to the JRootPane contained within the JFrame:

```
JRootPane rootPane = aJFrame.getRootPane();
Container contentPane = rootPane.getContentPane();
contentPane.add(...);
```

This can be shortened to

```
aJFrame.getContentPane().add(...);
```

> **WARNING** *If you do add components directly to the JFrame, it will result in an Error being thrown at runtime.*

Handling JFrame Events

The JFrame class supports the same set of events as an AWT Frame. You can register any of seven different listeners:

- ComponentListener — To find out when the frame moves or is resized

- ContainerListener — Normally not added to a JFrame because you add components to the content pane of its JRootPane

- FocusListener — To find out when the frame gets/loses input focus

> **WARNING** *If you register an InputMethodListener to the frame, your program will work only with the Java 2 platform.*

- KeyListener — Normally not added to a JFrame; instead, you'd register a keyboard action for its content pane

  ```
  JPanel content = (JPanel)frame.getContentPane();
  KeyStroke stroke = KeyStroke.getKeyStroke(KeyEvent.VK_ESCAPE, 0);
  content.registerKeyboardAction(actionListener, stroke,
  JComponent.WHEN_IN_FOCUSED_WINDOW);
  ```

- MouseListener and MouseMotionListener — To listen for mouse and mouse motion events

- WindowListener — To find out when a window is iconified/deiconified or a user is trying to open/close

With the help of the defaultCloseOperation property and the new ExitableJFrame class, you might find it unnecessary to add a WindowListener to help with frame closing as well as application stopping.

Extending JFrame

If you need to extend the JFrame frame class, this class has two important protected methods:

- protected void frameInit()

- protected JRootPane createRootPane()

By overriding either of these methods in a subclass, you can customize the initial appearance/behavior of the frame or that of its JRootPane. For example, in the ExitableJFrame class covered in Chapter 1, we initialized the default close operation to the new EXIT_ON_CLOSE state. Because you subclass JFrame, you don't need to add a call to the frameInit() method in either of the constructors. The parent class automatically calls the method.

```
public class ExitableJFrame extends JFrame {
  public static final int EXIT_ON_CLOSE = -1;
  public ExitableJFrame () {
  }
  public ExitableJFrame (String title) {
    super (title);
  }
  protected void frameInit() {
    super.frameInit();
    setDefaultCloseOperation(EXIT_ON_CLOSE);
  }
}
```

> **WARNING** *If you do override frameInit() of JFrame, remember to call super.frameInit() to reinitialize the default behaviors. If you forget and don't reimplement all the default behaviors yourself, your new frame will look and act differently.*

Class JWindow

The JWindow class is similar to Swing's JFrame class. It is the Swing equivalent to the appropriate AWT—in this case Window, a top-level window with no adornments. Like JFrame, JWindow uses a JRootPane for component management and implements the RootPaneContainer interface. Figure 8-6 shows these relationships for the JWindow class.

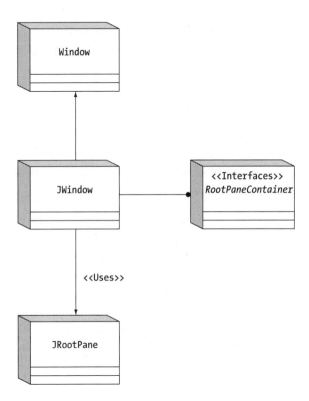

Figure 8-6: JWindow UML relationship diagram

Creating a JWindow

The JWindow class has three constructors, unlike the AWT Window class which lacks the first constructor in the list that follows. You can create a window without specifying a parent or by specifying the parent as a Frame or Window. If no parent is specified, an invisible one is used.

1. public JWindow()
    JWindow window = new JWindow();

2. `public JWindow(Frame owner)`
    `JWindow window = new JWindow(aFrame);`

3. `public JWindow(Window owner)`
    `JWindow window = new JWindow(anotherWindow);`

JWindow Properties

Table 8-6 lists the six properties of JWindow. These are similar in nature to the JFrame properties, except that JWindow has no property for a default close operation or a menu bar.

PROPERTY NAME	DATA TYPE	ACCESS
accessibleContext	AccessibleContext	read-only
contentPane	Container	read-write
glassPane	Component	read-write
layeredPane	JLayeredPane	read-write
layout	LayoutManager	write-only
rootPane	JRootPane	read-only

Table 8-6: JWindow properties

Handling JWindow Events

The JWindow class adds no additional event-handling capabilities beyond those of the JFrame and Window classes. See the section "Handling JFrame Events" earlier in this chapter for a list of listeners you can attach to a JWindow.

Extending JWindow

If you need to extend the JWindow class, the class has two protected methods of importance:

- `protected void windowInit()`

- `protected JRootPane createRootPane()`

Class `JDialog`

The `JDialog` class represents the standard pop-up window for displaying information related to a `Frame`. It acts like a `JFrame`, whereby its `JRootPane` contains a content pane and an optional `JMenuBar`, and it implements the `RootPaneContainer` and `WindowConstants` interfaces. Figure 8-7 shows these relationships.

Creating a JDialog

There are nine constructors for creating `JDialog` windows. Each allows you to customize the dialog owner, the window title, and the modality of the pop-up. When a `JDialog` is modal, it blocks input to the owner and the rest of the application. When a `JDialog` is nonmodal it allows a user to interact with the `JDialog` as well as the rest of your application.

> **WARNING** *For modality to work properly among the different Java versions, avoid mixing heavyweight AWT components with lightweight Swing components in a* `JDialog`.

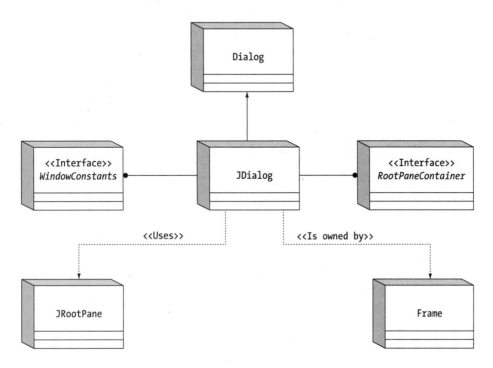

Figure 8-7: JDialog UML relationship diagram

The nine constructors for creating JDialog windows are:

1. ```
   public JDialog()
   JDialog dialog = new JDialog();
   ```

2. ```
   public JDialog(Dialog owner)
   JDialog dialog = new JDialog(anotherDialog);
   ```

3. ```
   public JDialog(Dialog owner, boolean modal)
   JDialog dialog = new JDialog(anotherDialog, true);
   ```

4. ```
   public JDialog(Dialog owner, String title)
   JDialog dialog = new JDialog(anotherDialog, "Hello");
   ```

5. ```
   public JDialog(Dialog owner, String title, boolean modal)
   JDialog dialog = new JDialog(anotherDialog, "Hello", true);
   ```

6. ```
   public JDialog(Frame owner)
   JDialog dialog = new JDialog(aFrame);
   ```

7. ```
   public JDialog(Frame owner, String windowTitle)
   JDialog dialog = new JDialog(aFrame, "Hello");
   ```

8. ```
   public JDialog(Frame owner, boolean modal)
   JDialog dialog = new JDialog(aFrame, false);
   ```

9. ```
   public JDialog(Frame owner, String title, boolean modal)
   JDialog dialog = new JDialog(aFrame, "Hello", true);
   ```

> **NOTE** *Instead of manually creating a JDialog and populating it, you may find yourself having JOptionPane automatically create and fill the JDialog for you. We'll look at JOptionPane in greater detail in Chapter 9.*

JDialog Properties

The JDialog class has the same eight properties as JFrame. In addition, JDialog contains a ninth one for positioning the dialog. These properties are listed in Table 8-7.
   ```

PROPERTY NAME	DATA TYPE	ACCESS
accessibleContext	AccessibleContext	read-only
contentPane	Container	read-write
defaultCloseOperation	int	read-write
glassPane	Component	read-write
jMenuBar	JMenuBar	read-write
layeredPane	JLayeredPane	read-write
layout	LayoutManager	write-only
locationRelativeTo	Component	write-only
rootPane	JRootPane	read-only

Table 8-7: JDialog properties

Setting the locationRelativeTo property of JDialog would be done prior to displaying the pop-up window. This causes the position of the JDialog to be centered over the component.

The constants to use for specifying the default close operation are shown back in Table 8-5. By default, the defaultCloseOperation property is set to HIDE_ON_CLOSE, which for a dialog pop-up is desirable default behavior.

Handling JDialog Events

There are no special JDialog events for you to deal with — only the same events as those for the JFrame class.

One thing that you may want to do with a JDialog is specify that pressing the ESCAPE key cancels the dialog. The easiest way to do this is to register an ESCAPE keystroke to a keyboard action within the JRootPane of the dialog, causing the JDialog to become hidden when pressed. The following source demonstrates this behavior. Most of the source duplicates the constructors of JDialog:

```java
import javax.swing.*;
import java.awt.*;
import java.awt.event.*;

public class EscapeDialog extends JDialog {
  public EscapeDialog() {
    this((Frame)null, false);
  }
  public EscapeDialog(Frame owner) {
    this(owner, false);
  }
  public EscapeDialog(Frame owner, boolean modal) {
```

```
        this(owner, null, modal);
    }
    public EscapeDialog(Frame owner, String title) {
      this(owner, title, false);
    }
    public EscapeDialog(Frame owner, String title, boolean modal) {
      super(owner, title, modal);
    }
    public EscapeDialog(Dialog owner) {
      this(owner, false);
    }
    public EscapeDialog(Dialog owner, boolean modal) {
      this(owner, null, modal);
    }
    public EscapeDialog(Dialog owner, String title) {
      this(owner, title, false);
    }
    public EscapeDialog(Dialog owner, String title, boolean modal) {
      super(owner, title, modal);
    }
    protected JRootPane createRootPane() {
      ActionListener actionListener = new ActionListener() {
        public void actionPerformed(ActionEvent actionEvent) {
          setVisible(false);
        }
      };
      JRootPane rootPane = new JRootPane();
      KeyStroke stroke = KeyStroke.getKeyStroke(KeyEvent.VK_ESCAPE, 0);
      rootPane.registerKeyboardAction(actionListener, stroke,
JComponent.WHEN_IN_FOCUSED_WINDOW);
      return rootPane;
    }
}
```

> **NOTE** *If you use the static creational methods of* JOptionPane, *pressing the Escape key to close the dialog box is automatically done to the* JDialog *windows it creates.*

Extending JDialog

If you need to extend the JDialog class, the class has two protected methods of importance, with one demonstrated in the previous example:

- protected void dialogInit()

- protected JRootPane createRootPane()

Class JApplet

The JApplet class is an extension to the AWT Applet class. For event handling to work properly within applets that use Swing components, your applets must subclass JApplet instead of Applet.

The JApplet works the same as the other high-level containers by implementing the RootPaneContainer interface. One important difference between JApplet and Applet is the default layout manager. Because you add components to the content pane of a JApplet, its default layout manager is BorderLayout. This is unlike the default layout manager of Applet, which is FlowLayout. In addition, Swing applets can also have a menu bar, or more specifically a JMenuBar, which is just another attribute of the JRootPane of the applet.

If you plan to deploy an applet that uses the Swing components, it is best to use the Java Plug-in from Sun Microsystems, because that will install the Swing libraries with a standard runtime.

Testing JApplet Solutions

If you'd like to test your Swing applet in a real browser without using the Java Plug-in, your 4.0+ browser can be manually configured for Swing support. For Internet Explorer, you need to find the registry entry for the Microsoft Java VM (My Computer\HKEY_LOCAL_MACHINE_SOFTWARE\Microsoft\Java VM) and add the location of the swingall.jar file from the Swing distribution to its CLASSPATH setting, as demonstrated in Figure 8-8.

For Netscape Navigator 4.06+ or Communicator 4.5+, you only need to copy the swingall.jar file to the appropriate Java directory. Look for the java40.jar file and place the swingall.jar file there. On Windows platforms, the default location is C:\ProgramFiles\Netscape\Communicator\Program\Java\Classes. However, your environment could be different.

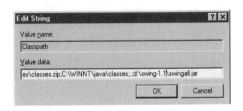

Figure 8-8: Setting CLASSPATH for Internet Explorer

In both cases, the next time you start up the browser, the Swing class libraries will now be available.

You can use the following applet to test for success. Look in the Java console for a message when the button is selected. You might also see a different message when the applet first starts up.

```java
import javax.swing.*;
import java.awt.event.*;
import java.awt.*;
public class TestApplet extends JApplet {
  protected JRootPane createRootPane() {
    JRootPane pane = new JRootPane();
    pane.putClientProperty("defeatSystemEventQueueCheck", Boolean.TRUE);
    return pane;
  }
  public void init() {
    JButton button = new JButton("Select");
    ActionListener actionListener = new ActionListener() {
      public void actionPerformed(ActionEvent actionEvent) {
        System.out.println("Selected");
      }
    };
    button.addActionListener(actionListener);
    Container container = getContentPane();
    container.add(button, BorderLayout.SOUTH);
  }
}
```

The client property `defeatSystemEventQueueCheck` used in the previous example is mentioned in the `JApplet` documentation as a way to remove a warning message to the Java console at startup time. But, it seems that it no longer removes the warning message. It's possible that in a later Swing release this will be corrected by either fixing the documentation or adding back support for the property. Another option for getting the message removed is to ask the browser vendors to permit the desired behavior that's causing the problem.

Extending JApplet

If you need to extend the `JApplet` class, the class has only one `protected` method of importance:

```java
protected JRootPane createRootPane()
```

Working with a Desktop

Swing provides for the management of a set of frames within a common window or desktop. This management is commonly called the multi-document interface, or MDI. The frames can be layered on top of one another or dragged around and their appearance is specific to the current look and feel. The frames are instances of the JInternalFrame class, whereas the desktop is a specialized JLayeredPane called JDesktopPane. The management of the frames within a desktop is the responsibility of a DesktopManager, in which the default implementation that's provided is DefaultDesktopManager. The iconified form of a JInternalFrame on the desktop is represented by the JDesktopIcon inner class of JInternalFrame. Figure 8-9 shows these relationships, including the InternalFrameListener, InternalFrameAdapter, and InternalFrameEvent introduced for event handling.

We'll first look at the parts that make up the desktop, and then we'll provide a complete example that uses all the parts.

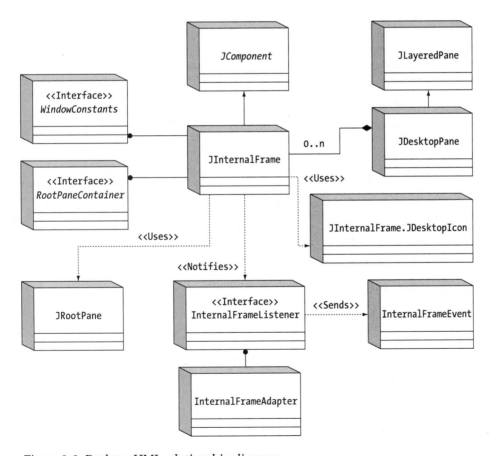

Figure 8-9: Desktop UML relationship diagram

> **NOTE** *The Swing libraries provide only those tools necessary to build an application using MDI. You use these tools in whatever manner you see fit.*

Class JInternalFrame

The JInternalFrame class is similar to the JFrame class. It acts as a high-level container, using the RootPaneContainer interface, but it isn't a top-level window. You must place internal frames within another top-level window. When dragged around, internal frames stay within the bounds of their container, which is usually a JDesktopPane. In addition, internal frames are lightweight and therefore offer a UI-delegate to make internal frames appear as the currently configured look and feel.

Creating a JInternalFrame

There are six constructors for JInternalFrame. They cascade in such a way that each adds a parameter to another constructor. With no arguments, the created JInternalFrame has no title and can't be resized, closed, maximized, or iconified. Internal frames can always be dragged, however.

1.  ```
    public JInternalFrame()
    JInternalFrame frame = new JInternalFrame();
    ```

2.  ```
    public JInternalFrame(String title)
    JInternalFrame frame = new JInternalFrame("The Title");
    ```

3.  ```
    public JInternalFrame(String title, boolean resizable)
    JInternalFrame frame = new JInternalFrame("The Title", true);
    ```

4.  ```
    public JInternalFrame(String title, boolean resizable, boolean
    closable)
    JInternalFrame frame = new JInternalFrame("The Title", false, true);
    ```

5.  ```
    public JInternalFrame(String title, boolean resizable, boolean
    closable, boolean maximizable)
    JInternalFrame frame = new JInternalFrame("The Title", true, false, true);
    ```

6.  ```
    public JInternalFrame(String title, boolean resizable, boolean
    closable, boolean maximizable, boolean iconifiable)
    JInternalFrame frame = new JInternalFrame("The Title", false, true,
    false, true);
    ```

> **NOTE** *In addition to your creating a* `JInternalFrame` *directly, you can rely on the* `JOptionPane` *to create an internal frame for common pop-up dialog boxes hosted by a* `JInternalFrame` *instead of being hosted by the standard* `JDialog`.

JInternalFrame Properties

The 27 different properties for the `JInternalFrame` class are listed in Table 8-8.

PROPERTY NAME	DATA TYPE	ACCESS
accessibleContext	AccessibleContext	read-only
background	Color	read-write bound
closable	boolean	read-write bound
closed	boolean	read-write bound constrained
contentPane	Container	read-write bound
defaultCloseOperation	int	read-write
desktopIcon	JInternalFrame.JDesktopIcon	read-write bound
desktopPane	JDesktopPane	read-only
foreground	Color	read-write bound
frameIcon	Icon	read-write bound
glassPane	Component	read-write bound
icon	boolean	read-write bound constrained
iconifiable	boolean	read-write
jMenuBar	JMenuBar	read-write bound
layer	Integer	read-write
layeredPane	JLayeredPane	read-write bound
layout	LayoutManager	write-only
maximizable	boolean	read-write bound
maximum	boolean	read-write bound constrained
resizable	boolean	read-write bound
rootPane	JRootPane	read-only bound
selected	boolean	read-write bound constrained
title	String	read-write bound
UI	InternalFrameUI	read-write
UIClassID	String	read-only
visible	boolean	write-only
warningString	String	read-only

Table 8-8: JInternalFrame properties

> **NOTE** *A 28th property also exists, a read-write bound* menuBar *property that's deprecated in favor of the* jMenuBar *property. They both control the same setting.*

The JInternalFrame contains the only four constrained properties within the Swing classes: closed, icon, maximum, and selected. They're directly related to the four boolean constructor parameters. Each allows you to check on the current state of the property as well as change its setting. However, because the properties are constrained, whenever you try to set one, the attempt must be in a try-catch block, catching PropertyVetoException:

```
try {
  // Try to iconify internal frame
  internalFrame.setIcon(false);
} catch (PropertyVetoException propertyVetoException) {
  System.out.println("Rejected");
}
```

To help you work with some of the bound properties, the JInternalFrame class defines 11 constants, as listed in Table 8-9. They represent the string that should be returned by getPropertyName() for a PropertyChangeEvent within a PropertyChangeListener.

PROPERTY NAME CONSTANT	ASSOCIATED PROPERTY
CONTENT_PANE_PROPERTY	contentPane
FRAME_ICON_PROPERTY	frameIcon
GLASS_PANE_PROPERTY	glassPane
IS_CLOSED_PROPERTY	closed
IS_ICON_PROPERTY	icon
IS_MAXIMUM_PROPERTY	maximum
IS_SELECTED_PROPERTY	selected
LAYERED_PANE_PROPERTY	layeredPane
MENU_BAR_PROPERTY	menuBar/jMenuBar
ROOT_PANE_PROPERTY	rootPane
TITLE_PROPERTY	title

Table 8-9: JInternalFrame property constants

The following class example demonstrates the use of the constants within a PropertyChangeListener.

```
import java.beans.*;
import javax.swing.*;

public class InternalFramePropertyChangeHandler implements PropertyChangeListener
{
  public void propertyChange(PropertyChangeEvent propertyChangeEvent) {
    String propertyName = propertyChangeEvent.getPropertyName();
    if (propertyName.equals(JInternalFrame.IS_ICON_PROPERTY)) {
      System.out.println("Icon property changed. React.");
    }
  }
}
```

> **WARNING** *The number of bound properties for the JInternalFrame class seems to be in a state of flux. Some properties are designated as bound for purposes of JavaBeans beans info but aren't bound within the source. Other properties are bound but send the wrong property name to the PropertyChangeListener. (In Swing 1.1, changing the frame icon requires the use of the menu bar property name.) I hope that all of this will be corrected in future Swing releases. But then you'll have to worry about which properties are bound in which Swing release. Bottom line: Use bound JInternalFrame properties with great care.*

Handling JInternalFrame Events

To help you use a JInternalFrame as you would use a JFrame, there's a new event listener for responding to internal frame opening- and closing-related events. The interface is called InternalFrameListener, and its definition is shown below. It works similarly to the AWT WindowListener interface, but with a JInternalFrame instead of an AWT Window class.

```
public interface InternalFrameListener extends EventListener {
  public void internalFrameActivated(InternalFrameEvent internalFrameEvent);
  public void internalFrameClosed(InternalFrameEvent internalFrameEvent);
  public void internalFrameClosing(InternalFrameEvent internalFrameEvent);
  public void internalFrameDeactivated(InternalFrameEvent internalFrameEvent);
  public void internalFrameDeiconified(InternalFrameEvent internalFrameEvent);
  public void internalFrameIconified(InternalFrameEvent internalFrameEvent);
  public void internalFrameOpened(InternalFrameEvent internalFrameEvent);
}
```

In addition, like the WindowAdapter class that has all the WindowListener methods stubbed out, there exists an InternalFrameAdapter class with all the InternalFrameListener methods stubbed out. If you're not interested in all the event happenings of a JInternalFrame, you can subclass InternalFrameAdapter and override only those methods you're interested in. For instance, the following listener is only interested in the iconification methods. Instead of providing stubs for the other five methods of InternalFrameListener, you'd only have to subclass InternalFrameAdapter and override the two relevant methods.

```
import javax.swing.*;
import javax.swing.event.*;

public class InternalFrameIconifyListener extends InternalFrameAdapter {
  public void internalFrameIconified(InternalFrameEvent internalFrameEvent) {
    JInternalFrame source = (JInternalFrame)internalFrameEvent.getSource();
    System.out.println ("Iconified: " + source.getTitle());
  }
  public void internalFrameDeiconified(InternalFrameEvent internalFrameEvent){
    JInternalFrame source = (JInternalFrame)internalFrameEvent.getSource();
    System.out.println ("Deiconified: " + source.getTitle());
  }
}
```

The InternalFrameEvent class is a subclass of AWTEvent. To define the values returned by the public int getID() method of AWTEvent, the InternalFrameEvent class defines a constant for each of the specific event subtypes that can be used. In addition, two other constants designate the range of valid values. Table 8-10 lists the nine constants.

EVENT SUBTYPE ID	ASSOCIATED INTERFACE METHOD
INTERNAL_FRAME_ACTIVATED	internalFrameActivated
INTERNAL_FRAME_CLOSED	internalFrameClosed
INTERNAL_FRAME_CLOSING	internalFrameClosing
INTERNAL_FRAME_DEACTIVATED	internalFrameDeactivated
INTERNAL_FRAME_DEICONIFIED	internalFrameDeiconified
INTERNAL_FRAME_FIRST	n/a
INTERNAL_FRAME_ICONIFIED	internalFrameIconified
INTERNAL_FRAME_LAST	n/a
INTERNAL_FRAME_OPENED	internalFrameOpened

Table 8-10: InternalFrameEvent event subtypes

Customizing a JInternalFrame Look and Feel

Because the JInternalFrame is a lightweight component, it has an installable look and feel. Each installable Swing look and feel provides a different JInternalFrame appearance and set of default UIResource values. Figure 8-10 shows the appearance of the JWindow container for the preinstalled set of look and feels.

The available set of UIResource-related properties for a JInternalFrame is shown in Table 8-11. For the JInternalFrame component, there are 22 different properties.

PROPERTY STRING	OBJECT TYPE
InternalFrame.activeTitleBackground	Color
InternalFrame.activeTitleForeground	Color
InternalFrame.border	Border
InternalFrame.closeIcon	Icon
InternalFrame.closePressed	Icon
InternalFrame.font	Font
InternalFrame.icon	Icon
InternalFrame.iconifyIcon	Icon
InternalFrame.iconifyPressed	Icon
InternalFrame.iconizeIcon	Icon
InternalFrame.inactiveTitleBackground	Color
InternalFrame.inactiveTitleForeground	Color
InternalFrame.maximizeIcon	Icon
InternalFrame.maximizePressed	Icon
InternalFrame.minimizeIcon	Icon
InternalFrame.minimizeIconBackground	Color
InternalFrame.paletteBorder	Border
InternalFrame.paletteCloseIcon	Icon
InternalFrame.paletteTitleHeight	Integer
InternalFrame.titleFont	Font
InternalFrame.windowShadeBorder	Border
InternalFrameUI	InternalFrameUI

Table 8-11: JInternalFrame UIResource elements

In addition to the many configurable properties in Table 8-11, with the Metal look and feel you can designate an internal frame to be a "palette" by using a special client property, JInternalFrame.isPalette. When set to Boolean.TRUE, this internal frame will have a slightly different appearance from the others and a shorter title bar (see Figure 8-11).

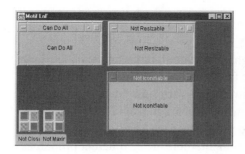

Motif

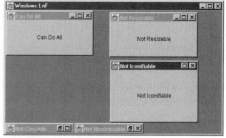

Windows

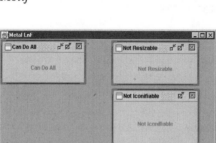

Metal

Macintosh

Figure 8-10: JInternalFrame under different look and feels

If you also add an internal frame to the PALETTE_LAYER of the desktop, the frame will always appear on top of all the other frames. Its appearance is noted in Figure 8-11. The complete source for creating the program in Figure 8-11 appears later in this chapter.

```
JInternalFrame palette = new JInternalFrame("Palette", true, false, true, false);
palette.setBounds(150, 0, 100, 100);
palette.putClientProperty("JInternalFrame.isPalette", Boolean.TRUE);
desktop.add(palette, JDesktopPane.PALETTE_LAYER);
```

> **NOTE** *If the current look and feel is something other than Metal, the palette layer will still be honored, but its appearance won't be quite as distinctive.*

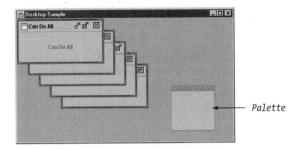

Figure 8-11: A JInternalFrame palette with other frames

Changing the JDesktopIcon

The JInternalFrame relies on an inner class, JDesktopIcon, to provide a UI delegate for the iconified view of the JInternalFrame. The class is merely a specialized
JComponent for providing this capability, and not a specialized Icon implementation. In fact, the JDesktopIcon class comments say that the class is temporary, so
you shouldn't try to customize it directly.

If you *do* want to customize the JDesktopIcon, you can change some of the
UIResource-related properties. Table 8-12 lists the five related properties for the
JDesktopIcon component.

PROPERTY STRING	OBJECT TYPE
DesktopIcon.background	Color
DesktopIcon.border	Border
DesktopIcon.font	Font
DesktopIcon.foreground	Color
DesktopIconUI	DesktopIconUI

Table 8-12: JInternalFrame.DesktopIcon UIResource elements

Class JDesktopPane

Another class for working with groups of internal frames is the JDesktopPane
class. The sole purpose of the desktop pane is to contain a set of internal frames.
When internal frames are contained within a desktop pane, they delegate most
of their behavior to the desktop manager of the desktop pane. I'll discuss the
DesktopManager interface in greater detail later in this chapter.

Creating a JDesktopPane

The JDesktopPane has a single no-argument constructor. Once it's created, you'd typically place the desktop in the center of a container managed by a BorderLayout. This ensures that the desktop takes up all the room in the container.

```
public JDesktopPane()
JDesktopPane desktop = new JDesktopPane ();
```

Adding Internal Frames to a JDesktopPane

The JDesktopPane doesn't implement RootPaneContainer. Instead of adding components to the different panes within a JRootPane, you add them directly to the JDesktopPane:

```
desktop.add(anInternalFrame);
```

JDesktopPane Properties

As Table 8-13 shows, there are six properties of JDesktopPane. The JInternalFrame at index 0 of the allFrames property array is the internal frame in front of the desktop (JInternalFrame f = desktop.getAllFrames()[0]). Besides getting all the frames within the JDesktopPane, you can get only those within a specific layer: public JInternalFrame[] getAllFramesInLayer(int layer). (Remember JLayeredPane, covered earlier in this chapter under "Working with Component Layers," the parent class of JDesktopPane?)

PROPERTY NAME	DATA TYPE	ACCESS
accessibleContext	AccessibleContext	read-only
allFrames	JInternalFrame[ ]	read-only
desktopManager	DesktopManager	read-write
opaque	boolean	read-only
UI	DesktopPaneUI	read-write
UIClassID	String	read-only

Table 8-13: JDesktopPane properties

Customizing JDesktopPane Look and Feel

Back in Figure 8-10 you can see JInternalFrame objects within a JDesktopPane. The basic appearance is the same from one look and feel to another. As Table

8-14 shows, there aren't many UIResource-related properties for a JDesktopPane to configure.

PROPERTY STRING	OBJECT TYPE
Desktop.background	Color
DesktopPaneUI	DesktopPaneUI

Table 8-14: JDesktopPane UIResource elements

One thing you can configure for a JDesktopPane is a special client property for configuring the drawing mode when dragging an internal frame around. When the JDesktopPane.dragMode client property is set to outline, only the outline of the internal frame will be drawn when the frame is moved. If this property isn't set, the internal frame will be repeatedly drawn as it's dragged around.

```
desktop.putClientProperty("JDesktopPane.dragMode", "outline");
// or
desktop.putClientProperty("JDesktopPane.dragMode", "faster");
```

Complete Desktop Example

Now that you have the major desktop-related classes under your belt, you can use the following example to demonstrate your understanding of the JInternalFrame and JDesktopPane. The basic process involves creating a group of JInternalFrame objects and putting them in a single JDesktopPane. Event handling can be done for individual components on each of the internal frames, if desired, or for individual frames. In this example, simply use the InternalFrameIconifyListener class, created earlier in this chapter in the section "Handling JInternal Frame Events," to listen for internal frames being iconified and deiconified.

Figure 8-11 shows how the program looks when it first starts. One particular internal frame has been designated a palette, and the outline drag mode is enabled.

The complete source for the example follows.

```
import javax.swing.*;
import javax.swing.event.*;
import java.awt.*;
import java.awt.event.*;

public class DesktopSample {

  public static void main(String[] args) {
    String title = (args.length==0 ? "Desktop Sample" : args[0]);
    JFrame frame = new ExitableJFrame(title);
```

```
    JDesktopPane desktop = new JDesktopPane();
    JInternalFrame internalFrames[] = {
      new JInternalFrame("Can Do All", true, true, true, true),
      new JInternalFrame("Not Resizable", false, true, true, true),
      new JInternalFrame("Not Closable", true, false, true, true),
      new JInternalFrame("Not Maximizable", true, true, false, true),
      new JInternalFrame("Not Iconifiable", true, true, true, false)
    };

    InternalFrameListener internalFrameListener = new
  InternalFrameIconifyListener();

    for(int i=0, n=internalFrames.length; i<n; i++) {
      // Add to desktop
      desktop.add(internalFrames[i]);

      // Position and size
      internalFrames[i].setBounds(i*25, i*25, 200, 100);

      // Add listener for iconification events
      internalFrames[i].addInternalFrameListener(internalFrameListener);

      JLabel label = new JLabel(internalFrames[i].getTitle(), JLabel.CENTER);
      Container content = internalFrames[i].getContentPane();
      content.add(label, BorderLayout.CENTER);
    }

    JInternalFrame palette = new JInternalFrame("Palette", true, false, true,
  false);
    palette.setBounds(150, 0, 200, 50);
    palette.putClientProperty("JInternalFrame.isPalette", Boolean.TRUE);
    desktop.add(palette, JDesktopPane.PALETTE_LAYER);

    desktop.putClientProperty("JDesktopPane.dragMode", "outline");

    Container content = frame.getContentPane();
    content.add(desktop, BorderLayout.CENTER);
    frame.setSize(500, 300);
    frame.setVisible(true);
  }
}
```

Interface DesktopManager

One remaining piece of the puzzle for working on a desktop is the desktop manager, which is an implementation of the DesktopManager interface, shown here:

```
public interface DesktopManager {
  public void activateFrame(JInternalFrame frame);
  public void beginDraggingFrame(JComponent frame);
  public void beginResizingFrame(JComponent frame, int direction);
  public void closeFrame(JInternalFrame frame);
  public void deactivateFrame(JInternalFrame frame);
  public void deiconifyFrame(JInternalFrame frame);
  public void dragFrame(JComponent frame, int newX, int newY);
  public void endDraggingFrame(JComponent frame);
  public void endResizingFrame(JComponent frame);
  public void iconifyFrame(JInternalFrame frame);
  public void maximizeFrame(JInternalFrame frame);
  public void minimizeFrame(JInternalFrame frame);
  public void openFrame(JInternalFrame frame);
  public void resizeFrame(JComponent frame, int newX, int newY, int newWidth, int
newHeight);
  public void setBoundsForFrame(JComponent frame, int newX, int newY, int
newWidth, int newHeight);
}
```

> **NOTE** *For the* DesktopManager *methods that accept a* JComponent *argument, the arguments are usually a* JInternalFrame *or another lightweight Swing component.*

When JInternalFrame objects are in a JDesktopPane, they shouldn't attempt operations such as iconifying or maximizing themselves. Instead, they should ask the desktop manager of the desktop pane in which they're installed to perform the operation:

```
getDesktopPane().getDesktopManager().iconifyFrame(anInternalFrame);
```

The DefaultDesktopManager class provides one such implementation of a DesktopManager. If the default isn't sufficient, a look and feel might provide its own DesktopManager implementation class, as the Windows look and feel does with the WindowsDesktopManager. You can also define your own manager, but this usually isn't necessary.

Summary

In this chapter, we explored the JRootPane class and how implementers of the RootPaneContainer interface rely on a JRootPane for internal component management. Instead of working directly with the main area of a Frame, Dialog, Window, or Applet, in Swing you work with the JRootPane of a JFrame, JDialog, JWindow, JApplet, or the new JInternalFrame class. The root pane can then layer components with the help of a JLayeredPane in such a way that tooltip text and pop-up menus will always appear above their associated components.

The JInternalFrame can also live within a desktop environment, in which a JDesktopPane and DesktopManager manage how and where the internal frames act and appear. You can also respond to internal frame events by associating InternalFrameListener implementations with a JInternalFrame.

In Chapter 9, we'll examine the specialized pop-up components within the Swing libraries: JColorChooser, JFileChooser, JOptionPane, and ProgressMonitor.

Pop-Ups and Choosers

IN CHAPTER 8, WE LOOKED AT THE top-level containers such as JFrame and JApplet. In addition, we explored the JDialog class that's used to create pop-up windows to display messages or get user input. Although the JDialog class works perfectly well, the Swing component set also offers several simpler approaches to get user input from pop-up windows.

The JOptionPane class is useful for displaying messages, obtaining textual user input, or getting the answer to a question. The ProgressMonitor and ProgressMonitorInputStream classes enable you to monitor the progress of lengthy tasks. In addition, the JColorChooser and JFileChooser classes come equipped with feature-filled pop-up windows for getting a color choice from a user or getting a file name or directory name. With the addition of these classes, your user interface development tasks can be accomplished much more quickly and easily.

Class JOptionPane

The JOptionPane is a special class for creating a panel to be placed in a pop-up window. The purpose of the panel is to display a message to a user and get a response back from that user. To accomplish its task, the panel presents content in four areas, as shown in the sample in Figure 9-1.

The four sections of the panel are the icon, message, input, and button areas. All the areas are optional, although having a panel without at least a message and a button makes the option pane virtually useless. Table 9-1 describes the purpose of the four areas.

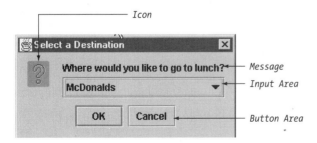

Figure 9-1: JOptionPane parts

AREA	DESCRIPTION
JOptionPane Icon	The icon area is for the display of an Icon to indicate the type of message being displayed to the user. It's the responsibility of the installed look and feel to provide default icons for certain types of messages, but you're free to provide your own if you need to display another icon type.
Message	The primary purpose of this area is to display a text message. In addition, the area can contain any optional set of objects to make the message more informational.
Input	The input area allows a user to provide a response to a message. The response can be free form, in a text field, or from a "pick list" in a combo box or list control. For "Yes" or "No" responses of the form, the button area would be used instead.
Button	The button area is also for getting user input. Selection of a button in this area signals the end of the usage of the JOptionPane. Default sets of button labels are available, or you can display any number of buttons, including none, with any labels you desire.

Table 9-1: JOptionPane area descriptions

Besides its being a panel with four sections within a pop-up window, the JOptionPane is capable of automatically placing itself in a pop-up window and managing the acquisition of the user's response. It can place itself in either a JDialog or a JInternalFrame, depending on the type of GUI you're providing to the user. With the help of an Icon and set of JButton components, the JOptionPane does its job. Figure 9-2 shows the interrelationships of all these components to the JOptionPane.

> **NOTE** *Because the JOptionPane can automatically place itself in a JDialog, you might never need to create a JDialog directly.*

Creating a JOptionPane

You can either manually create a JOptionPane through one of its seven constructors or go through one of the 23 factory methods discussed later in the section "Automatically Creating a JOptionPane in a Pop-Up Window."

You have the most control when manually creating the JOptionPane. However, you then must place it in a pop-up window, show the window, and finally manage getting the response. Because of the ease of use provided by the

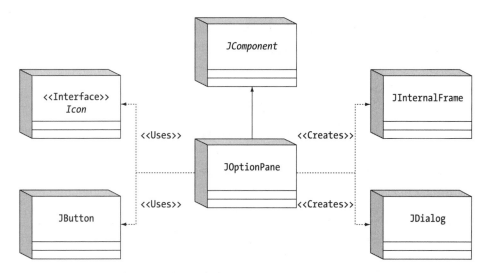

Figure 9-2: JOptionPane UML relationship diagram

automatically do-everything methods, you might think you'd *only* use the factory methods when working with JOptionPane. However, throughout this chapter you'll discover several other reasons why you might want to do things manually. In addition, when you use a visual-programming environment, the environment treats the JOptionPane as a JavaBean and will ignore the factory methods.

For the seven constructors, you can have different permutations of six different arguments. The arguments allow you to configure something in one of the four different areas shown in Figure 9-1. The six arguments are: the message, the message type, an option type, an icon, an array of options, and an initial option setting. The use of these arguments is shared with the factory methods.

The JOptionPane Constructors

Let's first look at the constructors, and then I'll explain the different arguments. Notice that the constructor arguments are cascading and only add additional arguments to the previous constructor.

1.  ```
    public JOptionPane()
    JOptionPane optionPane = new JOptionPane();
    ```

2.  ```
    public JOptionPane(Object message)
    JOptionPane optionPane = new JOptionPane("Printing complete");
    ```

3. `public JOptionPane(Object message, int messageType)`
    `JOptionPane optionPane = new JOptionPane("Printer out of paper",`
    `JOptionPane.WARNING_MESSAGE);`

4. `public JOptionPane(Object message, int messageType, int optionType)`
    `JOptionPane optionPane = new JOptionPane("Continue printing?",`
    `JOptionPane.QUESTION_MESSAGE, JOptionPane.YES_NO_OPTION);`

5. `public JOptionPane(Object message, int messageType, int optionType,`
    `Icon icon)`
    `Icon printerIcon = new ImageIcon("printer.jpg");`
    `JOptionPane optionPane = new JOptionPane("Continue printing?",`
    `JOptionPane.QUESTION_MESSAGE, JOptionPane.YES_NO_OPTION, printerIcon);`

6. `public JOptionPane(Object message, int messageType, int optionType, Icon`
    `icon, Object options[ ])`
    `Icon greenIcon = new DiamondIcon(Color.green);`
    `Icon redIcon = new DiamondIcon(Color.red);`
    `Object optionArray[] = new Object[] {greenIcon, redIcon};`
    `JOptionPane optionPane = new JOptionPane("Continue printing?",`
    `JOptionPane.QUESTION_MESSAGE, JOptionPane.YES_NO_OPTION, printerIcon,`
    `optionArray);`

7. `public JOptionPane(Object message, int messageType, int optionType, Icon`
    `icon, Object options[], Object initialValue)`
    `JOptionPane optionPane = new JOptionPane("Continue printing?",`
    `JOptionPane.QUESTION_MESSAGE, JOptionPane.YES_NO_OPTION, printerIcon,`
    `optionArray, redIcon);`

The JOptionPane Message Argument

The `message` argument is an `Object`, not a `String`. Whereas you normally pass only a quoted string as this argument, when dealing with an `Object` argument you can basically display anything you want in the message area. We'll look at the more advanced use of this argument later in this chapter in the section "Understanding the Message Property." Briefly, though, there are four basic rules to interpret the meaning of an `Object`-typed message argument. For elements within the array, recursively follow these rules.

- If the message is an array of objects (`Object[ ]`), make the `JOptionPane` place each entry onto a separate row.

- If the message is a Component, place the component in the message area.

- If the message is an Icon, place the Icon within a JLabel and display the label in the message area.

- If the message is an Object, convert it to a String with toString(), place the String in a JLabel, and display the label in the message area.

The JOptionPane Message Type and Icon Arguments

The messageType constructor argument is used to represent the type of message being displayed within the JOptionPane. If you don't provide a custom icon for the JOptionPane, the installed look and feel will use the messageType argument setting to determine which icon to display within the icon area. Five different types are available as JOptionPane constants.

MESSAGE TYPE	
ERROR_MESSAGE	For displaying an error message
INFORMATION_MESSAGE	For displaying an informational message
QUESTION_MESSAGE	For displaying a query message
WARNING_MESSAGE	For displaying a warning message
PLAIN_MESSAGE	For displaying any other type of message

Table 9-2: JOptionPane message types

If you're using a constructor with both messageType and icon arguments and want the JOptionPane to use the default icon for the messageType, just specify null as the value for the icon argument. If the icon argument is non-null, the specified icon will be used no matter what the message type is.

If the messageType constructor argument isn't specified, the default message type is PLAIN_MESSAGE.

The JOptionPane Option Type Argument

The optionType constructor argument is used to determine the configuration for the set of buttons in the button area. If the options argument described next is provided, then the optionType argument is ignored and configuration for the set of buttons is acquired from the options argument. Four different types are available as shown by the following list of JOptionPane constants.

- DEFAULT_OPTION—For a single "OK" button

- OK_CANCEL_OPTION—For "OK" and "Cancel" buttons

- YES_NO_CANCEL_OPTION—For "Yes," "No," and "Cancel" buttons

- YES_NO_OPTION—For "Yes" and "No" buttons

If the optionType constructor argument isn't specified, the default option type is DEFAULT_OPTION.

The JOptionPane Options and Initial Value Arguments

The options argument is an Object array used to construct a set of JButton objects for the button area of the JOptionPane. If this argument is null (or a constructor without this argument is used), the button labels will be determined by the optionType argument. Otherwise, the array works similarly to the message argument, but without supporting recursive arrays:

- If an options array element is a Component, place the component in the button area.

- If an options array element is an Icon, place the Icon within a JButton and place the button in the button area.

- If an options array element is an Object, convert it to a String with toString(), place the String in a JButton, and place the button in the button area.

Normally, the options argument will be an array of String objects. You may want to have an Icon on the JButton, although the resulting button won't have label. If you want to have both an icon and a text label on the button, you can manually create a JButton and place it in the array. Alternatively, you can directly include any other Component within the array. There's one minor problem with these last two approaches, however. It's *your* responsibility to handle responding to component selection and tell the JOptionPane when this component was selected. The "Adding Components to the Button Area" section later in this chapter shows how to properly handle this behavior.

When the options argument is non-null, the initialValue argument specifies which of the buttons will be the default button when the pane is initially displayed. If null, the first component in the button area will be the default button. In either case, the first button will have the input focus, unless there's an input component in the message area, in which case the input component will have the initial input focus.

> **NOTE** *To have no buttons on the option pane, pass an empty array as the options setting:* new Object[] {}.

Displaying a JOptionPane

After you've created the JOptionPane with one of the constructors, what you have is a panel filled with components. In other words, the obtained JOptionPane is not yet in a pop-up window. You need to create a JDialog, a JInternalFrame, or another pop-up window and then place the JOptionPane within it. In addition, if you pick this manual style of JOptionPane construction, you need to handle the closing of the pop-up window and listen for selection of a component in the button area. After selection, you then have to hide the pop-up window. Because there's so much to do here, the JOptionPane includes two helper methods to place a JOptionPane within either a modal JDialog or a JInternalFrame and take care of all the previously described behavior:

- public JDialog createDialog(Component parentComponent, String title)

- public JInternalFrame createInternalFrame(Component parentComponent, String title)

> **NOTE** *When using the* createDialog() *and* createInternalFrame() *methods to create a pop-up window, selection of an automatically created button results in the closing of the created pop-up. You'd then need to ask the* JOptionPane *which option the user selected with* getValue() *and, if appropriate, get the input value with* getInputValue().

The first argument to the method is a component over which the pop-up window will be centered. The second argument is the title for the pop-up window. Once you create the pop-up window, whether it's a JDialog or JInternalFrame, you show it. The pop-up is then close after one of the components in the button area is selected, at which point your program still continues. The following lines of source code show the creation of one such JOptionPane shown within a JDialog. The resulting pop-up window is shown in Figure 9-3.

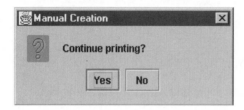

Figure 9-3: Sample JOptionPane in a JDialog

```
JOptionPane optionPane = new JOptionPane("Continue printing?",
JOptionPane.QUESTION_MESSAGE, JOptionPane.YES_NO_OPTION);

JDialog dialog = optionPane.createDialog(source, "Manual Creation");
dialog.show();
```

After you create the JOptionPane, place it in a pop-up window, and show it, and the user has responded, you need to find out what the user selected. The selection is provided via the public Object getValue() method of JOptionPane. The value returned by getValue() is determined by whether an options array was provided to the JOptionPane constructor. If the array was provided, the argument selected would be returned. In the event the array wasn't provided, an Integer object is returned, and its value represents the position of the button selected within the button area. In another case, getValue() could return null if nothing was selected, such as when the JDialog is closed by selecting the appropriate window decoration from the title bar of the pop-up window.

To make this multifaceted response easier to grasp, the following OptionPaneUtils class defines a method [public static int getSelection(JOptionPane optionPane)] that, given an option pane, returns the position of the selected value as an int, whether an options array was provided or not. To indicate that nothing was selected, JOptionPane.CLOSED_OPTION (-1) is returned.

```
import javax.swing.*;

public final class OptionPaneUtils {

  private OptionPaneUtils() {
  }

  public static int getSelection(JOptionPane optionPane) {
    // Default return value, signals nothing selected
    int returnValue = JOptionPane.CLOSED_OPTION;

    // Get selected Value
    Object selectedValue = optionPane.getValue();
```

```
    // If none, then nothing selected
    if (selectedValue != null) {
      Object options[] = optionPane.getOptions();
      if (options == null) {
        // default buttons, no array specified
        if(selectedValue instanceof Integer) {
          returnValue = ((Integer)selectedValue).intValue();
        }
      } else {
        // Array of option buttons specified
        for (int i=0, n = options.length; i < n; i++) {
          if(options[i].equals(selectedValue)) {
            returnValue = i;
            break; // out of for loop
          }
        }
      }
    }
    return returnValue;
  }
}
```

> **WARNING** *Because of a bug (4137962) in Sun's Solaris operating system, you shouldn't manually create modal dialog boxes and place JOptionPane components in them. The createDialog() version for Sun's Java 2 platform (and JDK 1.1) includes a workaround that recycles the dialog box windows instead of disposing of them.*

With the help of this new OptionPaneUtils.getSelection(JOptionPane) helper method, you can now find out the option pane selection with one line of code and then act accordingly based on the response.

```
int selection = OptionPaneUtils.getSelection(optionPane);
switch (selection) {
  case ...: ...
    break;
  case ...: ...
    break;
  default: ...
}
```

If you create a JOptionPane with a null options array, you can use the constants within the JOptionPane class to indicate the position of the default button labels and their return values from the OptionPaneUtils.getSelection(JOptionPane) method. These constants are found in Table 9-3. The usage of these constants enables you to avoid hard-coding constants such as 0, 1, 2, or –1.

POSITION	DESCRIPTION
CANCEL_OPTION	Used when the Cancel button is pressed
CLOSED_OPTION	Used when the pop-up window closed without the user pressing a button
NO_OPTION	Used when the No button is pressed
OK_OPTION	Used when the OK button is pressed
YES_OPTION	Used when the Yes button is pressed

Table 9-3: JOptionPane option position constants

Automatically Creating a JOptionPane in a Pop-up Window

Although you can manually create a JOptionPane, place it in a JDialog/JInternalFrame (or any other container), and fetch the response, the JOptionPane includes 23 factory methods for creating JOptionPane components directly within either a JDialog or a JInternalFrame. The 23 methods are first broken down into two sets: those that create the JOptionPane and show it within a JDialog, and those that show the pane within a JInternalFrame. Methods that show the JOptionPane within a JInternalFrame are named showInternal*XXX*Dialog(), and methods that create the pane within a JDialog are named show*XXX*Dialog().

The second group of factory methods for JOptionPane is what fills in the *XXX* of the prior names. This represents the various message types of option panes that you can create and display. In addition, the message type defines what's returned after the user selects something on the option pane. The four different message types are Message, Input, Confirm, and Option.

- With a message pop-up, there's no return value. Therefore, the method is defined void show[Internal]MessageDialog(...).

- With an input pop-up, the return value is either what the user typed in a text field (a String) or what the user picked from a list of options (an Object). Therefore, the show[Internal]InputDialog(...) methods return either a String or Object, depending on which version you use.

- With the confirm pop-up, the return value signifies which, if any, button the user picked within the option pane. After a button is picked, the pop-up window is dismissed, and the returned value is one of the integer constants from Table 9-3. Therefore, the method here is defined as `int show[Internal]ConfirmDialog(...)`.

- With the option pop-up, the return value is an `int`, the same type as the confirm pop-up so the methods are defined `int show[Internal]OptionDialog(...)`. If the button labels are manually specified with a non-`null` argument, the integer represents the selected button position.

The information in Table 9 should help you to visualize the 23 methods and their arguments. The method names (and return types) are found on the left side of the table, and their argument lists (and data types) are on the right. The numbers that repeat across the columns for each method name indicate a specific set of arguments for that method. For instance, the `showInputDialog` row shows a 3 in the Parent Component column, Message column, Title column, and Message Type column. Therefore, the `showInputDialog` method has one version defined as such: `public static String showInputDialog(Component parentComponent, Object message, String title, int messageType)`.

> **NOTE** *With the exception of one of the `showInputDialog(Object message)` methods, the parent component argument is required for all method varieties. The message argument is the only one required for all without exception.*

With the way the different `showXXXDialog()` methods are defined, you don't have to bother with discovering the selected button yourself, or even the user input. The return value for the various methods is one of the following: nothing (`void` return type), an `int` from Table 9-3, a `String`, or an `Object`, depending on the type of dialog box shown.

> **WARNING** *A significant difference exists between the `JOptionPane` constructors and the factory methods: The option type and message type arguments are reversed.*

METHOD NAME *Return Type*	PARENT COMPONENT *Component*	MESSAGE *Object*	TITLE *String*	OPTION TYPE *int*	MESSAGE TYPE *int*	ICON *Icon*	OPTIONS OBJECT[]	INITIAL VALUE OBJECT	SELECTION VALUES OBJECT[]	INITIAL SELECTION OBJECT
showMessageDialog *return type: void[123]*	1 2 3	1 2 3	2 3		2 3	3				
showInternalMessageDialog *return type: void[123]*	1 2 3	1 2 3	2 3		2 3	3				
showConfirmDialog *return type: int [1234]*	1 2 3 4	1 2 3 4	2 3 4	2 3 4	3 4	4				
showInternalConfirmDialog *return type: int [1234]*	1 2 3 4	1 2 3 4	2 3 4	2 3 4	3 4	4				
showInputDialog *return type: String[123]/Object[4]*	2 3 4	1 2 3 4	3 4		3 4	4			4	4
showInternalInputDialog *return type: String[12]/Object[3]*	1 2 3	1 2 3	2 3		2 3	3	3	3		
showOptionDialog *return type int[1]*	1	1	1	1	1	1	1	1		
showInternalOptionDialog *return type int[1]*	1	1	1	1	1	1	1	1		

Table 9-4: JOptionPane static create-and-show methods

JOptionPane Arguments for Factory Methods

Almost all the arguments for the factory methods match the JOptionPane constructor arguments. Two lists in the section "Creating a JOptionPane" earlier in this chapter describe the acceptable values for the message type and option type arguments. In addition, the usage of the message, options, and initial value arguments are also described. The parent component and title argument are passed along to one of the createDialog() or createInternalFrame() methods, depending on the type of pop-up in which the JOptionPane is embedded.

You next need to consider the selection values argument and the initial selection value argument of the showInputDialog() method. With an input dialog box, you can ask the user for text input and allow the user to type in anything, or you can present the user with a list of predefined choices. The selection values argument to showInputDialog() determines how you'd provide that set of choices, where the initial selection value represents the specific option to be chosen when the JOptionPane first appears. The look and feel will determine the appropriate Swing component to be used based on the number of choices presented. For small lists, a JComboBox is used. For larger lists, starting at 20 with the Motif, Metal, Windows, and Macintosh look and feels, a JList is used.

> **WARNING** *The* JList *is in multi-select mode. Double-clicking on a single item returns that single item. If a user selects multiple items and presses OK, the earliest selection in the array of selected values is returned.*

> **NOTE** *When the parent component argument is* null, *a hidden frame is used and the pop-up is centered on the screen.*

Example Factory Usage

Using the many factory methods, you can create the option pane, place it in a pop-up window, and get the response with a single line of source code.

The showMessageDialog() and showInternalMessageDialog() methods create an INFORMATION_MESSAGE pop-up with the pop-up title "Message," unless different argument settings are specified for message type and window title. Because the sole purpose of the message dialog box is to display a message, these dialog boxes only provide an OK button and return no value. Figure 9-4 shows sample message pop-ups created from the following lines of source.

```
JOptionPane.showMessageDialog(parent, "Printing complete");
JOptionPane.showInternalMessageDialog(desktop, "Printing complete");
```

The showConfirmDialog() and showInternalConfirmDialog() methods, by default, create a pop-up with a QUESTION_MESSAGE type and the pop-up title "Select an Option." Because confirm dialog boxes ask a question, their default option type is YES_NO_CANCEL_OPTION, giving them Yes, No, and Cancel buttons. The return value from a call to any of these methods is one of the JOptionPane class constants

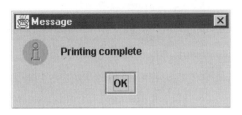

Dialog

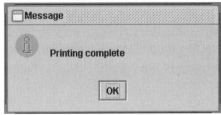

Internal frame

Figure 9-4: Sample message JOptionPane

YES_OPTION, NO_OPTION, or CANCEL_OPTION. No prizes for guessing which constant maps to which option pane button! Figure 9-5 shows sample confirm pop-ups created from the following lines of source.

```
JOptionPane.showConfirmDialog(parent, "Continue printing?");
JOptionPane.showInternalConfirmDialog(desktop, "Continue printing?");
```

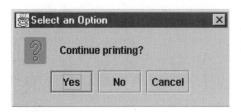 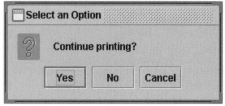

Dialog   *Internal frame*

Figure 9-5: Sample confirm JOptionPane

By default, the showInputDialog() and showInternalInputDialog() methods create a QUESTION_MESSAGE pop-up with the pop-up title "Input." The option type for input dialogs is OK_CANCEL_OPTION, giving them an OK and a Cancel button, and the option type isn't changeable. The return data type for these methods is either a String or an Object. If you don't specify selection values, the pop-up prompts you with a text field and returns the input as a String. If you do specify selection values, you get back an Object from the selection values array. Figure 9-6 shows some input pop-ups created from the following lines of source.

```
JOptionPane.showInputDialog(parent, "Enter printer name:");

// Moons of Neptune
String smallList[] = {"Naiad", "Thalassa", "Despina", "Galatea", "Larissa",
"Proteus", "Triton", "Nereid"};
JOptionPane.showInternalInputDialog(desktop, "Pick a printer", "Input",
JOptionPane.QUESTION_MESSAGE, null, smallList, "Triton");

// Moons of Saturn - includes two provisional designations to make 20
String bigList[] = {"Pan", "Atlas", "Prometheus", "Pandora", "Epimetheus",
"Janus", "Mimas", "Enceladus", "Tethys", "Telesto", "Calypso", "Dione", "Helene",
"Rhea", "Titan", "Hyperion", "Iapetus", "Phoebe", "S/1995 S 2", "S/1981 S 18"};
JOptionPane.showInputDialog(parent, "Pick a printer", "Input",
JOptionPane.QUESTION_MESSAGE, null, bigList, "Titan");
```

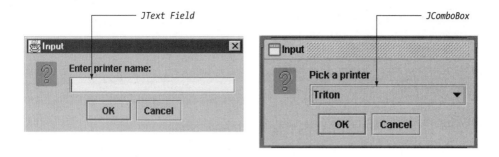

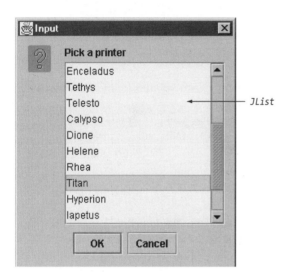

Figure 9-6: Sample input JOptionPane pop-ups

> **NOTE** *It is the responsibility of the look and feel to determine the type of input component. A look and feel can use something other than a JTextField, JComboBox, or JList. It's just that all the system-provided look and feels (from Sun) use these three components.*

The showOptionDialog() and showInternalOptionDialog() methods provide the most flexibility because they allow you to configure all the arguments. There are no default arguments and the return value is an int. If an options argument is not specified, the return value would be one of the constants found in Table 9-3. Otherwise, the value returned would represent the component position of the selected option from the options argument. Figure 9-7 shows a couple of input pop-ups created from the following lines of source, in which icons (instead of text) are provided on the buttons.

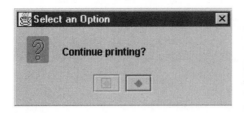 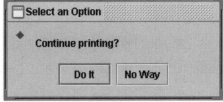

Dialog   *Internal frame*

Figure 9-7: Sample JOptionPane pop-ups

```
Icon greenIcon = new DiamondIcon(Color.green);
Icon redIcon = new DiamondIcon(Color.red);
Object iconArray[] = {greenIcon, redIcon};
JOptionPane.showOptionDialog(source, "Continue printing?", "Select an Option",
JOptionPane.YES_NO_OPTION, JOptionPane.QUESTION_MESSAGE, null, iconArray,
iconArray[1]);

Icon blueIcon = new DiamondIcon(Color.blue);
Object stringArray[] = {"Do It", "No Way"};
JOptionPane.showInternalOptionDialog(desktop, "Continue printing?", "Select an
Option", JOptionPane.YES_NO_OPTION, JOptionPane.QUESTION_MESSAGE, blueIcon,
stringArray, stringArray[0]);
```

> **WARNING**   *When using a factory method to show a JOptionPane within a
> JDialog, the dialog box is automatically modal, preventing another win-
> dow from getting the input focus. When showing the JOptionPane within a
> JInternalFrame, the internal frame might be modal but other windows
> might not be. Therefore, a user could do something within one of the other
> windows of the application, including an action on the JDesktopPane.*

JOptionPane Properties

Table 9-5 shows the 15 properties of JOptionPane. These properties are accessible
only if you don't use one of the factory methods of JOptionPane. For most of the
arguments, their meaning maps directly to one of the constructor arguments.

PROPERTY NAME	DATA TYPE	ACCESS
accessibleContext	AccessibleContext	read-only
icon	Icon	read-write bound
initialSelectionValue	Object	read-write bound
initialValue	Object	read-write bound
inputValue	Object	read-write bound
maxCharactersPerLineCount	int	read-only
message	Object	read-write bound
messageType	int	read-write bound
options	Object[]	read-write bound
optionType	int	read-write bound
selectionValues	Object[]	read-write bound
UI	OptionPaneUI	read-write bound
UIClassID	String	read-only
value	Object	read-write bound
wantsInput	boolean	read-write

Table 9-5: JOptionPane properties

The wantsInput property is automatically set to true for the input dialog boxes or when the selectionValues property is non-null. The inputValue property is the item picked from an input dialog box. The value property indicates the option selected from the button area.

Displaying Multi-line Messages

The maxCharactersPerLineCount property is set to an extremely large value, Integer.MAX_VALUE, by default. For some strange reason, the Swing developers chose not to provide a setter method for this property. If you want to change the setting, you must subclass JOptionPane and override the public int getMaxCharactersPerLineCount() method. This causes a long text message to be broken up into multiple lines for you within an option pane. In addition, you can't use any of the factory methods because they don't know about your subclass.

To help you create narrow JOptionPane components, you can add the following source to the OptionPaneUtils class definition shown earlier in this chapter in the section "Displaying a JOptionPane." The new method provides a way of specifying the desired option pane character width.

```
public static JOptionPane getNarrowOptionPane(int maxCharactersPerLineCount) {
    // Our inner class definition
    class NarrowOptionPane extends JOptionPane {
      int maxCharactersPerLineCount;
```

```
NarrowOptionPane(int maxCharactersPerLineCount) {
  this.maxCharactersPerLineCount = maxCharactersPerLineCount;
}
public int getMaxCharactersPerLineCount() {
  return maxCharactersPerLineCount;
}
}
return new NarrowOptionPane(maxCharactersPerLineCount);
}
```

Once the method and new class are defined, you can create an option pane of controlled character width, manually configure all the properties, place it in a pop-up window, show it, and then determine the user's response. The following source demonstrates usage of these new capabilities, with the long message trimmed a bit.

```
String msg = "this is a really long message ... this is a really long message";
JOptionPane optionPane = OptionPaneUtils.getNarrowOptionPane(72);
optionPane.setMessage(msg);
optionPane.setMessageType(JOptionPane.INFORMATION_MESSAGE);
JDialog dialog = optionPane.createDialog(source, "Width 72");
dialog.show();
```

Figure 9-8 demonstrates what would happen if you didn't change the maxCharactersPerLineCount property. Figure 9-8 also shows the new narrow JOptionPane.

Although this seems like a lot of work, it's the best way of creating multi-line option panes, unless you want to manually parse the message into separate lines.

> **NOTE** *Including a "\n" in the message text will force the message to be displayed on multiple lines. Then it's your responsibility to count the number of characters in each message line. The message text can't be formatted as HTML, as it can in other Swing components.*

Understanding the Message Property

In all the previous examples in this chapter of using the message argument to the JOptionPane constructors and using the factory methods, the message was a single string. As described earlier in the section "The JOptionPane Message Argument," this argument doesn't need to be a single string. For instance, if the

Default

Narrow

Figure 9-8: Default JOptionPane and a narrow JOptionPane

argument were an array of strings, each string would be on a separate line. This eliminates the need to use the narrow `JOptionPane`, but requires you to count the characters yourself. However, because you're splitting apart the message, you can again use one of the 23 factory methods. For instance, the following source creates the pop-up window shown in Figure 9-9.

Figure 9-9: Using JOptionPane with a string array

```
String multiLineMsg[] = {"Hello", "World"};
JOptionPane.showMessageDialog(source, multiLineMsg);
```

> **WARNING** *If you manually count the characters within a long message to split it into a multi-line message, the output may not be the best. For instance, when using a proportional font in which character widths vary, a line of 20 w's would be much wider than a line of 20 i's.*

The message argument not only supports displaying an array of strings, but can also support an array of any type of object. If an element in the array is a `Component`, it's placed directly into the message area. If the element is an `Icon`, the icon is placed within a `JLabel` and the `JLabel` is placed into the message area. All other objects are converted to a `String`, placed into a `JLabel`, and displayed in the message area, unless the object is itself an array, in which case these rules are applied recursively.

To demonstrate the possibilities, Figure 9-10 shows off the true capabilities of the JOptionPane. The actual content isn't meant to show anything in particular — just that you can display lots of different stuff. The message argument is made up of the following array:

```
Object complexMsg[] = {"Above Message", new DiamondIcon(Color.red), new
JButton("Hello"), new JSlider(), new DiamondIcon(Color.blue), "Below Message"};
```

Adding Components to the Message Area

If you were to display the pop-up in Figure 9-10, you'd notice a slight problem. The option pane doesn't know about the embedded JSlider setting, unlike the way it automatically knows about input to the automatic JTextField, JComboBox, or JList components. If you want the JOptionPane (or for that matter any input component) to get the JSlider value, you need to have your input component change the inputValue property of the JOptionPane. When this value is changed, the option pane tells the pop-up window to close because the JOptionPane has acquired its input value.

Attaching a ChangeListener to the JSlider component slider enables you to find out when its value has changed. Adding yet another method to the OptionPaneUtils class allows you to reuse this specialized JSlider with multiple JOptionPane objects. The important method call is shown in boldface in the following code. A similar line would need to be added for any input component that you wanted to place within a JOptionPane. The line notifies the option pane when the user has changed the value of the input component.

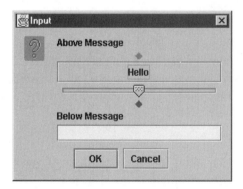

Figure 9-10: Using JOptionPane with a complex message property

```
public static JSlider getSlider(final JOptionPane optionPane) {
  JSlider slider = new JSlider();
  slider.setMajorTickSpacing (10);
  slider.setPaintTicks(true);
  slider.setPaintLabels(true);
  ChangeListener changeListener = new ChangeListener() {
    public void stateChanged(ChangeEvent changeEvent) {
      JSlider theSlider = (JSlider)changeEvent.getSource();
      if (!theSlider.getValueIsAdjusting()) {
        optionPane.setInputValue(new Integer(theSlider.getValue()));
      }
    }
  };
  slider.addChangeListener(changeListener);
  return slider;
}
```

Now that the specialized JSlider is created, you need to place it on a JOptionPane. This requires the manual creation of a JOptionPane component and surprisingly doesn't require the setting of the wantsInput property. The wantsInput property is set to true only when you want the JOptionPane to provide its own input component. Because we're providing one, this isn't necessary. The resulting pop-up window is shown in Figure 9-11.

```
JOptionPane optionPane = new JOptionPane();
JSlider slider = OptionPaneUtils.getSlider(optionPane);
optionPane.setMessage(new Object[] {"Select a value: " , slider});
optionPane.setMessageType(JOptionPane.QUESTION_MESSAGE);
optionPane.setOptionType(JOptionPane.OK_CANCEL_OPTION);
JDialog dialog = optionPane.createDialog(source, "My Slider");
dialog.show();
System.out.println ("Input: " + optionPane.getInputValue());
```

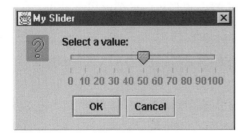

Figure 9-11: Using JOptionPane with a JSlider

> **NOTE** *If the user doesn't move the slider,* `JOptionPane.getInputValue()` *returns* `JOptionPane.UNINITIALIZED_VALUE`*. If you want the user to be able to slide the component multiple times and select the OK button when done, you'd need to provide your own user interface delegate for the* `JOptionPane`*, because the default delegate automatically shuts down once the slider value has been passed to the option pane. Customizing the user interface delegate is described in Chapter 18.*

> **NOTE** *The* `JSlider` *component will be more fully described in Chapter 12.*

Adding Components to the Button Area

In "The JOptionPane Options and Initial Value Arguments" section earlier in this chapter, I mentioned that if you have a `Component` in the array of options for the `JOptionPane`, you must configure the component yourself to handle selection. The same holds true for any components you add via the `options` property. When a component is configured to handle selection, the pop-up window that a `JOptionPane` is embedded in will disappear when the component is selected. The default set of buttons works this way. When installing your own components, you must notify the option pane when one of the components has been selected by setting the `value` property of the option pane.

To demonstrate this mechanism, let's create a `JButton` with both an icon and a text label that can be placed in an option pane. Without defining this component ourselves, the option pane supports only the display of a label or an icon on the button. When the button is selected, it tells the option pane it was selected by setting the option pane's `value` property to the current text label of the button. Adding yet another method to `OptionPaneUtils` allows you to create such a button. The boldfaced line in the following source is the important method call to add to any other such component that you want to combine with the component array for the options property of a `JOptionPane`. The line would be called after selection of such a component.

```
public static JButton getButton(final JOptionPane optionPane, String text, Icon
icon) {
  final JButton button = new JButton (text, icon);
  ActionListener actionListener = new ActionListener() {
    public void actionPerformed(ActionEvent actionEvent) {
      // Return current text label, instead of argument to method
      optionPane.setValue(button.getText());
    }
  };
  button.addActionListener(actionListener);
  return button;
}
```

After the specialized JButton is created, you need to place it in a JOptionPane.
Unfortunately, this, too, requires the long form of the JOptionPane usage. The
resulting pop-up window is shown in Figure 9-12.

```
JOptionPane optionPane = new JOptionPane();
optionPane.setMessage("I got an icon and a text label");
optionPane.setMessageType(JOptionPane.INFORMATION_MESSAGE);
Icon icon = new DiamondIcon (Color.blue);
JButton jButton = OptionPaneUtils.getButton(optionPane, "OK", icon);
optionPane.setOptions(new Object[] {jButton});
JDialog dialog = optionPane.createDialog(source, "Icon/Text Button");
dialog.show();
```

Figure 9-12: Using JOptionPane with a JButton containing a text label and an icon

Listening for Property Changes

The JOptionPane class defines 11 constants to assist with listening for bound property changes. These constants are listed in Table 9-6.

PROPERTY CHANGE CONSTANT
ICON_PROPERTY
INITIAL_SELECTION_VALUE_PROPERTY
INITIAL_VALUE_PROPERTY
INPUT_VALUE_PROPERTY
MESSAGE_PROPERTY
MESSAGE_TYPE_PROPERTY
OPTION_TYPE_PROPERTY
OPTIONS_PROPERTY
SELECTION_VALUES_PROPERTY
VALUE_PROPERTY
WANTS_INPUT_PROPERTY

Table 9-6: JOptionPane PropertyChangeListener support constants

If you don't use the factory methods of JOptionPane, you can instead use a PropertyChangeListener to listen for changes to the bound properties. This would allow you to passively listen for changes to bound properties, instead of actively getting them after the change.

Customizing a JOptionPane Look and Feel

Each installable Swing look and feel provides a different JOptionPane appearance and set of default UIResource values. Figure 9-13 shows the appearance of the JOptionPane container for the preinstalled set of look and feels: Motif, Windows, Metal, as well as the separate Macintosh look and feel.

The message type of the JOptionPane helps determine the default icon to display in the icon area of the option pane. For plain messages, there are no icons. The remaining four default icons—for informational, question, warning, and error messages—are shown in Figure 9-14 for the same look and feels.

The available set of UIResource-related properties for a JOptionPane is shown in Table 9-7. For the JOptionPane component, there are 17 different properties.

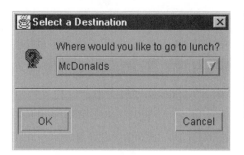

Motif

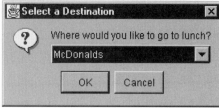

Windows

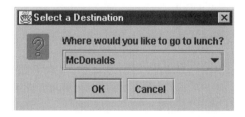

Metal

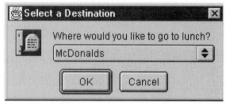

Macintosh

Figure 9-13: JOptionPane under different look and feels

	INFORMATIONAL	QUESTION	WARNING	ERROR
Motif				
Windows				
Metal				
Macintosh				

Figure 9-14: JOptionPane icons for the different look and feels

PROPERTY STRING	OBJECT TYPE
OptionPane.background	Color
OptionPane.border	Border
OptionPane.buttonAreaBorder	Border
OptionPane.cancelButtonText	String
OptionPane.errorIcon	Icon
OptionPane.font	Font
OptionPane.foreground	Color
OptionPane.informationIcon	Icon
OptionPane.messageAreaBorder	Border
OptionPane.messageForeground	Color
OptionPane.minimumSize	Dimension
OptionPane.noButtonText	String
OptionPane.okButtonText	String
OptionPane.questionIcon	Icon
OptionPane.warningIcon	Icon
OptionPane.yesButtonText	String
OptionPaneUI	OptionPaneUI

Table 9-7: JOptionPane UIResource elements

One good use of the resources in Table 9-7 is for customizing default button labels to match the locale or language of the user. For instance, to change the four labels for the Cancel, No, OK, and Yes buttons into French, add the following code to your program. (You may be able to get the translated text from a java.util.ResourceBundle.)

```
// Set JOptionPane button labels to French
UIManager.put("OptionPane.cancelButtonText", "Annuler");
UIManager.put("OptionPane.noButtonText", "Non");
UIManager.put("OptionPane.okButtonText", "D'accord");
UIManager.put("OptionPane.yesButtonText", "Oui");
```

Now when you display the option pane, the buttons will have localized button labels. Of course, this would require translating the messages for the option pane, too. Figure 9-15 shows how a pop-up would look for the following line of source that asks if the user is 18 or older. Because the pop-up window title isn't a property, you must pass the title to every created dialog box.

```
int result = JOptionPane.showConfirmDialog(aFrame, "Est-ce que vous avez 18 ans
ou plus?", "Choisisez une option", JOptionPane.YES_NO_CANCEL_OPTION);
```

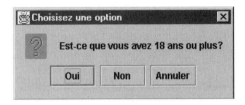

Figure 9-15: A JOptionPane in French

> **NOTE** *For a good resource on learning about using resource bundles for localization, see* Core Java 1.1, Volume II *(Sun Microsystems). At some point the* JOptionPane *will perhaps be redesigned to automatically provide localized button labels and title text.*

Class ProgressMonitor

The ProgressMonitor class is used to report on the status of a time-consuming task. The class is a special Swing class that's neither a component, an option pane, nor a JavaBean. Instead, you tell the progress monitor when each part of the task is done. If the task is taking an extended length of time to complete, the progress monitor displays a pop-up window like the one shown in Figure 9-16.

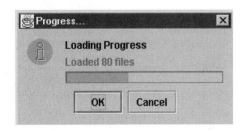

After the progress monitor displays the pop-up window, the user can do one of three things. The user can watch the progress monitor to see how much of the task has been completed; when the task is done, the progress monitor automatically disappears. Or, if the user can select the OK button, the pop-up window goes away and the task continues until completion without any visible clue of progress. Or, if the user can select the Cancel button, this tells the progress monitor that the task needs to be canceled. To

Figure 9-16: ProgressMonitor sample

detect the cancellation, the task needs to check the progress monitor periodically to see if the user canceled the task's operation. Otherwise, the task will continue.

The pop-up window that the ProgressMonitor displays is a JOptionPane with a maxCharactersPerLineCount property setting of 60, allowing the option pane to automatically word wrap any displayed messages. The option pane is embedded within a nonmodal JDialog whose title is "Progress." Because the JDialog isn't modal, a user can still interact with the main program. The JOptionPane for a ProgressMonitor will always get an informational icon within its icon area.

In addition, the message area of the option pane consists of three objects. At the top of the message area is a fixed message that stays the same throughout the life of the JOptionPane. The message can be a text string or an array of objects just like the message property of JOptionPane. In the middle of the message area is a note or variable message that can change as the task progresses. At the bottom of the message area is a progress bar (JProgressBar component) that fills as an increasing percentage of the task is completed. The button area of the option pane shows OK and Cancel buttons.

Creating a ProgressMonitor

When you create a ProgressMonitor, there are five arguments to the single constructor: public ProgressMonitor(Component parentComponent, Object message, String note, int minimum, int maximum).

The first argument represents the parent component for the JOptionPane for when the ProgressMonitor needs to appear. The parent component is the component over which the pop-up window would appear, and acts like the parentComponent argument for the createDialog() method of JOptionPane. You would then provide the static and variable message parts for the message area of the JOptionPane. Either of these message parts could be null, although null means that this part of the message area will never appear. Lastly, you provide minimum and maximum values as the range for the progress bar. The difference between these two values represents the expected number of operations to be performed, such as the number of files to load or the size of a file to read. Normally, the minimum setting is zero, but that isn't required. The number of completed operations determines how far the progress bar moves.

Initially, the pop-up window isn't displayed. By default, the progress monitor checks every half second to see if the task at hand will complete in two seconds. If the task has shown some progress and it still won't complete in two seconds, then the pop-up window appears. The time to completion is configurable by changing the millisToDecideToPopup and millisToPopup properties of the ProgressMonitor.

The following line of source demonstrates the creation of a ProgressMonitor with 200 steps in the operation. A reference to the progress monitor would need to be saved so that it can be notified as the task progresses.

```
monitor = new ProgressMonitor(parent, "Loading Progress", "Getting Started...",
0, 200);
```

Using a ProgressMonitor

Once you've created the ProgressMonitor, you need to begin the task whose progress is being monitored. As the task completes one or many steps, the

ProgressMonitor needs to be notified of the task's progress. Notification is done with a call to the `public void setProgress(int newValue)` method, where the argument represents the progress completed thus far and the `newValue` needs to be in the minimum...maximum range initially specified. This progress value needs to be maintained outside the progress monitor, because you can't ask the monitor how much progress has been made (no `public int getProgress()` method of `ProgressMonitor` exists). If the progress value were maintained in a variable named `progress`, the following two lines would update the progress value and notify the progress monitor.

```
progress += 5;
monitor.setProgress(progress);
```

The `progress` setting could represent the number of files loaded thus far, or the number of bytes read in from a file. In addition to updating the count, you should update the `note` to reflect the progress. If the difference between the `minimum` and `maximum` arguments used in the `ProgressMonitor` constructor was 100, then the current progress could be viewed as a percentage of the task. Otherwise, the progress property merely represents the progress completed so far.

```
monitor.setNote("Loaded " + progress + " files");
```

It's the responsibility of the executing task to check whether the user pressed the Cancel button on the progress monitor. If the task is canceled, the progress monitor automatically closes the dialog box, but the task must actively check for the change by adding a simple check at the appropriate place or places in the source:

```
if (monitor.isCanceled()) {
// Task canceled - cleanup
  ...
} else {
// Continue doing task
  ...
}
```

Most tasks requiring a `ProgressMonitor` will be implemented using separate threads to avoid blocking the responsiveness of the main program. A complete `ProgressMonitor` example appears a little later in this chapter.

ProgressMonitor Properties

Table 9-8 shows the seven properties of `ProgressMonitor`.

PROPERTY NAME	DATA TYPE	ACCESS
canceled	boolean	read-only
maximum	int	read-write
millisToDecideToPopup	int	read-write
millisToPopup	int	read-write
minimum	int	read-write
note	String	read-write
progress	int	write-only

Table 9-8: ProgressMonitor properties

The `millisToDecideToPopup` property represents the number of milliseconds that the monitor waits before deciding if it needs to display the pop-up window. If the `progress` property hasn't changed yet, the monitor waits for another increment of this time period before checking again. When the progress monitor checks and the progress property has changed, it estimates whether the task will be completed in the number of milliseconds in the `millisToPopup` property. If the progress monitor thinks the monitored task will complete on time, the pop-up window is never displayed. Otherwise, the pop-up will display after `millisToPopup` milliseconds have passed from the time the task started.

> **NOTE** *It's possible that multiple calls to `setProgress()` may not advance the progress bar on the option pane. The changes to the `progress` setting must be enough to make the progress bar advance at least one pixel in length. For instance, if the `minimum` and `maximum` settings were zero and 2 billion, increasing the progress setting 1,000 times by 5 would have no visible effect on the progress bar because the fractional amount would be negligible.*

> **TIP** *Although technically possible, it isn't a good practice to move the `minimum` and `maximum` properties after the pop-up has appeared. This could result in the progress bar increasing and decreasing in an erratic manner. The same behavior happens if you move the `progress` setting in a nonlinear fashion.*

Customizing ProgressMonitor Look and Feel

Changing the look and feel of the progress monitor requires changing the appearance of both the JProgressBar and the JLabel, as well as the JOptionPane the progress monitor uses. There are no UIResource-related properties for ProgressMonitor (or JDialog).

Complete ProgressMonitor Example

The following program creates a ProgressMonitor and allows you to either manually or automatically increase its progress property. These tasks are handled by on-screen buttons (see Figure 9-17). Selecting the Start button creates the ProgressMonitor. Selecting the Manual Increase button causes the progress to increase by 5. Selecting the Automatic Increase button causes the progress to increase by 3 every 250 milliseconds (1/4 second). Pressing the Cancel button on the pop-up window during the automatic increase demonstrates what should happen when the operation is canceled; the timer stops sending updates.

> **NOTE** *The pop-up window won't appear until some progress is shown.*

The ProgressMonitorHandler inner class at the start of the following program code is necessary to ensure that the ProgressMonitor is accessed only from the event thread. Otherwise, the access wouldn't be thread-safe in some random thread.

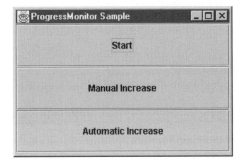

Figure 9-17: Main ProgressMonitor sample frame

```
import javax.swing.*;
import java.awt.*;
import java.awt.event.*;

public class SampleProgress {
  static ProgressMonitor monitor;
  static int progress;
  static Timer timer;

  static class ProgressMonitorHandler implements ActionListener {
    // Called by Timer
    public void actionPerformed(ActionEvent actionEvent) {
      if (monitor == null)
        return;
      if (monitor.isCanceled()) {
        System.out.println("Monitor canceled");
        timer.stop();
      } else {
        progress += 3;
        monitor.setProgress(progress);
        monitor.setNote("Loaded " + progress + " files");
      }
    }
  }

  public static void main(String args[]) {

    JFrame frame = new ExitableJFrame("ProgressMonitor Sample");
    Container contentPane = frame.getContentPane();
    contentPane.setLayout(new GridLayout (0, 1));

    // Define Start Button
    JButton startButton = new JButton ("Start");
    ActionListener startActionListener = new ActionListener() {
      public void actionPerformed(ActionEvent actionEvent) {
        Component parent = (Component)actionEvent.getSource();
        monitor = new ProgressMonitor(parent, "Loading Progress", "Getting
Started...", 0, 200);
        progress = 0;
      }
    };
    startButton.addActionListener(startActionListener);
    contentPane.add(startButton);
```

```java
    // Define Manual Increase Button
    // Pressing this button increases progress by 5
    JButton increaseButton = new JButton ("Manual Increase");
    ActionListener increaseActionListener = new ActionListener() {
      public void actionPerformed(ActionEvent actionEvent) {
        if (monitor == null)
          return;
        if (monitor.isCanceled()) {
          System.out.println("Monitor canceled");
        } else {
          progress += 5;
          monitor.setProgress(progress);
          monitor.setNote("Loaded " + progress + " files");
        }
      }
    };
    increaseButton.addActionListener(increaseActionListener);
    contentPane.add(increaseButton);

    // Define Automatic Increase Button
    // Start Timer to increase progress by 3 every 250 ms
    JButton autoIncreaseButton = new JButton ("Automatic Increase");
    ActionListener autoIncreaseActionListener = new ActionListener() {
      public void actionPerformed(ActionEvent actionEvent) {
        if (monitor != null) {
          if (timer == null) {
            timer = new Timer(250, new ProgressMonitorHandler());
          }
          timer.start();
        }
      }
    };
    autoIncreaseButton.addActionListener(autoIncreaseActionListener);
    contentPane.add(autoIncreaseButton);

    frame.setSize(300, 200);
    frame.setVisible(true);
  }
}
```

Class ProgressMonitorInputStream

The ProgressMonitorInputStream class represents an input stream filter that uses a ProgressMonitor to check the progress of the reading of an input stream. If the reading is taking too long to complete, a ProgressMonitor appears and the user can select the Cancel button on the pop-up window, causing the reading to be interrupted and the input stream to throw an InterruptedIOException. Figure 9-18 shows the relationships within the ProgressMonitorInputStream class.

Creating a ProgressMonitorInputStream

Like other filtering streams, the ProgressMonitorInputStream is created with a reference to the stream it needs to filter. Besides a reference to this filter, the single constructor for ProgressMonitorInputStream requires two arguments that its ProgressMonitor is going to need: a parent component and a message. As seen here, the constructor takes the ProgressMonitor arguments first:

```
public ProgressMonitorInputStream(Component parentComponent, Object message,
InputStream inputStream)
```

As with the JOptionPane and ProgressMonitor, the message argument is an Object, not a String, so you can display an array of components or strings on multiple lines. The following code creates one ProgressMonitorInputStream.

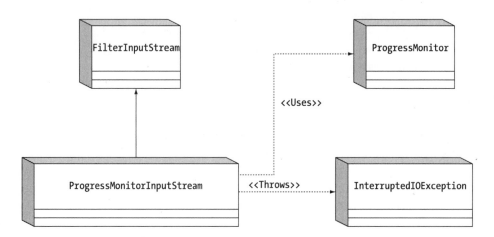

Figure 9-18: ProgressMonitorInputStream UML relationship diagram

```
FileInputStream fis = new FileInputStream(filename);
ProgressMonitorInputStream pmis = new ProgressMonitorInputStream(parent, "Reading
" + filename, fis);
```

> **NOTE** *The minimum...maximum range for the* ProgressMonitorInputStream
> *ProgressMonitor is [0, the size of the stream].*

Using a ProgressMonitorInputStream

As with all input streams, once you've created a ProgressMonitorInputStream, you
need to read from it. If the input stream isn't read quickly enough, the underlying
progress monitor causes the progress pop-up window to appear. Once that window appears, a user can monitor the progress, or cancel the reading by selecting
the Cancel button. If the Cancel button is selected, an InterruptedIOException is
thrown and the bytesTransferred field of the exception
would be set to the number of bytes successfully read.

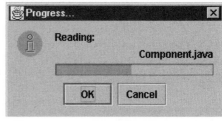

Figure 9-19 shows what one ProgressMonitorInputStream
pop-up might look like. For a little variety, the pop-up uses
two JLabel components in the message, instead of just one.

A complete source example follows. The boldfaced lines
are the keys to using the ProgressMonitorInputStream. They
set up the dialog box's message and create the input stream.
The program reads a file name from the command line,
reads the file, and copies the file to standard output (the
console). If the file is large enough, the progress monitor
will appear. If you press the Cancel button, the reading
stops and Canceled is printed to standard error.

*Figure 9-19: ProgressMonitorInputStream
pop-up*

```
import java.io.*;
import java.awt.*;
import javax.swing.*;

public class ProgressInputSample {
  public static final int NORMAL   = 0;
  public static final int BAD_FILE = 1;
  public static final int CANCELED = NORMAL;
  public static final int PROBLEM = 2;

  public static void main(String args[]) {
    int returnValue = NORMAL;
```

```
        if (args.length != 1) {
          System.err.println("Usage:");
          System.err.println("java ProgressInput filename");
        } else {
          try {
            FileInputStream fis = new FileInputStream(args[0]);
            JLabel filenameLabel = new JLabel(args[0], JLabel.RIGHT);
            filenameLabel.setForeground(Color.black);
            Object message[] = {"Reading:", filenameLabel};
            ProgressMonitorInputStream pmis = new ProgressMonitorInputStream(null,
message, fis);
            InputStreamReader isr = new InputStreamReader(pmis);
            BufferedReader br = new BufferedReader(isr);
            String line;
            while ((line = br.readLine()) != null) {
              System.out.println(line);
            }
            br.close();
          } catch (FileNotFoundException exception) {
            System.err.println("Bad File " + exception);
            returnValue = BAD_FILE;
          } catch (InterruptedIOException exception) {
            System.err.println("Canceled");
            returnValue = CANCELED;
          } catch (IOException exception) {
            System.err.println("I/O Exception " + exception);
            returnValue = PROBLEM;
          }
        }
        // AWT Thread created - must exit
        System.exit(returnValue);
      }
    }
```

> **NOTE** *Remember that having a null argument for the parent component to the ProgressMonitorInputStream constructor causes the pop-up window to appear centered on the screen.*

ProgressMonitorInputStream Properties

Table 9-9 shows the single property of ProgressMonitorInputStream. The progress monitor is created when the input stream is created. You shouldn't need to modify the progress monitor. However, you might want to provide a longer or shorter delay (the millisToDecideToPopup property of ProgressMonitor) before the pop-up window is displayed.

PROPERTY NAME	DATA TYPE	ACCESS
progressMonitor	ProgressMonitor	read-only

Table 9-9: ProgressMonitorInputStream property

Class JColorChooser

You can think of a JColorChooser as an input-only JOptionPane whose input field asks that you to choose a Color. Like a JOptionPane, the JColorChooser is just a bunch of components in a container, not a ready-to-use pop-up window. Figure 9-20 shows how a JColorChooser might appear in your own application window. At the top are three color chooser panels; at the bottom is a preview panel.

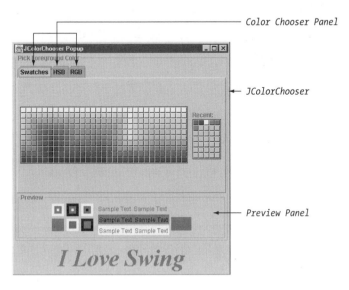

Figure 9-20: JColorChooser sample

In addition to appearing within your application windows, the JColorChooser class also provides support methods for automatically placing the group of components in a JDialog. Figure 9-21 shows one such automatically created pop-up.

In support of this behavior, the JColorChooser class requires the help of several support classes found in the javax.swing.colorchooser package. The data model for the JColorChooser is an implementation of the ColorSelectionModel interface. The javax.swing.colorchooser package provides the DefaultColorSelectionModel class as an implementation of the ColorSelectionModel interface. For the user interface, the JColorChooser class relies on the ColorChooserComponentFactory to create the default panels from which to choose a color. These panels are specific subclasses of the AbstractColorChooserPanel class, and if you don't like the default set, you can create your own.

By default, when multiple panels are in a JColorChooser, each panel is shown on a tab of a JTabbedPane. Nevertheless, the ColorChooserUI can deal with multiple panels in any way it desires. Figure 9-22 shows the relationships within all these classes.

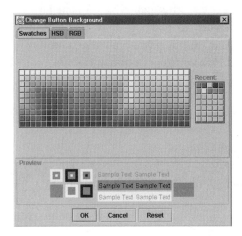

Figure 9-21: JColorChooser pop-up sample

Creating a JColorChooser

If you want to create a JColorChooser and place it in your own window, you'd use one of the three constructors for the JColorChooser class. By default, the initial color for the chooser is white. If you don't want white as the default, you can provide the initial color as a Color object or ColorSelectionModel. The different constructors follow, along with a sample creation usage.

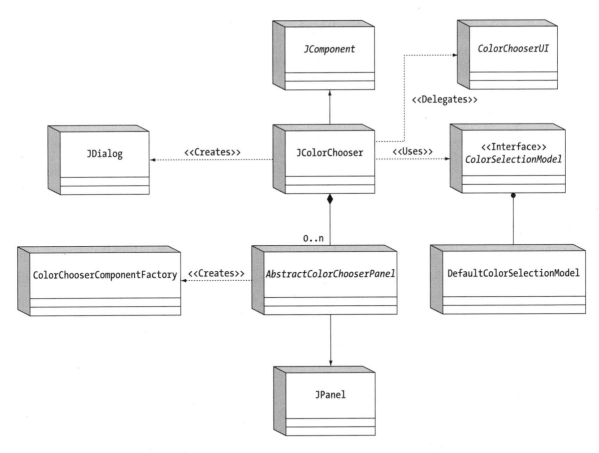

Figure 9-22: JColorChooser UML relationship diagram

1. `public JColorChooser()`
   `JColorChooser colorChooser = new JColorChooser();`

2. `public JColorChooser(Color initialColor)`
   `JColorChooser colorChooser = new`
   `JColorChooser(aComponent.getBackground());`

3. `public JColorChooser(ColorSelectionModel model)`
   `JColorChooser colorChooser = new JColorChooser(aColorSelectionModel);`

Using JColorChooser

Once you've created a JColorChooser from a constructor, you can place it in any
Container, just like any other Component. For instance, the following source created the GUI shown in Figure 9-20.

```
import java.awt.*;
import javax.swing.*;
import javax.swing.event.*;
import javax.swing.colorchooser.*;

public class ColorSample {

  public static void main(String args[]) {
    JFrame frame = new ExitableJFrame("JColorChooser Popup");
    Container contentPane = frame.getContentPane();

    final JLabel label = new JLabel("I Love Swing", JLabel.CENTER);
    label.setFont(new Font("Serif", Font.BOLD | Font.ITALIC, 48));
    contentPane.add(label, BorderLayout.SOUTH);

    final JColorChooser colorChooser = new JColorChooser(label.getBackground());
    colorChooser.setBorder(BorderFactory.createTitledBorder("Pick Foreground
Color"));
    // more source to come
    contentPane.add(colorChooser, BorderLayout.CENTER);

    frame.pack();
    frame.setVisible(true);
  }
}
```

Although this source code creates the GUI, selecting a different color within the JColorChooser doesn't do anything yet. Let's now add the code that causes color changes.

Listening for Color Selection Changes

The JColorChooser uses a ColorSelectionModel as its data model. As the following interface definition shows, the data model includes a single property, selectedColor, for managing the state of the color chooser.

```
public interface ColorSelectionModel {
  // Listeners
  public void addChangeListener(ChangeListener listener);
  public void removeChangeListener(ChangeListener listener);
  // Properties
  public Color getSelectedColor();
```

```
    public void setSelectedColor(Color newValue);
}
```

When a user changes the color within the JColorChooser, the selectedColor property changes, and the JColorChooser generates a ChangeEvent to notify any registered ChangeListener objects.

Therefore, to complete the earlier ColorSample example in the previous section, and have the foreground color of the label change when the user changes the color selection within the JColorChooser, you need to register a ChangeListener with the color chooser. This involves creating a ChangeListener and adding it to the ColorSelectionModel. Placing the following source code where the more source to come comment appears in the previous example is necessary for this example to work properly.

```
ColorSelectionModel model = colorChooser.getSelectionModel();
ChangeListener changeListener = new ChangeListener() {
  public void stateChanged(ChangeEvent changeEvent) {
    Color newForegroundColor = colorChooser.getColor();
    label.setForeground(newForegroundColor);
  }
};
model.addChangeListener(changeListener);
```

Once this source is added, the example is complete. Running the program brings up Figure 9-20, and selecting a new color alters the foreground of the label.

Creating and Showing a JColorChooser Pop-up Window

Although the previous example is sufficient if you want to include a JColorChooser within your own window, more often than not you want the JColorChooser to appear in a separate pop-up window. This window might appear as the result of selecting a button on the screen, or possibly even selecting a menu item. To support this behavior, the JColorChooser includes the following factory method:

```
public static Color showDialog(Component parentComponent, String title, Color
initialColor)
```

When called, showDialog() creates a modal dialog box with the given parent component and title. Within the dialog box is a JColorChooser whose initial color is the one provided. As Figure 9-21 shows, along the bottom are three buttons: OK, Cancel, and Reset. When OK is pressed, the pop-up window disappears and the showDialog() method returns the currently selected color. When Cancel is pressed, null is returned instead of the selected color or the initial color. Selection of the Reset button causes the JColorChooser to change its selected color to the initial color provided at startup.

What normally happens with the showDialog() method is that the initial color argument is some color property of an object. The returned value of the method call then becomes the new setting for the same color property. This usage pattern is shown in the following lines of code, where the changing color property is the background for a button. As with JOptionPane, the null parent-component argument causes the pop-up window to be centered on the screen instead of over any particular component.

```
Color initialBackground = button.getBackground();
Color background = JColorChooser.showDialog(null, "Change Button Background",
initialBackground);
if (background != null) {
  button.setBackground(background);
}
```

To place this code in the context of a complete example, the following source code offers a button that when selected displays a JColorChooser. The color selected within the chooser becomes the background color of the button after the OK button is selected.

```
import java.awt.*;
import java.awt.event.*;
import javax.swing.*;

public class ColorSamplePopup {

  public static void main(String args[]) {
    JFrame frame = new ExitableJFrame("JColorChooser Sample Popup");
    Container contentPane = frame.getContentPane();

    final JButton button = new JButton("Pick to Change Background");

    ActionListener actionListener = new ActionListener() {
      public void actionPerformed(ActionEvent actionEvent) {
        Color initialBackground = button.getBackground();
        Color background = JColorChooser.showDialog(null, "Change Button
Background", initialBackground);
        if (background != null) {
          button.setBackground(background);
```

```
        }
      }
    };
    button.addActionListener(actionListener);
    contentPane.add(button, BorderLayout.CENTER);

    frame.setSize(300, 100);
    frame.setVisible(true);
  }
}
```

Providing Your Own OK/Cancel Event Listeners

If the showDialog() method provides too much automatic behavior, you may prefer another JColorChooser method that allows you to customize the chooser before displaying it and define what happens when the OK and Cancel buttons are selected:

```
public static JDialog createDialog(Component parentComponent, String title,
boolean modal, JColorChooser chooserPane, ActionListener okListener,
ActionListener cancelListener)
```

In createDialog(), the parent component and title arguments are the same as showDialog(). The modal argument allows the pop-up window to be nonmodal, unlike showDialog() in which the pop-up is always modal. When the pop-up is nonmodal, the user can still interact with the rest of the application. The OK and Cancel buttons on the pop-up window automatically have one associated ActionListener that hides the pop-up window after selection. It's your responsibility to add your own listeners if you need any additional response from selection.

To demonstrate proper usage of createDialog(), the following program duplicates the functionality of the previously listed program. However, instead of automatically accepting the new color, the color change is rejected if the new background is the same color as the foreground. In addition, if the user selects the Cancel button, the button background color is set to red.

```
import java.awt.*;
import java.awt.event.*;
import javax.swing.*;

public class CreateColorSamplePopup {
```

```
public static void main(String args[]) {
  JFrame frame = new ExitableJFrame("JColorChooser Create Popup Sample");
  Container contentPane = frame.getContentPane();

  final JButton button = new JButton("Pick to Change Background");

  ActionListener actionListener = new ActionListener() {
    public void actionPerformed(ActionEvent actionEvent) {
      Color initialBackground = button.getBackground();

      final JColorChooser colorChooser = new JColorChooser(initialBackground);

      // For okay button selection, change button background to selected color
      ActionListener okActionListener = new ActionListener() {
        public void actionPerformed(ActionEvent actionEvent) {
          Color newColor = colorChooser.getColor();
          if (newColor.equals(button.getForeground())) {
            System.out.println("Color change rejected");
          } else {
            button.setBackground(colorChooser.getColor());
          }
        }
      };

      // For cancel button selection, change button background to red
      ActionListener cancelActionListener = new ActionListener() {
        public void actionPerformed(ActionEvent actionEvent) {
          button.setBackground(Color.red);
        }
      };

      final JDialog dialog = JColorChooser.createDialog(null, "Change Button
Background", true, colorChooser, okActionListener, cancelActionListener);

      // Wait until current event dispatching completes before showing dialog
      Runnable showDialog = new Runnable() {
        public void run() {
          dialog.show();
        }
      };
      SwingUtilities.invokeLater(showDialog);
    }
  };
  button.addActionListener(actionListener);
```

```
    contentPane.add(button, BorderLayout.CENTER);

    frame.setSize(300, 100);
    frame.setVisible(true);
  }
}
```

> **NOTE** *Notice that the* `actionPerformed()` *method that shows the color chooser uses the* `SwingUtilities.invokeLater()` *method to show the chooser. The current event dispatching needs to finish before showing the chooser. Otherwise, the previous action event processing won't complete before the chooser is shown.*

JColorChooser Properties

Table 9-10 lists information on the seven properties of the `JColorChooser`, including the three data types of the single property `color`.

PROPERTY NAME	DATA TYPE	ACCESS
accessibleContext	AccessibleContext	read-only
chooserPanels	AbstractColorChooserPanel[]	read-write bound
color	Color	read-write
color	int rgb	write-only
color	int red, int green, int blue	write-only
PreviewPanel	JComponent	read-write bound
SelectionModel	ColorSelectionModel	read-write bound
UI	ColorChooserUI	read-write bound
UIClassID	String	read-only

Table 9-10: JColorChooser properties

The `color` property is special in that it has three ways of setting itself:

- Directly from a `Color`

- From one integer representing its red-green-blue values combined into one `int` variable using the nibble allocation 0xAARRGGBB, where A is for alpha value (and unused in JRE 1.1)

- From three integers, separating the red, green, and blue color components into three separate `int` variables

If you don't use showDialog(), you can customize the JColorChooser before displaying it. Besides customizing the color property, which is settable in the JColorChooser constructor, you can customize the component to be displayed in the preview area and the color chooser panels.

Changing the Preview Panel

It's the responsibility of the ColorChooserComponentFactory class to provide the default component for the preview area of the JColorChooser. For the standard look and feels, the preview panel is in the bottom portion of the color chooser.

If you don't want a preview panel in the color chooser, you must change the previewPanel property to a component value that isn't null. When the property is set to null, the default preview panel is shown. Setting the property to an empty JPanel serves the purpose of not showing the preview panel. Figure 9-23 shows what one such color chooser might look like without the preview panel. Because the JPanel has no size when nothing is in it, this effectively removes the panel.

```
colorChooser.setPreviewPanel(new JPanel());
```

If you want the preview panel present, but just don't like the default appearance, you can add your own JComponent to the area. Configuration entails placing your new preview panel in a title-bordered container, and having the foreground of the preview panel change when the user selects a new color.

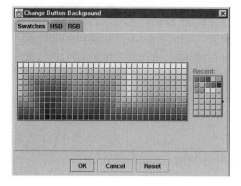

Figure 9-23: JColorChooser without preview panel

WARNING *A bug in the* ColorChooserUI *implementation class* (BasicColorChooserUI) *requires an extra step to properly install the preview panel. Besides calling* setPreviewPanel(newPanel), *you must call the* JColorChooser.updateUI() *method to enable the user interface to properly configure the new preview panel.*

The following source demonstrates the use of a JLabel as the custom preview panel with the necessary workaround. Figure 9-24 demonstrates what the JColorChooser that uses this preview panel would look like.

```
final JLabel previewLabel = new JLabel("I Love Swing", JLabel.CENTER);
previewLabel.setFont(new Font("Serif", Font.BOLD | Font.ITALIC, 48));
colorChooser.setPreviewPanel(previewLabel);
// Bug workaround
colorChooser.updateUI();
```

NOTE *Because the initial setting for the foreground of the preview panel is its background color, the panel will appear to be empty. This is one reason why the default preview panel shows text with contrasting background colors.*

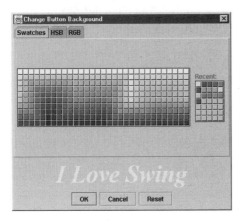

Figure 9-24: JColorChooser with custom preview panel

Adjusting the Color Chooser Panels

The various tabs in the upper part of the JColorChooser represent the AbstractColorChooserPanel implementations. Each allows the user to pick a color in a different manner. By default, the ColorChooserComponentFactory provides the JColorChooser with three panels (see Figure 9-25):

- The "Swatches" panel lets a user pick a color from a set of predefined color swatches, as if at a paint store.

- The "HSB" panel allows a user to pick a color using the Hue-Saturation-Brightness color model.

- The "RGB" panel is for picking colors using the Red-Green-Blue color model.

If you don't like the default chooser panels, or you just want to add other color chooser panels that work differently, you can create your own by subclassing the AbstractColorChooserPanel class. To add a new panel to the existing set, call public void addChooserPanel(AbstractColorChooserPanel panel). If you later decide that you no longer want the new panel, you can remove it with public AbstractColorChooserPanel removeChooserPanel(AbstractColorChooserPanel panel). To replace the existing set of panels, call setChooserPanels(AbstractColorChooserPanel panels[]).

Creating a new panel entails subclassing AbstractColorChooserPanel and filling in the details of choosing a color for the new panel. The class definition, shown in the following code lines, includes five abstract methods. These five methods are what must be overridden.

```
public abstract class AbstractColorChooserPanel extends JPanel {
  public AbstractColorChooserPanel();
  protected abstract void buildChooser();
  public abstract String getDisplayName();
  public abstract Icon getLargeDisplayIcon();
  public abstract Icon getSmallDisplayIcon();
  public abstract void updateChooser();
  protected Color getColorFromModel();
  public ColorSelectionModel getColorSelectionModel();
  public void installChooserPanel(JColorChooser);
  public void paint(Graphics);
  public void uninstallChooserPanel(JColorChooser);
}
```

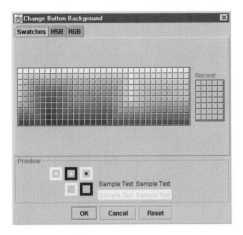

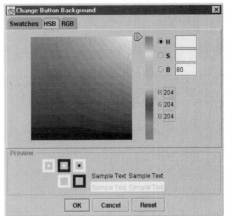

Swatches

HSB

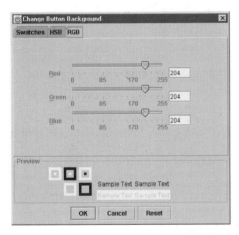

RGB

Figure 9-25: The default JColorChooser chooser panels

To demonstrate creating our own color chooser panel, we'll create one that displays a list of colors from the Color and SystemColor class. From this list, the user must pick one. We'll use a JComboBox to represent the list of colors. Figure 9-26 shows the finished panel. The panel is created and added with the following source:

```
SystemColorChooserPanel newChooser = new SystemColorChooserPanel();
AbstractColorChooserPanel chooserPanels[] = {newChooser};
colorChooser.setChooserPanels(chooserPanels);
```

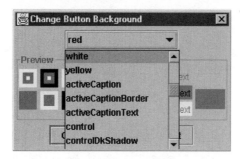

Figure 9-26: Replacing all panels with the new SystemColor chooser panel

> **NOTE** *Don't worry about the details of using the JComboBox. They are explained in depth in Chapter 13.*

The first method to define is public String getDisplayName(). This method returns a text label to display on the tab when multiple chooser panels are available. If there's only one chooser panel, this name isn't shown.

```
public String getDisplayName() {
  return "SystemColor";
}
```

The return values for the two Icon methods do nothing with the system look and feels. You can return null from them or return an Icon to check that nothing has been done with them. A custom ColorChooserUI could use the two Icon methods somewhere, possibly for the icon on a chooser panel tab.

```
public Icon getSmallDisplayIcon() {
  return new DiamondIcon(Color.blue);
}
```

```
public Icon getLargeDisplayIcon() {
  return new DiamondIcon(Color.green);
}
```

The protected void buildChooser() method is called by the installChooserPanel() method of AbstractColorChooserPanel when the panel is added to the chooser. You use this method to add the necessary components to the container. In our particular chooser, this involves creating the JComboBox and adding it to the panel. Because AbstractColorChooserPanel is a JPanel subclass, you can just add()

the combo box. The combo box must be filled with options and an event handler installed for when the user selects the component. The specifics of the event handling are described after the following block of source code.

```
protected void buildChooser() {
  comboBox = new JComboBox(labels);
  comboBox.addItemListener(this);
  add(comboBox);
}
```

> **NOTE** *In addition, if you choose to override* uninstallChooserPanel *(JColorChooserenclosingChooser), you need to call super.* uninstallChooserPanel (JColorChooser enclosingChooser) *last,* *instead* of first.

When a user changes the color value in an AbstractColorChooserPanel, the panel must notify the ColorSelectionModel of the change in color. In our panel, this equates to the user's selecting a new choice in the JComboBox. Therefore, when the combo box value changes, find the Color that equates to the choice and tell the model about the change.

```
public void itemStateChanged(ItemEvent itemEvent) {
  int state = itemEvent.getStateChange();
  if (state == ItemEvent.SELECTED) {
    int position = findColorLabel(itemEvent.getItem());
    // last position is bad (not selectable)
    if ((position != NOT_FOUND) && (position != labels.length-1)) {
      ColorSelectionModel selectionModel = getColorSelectionModel();
      selectionModel.setSelectedColor(colors[position]);
    }
  }
}
```

The final AbstractColorChooserPanel method to implement is the public void updateChooser() method. It, too, is called by installChooserPanel() at setup time. In addition, it's also called whenever the ColorSelectionModel of the JColorChooser changes. When updateChooser() is called, the chooser panel should update its display to show that the current color of the model is selected. Not all panels show which color is currently selected, so a call may do nothing. (The system-provided Swatches panel is one that doesn't display the current color.) In addition, it's possible that the current color isn't displayable on the panel. For instance, on our SystemColor panel, if the current selection isn't a SystemColor or

Color constant, you can either do nothing or display something to signify a custom color. Therefore, in our updateChooser() implementation, you need to get the current color from the ColorSelectionModel and change the color for the panel. The actual setting is done in a helper method called setColor(Color newValue).

```
public void updateChooser() {
  Color color = getColorFromModel();
  setColor(color);
}
```

The setColor(Color newColor) method simply looks up the color in a lookup table using the position returned from findColorPosition(Color newColor).

```
// Change combo box to match color, if possible
private void setColor(Color newColor) {
  int position = findColorPosition(newColor);
  comboBox.setSelectedIndex(position);
}
```

The specifics of the findColorLabel(Object label) and findColorPosition(Color newColor) methods are shown in the complete source coming up shortly.

If you don't use the showDialog() means of showing the chooser pop-up window, once the chooser panel has been defined, and you've created a chooser panel, it can be placed within a JColorChooser with addChooserPanel().

```
AbstractColorChooserPanel newChooser = new SystemColorChooserPanel();
colorChooser.addChooserPanel(newChooser);
```

After showing the JColorChooser and picking the appropriate tab, your new chooser will be available for use, as shown in Figure 9-27.

The complete source for the SystemColorChooserPanel follows. The program should use the ComboBoxModel to store the labels and colors arrays of the example in one data model. However, I thought it best to try to focus the example toward the AbstractColorChooserPanel details, instead of toward the MVC capabilities of the JComboBox. Feel free to change the example in order to use the appropriate data model for the JComboBox or some of the new Collections API classes found on the Java 2 platform.

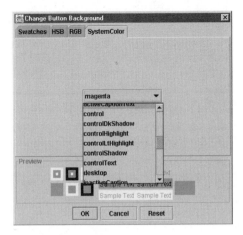

Figure 9-27: After adding the new SystemColor chooser panel

```java
import javax.swing.*;
import javax.swing.colorchooser.*;
import java.awt.*;
import java.awt.event.*;

public class SystemColorChooserPanel extends AbstractColorChooserPanel implements
ItemListener {
  private static int NOT_FOUND = -1;

  JComboBox comboBox;
  String labels[] = {
    "black",
    "blue",
    "cyan",
    "darkGray",
    "gray",
    "green",
    "lightGray",
    "magenta",
    "orange",
    "pink",
    "red",
```

```
                    "white",
                    "yellow",
                    "activeCaption",
                    "activeCaptionBorder",
                    "activeCaptionText",
                    "control",
                    "controlDkShadow",
                    "controlHighlight",
                    "controlLtHighlight",
                    "controlShadow",
                    "controlText",
                    "desktop",
                    "inactiveCaption",
                    "inactiveCaptionBorder",
                    "inactiveCaptionText",
                    "info",
                    "infoText",
                    "menu",
                    "menuText",
                    "scrollbar",
                    "text",
                    "textHighlight",
                    "textHighlightText",
                    "textInactiveText",
                    "textText",
                    "window",
                    "windowBorder",
                    "windowText",
                    "<Custom>"};

        Color colors[] = {
            Color.black,
            Color.blue,
            Color.cyan,
            Color.darkGray,
            Color.gray,
            Color.green,
            Color.lightGray,
            Color.magenta,
            Color.orange,
            Color.pink,
            Color.red,
            Color.white,
            Color.yellow,
```

```
    SystemColor.activeCaption,
    SystemColor.activeCaptionBorder,
    SystemColor.activeCaptionText,
    SystemColor.control,
    SystemColor.controlDkShadow,
    SystemColor.controlHighlight,
    SystemColor.controlLtHighlight,
    SystemColor.controlShadow,
    SystemColor.controlText,
    SystemColor.desktop,
    SystemColor.inactiveCaption,
    SystemColor.inactiveCaptionBorder,
    SystemColor.inactiveCaptionText,
    SystemColor.info,
    SystemColor.infoText,
    SystemColor.menu,
    SystemColor.menuText,
    SystemColor.scrollbar,
    SystemColor.text,
    SystemColor.textHighlight,
    SystemColor.textHighlightText,
    SystemColor.textInactiveText,
    SystemColor.textText,
    SystemColor.window,
    SystemColor.windowBorder,
    SystemColor.windowText,
    null};

  // Change combo box to match color, if possible
  private void setColor(Color newColor) {
    int position = findColorPosition(newColor);
    comboBox.setSelectedIndex(position);
  }

  // Given a label, find the position of the label in the list
  private int findColorLabel(Object label) {
    String stringLabel = label.toString();
    int position = NOT_FOUND;
    for (int i=0,n=labels.length; i<n; i++) {
      if (stringLabel.equals(labels[i])) {
        position=i;
        break;
      }
```

```
    }
    return position;
  }

  // Given a color, find the position whose color matches
  // This could result in a position different from original if two are equal
  // Since color is same, this is considered to be okay
  private int findColorPosition(Color color) {
    int position = colors.length-1;
    // Cannot use equals() to compare Color and SystemColor
    int colorRGB = color.getRGB();
    for (int i=0,n=colors.length; i<n; i++) {
      if ((colors[i] != null) && (colorRGB == colors[i].getRGB())) {
        position=i;
        break;
      }
    }
    return position;
  }

  public void itemStateChanged(ItemEvent itemEvent) {
    int state = itemEvent.getStateChange();
    if (state == ItemEvent.SELECTED) {
      int position = findColorLabel(itemEvent.getItem());
      // last position is bad (not selectable)
      if ((position != NOT_FOUND) && (position != labels.length-1)) {
        getColorSelectionModel().setSelectedColor(colors[position]);
      }
    }
  }

  public String getDisplayName() {
    return "SystemColor";
  }

  public Icon getSmallDisplayIcon() {
    return new DiamondIcon(Color.blue);
  }

  public Icon getLargeDisplayIcon() {
    return new DiamondIcon(Color.green);
  }
```

```
  protected void buildChooser() {
    comboBox = new JComboBox(labels);
    comboBox.addItemListener(this);
    add(comboBox);
  }

  public void updateChooser() {
    Color color = getColorFromModel();
    setColor(color);
  }
}
```

To demonstrate the use of the new chooser panel, the following program is provided. It's a slightly modified version of the CreateColorSamplePopup program listed in the section "Providing Your Own OK/Cancel Event Listeners" earlier in this chapter. You can uncomment the setChooserPanels() statement and comment out the addChooserPanel() call to go from adding one panel to replacing all of them.

```
import java.awt.*;
import java.awt.event.*;
import javax.swing.*;
import javax.swing.event.*;
import javax.swing.colorchooser.*;

public class CustomPanelPopup {

  public static void main(String args[]) {
    JFrame frame = new ExitableJFrame("JColorChooser Custom Panel Sample");
    Container contentPane = frame.getContentPane();

    final JButton button = new JButton("Pick to Change Background");

    ActionListener actionListener = new ActionListener() {
      public void actionPerformed(ActionEvent actionEvent) {
        Color initialBackground = button.getBackground();

        final JColorChooser colorChooser = new JColorChooser(initialBackground);
        AbstractColorChooserPanel newChooser = new SystemColorChooserPanel();
//        AbstractColorChooserPanel chooserPanels[] = {newChooser};
//        colorChooser.setChooserPanels(chooserPanels);
        colorChooser.addChooserPanel(newChooser);
```

```java
        // For okay button selection, change button background to selected color
        ActionListener okActionListener = new ActionListener() {
          public void actionPerformed(ActionEvent actionEvent) {
            Color newColor = colorChooser.getColor();
            if (newColor.equals(button.getForeground())) {
              System.out.println("Color change rejected");
            } else {
              button.setBackground(colorChooser.getColor());
            }
          }
        };

        // For cancel button selection, change button background to red
        ActionListener cancelActionListener = new ActionListener() {
          public void actionPerformed(ActionEvent actionEvent) {
            button.setBackground(Color.red);
          }
        };

        final JDialog dialog = JColorChooser.createDialog(null, "Change Button
Background", true, colorChooser, okActionListener, cancelActionListener);

        // Wait until current event dispatching completes before showing dialog
        Runnable showDialog = new Runnable() {
          public void run() {
            dialog.show();
          }
        };
        SwingUtilities.invokeLater(showDialog);
      }
    };
    button.addActionListener(actionListener);
    contentPane.add(button, BorderLayout.CENTER);

    frame.setSize(300, 100);
    frame.setVisible(true);
  }
}
```

Class *ColorChooserComponentFactory*

One class worthy of some special attention is ColorChooserComponentFactory. Normally, this class does its work behind the scenes and you never need to deal with it.

However, if you want to remove one of the default color choosers, you can't use the public AbstractColorChooserPanel removeChooserPanel(AbstractColorChooserPanel panel) method of JColorChooser. Initially, the chooserPanels property of JColorChooser is null. When this property is null, the default ColorChooserUI asks the ColorChooserComponentFactory for the default panels with the public static AbstractColorChooserPanel[] getDefaultChooserPanels() method. So, until you modify the property, no panels will appear. If you want to remove a default panel, you have to get the default array, place the panels you want to keep in a new array, and then change the chooserPanels property of the chooser to the new array.

The other method in the ColorChooserComponentFactory class is public static JComponent getPreviewPanel(), which gets the default preview panel when the previewPanel property of a JColorChooser is null. This is reason that providing a null argument to the setPreviewPanel() method of JColorChooser doesn't remove the preview panel. For the panel to be empty, you must provide a JComponent with no size.

```
colorChooser.setPreviewPanel(new JPanel());
```

Customizing a *JColorChooser* Look and Feel

The JColorChooser appearance is nearly the same for all the preinstalled look and feels. The only differences are related to how each look and feel displays the internal components, such as a JTabbedPane, JLabel, JButton, or JSlider. Changing the UIResource-related properties of those components affects the appearance of a newly created JColorChooser. In addition, the JColorChooser class has its own 27 UIResource-related properties available for customization, as listed in Table 9-11. Most of these resources are related to text labels appearing on the various default color chooser panels.

PROPERTY STRING	OBJECT TYPE
ColorChooser.background	Color
ColorChooser.cancelText	String
ColorChooser.font	Font
ColorChooser.foreground	Color
ColorChooser.hsbBlueText	String
ColorChooser.hsbBrightnessText	String
ColorChooser.hsbGreenText	String
ColorChooser.hsbHueText	String
ColorChooser.hsbNameText	String
ColorChooser.hsbRedText	String
ColorChooser.hsbSaturationText	String
ColorChooser.okText	String
ColorChooser.previewText	String
ColorChooser.resetText	String
ColorChooser.rgbBlueMnemonic	Integer
ColorChooser.rgbBlueText	String
ColorChooser.rgbGreenMnemonic	Integer
ColorChooser.rgbGreenText	String
ColorChooser.rgbNameText	String
ColorChooser.rgbRedMnemonic	Integer
ColorChooser.rgbRedText	String
ColorChooser.swatchesDefaultRecentColor	Color
ColorChooser.swatchesNameText	String
ColorChooser.swatchesRecentSwatchSize	Dimension
ColorChooser.swatchesRecentText	String
ColorChooser.swatchesSwatchSize	Dimension
ColorChooserUI	ColorChooserUI

Table 9-11: JColorChooser UIResource elements

Class JFileChooser

The Swing component set also provides a chooser for the selection of file names and/or directories: class JFileChooser. This chooser replaces the need for using the FileDialog from the original AWT component set. Like the other Swing chooser components, JFileChooser isn't automatically placed in a pop-up window, but it can be placed anywhere within the user interface of your program. Figure 9-28 shows a JFileChooser with the Metal look and feel that's been automatically placed in a modal JDialog.

In support of the JFileChooser class are a handful of classes in the javax. swing.filechooser package. The support classes include a FileFilter class for restricting files and directories to be listed in the FileView of the JFileChooser. The FileView controls how the directories and files are listed within the JFileChooser. The FileSystemView is an abstract class that tries to hide file-system related operating system specifics from the file chooser. Java 2 platform vendors will provide operating-system specific versions so that tasks such as listing root partitions can be done (with 100% Pure Java code). Figure 9-29 shows the relationships among these classes.

WARNING *Don't confuse the abstract javax.swing.filechooser.FileFilter class with the java.io.FileFilter interface. Although functionally similar, they're significantly different. The two probably coexist because the java.io. FileFilter interface doesn't exist in a Java 1.1 runtime. Because the Swing JFileChooser needs to run in both Java 1.1 and Java 2 environments, the chooser needed to define a replacement. Unless otherwise specified, all FileFilter references in this text are to the class in the javax.swing. filechooser package.*

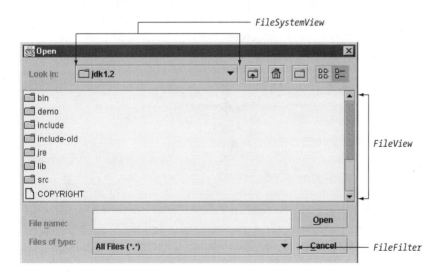

Figure 9-28: JFileChooser sample

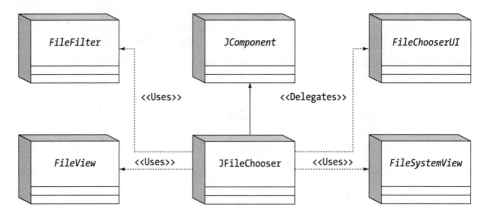

Figure 9-29: JFileChooser UML relationship diagram

Creating a JFileChooser

There are six constructors for JFileChooser. By default, the starting directory displayed is the user's home directory (system property user.home). If you want to start the JFileChooser pointing at another directory, the directory can be specified as either a String or a File object. In addition to your specifying a starting directory for the JFileChooser, you can specify a FileSystemView to specify a custom representation to the operating system's top-level directory structure. When the FileSystemView argument is not specified, the JFileChooser uses a FileSystemView appropriate for the user's operating system.

1. ```
   public JFileChooser()
   JFileChooser fileChooser = new JFileChooser();
   ```

2. ```
   public JFileChooser(File currentDirectory)
   File currentDirectory = new File("."); // starting directory of program
   JFileChooser fileChooser = new JFileChooser(currentDirectory);
   ```

3. ```
   public JFileChooser(File currentDirectory, FileSystemView fileSystemView)
   FileSystemView fileSystemView = new SomeFileSystemView(...);
   JFileChooser fileChooser = new JFileChooser(currentDirectory,
   fileSystemView);
   ```

4. ```
   public JFileChooser(FileSystemView fileSystemView)
   JFileChooser fileChooser = new JFileChooser(fileSystemView);
   ```

5. ```
   public JFileChooser(String currentDirectoryPath)
   String currentDirectoryPath = "."; // starting directory of program
   JFileChooser fileChooser = new JFileChooser(currentDirectoryPath);
   ```

6. ```
   public JFileChooser(String currentDirectoryPath, FileSystemView
   fileSystemView)
   JFileChooser fileChooser = new JFileChooser(currentDirectoryPath,
   fileSystemView);
   ```

Using JFileChooser

After creating a JFileChooser from a constructor, you can place it in any Container, because it's a JComponent. The JFileChooser object looks a little strange in an object that's not a pop-up window, but this may allow you to do a task without having to constantly bring up a new file chooser.

The following source demonstrates a simple window with two labels and a JFileChooser. Within *this* window, the Open and Cancel buttons are nonresponsive, but the buttons in the FileSystemView are live.

```java
import java.io.File;
import java.awt.*;
import java.awt.event.*;
import javax.swing.*;

public class FileSamplePanel {

  public static void main(String args[]) {
    JFrame frame = new ExitableJFrame("JFileChooser Popup");
    Container contentPane = frame.getContentPane();

    final JLabel directoryLabel = new JLabel(" ");
    directoryLabel.setFont(new Font("Serif", Font.BOLD | Font.ITALIC, 36));
    contentPane.add(directoryLabel, BorderLayout.NORTH);

    final JLabel filenameLabel = new JLabel(" ");
    filenameLabel.setFont(new Font("Serif", Font.BOLD | Font.ITALIC, 36));
    contentPane.add(filenameLabel, BorderLayout.SOUTH);

    JFileChooser fileChooser = new JFileChooser(".");
    contentPane.add(fileChooser, BorderLayout.CENTER);
```

```
      frame.pack();
      frame.setVisible(true);
   }
}
```

Adding an ActionListener to a JFileChooser

The JFileChooser allows you to add ActionListener objects to listen for selection of the approval or cancel buttons. To detect which button was selected, check the action command for the ActionEvent received by your ActionListener. Its action command setting would be either JFileChooser.APPROVE_SELECTION for selection of the approval button or JFileChooser.CANCEL_SELECTION for the Cancel button.

To complete the previous example, adding an action listener would allow you to set the text for the two labels when the user selects the Open button. On selection of the approval button, the text would become the current directory and file name. On selection of the Cancel button, text would be cleared.

```
// Create ActionListener
ActionListener actionListener = new ActionListener() {
   public void actionPerformed(ActionEvent actionEvent) {
      JFileChooser theFileChooser = (JFileChooser)actionEvent.getSource();
      String command = actionEvent.getActionCommand();
      if (command.equals(JFileChooser.APPROVE_SELECTION)) {
         File selectedFile = theFileChooser.getSelectedFile();
         directoryLabel.setText(selectedFile.getParent());
         filenameLabel.setText(selectedFile.getName());
      } else if (command.equals(JFileChooser.CANCEL_SELECTION)) {
         directoryLabel.setText(" ");
         filenameLabel.setText(" ");
      }
   }
};
fileChooser.addActionListener(actionListener);
```

With the addition of the action listener, the program is now complete in the sense that the Open and Cancel buttons are now active. Figure 9-30 shows what this window would look like after selection of the COPYRIGHT file in the jdk1.2 directory.

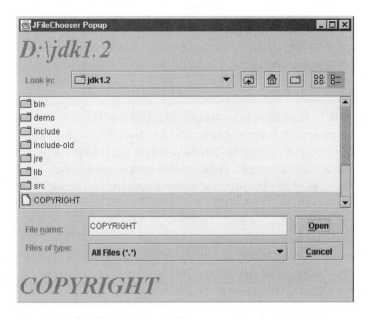

Figure 9-30: JFileChooser within a custom window

Creating and Showing a JFileChooser within a Pop-up Window

Instead of placing a JFileChooser panel within your own window, you'd more typically place it in a modal JDialog. There are three ways to do this, depending on the text you want to appear on the approval button.

- `public int showDialog(Component parentComponent, String approvalButtonText)`

- `public int showOpenDialog(Component parentComponent)`

- `public int showSaveDialog(Component parentComponent)`

Calling one of the previous methods will place the configured JFileChooser into a modal JDialog and show the dialog box centered over the parent component. Providing a null parent component centers the pop-up window on the screen. The call doesn't return until the user selects the approval or cancel button.

After selection of one of the two buttons, the call returns a status value, depending on which button was selected. This status would be one of three JFileChooser constants: APPROVE_OPTION, CANCEL_OPTION, or ERROR_OPTION.

> **WARNING** *If the user clicks the approval button without selecting anything,* CANCEL_OPTION *is returned.*

To perform the same task as the example in the previous section "Using JFileChooser," in which an ActionListener was attached to the JFileChooser, you can just show the dialog box and change the labels based on the return status, instead of relying on the action command. Here, the file chooser would be shown in another window, instead of within the window with the two labels.

```
JFileChooser fileChooser = new JFileChooser(".");
int status = fileChooser.showOpenDialog(null);
if (status == JFileChooser.APPROVE_OPTION) {
  File selectedFile = fileChooser.getSelectedFile();
  directoryLabel.setText(selectedFile.getParent());
  filenameLabel.setText(selectedFile.getName());
} else if (status == JFileChooser.CANCEL_OPTION) {
  directoryLabel.setText(" ");
  filenameLabel.setText(" ");
}
```

> **NOTE** *Notice that here we've switched from checking the* String *return values of the earlier example to checking* int *return values: [if* (command.equals(JFileChooser.APPROVE_SELECTION)) *versus if* (status == JFileChooser.APPROVE_OPTION)].

JFileChooser Properties

Once you understand the basic JFileChooser usage, you can customize the component's behavior and appearance by modifying its many properties. Table 9-12 shows the 22 properties of JFileChooser.

> **WARNING** *As of this writing, multi-selection of files isn't available through the system-provided look and feel classes.*

PROPERTY NAME	DATA TYPE	ACCESS
acceptAllFileFilter	FileFilter	read-only
accessibleContext	AccessibleContext	read-only
accessory	JComponent	read-write bound
approveButtonMnemonic	char	read-write bound
approveButtonText	String	read-write bound
approveButtonToolTipText	String	read-write bound
choosableFileFilters	FileFilter[ ]	read-only
currentDirectory	File	read-write bound
dialogTitle	String	read-write bound
dialogType	int	read-write bound
directorySelectionEnabled	boolean	read-only
fileFilter	FileFilter	read-write bound
fileHidingEnabled	boolean	read-write bound
fileSelectionEnabled	boolean	read-only
fileSelectionMode	int	read-write bound
fileSystemView	FileSystemView	read-write bound
fileView	FileView	read-write bound
multiSelectionEnabled	boolean	read-write bound
selectedFile	File	read-write bound
selectedFiles	File[ ]	read-write bound
UI	FileChooserUI	read-only
UIClassID	String	read-only

Table 9-12: JFileChooser properties

When the different showDialog() methods are used, the dialogType property is automatically set to one of three JOptionPane constants: OPEN_DIALOG, SAVE_DIALOG, CUSTOM_DIALOG. If you're not using showDialog(), you should set this property according to the type of dialog box you plan to work with.

Working with File Filters

The JFileChooser supports three ways of filtering its file and directory list. The first two involve working with the FileFilter class, and the last involves hidden files. First, let's look at the FileFilter.

FileFilter is an abstract class that works something like FilenameFilter in AWT. However, instead of working with strings for directory and file names, it works with a File object. For every File object that's to be displayed (both files and directories), the filter decides whether the File can appear within the JFileChooser. In addition to providing an acceptance mechanism, the filter also provides a description, or name, for when the description is displayed to a user.

These two capabilities are reflected in the two methods of the class definition that follow.

```
public abstract class FileFilter {
  public FileFilter();
  public abstract String getDescription();
  public abstract boolean accept(File file);
}
```

> **NOTE** *In my opinion, this abstract class should be an interface. I never got a definite answer from the Swing team on why it wasn't.*

To demonstrate a file filter, we'll create one that accepts an array of file extensions. If the file sent to accept() is a directory, we'll automatically accept it. Otherwise, the file extension must match one of the extensions in the array, and the character preceding the extension must be a period. For this particular filter, the comparisons will be case-insensitive.

```
import javax.swing.filechooser.*;
import java.io.File; // avoid FileFilter name conflict

public class ExtensionFileFilter extends FileFilter {
  String description;
  String extensions[];

  public ExtensionFileFilter(String description, String extension) {
    this(description, new String[] {extension});
  }

  public ExtensionFileFilter(String description, String extensions[]) {
    if (description == null) {
// Since no description, use first extension and # of extensions as description
      this.description = extensions[0]+"{"+extensions.length+"}" ;
    } else {
      this.description = description;
    }
    // Convert array to lowercase
    // Don't alter original entries
    this.extensions = (String[])extensions.clone();
    toLower(this.extensions);
  }
```

```
  private void toLower(String array[]) {
    for (int i=0, n=array.length; i<n; i++) {
      array[i] = array[i].toLowerCase();
    }
  }

  public String getDescription() {
    return description;
  }

  // ignore case, always accept directories
  // character before extension must be a period
  public boolean accept(File file) {
    if (file.isDirectory()) {
      return true;
    } else {
      String path = file.getAbsolutePath().toLowerCase();
      for (int i=0, n=extensions.length; i<n; i++) {
        String extension = extensions[i];
        if ((path.endsWith(extension)  &&
            (path.charAt(path.length()-extension.length()-1)) == '.')) {
          return true;
        }
      }
    }
    return false;
  }
}
```

Using the file filter entails creating it and associating it with the JFileChooser. If you just want to make the filter selectable by the user, but not the default initial selection, call public void addChoosableFileFilter(FileFilter filter). This will keep the default accept-all-files filter selected. If, instead, you want the filter to be set when the chooser first appears, call public void setFileFilter(FileFilter filter) and the file chooser will filter the initial set of files shown.

For example, the following source will add two filters to a file chooser:

```
FileFilter jpegFilter = new ExtensionFileFilter(null, new String[]{"JPG",
"JPEG"});
fileChooser.addChoosableFileFilter(jpegFilter);
FileFilter gifFilter = new ExtensionFileFilter("gif", new String[]{"gif"});
fileChooser.addChoosableFileFilter(gifFilter);
```

When no file filters have been associated with the JFileChooser, the filter from JFileChooser.getAcceptAllFileFilter() is used to provide a filter that accepts all files and that is also appropriate for the underlying operating system.

Figure 9-31 shows an open filter-selection combo box in a Motif file chooser.

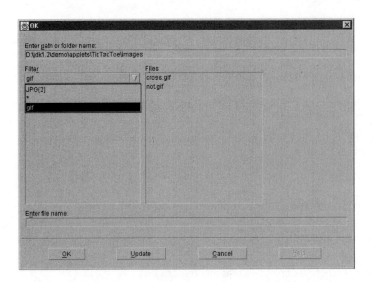

Figure 9-31: Using custom FileFilter with a JFileChooser

> **WARNING**   *Setting the FileFilter with setFileFilter() before adding filters with addChoosableFileFilter() causes the accept-all file filter to be unavailable. If you want to include multiple filters in the list and set the initial filter, add the additional filters first. The accept-all file filter is available from JFileChooser.getAcceptAllFileFilter(). You can always add it back if you lose it or need to temporarily remove it. In addition, you can reset the filter list with public void resetChoosableFileFilters().*

One built-in filter isn't a FileFilter. It concerns hidden files, such as those that begin with a period (.) on UNIX file systems. By default, hidden files aren't shown within the JFileChooser. To enable the display of hidden files, you must set the fileHidingEnabled property to false:

```
aFileChooser.setFileHidingEnabled(false);
```

> **TIP** *When creating javax.swing.filechooser.FileFilter subclasses, you may want to have the new class also implement the java.io.FileFilter interface. To do this, simply add "implements java.io.FileFilter" to the class definition because the method signature for the accept() method in the javax.swing.filechooser class matches the interface definition: public boolean accept(File file).*

Choosing Directories Instead of Files

The JFileChooser supports three selection modes: files only, directories only, and files and directories. The fileSelectionMode property setting determines the mode of the chooser. The available settings are specified by the three JFileChooser constants: FILES_ONLY, DIRECTORIES_ONLY, and FILES_AND_DIRECTORIES. Initially, the file chooser is in JFileChooser.FILES_ONLY mode. To change the mode, just call public void setFileSelectionMode(int newMode).

In addition to the fileSelectionMode property, you can use the read-only fileSelectionEnabled and directorySelectionEnabled properties to determine the type of input currently supported by the file chooser.

> **NOTE** *With the AWT FileDialog, it was impossible to enable directory selection.*

Adding Accessory Panels

The JFileChooser supports the addition of an accessory component. This component can enhance the functionality of the chooser, including previewing an image or document, or playing an audio file. To respond to file selection changes, the accessory component should attach itself as a PropertyChangeListener to the JFileChooser. When the JFileChooser.SELECTED_FILE_CHANGED_PROPERTY property changes, the accessory then changes to reflect the file selection. Figure 9-32 shows how an image previewer accessory component might appear. Configuring the accessory for a chooser is just like setting any other property.

```
fileChooser.setAccessory(new LabelAccessory(fileChooser));
```

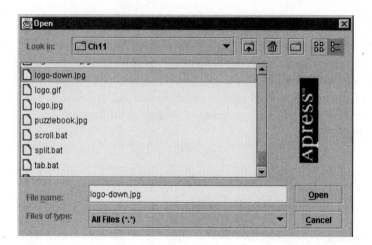

Figure 9-32: A JFileChooser with an accessory panel

The source for an Image component that displays an accessory icon follows. The selected image file becomes the icon for a JLabel component. The component does two scaling operations to make sure the dimensions of the image are sized to fit within the accessory.

```java
import javax.swing.*;
import java.beans.*;
import java.awt.*;
import java.io.*;

public class LabelAccessory extends JLabel implements PropertyChangeListener {
  private static final int PREFERRED_WIDTH = 125;
  private static final int PREFERRED_HEIGHT = 100;

  public LabelAccessory(JFileChooser chooser) {
    setVerticalAlignment(JLabel.CENTER);
    setHorizontalAlignment(JLabel.CENTER);
    chooser.addPropertyChangeListener(this);
    setPreferredSize(new Dimension(PREFERRED_WIDTH, PREFERRED_HEIGHT));
  }
  public void propertyChange(PropertyChangeEvent changeEvent) {
    String changeName = changeEvent.getPropertyName();
    if (changeName.equals(JFileChooser.SELECTED_FILE_CHANGED_PROPERTY)) {
      File file = (File)changeEvent.getNewValue();
      if (file != null) {
        ImageIcon icon = new ImageIcon(file.getPath());
        if (icon.getIconWidth() > PREFERRED_WIDTH) {
```

```
          icon = new ImageIcon(icon.getImage().getScaledInstance(PREFERRED_WIDTH,
-1, Image.SCALE_DEFAULT));
        if (icon.getIconHeight() > PREFERRED_HEIGHT) {
          icon = new ImageIcon(icon.getImage().getScaledInstance(-1, PRE-
FERRED_HEIGHT, Image.SCALE_DEFAULT));
        }
      }
      setIcon(icon);
    }
  }
 }
}
```

Class *FileSystemView*

The FileSystemView class localizes access to platform-specific file system information. Where the JDK 1.1 version of java.io.File was fairly crippled in this
respect, FileSystemView fills in to make it easier to design FileChooserUI objects.
The Swing FileSystemView class provides three custom views as package-private
subclasses of FileSystemView. They include support for UNIX and Windows, plus
a generic handler.

Although it isn't necessary to define your own FileSystemView, the class provides some features that can be used outside the context of JFileChooser. To
get the view specific to the user's runtime environment, call public static
FileSystemView getFileSystemView(). The class definition follows.

```
public abstract class FileSystemView {
  // Constructors
  public FileSystemView();  // Properties
  public File getHomeDirectory();
  public abstract File[] getRoots();
  // Class Methods
  public static FileSystemView getFileSystemView();
  // Other Methods
  public File createFileObject(File directory, String filename);
  public File createFileObject(String path);
  public abstract File createNewFolder(File containingDir) throws IOException;
  public File[] getFiles(File directory, boolean useFileHiding);
  public File getParentDirectory(File file);
  public abstract boolean isHiddenFile(File file);
  public abstract boolean isRoot(File file);
}
```

Class FileView

The final part of the JFileChooser we'll examine is the FileView area where all the file names are listed. Each of the custom look and feels has its own FileView area class. In addition, some of the predefined look and feels, such as Motif, aren't changeable. Nevertheless, at least in the Metal and Windows file choosers, you can customize the icons for different file types or change the display name for a file. The five methods of the FileView allow you to change the name, icon, or description (two forms) of each File in the view. In addition, the FileView actually controls whether a directory is traversable, allowing you to program in a weak level of access control. Nontraversable directories have a different default icon, because you can't do any further selection of them.

Here's the definition of the abstract FileView class.

```
public abstract class FileView {
  public FileView();
  public abstract String getDescription(File file);
  public abstract Icon getIcon(File file);
  public abstract String getName(File file);
  public abstract String getTypeDescription(File file);
  public abstract Boolean isTraversable(File file);
}
```

> **NOTE** *Notice that the isTraversable() method returns a Boolean value, not a boolean one, such as true or false.*

Customizing the FileView requires creating a subclass and overriding all the abstract methods. If you don't want to define custom behavior for a specific method, just have it return null. For instance, if you don't want to bother with modifying the traversability of directories, just place the following code in your FileView:

```
public Boolean isTraversable(File file) {
  return null;
}
```

Once you've defined the file view, simply change the fileView property of your JFileChooser:

```
fileChooser.setFileView(new JavaFileView());
```

Figure 9-33 shows the changed appearance of a Metal `JFileChooser` after installing a custom `FileView`.

The `JavaFileView` class provides a `FileView` implementation that customizes the appearance of files related to Java development — specifically, .java, .class, .jar, and .html or .htm files. For each of these file types, a special icon instead of the default icon is displayed next to the name. In addition, for Java source files, the length of the file is displayed. (Imagine all the file attributes being displayed!) Unfortunately, you can't modify the font or color from a `FileView`.

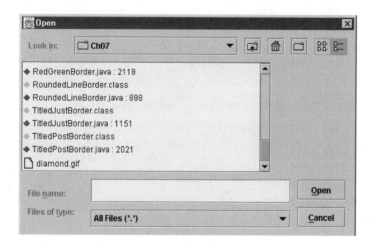

Figure 9-33: Changing the FileView

```java
import java.io.File;
import java.awt.*;
import javax.swing.*;
import javax.swing.filechooser.*;

public class JavaFileView extends FileView {
  Icon javaIcon = new DiamondIcon(Color.blue);
  Icon classIcon = new DiamondIcon(Color.green);
  Icon htmlIcon = new DiamondIcon(Color.red);
  Icon jarIcon = new DiamondIcon(Color.pink);

  public String getDescription(File file) {
    return null;
  }

  public String getName(File file) {
    String filename = file.getName();
    if (filename.endsWith(".java")) {
```

```
      String name = filename + " : " + file.length();
      return name;
    }
    return null;
  }

  public Boolean isTraversable(File file) {
    return null;
  }

  public String getTypeDescription(File file) {
    String typeDescription = null;
    String filename = file.getName().toLowerCase();

    if (filename.endsWith(".java")) {
      typeDescription = "Java Source";
    } else if (filename.endsWith(".class")){
      typeDescription = "Java Class File";
    } else if (filename.endsWith(".jar")){
      typeDescription = "Java Archive";
    } else if (filename.endsWith(".html") || filename.endsWith(".htm")) {
      typeDescription = "Applet Loader";
    }
    return typeDescription;
  }

  public Icon getIcon(File file) {
    if (file.isDirectory()) {
      return null;
    }
    Icon icon = null;
    String filename = file.getName().toLowerCase();
    if (filename.endsWith(".java")) {
      icon = javaIcon;
    } else if (filename.endsWith(".class")){
      icon = classIcon;
    } else if (filename.endsWith(".jar")){
      icon = jarIcon;
    } else if (filename.endsWith(".html") || filename.endsWith(".htm")) {
      icon = htmlIcon;
    }
    return icon;
  }
}
```

Customizing a JFileChooser Look and Feel

Each installable Swing look and feel provides a different JFileChooser appearance and set of default UIResource values. Figure 9-34 shows the appearance of the JFileChooser for the preinstalled set of look and feels: Motif, Windows, Metal, and the separate Macintosh look and feel.

The available set of UIResource-related properties for a JFileChooser is shown in Table 9-13. For the JFileChooser component, there are 42 different properties. Nearly all the properties relate to the button labels, mnemonics, icons, and tooltip text.

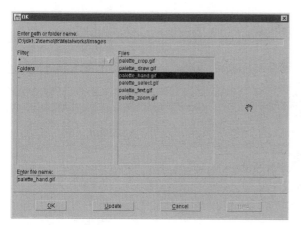

Motif

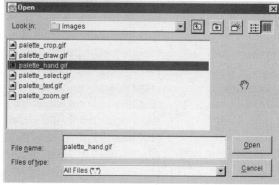

Windows

Metal

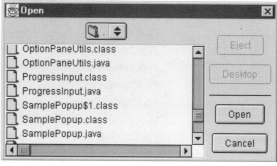

Macintosh

Figure 9-34: JFileChooser under different look and feels

PROPERTY STRING	OBJECT TYPE
FileChooser.acceptAllFileFilterText	String
FileChooser.cancelButtonMnemonic	Integer
FileChooser.cancelButtonText	String
FileChooser.cancelButtonToolTipText	String
FileChooser.detailsViewButtonAccessibleName	String
FileChooser.detailsViewButtonToolTipText	String
FileChooser.detailsViewIcon	Icon
FileChooser.directoryDescriptionText	String
FileChooser.fileDescriptionText	String
FileChooser.fileNameLabelMnemonic	Integer
FileChooser.fileNameLabelText	String
FileChooser.filesOfTypeLabelMnemonic	Integer
FileChooser.filesOfTypeLabelText	String
FileChooser.helpButtonMnemonic	Integer
FileChooser.helpButtonText	String
FileChooser.helpButtonToolTipText	String
FileChooser.homeFolderAccessibleName	String
FileChooser.homeFolderIcon	Icon
FileChooser.homeFolderToolTipText	String
FileChooser.listViewButtonAccessibleName	String
FileChooser.listViewButtonToolTipText	String
FileChooser.listViewIcon	Icon
FileChooser.lookInLabelMnemonic	Integer
FileChooser.lookInLabelText	String
FileChooser.newFolderAccessibleName	String
FileChooser.newFolderErrorSeparator	String
FileChooser.newFolderErrorText	String
FileChooser.newFolderIcon	Icon
FileChooser.newFolderToolTipText	String
FileChooser.openButtonMnemonic	Integer
FileChooser.openButtonText	String
FileChooser.openButtonToolTipText	String
FileChooser.saveButtonMnemonic	Integer
FileChooser.saveButtonText	String
FileChooser.saveButtonToolTipText	String
FileChooser.updateButtonMnemonic	Integer
FileChooser.updateButtonText	String
FileChooser.updateButtonToolTipText	String
FileChooser.upFolderAccessibleName	String
FileChooser.upFolderIcon	Icon
FileChooser.upFolderToolTipText	String
FileChooserUI	FileChooserUI

Table 9-13: JFileChooser UIResource elements

In addition to the more than 40 resources for JFileChooser, there are 5 additional ones as part of the FileView, which are shown in Table 9-14.

PROPERTY STRING	OBJECT TYPE
FileView.computerIcon	Icon
FileView.directoryIcon	Icon
FileView.fileIcon	Icon
FileView.floppyDriveIcon	Icon
FileView.hardDriveIcon	Icon

Table 9-14: FileView UIResource elements

NOTE *The beta4 release of the product code named JDK 1.2 had several other chooser components in preview mode. Unfortunately, none of them made it into the production release. With any luck, these or similar chooser components will be added to a later JFC/Project Swing release. The components included a font chooser, a date chooser with calendar, and a money chooser with a calculator.*

Summary

In this chapter, we explored the intricacies of Swing's pop-up and chooser classes. Instead of manually creating a JDialog and filling it with the necessary pieces, the Swing component set includes support for many different pop-up and chooser classes. Starting with the JOptionPane, we looked at how you can create informational, question, or input pop-ups. In addition, we explored how to monitor the progress of time-consuming tasks by using the ProgressMonitor and ProgressMonitorInputStream classes.

After looking at the more general pop-up classes, we explored the specifics of Swing's color and file chooser classes: JColorChooser and JFileChooser. From each of these two classes, you can prompt the user for the requested input and customize the display in more ways than you can imagine.

Now that you have a feel for the predefined pop-ups, let's move on in Chapter 10 to the specific LayoutManager classes provided in the Swing component set. With the help of the new layout managers, you can create even better user interfaces.

CHAPTER 10

Swing Layout Managers

IN CHAPTER 9, YOU LEARNED ABOUT THE various pop-up and chooser classes available from the Swing component set. In this chapter, you'll learn about the four Swing layout managers: BoxLayout and OverlayLayout, which are implementations of LayoutManager2, and ScrollPaneLayout and ViewportLayout, which are implementations of LayoutManager.

In addition to the layout managers, we'll look at the SizeRequirements class used by both the BoxLayout and OverlayLayout managers and examine the ScrollPaneConstants interface used as a support class by ScrollPaneLayout.

Besides the layout managers described in this chapter, AWT offers several other ones: FlowLayout, GridLayout, BorderLayout, CardLayout, and GridBagLayout. With the addition of the JTabbedPane component available to Swing, which is described in Chapter 11, the use of CardLayout is rarely necessary. Figure 10-1 shows the complete set of predefined layout managers.

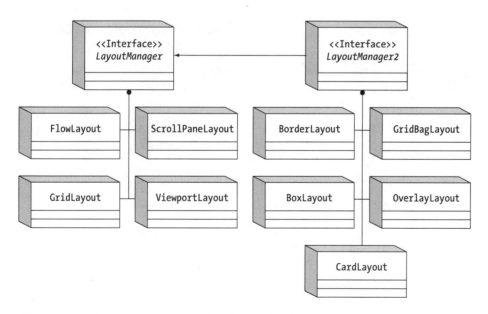

Figure 10-1: The LayoutManager class hierarchy diagram

> **NOTE** *If you're not familiar with the general concept of layout manage-*
> *ment, or if you need additional information about the layout managers*
> *found in the base AWT classes, check out another book of mine,* Java AWT
> Reference *(O'Reilly), which explains what a layout manager is, how it*
> *works, and how to create your own.*

Class BoxLayout

Swing's BoxLayout manager allows you to position components in either a horizontal row or a vertical column within your own container. In addition to using
BoxLayout within your own container, the Box class (described in the next chapter), offers a container that uses BoxLayout as its default layout manager. The
benefit of using a BoxLayout over something like FlowLayout or GridLayout is that
BoxLayout works to honor each component's x and y alignment properties as well
as its maximum size. Figure 10-2 demonstrates BoxLayout in action. Previously,
you would have had to figure out the necessary layout constraints to get
GridBagLayout to behave like this. You'll soon learn how much easier things are
with BoxLayout as compared with GridBagLayout.

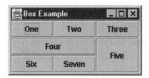

Before

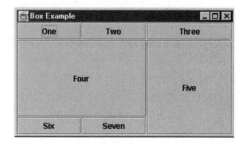

After

Figure 10-2: BoxLayout example, before and after resizing

Creating a BoxLayout

There's a single constructor for BoxLayout: public BoxLayout(Container target,
int axis). The constructor takes two arguments. The first argument is the container with which this instance of the layout manager is to be associated, and the
second is the layout direction. Valid directions are BoxLayout.X_AXIS for a left-to-
right layout and BoxLayout.Y_AXIS for a top-to-bottom layout.

WARNING *Trying to set the axis to something other than the equivalent value of these two constants will throw an AWTError. If the layout manager is associated to a container that isn't the container passed in to the constructor, an AWTError will be thrown when the layout manager tries to layout the other (that is, wrong) container.*

Once you create a BoxLayout instance, you can associate the layout manager with a container as you would with any other layout manager.

```
JPanel panel = new JPanel();
LayoutManager layout = new BoxLayout (panel, BoxLayout.X_AXIS);
panel.setLayout(layout);
```

Unlike all core AWT layout managers, a BoxLayout and container are bound together in two directions, from manager to container as well as from container to manager.

TIP *The Box class, described in Chapter 11, lets you create a container and set its layout manager to BoxLayout all in one step.*

Laying Out Components

Once you've set the layout manager of a container to BoxLayout, that's really all you do directly with the layout manager. Adding components to the container is done either with the add(Component component) method variety or with add(Component component, int index). Although BoxLayout implements the LayoutManager2 interface, implying the use of constraints, it currently uses none. Therefore, it isn't necessary to use add(Component component, Object constraints).

When it comes time to lay out the container, this is when BoxLayout does its work. The BoxLayout manager tries to satisfy the minimum and maximum sizes of the components within the container, as well as their x-axis and y-axis alignments. Alignment values range from 0.0f to 1.0f. (Alignment settings are floating-point constants, not doubles, hence the need for the "f".)

By default, all Component subclasses have an x-axis alignment of Component. CENTER_ALIGNMENT and a y-axis alignment of Component.CENTER_ALIGNMENT. However, all AbstractButton subclasses and JLabel have a default x-axis alignment of Component.LEFT_ALIGNMENT. Table 10-1 shows the constants available from Component for these component properties, settable with either setAlignmentX (float newValue) or setAlignmentY(float newValue). The different alignments work identically, except in different directions. In the case of horizontal alignments, this is similar to left-, center-, or right-justifying a paragraph.

DESCRIPTION	SETTING	VALUE
Vertical Alignment	Component.TOP_ALIGNMENT	0.0f
	Component.CENTER_ALIGNMENT	0.5f
	Component.BOTTOM_ALIGNMENT	1.0f
Horizontal Alignment	Component.LEFT_ALIGNMENT	0.0f
	Component.CENTER_ALIGNMENT	0.5f
	Component.RIGHT_ALIGNMENT	1.0f

Table 10-1: Component alignments

Laying Out Components with the Same Alignments

The BoxLayout manager acts differently depending on the alignment of the components within the container being managed. If all the alignments are the same, then those components whose maximumSize is smaller than the container will be aligned based on the alignment setting. For instance, if you have a wide area with a vertical BoxLayout and small buttons within it, the horizontal alignment will serve to left-, center-, or right-justify the buttons. Figure 10-3 shows how this looks.

The key point demonstrated here is that if all the components share the same alignment setting, then the actual alignment of all the components within the managed container is the components' alignment setting.

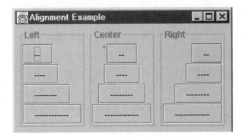

Figure 10-3: Three y-axis BoxLayout containers, each with components having the same horizontal alignments

The source used to generate Figure 10-3 follows:

```
import javax.swing.*;
import java.awt.*;
import java.awt.event.*;
```

```java
public class YAxisAlignX {
  private static Container makeIt(String title, float alignment) {
    String labels[] = {"-", "—", "——", "———"};

    JPanel container = new JPanel();
    container.setBorder(BorderFactory.createTitledBorder(title));
    BoxLayout layout = new BoxLayout(container, BoxLayout.Y_AXIS);
    container.setLayout(layout);

    for (int i=0,n=labels.length; i<n; i++) {
      JButton button = new JButton(labels[i]);
      button.setAlignmentX(alignment);
      container.add(button);
    }
    return container;
  }

  public static void main(String args[]) {
    JFrame frame = new ExitableJFrame("Alignment Example");

    Container panel1 = makeIt("Left",   Component.LEFT_ALIGNMENT);
    Container panel2 = makeIt("Center", Component.CENTER_ALIGNMENT);
    Container panel3 = makeIt("Right",  Component.RIGHT_ALIGNMENT);

    Container contentPane = frame.getContentPane();
    contentPane.setLayout(new FlowLayout());
    contentPane.add(panel1);
    contentPane.add(panel2);
    contentPane.add(panel3);

    frame.pack();
    frame.setVisible(true);
  }
}
```

An x-axis BoxLayout works similarly when all the components have the same vertical alignments. Instead of being left-, center-, and right-justified, the components would appear at the top, center, and bottom of the container. Figure 10-4 demonstrates this appearance.

The source for this figure requires that six lines be changed at the appropriate place in the code that was used to create Figure 10-3. Rather than list the entire source, I've supplied just the changes.

Figure 10-4: Three x-axis BoxLayout containers each having components with the same vertical alignments

```
String labels[] = {"-", "-", "-"};
...
BoxLayout layout = new BoxLayout(container, BoxLayout.X_AXIS);
...
Container panel1 = makeIt("Top",    Component.TOP_ALIGNMENT);
Container panel2 = makeIt("Center", Component.CENTER_ALIGNMENT);
Container panel3 = makeIt("Bottom", Component.BOTTOM_ALIGNMENT);
...
contentPane.setLayout(new GridLayout(1, 3));
```

Laying Out Components with Different Alignments

Although working with small components having the same alignment is relatively simple, if the components in a container managed by a BoxLayout have different alignments, things become more complex. In addition, the components won't necessarily be displayed the way you might expect. For a vertical box, the components appear as follows:

- If a component has its x alignment set to Component.LEFT_ALIGNMENT, then the left edge of the component will be aligned with the center of the container.

- If a component has its x alignment set to Component.RIGHT_ALIGNMENT, then the right edge of the component will be aligned with the center of the container.

- If a component has its x alignment set to Component.CENTER_ALIGNMENT, then the component will be centered within the container.

- Other alignment values would cause components to be placed in varying positions (depending on the value) relative to the center of the container.

To help you visualize this mixed alignment behavior, Figure 10-5 shows two
BoxLayout containers. The left container has two components, one with a left
alignment (the button labeled 0.0) and another with a right alignment (1.0). Here
you can see that the left edge of the right component is aligned to the right edge of
the left component, with the common edge being the center line of the container.
The right container shows additional components placed between the 0.0 and 1.0
alignment settings. The label of each button represents its alignment setting.

For a horizontal box, Figure 10-6 shows how the y alignment works the same
relative to the top and bottom of the components on an x-axis.

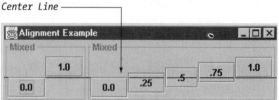

*Figure 10-6: Two x-axis BoxLayout containers
with mixed vertical alignments*

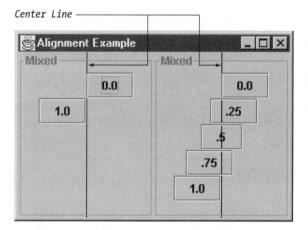

*Figure 10-5: Two y-axis BoxLayout containers
with mixed horizontal alignments*

Laying Out Larger Components

In the examples so far, the size of the components is always smaller than the
space available. Those examples demonstrate a subtle difference between Swing
and the original AWT components. The default maximum size of Swing components is the preferred size of the component, whereas with AWT components, the
default maximum size is a dimension with a width and height of Short.MAX_VALUE.
If the previous examples had used AWT Button components instead of Swing
JButton components, you'd see surprisingly different results. You'd also see different results if you manually set the maximum size property of the components to
some value wider or higher than the screen for the appropriate BoxLayout. Using
AWT Button components makes things a little easier to demonstrate.

In Figure 10-3, you can see three y-axis BoxLayout containers in which the
components inside the container share the same horizontal alignment setting and
the maximum size of each button is constrained. If the component's maximum
size is unconstrained, or just larger than the container, you see something like

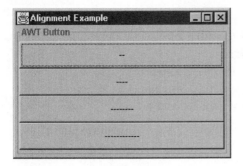

Figure 10-7: Y-axis BoxLayout containers with the same vertical alignments and unconstrained size

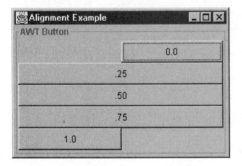

Figure 10-8: Y-axis BoxLayout containers with different vertical alignments, unconstrained size, and both minimum/maximum alignment present

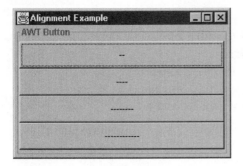

Figure 10-9: Y-axis BoxLayout containers with different vertical alignments, unconstrained size, and only one alignment at minimum/maximum

Figure 10-7, in which the y-axis BoxLayout container has four Button components with the same horizontal alignment. Notice that instead of aligning to the left, center, or right, the components grow to fill all available space.

If the components had different alignments *and* an unconstrained maximum size, you'd get yet another behavior. Any component with an alignment not at the minimum (0.0f) or maximum (1.0f) setting will grow to fill the entire space. If components with both the minimum and maximum alignment settings are present, the middle edges of those two components will align in the middle, as Figure 10-8 demonstrates.

If, however, only one component has an edge case and is in a container with components having other alignments, that edge-case component will grow toward somewhere other than the middle of the container. This behavior is shown in Figure 10-9. The x-axis BoxLayout containers work similarly with different horizontal alignments.

Class OverlayLayout

As its name implies, the OverlayLayout class is for layout management of components that lie on top of one another. When using add(Component component), the order in which you add components to a container with an OverlayLayout manager determines the component layering. If you use add(Component component, int index) instead, you can add components in any order. Although OverlayLayout implements the LayoutManager2 interface, like BoxLayout it currently doesn't use any constraints.

Determining the two-dimensional position of the components requires the layout manager to examine the x and y alignment properties of the components. Each component will be positioned such that its x and y alignment property defines a point shared by all the components, called the *axis point* of the layout manager. If you multiply the alignment value by the component's size in each appropriate direction, you'll get each part of the axis point for that component.

After the axis point is determined for each component, the OverlayLayout manager calculates the position of this shared point within the container. To calculate this position, the layout manager averages the different alignment properties of the components and then multiplies each setting by the width or height of the container. This position is where the layout manager places the axis point, and the components are then positioned over this shared point.

To demonstrate, let's look at how three buttons would be layered and positioned with different sizes and alignments. We'll have a 25-by-25 white button on top of a 50-by-50 gray button on top of a 100-by-100 black button. If the x and y alignment of each button was 0.0f, then the shared axis point for the three components would be their upper-left corner and the components would all be in the upper-left corner of the container. Figure 10-10a shows how this might appear. If the x and y alignment of each button was 1.0f, then the axis point for the three components would be their bottom-right corner and the components would be in the bottom-right corner of the container. Figure 10-10b shows this appearance. If the x and y alignment of each button was 0.5f, then the axis point for the three components would be their center and the components would be in the center of the container. Figure 10-10c shows this.

Having all components with the same alignment is relatively easy to visualize, but what would happen if the components had different alignments? For instance, if the small button had x and y alignments of 0.0f, the medium button had alignments of 0.5f, and the large button had alignments of 1.0f, where would everything appear? Well, the first thing the layout manager calculates is the axis point. Based on the specific alignment of each button, the axis point would be the upper-left corner of the small button, the middle of the medium button, and the bottom-right corner of the large button. The position of the axis point within the container would then be the average of the alignment values multiplied by the dimensions of the container. The average of 0, 0.5, and 1 for both directions places the axis point at the center of the container. It's from this position that the components are then placed and layered, as Figure 10-11 shows.

In addition to affecting positioning, the layering of components affects event handling. Only the component in the topmost layer where the event happened will receive an event. If each button has an associated `ActionListener`, only the topmost button at the position clicked would be notified,

10-10a. 0.0 x and y alignments

10-10b. 1.0 x and y alignments

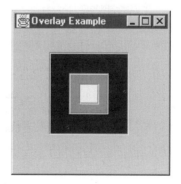

10-10c. 0.5 x and y alignments

Figure 10-10: Three examples of a trio of buttons managed by an OverlayLayout with the same alignments

no matter which button appeared on top. For instance, if you were to select the larger button in Figure 10-10, the larger button would be drawn to appear above the two smaller buttons. However, the larger button wouldn't be selected if you then clicked where the smaller button was currently buried.

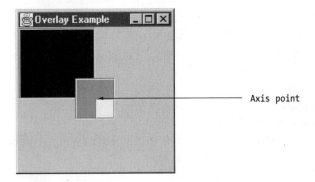

Figure 10-11: Three buttons managed by an OverlayLayout with 0.0, 0.5, and 1.0 x and y alignments

To try out the OverlayLayout manager, use the source that follows. It enhances the source code from the previous OverlayLayout examples to provide selectable buttons to demonstrate interactively the effect of varying the alignment values. Initially, the source has everything centered.

```
import javax.swing.*;
import java.awt.*;
import java.awt.event.*;

public class OverlaySample {
    public static final String SET_MINIMUM = "Minimum";
    public static final String SET_MAXIMUM = "Maximum";
    public static final String SET_CENTRAL = "Central";
    public static final String SET_MIXED   = "Mixed";

    static JButton smallButton = new JButton();
    static JButton mediumButton = new JButton();
    static JButton largeButton = new JButton();
```

```java
public static void setupButtons(String command) {
  if (SET_MINIMUM.equals(command)) {
    smallButton.setAlignmentX(0.0f);
    smallButton.setAlignmentY(0.0f);
    mediumButton.setAlignmentX(0.0f);
    mediumButton.setAlignmentY(0.0f);
    largeButton.setAlignmentX(0.0f);
    largeButton.setAlignmentY(0.0f);
  } else if (SET_MAXIMUM.equals(command)) {
    smallButton.setAlignmentX(1.0f);
    smallButton.setAlignmentY(1.0f);
    mediumButton.setAlignmentX(1.0f);
    mediumButton.setAlignmentY(1.0f);
    largeButton.setAlignmentX(1.0f);
    largeButton.setAlignmentY(1.0f);
  } else if (SET_CENTRAL.equals(command)) {
    smallButton.setAlignmentX(0.5f);
    smallButton.setAlignmentY(0.5f);
    mediumButton.setAlignmentX(0.5f);
    mediumButton.setAlignmentY(0.5f);
    largeButton.setAlignmentX(0.5f);
    largeButton.setAlignmentY(0.5f);
  } else if (SET_MIXED.equals(command)) {
    smallButton.setAlignmentX(0.0f);
    smallButton.setAlignmentY(0.0f);
    mediumButton.setAlignmentX(0.5f);
    mediumButton.setAlignmentY(0.5f);
    largeButton.setAlignmentX(1.0f);
    largeButton.setAlignmentY(1.0f);
  } else {
    throw new IllegalArgumentException("Illegal Command: " + command);
  }
  // Redraw panel
  ((JPanel)largeButton.getParent()).revalidate();
}

public static void main(String args[]) {
```

```
ActionListener generalActionListener = new ActionListener() {
  public void actionPerformed(ActionEvent actionEvent) {
    JComponent comp = (JComponent)actionEvent.getSource();
    System.out.println (actionEvent.getActionCommand() + ": " +
comp.getBounds());
  }
};

ActionListener sizingActionListener = new ActionListener() {
  public void actionPerformed(ActionEvent actionEvent) {
    setupButtons(actionEvent.getActionCommand());
  }
};

JFrame frame = new ExitableJFrame("Overlay Example");

JPanel panel = new JPanel();
LayoutManager overlay = new OverlayLayout(panel);
panel.setLayout(overlay);

Object settings[][] = {
  {"Small", new Dimension(25, 25), Color.white},
  {"Medium", new Dimension(50, 50), Color.gray},
  {"Large", new Dimension(100, 100), Color.black}
};
JButton buttons[] = {smallButton, mediumButton, largeButton};

for (int i=0, n=settings.length; i<n; i++) {
  JButton button = buttons[i];
  button.addActionListener(generalActionListener);
  button.setActionCommand((String)settings[i][0]);
  button.setMaximumSize((Dimension)settings[i][1]);
  button.setBackground((Color)settings[i][2]);
  panel.add(button);
}

setupButtons(SET_CENTRAL);
```

```
    JPanel actionPanel = new JPanel();
    actionPanel.setBorder(BorderFactory.createTitledBorder("Change Alignment"));
    String actionSettings[] = {SET_MINIMUM, SET_MAXIMUM, SET_CENTRAL,
SET_MIXED};
      for (int i=0, n=actionSettings.length; i<n; i++) {
        JButton button = new JButton(actionSettings[i]);
        button.addActionListener(sizingActionListener);
        actionPanel.add(button);
      }

    Container contentPane = frame.getContentPane();
    contentPane.add(panel, BorderLayout.CENTER);
    contentPane.add(actionPanel, BorderLayout.SOUTH);

    frame.setSize(400, 300);
    frame.setVisible(true);
  }
}
```

Class SizeRequirements

The BoxLayout and OverlayLayout managers rely on the SizeRequirements class to determine the exact positions of the contained components. The class contains various static methods to assist in the calculations necessary to position components in either an aligned or a tiled manner. The layout managers use this class to calculate their components' x coordinates and width and y coordinates and height. Each pair is calculated separately. If the layout manager needs both sets of attributes for positioning, the layout manager asks the SizeRequirements class separately for each.

Class ScrollPaneLayout

The ScrollPaneLayout manager is used by the JScrollPane class, a container class to be described in Chapter 11. Trying to use the layout manager outside JScrollPane isn't possible because the layout manager checks to see if the container object associated with the layout manager is an instance of JScrollPane.

Because the ScrollPaneLayout manager isn't available for usage outside a JScrollPane, Chapter 11 gives you a complete description of the layout manager (and the ScrollPaneConstants interface) in the context of the JScrollPane.

Class ViewportLayout

The ViewportLayout manager is used by the JViewport class, a container class (to be described in Chapter 11). The JViewport is also used within the ScrollPaneLayout/JScrollPane combination. Like ScrollPaneLayout, the ViewportLayout manager is closely tied to its component, JViewport in this case, and isn't usable outside the component, except in a subclass. In addition, rarely is the JViewport class used outside a JScrollPane.

Like the ScrollPaneLayout manager, the ViewportLayout manager will be discussed in the context of its container in Chapter 11, this time with JViewport.

Summary

This chapter introduced Swing's predefined layout managers BoxLayout, OverlayLayout, ScrollPaneLayout, and ViewportLayout. We saw how the various alignment settings affect the components within a container whenever you use a layout manager such as BoxLayout or OverlayLayout. In addition, I introduced the SizeRequirements class, a class used internally by BoxLayout and OverlayLayout.

In Chapter 11, we'll look at the Swing containers, JScrollPane and JViewport, that use the ScrollPaneLayout and ViewportLayout managers, plus several other of the more sophisticated Swing container classes.

CHAPTER 11

Advanced Swing Containers

CHAPTER 10 EXPLORED THE LAYOUT MANAGERS available within the Swing component set. In this chapter, we'll look at some of the containers that rely on these layout managers, and others that work without a layout manager.

Starting with the Box class, you'll discover the best way to use the BoxLayout manager to create a single row or column of components. Next, I cover the JSplitPane container, which is a bit like a specialized Box with just two components inside. The JSplitPane provides a splitter bar that acts as a divider you can drag to resize the components to suit your needs.

Then, we'll explore the JTabbedPane container, which works something like a container whose layout manager is a CardLayout, except with tabs built into the container that allow you to move from card to card. You'll be able to create multiple-screen, property-sheet dialog boxes for user input with JTabbedPane.

The last two advanced Swing containers covered are the JScrollPane and JViewport. Both of these components offer the ability to display a section of a large component within a limited amount of screen real estate. The JScrollPane adds scrollbars to a display area so that you can move around a large component that sits within a small area. In fact, the JScrollPane uses the JViewport to "clip away" the part of the larger component that shouldn't be seen.

So, let's get started and look at the first container, class Box.

Class Box

The Box class is a special Java Container for creating a single row or column of components with the help of the BoxLayout manager. The Box container works like a Panel (or JPanel), but has a different default layout manager, BoxLayout. Using BoxLayout can be a little cumbersome without a Box, which simplifies working with BoxLayout. You can associate the BoxLayout manager with a container in just three steps: manually creating the container, creating the layout manager, and associating the manager with the container. When you create an instance of Box, you perform the three steps at once. In addition, you can use an inner class of Box called Box.Filler to better position components within the container. Figure 11-1 shows these relationships of the Box class.

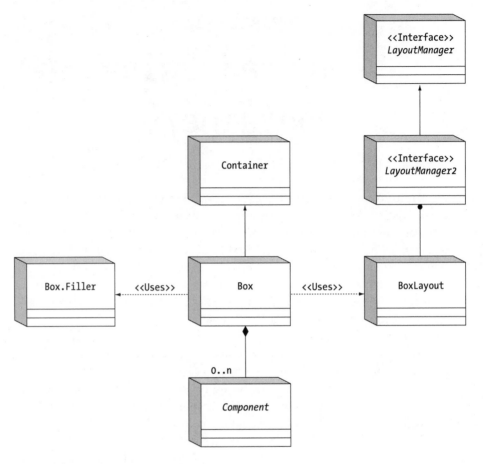

Figure 11-1: Box relationship diagram

Creating a Box

You have three ways to create a Box: one constructor and two static factory methods. The less frequently used constructor requires a direction for the main axis of the layout manager. The direction is specified by either of two BoxLayout constants, X_AXIS or Y_AXIS, to create a horizontal or vertical box, respectively. Instead of manually specifying the direction, simply create a Box with the desired orientation by using one of the factory methods that's been provided: createHorizontalBox() or createVerticalBox().

1. ```
   public Box(int direction)
   Box horizontalBox = new Box(BoxLayout.X_AXIS);
   Box verticalBox   = new Box(BoxLayout.Y_AXIS);
   ```
   ```

2. `public static Box createHorizontalBox()`
    `Box horizontalBox = Box.createHorizontalBox();`

3. `public static Box createVerticalBox()`
    `Box verticalBox   = Box.createVerticalBox();`

NOTE   *The Box class is not a JavaBean. Box lacks a no-argument constructor.*

Filling a horizontal and vertical Box with a JLabel, a JTextField, and a JButton demonstrates the flexibility of BoxLayout, as shown in Figure 11-2.

For the horizontal container, the label and button are at their preferred widths because their maximum size is the same as their preferred size. The text field uses up the remaining space. In the vertical container, the label and button heights are their preferred size, too, because their maximum size is still the same as their preferred size. As far as the text field goes, its height is the maximum container height.

For the vertical container, the label and button act the same way, but the width of the text field fills the height that the label and button don't use. In terms of its width, the text field is as wide as the container.

The source code for creating the screens shown in Figure 11-2 follows.

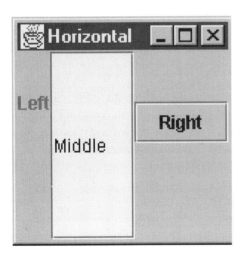 

Figure 11-2: A horizontal and a vertical box

```
import javax.swing.*;
import java.awt.*;

public class BoxSample {
  public static void main(String args[]) {
    JFrame verticalFrame = new ExitableJFrame("Vertical");
    Box verticalBox = Box.createVerticalBox();
    verticalBox.add(new JLabel("Top"));
    verticalBox.add(new JTextField("Middle"));
    verticalBox.add(new JButton("Bottom"));
    verticalFrame.getContentPane().add(verticalBox, BorderLayout.CENTER);
    verticalFrame.setSize(150, 150);
    verticalFrame.setVisible(true);

    JFrame horizontalFrame = new ExitableJFrame("Horizontal");
    Box horizontalBox = Box.createHorizontalBox();
    horizontalBox.add(new JLabel("Left"));
    horizontalBox.add(new JTextField("Middle"));
    horizontalBox.add(new JButton("Right"));
    horizontalFrame.getContentPane().add(horizontalBox, BorderLayout.CENTER);
    horizontalFrame.setSize(150, 150);
    horizontalFrame.setVisible(true);
  }
}
```

Box Properties

As Table 11-1 shows, there are only two Box properties. Although the layout property inherits a setLayout(LayoutManager) method from its parent Container class, if called on a Box object the class throws an AWTError. Once the BoxLayout manager is set during its construction, it can't be changed, nor can its direction.

PROPERTY NAME	DATA TYPE	ACCESS
accessibleContext	AccessibleContext	read-only
layout	LayoutManager	write-only

Table 11-1: Box properties

Working with Box.Filler

The Box class has an inner class Box.Filler to help you create invisible components for better component positioning within a container whose layout manager is BoxLayout. By directly manipulating the minimum, maximum, and preferred size of the created component, you can create components that grow to fill unused space or remain a fixed size, making screens more aesthetically pleasing to your users.

Instead of directly using the Box.Filler class, several static methods of the Box class can help you create the appropriate filler components. The factory methods allow you to categorize these components by type, instead of by minimum, maximum, or preferred size. We'll look at these methods in the next two sections.

If you're interested in this class definition, it's shown next. Like the Box class, Box.Filler isn't a JavaBean.

```
public class Box.Filler extends Component implements Accessible {
   public Filler(Dimension minSize, Dimension prefSize, Dimension maxSize);
   public void changeShape(Dimension minSize, Dimension prefSize, Dimension
maxSize);
   public AccessibleContext getAccessibleContext();
   public Dimension getMaximumSize();
   public Dimension getMinimumSize();
   public Dimension getPreferredSize();
}
```

Creating Areas That Grow

If a component has a dimensionless minimum and preferred size, and a maximum size bigger than the screen, the component will grow to take up unused space between components in the container along one or both axes. In the case of a Box, or more precisely a container whose layout manager is BoxLayout, the growth occurs along the layout manager's initially chosen direction (either BoxLayout.X_AXIS or BoxLayout.Y_AXIS). For a horizontal box, the growth affects the component's width. For a vertical box, the growth would be relected in the component's height. The name commonly given to this type of growing component is *glue*. The two flavors of glue are *direction-independent* glue and *direction-dependent glue*. The following factory methods of Box are used to create the glue components:

1.  ```
    public static Component createGlue()
    // Direction independent
    Component glue = Box.createGlue();
    aBox.add(glue);
    ```
    ```

2.  ```
    public static Component createHorizontalGlue();
    // Direction dependent: horizontal
    Component horizontalGlue = Box.createHorizontalGlue();
    aBox.add(horizontalGlue);
    ```

3.  ```
    public static Component createVerticalGlue()
    // Direction dependent: vertical
    Component verticalGlue  = Box.createVerticalGlue();
    aBox.add(verticalGlue);
    ```

> **NOTE** *You aren't limited to using these components within a* Box *or container with a layout manager of* BoxLayout. *You can use them anywhere you want to place invisible components.*

Once you create glue, you add it to a container like any other component by using Container.add(Component). Glue allows you to align components within a container, as Figure 11-3 shows.

You can add glue components to any container whose layout manager honors minimum, maximum, and preferred size properties of a component, such as BoxLayout. For instance, Figure 11-4 demonstrates what happens when you add a glue component to a JMenuBar right before adding the last JMenu. Because the layout manager for a JMenuBar is BoxLayout, this action pushes the last menu to the right edge of the menu bar, similar to the Motif/CDE style of help menus.

> **WARNING** *I recommend that you avoid using the capability described here to set up help menus on menu bars. Eventually, the* public void setHelpMenu(JMenu menu) *of* JMenuBar *will be implemented and won't throw an* Error.

Creating Rigid Areas

Because a glue component grows to fill the available space, if you want to have a fixed distance between components you need to create a rigid component, or *strut*. When doing so, you specify the strut's size. Struts can be two-dimensional, requiring you to specify the width *and* height of the component; or, they can be one-dimensional, requiring you to specify either width *or* height.

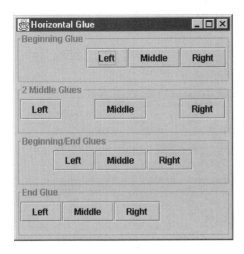

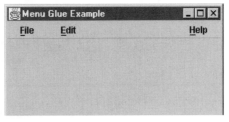

Figure 11-4: Using glue in a JMenuBar

Figure 11-3: Using glue in a Box

1. ```
   public static Component createRigidArea(Dimension dimension)
   // Two dimensional
   Component rigidArea = Box. createRigidArea(new Dimension(10, 10));
   aBox.add(rigidArea);
   ```

2. ```
   public static Component createHorizontalStrut(int width)
   // One-dimensional: horizontal
   Component horizontalStrut = Box. createHorizontalStrut(10);
   aBox.add(horizontalStrut);
   ```

3. ```
   public static Component createVerticalStrut(int height)
   // One-dimensional: vertical
   Component verticalStrut   = Box. createVerticalStrut(10);
   aBox.add(verticalStrut);
   ```

> **NOTE** *Although direction-independent glue created with* createGlue() *shows no side effects if you change container direction, creating a rigid area may cause layout problems if the axis is later changed. That's because the component has a dimension-less minimum size. Using* createRigidArea() *isn't recommended, unless you truly want a two-dimensional empty component. Besides the potential for problems if the box axis were to change, you need to create an extra object, a* Dimension, *when creating a rigid area.*
   ```

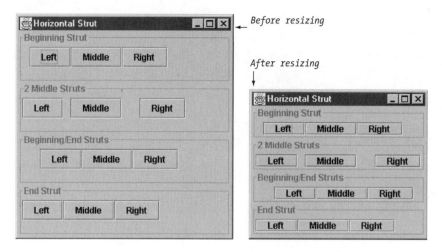

Figure 11-5: Using struts in a box

Figure 11-5 demonstrates several struts in action. Notice that you can have varying strut distances between different components, and struts at the end of a container may have no effect. After a user resizes a screen, the strut distance between components remains fixed, as the right-hand screen in Figure 11-5 shows.

Class JSplitPane

Similar to the Box, the JSplitPane container allows you to display components in a single row or column. Whereas a Box can contain any number of components, a JSplitPane is meant to display two — and only two — components. The components are of variable size and separated by a movable divider. The divider is specially constructed in that it can be grabbed by the end user and dragged to adjust the size of the contained components. The various parts of Figure 11-6 demonstrate both vertical and horizontal split panes, shown before and after moving the divider.

Creating a JSplitPane

There are five constructors for JSplitPane. With them, you can initialize the orientation of the contained component pair, set the continuousLayout property, or initialize the pair of components for the container. Unless otherwise specified, the orientation is horizontal. Orientation can be specified by either of the JSplitPane constants VERTICAL_SPLIT or HORIZONTAL_SPLIT. The continuousLayout property setting determines how the split pane reacts when the user drags the

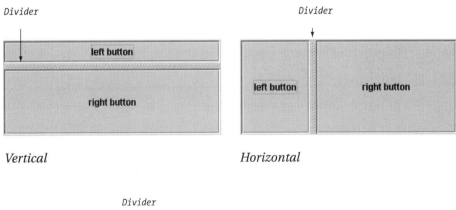

Figure 11-6: Examples of JSplitPane containers

divider. When the setting is false, the property's initial setting, only the divider is redrawn when dragged. When true, the JSplitPane resizes and redraws the components to each side of the divider as the user drags the divider.

If you're using the no-argument constructor, the initial set of components within the split pane is made up of buttons (two JButton components). Two other constructors explicitly set the initial two components. Surprisingly, the remaining two constructors provide no components by default within the container. To add or change the components within the JSplitPane, see the "Changing JSplitPane Components" section that's coming up.

1. public JSplitPane()
    ```
    JSplitPane splitPane = new JSplitPane();
    ```

2. public JSplitPane(int newOrientation)
    ```
    JSplitPane splitPane = new JSplitPane(JSplitPane.VERTICAL_SPLIT);
    ```

3. public JSplitPane(int newOrientation, boolean newContinuousLayout)
    ```
    JSplitPane splitPane = new JSplitPane(JSplitPane.VERTICAL_SPLIT, true);
    ```

4.  ```
    public JSplitPane(int newOrientation, Component newLeftComponent,
    Component newRightComponent)
    JComponent topComponent = new JButton("Top Button");
    JComponent bottomComponent = new JButton("Bottom Button");
    JSplitPane splitPane = new JSplitPane(JSplitPane.VERTICAL_SPLIT,
    topComponent, bottomComponent);
    ```

> **NOTE** *If the orientation is* `JSplitPane.VERTICAL_SPLIT`, *you can think of the top component as the left component and the bottom component as the right component.*

5.  ```
    public JSplitPane(int newOrientation, boolean newContinuousLayout,
    Component newLeftComponent, Component newRightComponent)
    JSplitPane splitPane = new JSplitPane(JSplitPane.VERTICAL_SPLIT, true,
    topComponent, bottomComponent);
    ```

JSplitPane Properties

Table 11-2 shows the 15 properties of `JSplitPane`.

PROPERTY NAME	DATA TYPE	ACCESS
accessibleContext	AccessibleContext	read-only
bottomComponent	Component	read-write
continuousLayout	boolean	read-write bound
dividerLocation	double	write-only
dividerLocation	int	read-write
dividerSize	int	read-write bound
lastDividerLocation	int	read-write bound
leftComponent	Component	read-write
maximumDividerLocation	int	read-only
minimumDividerLocation	int	read-only
oneTouchExpandable	boolean	read-write bound
orientation	int	read-write bound
rightComponent	Component	read-write
topComponent	Component	read-write
UI	SplitPaneUI	read-write
UIClassID	String	read-only

Table 11-2: JSplitPane properties

Setting Orientation

Besides initializing the orientation within the constructor, you can change the
JSplitPane orientation by changing the orientation property setting to either
JSplitPane.VERTICAL_SPLIT or JSplitPane.HORIZONTAL_SPLIT. If you try to change
the property to a nonequivalent setting, an IllegalArgumentException is thrown.

Dynamically changing the orientation at runtime is *not* recommended
because it can confuse a user. However, if you're using a visual development tool,
you can explicitly set the orientation after creating the JSplitPane with this
method. When not programming visually, you'd normally initialize the orientation when you create the JSplitPane.

Changing JSplitPane Components

There are four read-write properties for the different positions of a component
within a JSplitPane: bottomComponent, leftComponent, rightComponent, and
topComponent. In reality, these four properties represent two components internally: The left and top components are one; the right and bottom components
represent the other. You should use the properties that are appropriate for the
orientation of your JSplitPane. Everything will still work properly if, for instance,
you add a left component to a vertical JSplitPane, replacing the top component.
Using the inappropriate property methods can make life hell for the maintenance
programmer. Imagine, after creating a user interface, seeing something like the
following code six months later:

```
JComponent leftButton = new JButton("Left");
JComponent rightButton = new JButton("Right");
JSplitPane splitPane = new JSplitPane(JSplitPane.VERTICAL_SPLIT);
splitPane.setLeftComponent(leftButton);
splitPane.setRightComponent(rightButton);
```

If you glance at the source, you might think that the screen
will contain a button to the left and one to the right based
on the variable names and the set*XXX*Component() methods
used. But because the instantiated JSplitPane has a vertical
orientation, the interface that's created looks like Figure 11-
7. The variable names are used because of the button labels,
and not their position.

The code is more understandable if the setTopComponent()
and setBottomComponent() methods are used:

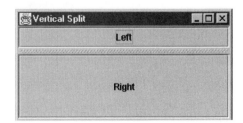

*Figure 11-7: Adding left/right buttons
to a vertical JSplitPane*

```
JComponent topButton = new JButton("Left");
JComponent bottomButton = new JButton("Right");
JSplitPane splitPane = new JSplitPane(JSplitPane.VERTICAL_SPLIT);
splitPane.setTopComponent(topButton);
splitPane.setBottomComponent(bottomButton);
```

Moving the JSplitPane Divider

Initially, the divider is shown below or to the right of the preferred size of the top/left component. At any time, you can reset the divider position to that position by calling the `public void resetToPreferredSizes()` method of `JSplitPane`. If you want to programmatically position the divider, you can change the `dividerLocation` property with `setDividerLocation(newLocation)`. This property can be changed to an `int` position, representing an absolute distance from the top/left side, or it can be set to a `double` value between 0.0 and 1.0 representing a percentage of the `JSplitPane` container width.

> **WARNING** *Changing the property setting to a double value outside the range of 0.0 and 1.0 results in an IllegalArgumentException being thrown.*

Although you can set the `dividerLocation` property with a `double` value, you only get an integer indicating its absolute position.

> **TIP** *With the predefined look and feel classes (Windows, Motif, Metal, and Macintosh), pressing the F8 key allows you to move the divider with keyboard keys such as HOME, END, or the arrows. F8 isn't a modifier like SHIFT or ALT. Instead, pressing F8 moves the focus to the divider so that it can be moved with keystrokes.*

Resizing Components and Working with a One-Touch Expandable Divider

Limitations exist on the resizing of components within the `JSplitPane`. The `JSplitPane` honors the minimum size of each contained component. If grabbing and moving the divider line will cause a component to shrink to less than its minimum size, the scroll pane won't let the user drag the divider past that minimum size.

NOTE *You can always programmatically position the divider to be any-where, even if it makes a component smaller than its minimum size. However, this isn't a good idea because the component has a minimum size for a good reason.*

If the minimum dimensions of a component are too large for a JSplitPane, you need to change the component's minimum size so that the divider can use some of that component's space. For AWT components, changing the minimum size of a standard component requires subclassing. With Swing components, you can simply call the setMinimumSize() method of JComponent with a new Dimension. Nevertheless, minimum sizes are set for a reason. The component probably won't look right if you reduce its minimum size.

A better approach is available for allowing one component to take up more space than another: Set the oneTouchExpandable property of the JSplitPane to true. When true, an icon is added to the divider, allowing a user to completely collapse one of the two components to give the other component the entire area. In the example here, the icon is a combination up-and-down arrow.

Figure 11-8 shows how this icon might appear (as rendered by the Metal look and feel) and illustrates what happens after selecting the up arrow on the divider to expand the lower component to its fullest size. Clicking again on the icon on the divider returns the components to their previous positions. Clicking on the divider somewhere other than on the icon will position the divider in such a way that the collapsed component is at its preferred size.

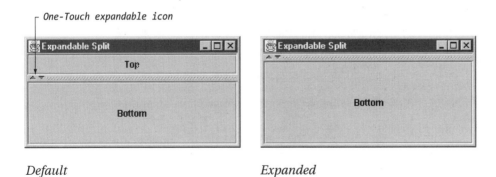

Default   *Expanded*

Figure 11-8: Setting and using the One-Touch Expandable option

> **NOTE** *There's no easy way to alter the icon or change how the divider is rendered. Both are defined by the* BasicSplitPaneDivider *subclass and created in the* public BasicSplitPaneDivider createDefaultDivider() *method of the* BasicSplitPaneUI *subclass for the specific look and feel.*

The lastDividerLocation property allows you or the system to inquire about the previous divider location. The JSplitPane uses this property when the user selects the maximizer icon to undo the minimization of one of the components in the JSplitPane.

> **WARNING** *Beware of components that base their minimum size on the container size or their initial size! Placing them in a* JSplitPane *may require you to manually set the minimum and/or preferred size of the components. The components that most frequently cause problems when used within a* JSplitPane *are* JTextArea *and* JScrollPane.

Listening for JSplitPane Property Changes

The JSplitPane class defines several constants to help with listening for bound property changes. These constants are listed in Table 11-3.

PROPERTY_CHANGE_CONSTANT
CONTINUOUS_LAYOUT_PROPERTY
DIVIDER_SIZE_PROPERTY
LAST_DIVIDER_LOCATION_PROPERTY
ONE_TOUCH_EXPANDABLE_PROPERTY
ORIENTATION_PROPERTY

Table 11-3: JSplitPane PropertyChangeListener support constants

One way of listening for when the user moves the divider is to watch for changes to the lastDividerLocation property. The following example attaches a PropertyChangeListener to a JSplitPane displaying the current divider location, and the current last location, and the previous last location. The component above and below the divider is the OvalPanel class (defined in Chapter 4), drawn to fill the dimensions of the component. This component helps to demonstrate the effect of having the continuousLayout property set to true.

```java
import javax.swing.*;
import java.awt.*;
import java.beans.*;

public class PropertySplit {
  public static void main(String args[]) {
    JFrame frame = new ExitableJFrame("Property Split");

    // Create/configure split pane
    JSplitPane splitPane = new JSplitPane(JSplitPane.VERTICAL_SPLIT);
    splitPane.setContinuousLayout(true);
    splitPane.setOneTouchExpandable(true);

    // Create top component
    JComponent topComponent = new OvalPanel();
    splitPane.setTopComponent(topComponent);

    // Create bottom component
    JComponent bottomComponent = new OvalPanel();
    splitPane.setBottomComponent(bottomComponent);

    // Create PropertyChangeListener
    PropertyChangeListener propertyChangeListener = new PropertyChangeListener()
{
      public void propertyChange (PropertyChangeEvent changeEvent) {
        JSplitPane sourceSplitPane = (JSplitPane)changeEvent.getSource();
        String propertyName = changeEvent.getPropertyName();
        if (propertyName.equals(JSplitPane.LAST_DIVIDER_LOCATION_PROPERTY)) {
          int current = sourceSplitPane.getDividerLocation();
          System.out.println ("Current: " + current);
          Integer last = (Integer)changeEvent.getNewValue();
          System.out.println ("Last: " + last);
          Integer priorLast = (Integer)changeEvent.getOldValue();
          System.out.println ("Prior last: " + priorLast);
        }
      }
    };

    // Attach listener
    splitPane.addPropertyChangeListener(propertyChangeListener);
```

```
        Container contentPane = frame.getContentPane();
        contentPane.add(splitPane, BorderLayout.CENTER);
        frame.setSize(300, 150);
        frame.setVisible(true);
    }
}
```

As the following sample output demonstrates, when you run the previous program, you'll notice that the lastDividerLocation property changes to reflect the divider's being dragged. When the user stops dragging the divider, the last setting is set to the initial last value (prior current value) when the drag started, and *not* to the prior setting for the dividerLocation property. As the divider is being dragged, the current value travels first to the last value and then to the prior last value. When the dragging stops, the final last setting (29 in this case) is set to the initial last setting to reflect the current value when the dragging started. The first current setting (31) is the new current setting after the divider is initially dragged (away from 29).

```
Current: 31
Last: 29
Prior last: 0
Current: 33
Last: 31
Prior last: 29
Current: 80
Last: 33
Prior last: 31
Current: 86
Last: 80
Prior last: 33
Current: 86
Last: 29
Prior last: 80
```

> **NOTE** *The BOTTOM, DIVIDER, LEFT, RIGHT, and TOP constants of the JSplitPane class aren't for PropertyChangeListener support. Instead, they're internal constraints used by the add(Component component, Object constraints) method.*

Customizing a JSplitPane Look and Feel

Each installable Swing look and feel provides a different JSplitPane appearance and set of default UIResource values for this component. Figure 11-9 shows the appearance of the JSplitPane container for the preinstalled set of look and feels: Motif, Windows, Metal, and Macintosh.

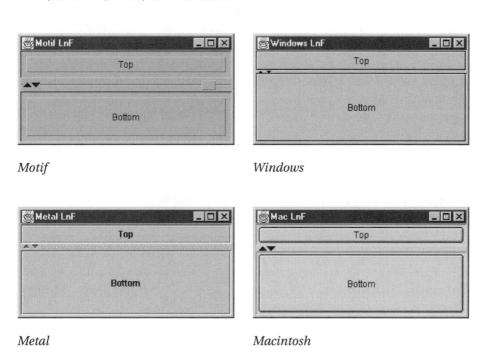

Motif *Windows*

Metal *Macintosh*

Figure 11-9: JSplitPane under the different look and feels

The available set of UIResource-related properties for a JSplitPane is shown in Table 11-4. For the JSplitPane component, there are seven different properties.

PROPERTY STRING	OBJECT TYPE
SplitPane.activeThumb	Color
SplitPane.background	Color
SplitPane.border	Border
SplitPane.dividerSize	Integer
SplitPane.highlight	Color
SplitPane.shadow	Color
SplitPaneUI	SplitPaneUI

Table 11-4: JSplitPane UIResource elements

> **NOTE** *Properties such as border, background, and shadow affect the divider's appearance, in addition to that of the JSplitPane.*

Class JTabbedPane

The JTabbedPane class represents the ever-popular *property sheet* to support input or output from multiple panels within a single window in which only one panel is shown at a time. Using JTabbedPane is like using the CardLayout manager from the core AWT classes, except with added support for changing cards built in. Whereas CardLayout is a LayoutManager, JTabbedPane is a full-fledged Container. In case you're not familiar with property sheets, tabbed dialog boxes, or tabbed panes (all alternate names for the same thing), Figure 11-10 shows a set of tabs, from the SwingSet demo that comes with the Swing classes.

> **TIP** *To get your hands on a tabbed panel for use with CardLayout for JDK 1.1, check out the Tab Splitter created by Scott Stanchfield, available at http://www.jguru.com/Bits/MSC/tabsplitter/tabsplitter.html.*

To help the JTabbedPane manage which Component (tab) is selected, the model for the container is an implementation of the SingleSelectionModel interface or, more precisely, a DefaultSingleSelectionModel instance. (SingleSelectionModel and DefaultSingleSelectionModel were described with the menuing classes in

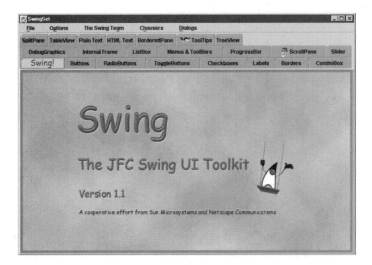

Figure 11-10: Sample JTabbedPane screen

Chapter 6.) Figure 11-11 shows how JTabbedPane **aggregates** Component objects as well as the other relationships to the JTabbedPane **class.**

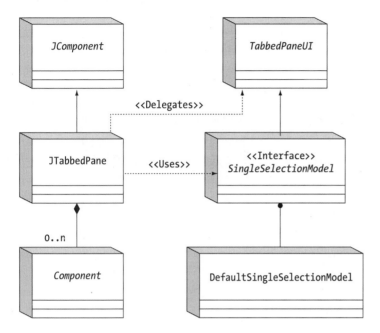

Figure 11-11: JTabbedPane UML relationship diagram

Creating a JTabbedPane

There are only two constructors for the JTabbedPane. The sole configurable option is the placement of the tabs used to change which component to display. By default, tabs are at the top of the container. However, you can explicitly specify a location with one of the following constants of JTabbedPane: TOP, BOTTOM, LEFT, or RIGHT. Figure 11-12 shows the screen from Figure 11-10 with the other three tab placements.

1. ```
   public JTabbedPane()
   JTabbedPane tabbedPane = new JTabbedPane();
   ```

2. ```
   public JTabbedPane(int tabPlacement)
   JTabbedPane tabbedPane = new JTabbedPane(JTabbedPane.RIGHT);
   ```

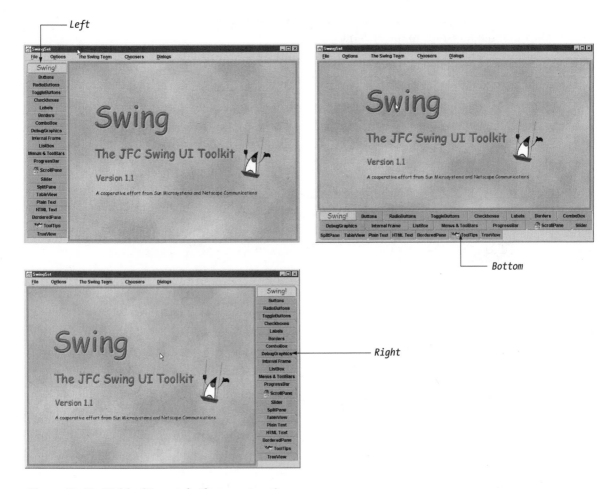

Figure 11-12: JTabbedPane tab placement options

> **WARNING** Setting the tab placement to something other than the equivalent values for the JTabbedPane constants of TOP, BOTTOM, LEFT, or RIGHT will cause an IllegalArgumentException to be thrown.

Adding and Removing Tabs

Once you've created the basic JTabbedPane container, you need to add panels that make up the sheets or pages of the JTabbedPane. You can add panels in either one of two basic ways.

If you're visually creating your interface with a tool like JBuilder or Visual Café, the user interface builder will use the familiar add() methods of Container to add a Component as a panel. You shouldn't use the various add() methods if you're programming by hand.

The more appropriate way to add components on panel to create tabs is with any of the addTab() or insertTab() methods listed next. Any or all of the arguments, besides the position index of insertTab(), can be null. If you don't provide the panel title, the JTabbedPane uses a default title of component.getName(). The displayed icon and tooltip settings have no default values. Providing a null component argument is relatively useless, but will add a panel with no component on it. If a user then selects the tab for the panel with the null component, the component for the previously selected panel remains visible while the selected tab changes.

- public void addTab(String title, Component component)

- public void addTab(String title, Icon icon, Component component)

- public void addTab(String title, Icon icon, Component component, String tip)

- public void insertTab(String title, Icon icon, Component component, String tip, int index)

When using addTab(), the tab is added to the end, which is the farthest right position for a set of top or bottom tabs, or at the very bottom for tabs positioned on the left or right side.

After creating a panel, you can change its title, icon, or component (but not its tooltip) on a particular tab with one of the set*XXX*At() methods:

- public void setTitleAt(int index, String title)

- public void setIconAt(int index, Icon icon)

- public void setComponentAt(int index, Component component)

In addition, you can change the background or foreground of a specific tab, enable/disable a specific tab, or have a different disabled icon with additional set*XXX*At() methods:

- `public void setBackgroundAt(int index, Color background)`

- `public void setForegroundAt(int index, Color foreground)`

- `public void setEnabledAt(int index, boolean enabled)`

- `public void setDisabledIconAt(int index, Icon disabledIcon)`

To remove a tab, you can remove a specific tab with `public void removeTabAt(int index)` or `public void remove(Component component)`. In addition, you can remove all tabs with `public void removeAll()`.

> **WARNING** *Make sure that components added to a JTabbedPane are opaque. If components are transparent, when the selected tab is changed the old selection won't be erased. Although this might sound good for doing something like creating overlays on a map, if part of the container display becomes corrupted, only the component on the selected tab is redrawn when the JTabbedPane is redrawn.*

JTabbedPane Properties

Table 11-5 shows the nine properties of `JTabbedPane`.

PROPERTY NAME	DATA TYPE	ACCESS
accessibleContext	AccessibleContext	read-only
model	SingleSelectionModel	read-write bound
selectedComponent	Component	read-write
selectedIndex	int	read-write
tabCount	int	read-only
tabPlacement	int	read-write bound
tabRunCount	int	read-only
UI	TabbedPaneUI	read-write bound
UIClassID	String	read-only

Table 11-5: JTabbedPane properties

You can programmatically change the displayed tab by setting either the `selectedComponent` or the `selectedIndex` property.

The `tabRunCount` property represents the number of rows (for top/bottom tab placement) or columns (for right/left placement) necessary to display all the tabs.

> **WARNING** *Changing the LayoutManager for the JTabbedPane will throw a ClassCastException when it comes time to display the container. In other words, don't do it.*

Listening for Changing Tab Selection

If you're interested in finding out when the selected tab changes, you need to listen for changes to the selection model. This is done by your attaching a ChangeListener to the JTabbedPane (or directly to the SingleSelectionModel). The registered ChangeListener reports when the selection model changes if the model changes when the selected panel changes.

The following program demonstrates listening for changes to the selected tab and displays the title of the newly selected tab.

```
import javax.swing.*;
import javax.swing.event.*;
import java.awt.*;

public class TabSample {
  static Color colors[] = {Color.red, Color.orange, Color.yellow, Color.green,
Color.blue,

Color.magenta};
  static void add(JTabbedPane tabbedPane, String label) {
    int count = tabbedPane.getTabCount();
    JButton button = new JButton(label);
    button.setBackground(colors[count]);
    tabbedPane.addTab(label, new DiamondIcon(colors[count]), button, label);
  }

  public static void main(String args[]) {
    JFrame frame = new ExitableJFrame("Tabbed Pane Sample");
    JTabbedPane tabbedPane = new JTabbedPane();
    String titles[] = {"General", "Security", "Content", "Connection",
"Programs",

"Advanced"};
    for (int i=0, n=titles.length; i<n; i++) {
      add(tabbedPane, titles[i]);
    }
```

```
        ChangeListener changeListener = new ChangeListener() {
          public void stateChanged(ChangeEvent changeEvent) {
            JTabbedPane sourceTabbedPane = (JTabbedPane)changeEvent.getSource();
            int index = sourceTabbedPane.getSelectedIndex();
            System.out.println ("Tab changed to: " +
sourceTabbedPane.getTitleAt(index));
          }
        };
        tabbedPane.addChangeListener(changeListener);

        Container contentPane = frame.getContentPane();
        contentPane.add(tabbedPane, BorderLayout.CENTER);
        frame.setSize(400, 150);
        frame.setVisible(true);
    }
}
```

Customizing a JTabbedPane Look and Feel

Each installable Swing look and feel provides a different JTabbedPane appearance
and set of default UIResource values for the JTabbedPane component. Figure 11-13
shows the appearance of the JTabbedPane container for the preinstalled set of look
and feels: Motif, Windows, Metal, and Macintosh. Specific to the look and feel is
how it responds when the set of available tabs is too wide for the display. Also specific to the look and feel is how it responds when a user selects a tab in a back row.

Motif

Windows

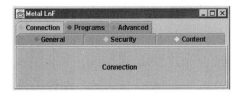

Metal

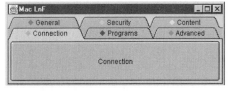

Macintosh

Figure 11-13: JTabbedPane under the different look and feels

The available set of UIResource-related properties for a JTabbedPane is shown in Table 11-6. For the JTabbedPane component, there are 22 different properties.

PROPERTY STRING	OBJECT TYPE
TabbedPane.background	Color
TabbedPane.contentBorderInsets	Insets
TabbedPane.darkShadow	Color
TabbedPane.focus	Color
TabbedPane.font	Font
TabbedPane.foreground	Color
TabbedPane.highlight	Color
TabbedPane.lightHighlight	Color
TabbedPane.selected	Color
TabbedPane.selectedTabPadInsets	Insets
TabbedPane.selectHighlight	Color
TabbedPane.shadow	Color
TabbedPane.tabAreaBackground	Color
TabbedPane.tabAreaInsets	Insets
TabbedPane.tabInsets	Insets
TabbedPane.tabRunOverlay	Integer
TabbedPane.textIconGap	Integer
TabbedPane.unselectedTabBackground	Color
TabbedPane.unselectedTabForeground	Color
TabbedPane.unselectedTabHighlight	Color
TabbedPane.unselectedTabShadow	Color
TabbedPaneUI	TabbedPaneUI

Table 11-6: JTabbedPane UIResource elements

Class JScrollPane

Swing's JScrollPane container is a direct replacement for AWT's ScrollPane component. They both provide for the display of a large component within a smaller display area, with scrolling support (if necessary) to get to the invisible parts. Figure 11-14 shows one such implementation, in which the large component is a JLabel with an ImageIcon on it.

Although one is a replacement for the other, several differences between the two components are worth noting. With AWT's ScrollPane component, you create the container and add the component to be scrolled directly to the container. By contrast, instead of adding the component to be scrolled directly to the JScrollPane container, you add the component to another component, a JViewport, within the scroll pane.

Figure 11-14: JScrollPane example

```
// AWT
Canvas canvas = new ImageCanvas("dog.jpg"); // fictitious custom class
ScrollPane scrollPane = new ScrollPane();
scrollPane.add(canvas);
//Swing
Icon icon = new ImageIcon("dog.jpg");
JLabel label = new JLabel(icon);
JScrollPane jScrollPane = new JScrollPane();
jScrollPane.setViewportView(label);
// or
JScrollPane jScrollPane2 = new JScrollPane(label);
```

Once you've added the component into the JScrollPane, you can use the scrollbars to see the parts of the large component that aren't visible within the inner area of the JScrollPane.

In addition to giving you the means to set the scrollable component for the JScrollPane, the other difference between a ScrollPane and JScrollPane has to do with the scrollbar display policy. The display policy determines if and when scrollbars are shown around the JScrollPane. With the AWT ScrollPane, the display policy was configurable, but you had to set the policy for both scrollbars to the same setting. By contrast, Swing's JScrollPane maintains separate policies for the horizontal and vertical scrollbars.

Besides enabling you to add the JViewport and two JScrollBar components for scrolling, the JScrollPane allows you to provide two more JViewport objects for row and column headers and four Component objects to display in the scroll pane corners. The placement of all these components is managed by the ScrollPaneLayout manager, introduced in Chapter 10 and described more fully here. The actual JScrollBar components used by JScrollPane are a subclass of JScrollBar called JScrollPane.ScrollBar. They're used instead of the regular JScrollBar to properly handle scrolling the component inside the inner

JViewport, when that component implements the Scrollable interface. Figure 11-15 illustrates these relationships.

To help you see how all the components fit within the JScrollPane, Figure 11-16 demonstrates how the ScrollPaneLayout positions the various pieces.

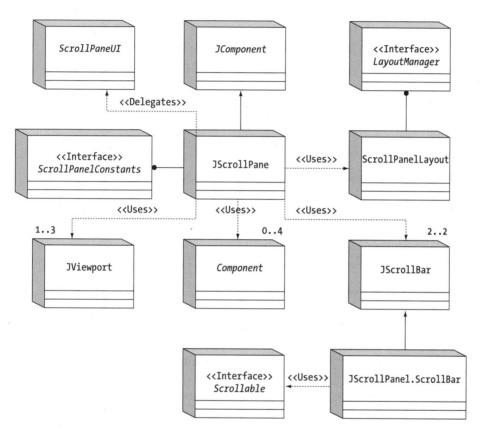

Figure 11-15: JScrollPane UML relationship diagram

Creating a JScrollPane

There are four JScrollPane constructors. They offer the options of preinstalling a component to scroll and configuring the scrolling policies of the individual scrollbars. By default, the scrollbars are shown only when needed. Table 11-7 shows the JScrollPane constants used to explicitly set the policies for each scrollbar. Using any other setting results in an IllegalArgumentException being thrown.

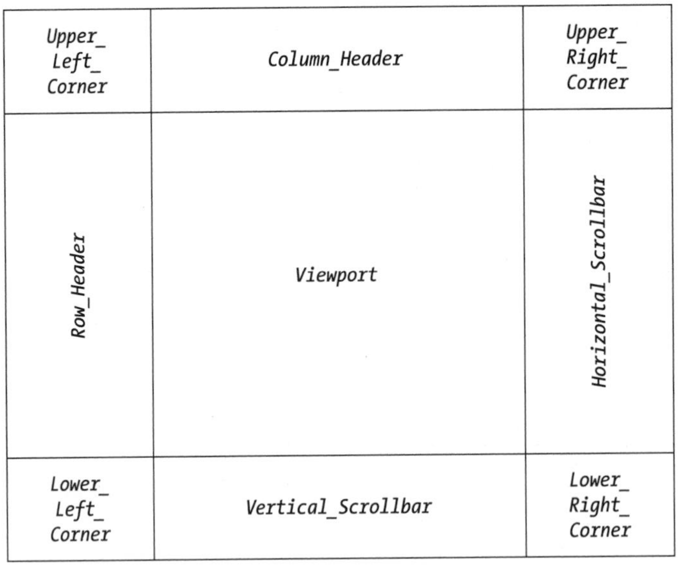

Upper_ Left_ Corner	Column_Header	Upper_ Right_ Corner
Row_Header	Viewport	Horizontal_Scrollbar
Lower_ Left_ Corner	Vertical_Scrollbar	Lower_ Right_ Corner

Figure 11-16: ScrollPaneLayout regions

POLICY TYPE	DESCRIPTION
VERTICAL_SCROLLBAR_AS_NEEDED	Displays designated scrollbar if viewport is too small to display its entire contents
HORIZONTAL_SCROLLBAR_AS_NEEDED	Displays designated scrollbar if viewport is too small to display its entire contents
VERTICAL_SCROLLBAR_ALWAYS	Always displays designated scrollbar
HORIZONTAL_SCROLLBAR_ALWAYS	Always displays designated scrollbar
VERTICAL_SCROLLBAR_NEVER	Never displays designated scrollbar
HORIZONTAL_SCROLLBAR_NEVER	Never displays designated scrollbar

Table 11-7: JScrollPane Scrollbar policies

To add or change the component after creating a JScrollPane, see the next section of this chapter.

1. ```
   public JScrollPane()
   JScrollPane scrollPane = new JScrollPane();
   ```

2. ```
   public JScrollPane(Component view)
   Icon icon = new ImageIcon("largeImage.jpg");
   JLabel imageLabel = new JLabel(icon);
   JScrollPane scrollPane = new JScrollPane(imageLabel);
   ```

3. ```
   public JScrollPane(int verticalScrollBarPolicy, int
   horizontalScrollBarPolicy)
   JScrollPane scrollPane = new
   JScrollPane(JScrollPane.VERTICAL_SCROLLBAR_ALWAYS,
   JScrollPane.HORIZONTAL_SCROLLBAR_ALWAYS);
   ```

4. ```
   public JScrollPane(Component view, int verticalScrollBarPolicy, int
   horizontalScrollBarPolicy)
   JScrollPane scrollPane = new JScrollPane(imageLabel,
   JScrollPane.VERTICAL_SCROLLBAR_ALWAYS,
   JScrollPane.HORIZONTAL_SCROLLBAR_ALWAYS);
   ```

Changing the Viewport View

If you've created a JScrollPane with an associated component to scroll, you just need to add the JScrollPane to the display and it's ready to go. If, however, you didn't associate a component at creation time, or just want to change it later, there are two ways to associate a new component to scroll. First, you can directly change the component to scroll by setting the viewportView property:

```
scrollPane.setViewportView(dogLabel);
```

The other way of changing the component to scroll involves centering the JViewport within the JScrollPane and changing its view property:

```
scrollPane.getViewport().setView(dogLabel);
```

You'll learn more about JViewport components in the section "Class JViewport" later in this chapter.

Interface Scrollable

Unlike the AWT components such as List, which automatically provide a scrollable area when the choices are too numerous to display at once, Swing components JList, JTable, JTextComponent, and JTree don't automatically provide scrolling support. You must create the component, add it to a JScrollPane, and then add the scroll pane to the screen.

```
JList list = new JList(...);
JScrollPane scrollPane = new JScrollPane(list);
aFrame.add(scrollPane, BorderLayout.CENTER);
```

The reason that adding a component to a JScrollPane works is that each of the Swing components that might be too large for the screen (and require scrolling support) implements the Scrollable interface. With this interface implemented, when you move the scrollbars of the Swing component within the JScrollPane, the JScrollPane asks the Scrollable component for its sizing information to properly position the component based on the current scrollbar positions.

The only time you need to worry about the Scrollable interface is when you're creating a new component that requires scrolling support. Although we don't create a new scrollable component here, the following is the Scrollable interface definition.

```
public interface Scrollable {
  public Dimension getPreferredScrollableViewportSize();
  public boolean getScrollableTracksViewportHeight();
  public boolean getScrollableTracksViewportWidth();
  public int getScrollableBlockIncrement(Rectangle visibleRect, int orientation,
int direction);
  public int getScrollableUnitIncrement(Rectangle visibleRect, int orientation,
int direction);
}
```

If you create a custom Scrollable component and then place that component in a JScrollPane, it will respond appropriately when the scrollbars for the JScrollPane are moved.

JScrollPane Properties

Table 11-8 shows the 18 properties of JScrollPane. The 7 properties marked with an "*" directly map to properties of the ScrollPaneLayout manager used by the JScrollPane. Changing one of these properties for a JScrollPane causes its layout manager to change accordingly. In addition, an attempt to change the layout property of JScrollPane to something other than a ScrollPaneLayout instance will throw a ClassCastException at runtime because the layout manager used by a JScrollPane must be a ScrollPaneLayout.

PROPERTY NAME	DATA TYPE	ACCESS
accessibleContext	AccessibleContext	read-only
columnHeader*	JViewport	read-write bound
columnHeaderView	Component	write-only
horizontalScrollBar*	JScrollBar	read-write bound
horizontalScrollBarPolicy*	int	read-write bound

(continued)

Table 11-8 (continued)

PROPERTY NAME	DATA TYPE	ACCESS
layout	LayoutManager	write-only
opaque	boolean	read-only
rowHeader*	JViewport	read-write bound
rowHeaderView	Component	write-only
UI	ScrollPaneUI	read-write
UIClassID	String	read-only
validateRoot	boolean	read-only
verticalScrollBar*	JScrollBar	read-write bound
verticalScrollBarPolicy*	int	read-write bound
viewport*	JViewport	read-write bound
viewportBorder	Border	read-write bound
viewportBorderBounds	Rectangle	read-only
viewportView	Component	write-only

Table 11-8: JScrollPane properties

Working with ScrollPaneLayout

The JScrollPane relies on the ScrollPaneLayout manager for the positioning of components within the container. Whereas most layout managers are designed to lay out any type of component, all but four regions of ScrollPaneLayout accept a component of a specific type. Table 11-9 shows what type of component can go into each of the regions shown in Figure 11-16.

LOCATION	DATA TYPE	DESCRIPTION
COLUMN_HEADER	JViewport	Usually empty. If main content is a table, serves as column headers that won't scroll as vertical scrollbar is moved.
HORIZONTAL_SCROLLBAR	JScrollBar	A scrollbar for the main content region placed below that region.
LOWER_LEFT_CORNER	Component	Usually empty. For a graphic in the lower-left corner.
LOWER_RIGHT_CORNER	Component	Usually empty. For a graphic in the lower-right corner.

(continued)

Table 11-9 (continued)

LOCATION	DATA TYPE	DESCRIPTION
ROW_HEADER	JViewport	Usually empty. If main content is a table, serves as row labels that won't scroll when horizontal scrollbar is moved.
UPPER_LEFT_CORNER	Component	Usually empty. For a graphic in the upper-left corner.
UPPER_RIGHT_CORNER	Component	Usually empty. For a graphic in the upper-right corner.
VERTICAL_SCROLLBAR	JScrollBar	A scrollbar for the main content region, placed to the right of the content area.
VIEWPORT	JViewport	The main content area.

Table 11-9: ScrollPaneLayout locations

As designed, the layout manager describes the screen layout necessary to support a main content area (VIEWPORT) that's too large for the available space. Scrollbars for navigating through the area can be placed to the right of the content area (VERTICAL_SCROLLBAR) or below it (HORIZONTAL_SCROLLBAR). Fixed headers that don't scroll can be placed above the content area (COLUMN_HEADER) or to its left (ROW_HEADER). The four corners (*_CORNER) are configurable to display any type of component, which are typically labels with images on them; however, any component can be placed there.

> **NOTE** *Some developers think of* ScrollPaneLayout *as a* GridBagLayout *with customized constraints (and restricted contents). How you think of it depends on the given circumstances. For most developers,* ScrollPaneLayout *won't be used outside a* JScrollPane.

Working with JScrollPane Headers and Corners

As Figure 11-16 and Table 11-9 demonstrate, many different regions exist within the JScrollPane. Normally, you only work with the central view and let the two scrollbars do their thing. In addition, when working with the JTable component, to be described in Chapter 17, the table automatically places the column labels within the column header region when placed within a JScrollPane.

You can also manually add/change the column header or add/change a row header for a JScrollPane. Although you can completely replace the JViewport in these areas, it's easier to just set the `columnHeaderView` or `rowHeaderView` property to the `Component` for the area. This action will place the component within a `JViewport` for you.

To place a component in one of the corners of the `JScrollPane`, you need to call the `public void setCorner(String key, Component corner)` method, where key is one of the following constants from `JScrollPane`: `LOWER_LEFT_CORNER`, `LOWER_RIGHT_CORNER`, `UPPER_LEFT_CORNER`, or `UPPER_RIGHT_CORNER`.

Working with corners can be tricky. A corner component is displayed only if the two components at a right angle from the corner are currently shown. For instance, if you were to place a company logo within a label in the lower-right corner, and the scrollbar policy for both scrollbars was as it should be, if one scrollbar wasn't needed, the logo in the corner wouldn't be shown. In another example, if a `JScrollPane` has a column header showing but doesn't have a row header, any component in the upper-left corner wouldn't be shown.

Therefore, just because you've set a corner to a component (as with `scrollPane.setCorner(JScrollPane.UPPER_LEFT_CORNER, logoLabel)`), don't expect it to be automatically shown. Moreover, as Figure 11-17 shows, the neighboring areas control the size of the corner. Don't assume a corner component can be as large as necessary. That's because its minimum, preferred, and maximum sizes are completely ignored. In Figure 11-17, the actual image used to create the corner component is larger than the space used.

Figure 11-17: A JScrollPane with a corner component and row and column headers

Resetting the Viewport Position

At times you may want to move the contents of the inner view to the upper-left corner of the `JScrollPane`. This change may be needed because the view changed, or because some event happened that requires the viewport component to return to the origin of the `JScrollPane`. The simplest way of moving the view is to adjust the position of the scrollbar thumbs of the `JScrollPane`. Setting each scrollbar to its minimum value effectively moves the view of the component to the component's upper-left corner. The following `ActionListener` can be associated with a button on the screen or in the corner of the `JScrollPane`, causing the contents of the `JScrollPane` to return to their origin.

```java
import java.awt.event.*;
import javax.swing.*;
```

```
public class JScrollPaneToTopAction implements ActionListener {
  JScrollPane scrollPane;
  public JScrollPaneToTopAction(JScrollPane scrollPane) {
    if (scrollPane == null) {
      throw new IllegalArgumentException("JScrollPaneToTopAction: null
JScrollPane");
    }
    this.scrollPane = scrollPane;
  }
  public void actionPerformed(ActionEvent actionEvent) {
    JScrollBar verticalScrollBar   = scrollPane.getVerticalScrollBar();
    JScrollBar horizontalScrollBar = scrollPane.getHorizontalScrollBar();
    verticalScrollBar.setValue(verticalScrollBar.getMinimum());
    horizontalScrollBar.setValue(horizontalScrollBar.getMinimum());
  }
}
```

Customizing a JScrollPane Look and Feel

Each installable Swing look and feel provides a different JScrollPane appearance and set of default UIResource values for the component. Figure 11-18 shows the appearance of the JScrollPane component for the preinstalled set of look and feels. With a JScrollPane, the primary difference among the look and feels is related to the scrollbar's appearance.

The available set of UIResource-related properties for a JScrollPane is shown in Table 11-10. For the JScrollPane component, there are six different properties.

PROPERTY STRING	OBJECT TYPE
ScrollPane.background	Color
ScrollPane.border	Border
ScrollPane.font	Font
ScrollPane.foreground	Color
ScrollPane.viewportBorder	Border
ScrollPaneUI	ScrollPaneUI

Table 11-10: JScrollPane UIResource elements

Class JViewport

The JViewport component is rarely used on its own outside a JScrollPane. It normally lives within the center of a JScrollPane and uses the ViewportLayout manager to respond to positioning requests to display a part of a large Component within a smaller space. Figure 11-19 shows these relationships. In addition to residing in the center of a JScrollPane, JViewport is also used for the row and column headers of a JScrollPane.

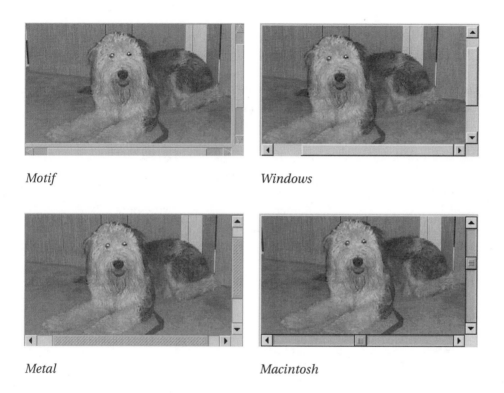

Motif   *Windows*

Metal   *Macintosh*

Figure 11-18: JScrollPane under the different look and feels

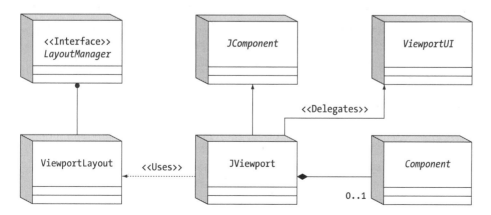

Figure 11-19: JViewport UML relationship diagram

Creating a JViewport

There's only one constructor for creating a JViewport: the no-argument JavaBeans version, public JViewport(). Once you've created the JViewport, you place a component within it by using setView(Component).

JViewport Properties

Table 11-11 shows the ten properties of JViewport. Setting the layout manager to something other than ViewportLayout is possible but not recommended because the layout manager makes the JViewport to do its work properly.

PROPERTY NAME	DATA TYPE	ACCESS
accessibleContext	AccessibleContext	read-only
backingStoreEnabled	boolean	read-write
border	Border	write-only
extentSize	Dimension	read-write
insets	Insets	read-only
optimizedDrawingEnabled	boolean	read-only
view	Component	read-write
viewPosition	Point	read-write
viewRect	Rectangle	read-only
viewSize	Dimension	read-write

Table 11-11: JViewport properties

Because of scrolling complexity and performance reasons, the JViewport doesn't support a border. Trying to change the border to a non-null value with setBorder(Border) throws an IllegalArgumentException. Because there can't be a border, the insets property setting is always (0, 0, 0, 0). Instead of displaying a border around the JViewport, you can display a border around the component within the view. Simply place a border around the component, or place the component inside a JPanel with a border. If you do place a border around the component, the border would be seen only if that part of the component is visible. If you don't want the border to scroll, you have to place the JViewport within a component such as a JScrollPane that has its own border.

The size of the view (viewSize property) is based on the size of the component (view property) within the JViewport. The view position (viewPosition property) is the upper-left corner of the view rectangle (viewRect property), where the rectangle's size is the extent size (extentSize property) of the view port. If that's confusing, Figure 11-20 should help you see where all these properties lie within the JViewport.

When the backingStoreEnabled property is set, the JViewport uses double-buffered rendering to improve performance when scrolling movement is one-dimensional (such as in a JScrollPane), basically allowing Graphics.copyArea() to be used. If the backingStoreEnabled property is disabled, no buffer is used and scrolling updates are done directly to the visible, on-screen bitmap. By default, the backingStoreEnabled property is false.

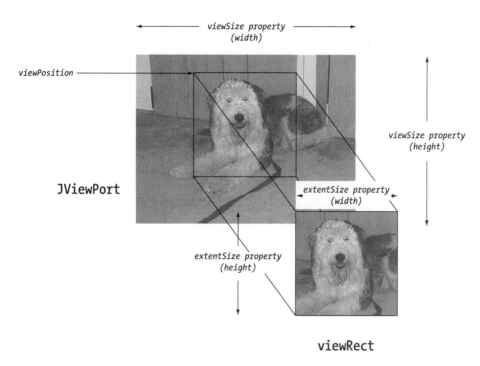

Figure 11-20: Visualizing JViewport properties

Scrolling the View

To move the visible part of the view around, just change the viewPosition property. This moves the viewRect, allowing you to see a different part of the view. To demonstrate this, the following program attaches keyboard accelerators to the JViewport so that you can use the arrow keys to move around the view. (Normally, the JScrollPane would get these keyboard actions.) The majority of the code is necessary to set up the appropriate keyboard accelerators. The bold-faced line of code is the one necessary to move the view.

```
import javax.swing.*;
import java.awt.*;
import java.awt.event.*;
```

```
public class MoveViewSample {

  public static final int INCREASE = 0; // direction
  public static final int DECREASE = 1; // direction
  public static final int X_AXIS   = 0; // axis
  public static final int Y_AXIS   = 1; // axis
  public static final int UNIT     = 0; // type
  public static final int BLOCK    = 1; // type

  static class MoveAction implements ActionListener {
    JViewport viewport;
    int direction;
    int axis;
    int type;
    public MoveAction(JViewport viewport, int direction, int axis, int type) {
      if (viewport == null) {
        throw new IllegalArgumentException ("null viewport not permitted");
      }
      this.viewport = viewport;
      this.direction = direction;
      this.axis = axis;
      this.type = type;
    }
    public void actionPerformed(ActionEvent actionEvent) {
      Dimension extentSize = viewport.getExtentSize();
      int horizontalMoveSize = 0;
      int verticalMoveSize = 0;
      if (axis == X_AXIS) {
        if (type == UNIT) {
          horizontalMoveSize = 1;
        } else { // type == BLOCK
          horizontalMoveSize = extentSize.width;
        }
      } else { // axis == Y_AXIS
        if (type == UNIT) {
          verticalMoveSize = 1;
        } else { // type == BLOCK
          verticalMoveSize = extentSize.height;
        }
      }
      if (direction == DECREASE) {
        horizontalMoveSize = -horizontalMoveSize;
        verticalMoveSize = -verticalMoveSize;
```

```
      }
      // Translate origin by some amount
      Point origin = viewport.getViewPosition();
      origin.x += horizontalMoveSize;
      origin.y += verticalMoveSize;
      // set new viewing origin
      viewport.setViewPosition(origin);
    }
  }

  public static void main(String args[]) {
    JFrame frame = new ExitableJFrame("JViewport Sample");
    Icon icon = new ImageIcon("dog.jpg");
    JLabel dogLabel = new JLabel(icon);
    JViewport viewport = new JViewport();
    viewport.setView(dogLabel);
    viewport.setBackingStoreEnabled(true);

    // Up key moves view up unit
    ActionListener upKeyAction = new MoveAction(viewport, DECREASE, Y_AXIS,
UNIT);
    KeyStroke upKey = KeyStroke.getKeyStroke(KeyEvent.VK_UP, 0);
    viewport.registerKeyboardAction(upKeyAction, upKey,
JComponent.WHEN_IN_FOCUSED_WINDOW);

    // Down key moves view down unit
    ActionListener downKeyAction = new MoveAction(viewport, INCREASE, Y_AXIS,
UNIT);
    KeyStroke downKey = KeyStroke.getKeyStroke(KeyEvent.VK_DOWN, 0);
    viewport.registerKeyboardAction(downKeyAction, downKey,
JComponent.WHEN_IN_FOCUSED_WINDOW);

    // Left key moves view left unit
    ActionListener leftKeyAction = new MoveAction(viewport, DECREASE, X_AXIS,
UNIT);
    KeyStroke leftKey = KeyStroke.getKeyStroke(KeyEvent.VK_LEFT, 0);
    viewport.registerKeyboardAction(leftKeyAction, leftKey,
JComponent.WHEN_IN_FOCUSED_WINDOW);

    // Right key moves view right unit
    ActionListener rightKeyAction = new MoveAction(viewport, INCREASE, X_AXIS,
UNIT);
    KeyStroke rightKey = KeyStroke.getKeyStroke(KeyEvent.VK_RIGHT, 0);
```

```
      viewport.registerKeyboardAction(rightKeyAction, rightKey,
  JComponent.WHEN_IN_FOCUSED_WINDOW);

      // PgUp key moves view up block
      ActionListener pgUpKeyAction = new MoveAction(viewport, DECREASE, Y_AXIS,
  BLOCK);
      KeyStroke pgUpKey = KeyStroke.getKeyStroke(KeyEvent.VK_PAGE_UP, 0);
      viewport.registerKeyboardAction(pgUpKeyAction, pgUpKey,
  JComponent.WHEN_IN_FOCUSED_WINDOW);

      // PgDn key moves view down block
      ActionListener pgDnKeyAction = new MoveAction(viewport, INCREASE, Y_AXIS,
  BLOCK);
      KeyStroke pgDnKey = KeyStroke.getKeyStroke(KeyEvent.VK_PAGE_DOWN, 0);
      viewport.registerKeyboardAction(pgDnKeyAction, pgDnKey,
  JComponent.WHEN_IN_FOCUSED_WINDOW);

      // Shift-PgUp key moves view left block
      ActionListener shiftPgUpKeyAction = new MoveAction(viewport, DECREASE,
  X_AXIS, BLOCK);
      KeyStroke shiftPgUpKey = KeyStroke.getKeyStroke(KeyEvent.VK_PAGE_UP,
  KeyEvent.SHIFT_MASK);
      viewport.registerKeyboardAction(shiftPgUpKeyAction, shiftPgUpKey,
  JComponent.WHEN_IN_FOCUSED_WINDOW);

      // Shift-PgDn key moves view right block
      ActionListener shiftPgDnKeyAction = new MoveAction(viewport, INCREASE,
  X_AXIS, BLOCK);
      KeyStroke shiftPgDnKey = KeyStroke.getKeyStroke(KeyEvent.VK_PAGE_DOWN,
  KeyEvent.SHIFT_MASK);
      viewport.registerKeyboardAction(shiftPgDnKeyAction, shiftPgDnKey,
  JComponent.WHEN_IN_FOCUSED_WINDOW);

      Container contentPane = frame.getContentPane();
      contentPane.add(viewport, BorderLayout.CENTER);
      frame.setSize(300, 200);
      frame.setVisible(true);
    }
  }
```

Customizing a JViewport Look and Feel

Each installable Swing look and feel shares the same JViewport appearance with the BasicViewportUI. There are no actual appearance differences. However, there still exists a set of UIResource-related properties for the JViewport, as shown in Table 11-12. For the JViewport component, there are four such properties.

PROPERTY STRING	OBJECT TYPE
Viewport.background	Color
Viewport.font	Font
Viewport.foreground	Color
ViewportUI	ViewportUI

Table 11-12: JViewport UIResource elements

Summary

In this chapter, we explored several high-level Swing containers. With the Box class, you can more easily utilize the BoxLayout manager to create a single row or column of components, honoring the minimum, preferred, and maximum size of the components the best way possible.

With the JSplitPane component, you can create a row or column consisting of two components with a divider in between them to allow an end user to alter the components' sizes manually by moving the divider.

The JTabbedPane container displays only one component from a set of contained components at a time. The displayed component is picked by the user's selecting a tab, which can contain a title and an icon. This is the popular property sheet metaphor commonly seen within newer applications.

The JScrollPane and JViewport containers allow you to display a large component within a small area. The JScrollPane adds scrollbars to enable an end user to move the visible part around, whereas the JViewport doesn't add these scrollbars.

In the Chapter 12, we'll once again examine the individual components within the Swing library, and specifically components including the JProgressBar, JScrollBar, and JSlider that share the BoundedRangeModel as their data model.

Bounded Range Components

IN THE PREVIOUS CHAPTER, YOU SAW how JScrollPane provides a scrollable region for those situations when there isn't sufficient space to display an entire component on screen. Swing also offers several components that support some type of scrolling or the display of a bounded range of values. The available components are JScrollBar, JSlider, JProgressBar, and, in a more limited sense, JTextField. What these components share is a BoundedRangeModel as their data model. The default implementation of this data model provided with the Swing classes is the DefaultBoundedRangeModel class. We'll look at the similarities (and differences) between these Swing components and the BoundedRangeModel.

Interface BoundedRangeModel

The BoundedRangeModel interface is the Model-View-Controller data model shared by the components described in this chapter. The interface contains four interrelated properties that are necessary to describe a range of values: minimum, maximum, value, and extent. The minimum and maximum properties define the limits of the value of the model. The value property defines what you might think of as the current setting of the model, where the maximum setting of the value property is not the value of the maximum property of the model. Instead, the maximum setting that the value property can take is the maximum property less the extent property. To help you visualize these properties, Figure 12-1 shows these settings in relation to a JScrollBar. Any other purpose of the extent property depends on the component acting as the model's view.

The settings for the four properties must abide by the following ordering:

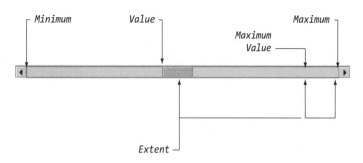

Figure 12-1: BoundedRange properties on a JScrollBar

```
minimum <= value <= value+extent <= maximum
```

When one of the settings changes, the change may trigger changes to other settings to keep the ordering valid. For instance, changing the minimum to a setting between the current value+extent setting and the maximum will decrease the extent and increase the value to keep the ordering valid. In addition, the original property change may result in a change to a new setting other than the requested setting. For instance, attempting to set the value below the minimum or maximum will set the value to the nearest limit of the range.

The BoundedRangeModel interface definition follows:

```
public interface BoundedRangeModel {
  // Properties
  public int  getExtent();
  public void setExtent(int newValue);
  public int  getMaximum();
  public void setMaximum(int newValue);
  public int  getMinimum();
  public void setMinimum(int newValue);
  public int  getValue();
  public void setValue(int newValue);
  public boolean getValueIsAdjusting();
  public void     setValueIsAdjusting(boolean newValue);
  // Listeners
  public void addChangeListener(ChangeListener listener);
  public void removeChangeListener(ChangeListener listener);
  // Other Methods
  public void setRangeProperties(int value, int extent, int minimum, int maximum,
boolean adjusting);
}
```

Although the different settings available for the model are JavaBean properties, when a property setting changes, the interface uses Swing's ChangeListener approach instead of a java.beans.PropertyChangeListener.

The model's valueIsAdjusting property comes into play when the user is performing a series of rapid changes to the model, probably as a result of dropping the slider's knob on the screen. For someone interested in only knowing when the final value is set for a model, a listener would ignore any changes until getValueIsAdjusting() returns false.

Class `DefaultBoundedRangeModel`

The Swing class actually implementing the `BoundedRangeModel` interface is `DefaultBoundedRangeModel`. This class takes care of the adjustments necessary to ensure the appropriate ordering of the different property values. It also manages a `ChangeListener` list to notify listeners when a change of the model happens.

    `DefaultBoundedRangeModel` has two constructors. The no-argument version, `public DefaultBoundedRangeModel()`, sets up the `minimum`, `value`, and `extent` properties of the model to have a setting of 0. The remaining `maximum` property gets a setting of 100. The second constructor version takes four integer parameters, explicitly setting four properties: `public DefaultBoundedRangeModel(int value, int extent, int minimum, int maximum)`. For both constructors, the initial value of the `valueIsAdjusting` property is `false` because the value of the model isn't yet changing beyond the initial value.

> **NOTE** *Unless you're sharing a model across multiple components, it generally isn't necessary to create a `BoundedRangeModel`. Even if you're sharing a model across multiple components, you can create just the first component and get its `BoundedRangeModel` model to share.*

Class `JScrollBar`

The simplest of the bounded range components is the `JScrollBar`. The `JScrollBar` component is used within the `JScrollPane` container, described in Chapter 11, to control the scrollable region. You can also use this component within your own containers, although with the flexibility of `JScrollPane` this usually isn't necessary. The one thing to remember about `JScrollBar`, however, is that it isn't used for the entry of a value, but solely for the scrolling of a region of screen real estate. For the entry of a value, you'd use the `JSlider` component discussed in the next section.

> **NOTE** *The `JScrollBar` within a `JScrollPane` is actually a specialized subclass of `JScrollBar` that properly deals with scrollable components that implement the `Scrollable` interface. Although you can change the scrollbars of a `JScrollPane`, it's usually unnecessary — and more work than you might think.*

As Figure 12-2 shows, the horizontal `JScrollBar` is composed of several parts. Starting from the middle and working outward, you find the scrollbar's *thumb*—also called a knob or slider. The width of the thumb is the `extent` property from the `BoundedRangeModel`. The current value of the scrollbar is at the left edge of the thumb. To the immediate left and right of the thumb are the block paging areas. Clicking to the left of the thumb will decrement the scrollbar's value, while clicking to the right increments it. The increased or decreased amount of the scrollbar's value is the scrollbar's `blockIncrement` property.

On the left and right edges of the scrollbar are arrow buttons. When the left arrow is pressed, the scrollbar decrements down a unit. The scrollbar's `unitIncrement` property specifies this "unit." To the immediate right of the left arrow is the minimum value of the scrollbar and the model. In addition to decreasing the value with the left arrow, clicking the right arrow causes the scrollbar to increment a unit. To the immediate left of the right arrow is the scrollbar's maximum range. The maximum value is actually a little farther to the left, where this "little farther" is specified by the model's `extent`. When the thumb is next to the right arrow, this places the scrollbar value of the scrollbar at the left edge of the thumb, which is the case with all other positions no matter where the thumb is.

A vertical `JScrollBar` is composed of the same parts as a horizontal `JScrollBar`, with the minimum and decrement parts at the top and the value designated by the top edge of the scrollbar's thumb. The maximum and increment parts are at the bottom.

Figure 12-3 shows the interrelationships of the `JScrollBar`. As previously mentioned, the model for the `JScrollBar` is the `BoundedRangeModel`. The delegate for the user interface is the `ScrollBarUI`.

Now that you've seen the different pieces of a `JScrollBar`, you'll next find out how to use them.

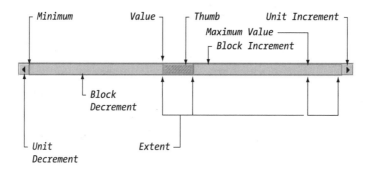

Figure 12-2: Horizontal JScrollBar anatomy

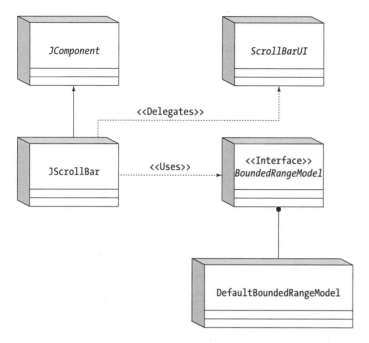

Figure 12-3: JScrollBar UML relationship diagram

Creating *JScrollBar* Components

There are three constructors for JScrollBar. Creating a JScrollBar with no arguments creates a vertical scrollbar with a default data model. The model has an
initial value of 0, a minimum of 0, a maximum of 100, and an extent of 10. This
default model offers a range of only 0–90. You can also explicitly set the orientation to JScrollBar.HORIZONTAL or JScrollBar.VERTICAL. If you don't like the initial
model settings provided by the other two constructors, you need to explicitly set
everything you want. If the data elements aren't properly constrained, as described
with BoundedRangeModel in the previous section, an IllegalArgumentException will
be thrown, causing the JScrollBar construction to be aborted.

1. ```
   public JScrollBar()
   JScrollBar aJScrollBar = new JScrollBar();
   ```

2. ```
   public JScrollBar(int orientation)
   // Vertical
   JScrollBar aJScrollBar = new JScrollBar(JScrollBar.VERTICAL);
   // Horizontal
   JScrollBar bJScrollBar = new JScrollBar(JScrollBar.HORIZONTAL);
   ```

3.  ```
    public JScrollBar(int orientation, int value, int extent,
    int minimum, int maximum)
    ```

To demonstrate the successful creation of a JScrollBar, the following line will create a horizontal scrollbar with an initial value of 500, a range of 0–1000, and an extent of 25.

JScrollBar aJScrollBar = new JScrollBar(JScrollBar.HORIZONTAL, 500, 25, 0, 1025);

> **NOTE** *Surprisingly missing from the list of constructors is one that accepts a BoundedRangeModel argument. If you have a model instance, you can either call setModel(BoundedRangeModel newModel) after creating the scrollbar or get the individual properties from the model when creating the scrollbar, as follows:*
>
> *JScrollBar aJScrollBar = new JScrollBar (JScrollBar.HORIZONTAL, aModel.getValue(), aModel.getExtent(), aModel.getMinimum(), aModel.getMaximum())*

Handling Scrolling Events

Once you've created your JScrollBar, it's necessary to listen for changes if you're interested in when the value changes. There are two ways of listening: the AWT 1.1 event model way and the Swing MVC way. The AWT way involves attaching an AdjustmentListener to the JScrollBar. The MVC way involves attaching a ChangeListener to the data model. Each works equally well, and both are notified if the model changes programmatically or by the user dragging the scrollbar thumb. The latter offers more flexibility, though — unless you're sharing a data model across components and need to know which one altered the model.

Listening to Scrolling Events with an AdjustmentListener

If you're porting a program from AWT that uses AWT's Scrollbar, the simplest porting strategy involves keeping the program using the AWT 1.1 event model. Attaching an AdjustmentListener to a Scrollbar was how one used to listen for the user to change the setting of the scrollbar. The Swing JScrollBar works no differently. The following code fragments, used for the example shown in Figure 12-4,
    ```

show how to attach an AdjustmentListener to a JScrollBar to listen for the user adjusting the value of the JScrollBar.

First, we'll define the appropriate AdjustmentListener that simply prints out the current value of the scrollbar:

```
AdjustmentListener adjustmentListener = new AdjustmentListener() {
  public void adjustmentValueChanged (AdjustmentEvent adjustmentEvent) {
    System.out.println ("Adjusted: " + adjustmentEvent.getValue());
  }
};
```

After you've created the listener, you can create the component and attach the listener:

```
JScrollBar oneJScrollBar = new JScrollBar (JScrollBar.HORIZONTAL);
oneJScrollBar.addAdjustmentListener(adjustmentListener);
```

This manner of listening for adjustment events works perfectly well even when you are *not* porting an AWT 1.1 program. However, attaching a ChangeListener to the data model, described next, provides more flexibility.

Listening to Scrolling Events with a ChangeListener

Attaching a ChangeListener to a JScrollBar data model provides more flexibility in your program designs. With an AWT AdjustmentListener, listeners are notified only when the value of the scrollbar changes. On the other hand, an attached ChangeListener is notified when there's any change in the minimum value, maximum value, current value, or extent. In addition, because the model has a valueIsAdjusting property, you can choose to ignore intermediate change events.

The following code fragment, used again in the program that follows, attaches a ChangeListener to the BoundedRangeModel of a JScrollBar. Attachment allows you to listen for when a user is adjusting the value of the JScrollBar.

To demonstrate, I'll define a ChangeListener that prints out the current value of the scrollbar when the model has finished adjusting. I'll enhance this BoundedChangeListener class throughout the chapter.

```
import javax.swing.*;
import javax.swing.event.*;

public class BoundedChangeListener implements ChangeListener {
  public void stateChanged(ChangeEvent changeEvent) {
    Object source = changeEvent.getSource();
    if (source instanceof BoundedRangeModel) {
```

```
        BoundedRangeModel aModel = (BoundedRangeModel)source;
        if (!aModel.getValueIsAdjusting()) {
          System.out.println ("Changed: " + aModel.getValue());
        }
      } else {
        System.out.println ("Something changed: " + source);
      }
    }
  }
}
```

Once you create the listener, you can create the component and attach the listener. In this particular case, you need to attach the listener to the data model of the component, instead of directly to the component.

```
ChangeListener changeListener = new BoundedChangeListener();
JScrollBar anotherJScrollBar = new JScrollBar (JScrollBar.HORIZONTAL);
BoundedRangeModel model = anotherJScrollBar.getModel();
model.addChangeListener(changeListener);
```

The source for the testing program follows:

```
import javax.swing.*;
import javax.swing.event.*;
import java.awt.*;
import java.awt.event.*;

public class ScrollBarSample {
  public static void main(String args[]) {
    AdjustmentListener adjustmentListener = new AdjustmentListener() {
      public void adjustmentValueChanged (AdjustmentEvent adjustmentEvent) {
        System.out.println ("Adjusted: " + adjustmentEvent.getValue());
      }
    };
    JScrollBar oneJScrollBar = new JScrollBar (JScrollBar.HORIZONTAL);
    oneJScrollBar.addAdjustmentListener(adjustmentListener);

    ChangeListener changeListener = new BoundedChangeListener();
    JScrollBar anotherJScrollBar = new JScrollBar (JScrollBar.HORIZONTAL);
    BoundedRangeModel model = anotherJScrollBar.getModel();
    model.addChangeListener(changeListener);

    JFrame theFrame = new ExitableJFrame("ScrollBars R Us");
    Container contentPane = theFrame.getContentPane();
```

```
        contentPane.add (oneJScrollBar, BorderLayout.NORTH);
        contentPane.add (anotherJScrollBar, BorderLayout.SOUTH);
        theFrame.setSize (300, 200);
        theFrame.setVisible (true);
    }
}
```

When run, this program shows the two horizontal scrollbars seen in Figure 12-4. The output of moving the scrollbars is sent to the console window.

Figure 12-4: Dual JScrollBar listening

JScrollBar Properties

After you've created a JScrollBar, it may become necessary to modify its underlying data model. You can get the model with the `public BoundedRangeModel getModel()` method and then modify the model directly. More likely, you'd just call the appropriate methods of the component: `setValue(int newValue)`, `setExtent(int newValue)`, `setMinimum(int newValue)`, and `setMaximum(int newValue)`. These methods act as proxies and redirect any calls to the equivalent model method.

> **WARNING**   *Although supported, it's not recommended that you modify a JScrollBar's orientation after displaying the component. This could seriously diminish the user's satisfaction and encourage the user to find a solution from another vendor!*

In addition to the data model properties, Table 12-1 shows the 15 properties of JScrollBar.

PROPERTY NAME	DATA TYPE	ACCESS
accessibleContext	AccessibleContext	read-only
blockIncrement	int	read-write bound
enabled	boolean	write-only
maximum	int	read-write
maximumSize	Dimension	read-only
minimum	int	read-write
minimumSize	Dimension	read-only
model	BoundedRangeModel	read-write bound
orientation	int	read-write bound
UI	ScrollBarUI	read-only
UIClassID	String	read-only
unitIncrement	int	read-write bound
value	int	read-write bound
valueIsAdjusting	boolean	read-write bound
visibleAmount	int	read-write

Table 12-1: JScrollBar properties

Customizing a JScrollBar Look and Feel

Each installable Swing look and feel provides a different JScrollBar appearance and set of default UIResource values. Figure 12-5 shows the appearance of the JScrollBar component for the preinstalled set of look and feels: Motif, Windows, Metal, and Macintosh.

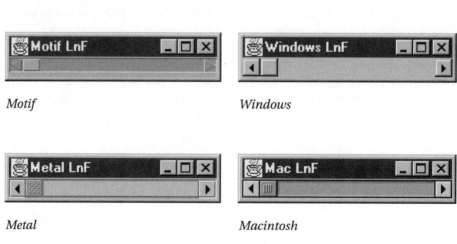

Motif

Windows

Metal

Macintosh

Figure 12-5: JScrollBar under different look and feels

The available set of UIResource-related properties for a JScrollBar is shown in Table 12-2. There are 34 different properties.

PROPERTY STRING	OBJECT TYPE
scrollbar	Color
ScrollBar.arrowBackground	Color
ScrollBar.arrowColor	Color
ScrollBar.arrowHighlight	Color
ScrollBar.arrowShadow	Color
ScrollBar.background	Color
ScrollBar.border	Border
ScrollBar.darkShadow	Color
ScrollBar.foreground	Color
ScrollBar.highlight	Color
ScrollBar.maximumThumbSize	Dimension
ScrollBar.minimumThumbSize	Dimension
ScrollBar.pressedArrowBackground	Color
ScrollBar.pressedArrowHighlight	Color
ScrollBar.pressedArrowShadow	Color
ScrollBar.pressedThumb	Color
ScrollBar.pressedThumbDarkShadow	Color
ScrollBar.pressedThumbHighlight	Color
ScrollBar.pressedThumbLightHighlight	Color
ScrollBar.pressedThumbShadow	Color
ScrollBar.shadow	Color
ScrollBar.thumb	Color
ScrollBar.thumbDarkShadow	Color
ScrollBar.thumbHighlight	Color
ScrollBar.thumbLightHighlight	Color
ScrollBar.thumbLightShadow	Color
ScrollBar.thumbShadow	Color
ScrollBar.track	Color
ScrollBar.trackDarkShadow	Color
ScrollBar.trackHighlight	Color
ScrollBar.trackLightHighlight	Color
ScrollBar.trackShadow	Color
ScrollBar.width	Integer
ScrollBarUI	ScrollBarUI

Table 12-2: JScrollBar UIResource elements

Class `JSlider`

Although the `JScrollBar` component is useful for scrolling regions of the screen, it's *not* a good component for getting user input for a range of values. For that purpose, Swing offers the `JSlider` component. In addition to a draggable thumb like the `JScrollBar` component, the `JSlider` component offers visible tick marks and labels to assist in showing the current setting and selecting a new one. Figure 12-6 shows several sample `JSlider` components.

The `JSlider` is made up of several pieces. The familiar `BoundedRangeModel` stores the data model for the component, and a `Dictionary` stores any labels for the tick marks. The user interface delegate is the `SliderUI`. Figure 12-7 shows the relationships of these components for the `JSlider`.

Now that you've seen the different pieces of a `JSlider`, let's find out how to use them.

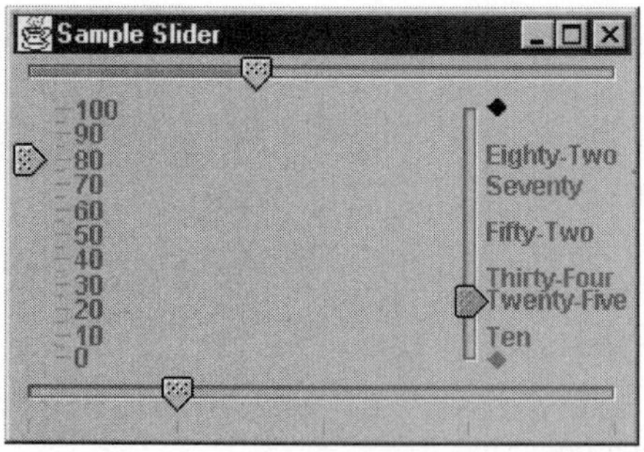

Figure 12-6: Sample JSlider components

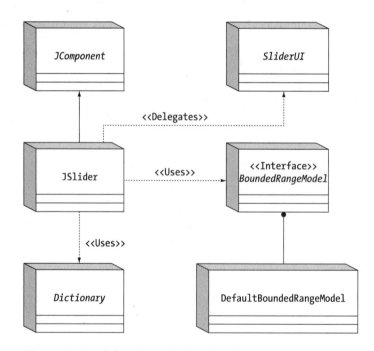

Figure 12-7: JSlider UML relationship diagram

Creating JSlider Components

There are six different constructors for JSlider. Creating a JSlider with no arguments creates a horizontal slider with a default data model. The model has an initial value of 50, a minimum of 0, a maximum of 100, and an extent of 0. You can also explicitly set the orientation with JSlider.HORIZONTAL or JSlider.VERTICAL, and any of the specific model properties, with the various constructors. In addition, you can explicitly set the data model for the component. If you're using a preconfigured BoundedRangeModel, remember to set the extent to 0 when creating the model.

> **NOTE** *If the extent property is greater than 0, then the maximum setting of the value property is decreased by that amount and the value setting will never reach the setting of the maximum property.*

1. ```
   public JSlider()
   JSlider aJSlider = new JSlider();
   ```

2. ```
   public JSlider(int orientation)
   // Vertical
   JSlider aJSlider = new JSlider(JSlider.VERTICAL);
   // Horizontal
   JSlider bJSlider = new JSlider(JSlider.HORIZONTAL);
   ```

> **WARNING** *Initializing the orientation to something not equivalent to VERTICAL or HORIZONTAL throws an IllegalArgumentException.*

3. ```
   public JSlider(int minimum, int maximum)
   // Initial value 50
   JSlider aJSlider = new JSlider(-100, 100);
   ```

> **WARNING** *All constructors that initialize the data model could throw an IllegalArgumentException if the range and initial value fail to abide by the rules of the BoundedRangeModel described earlier in the section "Interface BoundedRangeModel."*
   ```

4. `public JSlider(int minimum, int maximum, int value)`
   `JSlider aJSlider = new JSlider(-100, 100, 0);`

5. `public JSlider(int orientation, int minimum, int maximum, int value)`

   To demonstrate the creation of a vertical `JSlider`, the following line will create a vertical slider with an initial value of 6 and a range of 1–12, possibly for the months of a year.

   `JSlider aJSlider = new JSlider(JSlider.VERTICAL, 6, 1, 12);`

6. `public JSlider(BoundedRangeModel model)`

   For example, the following will create a data model with an initial value of 3, a range of 1–31, and an extent of 0. After creating the model, the `JSlider` direction is changed to vertical, prior to display on the screen.

   ```
   DefaultBoundedRangeModel model = new DefaultBoundedRangeModel(3, 0, 1, 31);
   JSlider aJSlider = new JSlider(model);
   aJSlider.setOrientation(JSlider.VERTICAL);
   ```

Handling JSlider Events

You track changes to a `JSlider` with a `ChangeListener`. There's no `AdjustmentListener` such as there is with `JScrollBar` and `Scrollbar`. The same `BoundedChangeListener` from the earlier `JScrollBar` example could be added to a data model of the `JSlider`, and you'll then be notified when the model changes.

```
ChangeListener aChangeListener = new BoundedChangeListener();
JSlider aJSlider = new JSlider ();
BoundedRangeModel model = aJSlider.getModel();
model.addChangeListener(changeListener);
```

In addition to attaching a `ChangeListener` to the model, you can associate the `ChangeListener` directly with the `JSlider`. This allows you to share the data model between views and listen independently for changes. This requires you to modify the above listener a little bit because the change event source will now be a `JSlider` instead of a `BoundedRangeModel`. The updated `BoundedChangeListener` will work for both associations, however. The changes are **boldfaced** in the code fragment that follows.

```java
import javax.swing.*;
import javax.swing.event.*;

public class BoundedChangeListener implements ChangeListener {
  public void stateChanged(ChangeEvent changeEvent) {
    Object source = changeEvent.getSource();
    if (source instanceof BoundedRangeModel) {
      BoundedRangeModel aModel = (BoundedRangeModel)source;
      if (!aModel.getValueIsAdjusting()) {
        System.out.println ("Changed: " + aModel.getValue());
      }
    } else if (source instanceof JSlider) {
      JSlider theJSlider = (JSlider)source;
      if (!theJSlider.getValueIsAdjusting()) {
        System.out.println ("Slider changed: " + theJSlider.getValue());
      }
    } else {
      System.out.println ("Something changed: " + source);
    }
  }
}
```

The association with the slider can now be direct, instead of indirect through the model.

```java
aJSlider.addChangeListener(changeListener);
```

JSlider Properties

After you've created a JSlider, you may want to modify its underlying data model. As is the case with JScrollBar, you can get the model with the public BoundedRangeModel getModel() method and then modify the model directly. You can also directly call the methods of the component: setValue(int newValue), setExtent(int newValue), setMinimum(int newValue), and setMaximum(int newValue). These methods act as proxies and redirect any calls to the equivalent model method.

Table 12-3 shows the 18 properties of JSlider.

PROPERTY NAME	DATA TYPE	ACCESS
accessibleContext	AccessibleContext	read-only
extent	int	read-write
inverted	boolean	read-write bound
labelTable	Dictionary	read-write bound
majorTickSpacing	int	read-write bound
maximum	int	read-write
minimum	int	read-write
minorTickSpacing	int	read-write bound
model	BoundedRangeModel	read-write bound
orientation	int	read-write bound
paintLabels	boolean	read-write bound
paintTicks	boolean	read-write bound
paintTrack	boolean	read-write bound
snapToTicks	boolean	read-write bound
UI	SliderUI	read-write bound
UIClassID	String	read-only
value	int	read-write
valueIsAdjusting	boolean	read-write

Table 12-3: JSlider properties

Displaying Tick Marks within a JSlider

The JSlider component allows you to add tick marks either below a horizontal slider or to the right of a vertical slider. These tick marks allow a user to get a rough estimate of the slider's value and scale. There can be both major and minor tick marks, in which the major ones are simply drawn to be a little longer. Either or both can be displayed, as well as neither of them, which is the default.

> **NOTE** *Technically, a custom look and feel could place the tick marks any-where. However, the predefined look and feels — Windows, Motif, Metal, and Macintosh — place the ticks below or to the right.*

To display the tick marks, the one thing you need to do is enable their painting with the `public void setPaintTicks(boolean newValue)` method. When called with a setting of `true`, this enables the painting of minor and major tick marks. By default, the tick spacing for both types of tick marks is set to zero. When either is set to zero, that particular tick type isn't displayed. Because both are initially zero, you have to change the value of either tick spacing to see any ticks. The public void setMajorTickSpacing(int newValue) and public void setMinorTickSpacing(int newValue) methods both support this change.

To demonstrate, Figure 12-8 shows four sliders: one with no ticks, one with aesthetically pleasing tick spacing, and two with unconventional tick spacing. It helps if the major tick spacing is a multiple of the minor tick spacing (just as a ruler shows inches, half-inches, quarter-inches, and so on with different tick lengths). In addition, the tick spacing shouldn't be so narrow that the ticks look like a solid block.

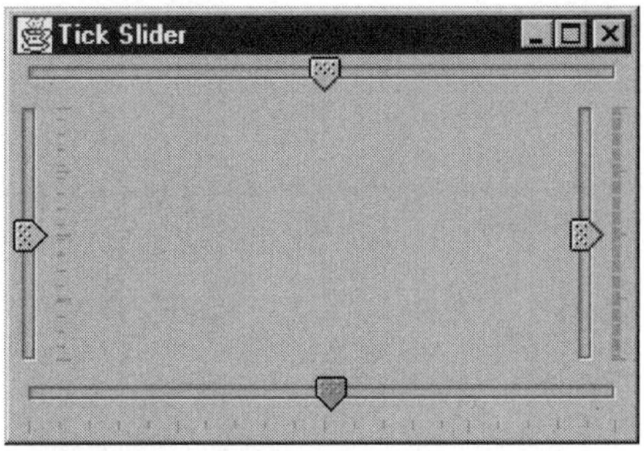

Figure 12-8: Four JSlider controls demonstrating ticks

The source for the example follows. The top slider has no ticks. The bottom slider has the aesthetically pleasing major/minor spacing, with minor ticks at 5 units and major ones at 25 units. The left slider displays poor spacing with minor ticks at 6 and major ticks at 25. The right slider has minor ticks at each individual unit, resulting in spacing that's much too tight.

```
import javax.swing.*;
import java.awt.*;

public class TickSliders {
  public static void main(String args[]) {
    JFrame f = new ExitableJFrame("Tick Slider");
    // No Ticks
    JSlider jSliderOne = new JSlider ();
    // Major Tick 25 - Minor 5
    JSlider jSliderTwo = new JSlider ();
    jSliderTwo.setMinorTickSpacing (5);
    jSliderTwo.setMajorTickSpacing (25);
    jSliderTwo.setPaintTicks (true);
    // Major Tick 25 - Minor 6
    JSlider jSliderThree = new JSlider (JSlider.VERTICAL);
    jSliderThree.setMinorTickSpacing (6);
    jSliderThree.setMajorTickSpacing (25);
    jSliderThree.setPaintTicks (true);
    JSlider jSliderFour = new JSlider (JSlider.VERTICAL);
    // Major Tick 25 - Minor 1
    jSliderFour.setMinorTickSpacing (1);
    jSliderFour.setMajorTickSpacing (25);
    jSliderFour.setPaintTicks (true);
```

```
        Container c = f.getContentPane();
        c.add (jSliderOne, BorderLayout.NORTH);
        c.add (jSliderTwo, BorderLayout.SOUTH);
        c.add (jSliderThree, BorderLayout.WEST);
        c.add (jSliderFour, BorderLayout.EAST);
        f.setSize (300, 200);
        f.setVisible (true);
    }
}
```

Snapping the JSlider Thumb into Position

One additional property of JSlider is related to tick marks: the snapToTicks property, set with public void setSnapToTicks(boolean newValue). When true and tick marks are displayed after you move the slider's thumb, the thumb will rest only on a tick. For instance, if a slider has a range of 0–100 with tick marks at every tenth unit, and you drop the thumb at the 33 mark, the thumb will snap to the position of the tick at 30. If tick marks aren't displayed, the property setting has no effect, including when labels are displayed without tick marks.

Labeling JSlider Positions

As Figure 12-6 shows, you can label any position within the JSlider with a Component. When a position is labeled, the component will be displayed next to it. The labels are stored within a lookup table that subclasses the Dictionary class, where the key is the Integer position and the value is the Component. Any AWT Component can be the label; however, the JLabel is best suited to the role. Figure 12-9 shows how the dictionary for the right slider of Figure 12-6 might look.

Normally, the Dictionary used to store the labels is a Hashtable. However, any class that extends the Dictionary class and that can use Integer keys will do. After you've created your dictionary of labels, you associate the dictionary with the slider with the public void setLabelTable(Dictionary newValue) method. The following source creates the label lookup table associated with Figure 12-9.

```
Hashtable table = new Hashtable();
table.put (new Integer (0), new JLabel(new DiamondIcon(Color.red)));
table.put (new Integer (10), new JLabel("Ten"));
table.put (new Integer (25), new JLabel("Twenty-Five"));
table.put (new Integer (34), new JLabel("Thirty-Four"));
table.put (new Integer (52), new JLabel("Fifty-Two"));
table.put (new Integer (70), new JLabel("Seventy"));
```

```
table.put (new Integer (82), new JLabel("Eighty-Two"));
table.put (new Integer (100), new JLabel(new DiamondIcon(Color.black)));
aJSlider.setLabelTable (table);
```

Simply associating the label table with the slider won't display the labels. To enable their painting, you need to call the `public void setPaintLabels(boolean newValue)` method with a parameter of `true`. If you haven't manually created a table of labels, the system will create one with an interval of values reflecting the major tick spacing. For example, the left slider of Figure 12-6 has a slider range of 0–100 and major tick spacing of 10. When `setPaintLabels(true)` is called on that slider, labels are created for 0, 10, 20, and so on, all the way up to 100. The minor tick spacing is irrelevant as far as automatic generation of labels. And the ticks don't have to be painted for the labels to appear — the `getPaintTicks()` method can return `false`.

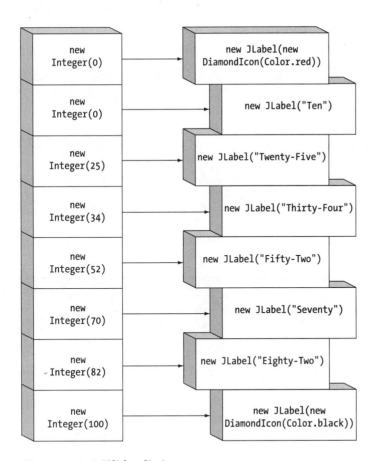

Figure 12-9: A JSlider dictionary

The automatic creation of labels is done through the public Hashtable createStandardLabels(int increment) method, where the increment is the major tick spacing. You don't have to call this method directly. If you want to create the labels from other than the minimum value, you can call the overloaded public Hashtable createStandardLabels(int increment, int start) variety, and associate the hash table with the slider yourself.

Customizing a JSlider Look and Feel

Each installable Swing look and feel provides a different JSlider appearance and set of default UIResource values. Figure 12-10 shows the appearance of the JSlider component for the preinstalled set of look and feels.

Two look-and-feel–related properties are part of the JSlider class definition. By default, the minimum slider value for a horizontal slider is at the left and for a vertical slider it's at the bottom.

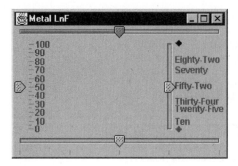

Motif

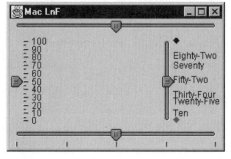

Windows

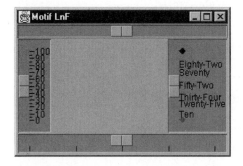

Metal

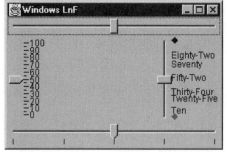

Macintosh

Figure 12-10: JSlider under different look and feels

To change the direction of a slider, call the `public void setInverted(boolean newValue)` method with an argument of `true`. In addition, the track that the slider moves along is displayed by default. You can turn it off with the `public void setPaintTrack(boolean newValue)` method. A value of `false` turns it off. Figure 12-11 identifies the `JSlider` track and points out the minimum and maximum positions of regular and inverted sliders.

Table 12-4 shows the 15 available `UIResource`-related properties for a `JSlider`.

PROPERTY STRING	OBJECT TYPE
Slider.background	Color
Slider.border	Border
Slider.darkShadow	Color
Slider.focus	Color
Slider.focusInsets	Insets
Slider.foreground	Color
Slider.highlight	Color
Slider.horizontalThumbIcon	Icon
Slider.majorTickLength	Integer
Slider.minorTickLength	Integer
Slider.shadow	Color
Slider.thumb	Color
Slider.trackWidth	Integer
Slider.verticalThumbIcon	Icon
SliderUI	SliderUI

Table 12-4: JSlider UIResource elements

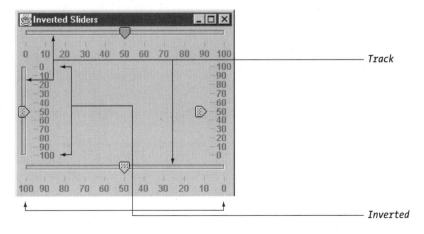

Figure 12-11: Identifying JSlider positions and tracks

445

Figure 12-12: A JSlider with a custom icon

To customize the `JSlider` appearance of your application, you may want to alter the icon used for the draggable thumb knob. With just a few lines of code, you can take any icon and make it the slider's icon for every slider in your application. Figure 12-12 shows the results. As with all `UIResource` properties, this change will affect all `JSlider` components created.

```
Icon icon = new ImageIcon("logo.jpg");
UIDefaults defaults = UIManager.getDefaults();
defaults.put("Slider.horizontalThumbIcon", icon);
```

> **NOTE** *The height and width of the icon are limited to the dimensions of the slider. Changing the icon property doesn't affect the slider size.*

JSlider Client Properties

By default, with the Metal look and feel, the track on which the slider moves does not change as the slider is moved over it. Nevertheless, you can enable a

Figure 12-13: Filled and unfilled JSlider

client property that will signal the slider to fill this track up to the point of the current value that the thumb has crossed. The name of this property is `JSlider.isFilled`, and a `Boolean` object represents the current setting. By default, this setting is `Boolean.FALSE`. Figure 12-13 demonstrates both a `Boolean.TRUE` and a `Boolean.FALSE` setting; the code fragment follows.

```
JSlider oneJSlider = new JSlider ();
oneJSlider.putClientProperty("JSlider.isFilled", Boolean.TRUE);
JSlider anotherJSlider = new JSlider ();
// Set to default setting
anotherJSlider.putClientProperty("JSlider.isFilled", Boolean.FALSE);
```

Class JProgressBar

Swing's `JProgressBar` is different from the other `BoundedRangeModel` components. Its main purpose is not to get input from the user but rather to present output. This output is in the form of a process completion percentage. As the percentage increases, a bar progresses across the component until the job is completed and the bar is filled. The movement of the bar is usually part of some multithreaded task, to avoid affecting the rest of the application. Figure 12-14 shows several sample JProgressBar components. The top bar uses all the display defaults. The bottom bar adds a border around the component and displays the completion percentage. The right bar removes the border and the left bar has a fixed string present instead of a completion percentage.

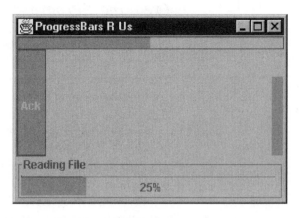

Figure 12-14: Sample JProgressBar components

From an object-oriented perspective, there are two primary parts to a JProgressBar. The familiar BoundedRangeModel stores the data model for the component, the ProgressUI is the user interface delegate. Figure 12-15 shows the relationships of these components for the JProgressBar.

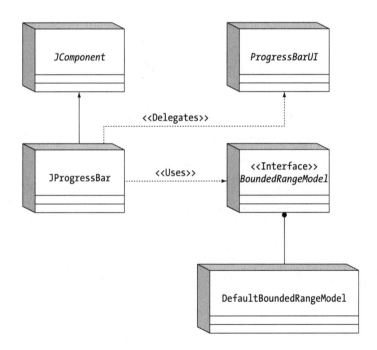

Figure 12-15: JProgressBar UML relationship diagram

Creating JProgressBar Components

There are five different constructors for JProgressBar. Creating a JProgressBar with no arguments creates a horizontal progress bar with a default data model. The model has an initial value of 0, a minimum value of 0, a maximum value of 100, and an extent of 0. The progress bar has an extent, it just doesn't use it, even though it's part of the data model.

You can explicitly set the orientation with JProgressBar.HORIZONTAL or JProgressBar.VERTICAL, as well as any of the specific model properties, with the different constructors. In addition, you can explicitly set the data model for the component.

Creating a JProgressBar from a BoundedRangeModel is a little awkward in the sense that the progress bar virtually ignores one setting and the initial value is normally initialized to the minimum. Assuming you want the JProgressBar to start as a user might expect it to, you need to remember to set the extent to 0 and the value to the minimum when creating the model. If you increase the extent property, then the maximum setting of the value property is decreased by that amount and the value setting will never reach the setting of the maximum property.

1. ```
   public JProgressBar()
   JProgressBar aJProgressBar = new JProgressBar();
   ```

2. ```
   public JProgressBar(int orientation)
   // Vertical
   JProgressBar aJProgressBar = new JProgressBar(JProgressBar.VERTICAL);
   // Horizontal
   JProgressBar bJProgressBar = new JProgressBar(JProgressBar.HORIZONTAL);
   ```

> **WARNING** *Initializing the orientation to a value not equivalent to* VERTICAL *or* HORIZONTAL *throws an* IllegalArgumentException.

3. ```
   public JProgressBar(int minimum, int maximum)
   JProgressBar aJProgressBar = new JProgressBar(0, 500);
   ```

4. ```
   public JProgressBar(int orientation, int minimum, int maximum)
   JProgressBar aJProgressBar = new JProgressBar(JProgressBar.VERTICAL, 0,
   1000);
   ```

5. ```
   public JProgressBar(BoundedRangeModel model)
   ```
   ```

For example, the following code will create a data model with an initial value of 0, a range of 0–250, and an extent of 0.

```
DefaultBoundedRangeModel model = new DefaultBoundedRangeModel(0, 0, 0, 250);
JProgressBar aJProgressBar = new JProgressBar(model);
```

JProgressBar Properties

After you've created a JProgressBar, you may want to modify it. Table 12-5 shows the 12 twelve properties of JProgressBar.

PROPERTY NAME	DATA TYPE	ACCESS
accessibleContext	AccessibleContext	read-only
borderPainted	boolean	read-write bound
maximum	int	read-write
minimum	int	read-write
model	BoundedRangeModel	read-write
orientation	int	read-write bound
percentComplete	double	read-only
string	String	read-write bound
stringPainted	boolean	read-write bound
UI	ProgressBarUI	read-write
UIClassID	String	read-only
value	int	read-write

Table 12-5: JProgressBar properties

Painting JProgressBar Borders

All JComponent subclasses feature a border property by default, and the JProgressBar has a special borderPainted property to easily enable or disable the painting of the border. Calling the public void setBorderPainted(boolean newValue) method with a parameter of false turns off the painting of the progress bar's border. The right-hand progress bar in Figure 12-14 has its border turned off. The source for its initialization follows:

```
JProgressBar cJProgressBar = new JProgressBar(JProgressBar.VERTICAL);
cJProgressBar.setBorderPainted(false);
```

Labeling a JProgressBar

The JProgressBar supports the displaying of text within the center of the component. There are three forms of this labeling:

- By default, no label exists.

- To display the percentage completed [100 x (value–minimum)/(maximum–minimum)], call the `public void setStringPainted(boolean newValue)` method with a parameter of `true`. This will result in a range from 0% to 100% displayed.

- To change the label to a fixed string, call the `public void setString(String newValue)` method and `setStringPainted(true)`. The dimensions of the string affect the size of the progress bar; therefore, a long string on a vertical progress bar will result in a wide bar.

The left-hand and bottom progress bars in Figure 12-14 demonstrate the fixed label and percentage label, respectively. The source code to create both progress bars follows:

```
JProgressBar bJProgressBar = new JProgressBar();
bJProgressBar.setStringPainted(true);
Border border = BorderFactory.createTitledBorder("Reading File");
bJProgressBar.setBorder(border);

JProgressBar dJProgressBar = new JProgressBar(JProgressBar.VERTICAL);
dJProgressBar.setString("Ack");
dJProgressBar.setStringPainted(true);
```

Stepping Along a JProgressBar

The main usage of the JProgressBar is to show progress as you step through a series of operations. Normally, you set the minimum value of the progress bar to zero and the maximum to the number of steps to perform. Starting with a value property of zero, you increase the value to the maximum as you perform each step. All these operations imply multithreading, which is, in fact, absolutely necessary. In addition, when updating the progress bar's value, you need to remember to update it only from within the event dispatching thread (with the help of `SwingUtilities.invokeAndWait()`, if appropriate, as described in Chapter 2).

The process of having a progress bar step through its range is as follows:

1. Initialize it.

   This is the basic process of creating a JProgressBar with the desired orientation and range. In addition, perform any bordering and labeling here.

   ```
   JProgressBar aJProgressBar = new JProgressBar(0, 50);
   aJProgressBar.setStringPainted(true);
   ```

2. Start up the thread to perform the desired steps.

   Probably as the result of performing some action on the screen, you'll
   need to start the thread to do the work the progress bar is reporting. You
   need to start a new thread so that the user interface remains responsive.

   ```
   Thread stepper = new BarThread (aJProgressBar);
   stepper.start();
   ```

3. Perform the steps.

   Ignore updating the progress bar, and instead write the appropriate
   code to perform each step.

   ```
   static class BarThread extends Thread {
     private static int DELAY = 500;
     JProgressBar progressBar;

     public BarThread (JProgressBar bar) {
       progressBar = bar;
     }

     public void run() {
       int minimum = progressBar.getMinimum();
       int maximum = progressBar.getMaximum();
       for (int i=minimum; i<maximum; i++) {
         try {
           // our job for each step is to just sleep
           Thread.sleep(DELAY);
         } catch (InterruptedException ignoredException) {
         } catch (InvocationTargetException ignoredException) {
           // The SwingUtilities.invokeAndWait() call
           // we'll add will throw this
         }
   ```

```
        }
      }
    }
```

4. For each step, have the thread update progress bar in the event thread.

    Create the Runnable class just once outside the for-loop. It isn't necessary to create one for each step.

```
Runnable runner = new Runnable() {
  public void run() {
    int value = progressBar.getValue();
    progressBar.setValue(value+1);
  }
};
```

    Within the loop, tell the runner to update the progress bar. This update must be done in the event thread using the special SwingUtilities method invokeAndWait() because you're updating a property of the JProgressBar.

```
SwingUtilities.invokeAndWait (runner);
```

    The complete working example is as follows:

```
import javax.swing.*;
import javax.swing.border.*;
import java.awt.*;
import java.awt.event.*;
import java.lang.reflect.InvocationTargetException;

public class ProgressBarStep {
  static class BarThread extends Thread {
    private static int DELAY = 500;
    JProgressBar progressBar;

    public BarThread (JProgressBar bar) {
      progressBar = bar;
    }

    public void run() {
      int minimum = progressBar.getMinimum();
      int maximum = progressBar.getMaximum();
      Runnable runner = new Runnable() {
```

```
      public void run() {
        int value = progressBar.getValue();
        progressBar.setValue(value+1);
      }
    };
    for (int i=minimum; i<maximum; i++) {
      try {
        SwingUtilities.invokeAndWait (runner);
        // our job for each step is to just sleep
        Thread.sleep(DELAY);
      } catch (InterruptedException ignoredException) {
      } catch (InvocationTargetException ignoredException) {
      }
    }
  }
}

public static void main(String args[]) {
  // Initialize
  final JProgressBar aJProgressBar = new JProgressBar(0, 50);
  aJProgressBar.setStringPainted(true);

  final JButton aJButton = new JButton ("Start");

  ActionListener ActionListener = new ActionListener() {
    public void actionPerformed(ActionEvent e) {
      aJButton.setEnabled(false);
      Thread stepper = new BarThread (aJProgressBar);
      stepper.start();
    }
  };

  aJButton.addActionListener(ActionListener);

  JFrame theFrame = new ExitableJFrame("Stepping Progress");
  Container contentPane = theFrame.getContentPane();
  contentPane.add (aJProgressBar, BorderLayout.NORTH);
  contentPane.add (aJButton, BorderLayout.SOUTH);
  theFrame.setSize (300, 200);
  theFrame.setVisible (true);
}
}
```

Figure 12-16 shows the demonstration program after selecting the button and at 22% completion.

By simply changing the sleep action in the previous example to the desired operation, this example should provide a suitable framework for reuse.

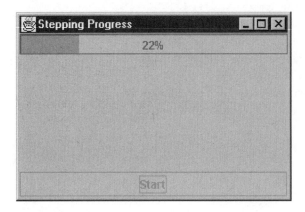

Figure 12-16: JProgressBar in action

NOTE   *To have the progress bar fill in the* opposite *direction, have the value start at the maximum and decrease it with each step. You probably don't want to display the percentage-completed string, as it will start at 100% and decrease to 0%.*

NOTE   *To display a progress bar in a dialog box, use the* ProgressMonitor *class from Chapter 9.*

Handling JProgressBar Events

Technically, the JProgressBar class supports notification of data model changes through a ChangeListener. In addition, you can attach a ChangeListener to its data model. Because the progress bar is meant more for visualization of output than for providing input, you typically won't find yourself attaching a ChangeListener.

However, there may be times when this is appropriate. To reuse the BoundedChangeListener from the section "Handling JSlider Events" earlier in this chapter, make one final change (shown in boldface) because the source of these change events is the JProgressBar.

```java
import javax.swing.*;
import javax.swing.event.*;

public class BoundedChangeListener implements ChangeListener {
  public void stateChanged(ChangeEvent changeEvent) {
    Object source = changeEvent.getSource();
    if (source instanceof BoundedRangeModel) {
      BoundedRangeModel aModel = (BoundedRangeModel)source;
      if (!aModel.getValueIsAdjusting()) {
        System.out.println ("Changed: " + aModel.getValue());
      }
    } else if (source instanceof JSlider) {
      JSlider theJSlider = (JSlider)source;
      if (!theJSlider.getValueIsAdjusting()) {
        System.out.println ("Slider changed: " + theJSlider.getValue());
      }
    } else if (source instanceof JProgressBar) {
      JProgressBar theJProgressBar = (JProgressBar)source;
      System.out.println ("ProgressBar changed: " + theJProgressBar.getValue());
    } else {
      System.out.println ("Something changed: " + source);
    }
  }
}
```

Customizing a JProgressBar Look and Feel

Each installable Swing look and feel provides a different JProgressBar appearance and set of default UIResource values. Figure 12-17 shows the appearance of the JProgressBar component for the preinstalled set of look and feels.

Table 12-6 shows the set of available UIResource-related properties for a JProgressBar. It has 11 different properties.

PROPERTY STRING	OBJECT TYPE
ProgressBar.background	Color
ProgressBar.backgroundHighlight	Color
ProgressBar.border	Border
ProgressBar.cellLength	Integer
ProgressBar.cellSpacing	Integer
ProgressBar.font	Font
ProgressBar.foreground	Color
ProgressBar.foregroundHighlight	Color
ProgressBar.selectionBackground	Color
ProgressBar.selectionForeground	Color
ProgressBarUI	ProgressBarUI

Table 12-6: JProgressBar UIResource elements

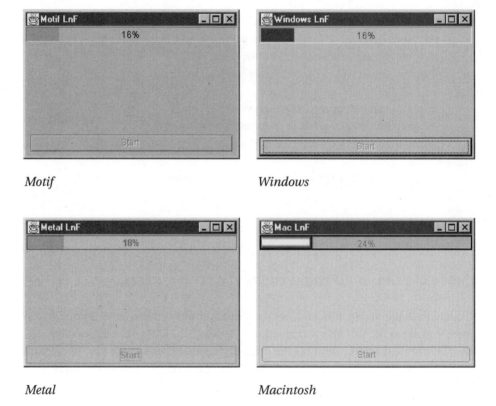

Motif

Windows

Metal

Macintosh

Figure 12-17: JProgressBar under different look and feels

Class `JTextField` and Interface `BoundedRangeModel`

The `JTextField` component is not technically a bounded-range component, but one that nevertheless uses `BoundedRangeModel`. Built inside the `JTextField` is a scrollable area used when the width of the component's contents exceeds its visible horizontal space. A `BoundedRangeModel` controls this scrolling area. We'll look at `JTextField` in more depth in Chapter 14. For now, the following example demonstrates how a `JScrollBar` can track the scrolling area of the `JTextField`. Figure 12-18 shows the example in action.

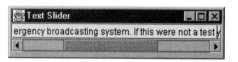

Figure 12-18: Tracking a JTextField width with a JScrollBar

Normally, the `JTextField` has no associated scrollbar. In fact, most look and feels don't offer it as an alternative. However, if this component is something you want to incorporate, you can reuse it in your own applications. Plenty of accessor methods should make reuse simpler and you can avoid having to access the internal pieces directly.

```
import javax.swing.*;
import java.awt.*;
import java.awt.event.*;
public class TextSlider extends JPanel {
  private JTextField textField;
  private JScrollBar scrollBar;
  public TextSlider() {
    setLayout (new BoxLayout (this, BoxLayout.Y_AXIS));
    textField = new JTextField();
    scrollBar = new JScrollBar(JScrollBar.HORIZONTAL);
    BoundedRangeModel brm = textField.getHorizontalVisibility();
    scrollBar.setModel (brm);
    add (textField);
    add (scrollBar);
  }
  public JTextField getTextField () {
    return textField;
  }
  public String getText() {
    return textField.getText();
  }
  public void addActionListener(ActionListener l) {
    textField.addActionListener(l);
  }
  public void removeActionListener(ActionListener l) {
    textField.removeActionListener(l);
```

```
  }
  public JScrollBar getScrollBar() {
    return scrollBar;
  }
  public static void main(String args[]) {
    JFrame f = new ExitableJFrame("Text Slider");
    final TextSlider ts = new TextSlider();
    ts.addActionListener (new ActionListener() {
      public void actionPerformed(ActionEvent e) {
        System.out.println ("Text: " + ts.getText());
      }
    });
    Container c = f.getContentPane();
    c.add (ts, BorderLayout.NORTH);
    f.setSize(300, 200);
    f.setVisible (true);
  }
}
```

Summary

In this chapter, you've learned how to use Swing's JScrollBar, JSlider, and JProgressBar components. You saw how each uses the BoundedRangeModel interface to control the internal data necessary to operate the component, and how the DefaultBoundedRangeModel class offers a default implementation of this data model.

Now that you know how to use the various bounded range components, you can move on to Chapter 13 that looks at the controls that offer data selection: JList and JComboBox.

List Model Controls

CHAPTER 12 EXPLORED THE BOUNDED RANGE controls that support scrolling and the input or display of some bounded range of values. In this chapter, we'll examine the data selection controls, JList and JComboBox, that present a list of choices to choose from. The primary difference between the two is that the JList component supports multiple selection whereas the JComboBox does not. Instead, it lets a user provide a choice that isn't among the available options. Figure 13-1 shows the two controls we'll be examining in more detail.

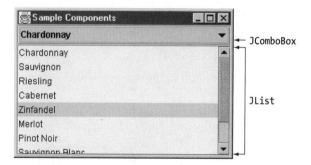

Figure 13-1: Sample JComboBox and JList controls

Interface ListModel

First, we'll examine the data model behind the two ListModel components. This data model originates with the ListModel interface. The AbstractListModel class provides an implementation basis by supporting the management and notification of a set of ListDataListener objects.

In the case of a JList component, the data model implementation is the DefaultListModel class. This class adds an actual data repository, which follows the API of a Vector, for the different elements to be displayed within the JList component.

In the JComboBox component, an extension of the ListModel interface called ComboBoxModel supports the notion of a selected item within the model. The DefaultComboBoxModel class implements the ComboBoxModel interface through yet another interface, the `MutableComboBoxModel`, which supplies methods to support adding and removing elements from the model.

Examining the class hierarchy of the `ListModel` component in Figure 13-2 will help you visualize this situation.

NOTE   *The `BasicDirectoryModel` class shown in Figure 13-2 is used by the file chooser component, `JFileChooser`, as described in Chapter 9.*

The actual `ListModel` interface is rather simple. It provides for management of a `ListDataListener`, and it accesses the size of a particular element of the model.

```java
public interface ListModel {
    // Properties
    public int getSize();
    // Listeners
    public void addListDataListener(ListDataListener l);
    public void removeListDataListener(ListDataListener l);
    // Other Methods
    public Object getElementAt(int index);
}
```

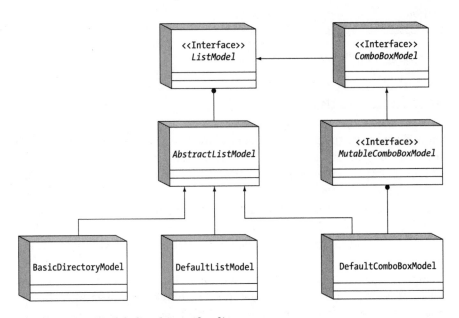

Figure 13-2: ListModel class hierarchy diagram

Class `AbstractListModel`

The `AbstractListModel` class provides a partial implementation of the `ListModel` interface. You need to only provide the data structure and the data. The class provides for the list management of `ListDataListener` objects and the framework for notification of those listeners when the data changes. When you modify the data model, you must then call the appropriate method of `AbstractListModel` to notify the listening `ListDataListener` objects:

- `protected void fireIntervalAdded(Object source, int index0, int index1)` — To be called after adding a contiguous range of values to the list

- `protected void fireIntervalRemoved(Object source, int index0, int index1)` — To be called after removing a contiguous range of values from the list

- `protected void fireContentsChanged(Object source, int index0, int index1)` — To be called if the modified range wasn't contiguous for insertion, removal, or both

> **NOTE** *The ranges specified by the fireXXX() methods of `AbstractListModel` are closed intervals. This simply means that the indices are the end points of the range modified. There's no implied order for the indices: index0, for example, doesn't have to be less than index1. The only requirement is that the methods be called* after *the data model has changed.*

If you have your data in an existing data structure, you need to convert it into a form that one of the Swing components understands, or implement the `ListModel` interface yourself. As you'll see, an array or `Vector` is directly supported by `JList` and `JComboBox`. You can also wrap your data structure into an `AbstractListModel`. For instance, if your initial data structure is an `ArrayList` from the Java 2 Collections framework, you can convert the data structure to a `ListModel` with the following code:

```
final List arrayList = ...;
ListModel model = new AbstractListModel() {
  public int getSize() { return arrayList.size(); }
  public Object getElementAt(int index) {
    return arrayList.get(index);
  }
}
```

Class *DefaultListModel*

The DefaultListModel class provides a data structure for you to store the data internally in the form of a Vector. You're just left with adding the data because the class already manages the ListDataListener list for you.

First, you create the data structure with the no-argument constructor [DefaultListModel model = new DefaultListModel()]. Then, you manipulate it. As shown in Table 13-1, there are only two properties of the DefaultListModel class.

PROPERTY NAME	DATA TYPE	ACCESS
empty	boolean	read-only
size	int	read-write

Table 13-1: DefaultListModel properties

The DefaultListModel class provides all its operational methods through a series of public methods, as shown in Table 13-2.

OPERATION	METHODS
Adding elements	public void add(int index, Object element)
	public void addElement(Object element)
	public void insertElementAt(Object element, int index)
Changing elements	public Object set(int index, Object element)
	public void setElementAt(Object element, int index)
Removing elements	public void clear()
	public Object remove(int index)
	public void removeAllElements()
	public boolean removeElement(Object element)
	public void removeElementAt(int index)
	public void removeRange(int fromIndex, int toIndex)

Table 13-2: DefaultListModel data model modifying methods

> **NOTE** *The addElement() method of DefaultListModel adds the element to the end of the data model. The removeElement() method returns a status: true if it found the object and removed it, and false otherwise.*

The DefaultListModel class is useful when you don't have your data in an existing data structure. For example, the results of a database query come back as a ResultSet. If you wish to use those results as the basis for what to display in a

JList, you must store them somewhere. That somewhere can be a DefaultListModel, as demonstrated by the following:

```
ResultSet results = aJDBCStatement.executeQuery("SELECT columnName FROM
tableName");
DefaultListModel model = new DefaultListModel();
while (results.next())
  model.addElement(result.getString(1));
}
```

Listening for ListModel Events with a ListDataListener

If you're interested in finding out when the contents of the list model change, you can register a ListDataListener with the model. Three separate methods of the interface tell you when contents are added, removed, or altered. Altering the data model means adding and/or removing contents from one or more regions of the data model *or* changing the preexisting contents without adding or removing anything. The interface definition follows.

```
public interface ListDataListener extends EventListener {
  public void contentsChanged(ListDataEvent e);
  public void intervalAdded(ListDataEvent e);
  public void intervalRemoved(ListDataEvent e);
}
```

Upon notification of the list-altering event you're passed a ListDataEvent instance, which contains three properties, as shown in Table 13-3.

PROPERTY NAME	DATA TYPE	ACCESS
index0	int	read-only
index1	int	read-only
type	int	read-only

Table 13-3: ListDataEvent properties

The indices aren't necessarily ordered and neither are the bounds of the altered region. In the case of the list model contents' changing, not everything within the region may have been altered. The area whose contents *did* change is the bounded region specified by the indices. The type property setting would be one of three constants, as shown in Table 13-4, that map directly to the specific interface method called.

TYPE CONSTANT	METHOD
CONTENTS_CHANGED	contentsChanged()
INTERVAL_ADDED	intervalAdded()
INTERVAL_REMOVED	intervalRemoved()

Table 13-4: ListDataEvent type constants

If any ListDataListener objects are attached to the data model when any one of the methods in Table 13-2 are called, each of the listeners will be notified of the data model change. To demonstrate the use of ListDataListener and the dynamic updating of the data model, the following ModifyModelSample program offers all the modifying methods shown in Table 13-2, sending the output in the form of the event and list contents to a JTextArea. Figure 13-3 shows the output for one such run, after several buttons were selected.

> **NOTE** *To help you decode the button labels in Figure 13-3, an F means the method affects the first cell, an M means it affects the middle cell, and an L means it affects the last cell. The removeElement 'Last' label will remove the first element in the data model whose contents is Last.*

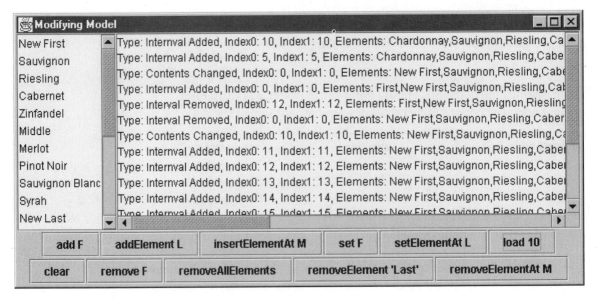

Figure 13-3: A listing for data model changes

The sample `ModifyModelSample` program source follows:

```
import javax.swing.*;
import javax.swing.event.*;
import java.awt.*;
import java.awt.event.*;
import java.io.*;
import java.util.Enumeration;

public class ModifyModelSample {
  static String labels[] = {"Chardonnay", "Sauvignon", "Riesling", "Cabernet",
    "Zinfandel", "Merlot", "Pinot Noir", "Sauvignon Blanc", "Syrah",
    "Gewürztraminer"};

  public static void main(String args[]) {
    JFrame frame = new ExitableJFrame("Modifying Model");
    Container contentPane = frame.getContentPane();

    // Fill model
    final DefaultListModel model = new DefaultListModel();
    for (int i=0, n=labels.length; i<n; i++) {
      model.addElement(labels[i]);
    }
    JList jlist = new JList(model);
    JScrollPane scrollPane1 = new JScrollPane(jlist);
    contentPane.add(scrollPane1, BorderLayout.WEST);

    final JTextArea textArea = new JTextArea();
    textArea.setEditable(false);
    JScrollPane scrollPane2 = new JScrollPane(textArea);
    contentPane.add(scrollPane2, BorderLayout.CENTER);

    ListDataListener listDataListener = new ListDataListener() {
      public void contentsChanged(ListDataEvent listDataEvent) {
        appendEvent(listDataEvent);
      }
      public void intervalAdded(ListDataEvent listDataEvent) {
        appendEvent(listDataEvent);
      }
      public void intervalRemoved(ListDataEvent listDataEvent) {
        appendEvent(listDataEvent);
      }
      private void appendEvent(ListDataEvent listDataEvent) {
        StringWriter sw = new StringWriter();
```

```java
      PrintWriter pw = new PrintWriter(sw);
      switch (listDataEvent.getType()) {
        case ListDataEvent.CONTENTS_CHANGED:
          pw.print("Type: Contents Changed");
          break;
        case ListDataEvent.INTERVAL_ADDED:
          pw.print("Type: Interval Added");
          break;
        case ListDataEvent.INTERVAL_REMOVED:
          pw.print("Type: Interval Removed");
          break;
      }
      pw.print(", Index0: " + listDataEvent.getIndex0());
      pw.print(", Index1: " + listDataEvent.getIndex1());
      DefaultListModel theModel = (DefaultListModel)listDataEvent.getSource();
      Enumeration elements = theModel.elements();
      pw.print(", Elements: ");
      while (elements.hasMoreElements()) {
        pw.print(elements.nextElement());
        pw.print(",");
      }
      pw.println();
      textArea.append(sw.toString());
    }
};

model.addListDataListener(listDataListener);

// Setup buttons
JPanel jp = new JPanel(new GridLayout(2, 1));
JPanel jp1 = new JPanel(new FlowLayout(FlowLayout.CENTER, 1, 1));
JPanel jp2 = new JPanel(new FlowLayout(FlowLayout.CENTER, 1, 1));
jp.add(jp1);
jp.add(jp2);
JButton jb = new JButton("add F");
jp1.add(jb);
jb.addActionListener(new ActionListener() {
  public void actionPerformed(ActionEvent actionEvent) {
    model.add(0, "First");
  }
});
jb = new JButton("addElement L");
jp1.add(jb);
jb.addActionListener(new ActionListener() {
```

```
    public void actionPerformed(ActionEvent actionEvent) {
      model.addElement("Last");
    }
});
jb = new JButton("insertElementAt M");
jp1.add(jb);
jb.addActionListener(new ActionListener() {
  public void actionPerformed(ActionEvent actionEvent) {
    int size = model.getSize();
    model.insertElementAt("Middle", size/2);
  }
});
jb = new JButton("set F");
jp1.add(jb);
jb.addActionListener(new ActionListener() {
  public void actionPerformed(ActionEvent actionEvent) {
    int size = model.getSize();
    if (size != 0)
      model.set(0, "New First");
  }
});
jb = new JButton("setElementAt L");
jp1.add(jb);
jb.addActionListener(new ActionListener() {
  public void actionPerformed(ActionEvent actionEvent) {
    int size = model.getSize();
    if (size != 0)
      model.setElementAt("New Last", size-1);
  }
});
jb = new JButton("load 10");
jp1.add(jb);
jb.addActionListener(new ActionListener() {
  public void actionPerformed(ActionEvent actionEvent) {
    for (int i=0, n=labels.length; i<n ;i++) {
      model.addElement(labels[i]);
    }
  }
});
jb = new JButton("clear");
jp2.add(jb);
jb.addActionListener(new ActionListener() {
  public void actionPerformed(ActionEvent actionEvent) {
```

```
      model.clear();
    }
});
jb = new JButton("remove F");
jp2.add(jb);
jb.addActionListener(new ActionListener() {
  public void actionPerformed(ActionEvent actionEvent) {
    int size = model.getSize();
    if (size != 0)
      model.remove(0);
  }
});
jb = new JButton("removeAllElements");
jp2.add(jb);
jb.addActionListener(new ActionListener() {
  public void actionPerformed(ActionEvent actionEvent) {
    model.removeAllElements();
  }
});
jb = new JButton("removeElement 'Last'");
jp2.add(jb);
jb.addActionListener(new ActionListener() {
  public void actionPerformed(ActionEvent actionEvent) {
    model.removeElement("Last");
  }
});
jb = new JButton("removeElementAt M");
jp2.add(jb);
jb.addActionListener(new ActionListener() {
  public void actionPerformed(ActionEvent actionEvent) {
    int size = model.getSize();
    if (size != 0)
      model.removeElementAt(size/2);
  }
});
jb = new JButton("removeRange FM");
jp2.add(jb);
jb.addActionListener(new ActionListener() {
  public void actionPerformed(ActionEvent actionEvent) {
    int size = model.getSize();
    if (size != 0)
      model.removeRange(0,size/2);
  }
});
```

```
        contentPane.add(jp, BorderLayout.SOUTH);
        frame.setSize(640, 300);
        frame.setVisible(true);
    }
}
```

The retrieving methods of the DefaultListModel class are quite varied in their capabilities. The class has the basic accessor methods public Object get(int index), public Object getElementAt(int index), and public Object elementAt(int index), which all do the same thing; it also has more specific methods. For instance, to work with all elements, you can obtain an instance of Enumeration using public Enumeration elements().

Or, if you want to work with all elements as an array, use either public Object[] toArray() or public void copyInto(Object anArray[]). You can also check for the existence of an element within a model with methods such as public boolean contains(Object element), public int indexOf(Object element), public int indexOf(Object element, int index), public int lastIndexOf(Object element), and public int lastIndexOf(Object element, int index).

> **TIP** *Once you're done adding elements to the data model, it's a good idea to trim its length with public void trimToSize(). This removes any extra space that was preallocated within the internal data structure. In addition, if you know the size of the data model in advance, you can call public void ensureCapacity(int minCapacity) to preallocate space. Both of these methods work only with DefaultListModel.*

Interface ComboBoxModel

The ComboBoxModel interface extends the ListModel interface. The key reason for this extension is that the classes that implement the ComboBoxModel interface need to manage the selected item internally through a selectedItem property, as shown by the interface definition.

```
public interface ComboBoxModel extends ListModel {
    // Properties
    public Object getSelectedItem();
    public void setSelectedItem(Object anItem);
}
```

Interface MutableComboBoxModel

In addition to the ComboBoxModel interface, another data model interface, MutableComboBoxModel, extends ComboBoxModel to make methods available to modify the data model.

```
public interface MutableComboBoxModel extends ComboBoxModel {
  // Other Methods
  public void addElement(Object obj);
  public void insertElementAt(Object obj, int index);
  public void removeElement(Object obj);
  public void removeElementAt(int index);
}
```

It's an implementation of *this* interface that the JComboBox component uses by default.

Class DefaultComboBoxModel

The DefaultComboBoxModel class extends the AbstractListModel class to provide an appropriate data model for the JComboBox. Because of this extension, it inherits the managing of the ListDataListener list.

Like DefaultListModel, DefaultComboBoxModel adds the necessary data structure for you to collect elements to show within a component. Also, because the model is modifiable, implementing MutableComboBoxModel causes the data model to call the various fileXXX() methods of the AbstractListModel class when the data elements within the model change.

> **NOTE** *If you create a DefaultComboBoxModel from an array, the elements of the array are copied into an internal data structure. If you use a Vector, they're not copied; instead, the actual Vector is used internally.*

To use the data model, you must first create the model with one of the three constructors:

1. `public DefaultComboBoxModel()`
   `DefaultComboBoxModel model = new DefaultComboBoxModel();`

2. ```
   public DefaultComboBoxModel(Object listData[])
   String labels[] = {"Chardonnay", "Sauvignon", "Riesling", "Cabernet",
   "Zinfandel", "Merlot", "Pinot Noir", "Sauvignon Blanc", "Syrah",
   "Gewürztraminer"};
   DefaultComboBoxModel model = new DefaultComboBoxModel(labels);
   ```

3. ```
   public DefaultComboBoxModel(Vector listData)
   Vector vector = aBufferedImage.getSources();
   DefaultComboBoxModel model = new DefaultComboBoxModel(vector);
   ```

Next, you manipulate the model. Two new properties are introduced in the
DefaultComboBoxModel class, as shown in Table 13-5.

PROPERTY NAME	DATA TYPE	ACCESS
selectedItem	Object	read-write
size	int	read-only

Table 13-5: DefaultComboBoxModel properties

The data model modification methods for the DefaultComboBoxModel are different
than those for DefaultListModel. They all come from the MutableComboBoxModel
interface: public void addElement(Object element), public void
insertElementAt(Object element, int index), public boolean
removeElement(Object element), and public void removeElementAt(int index).

Due to the flexibility (and functionality) of the DefaultComboBoxModel, it's usually unnecessary to create your own ComboBoxModel implementation. Just create
an instance of DefaultComboBoxModel and you're all set. Then, simply fill it up from
the appropriate data source.

> **NOTE** *One case in which you may wish to provide your own model is when
> you need to support the presence of the same item within the model multi-
> ple times. With the DefaultComboBoxModel, if you have two items in the list
> whose equals() methods will return true, the model won't work properly.*

If you really want to define your own model implementation, perhaps because
you have the data in your own data structure already, it works best to subclass
the AbstractListModel and implement the ComboBoxModel or MutableComboBoxModel
interface methods. When subclassing the AbstractListModel, you merely have to
provide the data structure and the access into it. Because the "selected item" part

of the data model is maintained outside the primary data structure, you need a place to store that, as well. The following program source demonstrates one such implementation using an `ArrayList` as the data structure. The program includes a `main()` method to demonstrate the usage of the model within a `JComboBox`. Figure 13-4 shows the model in action using the current system properties as the source for the data model elements.

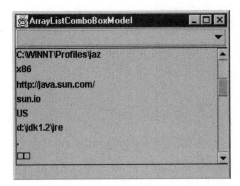

Figure 13-4: Using an ArrayListComboBoxModel

The program source follows:

```
import java.awt.*;
import javax.swing.*;
import java.util.Collection;
import java.util.ArrayList;
public class ArrayListComboBoxModel extends AbstractListModel implements
ComboBoxModel {
  private Object selectedItem;
  private ArrayList anArrayList;
  public ArrayListComboBoxModel(ArrayList arrayList) {
    anArrayList = arrayList;
  }
  public Object getSelectedItem() {
    return selectedItem;
  }
  public void setSelectedItem(Object newValue) {
    selectedItem = newValue;
  }
```

```
  public int getSize() {
    return anArrayList.size();
  }
  public Object getElementAt(int i) {
    return anArrayList.get(i);
  }

  public static void main(String args[]) {
    JFrame frame = new ExitableJFrame("ArrayListComboBoxModel");

    Collection col = System.getProperties().values();
    ArrayList arrayList = new ArrayList(col);
    ArrayListComboBoxModel model = new ArrayListComboBoxModel(arrayList);

    JComboBox comboBox = new JComboBox(model);

    Container contentPane = frame.getContentPane();
    contentPane.add(comboBox, BorderLayout.NORTH);
    frame.setSize(300, 225);
    frame.setVisible(true);
  }
}
```

Class JList

The JList component is the basic Swing component for selecting one or more items from a set of choices. You present the list of choices to the user and the user can pick one or several, depending on the selection mode of the component.

Three key elements and their implementations define the JList structure:

- A data model for holding the JList data, as defined by the ListModel interface

- A cell renderer for drawing the elements of the JList, as described by the ListCellRenderer interface

- A selection model for selecting elements of the JList, as described by the ListSelectionModel interface

Figure 13-5 shows the relationships of these objects to the JList.

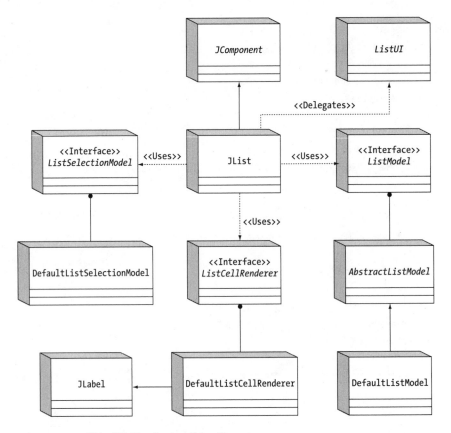

Figure 13-5: JList UML relationship diagram

Creating JList Components

The JList component has four constructors, which allow you to create a JList instance based on your initial data structure. If you use the no-argument constructor, you can fill in the data later. However, if you use the array or Vector constructor, you can't alter the contents.

1. ```
   public JList()
   JList jlist = new JList();
   ```

2. ```
   public JList(Object listData[])
   String labels[] = {"Chardonnay", "Sauvignon", "Riesling", "Cabernet",
   "Zinfandel", "Merlot", "Pinot Noir", "Sauvignon Blanc", "Syrah",
   "Gewürztraminer"};
   JList jlist = new JList(labels);
   ```

3. public JList(Vector listData)
```
Vector vector = aBufferedImage.getSources();
JList jlist = new JList(vector);
```

4. public JList(ListModel model)
```
ResultSet results = aJDBCStatement.executeQuery("SELECT columnName FROM
tableName");
DefaultListModel model = new DefaultListModel();
while (result.next())
  model.addElement(result.getString(1));
JList jlist = new JList(model);
```

> **NOTE** *If you want to display something other than the* toString() *results of each array element, see the section "Rendering JList Elements" later in this chapter.*

JList Properties

After creating a JList component, you can modify each of its many properties. Table 13-6 shows the 29 properties of JList.

PROPERTY NAME	DATA TYPE	ACCESS
accessibleContext	AccessibleContext	read-only
anchorSelectionIndex	int	read-only
cellRenderer	ListCellRenderer	read-write bound
firstVisibleIndex	int	read-only
fixedCellHeight	int	read-write bound
fixedCellWidth	int	read-write bound
lastVisibleIndex	int	read-only
leadSelectionIndex	int	read-only
listData	Vector	write-only
maxSelectionIndex	int	read-only
minSelectionIndex	int	read-only
model	ListModel	read-write bound
preferredScrollableViewportSize	Dimension	read-only
prototypeCellValue	Object	read-write bound
scrollableTracksViewportHeight	boolean	read-only
scrollableTracksViewportWidth	boolean	read-only

(continued)

Table 13-6 (continued)

PROPERTY NAME	DATA TYPE	ACCESS
selectedIndex	int	read-write
selectedIndices	int[ ]	read-write
selectedValue	Object	read-only
selectedValues	Object[ ]	read-only
selectionBackground	Color	read-write bound
selectionEmpty	boolean	read-only
selectionForeground	Color	read-write bound
selectionMode	int	read-write
selectionModel	ListSelectionModel	read-write bound
UI	ListUI	read-write
UIClassID	String	read-only
valueIsAdjusting	boolean	read-write
visibleRowCount	int	read-write bound

Table 13-6: JList properties

Many of the JList properties are related to the process of selection. For instance, anchorSelectionIndex, leadSelectionIndex, maxSelectionIndex, minSelectionIndex, selectedIndex, and selectedIndices deal with the indices of the selected rows, while selectedValue and selectedValues relate to the contents of the selected elements. The anchor selection index is the most recent index0 of a ListDataEvent, whereas the lead selection index is the most recent index1.

To control the preferred number of visible rows shown, set the visibleRowCount property of JList. The default setting for this property is 8.

Scrolling JList Components

When you're working with a JList component, you must place the component within a JScrollPane if you want to allow the user to pick from all available choices. If it's not placed within a JScrollPane and the default number of rows displayed is smaller than the size of the data model, or if there isn't sufficient space to display the rows, then the other choices aren't shown. When placed within a JScrollPane, the JList offers a vertical scrollbar to move through all the available choices.

If you don't place a JList in a JScrollPane and the number of choices exceeds the available space, only the first group of choices will be visible (see Figure 13-6).

Figure 13-6: A ten-element JList, in and out of a JScrollPane

> **TIP** *Whenever you see that a class implements the* Scrollable *interface, it should serve as a reminder to place that component within a* JScrollPane.

The JScrollPane relies on the dimensions provided by the preferredScrollable ViewportSize property setting to determine the preferred size of the pane contents. When the data model of a JList is empty, a default size of 16 pixels high by 256 pixels wide per visible row is used. Otherwise, the width is determined by looping through all the cells to find the widest one, and the height is determined by the height of the first cell.

To speed the sizing of the view port for the JScrollPane, you can define a prototype cell by setting the prototypeCellValue property. You must be sure the prototype toString() value is sufficiently wide and tall to accommodate all the contents of the JList. Then, the JScrollPane bases the sizing of its view port on the prototype and it won't be necessary for the JList to ask each cell for its size; instead, it will ask only for the prototype.

Another way of speeding performance is to assign a size to the fixedCellHeight and fixedCellWidth properties. Setting these properties is another way to avoid asking each cell for its rendered size. Setting both properties is the fastest way to have a JList sized within a view port. Of course, this is also the least flexible because it ensures that the JList choices aren't widened (or shortened) when the contents change. However, if you have a large number of entries in the data model, this loss of flexibility may be worthwhile to improve performance. Figure 13-7 helps you to visualize some of the sizing capabilities of a JList.

The source used to generate the output in Figure 13-7 follows. The center list in the figure contains more than 1,000 fixed-size cells. The top list shows that you can set the number of visible rows with setVisibleRowCount(). Notice that the bottom list in the figure also uses setVisibleRowCount(). However, because the list isn't in a JScrollPane, the request to limit the number of rows is ignored.

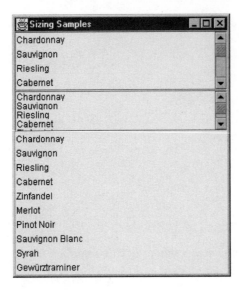

Figure 13-7: Sizing entries within a JList

```java
import javax.swing.*;
import java.awt.*;
public class SizingSamples {
  public static void main(String args[]) {
    String labels[] = {"Chardonnay", "Sauvignon", "Riesling", "Cabernet",
      "Zinfandel", "Merlot", "Pinot Noir", "Sauvignon Blanc", "Syrah",
      "Gewürztraminer"};

    JFrame frame = new ExitableJFrame("Sizing Samples");
    Container contentPane = frame.getContentPane();

    JList jlist1 = new JList(labels);
    jlist1.setVisibleRowCount(4);
    DefaultListModel model = new DefaultListModel();
    model.ensureCapacity(1000);
    for (int i=0;i<100;i++) {
      for (int j=0;j<10;j++) {
        model.addElement(labels[j]);
      }
    }
    JScrollPane scrollPane1 = new JScrollPane(jlist1);
    contentPane.add(scrollPane1, BorderLayout.NORTH);
```

```
    JList jlist2 = new JList(model);
    jlist2.setVisibleRowCount(4);
    jlist2.setFixedCellHeight(12);
    jlist2.setFixedCellWidth(200);
    JScrollPane scrollPane2 = new JScrollPane(jlist2);
    contentPane.add(scrollPane2, BorderLayout.CENTER);

    JList jlist3 = new JList(labels);
    jlist3.setVisibleRowCount(4);
    contentPane.add(jlist3, BorderLayout.SOUTH);

    frame.setSize(300, 350);
    frame.setVisible(true);
  }
}
```

In addition placing a JList within a JScrollPane, you can also find out which choices are visible or request that a specific element be made visible. The firstVisibleIndex and lastVisibleIndex properties allow you to find out which choices are currently visible within the JScrollPane. Both methods return –1 if nothing is visible; this usually happens where the data model is empty. To request that a specific element be made visible, just use the public void ensureIndexIsVisible(int index) method. For instance, to programmatically move the list to the top, use the following:

```
jlist.ensureIndexIsVisible(0);
```

Rendering JList Elements

Every element within the JList is called a cell. Every JList has an installed cell renderer that draws every cell when the list needs to be drawn. The default renderer, DefaultListCellRenderer, is a subclass of JLabel, which means you can use either text or an icon as the graphical depiction for the cell. This tends to suit most users' needs, but sometimes the cell's appearance can benefit from some customization. And, because every JList can have at most one renderer installed, customization requires that you replace the existing renderer.

Interface `ListCellRenderer`/Class `DefaultListCellRenderer`

The JList has an installed renderer. A class that implements the ListCellRenderer interface provides this renderer.

```
public interface ListCellRenderer {
  public Component getListCellRendererComponent(JList list, Object value, int
index, boolean isSelected, boolean cellHasFocus);
}
```

When it's time to draw each cell, the interface's sole method is called. The returned renderer provides the specific rendering for that one cell of the JList. The JList then uses the rendering to draw the element, and then gets the next renderer.

A reference to the enclosing JList is provided to the getListCellRendererComponent() method so that the renderer can share display characteristics. The value of the selection contains the object in the list's data model at position index. The index is zero-based from the beginning of the data model. The last two parameters allow you to customize the cell's appearance based on the cell's state, that is, whether it's selected or has the input focus.

We'll create a renderer to demonstrate this. The sole difference for this renderer is that the cell with the input focus has a titled border. After the renderer is created, you install it by setting the cellRenderer property of the JList. Figure 13-8 shows the output.

> **TIP** *For performance reasons, it is best not to create the actual renderer in the getListCellRendererComponent() method. Either subclass* Component *and return "this" or create a class variable to hold one instance of a* Component, *which then may be customized and returned.*

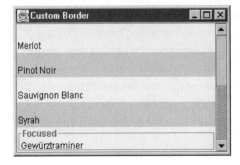

Figure 13-8: A JList with a custom focus border cell renderer

Source for the renderer follows.

```java
import java.awt.*;
import javax.swing.*;
import javax.swing.border.*;
public class FocusedTitleListCellRenderer implements ListCellRenderer {
  protected static Border noFocusBorder =
    new EmptyBorder(15, 1, 1, 1);
  protected static TitledBorder focusBorder =
    new TitledBorder(LineBorder.createGrayLineBorder(), "Focused");
  protected DefaultListCellRenderer defaultRenderer = new
DefaultListCellRenderer();

  public String getTitle() {
    return focusBorder.getTitle();
  }
  public void setTitle(String newValue) {
    focusBorder.setTitle(newValue);
  }

  public Component getListCellRendererComponent(JList list, Object value, int
index, boolean isSelected, boolean cellHasFocus) {
    JLabel renderer = (JLabel)defaultRenderer.getListCellRendererComponent(
      list, value, index, isSelected, cellHasFocus);
    renderer.setBorder(cellHasFocus ? focusBorder : noFocusBorder);
    return renderer;
  }
}
```

> **WARNING** *A common mistake when creating your own renderer is forgetting to make the renderer component opaque. This causes the background coloration of the renderer to be ignored and the list container's background to bleed through. With the DefaultListCellRenderer class, the renderer component is already opaque.*

A sample program that uses the new renderer follows. It doesn't do anything special other than install the custom cell renderer that was just created.

```java
import javax.swing.*;
import java.awt.*;
public class CustomBorderSample {
```

Learning Resource Centre

```
public static void main(String args[]) {
  String labels[] = {"Chardonnay", "Sauvignon", "Riesling", "Cabernet",
    "Zinfandel", "Merlot", "Pinot Noir", "Sauvignon Blanc", "Syrah",
    "Gewürztraminer"};
  JFrame frame = new ExitableJFrame("Custom Border");
  Container contentPane = frame.getContentPane();
  JList jlist = new JList(labels);
  ListCellRenderer renderer = new FocusedTitleListCellRenderer();
  jlist.setCellRenderer(renderer);
  JScrollPane sp = new JScrollPane(jlist);
  contentPane.add(sp, BorderLayout.CENTER);
  frame.setSize(300, 200);
  frame.setVisible(true);
}
}
```

Creating a Complex `ListCellRenderer`

More often than not, custom cell renderers (like that shown in Figure 13-8) are necessary when the data model consists of more-complex data in each element — something not representable by a text string. For instance, imagine that each element of the data model consists of a font, foreground color, icon, and text string. Ensuring the proper usage of these elements within the renderer simply involves a little more work in configuring the renderer component. In this particular example, we'll store within an array each element of the data model. A new class could have been defined or a hash table used just as easily.

The output of this example is shown in Figure 13-9.

This renderer merely customizes the renderer component returned by the `DefaultListCellRenderer`. The customization is based on the data model value being passed in as an array to the `value` argument of the `getListCellRendererComponent()` method.

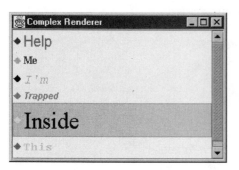

Figure 13-9: Using a more-complex list cell renderer

```
import java.awt.*;
import javax.swing.*;
import javax.swing.border.*;
public class ComplexCellRenderer implements ListCellRenderer {
  protected DefaultListCellRenderer defaultRenderer = new
DefaultListCellRenderer();
```

```
    public Component getListCellRendererComponent(JList list, Object value, int
index,
        boolean isSelected, boolean cellHasFocus) {
      Font theFont        = null;
      Color theForeground = null;
      Icon theIcon        = null;
      String theText      = null;

      JLabel renderer = (JLabel)defaultRenderer.getListCellRendererComponent(
        list, value, index, isSelected, cellHasFocus);

      if (value instanceof Object[]) {
        Object values[] = (Object[])value;
        theFont         = (Font)values[0];
        theForeground   = (Color)values[1];
        theIcon         = (Icon)values[2];
        theText         = (String)values[3];
      } else {
        theFont         = list.getFont();
        theForeground   = list.getForeground();
        theText         = "";
      }
      if (!isSelected) {
        renderer.setForeground(theForeground);
      }
      if (theIcon != null) {
        renderer.setIcon(theIcon);
      }
      renderer.setText(theText);
      renderer.setFont(theFont);
      return renderer;
    }
}
```

The following demonstration program reuses the DiamondIcon created in Chapter 4.
Most of the code is for initialization of the data model.

```
import javax.swing.*;
import java.awt.*;
public class ComplexRenderingSample {
  public static void main(String args[]) {
```

```
Object elements[][] = {
  {new Font("Helvetica", Font.PLAIN, 20), Color.red,
    new DiamondIcon(Color.blue), "Help"},
  {new Font("TimesRoman", Font.BOLD, 14), Color.blue,
    new DiamondIcon(Color.green), "Me"},
  {new Font("Courier", Font.ITALIC, 18), Color.green,
    new DiamondIcon(Color.black), "I'm"},
  {new Font("Helvetica", Font.BOLD | Font.ITALIC, 12), Color.gray,
    new DiamondIcon(Color.magenta), "Trapped"},
  {new Font("TimesRoman", Font.PLAIN, 32), Color.pink,
    new DiamondIcon(Color.yellow), "Inside"},
  {new Font("Courier", Font.BOLD, 16), Color.yellow,
    new DiamondIcon(Color.red), "This"},
  {new Font("Helvetica", Font.ITALIC, 8), Color.darkGray,
    new DiamondIcon(Color.pink), "Computer"}
};

JFrame frame = new ExitableJFrame("Complex Renderer");
Container contentPane = frame.getContentPane();

JList jlist = new JList(elements);
ListCellRenderer renderer = new ComplexCellRenderer();
jlist.setCellRenderer(renderer);
JScrollPane scrollPane = new JScrollPane(jlist);
contentPane.add(scrollPane, BorderLayout.CENTER);

frame.setSize(300, 300);
frame.setVisible(true);
  }
}
```

When you create your own rendering components, you'll find it's best to start with the default list cell renderer. This allows you to focus on the specific details you're interested in. Otherwise, you'd have to worry about everything, such as the default selection foreground and background colors, or whether you've remembered to make the component opaque. Of course, if you want to configure everything yourself, feel free to do so.

Selecting JList Elements

By default, every JList component is in multi-select mode. This means that you can select multiple elements within the component. How you select multiple elements depends on the user interface you're employing. For instance, with the Metal look and feel interface, CTRL-select (CTRL key and left mouse button on a right-handed mouse) acts as a selection toggle, and SHIFT-select acts as a means of range selection.

Interface ListSelectionModel/Class DefaultListSelectionModel

An implementation of the ListSelectionModel interface controls the selection mechanism for a JList component. The interface definition, shown here, defines constants for different selection modes and describes how to manage a list of ListSelectionListener objects. It also provides the means to describe several selection intervals.

```
public interface ListSelectionModel {
  // Constants
  public final static int MULTIPLE_INTERVAL_SELECTION;
  public final static int SINGLE_INTERVAL_SELECTION;
  public final static int SINGLE_SELECTION;
  // Properties
  public int getAnchorSelectionIndex();
  public void setAnchorSelectionIndex(int index);
  public int getLeadSelectionIndex();
  public void setLeadSelectionIndex(int index);
  public int getMaxSelectionIndex();
  public int getMinSelectionIndex();
  public boolean isSelectionEmpty();
  public int getSelectionMode();
  public void setSelectionMode(int selectionMode);
  public boolean getValueIsAdjusting();
  public void setValueIsAdjusting(boolean valueIsAdjusting);
  // Listeners
  public void addListSelectionListener(ListSelectionListener x);
  public void removeListSelectionListener(ListSelectionListener x);
  // Other Methods
  public void addSelectionInterval(int index0, int index1);
  public void clearSelection();
  public void insertIndexInterval(int index, int length, boolean before);
  public boolean isSelectedIndex(int index);
  public void removeIndexInterval(int index0, int index1);
  public void removeSelectionInterval(int index0, int index1);
  public void setSelectionInterval(int index0, int index1);
}
```

Three different selection modes are available. Table 13-7 contains the name of each mode and its description. Figure 13-10 shows you the results of each selection mode.

MODE	DESCRIPTION
SINGLE_SELECTION	One item at a time can be selected.
SINGLE_INTERVAL_SELECTION	One contiguous range of items can be selected.
MULTIPLE_INTERVAL_SELECTION	Any set of ranges can be selected.

Table 13-7: ListSelectionModel modes

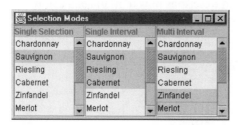

Figure 13-10: Visual representation of selection modes

To change the selection mode of a JList, set its selectionMode property to one of the ListSelectionModel constants shown in Table 13-7. For instance, the following would change a list to single selection mode:

```
JList list = new JList(...);
list.setSelectionMode(ListSelectionModel.SINGLE_SELECTION);
```

The DefaultListSelectionModel class is the default implementation of the ListSelectionModel interface. You can examine any of its eight properties, shown in Table 13-8, to learn about the currently selected range.

PROPERTY NAME	DATA TYPE	ACCESS
anchorSelectionIndex	int	read-write
leadAnchorNotificationEnabled	boolean	read-write
leadSelectionIndex	int	read-write
maxSelectionIndex	int	read-only
minSelectionIndex	int	read-only
selectionEmpty	boolean	read-only
selectionMode	int	read-write
valueIsAdjusting	boolean	read-write

Table 13-8: DefaultListSelectionModel properties

The selection model can show you what is currently being used in the multi-selection mode when the selectionEmpty property is false. Simply ask each index between the minimum and maximum selection indices if it's selected with public boolean isSelectedIndex(int index). Because multi-selection mode supports noncontiguous areas, this is the only way to find out what's selected. However, the selectedIndices property of JList provides this information for you without your having to check manually.

Listening to JList Events with a ListSelectionListener

If you want to know when elements of a JList have been selected, you need to attach a ListSelectionListener to the JList or the ListSelectionModel. The addListSelectionListener() and removeListenerListener() methods of the JList only delegate to the underlying ListSelectionModel. When the set of selected elements changes, attached listener objects get notified. The interface definition follows:

```
public interface ListSelectionListener extends EventListener {
  public void valueChanged(ListSelectionEvent e);
}
```

The ListSelectionEvent instance received by the listener describes the range of affected elements for *this* selection event, as well as whether or not the selection is still changing, as shown in Table 13-9. When a user is still altering selected elements, with a valueIsAdjusting setting of true, you might want to delay performing costly operations such as drawing a high-resolution graphics presentation.

PROPERTY NAME	DATA TYPE	ACCESS
firstIndex	int	read-only
lastIndex	int	read-only
valueIsAdjusting	boolean	read-only

Table 13-9: ListSelectionEvent properties

In order to demonstrate selection with a JList, the following program adds a JTextArea to a window to show the output of the selection listener. The listener prints out the currently selected items by item position and value. Figure 13-11 shows the appearance of the running program.

This example prints out only the currently selected items when it is not doing a rapid update (when isAdjusting reports false). Otherwise, the program merely reports the starting and ending range of selection changes, as well as the adjusting status. The example examines the selectedIndices and selectedValues properties of JList to get an ordered list of selected items. The selected indices array and `selected values` array are ordered in the same way, so a particular element of the data model will show up in the same position in both lists.

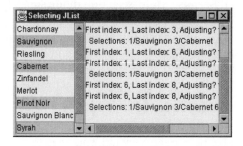

Figure 13-11: Listening for JList selections

```
import javax.swing.*;
import javax.swing.event.*;
import java.awt.*;
import java.io.*;

public class SelectingJListSample {
  public static void main(String args[]) {
    String labels[] = {"Chardonnay", "Sauvignon", "Riesling", "Cabernet",
      "Zinfandel", "Merlot", "Pinot Noir", "Sauvignon Blanc", "Syrah",
      "Gewürztraminer"};
    JFrame frame = new ExitableJFrame("Selecting JList");
    Container contentPane = frame.getContentPane();

    JList jlist = new JList(labels);
    JScrollPane scrollPane1 = new JScrollPane(jlist);
    contentPane.add(scrollPane1, BorderLayout.WEST);

    final JTextArea textArea = new JTextArea();
    textArea.setEditable(false);
    JScrollPane scrollPane2 = new JScrollPane(textArea);
    contentPane.add(scrollPane2, BorderLayout.CENTER);

    ListSelectionListener listSelectionListener = new ListSelectionListener() {
      public void valueChanged(ListSelectionEvent listSelectionEvent) {
        StringWriter sw = new StringWriter();
        PrintWriter pw = new PrintWriter(sw);
        pw.print("First index: " + listSelectionEvent.getFirstIndex());
        pw.print(", Last index: " + listSelectionEvent.getLastIndex());
```

```
        boolean adjust = listSelectionEvent.getValueIsAdjusting();
        pw.println(", Adjusting? " + adjust);
        if (!adjust) {
          JList list = (JList)listSelectionEvent.getSource();
          int selections[] = list.getSelectedIndices();
          Object selectionValues[] = list.getSelectedValues();
          for (int i=0, n=selections.length; i<n; i++) {
            if (i==0) {
              pw.print("  Selections: ");
            }
            pw.print(selections[i] + "/" + selectionValues[i] + " ");
          }
          pw.println();
        }
        textArea.append(sw.toString());
      }
    };
    jlist.addListSelectionListener(listSelectionListener);

    frame.setSize(350, 200);
    frame.setVisible(true);
  }
}
```

> **NOTE** *If you know that a* JList *is in single-selection mode, you can get the currently selected item with either the* selectedIndex *or* selectedValue *properties.*

There's no special selection event for double-clicking on an item in the list. If you're interested in double-click events, you have to fall back to the AWT MouseEvent-MouseListener pair. Adding the following code to the previous program will add appropriate text to the JTextArea for double-click events. The key method here is the public int locationToIndex(Point location) method of JList, which attempts to map screen coordinates to list elements.

```
import java.awt.event.*;
...
MouseListener mouseListener = new MouseAdapter() {
    public void mouseClicked(MouseEvent mouseEvent) {
      JList theList = (JList)mouseEvent.getSource();
      if (mouseEvent.getClickCount() == 2) {
```

```
        int index = theList.locationToIndex(mouseEvent.getPoint());
        if (index >= 0) {
          Object o = theList.getModel().getElementAt(index);
          textArea.append("Double-clicked on: " + o.toString());
          textArea.append(System.getProperty("line.separator"));
        }
      }
    }
  };
  jlist.addMouseListener(mouseListener);
```

> **NOTE** *The* JList *class also provides the* public Point indexToLocation(int index) *method, which produces the reverse behavior, returning a* Point *as the origin of the provided index.*

Manually Selecting JList Events

In addition to detecting when a user selects items in a list, you can also programmatically select or deselect items. If any ListSelectionListener objects are attached to the JList, they'll be notified when the set of selected items is programmatically altered.

- For a single item, public void setSelectedValue(Object element, boolean shouldScroll) selects the first item that matches the *element*. If the element wasn't previously selected, everything that *was* selected will be deselected first.

- For a range of items, public void setSelectedInterval(int index0, int index1) selects an inclusive range.

- For adding a range of selected items to the already selected set, use public void addSelectedInterval(int index0, int index1).

- You can clear all the selected items with the public void clearSelection() method.

- You can clear a range of selected items with the public void removeSelectedInterval(int index0, int index1) method.

Customizing a JList Look and Feel

Each installable Swing look and feel provides a different JList appearance and set of default UIResource value settings for the component. Figure 13-12 shows the appearance of the JList component for the preinstalled set of look and feels: Motif, Windows, Metal, and Macintosh.

Motif

Windows

Metal

Macintosh

Figure 13-12: JList under different look and feels

The available set of UIResource-related properties for a JList is shown in Table 13-10. For the JList component, there are nine different properties.

PROPERTY STRING	OBJECT TYPE
List.background	Color
List.border	Border
List.cellRenderer	ListCellRender
List.focusCellHighlightBorder	Border
List.font	Font
List.foreground	Color
List.selectionBackground	Color
List.selectionForeground	Color
ListUI	ListUI

Table 13-10: JList UIResource elements

DualListBox Example

In order to help you better understand the JList component, I've provided a complete JList example by creating a new Swing component called a DualListBox. The primary purpose of a dual list box is to create two lists of choices: one to pick from, and one that makes up your result set. This works great when the initial choice list is sizable. Trying to multi-select from a JList that contains many selections can be annoying, especially if you happen to deselect what you've already selected because you didn't have the SHIFT or CTRL key held down. With a dual list box, you select items in the first list and move them into the second. The user can easily scroll through the two lists without fear of accidentally deselecting anything. Figure 13-13 shows how the DualListBox might look like in use.

To use this custom component, create it by calling the constructor [DualListBox dual = new DualListBox()], and then fill it up with data by using either setSourceElements() or addSourceElements(), with each one taking either a ListModel or an array argument. The add version supplements the existing choices, whereas the

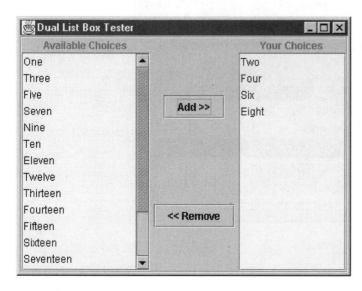

Figure 13-13: The DualListBox in action

set version clears out the choices first. When it's time to ask the component what the user selected, you can ask for an Enumeration of the chosen elements with destinationElements(). Additional properties you may want to configure include:

- The source choices' title defaulting to "Available Choices."

- The destination choices' title defaulting to "Your Choices."

- Changing the source or destination list cell renderer, visible row count, foreground color, or background color.

The complete source code for our new DualListBox component follows. The included main() method demonstrates the component.

```java
import java.awt.*;
import java.awt.event.*;
import javax.swing.*;
import java.util.Enumeration;

public class DualListBox extends JPanel {

  private static final Insets EMPTY_INSETS = new Insets(0,0,0,0);
  private static final String ADD_BUTTON_LABEL = "Add >>";
  private static final String REMOVE_BUTTON_LABEL = "<< Remove";
  private static final String DEFAULT_SOURCE_CHOICE_LABEL = "Available Choices";
  private static final String DEFAULT_DEST_CHOICE_LABEL = "Your Choices";
  private JLabel sourceLabel;
  private JList sourceList;
  private DefaultListModel sourceListModel;
  private JList destList;
  private DefaultListModel destListModel;
  private JLabel destLabel;
  private JButton addButton;
  private JButton removeButton;
  public DualListBox() {
    initScreen();
  }
  public String getSourceChoicesTitle() {
    return sourceLabel.getText();
  }
  public void setSourceChoicesTitle(String newValue) {
    sourceLabel.setText(newValue);
  }
```

```
public String getDestinationChoicesTitle() {
  return destLabel.getText();
}
public void setDestinationChoicesTitle(String newValue) {
  destLabel.setText(newValue);
}
public void clearSourceListModel() {
  sourceListModel.clear();
}
public void clearDestinationListModel() {
  destListModel.clear();
}
public void addSourceElements(ListModel newValue) {
  fillListModel(sourceListModel, newValue);
}
public void setSourceElements(ListModel newValue) {
  clearSourceListModel();
  addSourceElements(newValue);
}
public void addDestinationElements(ListModel newValue) {
  fillListModel(destListModel, newValue);
}
private void fillListModel(DefaultListModel model, ListModel newValues) {
  int size = newValues.getSize();
  for (int i=0; i<size; i++) {
    model.addElement(newValues.getElementAt(i));
  }
}
public void addSourceElements(Object newValue[]) {
  fillListModel(sourceListModel, newValue);
}
public void setSourceElements(Object newValue[]) {
  clearSourceListModel();
  addSourceElements(newValue);
}
public void addDestinationElements(Object newValue[]) {
  fillListModel(destListModel, newValue);
}
private void fillListModel(DefaultListModel model, Object newValues[]) {
  int size = newValues.length;
  for (int i=0; i<size; i++) {
    model.addElement(newValues[i]);
  }
```

```
  }
  public Enumeration sourceElements() {
    return sourceListModel.elements();
  }
  public Enumeration destinationElements() {
    return destListModel.elements();
  }
  public void setSourceCellRenderer(ListCellRenderer newValue) {
    sourceList.setCellRenderer(newValue);
  }
  public ListCellRenderer getSourceCellRenderer() {
    return sourceList.getCellRenderer();
  }
  public void setDestinationCellRenderer(ListCellRenderer newValue) {
    destList.setCellRenderer(newValue);
  }
  public ListCellRenderer getDestinationCellRenderer() {
    return destList.getCellRenderer();
  }
  public void setVisibleRowCount(int newValue) {
    sourceList.setVisibleRowCount(newValue);
    destList.setVisibleRowCount(newValue);
  }
  public int getVisibleRowCount() {
    return sourceList.getVisibleRowCount();
  }
  public void setSelectionBackground(Color newValue) {
    sourceList.setSelectionBackground(newValue);
    destList.setSelectionBackground(newValue);
  }
  public Color getSelectionBackground() {
    return sourceList.getSelectionBackground();
  }
  public void setSelectionForeground(Color newValue) {
    sourceList.setSelectionForeground(newValue);
    destList.setSelectionForeground(newValue);
  }
  public Color getSelectionForeground() {
    return sourceList.getSelectionForeground();
  }
  private void clearSourceSelected() {
    int selected[] = sourceList.getSelectedIndices();
    for (int i=selected.length-1; i >= 0; --i) {
```

```
                        sourceListModel.removeElementAt(selected[i]);
                }
        }
        private void clearDestinationSelected() {
            int selected[] = destList.getSelectedIndices();
            for (int i=selected.length-1; i >= 0; −i) {
                destListModel.removeElementAt(selected[i]);
            }
        }
        private void initScreen() {
            setBorder(BorderFactory.createEtchedBorder());
            setLayout(new GridBagLayout());
            sourceLabel = new JLabel(DEFAULT_SOURCE_CHOICE_LABEL);
            sourceListModel = new DefaultListModel();
            sourceList = new JList(sourceListModel);
            add(sourceLabel, new TheGridBagConstraints(0, 0, 1, 1, 0, 0,
                GridBagConstraints.CENTER, GridBagConstraints.NONE, EMPTY_INSETS, 0, 0));
            add(new JScrollPane(sourceList), new TheGridBagConstraints(0, 1, 1, 5, .5, 1,
                GridBagConstraints.CENTER, GridBagConstraints.BOTH, EMPTY_INSETS, 0, 0));

            addButton = new JButton(ADD_BUTTON_LABEL);
            add(addButton, new TheGridBagConstraints(1, 2, 1, 2, 0, .25,
                GridBagConstraints.CENTER, GridBagConstraints.NONE, EMPTY_INSETS, 0, 0));
            addButton.addActionListener(new AddListener());
            removeButton = new JButton(REMOVE_BUTTON_LABEL);
            add(removeButton, new TheGridBagConstraints(1, 4, 1, 2, 0, .25,
                GridBagConstraints.CENTER, GridBagConstraints.NONE, new Insets(0,5,0,5), 0,
0));
            removeButton.addActionListener(new RemoveListener());

            destLabel = new JLabel(DEFAULT_DEST_CHOICE_LABEL);
            destListModel = new DefaultListModel();
            destList = new JList(destListModel);
            add(destLabel, new TheGridBagConstraints(2, 0, 1, 1, 0, 0,
                GridBagConstraints.CENTER, GridBagConstraints.NONE, EMPTY_INSETS, 0, 0));
            add(new JScrollPane(destList), new TheGridBagConstraints(2, 1, 1, 5, .5, 1.0,
                GridBagConstraints.CENTER, GridBagConstraints.BOTH, EMPTY_INSETS, 0, 0));
        }

        public static void main(String args[]) {
            JFrame f = new ExitableJFrame("Dual List Box Tester");
            DualListBox dual = new DualListBox();
            dual.addSourceElements(new String[] {"One", "Two", "Three"});
```

```
      dual.addSourceElements(new String[] {"Four", "Five", "Six"});
      dual.addSourceElements(new String[] {"Seven", "Eight", "Nine"});
      dual.addSourceElements(new String[] {"Ten", "Eleven", "Twelve"});
      dual.addSourceElements(new String[] {"Thirteen", "Fourteen", "Fifteen"});
      dual.addSourceElements(new String[] {"Sixteen", "Seventeen", "Eighteen"});
      dual.addSourceElements(new String[] {"Nineteen", "Twenty", "Thirty"});
      f.getContentPane().add(dual, BorderLayout.CENTER);
      f.setSize(400, 300);
      f.setVisible(true);
    }
    private class AddListener implements ActionListener {
      public void actionPerformed(ActionEvent e) {
        Object selected[] = sourceList.getSelectedValues();
        addDestinationElements(selected);
        clearSourceSelected();
      }
    }
    private class RemoveListener implements ActionListener {
      public void actionPerformed(ActionEvent e) {
        Object selected[] = destList.getSelectedValues();
        addSourceElements(selected);
        clearDestinationSelected();
      }
    }
  }
}
```

I'll admit that there's room for improvement in the example in this section. For instance, the two lists could be sorted. Nevertheless, it demonstrates the JList capabilities quite well and provides a good starting point. If I weren't trying to let this program work under JDK 1.1, I would have used the Java Collections API for sorting and the new GridBagLayout constructor (instead of my TheGridBagConstraints class) for single-line initialization. You can also fix up the program to return choices to their original position in the source list after they're removed from the destination list.

Class JComboBox

The JComboBox component of the Swing component set is a multi-part component that allows a user to choose from a predefined set of choices with the help of a pull-down list. In its basic configuration, a JComboBox acts like a JLabel to display the current user selection. Embedded within the JLabel is a pop-up menu containing choices within a JList control. When the desired choice isn't available, the JComboBox can use a JTextField to enter a new choice. The JList part is automatically embedded within a `JScrollPane` when desired; you don't have to manually create the `JList` or place it in the `JScrollPane`. In addition, the text field for editing is disabled by default, permitting a user to select from the set of pre-defined choices. Figure 13-14 shows two `JComboBox` components, one showing its list of choices but which is not editable, the other not showing its choices but which is editable.

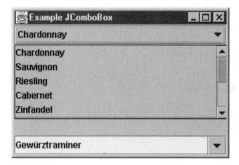

Figure 13-14: Sample JComboBox components

Four essential elements define the `JComboBox` component and their implementations:

- A data model for holding the `JComboBox` data, as defined by the `ListModel` interface

- A cell renderer for drawing the elements of the `JComboBox`, as described by the `ListCellRenderer` interface

- An editor for entering choices not part of the predefined data model, as defined by the `ComboBoxEditor` interface

- A keystroke manager for handling keyboard input to select elements of the `JComboBox`, as described by the `KeySelectionManager` interface

Figure 13-15 shows the relationships of these objects to the `JComboBox`.

Many of these capabilities are shared with the `JList` component. This isn't accidental; the two components are fairly similar. Let's now look at the `JComboBox` in more detail.

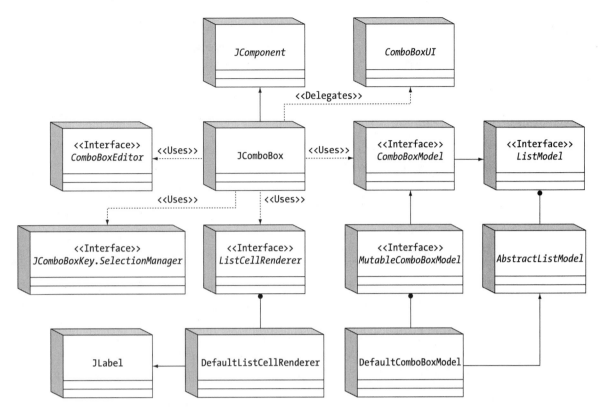

Figure 13-15: JComboBox UML relationship diagram

Creating JComboBox Components

Like the JList component, the JComboBox component has four constructors,
allowing you to create one based on your initial data structure. *Unlike* the JList
component, the default model used by the array and Vector constructor permits
the adding and removing of data elements.

1. public JComboBox()
    JComboBox comboBox = new JComboBox();

2. public JComboBox(Object listData[])
    String labels[] = {"Chardonnay", "Sauvignon", "Riesling", "Cabernet",
    "Zinfandel", "Merlot", "Pinot Noir", "Sauvignon Blanc", "Syrah",
    "Gewürztraminer"};
    JComboBox comboBox = new JComboBox(labels);

3. ```
   public JComboBox(Vector listData)
   Vector vector = aBufferedImage.getSources();
   JComboBox comboBox = new JComboBox(vector);
   ```

4. ```
   public JComboBox(ComboBoxModel model)
   ResultSet results = aJDBCStatement.executeQuery("SELECT columnName FROM
   tableName");
   DefaultComboBoxModel model = new DefaultComboBoxModel();
   while (result.next())
     model.addElement(results.getString(1));
   JComboBox comboBox = new JComboBox(model);
   ```

JComboBox Properties

After you create a JComboBox component, you can modify each of its many properties. Table 13-11 shows the 18 properties of JComboBox.

PROPERTY NAME	DATA TYPE	ACCESS
accessibleContext	AccessibleContext	read-only
actionCommand	String	read-write
editable	boolean	read-write bound
editor	ComboBoxEditor	read-write bound
enabled	boolean	write-only bound
focusTraversable	boolean	read-only
itemCount	int	read-only
keySelectionManager	JComboBox.KeySelectionManager	read-write
lightWeightPopupEnabled	boolean	read-write
maximumRowCount	int	read-write bound
model	ComboBoxModel	read-write bound
popupVisible	boolean	read-write
renderer	ListCellRenderer	read-write bound
selectedIndex	int	read-write
selectedItem	Object	read-write
selectedObjects	Object[ ]	read-only
UI	ComboBoxUI	read-write
UIClassID	String	read-only

Table 13-11: JComboBox properties

The significant properties of the JComboBox are concerned with the display of the pop-up. You can control the maximum number of visible entries in the pop-up by setting the maximumRowCount property. The lightWeightPopupEnabled property setting helps determine the type of window to use when displaying the pop-up menu of choices. If the component fits completely within the top-level window of the program, the component will be lightweight. If it doesn't fit, it will be heavyweight. If you're mixing AWT and Swing components in a program, you can force the pop-up menu of choices to be heavyweight by setting the lightWeightPopupEnabled property to true. This will force the pop-up to appear above other components. The remaining property related to the pop-up list is the popupVisible property, which allows you to programmatically display the pop-up list.

> **NOTE** *Besides setting the popupVisible property, you can use the public void hidePopup() and public void showPopup() methods to toggle the pop-up visibility status.*

Rendering JComboBox Elements

The rendering of elements within a JComboBox is done with a ListCellRenderer. This is the same renderer that is used for a JList component. Once you've created a renderer for either one of these two components, you can use that renderer for the other component. If we reused the ComplexCellRenderer from earlier in the chapter, we could add the following lines to the ComplexRenderingSample example to have the two components share the same renderer.

```
JComboBox comboBox = new JComboBox(elements);
comboBox.setRenderer(renderer);
contentPane.add(comboBox, BorderLayout.NORTH);
```

The output of adding these lines is shown in Figure 13-16.

> **NOTE** *You might notice that the pop-up for the JComboBox in Figure 13-16 is larger than it needs to be given the available choices. This happened because of the varying sizes of the different elements. The number of elements within the pop-up multiplied by the tallest element determines the height of the pop-up. To get rid of the extra space, you can limit the number of visible choices with setMaximumRowCount(). However, it also uses the maximum element height to calculate visible space, so more choices than required could be visible; consequently, you will lose the extra space at the bottom.*

Figure 13-16: A JComboBox with a custom renderer

Not all renderers will work as expected with both the JComboBox and JList components. For instance, the FocusedTitleListCellRenderer demonstrated earlier in Figure 13-8 wouldn't show the "Focused" title border in a JComboBox because the choices never had the input focus. In addition, different components may have different default colors (unselected background color in this case). It may be necessary to ask what color the component normally would be rendered in, and act accordingly.

Selecting JComboBox Elements

The JComboBox component supports at least three different events related to selection. You can listen for keyboard input to support key selection with the help of the JComboBox.KeySelectionManager class. You can also listen with an ActionListener or an ItemListener to find out when the selected item of the JComboBox changes.

If you want to programmatically select an element, use public void setSelectedItem(Object element) or public void setSelectedIndex(int index).

TIP   *To programmatically deselect the current choice of a* JComboBox, *call* setSelectedIndex() *with an argument of –1.*

Listening to Keyboard Events with a KeySelectionManager

The JComboBox has a public inner interface that's fairly important. KeySelectionManager, and its default implementation, manages selection from the keyboard of items within the JComboBox. The default manager locates the next element that corresponds to the pressed key. It has no memory, so it strictly matches the first letter of an element. If you don't like this behavior, you can either turn it off or create a new key selection manager.

NOTE   *The* KeySelectionManager *works only in combo boxes that are not editable.*

If you want to turn off the key selection capabilities, you can't do so by simply setting the keySelectionManager property to null. Instead, you must create an implementation of the interface with an appropriate method. The single method of the interface is public int selectionForKey(char aKey, ComboBoxModel aModel). In the event the pressed key doesn't match any elements, the routine needs to return –1. Otherwise, it should return the position of the matched element. So, to ignore keyboard input, the routine should always return –1, as shown here:

```
JComboBox.KeySelectionManager manager =
  new JComboBox.KeySelectionManager() {
    public int selectionForKey(char aKey, ComboBoxModel aModel) {
      return -1;
    }
  };
aJcombo.setKeySelectionManager(manager);
```

On the other hand, if you want to have a key selection manager remembering previous keystrokes so that it can allow the user to "home in" on a textual choice, there's a little more work involved.

All keys pressed without a three-second delay between keystrokes are considered part of the same input-matching group (unless a key is invalid). If what has been entered so far matches the beginning of an element within the JComboBox, then the selected item changes.

The selectionForKey() method makes up the bulk of the work. It converts input keys to uppercase and compares the results to the uppercase variant of the elements of the data model. The following example demonstrates multi-key support.

```
import javax.swing.*;
import java.awt.event.*;

public class MultiKeySelectionManager implements JComboBox.KeySelectionManager {
  private StringBuffer currentSearch = new StringBuffer();
  private Timer resetTimer;
  private final static int RESET_DELAY = 3000;
  public MultiKeySelectionManager() {
    resetTimer = new Timer(RESET_DELAY, new ActionListener() {
      public void actionPerformed(ActionEvent actionEvent) {
        currentSearch.setLength(0);
      }
    });
  }
  public int selectionForKey(char aKey, ComboBoxModel aModel) {
    // Reset if invalid character
    if (aKey == KeyEvent.CHAR_UNDEFINED) {
      currentSearch.setLength(0);
      return -1;
    }
    // Since search, don't reset search
    resetTimer.stop();
    // Convert input to uppercase
    char key = Character.toUpperCase(aKey);
    // Build up search string
    currentSearch.append(key);
    // Find selected position within model to starting searching from
    Object selectedElement = aModel.getSelectedItem();
    int selectedIndex = -1;
    if (selectedElement != null) {
      for (int i=0, n=aModel.getSize(); i<n; i++) {
        if (aModel.getElementAt(i) == selectedElement) {
          selectedIndex = i;
          break;
        }
      }
    }
    boolean found = false;
    String search = currentSearch.toString();
```

```
  // Search from selected forward, wrap back to beginning if not found
  for (int i=0, n=aModel.getSize(); i<n; i++) {
    String element =
aModel.getElementAt(selectedIndex).toString().toUpperCase();
    if (element.startsWith(search)) {
      found = true;
      break;
    }
    selectedIndex++;
    if (selectedIndex == n) {
      selectedIndex = 0; // wrap
    }
  }
  // Restart timer
  resetTimer.start();
  return(found ? selectedIndex : -1);
  }
}
```

After you've created the manager, you simply need to install it with something like the following:

```
JComboBox comboBox = new JComboBox(labels);
MultiKeySelectionManager mk = new MultiKeySelectionManager();
comboBox.setKeySelectionManager(mk);
```

Once installed, the manager automatically processes keystrokes. You can also programmatically signal the key selection manager to perform its duties with the selectWithKeyChar() method of JComboBox.

Listening to JComboBox Events with an ActionListener

The primary means of listening for selection events is through an ActionListener. It will tell you when an element has been selected within a JComboBox. Unfortunately, the listener doesn't know which element is selected.

Because the ActionListener can't identify the selected element, it must ask the JComboBox that served as the source of the event. To determine the selected element from the JComboBox, use either getSelectedItem() or getSelectedIndex(). If an index of –1 is returned, then the currently selected item isn't part of the model. This seemingly impossible situation happens when the JComboBox is editable and the user has entered a value that isn't part of the original model.

> **NOTE** *The text string comboBoxChanged is the action command for the ActionEvent sent to the ActionListener when an item within a JComboBox changes.*

Listening to JComboBox Events with an ItemListener

If you use an ItemListener to find out when the selected item within a JComboBox changes, you'll also learn which item was deselected.

To demonstrate both the ActionListener and the ItemListener, the following program attaches both of them to the same JComboBox. The ActionListener prints its "action command," as well as the currently selected item. The ItemListener prints the affected item and the state change for it, as well as the currently selected item. Figure 13-17 shows the results after the program has been running for some time.

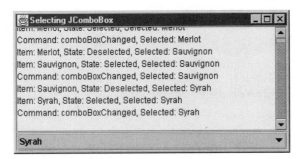

Figure 13-17: Listening for JComboBox selections

The source code for the example follows:

```java
import javax.swing.*;
import javax.swing.event.*;
import java.awt.*;
import java.awt.event.*;
import java.io.*;

public class SelectingComboSample {
  static private String selectedString(ItemSelectable is) {
    Object selected[] = is.getSelectedObjects();
    return((selected.length == 0) ? "null" : (String)selected[0]);
  }
```

```
public static void main(String args[]) {
  String labels[] = {"Chardonnay", "Sauvignon", "Riesling", "Cabernet",
    "Zinfandel", "Merlot", "Pinot Noir", "Sauvignon Blanc", "Syrah",
    "Gewürztraminer"};
  JFrame frame = new ExitableJFrame("Selecting JComboBox");
  Container contentPane = frame.getContentPane();

  JComboBox comboBox = new JComboBox(labels);
  contentPane.add(comboBox, BorderLayout.SOUTH);

  final JTextArea textArea = new JTextArea();
  textArea.setEditable(false);
  JScrollPane sp = new JScrollPane(textArea);
  contentPane.add(sp, BorderLayout.CENTER);

  ItemListener itemListener = new ItemListener() {
    public void itemStateChanged(ItemEvent itemEvent) {
      StringWriter sw = new StringWriter();
      PrintWriter pw = new PrintWriter(sw);
      int state = itemEvent.getStateChange();
      String stateString =
        ((state == ItemEvent.SELECTED) ? "Selected" : "Deselected");
      pw.print("Item: " + itemEvent.getItem());
      pw.print(", State: " + stateString);
      ItemSelectable is = itemEvent.getItemSelectable();
      pw.print(", Selected: " + selectedString(is));
      pw.println();
      textArea.append(sw.toString());
    }
  };
  comboBox.addItemListener(itemListener);

  ActionListener actionListener = new ActionListener() {
    public void actionPerformed(ActionEvent actionEvent) {
      StringWriter sw = new StringWriter();
      PrintWriter pw = new PrintWriter(sw);
      pw.print("Command: " + actionEvent.getActionCommand());
      ItemSelectable is = (ItemSelectable)actionEvent.getSource();
      pw.print(", Selected: " + selectedString(is));
      pw.println();
      textArea.append(sw.toString());
    }
```

```
    };
    comboBox.addActionListener(actionListener);

    frame.setSize(400, 200);
    frame.setVisible(true);
  }
}
```

Listening to JComboBox Events with a ListDataListener

You can attach a ListDataListener to the data model of the JComboBox. This listener would then be notified when the selected element of the model changes. Unfortunately, the listener would also be notified of other data model changes. In other words, using a ListDataListener to find out when an element of a JComboBox is selected is *not* a recommended option.

> **NOTE** *Mouse movement and cursor movement events within a JComboBox don't change the selected entry; mouse release events* do *change the selected entry. Any registered listeners would be notified when a selected mouse button is released over an element within the JComboBox pop-up.*

Editing JComboBox Elements

There will be times when you want to use a combo box like a text field in which you list the most likely text input from the user, but also allow the user to enter something else. By enabling the editable property of the JComboBox, you've added this capability. To demonstrate, Figure 13-18 shows an editable JComboBox. The screen also contains a text area that reports the current selected item and index. Even if you manually enter one of the choices within the JComboBox, getSelectedIndex() will report the proper position. Remember that if you enter a value that's not present, getSelectedIndex() returns –1. The source for the example follows.

```
import java.awt.*;
import javax.swing.*;
import java.awt.event.*;
public class EditComboBox {
  public static void main(String args[]) {
    String labels[] = {"Chardonnay", "Sauvignon", "Riesling", "Cabernet",
      "Zinfandel", "Merlot", "Pinot Noir", "Sauvignon Blanc", "Syrah",
```

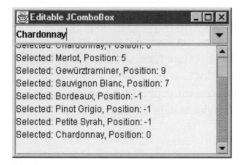

Figure 13-18: Using an editable JComboBox

```
      "Gewürztraminer"};
   JFrame frame = new ExitableJFrame("Editable JComboBox");
   Container contentPane = frame.getContentPane();

   final JComboBox comboBox = new JComboBox(labels);
   comboBox.setMaximumRowCount(5);
   comboBox.setEditable(true);
   contentPane.add(comboBox, BorderLayout.NORTH);

   final JTextArea textArea = new JTextArea();
   JScrollPane scrollPane = new JScrollPane(textArea);
   contentPane.add(scrollPane, BorderLayout.CENTER);

   ActionListener actionListener = new ActionListener() {
     public void actionPerformed(ActionEvent actionEvent) {
       textArea.append("Selected: " + comboBox.getSelectedItem());
       textArea.append(", Position: " + comboBox.getSelectedIndex());
       textArea.append(System.getProperty("line.separator"));
     }
   };
   comboBox.addActionListener(actionListener);

   frame.setSize(300, 200);
   frame.setVisible(true);
  }
}
```

By default, the input field provided for editing is a JTextField. The default JTextField serves as a good editor if your data model consists of text strings. However, once your model contains a different type of object (for example, colors), you need to provide a different editor. By default, once you type in the text field (editing the results of toString() for your element), the object is treated as a String. Technically, a different editor isn't always necessary. If you can parse the contents of the text field as a string to the proper data type, then do that. But, if you want to restrict the input in any manner (for example, allow only numeric input) or provide a better input mechanism, you must provide your own editor. The interface that defines the necessary behavior is called ComboBoxEditor and its definition is shown here.

```
public interface ComboBoxEditor {
  // Properties
  public Component getEditorComponent();
  public Object getItem();
  public void setItem(Object anObject);
  // Listeners
  public void addActionListener(ActionListener l);
  public void removeActionListener(ActionListener l);
  // Other Methods
  public void selectAll();
}
```

> **NOTE** *The default editor is the* BasicComboBoxEditor *implementation in the* javax.swing.plaf.basic *package.*

The add/remove listener methods are necessary for notifying any listeners when the ComboBoxEditor value has changed. It's not necessary for you to add a listener, and normally you won't. Nevertheless, the methods are part of the interface, so they'll need to be implemented if you want to provide your own editor.

The getEditorComponent() method returns the Component object used for the editor. You can use either an AWT or a Swing component for the editor (for example, a JColorChooser for color selection). The selectAll() method is called when the editor is first shown. It tells the editor to select everything within it. Selecting everything allows a user to merely type over the current input for the default JTextField case. Some editors may not require use of this method.

The item property methods demand the most work when you're providing a custom editor. You'll need to provide a method to map the specific pieces of the Object subclass to the components in order to present the data to be edited. You then need to get the data from the editor so that the data can be stored back in an instance of the original object.

To demonstrate, the following source code is a ComboBoxEditor for the Color class. A custom editor is necessary because there's no automatic way to parse the results of editing the default string shown for a Color. This editor will use a JColorChooser for the user to pick a new color value. The getItem() method needs to return only the current value, a Color. The setItem() method needs to convert the object passed to a Color object; the argument to setItem() is an Object. The setItem() method could be made to accept only Color arguments. However, for this example, any string that's decodable with the Color.decode() method is also supported.

```java
import java.awt.*;
import javax.swing.*;
import javax.swing.event.*;
import java.awt.event.*;
public class ColorComboBoxEditor implements ComboBoxEditor {
  final protected JButton editor;
  protected EventListenerList listenerList = new EventListenerList();
  public ColorComboBoxEditor(Color initialColor) {
    editor = new JButton("");
    editor.setBackground(initialColor);
    ActionListener actionListener = new ActionListener() {
      public void actionPerformed(ActionEvent e) {
        Color currentBackground = editor.getBackground();
        Color color = JColorChooser.showDialog(
          editor, "Color Chooser", currentBackground);
        if ((color != null) && (currentBackground != color)) {
          editor.setBackground(color);
          fireActionEvent(color);
        }
      }
    };
    editor.addActionListener(actionListener);
  }
  public void addActionListener(ActionListener l) {
    listenerList.add(ActionListener.class, l);
  }
  public Component getEditorComponent() {
    return editor;
  }
  public Object getItem() {
    return editor.getBackground();
  }
  public void removeActionListener(ActionListener l) {
    listenerList.remove(ActionListener.class, l);
  }
  public void selectAll() {
```

```
      // ignore
    }
    public void setItem(Object newValue) {
      if (newValue instanceof Color) {
        Color color = (Color)newValue;
        editor.setBackground(color);
      } else {
        // Try to decode
        try {
          Color color = Color.decode(newValue.toString());
          editor.setBackground(color);
        } catch (NumberFormatException e) {
          // ignore - value unchanged
        }
      }
    }
    protected void fireActionEvent(Color color) {
      Object listeners[] = listenerList.getListenerList();
      for (int i = listeners.length-2; i>=0; i-=2) {
        if (listeners[i] == ActionListener.class) {
          ActionEvent actionEvent =
            new ActionEvent(editor, ActionEvent.ACTION_PERFORMED,
color.toString());
          ((ActionListener)listeners[i+1]).actionPerformed(actionEvent);
        }
      }
    }
  }
```

To use the new editor, you need to associate it with a JComboBox. After you change the EditComboBox example listed earlier in this section to make the data model consist of an array of Color objects, you can then install the editor by adding the following:

```
Color color = (Color)comboBox.getSelectedItem();
ComboBoxEditor editor = new ColorComboBoxEditor(color);
comboBox.setEditor(editor);
```

A complete test program follows. It's different than the EditComboBox because I've added a JLabel below the JComboBox that stays in sync with the currently selected color of the JComboBox. There's also a custom cell renderer that sets the background color to the value of the cell. Figure 13-19 shows the screen and a visible editor.

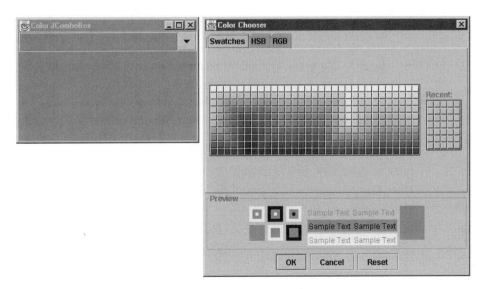

Figure 13-19: Using a custom ComboBoxEditor

```
import java.awt.*;
import javax.swing.*;
import java.awt.event.*;
public class ColorComboBox {
  static class ColorCellRenderer implements ListCellRenderer {
    protected DefaultListCellRenderer defaultRenderer = new
DefaultListCellRenderer();
    // width doesn't matter as combobox will size
    private final static Dimension preferredSize = new Dimension(0, 20);
    public Component getListCellRendererComponent(JList list, Object value, int
index,
        boolean isSelected, boolean cellHasFocus) {
      JLabel renderer = (JLabel)defaultRenderer.getListCellRendererComponent(
        list, value, index, isSelected, cellHasFocus);
      if (value instanceof Color) {
        renderer.setBackground((Color)value);
      }
      renderer.setPreferredSize(preferredSize);
      return renderer;
    }
  }
  public static void main(String args[]) {
    Color colors[] = {Color.black, Color.blue, Color.cyan, Color.darkGray,
      Color.gray, Color.green, Color.lightGray, Color.magenta, Color.orange,
```

```
              Color.pink, Color.red, Color.white, Color.yellow};
      JFrame frame = new ExitableJFrame("Color JComboBox");
      Container contentPane = frame.getContentPane();

      final JComboBox comboBox = new JComboBox(colors);
      comboBox.setMaximumRowCount(5);
      comboBox.setEditable(true);
      comboBox.setRenderer(new ColorCellRenderer());
      Color color = (Color)comboBox.getSelectedItem();
      ComboBoxEditor editor = new ColorComboBoxEditor(color);
      comboBox.setEditor(editor);
      contentPane.add(comboBox, BorderLayout.NORTH);

      final JLabel label = new JLabel();
      label.setOpaque(true);
      label.setBackground((Color)comboBox.getSelectedItem());
      contentPane.add(label, BorderLayout.CENTER);

      ActionListener actionListener = new ActionListener() {
        public void actionPerformed(ActionEvent actionEvent) {
          Color selectedColor = (Color)comboBox.getSelectedItem();
          label.setBackground(selectedColor);
        }
      };
      comboBox.addActionListener(actionListener);

      frame.setSize(300, 200);
      frame.setVisible(true);
    }
}
```

Customizing a JComboBox Look and Feel

Each installable Swing look and feel provides a different JComboBox appearance and set of default UIResource value settings for the component. Figure 13-20 shows the appearance of the JComboBox component for the preinstalled set of look and feels: Motif, Windows, Metal, and Macintosh.

The available set of UIResource-related properties for a JComboBox is shown in Table 13-12. The JComboBox component has 13 different properties.

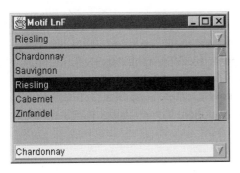

Motif

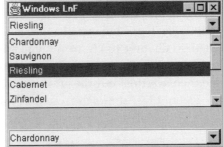

Windows

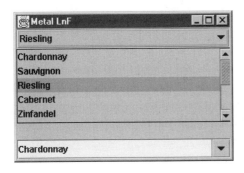

Metal

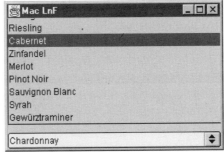

Macintosh

Figure 13-20: JComboBox under different look and feels

PROPERTY STRING	OBJECT TYPE
ComboBox.background	Color
ComboBox.border	Border
ComboBox.control	Color
ComboBox.controlForeground	Color
ComboBox.disabledBackground	Color
ComboBox.disabledForeground	Color
ComboBox.font	Font
ComboBox.foreground	Color
ComboBox.listBackground	Color
ComboBox.listForeground	Color
ComboBox.selectionBackground	Color
ComboBox.selectionForeground	Color
ComboBoxUI	ComboBoxUI

Table 13-12: JComboBox UIResource elements

Changing the pop-up icon is one example of customizing the look and feel. To do this, you'll need to install a new user interface. (This process is discussed at length in Chapter 18.) Basically, you are going to inherit the default functionality from either the BasicComboBoxUI or MetalComboBoxUI user interface delegates, and then override only the protected JButton createArrowButton() method.

Figure 13-21 shows the results of this change to the JComboBox user interface.

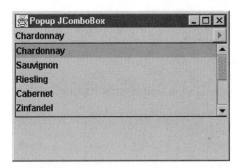

Figure 13-21: Altering the JComboBox pop-up button

The source for the JComboBox example follows:

```
import java.awt.*;
import javax.swing.*;
import javax.swing.plaf.*;
import javax.swing.plaf.basic.*;
public class PopupComboSample {
  public static void main(String args[]) {
    String labels[] = {"Chardonnay", "Sauvignon", "Riesling", "Cabernet",
      "Zinfandel", "Merlot", "Pinot Noir", "Sauvignon Blanc", "Syrah",
      "Gewürztraminer"};
    JFrame frame = new ExitableJFrame("Popup JComboBox");
    Container contentPane = frame.getContentPane();

    JComboBox comboBox = new JComboBox(labels);
    comboBox.setMaximumRowCount(5);
    comboBox.setUI((ComboBoxUI)MyComboBoxUI.createUI(comboBox));
    contentPane.add(comboBox, BorderLayout.NORTH);

    frame.setSize(300, 200);
    frame.setVisible(true);
    comboBox.showPopup();
  }
```

```
   static class MyComboBoxUI extends BasicComboBoxUI {
     public static ComponentUI createUI(JComponent c) {
       return new MyComboBoxUI();
     }
     protected JButton createArrowButton() {
       JButton button = new BasicArrowButton(BasicArrowButton.EAST);
       return button;
     }
   }
 }
}
```

Shared Data Model Example

You may have noticed several similarities between the parts that make up the
JComboBox and JList. You can use the same data model and same renderer for
both components. Ignoring the use of a shared renderer between components,
which was already shown, I'll demonstrate how you'd share the same data model
across several components.

The example has two editable combo boxes and one JList, all sharing one
data model. There'll also be a button on the screen that will dynamically add
items to the data model. Because the data model will be associated with several
components, you'll notice that each of them has additional options to choose
from after selecting the button. Figure 13-22 shows what the screen might look
like after adding several elements.

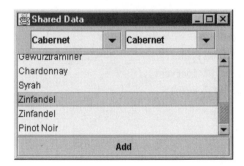

Figure 13-22: Sharing a data model across components

And, here is the source:

```
import java.awt.*;
import java.awt.event.*;
```

```java
import javax.swing.*;
public class SharedDataSample {
  public static void main(String args[]) {
    final String labels[] = {"Chardonnay", "Sauvignon", "Riesling", "Cabernet",
      "Zinfandel", "Merlot", "Pinot Noir", "Sauvignon Blanc", "Syrah",
      "Gewürztraminer"};
    final DefaultComboBoxModel model = new DefaultComboBoxModel(labels);

    JFrame frame = new ExitableJFrame("Shared Data");
    Container contentPane = frame.getContentPane();

    JPanel panel = new JPanel();
    JComboBox comboBox1 = new JComboBox(model);
    comboBox1.setMaximumRowCount(5);
    comboBox1.setEditable(true);

    JComboBox comboBox2 = new JComboBox(model);
    comboBox2.setMaximumRowCount(5);
    comboBox2.setEditable(true);
    panel.add(comboBox1);
    panel.add(comboBox2);
    contentPane.add(panel, BorderLayout.NORTH);

    JList jlist = new JList(model);
    JScrollPane scrollPane = new JScrollPane(jlist);
    contentPane.add(scrollPane, BorderLayout.CENTER);

    JButton button = new JButton("Add");
    contentPane.add(button, BorderLayout.SOUTH);
    ActionListener actionListener = new ActionListener() {
      public void actionPerformed(ActionEvent actionEvent) {
        int index = (int)(Math.random()*labels.length);
        model.addElement(labels[index]);
      }
    };
    button.addActionListener(actionListener);

    frame.setSize(300, 200);
    frame.setVisible(true);
  }
}
```

> **NOTE** *When running the previous program, if you share a data model across multiple* JComboBox *components, there can't be a different selected element within each component. When an element is "selected" in one, it's selected in all. This seems to be a bug in the MVC design of the* JComboBox. *In addition, because a* ListSelectionModel *manages selection for the* JList, *changing the selected element of a* JComboBox *has no effect on the selected elements within a* JList *sharing the same model.*

Summary

This chapter has demonstrated how to use Swing's JList and JComboBox components. You've seen how each component supports its own data model, renderer, selection capabilities, and even a custom editor for the JComboBox component. Although all these capabilities are customizable, each of the components is readily usable with its default configuration.

In Chapter 14, we'll explore the Swing text components.

CHAPTER 14

Basic Text Components

CHAPTER 13 EXPLORED THE DATA SELECTION controls within the Swing component set. In this chapter, we'll look at the basic capabilities of the Swing text components. (The more-advanced text component capabilities are covered in Chapter 15.)

The Swing component set features five text components. Two replace their AWT counterparts and three are brand new. Just like in the AWT world, they all share a common parent class. I'll start off by discussing that parent class, JTextComponent. It defines the common behavior that's necessary for all text controls.

The direct subclasses of JTextComponent are JTextField, JTextArea, and JEditorPane. The JTextField is used for a single line of single-attributed text (that is, a single font and a single color). It is a direct replacement for the AWT TextField component. JTextField has a single subclass JPasswordField for those times when a JTextField needs to be used with an input mask for the entry of a password. (This is unlike the AWT world, in which TextField is used directly for that purpose.) The other replacement AWT component is JTextArea, which replaces the TextArea component. The JTextArea is used for multiple lines of single-attributed text input.

The remaining two text components are the JEditorPane and its subclass JTextPane. Neither one of them replaces any of the standard AWT components. The JEditorPane is a generic editor that can support the editing of multi-attributed input. The JTextPane is customized for plain text input. In both cases, the input can be images as well as components. Figure 14.1 should help you visualize this class hierarchy.

> **NOTE** *All JTextComponent subclasses are in the javax.swing package. With the exception of the event-related pieces, the remaining support interfaces and classes discussed in this chapter are found in the javax.swing.text package (or a subpackage). Like all event-related pieces, the text pieces are found in the javax.swing.event package.*

Like all other Swing components, text components live in an MVC world. The components shown in Figure 14-1 are the various available UI delegates. The remaining part of the UI-delegate is the text view, which is based on the View class and discussed further in Chapter 15. The data model for each of the components

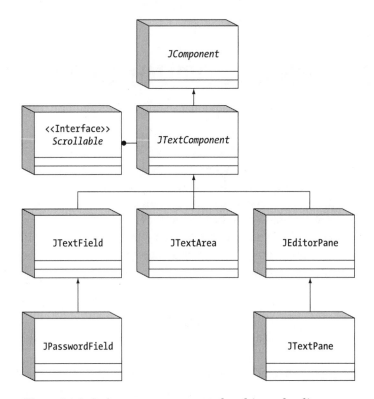

Figure 14-1: Swing text component class hierarchy diagram

is an implementation of the Document interface, of which there are five extensions (or implementations). The single-attributed components use the PlainDocument class as their data model, while the multi-attributed components use DefaultStyledDocument as their model. Both of these classes subclass the AbstractDocument class, which defines their common Document interface implementation. The DefaultStyledDocument class also implements the StyledDocument interface, which is an extension of Document for supporting multi-attributed content. An additional Document implementation, HTMLDocument, is available for the JEditorPane when its content type is text/html.

Many other classes to be discussed in this chapter and in Chapter 15 are common among the text components. As with many of the other Swing components, you can customize the look and feel of the components without creating a new UI delegate. For the text components, the Highlighter and Caret interfaces describe how text is highlighted and where text is inserted, and allow you to customize the text component appearance. In addition, the Keymap class defines the bindings between keystrokes and text actions, letting you alter the feel of text components without your having to do much of anything.

Other text components worth mentioning in this chapter are designed for event handling. No longer do you have to use the KeyListener/KeyEvent or TextEvent/TextListener combination for dealing with input validation. Instead, the Swing components use the DocumentEvent/DocumentListener combination. This combination provides a much more flexible manner of input validation, especially in the MVC environment of the Swing text components. Additional event handling is done through an extension of the AbstractAction capabilities introduced in Chapter 2. This is the TextAction class for tying key bindings to Action implementations. This class will be briefly touched on in this chapter and discussed more fully in Chapter 15. Many of the text framework pieces are tied together by what is called an EditorKit. This will be discussed in Chapter 15, as well.

> **NOTE** *Due to the many interconnections among the Swing text component classes, you'll probably find a number of references in this chapter to information found in Chapter 15. Feel free to jump between this chapter and the next to read up on the full details of a particular capability.*

Class JTextComponent

The JTextComponent class is the parent class for all the components used as textual views. It describes the common behavior shared by all text components. Among other things, this common behavior includes a Highlighter for selection support, a Caret for navigation throughout the content, a set of commands supported through the actions property (an array of Action implementers), a set of key bindings through a Keymap, an implementation of the Scrollable interface so that each of the specific text components can be placed within a JScrollPane, and the text stored within the component. If that all sounds like a lot to manage, don't worry. We'll look at everything in pieces *after* describing the first subclass of JTextComponent, the JTextField class.

JTextComponent Properties

Table 14-1 shows the 26 properties of JTextComponent. These properties cover the range of capabilities you'd expect from text components.

PROPERTY NAME	DATA TYPE	ACCESS
accessibleContext	AccessibleContext	read-only
actions	Action[ ]	read-only
caret	Caret	read-write bound
caretColor	Color	read-write bound
caretPosition	int	read-write
disabledTextColor	Color	read-write bound
document	Document	read-write bound
editable	boolean	read-write
enabled	boolean	write-only
focusAccelerator	char	read-write bound
focusTraversable	boolean	read-only
highlighter	Highlighter	read-write bound
inputMethodRequests*	InputMethodRequests	read-only
keymap	Keymap	read-write bound
margin	Insets	read-write bound
opaque	boolean	read-write
preferredScrollableViewportSize	Dimension	read-only
scrollableTracksViewportHeight	boolean	read-only
scrollableTracksViewportWidth	boolean	read-only
selectedText	String	read-only
selectedTextColor	Color	read-write bound
selectionColor	Color	read-write bound
selectionEnd	int	read-write
selectionStart	int	read-write
text	String	read-write
UI	TextUI	read-write

Table 14-1: JTextComponent properties

* The inputMethodsRequests property is available only on the Java 2 platform. JDK 1.1 doesn't provide the java.awt.im package.

These properties can be broken up into eight groupings:

- Data model — The document property is for the data model of all text components. The text property is used for treating this data model as a String.

- Color — The caretColor, disabledTextColor, selectedTextColor, and selectionColor properties, as well as the inherited foreground and background properties, specify the color for rendering the cursor, disabled text, selected text, selected text background, regular text, and regular text background.

- Caret — The caret and caretPosition properties are for navigating through the document.

- Highlighter — The highlighter, selectionStart, and selectionEnd properties are responsible for highlighting the selectedText section of the document.

- Margin — The margin property is for specifying how far the text contents appear from the edges of the text component.

- Events — The actions and keymap properties describe which capabilities the text component supports. In the case of the Action[ ] for the actions property, the capabilities are a series of ActionListener implementations that you can associate with components for event handling. For instance, instead of creating an ActionListener to perform cut, copy, and paste operations, you find the appropriate Action within the actions property and associate it with a component. The keymap property works in a similar manner, but it associates Action implementations with specific keys. For instance, it contains an entry in the key map of what to do when the PAGEUP key is pressed.

- Scrollable interface — The preferredScrollableViewportSize, scrollableTracksViewportHeight, and scrollableTracksViewportWidth properties are implementations of the respective Scrollable interface methods.

- State — The editable, enabled, opaque, and focusTraversable properties describe various states of the text components. The editable property allows you to make a text component read-only when it is set to false. When the enabled property is false, the content is read-only and you can't scroll around the component to see areas of the text that aren't currently visible. When the opaque property is set to false, the contents of the area behind the text component bleed through, allowing you to have an image background if desired. See Figure 14-2 for how this might appear. For the read-only focusTraversable property, text components are in the focus cycle (that is, they can be tabbed into) when they're enabled. The focusAccelerator is used when a neighboring JLabel has the text component set in its labelFor property, allowing you to use the visible mnemonic of the JLabel to move focus into the text component.

The following is the source code used to generate Figure 14-2. If you comment out the setOpaque(false) line, a background image will not be shown.

```java
import javax.swing.*;
import java.awt.*;

public class BackgroundSample {
  public static void main(String args[]) {
    JFrame frame = new ExitableJFrame("Background Example");
    final ImageIcon imageIcon = new ImageIcon("draft.gif");
    JTextArea textArea = new JTextArea() {
      Image image = imageIcon.getImage();
      Image grayImage = GrayFilter.createDisabledImage(image);
      {setOpaque(false);}  // instance initializer
      public void paint (Graphics g) {
        g.drawImage(grayImage, 0, 0, this);
        super.paint(g);
      }
    };
    JScrollPane scrollPane = new JScrollPane(textArea);
    Container content = frame.getContentPane();
    content.add(scrollPane, BorderLayout.CENTER);
    frame.setSize(250, 250);
    frame.setVisible(true);
  }
}
```

Figure 14-2: An opaque text component with an image background

JTextComponent Operations

The JTextComponent defines the basic framework for many of the operations performed on the text controls.

- I/O—The public void read(Reader in, Object description) and public void write(Writer out) methods (both throwing IOException) allow you to read/write the text component contents with ease.

- Clipboard access—The public void cut(), public void copy(), and public void paste() methods provide access to the system clipboard.

- Positioning—The public void moveCaretPosition(int position) method allows you to position the caret. The position represents a one-dimensional position indicating the number of characters to precede the caret from the beginning of the text component.

- Selection—The public void replaceSelection(String content), public void selectAll(), and public void select(int selectionStart, int selectionEnd) methods allow you to select part of the content within the component and replace the content that is selected.

- Conversion—The public Rectangle modelToView(int position) throws BadLocationException and public int viewToModel(Point point) methods allow you (or more likely allow the *system*) to map a position within the JTextComponent to a physical mapping within the representation of the contents for the specific text UI delegate.

Now that you've had an overview of the JTextComponent class, we'll look at its different subclasses. First is the JTextField, which will be used to demonstrate the operations listed here.

Class JTextField

The JTextField component is the text component for a single line of input, like its AWT counterpart TextField. The data model for a JTextField is the PlainDocument implementation of the Document interface. The PlainDocument model limits input to single-attributed text, meaning that it must be a single font and color. When the ENTER key is pressed within the JTextField, it automatically notifies any registered ActionListener implementations. Figure 14-3 shows these relationships.

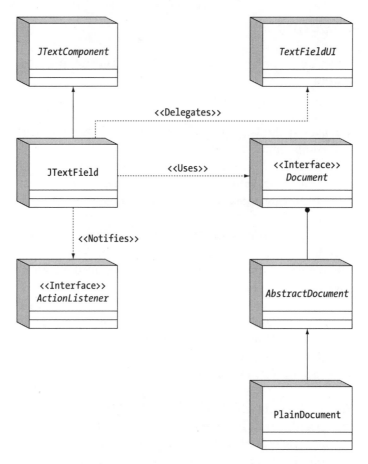

Figure 14-3: Swing JTextField UML relationship diagram

Creating a JTextField

There are five constructors for the JTextField component. By default, you get an empty text field zero columns wide with a default initial model. You can specify the initial text for the JTextField and how wide you want the component to be. Width is specified as the number of "m" characters in the current font that will fit within the component. There's no restriction on the number of characters that can be input. If you specify the Document data model in the constructor, you will probably want to specify a null initial-text argument. Otherwise, the current contents of the document will be replaced by the initial text for the text field.

1. `public JTextField()`
    `JTextField textField = new JTextField();`

2.  ```
    public JTextField(String text)
    JTextField textField = new JTextField("Initial Text");
    ```

3.  ```
    public JTextField(int columnWidth)
    JTextField textField = new JTextField(14);
    ```

4.  ```
    public JTextField(String text, int columnWidth)
    JTextField textField = new JTextField("Initial Text", 14);
    ```

5.  ```
    public JTextField(Document model, String text, int columnWidth)
    JTextField textField = new JTextField(aModel, null, 14);
    ```

Using JLabel Mnemonics

In the discussion of mnemonics in Chapter 4, I stated that the various button classes can have a keyboard shortcut to cause the button component to be selected. This is usually indicated visually by the special mnemonic character being underlined. If the user presses the mnemonic character along with a platform-specific mnemonic activation key, such as ALT for both Windows and UNIX, the button is activated/selected.

In the case of the JTextField, and all other text components, a similar capability can be utilized with the help of a JLabel. You can set the display mnemonic for a label, but instead of selecting the label when the mnemonic key is pressed, selection causes an associated component to get the input focus. The display mnemonic is set with the public void setDisplayedMnemonic(character) method in which the character is either an int or a char. Using the KeyEvent constants when changing the mnemonic setting simplifies initialization considerably.

The following source demonstrates how to interconnect a specific JLabel and JTextField. In addition to calling the setDisplayedMnemonic() method, you must also call the public void setLabelFor(Component component) method. This configures the JLabel to move input focus to the text field when the special mnemonic value is pressed.

```
JLabel label = new JLabel("Name: ");
label.setDisplayedMnemonic(KeyEvent.VK_N);
JTextField textField = new JTextField();
label.setLabelFor(textField);
```

Figure 14-4 shows what this sample program might look like. The complete source for the program follows.

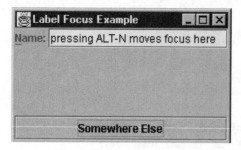

Figure 14-4: Connecting a JLabel and a JTextField

```java
import javax.swing.*;
import java.awt.*;
import java.awt.event.*;

public class LabelSample {
  public static void main(String args[]) {
    JFrame frame = new ExitableJFrame("Label Focus Example");
    Container content = frame.getContentPane();
    JPanel panel = new JPanel(new BorderLayout());
    JLabel label = new JLabel("Name: ");
    label.setDisplayedMnemonic(KeyEvent.VK_N);
    JTextField textField = new JTextField();
    label.setLabelFor(textField);
    panel.add(label, BorderLayout.WEST);
    panel.add(textField, BorderLayout.CENTER);
    content.add(panel, BorderLayout.NORTH);
    content.add(new JButton("Something Else"), BorderLayout.SOUTH);
    frame.setSize(250, 150);
    frame.setVisible(true);
  }
}
```

JTextField Properties

Table 14-2 lists the 11 properties of JTextField.

PROPERTY NAME	DATA TYPE	ACCESS
accessibleContext	AccessibleContext	read-only
actionCommand	String	write-only
actions	Action[]	read-only

(continued)

Table 14-2 (continued)

PROPERTY NAME	DATA TYPE	ACCESS
columns	int	read-write
font	Font	write-only
horizontalAlignment	int	read-write bound
horizontalVisibility	BoundedRangeModel	read-only
preferredSize	Dimension	read-only
scrollOffset	int	read-write
UIClassID	String	read-only
valdiateRoot	boolean	read-only

Table 14-2: JTextField properties

There's a tight coupling between the horizontalVisibility and the scrollOffset properties. The BoundedRangeModel for the horizontalVisibility property of JTextField represents the width range required for displaying the contents of the text field. If there isn't enough space to display the contents, the scrollOffset setting reflects how far off to the left the text has scrolled. As the user navigates through the text within the JTextField, the scrollOffset is automatically updated.

By changing the scrollOffset setting, you can control which part of the text field contents is visible. To ensure that the beginning of the contents for the text field is visible, set the scrollOffset setting to zero. To make sure that the *end* of the contents is visible, you need to ask the horizontalVisibility property what the extent of the BoundedRangeModel is. The extent represents how wide the range is, while the scrollOffset setting would be set to the extent setting to ensure that the end of the text field contents is visible.

```
BoundedRangeModel model = textField.getHorizontalVisibility();
int extent = model.getExtent();
textField.setScrollOffset(extent);
```

The text field in Figure 14-5 contains the 26 letters of the alphabet plus the ten cardinal numbers: ABCDEFGHIJKL MNOPQRSTUVWXYZ1234567890. Not all these characters fit on the screen; therefore the letters A–K have scrolled off to the left. Because something has scrolled off to the left, the scrollOffset property is not at zero.

By changing the horizontalAlignment property setting, you can right-, left-, or center-justify the contents of a JTextField. This capability is new to Swing and is not a part of the original AWT TextField component. By default, the text alignment is left-justified, which is how it appeared under AWT.

Figure 14-5: Visualizing the ScrollOffset

The `public void setHorizontalAlignment(int alignment)` method takes an argument of `JTextField.LEFT`, `JTextField.CENTER`, or `JTextField.RIGHT` to specify the contents alignment. Figure 14-6 shows how the alignment setting affects the contents.

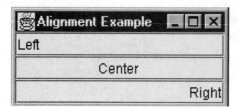

Figure 14-6: Text field alignments

> **NOTE** *You can set the document property, inherited from* `JTextComponent`, *to any implementation of the* `Document` *interface. If you use a* `StyledDocument` *with a* `JTextField`, *the UI delegate will ignore all style attributes. The* `StyledDocument` *interface will be further discussed in Chapter 15.*

JTextComponent Operations with a JTextField

The following operations are possible with all `JTextComponent` subclasses. They're shown here specifically for the `JTextField` because they need a specific implementation to be truly demonstrated. You can perform the same tasks with the `JPasswordField`, `JTextArea`, `JEditorPane`, and `JTextPane`.

Loading and Saving Content

Have you ever looked for an easy way to load or save the contents of a text component? With the `public void read(Reader in, Object description)` and `public void write(Writer out)` methods from `JTextComponent` (both throwing an `IOException`), you can easily load and save the contents from any text component.

With the `read()` method, the description argument is added as a property of the `Document` data model. This allows you to retain information about where the data came from. The following example demonstrates how you'd read in the contents of filename and store it in `textComponent`. The filename is automatically retained as the description.

```
FileReader reader = null;
try {
  reader = new FileReader(filename);
  textComponent.read(reader, filename);
} catch (IOException exception) {
  System.out.println("Load oops");
} finally {
  if (reader != null) {
    try {
      reader.close();
    } catch (IOException ignoredException) {
    }
  }
}
```

If you later wanted to get the "description" back from the data model, which happens to be the filename in this case, you would just ask. The properties of the Document are simply another key-value lookup table. The key in this particular case is the class constant Document.StreamDescriptionProperty. If you don't want a description stored, you pass null as the description argument to the read() method. The following two lines show how you'd get back this description.

```
Document document = textComponent.getDocument();
String filename =
(String)document.getProperty(Document.StreamDescriptionProperty);
```

> **NOTE** *The Document interface will be discussed in more detail later in this chapter.*

Before you can read a file into a text component, you need to create the file to read. This could be done outside a Java program, or you could use the write() method of JTextComponent to create the file. The following demonstrates how to use the write() method to write the contents. For simplicity's sake, it doesn't deal with getting the filename from the Document because initially this would be "unset."

```
FileWriter writer = null;
try {
  writer = new FileWriter(filename);
  textComponent.write(writer);
} catch (IOException exception) {
  System.out.println("Save oops");
```

```
    } finally {
      if (writer != null) {
        try {
          writer.close();
        } catch (IOException ignoredException) {
        }
      }
    }
  }
```

Figure 14-7 shows a sample program that uses the loading and saving capabilities. Loading and saving options on buttons are more commonly seen under a File menu. The Clear button clears the contents of the text field.

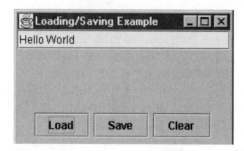

Figure 14-7: Loading and saving a text component

The following source code puts all the pieces together in a sample program to demonstrate loading and saving.

```
import java.awt.*;
import java.awt.event.*;
import javax.swing.*;
import javax.swing.text.*;
import java.io.*;

public class LoadSave {

  public static void main (String args[]) {
    final String filename = "text.out";
    JFrame frame = new ExitableJFrame("Loading/Saving Example");
    Container content = frame.getContentPane();

    final JTextField textField = new JTextField();
    content.add(textField, BorderLayout.NORTH);
```

```
      JPanel panel = new JPanel();

      // Setup actions
      JButton loadButton = new JButton ("Load");
      panel.add(loadButton);
      ActionListener loadAction = new ActionListener() {
        public void actionPerformed(ActionEvent e) {
          doLoadCommand(textField, filename);
        }
      };
      loadButton.addActionListener(loadAction);

      JButton saveButton = new JButton ("Save");
      panel.add(saveButton);
      ActionListener saveAction = new ActionListener() {
        public void actionPerformed(ActionEvent e) {
          doSaveCommand(textField, filename);
        }
      };
      saveButton.addActionListener(saveAction);

      JButton clearButton = new JButton ("Clear");
      panel.add(clearButton);
      ActionListener clearAction = new ActionListener() {
        public void actionPerformed(ActionEvent e) {
          textField.setText("");
        }
      };
      clearButton.addActionListener(clearAction);

      content.add(panel, BorderLayout.SOUTH);

      frame.setSize(250, 150);
      frame.setVisible(true);
    }

  public static void doSaveCommand(JTextComponent textComponent, String filename)
{
      FileWriter writer = null;
      try {
        writer = new FileWriter(filename);
        textComponent.write(writer);
      } catch (IOException exception) {
```

```
          System.out.println("Save oops");
          exception.printStackTrace();
        } finally {
          if (writer != null) {
            try {
              writer.close();
            } catch (IOException ignoredException) {
            }
          }
        }
      }
    }

  public static void doLoadCommand(JTextComponent textComponent, String filename)
{
      FileReader reader = null;
      try {
        reader = new FileReader(filename);
        textComponent.read(reader, filename);
      } catch (IOException exception) {
        System.out.println("Load oops");
        exception.printStackTrace();
      } finally {
        if (reader != null) {
          try {
            reader.close();
          } catch (IOException ignoredException) {
          }
        }
      }
    }
}
```

> **NOTE** *By default, file reading and writing deals only with plain text. If the contents are styled (although this is not useful in a* JTextField*), the styled attributes aren't saved. This loading and saving behavior can be customized by the* EditorKit, *a class discussed in Chapter 15.*

Accessing the Clipboard

The Swing text components have built-in support to access the system clipboard for cut, copy, and paste operations. No longer do you have to manually concoct a Transferable clipboard object. Now, you just call one of the three public void

cut(), public void copy(), and public void paste() methods of the
JTextComponent class.

You can call these methods directly from ActionListener implementations
associated with buttons or menu items, which isn't the easiest way to do it. You can
create your own ActionListener, like the following, to perform a cut operation.

```
ActionListener cutListener = new ActionListener() {
  public void actionPerformed(ActionEvent actionEvent) {
    aTextComponent.cut();
  }
};
```

Or, you can do it the easy way: Find an existing cut Action by asking the text
component. If you look at the set of JTextComponent properties in Table 14-1,
you'll notice one property named actions that's an array of Action objects. This
property contains a predefined set of Action implementations that you can
directly associate as an ActionListener with any button or menu item. If you
find the right one for cut, copy, and paste, you won't have to manually create
the ActionListener implementations.

Once you get the current actions for the text component, you can go through
the array until you find the appropriate one. Because actions are named, you
merely need to know the text string for the name. The DefaultEditorKit class has
about 40 keys as public constants.

```
Action actions[] = textField.getActions();
Action cutAction = TextUtilities.findAction(actions, DefaultEditorKit.cutAction);
```

All actions in the set for a text component are a type of
TextAction, which is an extension of the AbstractAction
class. The essential thing to know about a TextAction is that
it acts on the last focused text component. So, even though
we acquired the cut action from a text field in the above
source fragment, the same cut action would work for a text
area on the same screen. Whichever text component had
the input focus last would be the one cut when the specific
cutAction is activated.

To help you visualize this behavior, Figure 14-8 shows a
screen with a JTextField at the top and a JTextArea in the
middle. There are buttons on the bottom for the cut, copy,
and paste operations. If you run the program, you'll notice
that the cut, copy, and paste actions act on the last focused
text component.

*Figure 14-8: Accessing the system
clipboard from a text component*

> **NOTE** *The TextAction class will be discussed more extensively in Chapter 15 along with the* DefaultEditorKit.

The following source code is the complete example for finding an Action in the actions property array and using cut, copy, and paste.

```
import java.awt.*;
import java.awt.event.*;
import java.util.*;
import javax.swing.*;
import javax.swing.text.*;

public class CutPasteSample {
  public static void main (String args[]) {
    JFrame frame = new ExitableJFrame("Cut/Paste Example");
    Container content = frame.getContentPane();

    JTextField textField = new JTextField();
    JTextArea textArea = new JTextArea();
    JScrollPane scrollPane = new JScrollPane(textArea);

    content.add(textField, BorderLayout.NORTH);
    content.add(scrollPane, BorderLayout.CENTER);

    Action actions[] = textField.getActions();

    Action cutAction   = TextUtilities.findAction(actions,
DefaultEditorKit.cutAction);
    Action copyAction  = TextUtilities.findAction(actions,
DefaultEditorKit.copyAction);
    Action pasteAction = TextUtilities.findAction(actions,
DefaultEditorKit.pasteAction);

    JPanel panel = new JPanel();
    content.add(panel, BorderLayout.SOUTH);

    JButton cutButton = new ActionButton(cutAction);
    cutButton.setText("Cut");
    panel.add(cutButton);

    JButton copyButton = new ActionButton(copyAction);
```

```
    copyButton.setText("Copy");
    panel.add(copyButton);

    JButton pasteButton = new ActionButton(pasteAction);
    pasteButton.setText("Paste");
    panel.add(pasteButton);

    frame.setSize(250, 250);
    frame.setVisible(true);
  }
}
```

> **NOTE**   *The ActionButton class used in this example was created in Chapter 2.*

The previous example uses the following TextUtilities support class. There's no direct way to find out if a specific action for a specific key exists in the actions property array. Instead, you must manually search for it. The public static Action findAction(Action actions[], String key) method does the searching for you.

```
import javax.swing.*;
import javax.swing.text.*;
import java.util.Hashtable;
public class TextUtilities {
  private TextUtilities() {
  }

  public static Action findAction(Action actions[], String key) {
    Hashtable commands = new Hashtable();
    for (int i = 0; i < actions.length; i++) {
      Action action = actions[i];
      commands.put(action.getValue(Action.NAME), action);
    }
    return (Action)commands.get(key);
  }
}
```

> **NOTE**   *The cut() and copy() methods of the JPasswordField class cause the system to beep, instead of placing the current contents onto the system password. You can still paste() something from the clipboard into a JPasswordField, though. This is done for security reasons.*

Document Interface

The Document interface defines the data model for the different text components. Implementations of the interface are meant to store both the actual content as well as any information to mark up the content (bold/italics). While all the content will be text, the way in which the text component displays the content could result in nontextual output, such as an HTML renderer.

The data model is stored apart from the text component (the view). Therefore, if you're interested in monitoring changes to the content of a text component, you must watch the Document itself for changes and not the text component. If the changes reach the text component, it's too late — the model has already changed. To listen for changes, attach a DocumentListener to the model. However, the more likely scenario for restricting input is to provide a custom model.

In addition to accessing the textual content through the Document interface, a framework is defined to support undo/redo capabilities. This will be explored in Chapter 19.

Now let's walk through the pieces that make up a Document to get an understanding of how to use the basics of the different text components. First, here's the interface definition:

```
public interface Document {
    // Constants
    public final static String StreamDescriptionProperty;
    public final static String TitleProperty;
    // Listeners
    public void addDocumentListener(DocumentListener listener);
    public void removeDocumentListener(DocumentListener listener);
    public void addUndoableEditListener(UndoableEditListener listener);
    public void removeUndoableEditListener(UndoableEditListener listener);
    // Properties
    public Element getDefaultRootElement();
    public Position getEndPosition();
    public int getLength();
    public Element[ ] getRootElements();
    public Position getStartPosition();
    // Other Methods
    public Position createPosition(int offset) throws BadLocationException;
    public Object getProperty(Object key);
    public String getText(int offset, int length) throws BadLocationException;
    public void getText(int offset, int length, Segment txt) throws
BadLocationException;
    public void insertString(int offset, String str, AttributeSet a) throws
```

```
BadLocationException;
    public void putProperty(Object key, Object value);
    public void remove(int offset, int len) throws BadLocationException;
    public void render(Runnable r);
}
```

The content within a Document is described by a series of elements in which each
element implements the Element interface. Within each element, you can store
attributes so that select content can be made bold, italic, or colorized. The elements don't store the content—just the attributes—therefore one Document can
be rendered differently from different Element sets.

The following is an example of a basic HTML document with a title and a
bulleted list for content.

```
<html>

<head>
<title>Cards</title>
</head>

<body>

<h1>Suits:</h1>

<ul>
    <li>Clubs</li>
    <li>Diamonds</li>
    <li>Hearts</li>
    <li>Spades</li>
</ul>
</body>
</html>
```

Looking at the structure of the elements in this HTML document, you get a hierarchy as shown in Figure 14-9.

Although this particular document might not warrant it, multiple element
hierarchies are possible. Each would store different attributes because a particular
text component could have an alternative rendering of the content. Alternatively,
different style sheets could be used to render the same HTML markup differently.

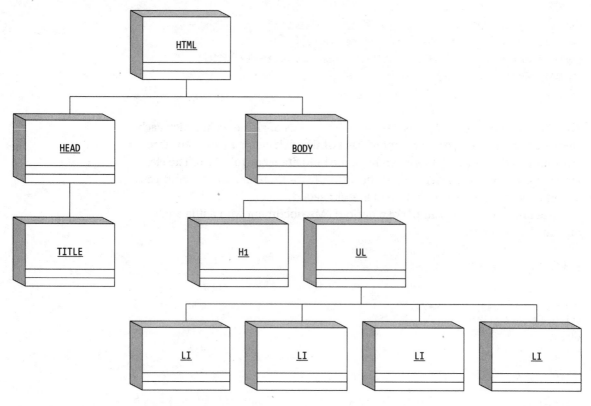

Figure 14-9: Examining the Element makeup of a Document

Class AbstractDocument

The AbstractDocument class provides the basic implementation of the Document interface. It defines the management of the listener lists, provides a read-write locking mechanism to ensure that content isn't corrupted, and enables a Dictionary for storing document properties.

Table 14-3 lists the eight properties of the AbstractDocument class, of which five are defined by the Document interface itself. For the most part, you don't access any of these directly. In the case of the documentProperties property, you get and set individual properties with the public Object getProperty(Object key) and public void putProperty(Object key, Object value) methods. For the length, in most cases you can simply ask for the text within a text component and then get *its* length [textComponent.getText().length()].

PROPERTY NAME	DATA TYPE	ACCESS
asynchronousLoadPriority*	int	read-write
bidiRootElement*	Element	read-only
defaultRootElement	Element	read-only
documentProperties*	Dictionary	read-write
endPosition	Position	read-only
length	int	read-only
rootElements	Element[ ]	read-only
startPosition	Position	read-only

Table 14-3: AbstractDocument properties

* These properties are specific to the AbstractDocument class. The remaining five are defined in the Document interface.

The bidiRootElement property is for the bidirectional root element, which may be appropriate in certain Unicode character sets. You'd normally just use the defaultRootElement. However, neither of these are accessed all that much.

Class PlainDocument

The PlainDocument class is a specific implementation of the AbstractDocument class. It stores no character-level attributes for the content. Instead, the elements describe where the content and each line in the content begins.

Element will be further explained more in the Chapter 15. In the meantime, the following program walks through the Element tree for a PlainDocument, the model used for both the JTextField and the JTextArea.

```java
import java.awt.*;
import java.awt.event.*;
import java.util.*;
import javax.swing.*;
import javax.swing.text.*;

public class ElementSample {
  public static void main (String args[]) {
    JFrame frame = new ExitableJFrame("Cut/Paste Example");
    Container content = frame.getContentPane();

    final JTextArea textArea = new JTextArea();
    JScrollPane scrollPane = new JScrollPane(textArea);
```

```
        JButton button = new JButton("Show Elements");
        ActionListener actionListener = new ActionListener() {
          public void actionPerformed(ActionEvent actionEvent) {
            Document document = textArea.getDocument();
            ElementIterator iterator = new ElementIterator(document);
            Element element = iterator.first();
            while (element != null) {
              System.out.println(element.getStartOffset());
              element = iterator.next();
            }
          }
        };
        button.addActionListener(actionListener);

        content.add(scrollPane, BorderLayout.CENTER);
        content.add(button, BorderLayout.SOUTH);

        frame.setSize(250, 250);
        frame.setVisible(true);
      }
    }
```

Assume the contents of the JTextArea are as follows:

```
Hello World
Welcome Home
Adios
```

The program would report Element objects starting at 0, 0, 12, and 25. The first 0 represents the start of the content, while the second represents the start of the first line.

Creating Custom Documents

In the AWT world, if you want to restrict input into a text field, you attach a KeyListener and consume() keystrokes that you don't want to appear with the component. With the Swing text components, you instead create a new Document implementation and customize what's accepted in the Document.

If you create a subclass of AbstractDocument, the overriding of the public void insertString(int offset, String string, AttributeSet attributes) and public void remove(int offset, int length) methods allows you to customize input.

The insertString() method is called when a text string is inserted into the Document, and the remove() method is called when something's deleted. To restrict input, just override each method and check to see if the new content would be valid. If the content isn't, reject it and leave things be.

To demonstrate, I've created a custom document that only accepts integer numeric input within a certain range. Since you don't need to store character level attributes, only an integer value, you can create a subclass of PlainDocument.

When you subclass PlainDocument, you need to override the behavior of insertString() and remove(). Because you're ensuring that the input is numeric and within a valid range, you must validate the proposed input to see if it's acceptable. If it is acceptable, then you can really modify the document model by calling super.insertString() or super.remove(). Once you create the new Document, you associate it with a text component with public void setDocument(Document).

What follows is the new IntegerRangeDocument class definition. Following the class definition is Figure 14-10, which shows the document in use.

```java
import javax.swing.text.*;
import java.awt.Toolkit;

public class IntegerRangeDocument extends PlainDocument {

  int minimum, maximum;
  int currentValue = 0;

  public IntegerRangeDocument(int minimum, int maximum) {
    this.minimum = minimum;
    this.maximum = maximum;
  }

  public int getValue() {
    return currentValue;
  }

  public void insertString(int offset, String string, AttributeSet attributes)
      throws BadLocationException {

    if (string == null) {
      return;
    } else {
      String newValue;
      int length = getLength();
      if (length == 0) {
```

```
          newValue = string;
        } else {
          String currentContent = getText(0, length);
          StringBuffer currentBuffer = new StringBuffer(currentContent);
          currentBuffer.insert(offset, string);
          newValue = currentBuffer.toString();
        }
        try {
          currentValue = checkInput(newValue);
          super.insertString(offset, string, attributes);
        } catch (Exception exception) {
          Toolkit.getDefaultToolkit().beep();
        }
      }
    }
  public void remove(int offset, int length) throws BadLocationException {
    int currentLength = getLength();
    String currentContent = getText(0, currentLength);
    String before = currentContent.substring(0, offset);
    String after = currentContent.substring(length+offset, currentLength);
    String newValue = before + after;
    try {
      currentValue = checkInput(newValue);
      super.remove(offset, length);
    } catch (Exception exception) {
      Toolkit.getDefaultToolkit().beep();
    }
  }
  public int checkInput(String proposedValue) throws NumberFormatException {
    int newValue = 0;
    if (proposedValue.length() > 0) {
      newValue = Integer.parseInt(proposedValue);
    }
    if ((minimum <= newValue) && (newValue <= maximum)) {
      return newValue;
    } else {
      throw new NumberFormatException();
    }
  }
}
```

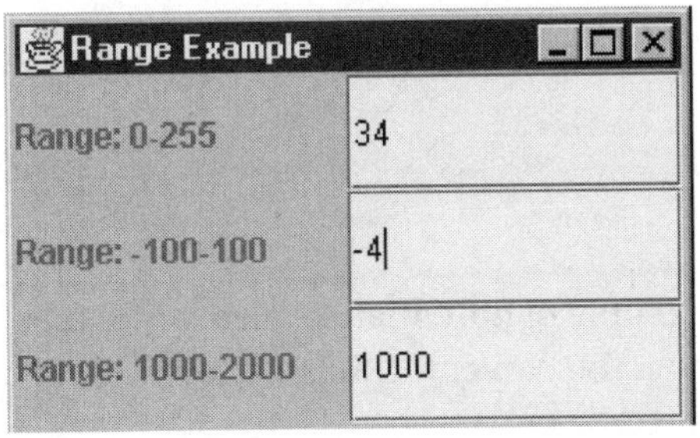

Figure 14-10: Using a Document that restricts input to a range of values

The sample program using the new IntegerRangeDocument follows:

```java
import javax.swing.*;
import javax.swing.text.*;
import java.awt.*;
import java.awt.event.*;

public class RangeSample {
  public static void main(String args[]) {
    JFrame frame = new ExitableJFrame("Range Example");
    Container content = frame.getContentPane();
    content.setLayout(new GridLayout(3, 2));

    content.add(new JLabel("Range: 0-255"));
    Document rangeOne = new IntegerRangeDocument(0, 255);
    JTextField textFieldOne = new JTextField();
    textFieldOne.setDocument(rangeOne);
    content.add(textFieldOne);

    content.add(new JLabel("Range: -100-100"));
    Document rangeTwo = new IntegerRangeDocument(-100, 100);
    JTextField textFieldTwo = new JTextField();
    textFieldTwo.setDocument(rangeTwo);
    content.add(textFieldTwo);

    content.add(new JLabel("Range: 1000-2000"));
    Document rangeThree = new IntegerRangeDocument(1000, 2000);
    JTextField textFieldThree = new JTextField();
    textFieldThree.setDocument(rangeThree);
    content.add(textFieldThree);
```

```
        frame.setSize(250, 150);
        frame.setVisible(true);
    }
}
```

If you try out this program, you'll notice a couple of potential problems. The first text field, with a range of 0 to 255, works fine. You can enter/delete characters at will, as long as the content is within the range.

In the second text field, the valid range is –100 to +100. Although you can enter any of the 201 numbers into the text field, if you want a negative number you need to enter something like 3, left-arrow, -. Because the text field validates input with each key, the - by itself isn't valid. You'd have to either specifically accept a - as valid input in the checkInput() method shown earlier in this section, or force users to enter negative numbers in an awkward manner.

The third text field presents an even more troublesome situation. The valid range of input is 1000–2000. As you press each key to enter a number, such as 1500, it's rejected. You can't build up the input to 1500 because 1 isn't a valid input, nor is 5, nor is 0, by themselves. Instead, to enter a number into this text field, you must enter it somewhere *else,* place it into the system clipboard, and then use Ctrl-V to paste it into the text field as the field's final value. You can't use Backspace to correct a mistake, because no three-digit numbers are valid.

While the IntegerRangeDocument class shown earlier in this section of the chapter presents a workable Document class for any integer range, it works best with ranges of positive numbers that begin at zero.

Interface DocumentListener/Interface DocumentEvent

If you're interested in finding out when the content of a text component changes, you can attach an implementation of the DocumentListener interface to the Document model of the component. From the three interface methods, you can find out if the contents were added to (insertUpdate()), removed from (removeUpdate()), or stylistically changed (changeUpdate()) — the last being an attribute change versus a content change.

```
public interface DocumentListener implements EventListener {
  public void changedUpdate(DocumentEvent documentEvent);
  public void insertUpdate(DocumentEvent documentEvent);
  public void removeUpdate(DocumentEvent documentEvent);
}
```

The interface method will receive an instance of DocumentEvent, from which you can find out where the change occurred as well as the type of change.

```
public interface DocumentEvent {
  public Document getDocument();
  public int getLength();
  public int getOffset();
  public DocumentEvent.EventType getType();
  public DocumentEvent.ElementChange getChange(Element element);
}
```

The offset property of the event is where the change started. The length property of the event tells the length of the change that happened. The type of the event can be derived from whichever one of the three DocumentListener methods were called. In addition, the DocumentEvent.EventType class has three constants of CHANGE, INSERT, and REMOVE, so you can find out which event type happened directly from the type property.

With regard to the getChange() method of DocumentEvent, it requires an Element to return a DocumentEvent.ElementChange. You normally use the default root element from the Document, as in the following example.

```
Document documentSource = documentEvent.getDocument();
Element rootElement = documentSource.getDefaultRootElement();
DocumentEvent.ElementChange change = documentEvent.getChange(rootElement);
```

Once you have your DocumentEvent.ElementChange instance, you can find out the added and removed elements, if you need that level of information.

```
public interface DocumentEvent.ElementChange {
  public Element[ ] getChildrenAdded();
  public Element[ ] getChildrenRemoved();
  public Element getElement();
  public int getIndex();
}
```

> **TIP** *What happened to* TextListener *and* TextEvent*? If you're porting an AWT program to use the Swing text components, you can no longer use the* TextListener–TextEvent *pair. They've been replaced by the more flexible* DocumentListener–DocumentEvent *pair.*

Interface Caret and Interface Highlighter

Now that you understand the data model aspect of a text component, you can look at some aspects of its selection rendering through the Caret and Highlighter interfaces. Remember that these are properties of the text component, not the data model.

The Caret interface describes what's usually referred to as the cursor: the location in the document where you can insert text. The Highlighter interface provides the basis for how to paint selected text. These two interfaces, their related interfaces, and their implementations are rarely altered. The text components simply use their default implementations with the DefaultCaret and DefaultHighlighter classes.

Although you probably won't alter the caret and highlighter behavior for a text component, you should know that there are many interrelated classes working together, as shown in Figure 14-11. For the Highlighter interface, the predefined implementation is called DefaultHighlighter, which extends another implementation called LayeredHighlighter. The Highlighter also manages a collection of Highlighter.Highlight objects to designate highlighted sections.

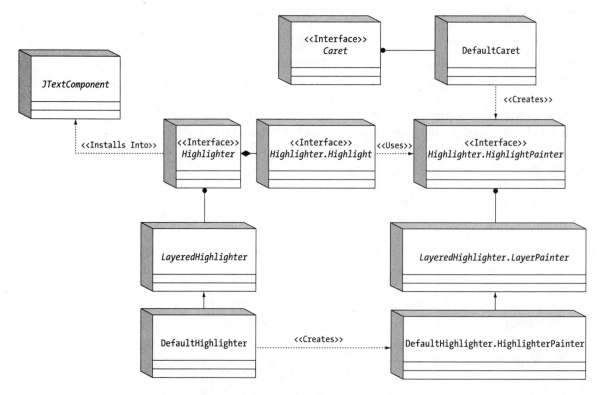

Figure 14-11: Caret/Highlighter UML relationship diagram

The DefaultHighlighter creates a DefaultHighlighter.HighlightPainter to paint the highlighted section(s) of text. The HighlightPainter is an implementation of the Highlighter.HighlightPainter interface and extends the LayeredHighlighter.LayerPainter class. Each section to paint is described by a Highlighter.Highlight, where the Highlighter manages the set. The actual HighlightPainter is created by the DefaultCaret implementation.

The Highlighter interface describes how to paint selected text within a text component. If you don't like the color, you can simply change the TextField.selectionBackground UI property setting to a different color.

```
public interface Highlighter {
  // Properties
  public Highlighter.Highlight[ ] getHighlights();
  // Other Methods
  public Object addHighlight(int p0, int p1, Highlighter.HighlightPainter p)
throws BadLocationException;
  public void changeHighlight(Object tag, int p0, int p1) throws
BadLocationException;
  public void deinstall(JTextComponent component);
  public void install(JTextComponent component)
  public void paint(Graphics g);
  public void removeAllHighlights();
  public void removeHighlight(Object tag);
}
```

The Caret interface describes the current cursor, as well as several selection attributes. Of the Highlighter and Caret interfaces, the latter is the one that you'd actually use, although it isn't necessary to subclass it.

```
public interface Caret {
  // Properties
  public int getBlinkRate();
  public void setBlinkRate(int newValue);
  public int getDot();
  public void setDot(int newValue);
  public Point getMagicCaretPosition();
  public void setMagicCaretPosition(Point newValue);
  public int getMark();
  public boolean isSelectionVisible();
  public void setSelectionVisible(boolean newValue);
  public boolean isVisible();
  public void setVisible(boolean newValue);
  // Listeners
```

```
    public void addChangeListener(ChangeListener l);
    public void removeChangeListener(ChangeListener l);
    // Other Methods
    public void deinstall(JTextComponent c);
    public void install(JTextComponent c);
    public void moveDot(int dot);
    public void paint(Graphics g);
}
```

Table 14-4 lists the six attributes of a Caret. The blinkRate is the millisecond delay between the flashes of the caret. The dot property is the current position within the text component of the cursor. To move the cursor to another position so that some text will be highlighted, add a call to the moveDot(int newPosition) method. This sets the mark property to the old dot position and sets the new dot setting to the new position.

PROPERTY NAME	DATA TYPE	ACCESS
blinkRate	int	read-write
dot	int	read-write
magicCaretPosition	Point	read-write
mark	int	read-only
selectionVisible	boolean	read-write
visible	boolean	read-write

Table 14-4: Caret properties

Other than the self-explanatory visibility properties, the one remaining property is the magicCaretPosition property. This property deals with moving up and down lines of different lengths. For instance, in the following lines of text that follow this paragraph, imagine that the current cursor position is between the n and g on the first line. If you pressed the down arrow twice, you'd want the cursor to stay at the same horizontal position, instead of moving to the end of the shorter second line. It's the magicCursorPosition property that retains this information, such that the cursor ends up being between the D and the o in the third line. Without the magic position retained, the cursor would fall in between the p and the word space of the last line.

```
Friz Freleng
Mel Blanc
What's up Doc?
```

One useful instance of using the caret is finding the current screen location in response to a keystroke. That way, you can pop up a menu at the current cursor position. This would be similar to the Code Insights option in JBuilder or IntelliSense in Visual J++ in which the tool helps you complete method calls by popping up a menu of methods to choose.

Given the current dot location in the model, map it to the position in the view with the `public Rectangle modelToView(int position)` method of `JTextComponent` (which can throw a `BadLocationException`). Then, use the `Rectangle` returned as the location to pop up the menu, as shown in Figure 14-12.

The following program will show a `JPopupMenu` at the location where the period (".") key is pressed in the text field.

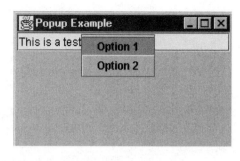

Figure 14-12: Using the Caret to determine a pop-up location

```
import javax.swing.*;
import javax.swing.text.*;
import javax.swing.plaf.*;
import java.awt.*;
import java.awt.event.*;

public class PopupSample {
  public static void main(String args[]) {
    JFrame frame = new ExitableJFrame("Popup Example");
    Container content = frame.getContentPane();

    final JPopupMenu popup = new JPopupMenu();
    JMenuItem menuItem1 = new JMenuItem("Option 1");
    popup.add(menuItem1);

    JMenuItem menuItem2 = new JMenuItem("Option 2");
    popup.add(menuItem2);

    final JTextField textField = new JTextField();
    content.add(textField, BorderLayout.NORTH);

    ActionListener actionListener = new ActionListener() {
      public void actionPerformed(ActionEvent actionEvent) {
        try {
          int dotPosition = textField.getCaretPosition();
          Rectangle popupLocation = textField.modelToView(dotPosition);
          popup.show(textField, popupLocation.x, popupLocation.y);
        } catch (BadLocationException badLocationException) {
          System.out.println("Oops");
        }
```

```
      }
    };
    KeyStroke keystroke = KeyStroke.getKeyStroke(KeyEvent.VK_PERIOD, 0, false);
      textField.registerKeyboardAction(actionListener, keystroke,
JComponent.WHEN_FOCUSED);

    frame.setSize(250, 150);
    frame.setVisible(true);
  }
}
```

Interface *CaretListener/Class CaretEvent*

If you want to listen for cursor movements, you have two ways to do so. You can associate either a ChangeListener with the Caret or a CaretListener with the JTextComponent. Working directly with the JTextComponent is the easier approach, though both will function equally well.

In the case of the CaretListener, there's a single method defined by the interface:

```
public interface CaretListener implements EventListener {
  public void caretUpdate(CaretEvent caretEvent);
}
```

When the listener is notified, a CaretEvent is sent, which reports on the new dot and mark locations.

```
public abstract class CaretEvent extends EventObject {
  public CaretEvent(Object source);
  public abstract int getDot();
  public abstract int getMark();
}
```

To demonstrate, Figure 14-13 shows a program with a CaretListener attached to the inner JTextArea. When the CaretEvent happens, the current dot value is sent to the top text field and the current mark setting is sent to the button. In the current situation, the cursor dot is at the beginning of the second line, with the mark at the end.

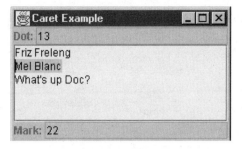

Figure 14-13: CaretListener sample

The following program is the demonstration of the CaretListener.

```java
import javax.swing.*;
import javax.swing.event.*;
import java.awt.*;

public class CaretSample {
  public static void main(String args[]) {
    JFrame frame = new ExitableJFrame("Caret Example");

    Container content = frame.getContentPane();
    JTextArea textArea = new JTextArea();
    JScrollPane scrollPane = new JScrollPane(textArea);
    content.add(scrollPane, BorderLayout.CENTER);

    final JTextField dot = new JTextField();
    dot.setEditable(false);
    JPanel dotPanel = new JPanel(new BorderLayout());
    dotPanel.add(new JLabel("Dot: "), BorderLayout.WEST);
    dotPanel.add(dot, BorderLayout.CENTER);
    content.add(dotPanel, BorderLayout.NORTH);

    final JTextField mark = new JTextField();
    mark.setEditable(false);
    JPanel markPanel = new JPanel(new BorderLayout());
    markPanel.add(new JLabel("Mark: "), BorderLayout.WEST);
    markPanel.add(mark, BorderLayout.CENTER);
    content.add(markPanel, BorderLayout.SOUTH);

    CaretListener listener = new CaretListener() {
      public void caretUpdate(CaretEvent caretEvent) {
        dot.setText("" + caretEvent.getDot());
```

```
        mark.setText("" + caretEvent.getMark());
      }
    };

    textArea.addCaretListener(listener);

    frame.setSize(250, 150);
    frame.setVisible(true);
  }
}
```

Interface Keymap

In "MVC-speak," the keymap property of the text component is the Controller part. It maps KeyStroke objects to individual actions through the Keymap interface. (The KeyStroke class was discussed in Chapter 2.) When you register the KeyStroke to the JTextComponent with registerKeyboardAction(), as in the PopupSample program shown earlier in this chapter, the text component stores this mapping from KeyStroke to Action in a Keymap. For instance, the BACKSPACE key is mapped to delete the previous character. If you want to add another binding, you just register another keystroke.

While you can register keystrokes with a text component, you can also add actions for keystrokes directly to the Keymap. This allows you to share a keymap across multiple text components as long as they all share the same extended behavior.

```
public interface Keymap {
  // Properties
  public Action[ ] getBoundActions();
  public KeyStroke[ ] getBoundKeyStrokes();
  public Action getDefaultAction();
  public void setDefaultAction(Action action);
  public String getName();
  public Keymap getResolveParent();
  public void setResolveParent(Keymap parent);
  // Other Methods
  public void addActionForKeyStroke(KeyStroke keystroke, Action action);
  public Action getAction(KeyStroke keystroke);
  public KeyStroke[ ] getKeyStrokesForAction(Action action);
  public boolean isLocallyDefined(KeyStroke keystroke);
  public void removeBindings();
  public void removeKeyStrokeBinding(KeyStroke keystroke);
}
```

While you tend to think of only adding keystrokes to the keymap, there are times when you want to remove them, too. For instance, the JTextField has an entry in the keymap for the ENTER key so that any registered ActionListener objects are notified. If the JTextField is on a screen where a button has been designated as the *default,* pressing ENTER won't select the default button, as desired. Removal of the default behavior is a simple process of requesting the removal of the single KeyStroke from the Keymap, as shown here:

```
Keymap keymap = textField.getKeymap();
KeyStroke keystroke = KeyStroke.getKeyStroke(KeyEvent.VK_ENTER, 0, false);
keymap.removeKeyStrokeBinding(keystroke);
```

Then, when you press ENTER in the text field, the default button is activated, as shown in Figure 14-14.

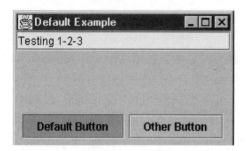

Figure 14-14: Using the default button after removing the Enter binding from the Keymap

The following program provides an example of removing a key binding from the Keymap.

```
import javax.swing.*;
import javax.swing.text.*;
import java.awt.*;
import java.awt.event.*;

public class DefaultSample {
  public static void main(String args[]) {
    JFrame frame = new ExitableJFrame("Default Example");
    Container content = frame.getContentPane();

    JTextField textField = new JTextField();
    content.add(textField, BorderLayout.NORTH);
```

```
ActionListener actionListener = new ActionListener() {
  public void actionPerformed(ActionEvent actionEvent) {
    System.out.println(actionEvent.getActionCommand() + " selected");
  }
};

JPanel panel = new JPanel();
JButton defaultButton = new JButton("Default Button");
defaultButton.addActionListener(actionListener);
panel.add(defaultButton);

JButton otherButton = new JButton("Other Button");
otherButton.addActionListener(actionListener);
panel.add(otherButton);

content.add(panel, BorderLayout.SOUTH);

Keymap keymap = textField.getKeymap();
KeyStroke keystroke = KeyStroke.getKeyStroke(KeyEvent.VK_ENTER, 0, false);
keymap.removeKeyStrokeBinding(keystroke);

frame.getRootPane().setDefaultButton(defaultButton);

frame.setSize(250, 150);
frame.setVisible(true);
  }
}
```

Class *JTextComponent.KeyBinding*

The JTextComponent class stores the specific key bindings with the help of the JTextComponent.KeyBinding class. The current look and feel defines what the default set of the key bindings are for text components, such as the familiar CTRL-X for Cut, CTRL-C for Copy, and CTRL-V for Paste on a Windows platform.

Handling *JTextField* Events

Dealing with events in Swing text components is completely different than dealing with events in AWT text components. Although you can still attach an ActionListener to listen for when the user presses the ENTER key in the text field, attaching a KeyListener or a TextListener is no longer useful.

Feel free to keep on using a FocusListener to find out when a text field gets or loses the input focus. However, it may not be the most opportune time to do so if you're waiting for a lost focus to validate input. Do you *really* want an error message to pop up when the window loses focus (causing the text field itself to lose focus)? Input validation is best left to the Document to accomplish or when a user submits a form.

Listening to JTextField Events with an ActionListener

Like the AWT TextField component, the JTextField will notify any registered ActionListener objects when the user presses ENTER from within the text field. There is one major difference between the two components. Both components send an ActionEvent to the ActionListener objects. Part of this ActionEvent is an action command. For the TextField, the action command was always the current contents of the component. With the Swing JTextField, you can now set this action command to be something separate from the content. The JTextField has an actionCommand property. When it is set to null (the default setting), the action command for the ActionEvent still makes up the contents of the component. However, if you set the actionCommand property for the JTextField, then that actionCommand setting is part of the ActionEvent.

The following code demonstrates this difference. There are two text fields. When ENTER is pressed in the first, causing the registered ActionListener to be notified, "Yo" is printed out. For the second text field, the contents are printed out when ENTER is pressed within it.

```
JTextField nameTextField = new JTextField();
JTextField cityTextField = new JTextField();
ActionListener actionListener = new ActionListener() {
  public void actionPerformed(ActionEvent actionEvent) {
    System.out.println("Command: " + actionEvent.getActionCommand());
  }
};
nameTextField.setActionCommand("Yo");
nameTextField.addActionListener(actionListener);
cityTextField.addActionListener(actionListener);
```

Listening to JTextField Events with an KeyListener

With the Swing text components, you normally don't listen for key events with a KeyListener — at least not to validate input. Running the following example demonstrates that you can still find out when a key has been pressed or released, and just not when it's been typed.

```
KeyListener keyListener = new KeyListener() {
  public void keyPressed(KeyEvent keyEvent) {
    printIt("Pressed", keyEvent);
  }
  public void keyReleased(KeyEvent keyEvent) {
    printIt("Released", keyEvent);
  }
  public void keyTyped(KeyEvent keyEvent) {
    printIt("Typed", keyEvent);
  }
  private void printIt(String title, KeyEvent keyEvent) {
    int keyCode = keyEvent.getKeyCode();
    String keyText = KeyEvent.getKeyText(keyCode);
    System.out.println(title + " : " + keyText);
  }
};
nameTextField.addKeyListener(keyListener);
cityTextField.addKeyListener(keyListener);
```

> **NOTE** *JFC/Swing 1.1.1 and the Java 2 SDK version 1.2.2 report "typed" events. Prior versions do not.*

Listening to JTextField Events with a FocusListener

The use of the FocusListener didn't change from the TextField to the JTextField. But, as previously stated, you still have to be careful when using them.

In the following example, if the text field gains the input focus, all text field content is selected. If you try to move the input focus beyond the text field, you'll find that you can't, unless the contents of the text field are empty or the contents consist of the string "Exit".

```
FocusListener focusListener = new FocusListener() {
  public void focusGained(FocusEvent focusEvent) {
    JTextComponent source = (JTextComponent)focusEvent.getSource();
    source.selectAll();
  }
  public void focusLost(FocusEvent focusEvent) {
    final JTextComponent source = (JTextComponent)focusEvent.getSource();
    String text = source.getText();
    if ((text.length() != 0) && !(text.equals("Exit"))) {
```

```
      Runnable runnable = new Runnable() {
        public void run() {
          JOptionPane.showMessageDialog (source, "Can't leave.", "Error Dialog",
JOptionPane.ERROR_MESSAGE);
          source.requestFocus();
        }
      };
      SwingUtilities.invokeLater(runnable);
    }
  }
};
nameTextField.addFocusListener(focusListener);
cityTextField.addFocusListener(focusListener);
```

> **TIP** *See what happens when the main window no longer has the input focus. This triggers the notification of the focus listener because focus has been lost.*

Listening to JTextField Events with a DocumentListener

With the AWT TextField, if you wanted to find out when the contents of the component changed, you associated a TextListener with the TextField. To get the same behavior with the Swing JTextField, you instead need to associate a listener with the data model. In this case, the data model is Document and the listener is a DocumentListener. The following example is meant to duplicate the AWT capabilities. This normally wouldn't be done for validation purposes. For validation, you create a new Document type, as shown in the earlier section "Creating Custom Documents."

```
DocumentListener documentListener = new DocumentListener() {
  public void changedUpdate(DocumentEvent documentEvent) {
    printIt(documentEvent);
  }
  public void insertUpdate(DocumentEvent documentEvent) {
    printIt(documentEvent);
  }
  public void removeUpdate(DocumentEvent documentEvent) {
    printIt(documentEvent);
  }
  private void printIt(DocumentEvent documentEvent) {
```

```
DocumentEvent.EventType type = documentEvent.getType();
String typeString = null;
if (type.equals(DocumentEvent.EventType.CHANGE)) {
  typeString = "Change";
} else if (type.equals(DocumentEvent.EventType.INSERT)) {
  typeString = "Insert";
} else if (type.equals(DocumentEvent.EventType.REMOVE)) {
  typeString = "Remove";
}
System.out.print("Type :    " + typeString + " / ");
Document source = documentEvent.getDocument();
int length = source.getLength();
try {
  System.out.println("Contents: " + source.getText(0, length));
} catch (BadLocationException badLocationException) {
  System.out.println("Contents: Unknown");
}
  }
};
nameTextField.getDocument().addDocumentListener(documentListener);
cityTextField.getDocument().addDocumentListener(documentListener);
```

Putting It All Together

Now that we've examined the usage of the listeners separately, let's put them all together within one example. Figure 14-15 shows the end result of this endeavor. Keep in mind that the magic word to tab out of a component is "Exit."

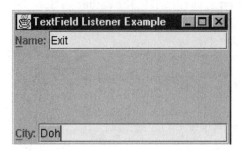

Figure 14-15: JTextField event demonstration

And, here's the source for the example in Figure 14-15:

```
import javax.swing.*;
import javax.swing.text.*;
import javax.swing.event.*;
import java.awt.*;
import java.awt.event.*;

public class JTextFieldSample {
  public static void main(String args[]) {
    JFrame frame = new ExitableJFrame("TextField Listener Example");
    Container content = frame.getContentPane();

    JPanel namePanel = new JPanel(new BorderLayout());
    JLabel nameLabel = new JLabel("Name: ");
    nameLabel.setDisplayedMnemonic(KeyEvent.VK_N);
    JTextField nameTextField = new JTextField();
    nameLabel.setLabelFor(nameTextField);
    namePanel.add(nameLabel, BorderLayout.WEST);
    namePanel.add(nameTextField, BorderLayout.CENTER);
    content.add(namePanel, BorderLayout.NORTH);

    JPanel cityPanel = new JPanel(new BorderLayout());
    JLabel cityLabel = new JLabel("City: ");
    cityLabel.setDisplayedMnemonic(KeyEvent.VK_C);
    JTextField cityTextField = new JTextField();
    cityLabel.setLabelFor(cityTextField);
    cityPanel.add(cityLabel, BorderLayout.WEST);
    cityPanel.add(cityTextField, BorderLayout.CENTER);
    content.add(cityPanel, BorderLayout.SOUTH);

    ActionListener actionListener = new ActionListener() {
      public void actionPerformed(ActionEvent actionEvent) {
        System.out.println("Command: " + actionEvent.getActionCommand());
      }
    };
    nameTextField.setActionCommand("Yo");
    nameTextField.addActionListener(actionListener);
    cityTextField.addActionListener(actionListener);

    KeyListener keyListener = new KeyListener() {
      public void keyPressed(KeyEvent keyEvent) {
        printIt("Pressed", keyEvent);
```

```
      }
      public void keyReleased(KeyEvent keyEvent) {
        printIt("Released", keyEvent);
      }
      public void keyTyped(KeyEvent keyEvent) {
        printIt("Typed", keyEvent);
      }
      private void printIt(String title, KeyEvent keyEvent) {
        int keyCode = keyEvent.getKeyCode();
        String keyText = KeyEvent.getKeyText(keyCode);
        System.out.println(title + " : " + keyText + "/" +
KeyEvent.getKeyChar());
      }
    };
    nameTextField.addKeyListener(keyListener);
    cityTextField.addKeyListener(keyListener);

    FocusListener focusListener = new FocusListener() {
      public void focusGained(FocusEvent focusEvent) {
        JTextComponent source = (JTextComponent)focusEvent.getSource();
        source.selectAll();
      }
      public void focusLost(FocusEvent focusEvent) {
        final JTextComponent source = (JTextComponent)focusEvent.getSource();
        String text = source.getText();
        if ((text.length() != 0) && !(text.equals("Exit"))) {
          Runnable runnable = new Runnable() {
            public void run() {
              JOptionPane.showMessageDialog (source, "Can't leave.", "Error
Dialog",

JOptionPane.ERROR_MESSAGE);
              source.requestFocus();
            }
          };
          SwingUtilities.invokeLater(runnable);
        }
      }
    };
    nameTextField.addFocusListener(focusListener);
    cityTextField.addFocusListener(focusListener);

    DocumentListener documentListener = new DocumentListener() {
      public void changedUpdate(DocumentEvent documentEvent) {
```

```
      printIt(documentEvent);
    }
    public void insertUpdate(DocumentEvent documentEvent) {
      printIt(documentEvent);
    }
    public void removeUpdate(DocumentEvent documentEvent) {
      printIt(documentEvent);
    }
    private void printIt(DocumentEvent documentEvent) {
      DocumentEvent.EventType type = documentEvent.getType();
      String typeString = null;
      if (type.equals(DocumentEvent.EventType.CHANGE)) {
        typeString = "Change";
      } else if (type.equals(DocumentEvent.EventType.INSERT)) {
        typeString = "Insert";
      } else if (type.equals(DocumentEvent.EventType.REMOVE)) {
        typeString = "Remove";
      }
      System.out.print("Type  :   " + typeString + " / ");
      Document source = documentEvent.getDocument();
      int length = source.getLength();
      try {
        System.out.println("Contents: " + source.getText(0, length));
      } catch (BadLocationException badLocationException) {
        System.out.println("Contents: Unknown");
      }
    }
  };
  nameTextField.getDocument().addDocumentListener(documentListener);
  cityTextField.getDocument().addDocumentListener(documentListener);

  frame.setSize(250, 150);
  frame.setVisible(true);
  }
}
```

WARNING   *Oddly enough, it's possible (especially on a slow system) to enter text in one field, transfer focus to the other text component, and then enter text in it before the first dialog box appears. This results in a nasty situation in which you have two dialog boxes on the screen and can't close either of them.*

Customizing a JTextField Look and Feel

Each installable Swing look and feel provides a different JTextField appearance and set of default UIResource values. The available set of 17 UIResource-related properties for a JTextField is shown in Table 14-5.

PROPERTY STRING	OBJECT TYPE
text	Color
TextField.background	Color
TextField.border	Border
TextField.caretBlinkRate	Integer
TextField.caretForeground	Color
TextField.font	Font
TextField.foreground	Color
TextField.inactiveForeground	Color
TextField.keyBindings	KeyBinding[ ]
TextField.margin	Insets
TextField.selectionBackground	Color
TextField.selectionForeground	Color
TextFieldUI	TextFieldUI
textHighlight	Color
textHighlightText	Color
textInactiveText	Color
textText	Color

Table 14-5: JTextField UIResource elements

Figure 14-16 shows the appearance of the JTextField component for the preinstalled set of look and feels: Motif, Windows, Metal, and Macintosh.

Class JPasswordField

The JPasswordField component is designed for input of passwords. Instead of echoing what the user types, a special input mask is displayed back. It works like an AWT TextField with an input mask of "*". The major differences between the two components can enhance security. You can't unset the mask, nor can you cut or copy the contents of the password component.

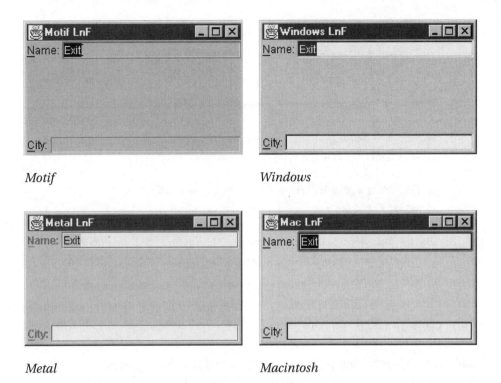

Motif

Windows

Metal

Macintosh

Figure 14-16: JTextField under different look and feels

Creating a JPasswordField

The JPasswordField class has the same five constructors as the JTextField. With the no-argument constructor, you get an empty input field zero columns wide, a default initial Document model, and an echo character of "*". Although you can specify the initial text in the constructor, you're usually prompting a user for a password to verify the user's identity, not to see if the user can submit a form. Therefore, a JPasswordField tends to be empty at startup. As with the JTextField, you can also specify the initial width, assuming that the layout manager of the container in which the JPasswordField is placed will honor this request.

You can also specify the Document data model for the password field in a constructor. When specifying the Document data model, you should specify a null initial-text argument; otherwise, the current contents of the document will be replaced by the initial text for the password field. In addition, you should *not* try to use a custom Document with a JPasswordField. Because the component doesn't display any visual feedback besides how many characters have been entered, it can be confusing to a user if you tried to restrict input to only numerical data.

```
1.  public JPasswordField()
    JPasswordField passwordField = new JPasswordField();

2.  public JPasswordField(String text)
    JPasswordField passwordField = new JPasswordField("Initial Password");

3.  public JPasswordField(int columnWidth)
    JPasswordField passwordField = new JPasswordField(14);

4.  public JPasswordField(String text, int columnWidth)
    JPasswordField passwordField = new JPasswordField("Initial Password", 14);

5.  public JPasswordField(Document model, String text, int columnWidth)
    JPasswordField passwordField = new JPasswordField(aModel, "Initial
    Password", 14);
```

JPasswordField Properties

Table 14-6 shows the four properties of JPasswordField. Setting the echoChar property allows you to use a mask character other than the default "*" character.

PROPERTY NAME	DATA TYPE	ACCESS
accessibleContext	AccessibleContext	read-only
echoChar	char	read-write
password	char[ ]	read-only
UIClassID	String	read-only

Table 14-6: JPasswordField properties

If the echoChar property is set to the character "\u0000" (0), the public boolean echoCharIsSet() method returns false. In all other cases, the method returns true.

> **WARNING** *Avoid using the deprecated read-only text property that is a String. You should use the password property instead because it's a char[ ] that can be cleared immediately after usage. A String must wait for the garbage collector to dispose of it.*

Customizing JPasswordField Look and Feel

The JPasswordField is a subclass of a JTextField. It has the same appearance under all the predefined look and feels as the JTextField. Examine Figure 14-16 to see how the JPasswordField appears under each of the look and feels. The one difference is that the content is masked by the current echoChar property setting. This is shown in Figure 14-17. The top text component is a JTextField; the bottom one is a JPasswordField.

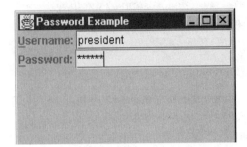

Figure 14-17: JPasswordField sample

The set of 12 UIResource-related properties for a JPasswordField is shown in Table 14-7.

PROPERTY STRING	OBJECT TYPE
PasswordField.background	Color
PasswordField.border	Border
PasswordField.caretBlinkRate	Integer
PasswordField.caretForeground	Color
PasswordField.font	Font
PasswordField.foreground	Color
PasswordField.inactiveForeground	Color
PasswordField.keyBindings	KeyBinding[ ]
PasswordField.margin	Insets
PasswordField.selectionBackground	Color
PasswordField.selectionForeground	Color
PasswordFieldUI	PasswordFieldUI

Table 14-7: JPasswordField UIResource elements

Class `JTextArea`

Like the AWT `TextArea`, the `JTextArea` component is the text component for multi-line input. Similar to the `JTextField`, the data model for a `JTextArea` is the `PlainDocument` implementation of the `Document` interface. Therefore, the `JTextArea` is limited to single-attributed text. Figure 14-18 illustrates these relationships.

> **NOTE**   *One thing isn't shown in Figure 14-8: As with other Swing compo-nents that may require scrolling, the `JTextArea` doesn't support scrolling itself. You need to place each `JTextArea` within a `JScrollPane` to allow a user to properly scroll through the contents of a `JTextArea`.*

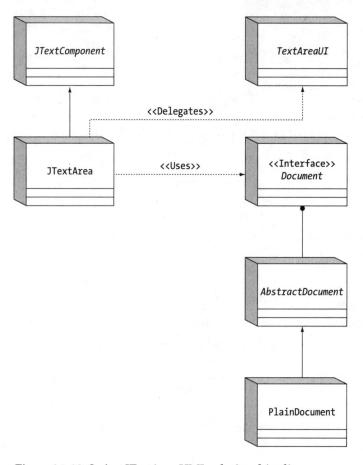

Figure 14-18: Swing JTextArea UML relationship diagram

Creating a JTextArea

There are six constructors for creating a JTextArea. Unless otherwise specified, the text area is able to hold zero rows and columns of content. Although this might sound like a serious limitation, you're just telling the text area to let the current LayoutManager worry about the size of your text area. The contents of the JTextArea are initially empty unless specified from either the starting text string or the Document model.

The six JTextArea constructors are:

1. ```
   public JTextArea()
   JTextArea textArea = new JTextArea();
   ```

2. ```
   public JTextArea(Document document)
   Document document = new PlainDocument();
   JTextArea textArea = new JTextArea(document);
   ```

3. ```
   public JTextArea(String text)
   JTextArea textArea = new JTextArea("...");
   ```

4. ```
   public JTextArea(int rows, int columns)
   JTextArea textArea = new JTextArea(10, 40);
   ```

5. ```
   public JTextArea(String text, int rows, int columns)
   JTextArea textArea = new JTextArea("...", 10, 40);
   ```

6. ```
   public JTextArea(Document document, String text, int rows, int columns)
   JTextArea textArea = new JTextArea(document, null, 10, 40);
   ```

> **NOTE** *Other initial settings for a JTextArea include having a tab stop every eight positions and turning off word wrap. For more on tab stops, see the TabStop and TabSet class descriptions in Chapter 15.*

After creating a JTextArea, remember to place the JTextArea into a JScrollPane. Then if there isn't sufficient space on the screen, the JScrollPane will manage the scrolling for you. Figure 14-19 shows how a JTextArea looks within a JScrollPane, and outside of a JScrollPane. In the JTextArea not in the JScrollPane, there's no way to see the text that falls below the bottom screen border. Unfortunately, moving the cursor into that area doesn't cause the content at the top to move up.

```
JTextArea textArea = new JTextArea();
JScrollPane scrollPane = new JScrollPane(textArea);
content.add(scrollPane);
```

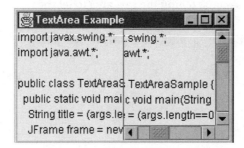

Figure 14-19: A JTextArea without a JScrollPane and one within a JScrollPane

JTextArea Properties

Table 14-8 shows the 13 properties of JTextArea.

PROPERTY NAME	DATA TYPE	ACCESS
accessibleContext	AccessibleContext	read-only
columns	int	read-write
font	Font	write-only
lineCount	int	read-only
lineWrap	boolean	read-write bound
managingFocus	boolean	read-only
preferredScrollableViewportSize	Dimension	read-only
preferredSize	Dimension	read-only
rows	int	read-write
scrollableTracksViewportWidth	boolean	read-only
tabSize	int	read-write bound
UIClassID	String	read-only
wrapStyleWord	boolean	read-write bound

Table 14-8: JTextArea properties

The rows and columns properties come directly from the constructor arguments. The preferredScrollableViewportSize and scrollableTracksViewportWidth properties come from implementing the Scrollable interface for scrolling support. The font and preferredSize properties merely customize the behavior inherited from JTextComponent.

That leaves the more-interesting properties of lineCount, tabSize, lineWrap with wrapStyleWord, and managingFocus to examine.

- The lineCount property allows you to find out how many lines are in the text area. This is useful for sizing purposes.

- The tabSize property allows you to control the tab position interval within the text area. By default this value is 8.

- The lineWrap and wrapStyleWord properties work together. By default, the wrapping of long lines is disabled. If you enable line wrapping (by setting the lineWrap property to true), the point at which long lines wrap depends on the wrapStyleWord property setting. Initially, this property is false, which means that if the lineWrap property is true, line wrapping happens at character boundaries. If both lineWrap and wrapStyleWord are true, then each word from a line that doesn't fit is wrapped to another line, as it is in a word processor. So, to get the word wrap capabilities that most people want, you have to set both properties to true for your JTextArea:

```
JTextArea textArea = new JTextArea("...");
textArea.setLineWrap(true);
textArea.setWrapStyleWord(true);
JScrollPane scrollPane = new JScrollPane(textArea);
```

- The managingFocus property can be interesting, although many programmers leave this property alone, especially becuase it is a read-only property. To change the setting, you must subclass the JTextArea class. The initial setting of this property value is true, which means that the JTextArea keeps all the tab events to itself. Because no other components are within the JTextArea, this leaves the JTextArea to deal with managing focus itself. If you subclass JTextArea to return false for isManagingFocus(), then you have effectively permitted the tab character to guide a user from a JTextArea to the next component in the current focus cycle.

```
JTextArea textArea = new JTextArea() {
  public boolean isManagingFocus() {
    return false;
  }
};
JScrollPane scrollPane = new JScrollPane(textArea);
```

NOTE   *The CTRL-TAB and SHIFT-CTRL-TAB key combinations allow users to change focus from within* JTextArea *components without having to subclass the component.*

Handling JTextArea Events

No events are specific to a JTextArea. You can use one of the inherited listeners, such as a FocusListener, from JTextComponent (or one of its parents).

At times, you'll just have a JTextArea on the screen and get its contents after the user presses a button on his screen. Other times, there's a bit more planning involved.

Customizing a JTextArea Look and Feel

Each installable Swing look and feel provides a different JTextArea appearance and set of default UIResource values. Figure 14-20 shows the appearance of the JTextArea component for the preinstalled set of look and feels. Notice that the primary difference in the appearance of each is the scrollbar from the JScrollPane, which is not a part within the actual JTextArea.

The available set of 12 UIResource-related properties for a JTextArea is listed in Table 14-9.

PROPERTY STRING	OBJECT TYPE
TextArea.background	Color
TextArea.border	Border
TextArea.caretBlinkRate	Integer
TextArea.caretForeground	Color
TextArea.font	Font
TextArea.foreground	Color
TextArea.inactiveForeground	Color
TextArea.keyBindings	KeyBinding[ ]
TextArea.margin	Insets
TextArea.selectionBackground	Color
TextArea.selectionForeground	Color
TextAreaUI	TextAreaUI

Table 14-9: JTextArea UIResource elements

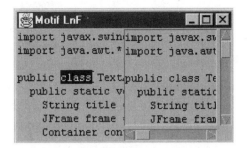

Motif

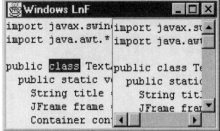

Windows

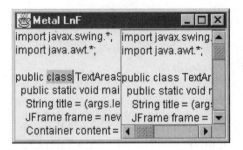

Metal

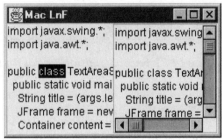

Macintosh

Figure 14-20: JTextArea under different look and feels

Class JEditorPane

The JEditorPane class offers your first exposure to capabilities beyond that of the basic AWT text components. It provides the ability to display *and edit* multi-attributed text. Where the JTextField and JTextArea only supported single-color, single-font content, the JEditorPane allows you to tag your content with various styles, such as bold, italics, 14-point Helvetica, right-justified paragraphs, or with the appearance of an HTML viewer, as shown in Figure 14-21.

> **NOTE** *If you compare Figure 14-21 to the display of* www.apress.com *with a current 4.0+ browser, you'll notice some differences. The HTML support for JEditorPane is only at the HTML 3.2 level, whereas HTML 4.0 is the current version as of this writing. Advanced capabilities such as background images for table cells aren't supported.*

Figure 14-21: Sample JEditorPane as an HTML viewer

The JEditorPane supports the display and editing of multi-attributed text through the help of an EditorKit specific to the text markup mechanism. Predefined kits exist to support raw text, HTML documents, and Rich Text Format (RTF) documents. Because the content is multi-attributed, the PlainDocument model is no longer sufficient. Instead, Swing provides a StyledDocument in the form of the DefaultStyledDocument class for maintaining the document model. The remaining part of the mix is the new HyperlinkListener/HyperlinkEvent event-handling pair for monitoring hyperlink operations within the document. Figure 14-22 shows the relationships among the JEditorPane class.

> **NOTE** *The JEditorPane will be explained in more depth in Chapter 15.*

Creating a JEditorPane

The JEditorPane has four constructors. The no-argument constructor creates an empty JEditorPane. If you want to initialize the contents, you can directly specify the text and its MIME type. Or, you can specify the URL for where to get the contents. The URL can be specified as either a String or a URL object. When you specify the contents as a URL, the JEditorPane determines the MIME type from the response.

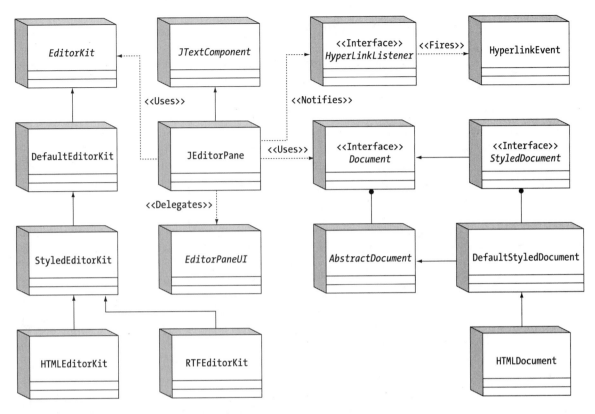

Figure 14-22: Swing JEditorPane UML relationship diagram

```
1.   public JEditorPane()
     JEditorPane editorPane = new JEditorPane();


2.   public JEditorPane(String type, String text)
     String content = "<H1>Got Java?</H1>";
     String type = "text/html";
     JEditorPane editorPane = new JEditorPane(type, content);


3.   public JEditorPane(String urlString) throws IOException
     JEditorPane editorPane = new JEditorPane("http://java.miningco.com");


4.   public JEditorPane(URL url) throws IOException
     URL url = new URL("http://java.miningco.com");
     JEditorPane editorPane = new JEditorPane(url);
```

JEditorPane Properties

Table 14-10 shows the ten properties of JEditorPane. Most of the properties just customize the behavior of the parent classes.

PROPERTY NAME	DATA TYPE	ACCESS
accessibleContext	AccessibleContext	read-only
contentType	String	read-write
editorKit	EditorKit	read-write bound
managingFocus	boolean	read-only
page	URL	read-write bound
page	String	write-only bound
preferredSize	Dimension	read-only
scrollableTracksViewportHeight	boolean	read-only
scrollableTracksViewportWidth	boolean	read-only
text	String	read-write
UIClassID	String	read-only

Table 14-10: JEditorPane properties

> **NOTE** *The page property is non-standard in the sense it has two setter methods, but only one getter.*

Four interesting properties of JEditorPane are the editorKit, which I'll talk about in Chapter 15, contentType, page, and text.

The contentType property represents the MIME-type of the content inside the document. This property tends to be automatically set when you set up the content in the constructor (or elsewhere). In the event the editor kit is unable to determine the MIME-type, you can manually set it. The three MIME-types with built-in support are text/html, text/plain, and text/rtf, as reported by the getContentType() method of the predefined editor kits.

The page property allows you to change the displayed contents to reflect the contents of a specific URL so that you can use the contents in some manner not programmed into the environment.

The text property allows you to find out what the textual content is based on the current Document model.

Handling JEditorPane Events

Because JEditorPane is just another text area component with some special display characteristics, it supports the same set of listeners for event handling as does the JTextArea component. In addition, the JEditorPane provides a special listener-event combination to deal with hyperlinks within a document.

Interface HyperlinkListener/Class HyperlinkEvent

The HyperlinkListener interface defines one method, public void hyperlinkUpdate (HyperlinkEvent hyperlinkEvent) that works with a HyperlinkEvent to respond to, not surprisingly, a hyperlink event. The event includes a HyperlinkEvent. EventType that reports on the type of event and allows you to report differently, either by following the link when selected or possibly changing the cursor when moving the mouse over (or off) the hyperlink.

Here's the HyperlinkListener definition:

```
public interface HyperlinkListener implements EventListener {
  public void hyperlinkUpdate(HyperlinkEvent hyperlinkEvent);
}
```

And, here's the HyperlinkEvent definition:

```
public class HyperlinkEvent extends EventObject {
  // Constructors
  public HyperlinkEvent(Object source, HyperlinkEvent.EventType type, URL url);
  public HyperlinkEvent(Object source, HyperlinkEvent.EventType type, URL url,
String description);
  // Properties
  public String getDescription();
  public HyperlinkEvent.EventType getEventType();
  public URL getURL();
}
```

The hyperlink event types will be one of three constants within the HyperlinkEvent. EventType class:

- ACTIVATED — Usually involving a mouse click over the appropriate content.

- ENTERED — Moving the mouse over the hyperlink content

- EXITED — Moving the mouse out of the hyperlink content

Therefore, if you want to create a HyperlinkListener that changes the cursor while it's over the hyperlink and follows the hyperlink when activated, you can create your own miniature HTML help viewer. Unfortunately, the HTMLEditorKit that comes with Swing doesn't generate ENTERED and EXIT HyperlinkEvent objects, only ACTIVATED ones. So, all you can do is provide the following hyperlink capabilities. The editor kit is even more picky because activation of a hyperlink involves clicking on a link *without* moving the mouse.

The following HyperlinkListener implementation will do the trick for you. There are println statements present in the listener should a later version of the Swing release add the capabilities for ENTERED and EXITED support. You can remove them if you don't want to have this hidden notification mechanism in place.

```java
import java.awt.*;
import javax.swing.*;
import javax.swing.text.*;
import javax.swing.event.*;
import java.io.*;
import java.net.*;

public class ActivatedHyperlinkListener implements HyperlinkListener {

  Frame frame;
  JEditorPane editorPane;

  public ActivatedHyperlinkListener(Frame frame, JEditorPane editorPane) {
    this.frame = frame;
    this.editorPane = editorPane;
  }

  public void hyperlinkUpdate(HyperlinkEvent hyperlinkEvent) {
    HyperlinkEvent.EventType type = hyperlinkEvent.getEventType();
    final URL url = hyperlinkEvent.getURL();
    if (type == HyperlinkEvent.EventType.ENTERED) {
      System.out.println("Entered");
    } else if (type == HyperlinkEvent.EventType.EXITED) {
      System.out.println("Exited");
    } else if (type == HyperlinkEvent.EventType.ACTIVATED) {
      System.out.println("Activated");
      Runnable runner = new Runnable() {
        public void run() {
          // Retain reference to original
          Document doc = editorPane.getDocument();
          try {
            editorPane.setPage(url);
```

```
        } catch (IOException ioException) {
          JOptionPane.showMessageDialog(frame, "Error following link", "Invalid
link", JOptionPane.ERROR_MESSAGE);
          editorPane.setDocument(doc);
        }
      }
    };
    SwingUtilities.invokeLater(runner);
    }
  }
}
```

> **TIP** *Don't forget to make the* JEditorPane *read-only with a call to* setEditable(false). *Otherwise, the viewer acts as an editor.*

The following is a complete example using our new ActivatedHyperlinkListener class. The frame it creates looks like Figure 14-21.

```
import javax.swing.*;
import javax.swing.event.*;
import java.awt.*;
import java.io.*;

public class EditorPaneSample {
  public static void main(String args[]) throws IOException {
    JFrame frame = new ExitableJFrame("EditorPane Example");
    Container content = frame.getContentPane();

    JEditorPane editorPane = new JEditorPane("http://www.apress.com");
    editorPane.setEditable(false);

    HyperlinkListener hyperlinkListener = new ActivatedHyperlinkListener(frame,
editorPane);
    editorPane.addHyperlinkListener(hyperlinkListener);

    JScrollPane scrollPane = new JScrollPane(editorPane);
    content.add(scrollPane);

    frame.setSize(640, 480);
    frame.setVisible(true);
  }
}
```

Customizing a *JEditorPane* Look and Feel

The appearance of the JEditorPane is similar to that of a JTextArea. Although the supported contents differ, the look-and-feel–related attributes usually aren't different. See Figure 14-20 for how the JEditorPane looks under the various pre-defined look and feels.

The available set of 12 UIResource-related properties for a JEditorPane is shown in Table 14-11. Their names are similar to those of the JTextArea settings.

PROPERTY STRING	OBJECT TYPE
EditorPane.background	Color
EditorPane.border	Border
EditorPane.caretBlinkRate	Integer
EditorPane.caretForeground	Color
EditorPane.font	Font
EditorPane.foreground	Color
EditorPane.inactiveForeground	Color
EditorPane.keyBindings	KeyBinding[ ]
EditorPane.margin	Insets
EditorPane.selectionBackground	Color
EditorPane.selectionForeground	Color
EditorPaneUI	EditorPaneUI

Table 14-11: JEditorPane UIResource elements

Class **JTextPane**

The JTextPane is a specialized form of the JEditorPane designed especially for the editing (and display) of styled text. It differs from the JEditorPane only in its manner of providing the content to display because the text isn't tagged with the styles as it would be in an HTML or RTF document.

The JTextPane relies on three interfaces (to be discussed in Chapter 15) for the setting of text attributes. The interfaces are AttributeSet for a basic collection of attributes, MutableAttributeSet for a changeable collection of attributes, and Style for a set of attributes to be associated with a part of a StyledDocument. Figure 14-23 shows these relationships for the JTextPane class.

The rest of this section will touch on the usage of the JTextPane. See Chapter 15 for additional information about configuring styles for different parts of the styled content within a JTextPane.

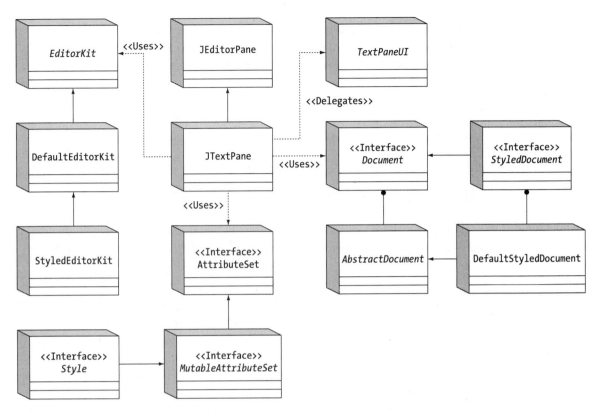

Figure 14-23: Swing JTextPane UML relationship diagram

Creating a JTextPane

There are only two constructors for the JTextPane. The no-argument constructor initially has zero contents. The second constructor allows you to create the Document first, and then use it in the JTextPane.

1.  ```
    public JTextPane()
    JTextPane textPane = new JTextPane();
    JScrollPane scrollPane = new JScrollPane(textPane);
    ```

2.  ```
    public JTextPane(StyledDocument document)
    StyledDocument document = new DefaultStyledDocument();
    JTextPane textPane = new JTextPane(document);
    JScrollPane scrollPane = new JScrollPane(textPane);
    ```

> **TIP** *Remember to place your JTextPane within a JScrollPane if the contents will be larger than the available screen space.*

JTextPane Properties

Table 14-12 shows the nine properties of JTextPane. We'll look at these in greater detail in Chapter 15.

PROPERTY NAME	DATA TYPE	ACCESS
characterAttributes	AttributeSet	read-only
document	Document	write-only
editorKit	EditorKit	write-only
inputAttributes	MutableAttributeSet	read-only
logicalStyle	Style	read-write
paragraphAttributes	AttributeSet	read-only
scrollableTracksViewportWidth	boolean	read-only
styledDocument	StyledDocument	read-write
UIClassID	String	read-only

Table 14-12: JTextPane properties

Customizing a JTextPane Look and Feel

The JTextPane is a subclass of a JEditorPane. It has the same appearance under all the predefined look and feels as the JTextArea. Although the contents might differ, the look and feel is the same. See Figure 14-20 for how the JTextPane looks under the different predefined look and feels.

The available set of UIResource-related properties for a JTextPane is shown in Table 14-13. For the JTextPane component, there are 12 different properties. Their names are similar to the JTextArea settings.

PROPERTY STRING	OBJECT TYPE
TextPane.background	Color
TextPane.border	Border
TextPane.caretBlinkRate	Integer
TextPane.caretForeground	Color
TextPane.font	Font
TextPane.foreground	Color

(continued)

Table 14-13 (continued)

PROPERTY STRING	OBJECT TYPE
TextPane.inactiveForeground	Color
TextPane.keyBindings	KeyBinding[ ]
TextPane.margin	Insets
TextPane.selectionBackground	Color
TextPane.selectionForeground	Color
TextPaneUI	TextPaneUI

Table 14-13: JTextPane UIResource elements

Sample JTextPane

Although I'm not going to go into all the details of loading the content for a StyledDocument for a JTextPane in this chapter, I'll nevertheless provide an example that does that. (For more details, flip over to Chapter 15.) Figure 14-24 shows how a JTextPane might look like with a few paragraphs of content. Notice that the content is *not* restricted to just text. It can have images as well. The key line of the source code is the call to insertString() and its style argument:

```
document.insertString(document.getLength(), message, style);
```

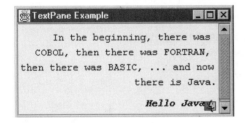

Figure 14-24: Sample JTextPane

The following program demonstrates the setup of a StyledDocument for a JTextPane with multi-attributed text. The details of using Style, SimpleAttributeSet, and StyleConstants will be discussed in Chapter 15.

```
import javax.swing.*;
import javax.swing.text.*;
import javax.swing.event.*;
import java.awt.*;
```

```
public class TextPaneSample {
  private static String message =
    "In the beginning, there was COBOL, then there was FORTRAN, " +
    "then there was BASIC, ... and now there is Java.\n";

  public static void main(String args[]) {
    String title = (args.length==0 ? "TextPane Example" : args[0]);
    JFrame frame = new ExitableJFrame(title);
    Container content = frame.getContentPane();

    StyleContext context = new StyleContext();
    StyledDocument document = new DefaultStyledDocument(context);

    Style style = context.getStyle(StyleContext.DEFAULT_STYLE);
    StyleConstants.setAlignment(style, StyleConstants.ALIGN_RIGHT);
    StyleConstants.setFontSize(style, 14);
    StyleConstants.setSpaceAbove(style, 4);
    StyleConstants.setSpaceBelow(style, 4);

    // Insert content
    try {
      document.insertString(document.getLength(), message, style);
    } catch (BadLocationException badLocationException) {
      System.err.println("Oops");
    }

    SimpleAttributeSet attributes = new SimpleAttributeSet();
    StyleConstants.setBold(attributes, true);
    StyleConstants.setItalic(attributes, true);

    // Insert content
    try {
      document.insertString(document.getLength(), "Hello Java", attributes);
    } catch (BadLocationException badLocationException) {
      System.err.println("Oops");
    }

    // Third style for icon/component
    Style labelStyle = context.getStyle(StyleContext.DEFAULT_STYLE);

    Icon icon = new ImageIcon("Computer.gif");
    JLabel label = new JLabel(icon);
    StyleConstants.setComponent(labelStyle, label);
```

```
// Insert content
try {
  document.insertString(document.getLength(), "Ignored", labelStyle);
} catch (BadLocationException badLocationException) {
  System.err.println("Oops");
}

JTextPane textPane = new JTextPane(document);
textPane.setEditable(false);
JScrollPane scrollPane = new JScrollPane(textPane);
content.add(scrollPane, BorderLayout.CENTER);

frame.setSize(300, 150);
frame.setVisible(true);
  }
}
```

Summary

In this chapter, we began to explore the details of the Swing text components. We initially looked at the root text component, JTextComponent, and the many operations it defines for all other text components. We then explored the specific text components of JTextField, JPasswordField, JTextArea, JEditorPane, and JTextPane.

We also explored the various pieces that make up the different components. We delved into the data model for the text components, based on the Document interface, for the AbstractDocument and PlainDocument classes. We also looked at creating a custom document for restricting input to a text component. In addition, we explored the Caret and Highlighter interfaces for displaying the cursor and highlighted text as well as the Keymap to make the text components act as the controller. As the controller, the Keymap converts a user's keystrokes into specific actions that affect the model for the text component.

We also looked at how events are handled and how event handling differs between AWT and Swing text components. In addition to the AWT event handling classes, Swing adds some new ones designed for listening for cursor movement with the CaretListener and document content changes with the DocumentListener. The JEditorPane also provides another event handler with the HyperlinkListener.

In Chapter 15, we'll further explore the Swing text components. This chapter touched on the basic features of all the components, while the next chapter goes into all the gory details of working with the TextAction and configuring Style objects to work with a StyledDocument.

CHAPTER 15

Advanced Text Capabilities

IN CHAPTER 14, YOU WERE INTRODUCED TO the myriad capabilities of the Swing text components. In this chapter, we'll continue on the same path by looking at more-advanced capabilities that will prove useful in special situations.

The Swing text components ship with many prefabricated features. For instance, as you saw in Chapter 14, although text components have methods such as cut(), copy(), and paste() to work with the system clipboard, you really don't need to ever to use them. This is because the Swing text components come with their own predefined set of Action objects. To use Action objects, just attach them to a component, such as a button or menu item, and then simply select the component that triggers the Action. For text components, the Action object is an instance of TextAction, which has a nice additional feature of knowing which text component last had the input focus.

We'll also look at how to create stylized text for display in a JTextPane. If you want to display multicolored text documents or different font styles, the JTextPane component provides a series of interfaces and classes to describe the attributes attached to the document. The AttributeSet interface gives you these on a read-only basis, and the MutableAttributeSet interface extends AttributeSet in order to set attributes. You'll see how the SimpleAttributeSet class implements both of these interfaces by offering a Hashtable to store the text attributes, and how the StyleConstants class helps to configure the many text attributes you can apply.

You'll also see how to work with tab stops within your text documents. These tab-stop techniques also enable you to define leader characters and how text is aligned. (The word *leader* comes from the expression "to lead the eye.") In addition, you'll get a glimpse of the different editor kits that Swing provides and the many different views the basic Swing text delegate can render in order to draw your document content.

Class TextAction

The TextAction class is a special case of the Action interface that was defined with the other Swing event-handling capabilities in Chapter 2 and briefly reviewed in Chapter 14. The purpose of the TextAction class is to provide concrete Action implementations that can work with text components. These implementations are smart enough to know which text component most recently had the input focus and therefore should be the subject of the action.

For every text component, you obviously need a way to associate keystrokes with specific actions. This is done via the Keymap interface, whose methods either tell you or allow you to set the Action that will be associated to a keystroke. The Keymap interface maps a KeyStroke to a TextAction so that separate KeyListener objects don't have to be associated with the text component for each keystroke in order to listen for it. These maps can be shared across multiple components and/or customized for a particular look and feel. As you will soon see, the JTextComponent also has getKeymap() and setKeymap() methods that allow you to read or customize the keymap. Figure 15-1 helps you visualize these relationships.

> **NOTE** *Although the Swing text components use TextAction, KeyStroke, and Keymap, they still support the ability to attach a KeyListener. Using a KeyListener, however, usually isn't appropriate, especially when you want to restrict input to match certain criteria. The better approach for restricting input is to come up with a custom Document model, as demonstrated in Chapter 14.*

The text components come with many predefined TextAction implementations. Through a default key map, the text components know about these predefined actions and therefore know how to insert and remove content and how to track the positions of both the cursor and caret. If the text component supports stylized content, as JTextPane does, there are additional default actions to support this content. All these implementations derive from the JFC/Swing technology editor kits. An EditorKit provides a logical grouping of the various ways to edit a text component, described later in this chapter.

Listing Actions

To find out which actions a JTextComponent supports, you merely ask using the public Action[ ] getActions() method. This will return an array of Action objects, usually of type TextAction, that can be used like any other Action, such as for creating buttons on a JToolBar.

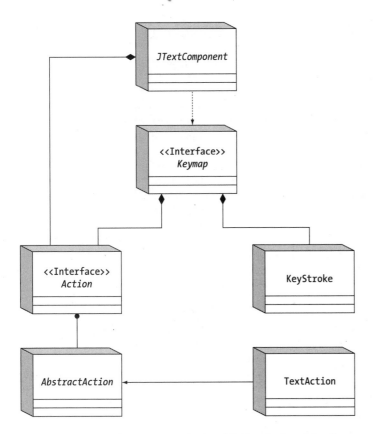

Figure 15-1: JTextComponent-Action UML relationship diagram

Figure 15-2 shows a program that will list the actions for the different predefined components. Pick a component from the JRadioButton group, and its list of text actions will be displayed in the text area. For each action, the action name and class name will be shown.

> **NOTE** *You might have observed that* JTextField *and* JPasswordField *have one more* TextAction *than* JTextArea *and* JEditorPane. *It's used for depressing the* ENTER *key while in the text component and is called* notify-field-accept.

The listing for the program used to generate Figure 15-2 follows.

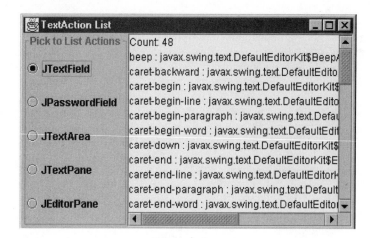

Figure 15-2: TextAction list demonstration

```java
import javax.swing.*;
import javax.swing.text.*;
import java.awt.*;
import java.awt.event.*;
import java.io.*;
import java.util.*;

public class ListActions {
  public static void main(String args[]) {
    JFrame frame = new ExitableJFrame("TextAction List");
    Container contentPane = frame.getContentPane();

    String components[] =
      {"JTextField", "JPasswordField", "JTextArea", "JTextPane", "JEditorPane"};

    final JTextArea textArea = new JTextArea();
    textArea.setEditable(false);
    JScrollPane scrollPane = new JScrollPane(textArea);
    contentPane.add(scrollPane, BorderLayout.CENTER);

    ActionListener actionListener = new ActionListener() {
      public void actionPerformed(ActionEvent actionEvent) {
        // Determine which component selected
        String command = actionEvent.getActionCommand();
        JTextComponent component = null;
        if (command.equals("JTextField")) {
          component = new JTextField();
```

```
    } else if (command.equals("JPasswordField")) {
      component = new JPasswordField();
    } else if (command.equals("JTextArea")) {
      component = new JTextArea();
    } else if (command.equals("JTextPane")) {
      component = new JTextPane();
    } else {
      component = new JEditorPane();
    }

    // Process action list
    Action actions[] = component.getActions();
    // Java 2 specific code to sort
    Comparator comparator = new Comparator() {
      public int compare(Object a1, Object a2) {
        int returnValue = 0;
        if ((a1 instanceof Action) && (a2 instanceof Action)) {
          String firstName = (String)((Action)a1).getValue(Action.NAME);
          String secondName = (String)((Action)a2).getValue(Action.NAME);
          returnValue = firstName.compareTo(secondName);
        }
        return returnValue;
      }
    };
    Arrays.sort(actions, comparator);
    // end Java 2 specific code
    StringWriter sw = new StringWriter();
    PrintWriter pw = new PrintWriter(sw, true);
    int count = actions.length;
    pw.println("Count: " + count);
    for (int i=0; i<count; i++) {
      pw.print  (actions[i].getValue(Action.NAME));
      pw.print  (" : ");
      pw.println(actions[i].getClass().getName());
    }
    pw.close();
    textArea.setText(sw.toString());
    textArea.setCaretPosition(0);
  }
};

final Container componentsContainer =
  RadioButtonUtils.createRadioButtonGrouping(components, "Pick to List
```

```
Actions", actionListener);

    contentPane.add(componentsContainer, BorderLayout.WEST);
    frame.setSize(400, 250);
    frame.setVisible(true);
  }
}
```

> **WARNING**   *If you're using JFC/Swing with JDK 1.1, you'll need to comment out the code that sorts the Action list. In the preceding example code, the Collections API of the Java 2 SDK is used.*

Using Actions

So far, you've seen that there are many predefined TextAction implementations available for the various text components. Yet thus far we haven't done anything to really *use* them.

By making a few minor changes to the program listed in the previous section, you can enhance the program somewhat in order to activate it. When one of the radio buttons is selected, that type of text component is displayed where the text list of Action objects appears in Figure 15-2. In addition, the different Action objects are added to a new JMenuBar placed at the top of the display window. This technique is useful because it shows that you can readily discover the supported operations of a text component and provide access to that behavior without having to know precisely what the actual behavior is. This is just one demonstration of the many ways you can use TextAction objects.

Figure 15-3 shows some of the available operations for a JTextArea. When you select the different menu options, the JTextComponent is appropriately affected.

The following program elicits the behavior shown in Figure 15-3. After all the menu buttons are activated, we're stuck with a text label that might not be exactly what we want. This can, however, easily be changed with the public void setText(String label) method of JMenuItem. If you do this remember that you have to know what's in the menu item to change the label to something meaningful.

```
import javax.swing.*;
import javax.swing.text.*;
import java.awt.*;
import java.awt.event.*;
import java.io.*;
import java.util.*;
```

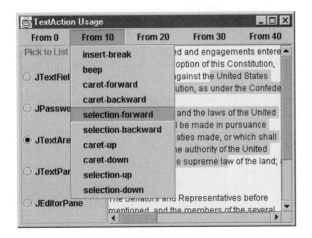

Figure 15-3: TextAction list usage demonstration

```java
public class ActionsMenuBar {
  public static void main(String args[]) {
    final JFrame frame = new ExitableJFrame("TextAction Usage");
    Container contentPane = frame.getContentPane();
    final JScrollPane scrollPane = new JScrollPane();
    contentPane.add(scrollPane, BorderLayout.CENTER);

    final JMenuBar menuBar = new JMenuBar();
    frame.setJMenuBar(menuBar);

    ActionListener actionListener = new ActionListener() {
      JTextComponent component;
      public void actionPerformed(ActionEvent actionEvent) {
        // Determine which component selected
        String command = actionEvent.getActionCommand();
        if (command.equals("JTextField")) {
          component = new JTextField();
        } else if (command.equals("JPasswordField")) {
          component = new JPasswordField();
        } else if (command.equals("JTextArea")) {
          component = new JTextArea();
        } else if (command.equals("JTextPane")) {
          component = new JTextPane();
        } else {
          component = new JEditorPane();
        }
        scrollPane.setViewportView(component);
```

```
        // Process action list
        Action actions[] = component.getActions();
        menuBar.removeAll();
        menuBar.revalidate();
        JMenu menu = null;
        for (int i=0, n=actions.length; i<n; i++) {
          if ((i % 10) == 0) {
            menu = new JMenu("From " + i);
            menuBar.add(menu);
          }
          menu.add(actions[i]);
        }
        menuBar.revalidate();
      }
    };

    String components[] =
      {"JTextField", "JPasswordField", "JTextArea", "JTextPane", "JEditorPane"};
    final Container componentsContainer =
      RadioButtonUtils.createRadioButtonGrouping(components, "Pick to List
Actions", actionListener);
    contentPane.add(componentsContainer, BorderLayout.WEST);

    frame.setSize(400, 300);
    frame.setVisible(true);
  }
}
```

Finding Actions

Although listing and using Action objects related to a text component is a fairly
malleable process, unless you know what you're looking for, it isn't very useful.
Thankfully, the DefaultEditorKit has 46 class constants that match the shared 46
(out of 47) Action objects of all the text components. The class constants' names
more or less reflect their functionality. The JTextField adds an additional constant for the Action shared with JPasswordField. Unfortunately, the remaining
constants available to the JTextPane aren't class constants of the StyledEditorKit,
which defines the additional Action implementations.

> **NOTE** *One additional* Action *exists primarily for debugging purposes. Its* Action *name is "dump-model" and it lacks a class constant to go with it. When initiated, the method literally dumps out the* Document *model* Element *structure for the text component.*

Table 15-1 lists the 47 constants available to help you locate the predefined Action you're seeking.

ACTION CONSTANTS

DefaultEditorKit.backwardAction
DefaultEditorKit.beepAction
DefaultEditorKit.beginAction
DefaultEditorKit.beginLineAction
DefaultEditorKit.beginParagraphAction
DefaultEditorKit.beginWordAction
DefaultEditorKit.copyAction
DefaultEditorKit.cutAction
DefaultEditorKit.defaultKeyTypedAction
DefaultEditorKit.deleteNextCharAction
DefaultEditorKit.deletePrevCharAction
DefaultEditorKit.downAction
DefaultEditorKit.endAction
DefaultEditorKit.endLineAction
DefaultEditorKit.endParagraphAction
DefaultEditorKit.endWordAction
DefaultEditorKit.forwardAction
DefaultEditorKit.insertBreakAction
DefaultEditorKit.insertContentAction
DefaultEditorKit.insertTabAction
DefaultEditorKit.nextWordAction
DefaultEditorKit.pageDownAction
DefaultEditorKit.pageUpAction
DefaultEditorKit.pasteAction
DefaultEditorKit.previousWordAction
DefaultEditorKit.readOnlyAction
DefaultEditorKit.selectAllAction
DefaultEditorKit.selectionBackwardAction
DefaultEditorKit.selectionBeginAction
DefaultEditorKit.selectionBeginLineAction

(continued)

Table 15-1 (continued)

ACTION CONSTANTS

DefaultEditorKit.selectionBeginParagraphAction

DefaultEditorKit.selectionBeginWordAction

DefaultEditorKit.selectionDownAction

DefaultEditorKit.selectionEndAction

DefaultEditorKit.selectionEndLineAction

DefaultEditorKit.selectionEndParagraphAction

DefaultEditorKit.selectionEndWordAction

DefaultEditorKit.selectionForwardAction

DefaultEditorKit.selectionNextWordAction

DefaultEditorKit.selectionPreviousWordAction

DefaultEditorKit.selectionUpAction

DefaultEditorKit.selectLineAction

DefaultEditorKit.selectParagraphAction

DefaultEditorKit.selectWordAction

DefaultEditorKit.upAction

DefaultEditorKit.writableAction

JTextField.notifyAction

Table 15-1: TextAction name constants

With such a huge list of constants, what on earth do you *do* with them? Well, first you find the constant for the predefined TextAction you want to use. This is relatively easy because the names are fairly self-explanatory.

To demonstrate, let's create a program that shows how to work with these constants. The program will have two text areas to show that TextAction objects really know to work with the last text component that had the input focus. One set of menu items will include two options that are used to switch the text area from read-only to writable. This action will be done using the DefaultEditorKit.readOnlyAction and DefaultEditorKit.writableAction names. The other set of menu items includes options for cut, copy, and paste support whose constants are DefaultEditorKit.cutAction, DefaultEditorKit.copyAction, and DefaultEditorKit.pasteAction.

Because the constants are String values, you have to "look up" the actual Action object to use. The look up-process requires first getting the array of all Action objects supported by the text component via getActions(), and then finding the one with the right name. The following helper class provides just such a method to help you find the Action from a name and text component. Alas, it isn't optimized to speed up repeated requests.

```
import javax.swing.*;
import javax.swing.text.*;
```

```
public class FindAction {
  private FindAction() {
  }

  public static Action locate(JTextComponent component, String name) {
    Action returnValue = null;
    Action actions[] = component.getActions();
    for (int i = 0, n=actions.length; i<n; i++) {
      Action action = actions[i];
      String actionName = (String)action.getValue(Action.NAME);
      if (actionName.equals(name)) {
        returnValue = action;
        break;
      }
    }
    return returnValue;
  }
}
```

When you want to find an action, call the locate() method with the appropriate action name (and text component) as the argument:

```
Action anAction = FindAction.locate(textComponent,
DefaultEditorKit.readOnlyAction);
```

Figure 15-4 shows the program at work. By asking for specific TextAction instances, you don't have to constantly recode repetitive operations. In fact, if

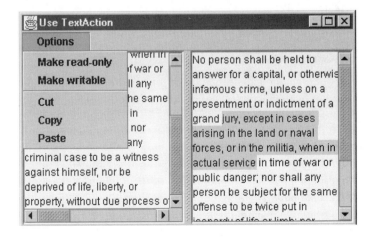

Figure 15-4: Specific TextAction usage demonstration

you constantly find yourself repeating the same operations over and over with a text component, it's probably time for *you* to create your own TextAction objects.

The complete program to find and use various TextAction objects follows. It corresponds to the screen in Figure 15-4. Notice that for each JMenuItem created, the text label changes to give it a more user-friendly setting.

```java
import javax.swing.*;
import javax.swing.text.*;
import java.awt.*;
import java.awt.event.*;
import java.io.*;
import java.util.*;

public class UseActions {
  public static void main(String args[]) {
    JFrame frame = new ExitableJFrame("Use TextAction");
    Container contentPane = frame.getContentPane();
    Dimension empty = new Dimension(0,0);

    final JTextArea leftArea = new JTextArea();
    JScrollPane leftScrollPane = new JScrollPane(leftArea);
    leftScrollPane.setPreferredSize(empty);

    final JTextArea rightArea = new JTextArea();
    JScrollPane rightScrollPane = new JScrollPane(rightArea);
    rightScrollPane.setPreferredSize(empty);

    JSplitPane splitPane = new JSplitPane(JSplitPane.HORIZONTAL_SPLIT,
      leftScrollPane, rightScrollPane);

    JMenuBar menuBar = new JMenuBar();
    frame.setJMenuBar(menuBar);
    JMenu menu = new JMenu("Options");
    menuBar.add(menu);
    JMenuItem menuItem;

    Action readAction = FindAction.locate(leftArea,
DefaultEditorKit.readOnlyAction);
    menuItem = menu.add(readAction);
    menuItem.setText("Make read-only");
    Action writeAction = FindAction.locate(leftArea,
DefaultEditorKit.writableAction);
    menuItem = menu.add(writeAction);
    menuItem.setText("Make writable");
```

```
    menu.addSeparator();

    Action cutAction = FindAction.locate(leftArea, DefaultEditorKit.cutAction);
    menuItem = menu.add(cutAction);
    menuItem.setText("Cut");
    Action copyAction = FindAction.locate(leftArea, DefaultEditorKit.copyAction);
    menuItem = menu.add(copyAction);
    menuItem.setText("Copy");
    Action pasteAction = FindAction.locate(leftArea,
DefaultEditorKit.pasteAction);
    menuItem = menu.add(pasteAction);
    menuItem.setText("Paste");

    contentPane.add(splitPane, BorderLayout.CENTER);
    frame.setSize(400, 250);
    frame.setVisible(true);
    splitPane.setDividerLocation(.5);
  }
}
```

Creating Styled Text

In Chapter 14, we looked at displaying plain text (and HTML). With the Swing
text components — or at least the JTextPane — you can also display stylized text,
in which different blocks of text can have multiple attributes. These attributes
might include boldface, italics, or a different font or color at the character level,
or perhaps justification at the paragraph level, just as with any of the modern
word processors.

To support these capabilities, Swing supplies many different interfaces and
classes, all of which start with the specialized Document interface extension of
StyledDocument. The StyledDocument interface, or more precisely the
DefaultStyledDocument implementation, manages a series of styles and attribute
sets for the contents of a Document.

> **NOTE** *The Document interface was first discussed in Chapter 14 with the*
> *PlainDocument implementation class coverage.*

The various styles used by a StyledDocument are described initially by the
AttributeSet interface, which is a set of key-value pairs of read-only attributes.
The key for an attribute might be "current font," in which the setting would be

the font to use. To actually change the font, you need to move on to the MutableAttributeSet interface, which supplies the ability to add and remove attributes. For instance, if you had an AttributeSet for "bold," you could use MutableAttributeSet to also add italics, underlining, or colorization (or all three) to the set.

For a simple implementation of AttributeSet, there is the StyleContext.SmallAttributeSet class, which uses an array to manage the set of attributes. For an implementation of the MutableAttributeSet interface, there is the SimpleAttributeSet class, which uses a Hashtable to manage the attributes. More complex attribute sets move on to the Style interface, which adds a name to the set of attributes as defined by a MutableAttributeSet. The actual Style implementation class is the StyleContext.NamedStyle class. Besides adding a name, the Style interface adds the ability to have a ChangeListener monitor a set of attributes for changes.

The class that manages the set of Style objects for a StyledDocument is the StyleContext class. An implementation of the AbstractDocument.AttributeContext class, it uses the StyleConstants class, which defines various attributes for commonly used styles.

To help you to keep some semblance of order among all these classes and interfaces, Figure 15-5 shows their relationships.

> **NOTE** *Keep in mind that all of the classes and interfaces presented in Figure 15-5 are required just to set up the Document data model for a particular JTextPane.*

Interface StyledDocument/ Class DefaultStyledDocument

The StyledDocument interface extends the Document interface by adding the ability to store styles for the content of the document. These styles can describe the character or paragraph attributes, such as color, orientation, or font.

```
public interface StyledDocument extends Document {
    public Style addStyle(String nm, Style parent);
    public Color getBackground(AttributeSet attribute);
    public Element getCharacterElement(int position);
    public Font getFont(AttributeSet attribute);
    public Color getForeground(AttributeSet attribute);
    public Style getLogicalStyle(int position);
    public Element getParagraphElement(int position);
    public Style getStyle(String name);
```

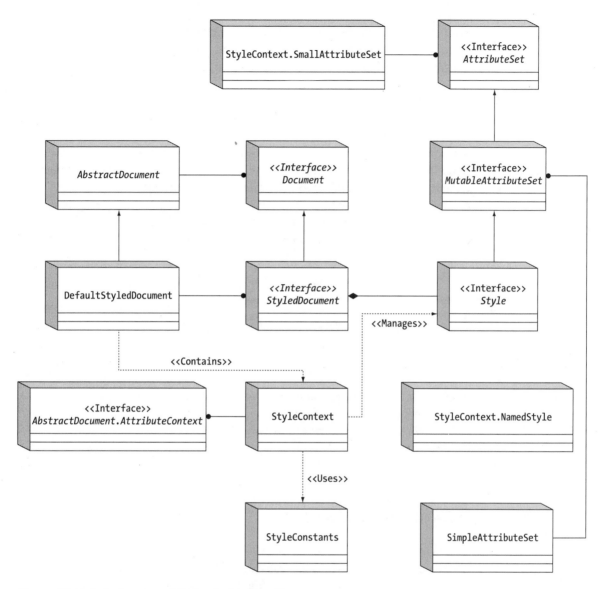

Figure 15-5: StyledDocument UML relationship diagram

```
    public void removeStyle(String name);
    public void setCharacterAttributes(int offset, int length, AttributeSet s,
boolean replace);
    public void setLogicalStyle(int position, Style style);
    public void setParagraphAttributes(int offset, int length, AttributeSet s,
boolean replace);
}
```

The DefaultStyledDocument class is the implementation of the StyledDocument interface provided with the Swing components. It serves as the data model for the JTextPane component.

Creating a DefaultStyledDocument

You can create a DefaultStyledDocument in any one of the three ways listed here. You can share the StyleContext between multiple documents or use the default context. In addition, you can predefine the content using one of the AbstractDocument.Content implementations, either GapContent or StringContent. Although you can use the third constructor, try to avoid it because the implementation classes seem to be meant more for internal use.

1. ```
   public DefaultStyledDocument()
   DefaultStyledDocument document = new DefaultStyledDocument();
   ```

2. ```
   public DefaultStyledDocument(StyleContext styles)
   StyleContext context = new StyleContext();
   DefaultStyledDocument document = new DefaultStyledDocument(context);
   ```

3. ```
   public DefaultStyledDocument(AbstractDocument.Content content,
   StyleContext styles)
   AbstractDocument.Content content = new StringContent();
   DefaultStyledDocument document = new DefaultStyledDocument(content,
   context);
   ```

DefaultStyledDocument Properties

Besides having a default root element to describe the contents of the document, the DefaultStyledDocument makes available the style names as an Enumeration. These are the only two properties defined at the DefaultStyledDocument level, as shown in Table 15-2.

PROPERTY NAME	DATA TYPE	ACCESS
defaultRootElement	Element	read-only
styleNames	Enumeration	read-only

Table 15-2: DefaultStyledDocument properties
   ```

Interface AttributeSet

The AttributeSet interface describes a read-only set of key-value attributes, allowing you access to the description content of a series of attributes. If the set of attributes lacks a specific key defined for it, the AttributeSet supports the ability to look elsewhere by travelling up a chain to a "resolving parent" for the parent's definition of the attribute. This allows the AttributeSet to define a core set of attributes and lets developers (or possibly even users) modify only the set of attributes they want. Unless you want someone to change the defaults globally, you shouldn't provide direct access to the resolving parent. That way, you never lose any of the original settings.

```
public interface AttributeSet {
  // Constants
  public final static Object NameAttribute;
  public final static Object ResolveAttribute;
  // Properties
  public int getAttributeCount();
  public Enumeration getAttributeNames();
  public AttributeSet getResolveParent();
  // Other Methods
  public boolean containsAttribute(Object name, Object value);
  public boolean containsAttributes(AttributeSet attributes);
  public AttributeSet copyAttributes();
  public Object getAttribute(Object key);
  public boolean isDefined(Object attrName);
  public boolean isEqual(AttributeSet attr);
}
```

Interface MutableAttributeSet

The MutableAttributeSet interface describes how you'd go about adding to or removing from the set of attributes, as well as how to set the resolving parent.

```
public interface MutableAttributeSet extends AttributeSet {
  public void addAttribute(Object name, Object value);
  public void addAttributes(AttributeSet attributes);
  public void removeAttribute(Object name);
  public void removeAttributes(AttributeSet attributes);
  public void removeAttributes(Enumeration names);
  public void setResolveParent(AttributeSet parent);
}
```

Class *SimpleAttributeSet*

The SimpleAttributeSet class is the first implementation of the AttributeSet interface. When you begin using it, you'll finally be able to see just how to create the multi-attributed text for display in the JTextPane. The SimpleAttributeSet class is a specific implementation of AttributeSet that relies on a standard Java Hashtable for managing the key/attribute pairs.

Creating a *SimpleAttributeSet*

You would typically create an empty SimpleAttributeSet and then set its attributes, as in the first constructor that follows. Or, you can instead provide the initial settings for the set of attributes in the constructor. Note that this is *not* the resolving parent — it's just an initialized data structure.

1. public SimpleAttributeSet()
   SimpleAttributeSet attributeSet1 = new SimpleAttributeSet();

2. public SimpleAttributeSet(AttributeSet source)
   SimpleAttributeSet attributeSet2 = new SimpleAttributeSet(attributeSet1);

SimpleAttributeSet Properties

Table 15-3 displays the four properties of SimpleAttributeSet. They provide access to the set of attributes whether any attributes exist, as well as who the resolving parent is (if any).

PROPERTY NAME	DATA TYPE	ACCESS
attributeCount	int	read-only
attributeNames	Enumeration	read-only
empty	boolean	read-only
resolveParent	AttributeSet	read-write

Table 15-3: SimpleAttributeSet properties

Using *SimpleAttributeSet*

To demonstrate the use of SimpleAttributeSet and display some multi-attributed text, let's populate the StyledDocument for a JTextPane. After creating the DefaultStyledDocument, you add content to it by calling the public void insertString(int offset, String contents, AttributeSet attributes) method, which happens to throw a BadLocationException. You can then change the attribute set and add more attributes.

To create an appropriate AttributeSet, you need to discover the keys for the attributes you want to alter. We'll see some helper methods shortly in the StyleConstants class covered in the next section. All the keys are hidden away in four public inner classes of StyleConstants: CharacterConstants, ColorConstants, FontConstants, and ParagraphConstants, as shown in Table 15-4.

ATTRIBUTESET KEY CONSTANTS	VALUE TYPE	DEFAULT SETTING
CharacterConstants.Background	Color	Color.black
ColorConstants.Background	Color	Color.black
CharacterConstants.BidiLevel	Integer	0
CharacterConstants.Bold	Boolean	false
FontConstants.Bold	Boolean	false
CharacterConstants.ComponentAttribute	Component	null
CharacterConstants.Family	String	"Monospaced"
FontConstants.Family	String	"Monospaced"
CharacterConstants.Foreground	Color	Color.black
ColorConstants.Foreground	Color	Color.black
CharacterConstants.IconAttribute	Icon	null
CharacterConstants.Italic	Boolean	false
FontConstants.Italic	Boolean	false
CharacterConstants.Size	Integer	12
FontConstants.Size	Integer	12
CharacterConstants.StrikeThrough	Boolean	false
CharacterConstants.Subscript	Boolean	false
CharacterConstants.Superscript	Boolean	false
CharacterConstants.Underline	Boolean	false
ParagraphConstants.Alignment	Integer	ALIGN_LEFT
ParagraphConstants.FirstLineIndent	Float	0
ParagraphConstants.LeftIndent	Float	0
ParagraphConstants.LineSpacing	Float	0
ParagraphConstants.Orientation	unknown	unknown
ParagraphConstants.RightIndent	Float	0
ParagraphConstants.SpaceAbove	Float	0
ParagraphConstants.SpaceBelow	Float	0
ParagraphConstants.TabSet	TabSet	null

Table 15-4: Key constants for storing AttributeSet values

So, if you wanted to create content that was both bold *and* italic, you'd add two attributes to a SimpleAttributeSet and insert the content into the document:

```
SimpleAttributeSet attributes = new SimpleAttributeSet();
attributes.addAttribute(StyleConstants.CharacterConstants.Bold, Boolean.TRUE);
attributes.addAttribute(StyleConstants.CharacterConstants.Italic, Boolean.TRUE);

// Insert content
try {
  document.insertString(document.getLength(), "Hello Java", attributes);
} catch (BadLocationException badLocationException) {
  System.err.println("Oops");
}
```

To summarize how to specify the style of the content, simply set up the attribute set, insert the content, and then repeat the steps for each bit of content you add.

Figure 15-6 shows how a JTextPane would appear with the words "Hello Java" and a second insertion displayed.

The source for the program follows.

```
import javax.swing.*;
import javax.swing.text.*;
import javax.swing.event.*;
import java.awt.*;

public class SimpleAttributeSample {
  public static void main(String args[]) {
    JFrame frame = new ExitableJFrame("Simple Attributes");
    Container content = frame.getContentPane();
```

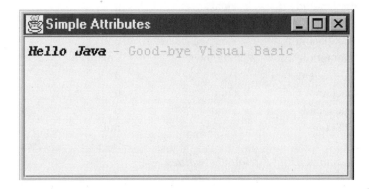

Figure 15-6: Demonstrating SimpleAttributeSet

```java
    StyledDocument document = new DefaultStyledDocument();

    SimpleAttributeSet attributes = new SimpleAttributeSet();
    attributes.addAttribute(StyleConstants.CharacterConstants.Bold,
Boolean.TRUE);
    attributes.addAttribute(StyleConstants.CharacterConstants.Italic,
Boolean.TRUE);

    // Insert content
    try {
      document.insertString(document.getLength(), "Hello Java", attributes);
    } catch (BadLocationException badLocationException) {
      System.err.println("Oops");
    }

    attributes = new SimpleAttributeSet();
    attributes.addAttribute(StyleConstants.CharacterConstants.Bold,
Boolean.FALSE);
    attributes.addAttribute(StyleConstants.CharacterConstants.Italic,
Boolean.FALSE);
    attributes.addAttribute(StyleConstants.CharacterConstants.Foreground,
Color.lightGray);

    // Insert content
    try {
      document.insertString(document.getLength(), " - Good-bye Visual Basic",
attributes);
    } catch (BadLocationException badLocationException) {
      System.err.println("Oops");
    }

  JTextPane textPane = new JTextPane(document);
  textPane.setEditable(false);
  JScrollPane scrollPane = new JScrollPane(textPane);
  content.add(scrollPane, BorderLayout.CENTER);

  frame.setSize(300, 150);
  frame.setVisible(true);
  }
}
```

> **NOTE** *The StyleContext class uses another class called StyleContext. SmallAttributeSet for the creation of attribute sets. Although the class itself is public, it's a nonstatic inner class. Therefore, only StyleContext can create it.*

Class StyleConstants

The StyleConstants class is chock-full of helper methods to simplify setting attribute sets. Yet, instead of your having to burrow into the constants of the inner classes of StyleConstants, the class makes them available through class constants at the StyleConstants level.

```
public final static Object Alignment;
public final static Object Background;
public final static Object BidiLevel;
public final static Object Bold;
public final static Object ComponentAttribute;
public final static String ComponentElementName;
public final static Object ComposedTextAttribute;
public final static Object FirstLineIndent;
public final static Object FontFamily;
public final static Object FontSize;
public final static Object Foreground;
public final static Object IconAttribute;
public final static String IconElementName;
public final static Object Italic;
public final static Object LeftIndent;
public final static Object LineSpacing;
public final static Object ModelAttribute;
public final static Object NameAttribute;
public final static Object Orientation;
public final static Object ResolveAttribute;
public final static Object RightIndent;
public final static Object SpaceAbove;
public final static Object SpaceBelow;
public final static Object StrikeThrough;
public final static Object Subscript;
public final static Object Superscript;
public final static Object TabSet;
public final static Object Underline;
```

Several static methods allow you to modify a `MutableAttributeSet` using more logical method names, without requiring you to know the more obscure `AttributeSet` name. Use the `StyleConstants` variables of `ALIGN_CENTER`, `ALIGN_JUS-TIFIED`, `ALIGN_LEFT`, and `ALIGN_RIGHT` for the `int` argument to `setAlignment()`.

```
public static void setAlignment(MutableAttributeSet a, int align);
public static void setBackground(MutableAttributeSet a, Color fg);
public static void setBidiLevel(MutableAttributeSet a, int o);
public static void setBold(MutableAttributeSet a, boolean b);
public static void setComponent(MutableAttributeSet a, Component c);
public static void setFirstLineIndent(MutableAttributeSet a, float i);
public static void setFontFamily(MutableAttributeSet a, String fam);
public static void setFontSize(MutableAttributeSet a, int s);
public static void setForeground(MutableAttributeSet a, Color fg);
public static void setIcon(MutableAttributeSet a, Icon c);
public static void setItalic(MutableAttributeSet a, boolean b);
public static void setLeftIndent(MutableAttributeSet a, float i);
public static void setLineSpacing(MutableAttributeSet a, float i);
public static void setRightIndent(MutableAttributeSet a, float i);
public static void setSpaceAbove(MutableAttributeSet a, float i);
public static void setSpaceBelow(MutableAttributeSet a, float i);
public static void setStrikeThrough(MutableAttributeSet a, boolean b);
public static void setSubscript(MutableAttributeSet a, boolean b);
public static void setSuperscript(MutableAttributeSet a, boolean b);
public static void setTabSet(MutableAttributeSet a, TabSet tabs);
public static void setUnderline(MutableAttributeSet a, boolean b);
```

For instance, instead of calling `attributes.addAttribute(StyleConstants.CharacterConstants.Bold, Boolean.TRUE)` and `attributes.addAttribute(StyleConstants.CharacterConstants.Italic, Boolean.TRUE)` to make the `SimpleAttributeSet` both bold *and* italic, you could do the following:

```
StyleConstants.setBold(attributes, true);
StyleConstants.setItalic(attributes, true);
```

The latter form shown in the previous two lines of code is much more readable and easier to maintain!

> **TIP** *Besides methods to change `AttributeSet` objects, the `StyleConstants` class provides many other methods that let you check on the status of an `AttributeSet` to see if a setting is currently enabled or disabled.*

Class TabStop and TabSet

Table 15-4 listed the ParagraphConstants.TabSet attribute for an AttributeSet. The TabSet class represents a collection of TabStop objects, each defining a tab position, alignment, and leader. If you wanted to define your own tab stops for a JTextPane, you could create a set of TabStop objects, one for each tab stop, create the TabSet, and then associate the TabSet with a MutableAttributeSet.

Creating a TabStop

The TabStop class isn't a JavaBean and therefore lacks a no-argument constructor. Instead, you must specify the position, in pixels, at which to place the tab stop.

1. `public TabStop(float position)`
    `TabStop stop = new TabStop(40);`

2. `public TabStop(float position, int align, int leader)`
    `TabStop stop = new TabStop(40, TabStop.ALIGN_DECIMAL,`
    `TabStop.LEAD_DOTS);`

> **NOTE** *Although theoretically it can be specified, the* leader *argument to the* TabStop *constructor is currently ignored by the predefined text components.*

TabStop Properties

Table 15-5 displays the three properties of TabStop. Each was configured by the constructor.

PROPERTY NAME	DATA TYPE	ACCESS
alignment	int	read-only
leader	int	read-only
position	int	read-only

Table 15-5: TabStop properties

Four alignment settings are specified by the five constants listed in Table 15-6. Figure 15-7 shows how the different settings are displayed.

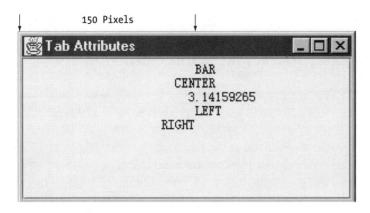

Figure 15-7: TabStop alignment

ALIGNMENT	DESCRIPTION
ALIGN_BAR	Starts at tab position
ALIGN_LEFT	Starts at tab position
ALIGN_CENTER	Centers over tab position
ALIGN_DECIMAL	Places decimal point at tab position
ALIGN_RIGHT	Ends at tab position

Table 15-6: TabStop alignment settings

NOTE *Although the* ALIGN_BAR *and* ALIGN_LEFT *are technically different constants, their alignment setting currently yields the same result.*

The source for the TabStop alignment program follows. Once you have a TabStop object, or a group of them, you pass the object to the TabSet constructor in an array of TabStop objects like this: TabSet tabset = new TabSet(new TabStop[] {tabstop}).

```
import javax.swing.*;
import javax.swing.text.*;
import javax.swing.event.*;
import java.awt.*;

public class TabSample {
  public static void main(String args[]) {
    JFrame frame = new ExitableJFrame("Tab Attributes");
    Container content = frame.getContentPane();
```

```
        StyledDocument document = new DefaultStyledDocument();

        int positions[] = {TabStop.ALIGN_BAR, TabStop.ALIGN_CENTER,
TabStop.ALIGN_DECIMAL,
           TabStop.ALIGN_LEFT, TabStop.ALIGN_RIGHT};
        String strings[] = {"\tBAR\n", "\tCENTER\n", "\t3.14159265\n", "\tLEFT\n",
"\tRIGHT\n"};

        SimpleAttributeSet attributes = new SimpleAttributeSet();

        for (int i=0, n=positions.length; i<n; i++) {
          TabStop tabstop = new TabStop(150, positions[i], TabStop.LEAD_NONE);
          try {
            int position = document.getLength();
            document.insertString(position, strings[i], null);
            TabSet tabset = new TabSet(new TabStop[] {tabstop});
            StyleConstants.setTabSet(attributes, tabset);
            document.setParagraphAttributes(position, 1, attributes, false);
          } catch (BadLocationException badLocationException) {
            System.err.println("Oops");
          }
        }

      JTextPane textPane = new JTextPane(document);
      textPane.setEditable(false);
      JScrollPane scrollPane = new JScrollPane(textPane);
      content.add(scrollPane, BorderLayout.CENTER);

      frame.setSize(300, 150);
      frame.setVisible(true);
    }
}
```

> **WARNING**   *It seems that the Java 2 platform doesn't work properly with tab stops, although the JDK 1.1 environment does. If you run the* TabSample *program with the Java 2 platform, everything will appear left-justified. The Bug ID for this problem is 4191750.*

In addition to specifying a position and alignment, you can specify which character you want to appear as a leader in the white space created by the tab character. By default, nothing exists there; therefore the constant is LEAD_NONE. However, you can assign another value to the TabStop, including a line of periods (dots), or thick lines, and so on. Unfortunately, this option is available but unsupported. While a nonstandard Swing component *might* support this capability, the standard ones currently don't. Table 15-7 lists the ignored settings for the leader property.

LEADER

LEAD_DOTS
LEAD_EQUALS
LEAD_HYPHENS
LEAD_NONE
LEAD_THICKLINE
LEAD_UNDERLINE

Table 15-7: TabStop leader settings

Interface Style

The Style interface is one more of the enhanced ways to specify an AttributeSet. It adds a name to the MutableAttributeSet, and the ability to attach a ChangeListener to a Style in order to monitor changes to the attribute settings.

```
String BOLD_ITALIC = "BoldItalic";
Style style = (Style)document.getStyle(StyleContext.DEFAULT_STYLE);
StyleConstants.setBold(style, true);
StyleConstants.setItalic(style, true);
document.addStyle(BOLD_ITALIC, null);
```

Then, later, you can find the style and use it:

```
style = document.getStyle(BOLD_ITALIC);
document.insertString(document.getLength(), "Hello Java", style);
```

Class StyleContext

The StyleContext class manages the styles for a styled document. With the help of the StyleContext.NamedStyle class, you can leave the JTextPane to do its own thing because the StyleContext knows when something needs to be done.

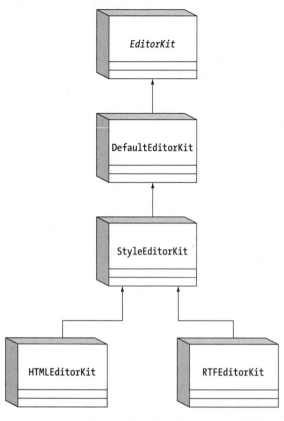

Figure 15-8: EditorKit class hierarchy diagram

The Editor Kits

You briefly saw some of the default EditorKit capabilities of TextAction objects earlier in this chapter in the section "Class TextAction." The EditorKit class serves as the mastermind for pulling together all the different aspects of the text components. It creates documents, manages actions, and creates the visual representation of the document or View. In addition, an EditorKit knows how to read or write the document to a stream. Each document type requires its own EditorKit, so different ones are provided with the JFC/Project Swing components. As shown in Figure 15-8, there are several predefined editor kits for both HTML and RTF text, as well as plain and styled text.

Working with Views

The actual display of the Document contents is done through the EditorKit with the help of a ViewFactory. For each Element of the Document, the ViewFactory determines which View is created for that element and rendered by the text component delegate. For each different type of element, there is a different View subclass. And, as shown in Figure 15-9, quite a few different View subclasses are available.

> **NOTE**   *For additional information about the Swing text package, be sure to stop by The Swing Connection at http://java.sun.com/products/jfc/tsc/text/text_main.html.*

Summary

In this chapter, you saw several of the more advanced aspects of working with the JFC/Project Swing text components. We looked into how to utilize the predefined TextAction objects to create working user interfaces without defining any of your own event-handling capabilities. In addition, we explored the JTextPane and

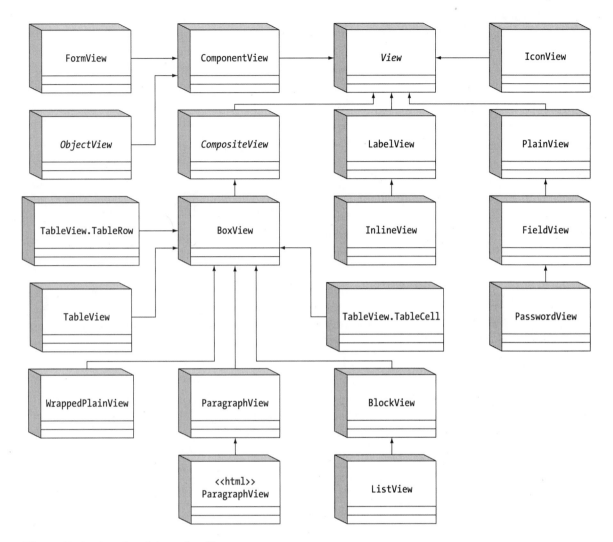

Figure 15-9: View class hierarchy diagram

how to create multi-attributed text within JTextPane through the AttributeSet, MutableAttributeSet, SimpleAttributeSet, and StyleConstants. You also saw how to create tab stops within a Document and glanced at both the EditorKit and View facilities of Swing.

In Chapter 16, we'll explore the Swing component for displaying hierarchical data: the JTree.

CHAPTER 16

Sculpting Trees

IN CHAPTER 15, WE LOOKED AT HOW TO work with the text document capabilities within the Swing component set. In this chapter, you'll learn how to work with Swing's tree class, the JTree component.

The JTree component is the visual component for displaying hierarchical data elements, also known as *nodes*. Using this tree metaphor, imagine the tree is flipped upside down. The node at the top of the tree is called the *root*. Extending out of the root node of the tree are branches to other nodes. If a node has no branches coming out of it, that node is called a *leaf node*. See Figure 16-1 for a simple JTree.

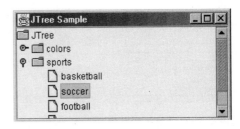

Figure 16-1: Sample JTree

Introducing Trees

Many interconnected classes are used in the composition of the JTree. First, the JTree implements the Scrollable interface so that you can place the tree within a JScrollPane for scroll management. The display of each node within the tree is controlled by implementations of the TreeCellRenderer interface; by default, the implementation is the DefaultTreeCellRenderer class. Nodes of a tree are editable with implementations of TreeCellEditor. Two editor implementations are available, one offering a text field with DefaultTreeCellEditor, and one offering a check box or combo box with DefaultCellEditor. If either of these two classes isn't enough, you can place custom editors within an EditorContainer. Figure 16-2 shows this set of JTree relationships. The elements of Figure 16-2 control the appearance if the JTree, whereas the elements of Figure 16-3 control the contents of the JTree.

> **NOTE** *The DefaultCellEditor class can also be used with the JTable component, which will be described in Chapter 17.*

By default, the actual nodes of the JTree are implementations of the TreeNode interface or its subinterface MutableTreeNode. The DefaultMutableTreeNode class is one such implementation that's commonly used, with the JTree.DynamicUtilTreeNode inner

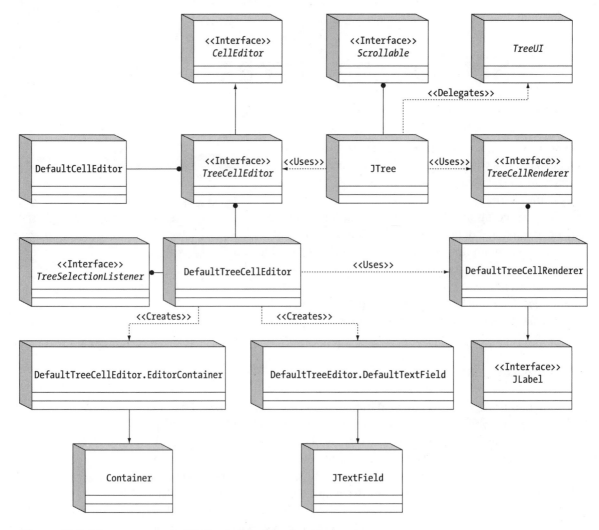

Figure 16-2: JTree appearance UML relationship diagram

class helping to create the tree nodes. The many tree nodes make up the TreeModel for the JTree, stored by default into an instance of the DefaultTreeModel class.

Tree selection is managed by a TreeSelectionModel implementation, with a default implementation of DefaultTreeSelectionModel available. The path of nodes from the root of the tree to the selected node is maintained within a TreePath, with the help of a RowMapper implementation to map rows to paths. All these interconnections describing the model contents of the JTree are shown in Figure 16-3.

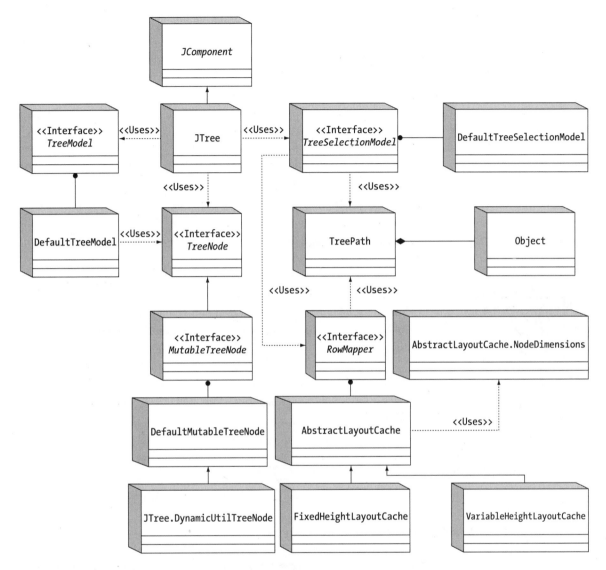

Figure 16-3: JTree contents UML relationship diagram

In addition to all the previously mentioned interfaces and classes, many event classes and event listener interfaces are available. These are shown in Figure 16-4 and will be discussed later in this chapter.

> **NOTE** *The tree-specific classes are found in the* javax.swing.tree *package.*
> *The event-related classes are in the* javax.swing.event *package.*

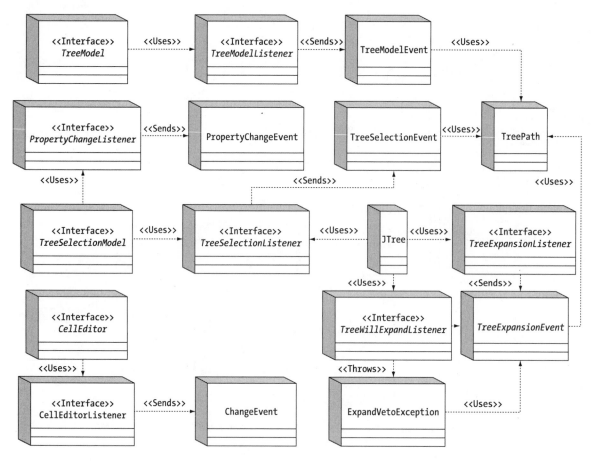

Figure 16-4: JTree events UML relationship diagram

Class JTree

To get started, let's look at the JTree class. It forms the basis for visually displaying a set of hierarchical data elements.

Creating a JTree

There are seven different ways to create a JTree, with five different ways to specify the nodes. The first of the constructors is the no-argument JavaBeans variety. Surprisingly, it has a default data model with some nodes in it. This data model was shown in Figure 16-1. Normally, you'd change the data model of the default tree after creation with setModel(TreeModel newModel).

The next three constructors (items 2 through 4 in the following list) seem to belong together. Creation of a JTree from a Hashtable made up of key-value pairs uses the set of keys for the nodes and values for the children, whereas creation from an array or Vector uses the elements as the nodes. This may seem to imply that the tree is only one level deep, when in fact the tree can be infinitely deep if the key or element was in turn a Hashtable, an array, or a Vector.

The remaining three constructors use the custom data structures of JTree, which will be explained later in this chapter. By default, only those nodes that have children are leaf nodes. However, trees can be constructed with partial nodes that won't get children until later. The last constructor causes a method to be called when you try to open a parent node, instead of the parent node just looking for child nodes.

> **TIP** *If the value for a key in a Hashtable is another Hashtable, array, or Vector, you can create a multi-level tree by using the top-level Hashtable as the constructor argument.*

1.  ```
    public JTree()
    JTree tree = new JTree();
    ```

2.  ```
    public JTree(Hashtable value)
    JTree tree = new JTree(System.getProperties());
    ```

3.  ```
    public JTree(Object value[])
    public static void main (String args[]) {
       JTree tree = new JTree(args);

       ...

    }
    ```

4.  ```
    public JTree(Vector value)
    Vector vector = new Vector();
    vector.add("One");
    vector.add("Two");
    JTree tree = new JTree(vector);
    ```

5.  ```
    public JTree(TreeModel value)
    JTree tree = new JTree(aTreeModel);
    ```

6.  ```
    public JTree(TreeNode value)
    JTree tree = new JTree(aTreeNode);
    ```

7.  ```
    public JTree(TreeNode value, boolean asksAllowsChildren)
    JTree tree = new JTree(aTreeNode, true);
    ```
    ```

Using a Hashtable, an array, or a Vector as the argument in the constructor tree does, in fact, allow you to create multi-level trees. There are two minor problems with this, however. The root node isn't visible, and it automatically has a data element of "root." The text label for any other nodes of type Hashtable, array, or Vector is the result of toString(). The default text is not desirable in any of these three instances. You either get the results of the toString() method of the Object class for an array, or a label that includes a list of all the elements in the Hashtable or Vector. In the case of an Object array, the output would look something like [Ljava.lang.Object;@fa8d8993.

Although no array class exists to subclass so that you can override toString(), you can subclass Hashtable or Vector to provide a different toString() behavior. Offering a name to the constructor of this new class allows you to provide a text label to use in the tree when the Hashtable or Vector is not the root node. The following class defines this behavior for a Vector subclass. In addition to the constructor's providing a name, the class also adds a constructor that initializes the vector to the contents of an array.

```java
import java.util.Vector;
public class NamedVector extends Vector {
  String name;
  NamedVector(String name) {
    this.name = name;
  }
  NamedVector(String name, Object elements[]) {
    this.name = name;
    for (int i=0, n=elements.length; i<n; i++) {
      add(elements[i]);
    }
  }
  public String toString() {
    return "[" + name + "]";
  }
}
```

Figure 16-5 displays a demonstration of the NamedVector class in action. The source for the example shown in Figure 16-5 follows.

```java
import javax.swing.*;
import javax.swing.tree.*;
import java.awt.*;
import java.util.Vector;

public class TreeArraySample {
  public static void main(String args[]) {
```

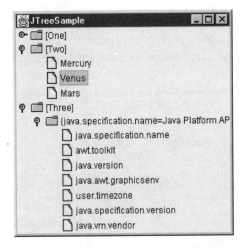

Figure 16-5: Sample JTree with the Vector subclass node

```
    JFrame frame = new ExitableJFrame("JTreeSample");
    Vector oneVector = new NamedVector("One", args);
    Vector twoVector = new NamedVector("Two", new String[]{"Mercury", "Venus",
"Mars"});
    Vector threeVector = new NamedVector("Three");
    threeVector.add(System.getProperties());
    threeVector.add(twoVector);
    Object rootNodes[] = {oneVector, twoVector, threeVector};
    Vector rootVector = new NamedVector("Root", rootNodes);
    JTree tree = new JTree(rootVector);
    frame.getContentPane().add(tree, BorderLayout.CENTER);
    frame.setSize(300, 300);
    frame.setVisible(true);
  }
}
```

Scrolling Trees

If you created and ran the previous program, you'd notice one small problem.
When all the parent nodes are open, the tree is too big for the initial screen size.
Not only that, you can't see the nodes at the bottom of the tree. To fix this situa-
tion, it's necessary to place instances of the JTree class within a JScrollPane so
that the scroll pane can manage the scrolling aspects of the tree. Similar to the
JTextArea class described in Chapter 15, the JTree class implements the
Scrollable interface for scrolling support.

Replacing the two boldfaced lines in the example on the previous page with the two boldfaced lines in the following example will place the tree within a scroll pane. This will cause the tree to appear in a scrollable region when the tree is too large for the available display space.

```
// from
JTree tree = new JTree(rootVector);
frame.getContentPane().add(tree, BorderLayout.CENTER);
// to
JTree tree = new JTree(rootVector);
JScrollPane scrollPane = new JScrollPane(tree);
frame.getContentPane().add(scrollPane, BorderLayout.CENTER);
```

In addition to using a JScrollPane for scrolling, you can manually scroll what's visible in the scrolling region. Use the `public void scrollPathToVisible(TreePath path)` and `public void scrollRowToVisible(int row)` methods to move a particular tree path or row into some part of the visible area. The *row* of a node indicates the number of nodes above the current node to the top of the tree. This differs from the *level* of the tree, which is the number of ancestors (or parent nodes) a node has. Figures 16-6a and 16-6b should help you visualize this difference. In Figure 16-6a, the "soccer" node is at level 2 and row 8. When the "colors" node is closed in Figure 16-6b, the soccer node remains on level 2 but moves to row 4 because the "blue," "violet," "red," and "yellow" rows are no longer visible.

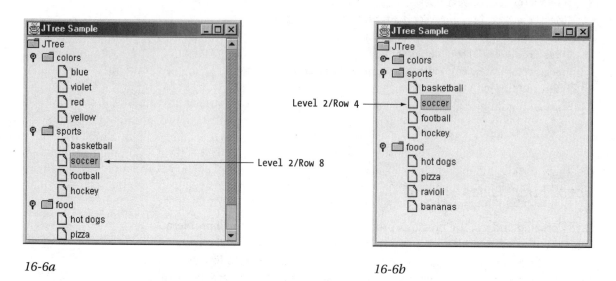

16-6a

16-6b

Figure 16-6: Rows versus levels of a tree

JTree Properties

There are many JavaBeans properties for the JTree. Table 16-1 lists the 33 specific properties of JTree. We'll explore many of these as we look at the different classes that make up the JTree.

PROPERTY NAME	DATA TYPE	ACCESS
accessibleContext	AccessibleContext	read-only
cellEditor	TreeCellEditor	read-write bound
cellRenderer	TreeCellRenderer	read-write bound
editable	boolean	read-write bound
editing	boolean	read-only
editingPath	TreePath	read-only
fixedRowHeight	boolean	read-only
invokesStopCellEditing	boolean	read-write bound
largeModel	boolean	read-write bound
lastSelectedPathComponent	Object	read-only
leadSelectionPath	TreePath	read-only
leadSelectionRow	int	read-only
maxSelectionRow	int	read-only
minSelectionRow	int	read-only
model	TreeModel	read-write bound
preferredScrollableViewportSize	Dimension	read-only
rootVisible	boolean	read-write bound
rowCount	int	read-only
rowHeight	int	read-write bound
scrollableTracksViewportHeight	boolean	read-only
scrollableTracksViewportWidth	boolean	read-only
scrollsOnExpand	boolean	read-write
selectionCount	int	read-only
selectionEmpty	boolean	read-only
selectionModel	TreeSelectionModel	read-write bound
selectionPath	TreePath	read-write
selectionPaths	TreePath[ ]	read-write
selectionRow	int	write-only
selectionRows	int[ ]	read-write
showsRootHandles	boolean	read-write bound
UI	TreeUI	read-write
UIClassID	String	read-only
visibleRowCount	int	read-write bound

Table 16-1: JTree properties

Some JTree properties are interrelated. For instance, when the rowHeight property is positive, it means that the node at each row is displayed with a fixed height, no matter what size the nodes within the tree should be. When the rowHeight property is negative, the cellRenderer property determines the rowHeight. So, the value of rowHeight determines the setting of the fixedRowHeight property. Changing the value of rowHeight to a value such as 12 pixels high results in the fixedRowHeight property having a setting of true.

The largeModel property setting is a suggestion to the TreeUI to help it display the tree. Initially this setting is false because a tree has many data elements and you don't want the user interface component to cache excessive information (such as node renderer sizes) about the tree. For smaller models, caching information about a tree doesn't require as much memory.

The current setting of lastSelectedPathComponent property is the contents of the last selected node. At any time, you can ask a tree what's selected. If nothing is selected, this property value will be null. Because trees support multiple selection, the lastSelectedPathComponent property doesn't return all selected nodes.

The three selection row properties, leadSelectionRow, minSelectionRow, and maxSelectionRow, are interesting in that the row values can change based on another parent node's opening or closing. When a single node in the tree is selected, all three properties have the same setting. You can get an array of all selected row indices with the selectionRows property. However, there's no way to map a row number to a node in the tree. Instead, use the selectionPaths property, which provides an array of TreePath elements. As you'll soon see, each TreePath includes the selected node, and all nodes on the path from the root node to the selected node.

There are three visibility-related settings of a tree. You can adjust the preferred number of rows to display for the tree by setting the visibleRowCount property. By default, the setting is 20. This setting is valid only when a particular tree is within a JScrollPane or some other component that uses the Scrollable interface. The second visibility-related setting has to do with whether the root node is visible. When the tree is created from a Hashtable, array, or Vector constructor, the root isn't visible. Otherwise, initially it will be visible. Changing the rootVisible property allows you to alter this setting. The final setting has to do with the icon next to the root node. By default, there's no icon at the root level to show the open or closed state of the root of the tree. All nonroot nodes always have this type of icon. To show the root icon, set the showsRootHandles property to true.

Customizing a JTree Look and Feel

Each installable Swing look and feel provides a different JTree appearance and set of default UIResource values. Figure 16-7 shows the appearance of the JTree container for the preinstalled set of look and feels: Motif, Windows, Metal, and Macintosh.

The available set of `UIResource`-related properties for a `JTree` is shown in Table 16-2. For the `JTree` component, there are 30 different properties.

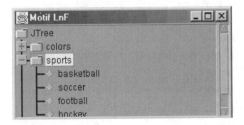

Motif

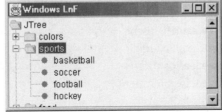

Windows

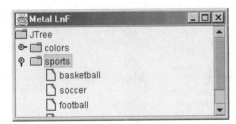

Metal

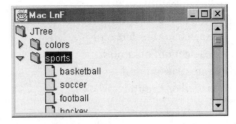

Macintosh

Figure 16-7: JTree under different look and feels

PROPERTY STRING	OBJECT TYPE
Tree.background	Color
Tree.changeSelectionWithFocus	Boolean
Tree.closedIcon	Icon
Tree.collapsedIcon	Icon
Tree.darkCollapsedIcon	Icon
Tree.darkExpandedIcon	Icon
Tree.drawsFocusBorderAroundIcon	Boolean
Tree.editorBorder	Border
Tree.editorBorderSelectionColor	Color
Tree.expandedIcon	Icon
Tree.font	Font

(continued)

Table 16-2 (continued)

PROPERTY STRING	OBJECT TYPE
Tree.foreground	Color
Tree.hash	Color
Tree.iconBackground	Color
Tree.iconForeground	Color
Tree.iconHighlight	Color
Tree.iconShadow	Color
Tree.leafIcon	Icon
Tree.leftChildIndent	Integer
Tree.line	Color
Tree.openIcon	Icon
Tree.rightChildIndent	Integer
Tree.rowHeight	Integer
Tree.scrollsOnExpand	Boolean
Tree.selectionBackground	Color
Tree.selectionBorderColor	Color
Tree.selectionForeground	Color
Tree.textBackground	Color
Tree.textForeground	Color
TreeUI	TreeUI

Table 16-2: JTree UIResource elements

Of the many different JTree resources, five are for the various icons displayed within the JTree. To see how the five icons are postitioned, examine Figure 16-8. If you just want to change the icons (and possibly the colors) of a tree, all you need to do is change the icon properties with lines such as the following:

```
UIManager.put("Tree.openIcon", new DiamondIcon(Color.red, false));
```

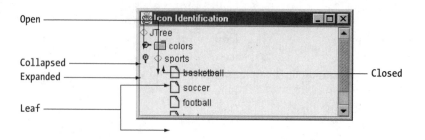

Figure 16-8: JTree icons

The purpose of one property, Tree.hash color, may not be immediately obvious. This color is for the lines drawn to connect nodes. With the Metal look and feel, by default no lines connect the nodes. To enable the drawing of these lines, you must set the JTree.lineStyle client property. This property isn't a UIResource property, but rather a client property set with the public final void putClientProperty(Object key, Object value) method of JComponent.

There are three valid settings for the JTree.lineStyle property:

- None — the default setting, for drawing no lines to connect nodes

- Angled — for drawing lines in the Tree.hash color to connect the nodes

- Horizontal — for drawing horizontal lines between first-level nodes in the Tree.line color

With client properties, you must create the tree first and then set the property. Client properties are specific to tree components, and are not set for all trees. Therefore, creating a tree with angled lines entails using the following lines of code. (See the screen shown in Figure 16-9. The third line was added to change the hash color.)

```
JTree tree = new JTree();
tree.putClientProperty("JTree.lineStyle", "Angled");
UIManager.put("Tree.hash", Color.red);
```

Figure 16-10 shows what the horizontal lines between level-one nodes look like, produced from the following source code.

```
JTree tree = new JTree();
tree.putClientProperty("JTree.lineStyle", "Horizontal");
UIManager.put("Tree.line", Color.green);
```

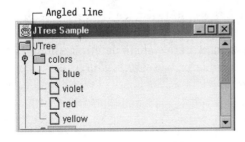

Figure 16-9: A JTree with angled connection lines

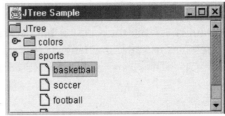

Figure 16-10: A JTree with horizontal level lines

631

> **NOTE** *The* JTree.lineStyle *client property is only used by the Metal look and feel. If the current look and feel isn't Metal, the property setting will be ignored if set, unless another custom look and feel took advantage of the setting. The other system-provided look and feels don't use this setting.*

Interface TreeCellRenderer

Each of the nodes within the JTree has an installed cell *renderer*. It's the responsibility of the renderer to draw the node and clearly display its state. The default renderer is basically a JLabel, which allows you to have both text and an icon within the node. However, any component can serve as the node renderer. When the renderer is the default, its icon is used to represent the state of the node — say, whether it's a leaf node or an open/closed node — not if a node is collapsed, expanded, or for some other setting.

> **NOTE** *The tree cell renderer is just that — a renderer. If the renderer were, say, a* JButton, *it wouldn't be selectable but would nevertheless be drawn to look just like a* JButton.

The configuration of each node renderer is defined by the TreeCellRenderer interface. Any class implementing this interface can serve as a renderer for your JTree.

```
public interface  TreeCellRenderer {
  public Component getTreeCellRendererComponent(JTree tree, Object value, boolean
selected, boolean expanded, boolean leaf, int row, boolean hasFocus);
}
```

When it's time to draw a node of a tree, that tree asks its registered TreeCellRenderer how to display that specific node. The node itself is passed in as the value argument so that the renderer has access to its current state to determine how to render this state. To change the installed renderer, use public void setCellRenderer(TreeCellRenderer renderer).

Class *DefaultTreeCellRenderer*

The DefaultTreeCellRenderer class serves as the default tree cell renderer. This class is a JLabel subclass, so it can support capabilities such as displaying tooltip text or pop-up menus specific to a node. It has only a no-argument constructor.

When used by a JTree, the DefaultTreeCellRenderer uses the various default icons (as shown in Figure 16-8) to display the current state of the node, and a text representation of the data for the node. The text representation is acquired by calling the toString() method for each node of the tree.

DefaultTreeCellRenderer Properties

Table 16-3 shows the 14 properties added (or altered) with DefaultTreeCellRenderer. Because the default renderer happens to be a JLabel, you also acquire many additional properties from it.

PROPERTY NAME	DATA TYPE	ACCESS
background	Color	write-only
backgroundNonSelectionColor	Color	read-write
backgroundSelectionColor	Color	read-write
borderSelectionColor	Color	read-write
closedIcon	Icon	read-write
defaultClosedIcon	Icon	read-only
defaultLeafIcon	Icon	read-only
defaultOpenIcon	Icon	read-only
font	Font	write-only
leafIcon	Icon	read-write
openIcon	Icon	read-write
preferredSize	Dimension	read-only
textNonSelectionColor	Color	read-write
textSelectionColor	Color	read-write

Table 16-3: DefaultTreeCellRenderer properties

If you don't like working with the UIManager or only want to change the icons, font, or colors for a single tree, you don't need to create a custom tree cell renderer. Instead, you can ask the tree for its renderer and customize it to display the icons, font, or colors you want. Figure 16-11 shows a JTree with an altered renderer. Instead of creating a new renderer, the existing default renderer was customized with the following source:

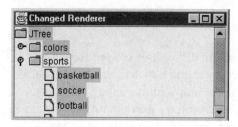

Figure 16-11: A JTree with an altered default renderer

```
JTree tree = new JTree();
DefaultTreeCellRenderer renderer =
(DefaultTreeCellRenderer)tree.getCellRenderer();
// Swap background colors
Color backgroundSelection = renderer.getBackgroundSelectionColor();
renderer.setBackgroundSelectionColor(renderer.getBackgroundNonSelectionColor());
renderer.setBackgroundNonSelectionColor(backgroundSelection);
// Swap text colors
Color textSelection = renderer.getTextSelectionColor();
renderer.setTextSelectionColor(renderer.getTextNonSelectionColor());
renderer.setTextNonSelectionColor(textSelection);
```

Remember that TreeUI caches renderer size information. If a change to the renderer changes the renderer size, this cache isn't updated. This appears to be a bug that might be corrected in a future release of Swing. However, to get around the problem now, it's necessary to signal to the tree that the cache is invalid. One such signal is to change the rowHeight property. As long as the current rowHeight property setting isn't positive, the TreeUI must ask the renderer for its height. Therefore, decreasing the value by 1 has a side effect of invalidating the cached renderer size information, causing the tree to be displayed with the proper initial sizes for all the renderers. Adding the following source to the previous example demonstrates this.

```
renderer.setFont(new Font("Dialog", Font.BOLD | Font.ITALIC, 32));
int rowHeight = tree.getRowHeight();
if (rowHeight <= 0) {
  tree.setRowHeight(rowHeight - 1);
}
```

The left-hand box in Figure 16-2 shows the effect this addition has on Figure 16-11. If you didn't change the rowHeight property to invalidate the display cache, you would get the right-hand box instead.

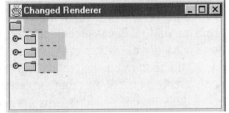

With size-change notification   *Without size-change notification*

Figure 16-12: Properly modifying the size of a tree renderer, and not

Creating a Custom Renderer

If the nodes of your JTree consist of information that is too complex to display within the text of a single JLabel, you can create your own renderer. For instance, if the nodes of your tree describe books by their title, author, and price, you can use a container as your renderer in which a separate component in the container displays each part.

To describe each book in this example, you need to define a class for storing the necessary information.

```java
public class Book {
  String title;
  String authors;
  float price;
  public Book(String title, String authors, float price) {
    this.title = title;
    this.authors = authors;
    this.price = price;
  }
  public String getTitle() {
    return title;
  }
  public String getAuthors() {
    return authors;
  }
  public float getPrice() {
    return price;
  }
}
```

To render a book as a node in the tree, you need to create a TreeCellRenderer implementation. Because the books are going to be leaf nodes, our custom renderer will use a DefaultTreeCellRenderer to render all the other nodes. The key part of the renderer is the getTreeCellRendererComponent(). In the event that the node data received by this method is a Book, it stores the appropriate information in the different labels and returns a JPanel as the renderer, with labels for each of the book titles, authors, and prices. Otherwise, the getTreeCellRendererComponent() method returns the default renderer, having had its label set accordingly.

Here's the source for our renderer. Notice that we use the same selection colors as the remaining nodes of the tree so that the book nodes don't appear out of place.

```java
import javax.swing.*;
import javax.swing.tree.*;
import java.awt.*;

public class BookCellRenderer implements TreeCellRenderer {
  JLabel titleLabel;
  JLabel authorsLabel;
  JLabel priceLabel;
  JPanel renderer;
  DefaultTreeCellRenderer defaultRenderer = new DefaultTreeCellRenderer();
  Color backgroundSelectionColor;
  Color backgroundNonSelectionColor;
  public BookCellRenderer() {
    renderer = new JPanel(new GridLayout(0, 1));
    titleLabel = new JLabel(" ");
    titleLabel.setForeground(Color.blue);
    renderer.add(titleLabel);
    authorsLabel = new JLabel(" ");
    authorsLabel.setForeground(Color.blue);
    renderer.add(authorsLabel);
    priceLabel = new JLabel(" ");
    priceLabel.setHorizontalAlignment(JLabel.RIGHT);
    priceLabel.setForeground(Color.red);
    renderer.add(priceLabel);
    renderer.setBorder(BorderFactory.createLineBorder(Color.black));
    backgroundSelectionColor = defaultRenderer.getBackgroundSelectionColor();
    backgroundNonSelectionColor =
defaultRenderer.getBackgroundNonSelectionColor();
  }
  public Component getTreeCellRendererComponent(JTree tree, Object value,
      boolean selected, boolean expanded, boolean leaf, int row, boolean
```

```
hasFocus) {
    Component returnValue = null;
    if ((value != null) && (value instanceof DefaultMutableTreeNode)) {
      Object userObject = ((DefaultMutableTreeNode)value).getUserObject();
      if (userobject instanceof Book) {
        Book book = (Book)userObject;
        titleLabel.setText(book.getTitle());
        authorsLabel.setText(book.getAuthors());
        priceLabel.setText("" + book.getPrice());
        if (selected) {
          renderer.setBackground(backgroundSelectionColor);
        } else {
          renderer.setBackground(backgroundNonSelectionColor);
        }
        renderer.setEnabled(tree.isEnabled());
        returnValue = renderer;
      }
    }
    if (returnValue == null) {
      returnValue = defaultRenderer.getTreeCellRendererComponent(tree, value,
selected, expanded, leaf, row, hasFocus);
    }
    return returnValue;
  }
}
```

> **TIP** *The JLabel components are created with an initial text label consisting of a space. Having a non-empty label gives each component some dimensions. The TreeUI caches node sizes to improve performance. Having an initial size for the labels ensures that the cache is initialized properly.*

The last remaining part is the test program. The majority of it just creates arrays of Book objects. You'll reuse the NamedVector class used earlier in this chapter to help create the tree branches. The code lines necessary for changing the tree cell renderer are boldfaced. Running the program demonstrates the custom renderer, as shown in Figure 16-13.

```
import javax.swing.*;
import javax.swing.tree.*;
import java.awt.*;
import java.util.*;
```

```
public class BookTree {
  public static void main(String args[]) {
    JFrame frame = new ExitableJFrame("Book Tree");
    Book javaBooks[] = {
      new Book("Core Java 1.2 Fundamentals", "Cornell/Horstmann", 42.99f),
      new Book("Java Servlets", "Moss", 44.95f),
      new Book("Essential JNI", "Schneier", 49.95f)
    };
    Book htmlBooks[] = {
      new Book("Dynamic HTML", "Goodman", 39.95f),
      new Book("HTML 4 Bible", "Pfaffenberger/Gutzman", 49.99f)
    };
    Vector javaVector = new NamedVector("Java Books", javaBooks);
    Vector htmlVector = new NamedVector("HTML Books", htmlBooks);
    Object rootNodes[] = {javaVector, htmlVector};
    Vector rootVector = new NamedVector("Root", rootNodes);
    JTree tree = new JTree(rootVector);
    TreeCellRenderer renderer = new BookCellRenderer();
    tree.setCellRenderer(renderer);
    JScrollPane scrollPane = new JScrollPane(tree);
    frame.getContentPane().add(scrollPane, BorderLayout.CENTER);
    frame.setSize(300, 300);
    frame.setVisible(true);
  }
}
```

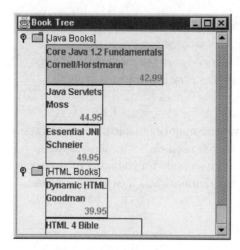

Figure 16-13: A JTree with a custom renderer

> **NOTE** *Don't worry about the details of* DefaultMutableTreeNode
> *just yet. Unless otherwise directed, all the nodes of every tree are a*
> DefaultMutableTreeNode. *Each array element we've placed in a* Vector
> *in the previous example defines the data for that specific node. This data*
> *is then stored in the* userObject *property of its* DefaultMutableTreeNode.

Working with Tree Tooltips

If you want a tree to display tooltips for the nodes, you must register the component with the ToolTipManager. If you don't register the component, the renderer will never get the opportunity to display tooltips. The renderer displays the tip, not the tree, so setting tooltip text for the tree is ignored. The following line shows how you'd register a specific tree with the ToolTipManager.

```
ToolTipManager.sharedInstance().registerComponent(aTree);
```

Once you've notified the ToolTipManager that you want the tree to display tooltip text, you must tell the renderer what text to display. Although you can directly set the text with the following lines, this results in a constant setting for all nodes.

```
DefaultTreeCellRenderer renderer =
(DefaultTreeCellRenderer)aTree.getCellRenderer();
renderer.setToolTipText("Constant Tool Tip Text");
```

Instead of providing a constant setting, one alternative is to provide the renderer with a table of tooltip strings so that it can determine at runtime which string to display as the tooltip text. The following renderer is one example that relies on a java.util.Dictionary implementation (like a Hashtable) to store a mapping from nodes to tooltip text. If a tip exists for a specific node, the renderer associates the tip with it.

Although this example is creating a new tree cell renderer, the behavior is only customizing what has already been done for the DefaultTreeCellRenderer. Instead of having to configure the icons and text yourself, let the default renderer do it for you. Then, add the tooltip text.

```
import javax.swing.*;
import javax.swing.tree.*;
import java.awt.*;
import java.util.*;
```

```
public class ToolTipTreeCellRenderer implements TreeCellRenderer {
  DefaultTreeCellRenderer renderer = new DefaultTreeCellRenderer();
  Dictionary tipTable;

  public ToolTipTreeCellRenderer (Dictionary tipTable) {
    this.tipTable = tipTable;
  }

  public Component getTreeCellRendererComponent(JTree tree, Object value,
      boolean selected, boolean expanded, boolean leaf, int row, boolean
hasFocus) {
    renderer.getTreeCellRendererComponent(tree, value, selected, expanded, leaf,
row, hasFocus);
    if (value != null) {
      Object tipKey;
      if (value instanceof DefaultMutableTreeNode) {
        tipKey = ((DefaultMutableTreeNode)value).getUserObject();
      } else {
        tipKey = tree.convertValueToText(value, selected, expanded, leaf, row,
hasFocus);
      }
      Object tip = tipTable.get(tipKey);
      if (tip != null) {
        renderer.setToolTipText(tip.toString());
      } else {
        renderer.setToolTipText(null);
      }
    }
    return renderer;
  }
}
```

NOTE *This example takes advantage of the* `JTree` *method* `public String` `convertValueToText(Object value, boolean selected, boolean expanded,` `boolean leaf, int row boolean hasFocus)` *to convert the tree node value to a text string. The value parameter is normally a* `DefaultMutableTreeNode`, *to be described later in this chapter. When the value parameter is not a* `DefaultMutableTreeNode`, *using* `convertValueToText()` *allows the renderer to support other types of tree nodes.*

Using the new `ToolTipTreeCellRenderer` class simply involves creating the `Properties` list, filling it up with tooltip text for the necessary nodes, and then associating the renderer with the tree. Figure 16-14 shows the renderer in action.

The complete sample program used to generate the screen in Figure 16-14 is shown next. This tree uses the list of system properties as the tree nodes. The tooltip text is the current setting for the specific property. When using the `ToolTipTreeCellRenderer`, be sure to register the tree with the `ToolTipManager`.

```java
import javax.swing.*;
import javax.swing.tree.*;
import java.awt.*;
import java.util.*;

public class TreeTips {
  public static void main(String args[]) {
    JFrame frame = new ExitableJFrame("Tree Tips");
    Properties props = System.getProperties();
    JTree tree = new JTree(props);
    ToolTipManager.sharedInstance().registerComponent(tree);
    TreeCellRenderer renderer = new ToolTipTreeCellRenderer(props);
    tree.setCellRenderer(renderer);
    JScrollPane scrollPane = new JScrollPane(tree);
    frame.getContentPane().add(scrollPane, BorderLayout.CENTER);
    frame.setSize(300, 150);
    frame.setVisible(true);
  }
}
```

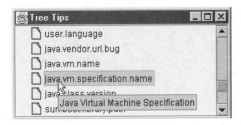

Figure 16-14: A JTree with tooltips, using the new ToolTipTreeCellRenderer

Editing Tree Nodes

In addition to supporting individualized tree cell renderers, `JTree` components can be editable, allowing users to change the contents of any node of the tree. To make a tree editable, just change the editable property setting to true. By default, trees are read-only.

```
aTree.setEditable(true);
```

When a tree is editable, it can have customized editors, just like renderers. By default, the editor is a text field. In addition, there is built-in support for picking choices from combo boxes, as well as using check boxes.

> **NOTE** *Unfortunately, the built-in check box editor works better within a table than within a tree, where the column label is the name and the value is the cell.*

Figure 16-15 shows a tree using the default editor. To enable the editor, you need to double-click on a node. If a node isn't selected yet, this would effectively be a triple-click; the first click would select the node and the other two would enable the text field editor. If the node isn't a leaf node, the first selection will also display/hide the children of the node.

A series of classes is available to support editing tree nodes. Many are shared with the JTable component because both can support editable cells. The CellEditor interface forms the basis for the TreeCellEditor interface. Any editor implementation for a JTree must implement the TreeCellEditor interface. The DefaultCellEditor offers one such editor implementation, and the DefaultTreeCellEditor offers another. Let's now look at the interfaces and classes in more detail.

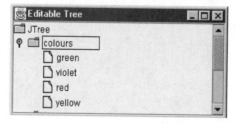

Figure 16-15: An editable JTree with the default editor

Interface CellEditor

The CellEditor interface defines the necessary basics for any editor used with a JTree or JTable, and for any third-party components that need an editor. Besides defining how to manage a list of CellEditorListener objects, the interface describes how to determine if a particular node or cell is editable and what the new value is after the editor has changed its value.

```
public interface CellEditor {
  // Properties
  public Object getCellEditorValue();
  // Listeners
  public void addCellEditorListener(CellEditorListener l);
  public void removeCellEditorListener(CellEditorListener l);
  // Other Methods
  public void cancelCellEditing();
  public boolean isCellEditable(EventObject event);
  public boolean shouldSelectCell(EventObject event);
  public boolean stopCellEditing();
}
```

Interface TreeCellEditor

The TreeCellEditor interface works similarly to the TreeCellRenderer interface. The sole argument missing from the get*XXX*Component() method is one that tells the editor it has the input focus. In the case of an editor, it must already have the input focus. Any class implementing the TreeCellEditor interface can serve as an editor for your JTree.

```
public interface TreeCellEditor implements CellEditor {
  public Component getTreeCellEditorComponent(JTree tree, Object value, boolean
isSelected, boolean expanded, boolean leaf, int row);
}
```

Class DefaultCellEditor

The DefaultCellEditor class serves as an editor for both tree nodes and table cells. The class allows you to easily provide a text editor, combo box editor, or check box editor to modify the contents of a node or cell.

The DefaultTreeCellEditor class, described next, uses this class to provide an editor for a customized text field, maintaining the appropriate node-type icon based on a TreeCellRenderer.

Creating a *DefaultCellEditor*

When you create a `DefaultCellEditor` instance, you provide the `JTextField`, `JComboBox`, or `JCheckBox` to use as the editor. With a `JTree`, you should use the `DefaultTreeCellEditor` if you want a `JTextField` editor. That text field will share the same font and use the appropriate editor border for the tree. When a `JCheckBox` is used as the editor, the node for the tree should be either a `Boolean` value or a `String` that can be converted to a `Boolean`.

> **NOTE**   *See the constructor for `Boolean` that accepts a `String` to find out how the `String` is converted to a `Boolean` value.*

1.  ```
    public DefaultCellEditor(JTextField editor)
    JTextField textField = new JTextField();
    TreeCellEditor editor = new DefaultCellEditor(textField);
    ```

2.  ```
    public DefaultCellEditor(JComboBox editor)
    public static void main (String args[]) {
        JComboBox comboBox = new JComboBox(args);
         TreeCellEditor editor = new DefaultCellEditor(comboBox);
         ...
    }
    ```

3.  ```
    public DefaultCellEditor(JCheckBox editor)
    JCheckBox checkBox = new JCheckBox();
    TreeCellEditor editor = new DefaultCellEditor(checkBox);
    ```

After creating an editor, you tell the tree to use it with a call similar to `tree.setCellEditor(editor)`. And don't forget to make the tree editable with `tree.setEditable(true)`. For instance, if you wanted an editable combo box as your editor, the following source code would work. It produces the screen shown in Figure 16-16 when editing the "basketball" node shown in the figure.

```
JTree tree = new JTree(...);
tree.setEditable(true);
String elements[] = {"Root", "chartreuse", "rugby", "sushi"};
JComboBox comboBox = new JComboBox(elements);
comboBox.setEditable(true);
TreeCellEditor editor = new DefaultCellEditor(comboBox);
tree.setCellEditor(editor);
```
```

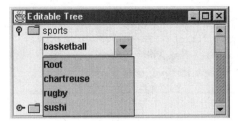

Figure 16-16: An editable JTree with a JComboBox editor

> **TIP** *Notice that no icon indicates the type of node being edited. This is rectified with the DefaultTreeCellEditor class. The DefaultCellEditor is primarily for use within a JTable, not a JTree.*

> **TIP** *When you use a noneditable JComboBox as the cell editor, if the set of choices doesn't include the original node setting, it's impossible to get back to the original setting once the node value changes.*

To see how awkward the appearance of a JCheckBox is with the DefaultCellEditor as a TreeCellEditor, look at Figure 16-17, which uses the following source:

```
Object array[] = {Boolean.TRUE, Boolean.FALSE, "Hello"}; // Hello maps to false
JTree tree = new JTree(array);
tree.setEditable(true);
tree.setRootVisible(true);
JCheckBox checkBox = new JCheckBox();
TreeCellEditor editor = new DefaultCellEditor(checkBox);
tree.setCellEditor(editor);
```

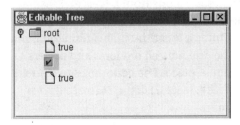

Figure 16-17: An editable JTree with a JCheckBox editor

> **NOTE**   *Use of the JCheckBox with the DefaultCellEditor isn't recommended with a JTree. See the "Creating a Better Check Box Node Editor" section later on for an implementation that's more appropriate to a tree.*

The awkwardness of the JCheckBox editor and custom text field editor within the DefaultTreeCellEditor leaves the JComboBox as the only TreeCellEditor you'll get from DefaultCellEditor. However, you might want to place the combo box editor within a DefaultTreeCellEditor to display the appropriate icon next to the node.

DefaultCellEditor Properties

The DefaultCellEditor has only three properties, which are listed in Table 16-4. The editor can be any AWT component, not just a lightweight Swing component. Keep in mind the hazards of mixing heavyweight and lightweight components if you do choose to use a heavyweight component as the editor. If you want to find out what the current setting is for the editor component, ask for the setting of the cellEditorValue property.

PROPERTY NAME	DATA TYPE	ACCESS
cellEditorValue	Object	read-only
clickCountToStart	int	read-write
component	Component	read-only

Table 16-4: DefaultCellEditor properties

Class DefaultTreeCellEditor

The DefaultTreeCellEditor class is the TreeCellEditor that's automatically used by a JTree when you make a tree editable but you don't associate an editor to that tree. The DefaultTreeCellEditor combines the icons from a TreeCellRenderer with a TreeCellEditor to return a combined editor.

The default component used as the editor is a JTextField. This text editor is special in that it tries to limit its height to the original cell renderer and prefers the font of the tree so that it won't appear out of place. The editor uses two public inner classes to accomplish this feat: DefaultTreeCellEditor.EditorContainer and DefaultTreeCellEditor.DefaultTextField.

There are two constructors for DefaultTreeCellEditor. Normally, you don't need to call the first constructor because it's automatically created for you by the user interface when it determines that the node is editable. Nevertheless, it may be necessary if you want to customize the default editor in some manner.

1. ```
   public DefaultTreeCellEditor(JTree tree, DefaultTreeCellRenderer renderer)
   JTree tree = new JTree(...);
   DefaultTreeCellRenderer renderer =
   (DefaultTreeCellRenderer)tree.getCellRenderer();
   TreeCellEditor editor = new DefaultTreeCellEditor(tree, renderer);
   ```

2. ```
   public DefaultTreeCellEditor(JTree tree, DefaultTreeCellRenderer renderer,
   TreeCellEditor editor)
   public static void main (String args[]) {
     JTree tree = new JTree(...);
     DefaultTreeCellRenderer renderer =
   (DefaultTreeCellRenderer)tree.getCellRenderer();
     JComboBox comboBox = new JComboBox(args);
     TreeCellEditor comboEditor = new DefaultCellEditor(comboBox);
     TreeCellEditor editor = new DefaultTreeCellEditor(tree, renderer,
   comboEditor);
     ...
   }
   ```

Creating a Proper ComboBox Editor for a Tree

As Figure 16-16 showed, using a JComboBox as the TreeCellEditor via a
DefaultCellEditor doesn't place the appropriate node-type icon next to the editor. If you want the icons present, you have to combine the DefaultCellEditor
with a DefaultTreeCellEditor to get an editor with both an icon and an editor. It's
really not as hard as it sounds. It just involves two extra steps: getting the renderer for the tree (from which to get the icons), and then combining the icon
with the editor to get a new editor. The following source demonstrates this, with
the improved output shown in Figure 16-18.

```
JTree tree = new JTree();
tree.setEditable(true);
DefaultTreeCellRenderer renderer =
(DefaultTreeCellRenderer)tree.getCellRenderer();
String elements[] = {"Root", "chartreuse", "rugby", "sushi"};
JComboBox comboBox = new JComboBox(elements);
comboBox.setEditable(true);
TreeCellEditor comboEditor = new DefaultCellEditor(comboBox);
TreeCellEditor editor = new DefaultTreeCellEditor(tree, renderer, comboEditor);
tree.setCellEditor(editor);
```

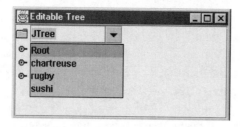

Figure 16-18: An editable JTree with a JComboBox editor and tree icons

Creating an Editor Just for Leaf Nodes

Sometimes when editing a tree you want only the leaf nodes to be editable. Returning null from the getTreeCellEditorComponent() request effectively makes the node not editable. Unfortunately this causes a NullPointerException to be thrown by the user interface class.

Instead of returning null, what you *can* do is override the default behavior of the public boolean isCellEditable(EventObject object) method, which is part of the CellEditor interface. If the original return value is true, you can do an additional check to see if the selected node of the tree is a leaf or not. Nodes of a tree implement the TreeNode interface, which I'll describe later in this chapter in the section "Interface Treenode." This interface happens to have a method public boolean isLeaf() that provides the answer you're looking for. The class definition for our new leaf cell editor follows.

```
import javax.swing.*;
import javax.swing.tree.*;
import java.awt.*;
import java.util.EventObject;

public class LeafCellEditor extends DefaultTreeCellEditor {

  public LeafCellEditor(JTree tree, DefaultTreeCellRenderer renderer) {
    super(tree, renderer);
  }

  public LeafCellEditor(JTree tree, DefaultTreeCellRenderer renderer,
TreeCellEditor editor) {
    super(tree, renderer, editor);
  }

  public boolean isCellEditable(EventObject event) {
    // Get initial setting
```

```
    boolean returnValue = super.isCellEditable(event);
    // If still possible, check if current tree node is a leaf
    if (returnValue) {
      Object node = tree.getLastSelectedPathComponent();
      if ((node != null) &&  (node instanceof TreeNode)) {
        TreeNode treeNode = (TreeNode)node;
        returnValue = treeNode.isLeaf();
      }
    }
    return returnValue;
  }
}
```

Use of the LeafCellRenderer is just like a DefaultTreeCellRenderer. It requires a JTree and DefaultTreeCellRenderer for its constructor. In addition, it supports an optional TreeCellEditor. If one isn't provided, a JTextField is used as the editor.

```
JTree tree = new JTree();
tree.setEditable(true);
DefaultTreeCellRenderer renderer =
(DefaultTreeCellRenderer)tree.getCellRenderer();
TreeCellEditor editor = new LeafCellEditor(tree, renderer);
tree.setCellEditor(editor);
```

Interface CellEditorListener/Class ChangeEvent

Before exploring the creation of a complete TreeCellEditor, we'll look at the CellEditorListener interface. The interface, whose definition follows, contains two methods that are used with a CellEditor.

```
public interface CellEditorListener implements EventListener {
  public void editingCanceled(ChangeEvent changeEvent);
  public void editingStopped(ChangeEvent changeEvent);
}
```

The editor calls the editingCanceled() method of the registered listeners to signal that the editing of the node's value has been aborted. By contrast, the editingStopped() method is called to signal the completion of an editing session.

Normally, it's not necessary to create a CellEditorListener. However, when creating a TreeCellEditor (or any CellEditor), it *is* necessary to manage a list of its listeners and notify said listeners when necessary.

Creating a Better Check Box Node Editor

Using the JCheckBox editor provided by the DefaultCellEditor class isn't a good option when working with a JTree. Although the editor can be wrapped into a DefaultTreeCellEditor to get the appropriate tree icon next to it, there's no way to display text within the check box, besides "true" or "false" that is. Other text strings can be displayed within the tree, but once a node is edited, the text label for the edited node can only be "true" or "false."

To have an editable check box with a text label as the tree cell editor, you have to create your own. The complete process involves creating three classes, and a test program to connect them all. The three classes include a data model for each node of the tree, a tree cell renderer to render this custom data structure, and the actual editor.

> **NOTE** *The renderer and editor created here will only support check-box–like data as the leaf nodes. If you want to support check boxes as nonleaf nodes, you have to pull out the unnecessary code.*

Creating the CheckBoxNode Class

The first class to be created is for the data model for each leaf node of the tree. We could use the same data model as the JCheckBox class, but that uses extraneous information at each node that you don't need. The only information necessary is the selected state of the node and its text label. With the addition of some setter and getter methods for the state and label, our class is basically defined. The other classes won't be quite this easy.

```
public class CheckBoxNode {
  String text;
  boolean selected;
  public CheckBoxNode(String text, boolean selected) {
    this.text = text;
    this.selected = selected;
  }
  public boolean isSelected() {
    return selected;
  }
  public void setSelected(boolean newValue) {
    selected = newValue;
  }
```

```
  public String getText() {
    return text;
  }
  public void setText(String newValue) {
    text = newValue;
  }
  public String toString() {
    return getClass().getName() + "[" + text + "/" + selected + "]";
  }
}
```

Creating the CheckBoxNodeRenderer Class

The renderer will have two parts. For nonleaf nodes, you can use the
DefaultTreeCellRenderer because those nodes aren't meant to be CheckBoxNode
elements. For the renderer for leaf nodes of type CheckBoxNode, you need to map the
data structure into an appropriate renderer. Because these nodes contain a selection
state and a text label, the JCheckBox acts as a good renderer for the leaf nodes.

The easier of the two to explain is the nonleaf node renderer. Here it simply
configures a DefaultTreeCellRenderer as it would normally. Nothing special is done.

The renderer for the leaf nodes requires a bit more work. Before even configuring any nodes, you have to make it look like the default renderer. The
constructor acquires the necessary fonts and various colors from the look and
feel for the renderer, ensuring that the two renderers will appear similar.

The definition for the tree cell renderer, class CheckBoxNodeRenderer, follows:

```
import javax.swing.*;
import javax.swing.border.*;
import javax.swing.tree.*;
import java.awt.*;

public class CheckBoxNodeRenderer implements TreeCellRenderer {
  protected JCheckBox leafRenderer = new JCheckBox();
  protected DefaultTreeCellRenderer nonLeafRenderer = new
DefaultTreeCellRenderer();
  Color selectionBorderColor, selectionForeground, selectionBackground,
textForeground, textBackground;

  public CheckBoxNodeRenderer() {
    Font fontValue;
    fontValue = UIManager.getFont("Tree.font");
    if (fontValue != null) {
```

```
        leafRenderer.setFont(fontValue);
      }
      Boolean booleanValue =
(Boolean)UIManager.get("Tree.drawsFocusBorderAroundIcon");
      leafRenderer.setFocusPainted((booleanValue != null) &&
(booleanValue.booleanValue()));

      selectionBorderColor = UIManager.getColor("Tree.selectionBorderColor");
      selectionForeground = UIManager.getColor("Tree.selectionForeground");
      selectionBackground = UIManager.getColor("Tree.selectionBackground");
      textForeground = UIManager.getColor("Tree.textForeground");
      textBackground = UIManager.getColor("Tree.textBackground");
    }

  public Component getTreeCellRendererComponent(JTree tree, Object value,
       boolean selected, boolean expanded, boolean leaf, int row, boolean
hasFocus) {

    Component returnValue;
    if (leaf) {

       String stringValue = tree.convertValueToText(value, selected, expanded,
leaf, row, false);
       leafRenderer.setText(stringValue);
       leafRenderer.setSelected(false);

       leafRenderer.setEnabled(tree.isEnabled());

       if(selected) {
         leafRenderer.setForeground(selectionForeground);
         leafRenderer.setBackground(selectionBackground);
       } else {
         leafRenderer.setForeground(textForeground);
         leafRenderer.setBackground(textBackground);
       }

       if ((value != null) && (value instanceof DefaultMutableTreeNode)) {
         Object userObject = ((DefaultMutableTreeNode)value).getUserObject();
         if (userObject instanceof CheckBoxNode) {
           CheckBoxNode node = (CheckBoxNode)userObject;
           leafRenderer.setText(node.getText());
           leafRenderer.setSelected(node.isSelected());
         }
```

```
        }
        returnValue = leafRenderer;
    } else {
        returnValue = nonLeafRenderer.getTreeCellRendererComponent(tree, value,
selected, expanded, leaf, row, hasFocus);
    }
    return returnValue;;
  }
}
```

Creating the CheckBoxNodeEditor Class

The CheckBoxNodeEditor class is the last part of our creating a better check box node editor. It serves as the TreeCellEditor implementation, allowing you to support editing of trees whose leaf node data are of type CheckBoxNode. The TreeCellEditor interface is an extension of the CellEditor implementation, so you must implement the methods of both interfaces. You can't extend DefaultCellEditor or DefaultTreeCellEditor because they would require you to use the JCheckBox editor implementation they provide, instead of the new one we're trying to create here.

To help you understand our new TreeCellEditor, we'll look at the implementation of the two interfaces in pieces. But first, one more thing needs to be done.

Because the editor acts as the renderer, when the node is selected it's easiest to create the editor as a subclass of the CheckBoxNodeRenderer. This will ensure that the editor appears similar in appearance to the renderer. Because the renderer for the leaf nodes will be a JCheckBox, this works perfectly well to enable you to change the node state. The editor JCheckBox will be active and changeable, allowing a user to change from a selected state to an unselected state, and vice versa. If the editor were the standard DefaultTreeCellRenderer, then you'd need to manage the creation of selection changes.

Now that the class hierarchy has been set up, the first method to examine is the public Object getCellEditorValue() method of CellEditor. The purpose of this method is to convert the data as stored within the node editor into the data as stored within the node. The user interface calls this method to get the editor's value after it has determined that the user has successfully changed the data within the editor. In this method, you need to create a new object each time. Otherwise, the same node will be in the tree multiple times, causing all nodes to be equal to the renderer for the last edited node. To convert the editor to the data model, it's necessary to ask the editor what its current label and selected state are and then create and return a new node.

```
public Object getCellEditorValue() {
  CheckBoxNode checkBoxNode = new CheckBoxNode(editor.getText(),
editor.isSelected());
  return checkBoxNode;
}
```

> **NOTE** *It's not the job of the editor to directly access the node within the tree to update it. The getCellEditorValue() method returns the appropriate node object so that the user interface can notify the tree of any changes.*

The next set of methods relates to the CellEditorListener. You need to manage a list of listeners with the addCellEditorListener() and removeCellEditorListener() methods, and provide methods that notify the list of listeners for each method in the interface. The event-firing methods aren't part of any interface, so their names aren't locked into anything. Nevertheless, the naming convention seems to involve prefixing the method with fire, and then tacking on the interface method name.

```
EventListenerList listenerList = new EventListenerList();
ChangeEvent changeEvent = null;

public void addCellEditorListener(CellEditorListener listener) {
  listenerList.add(CellEditorListener.class, listener);
}

public void removeCellEditorListener(CellEditorListener listener) {
  listenerList.remove(CellEditorListener.class, listener);
}

protected void fireEditingCanceled() {
  Object listeners[] = listenerList.getListenerList();
  for (int i = listeners.length-2; i>=0; i-=2) {
    if (listeners[i]==CellEditorListener.class) {
      // Lazily create the change event
      if (changeEvent == null) {
        changeEvent = new ChangeEvent(this);
      }
      ((CellEditorListener)listeners[i+1]).editingCanceled(changeEvent);
    }
  }
}

protected void fireEditingStopped() {
```

```
  Object listeners[] = listenerList.getListenerList();
  for (int i = listeners.length-2; i>=0; i-=2) {
    if (listeners[i]==CellEditorListener.class) {
      // Lazily create the change event
      if (changeEvent == null) {
        changeEvent = new ChangeEvent(this);
      }
      ((CellEditorListener)listeners[i+1]).editingStopped(changeEvent);
    }
  }
}
```

The next CellEditor method, cancelCellEditing(), is called when a new node of the tree is selected, announcing that the editing process of the prior selection has stopped and any interim update has been aborted. The method is capable of doing anything, such as destroying any necessary interim objects used by the editor. However, what the method should do is call fireEditingCanceled(); this ensures that any registered CellEditorListener objects are notified of the cancellation.

```
public void cancelCellEditing() {
  fireEditingCanceled();
}
```

The stopCellEditing() method of the CellEditor interface returns a boolean. This method is called to see if editing of the current node can stop. If any validation needs to be done to determine whether editing can stop, you'd check here. For our CheckBoxNodeEditor, there's no validation check necessary. Therefore, editing can always stop, allowing the method to always return true.

```
public boolean stopCellEditing() {
  // validation if appropriate
  return true;
}
```

The stopCellEditing() method doesn't call fireEditingStopped(). Instead, the fireEditingStopped() method would be called when you want to have the editor stop editing. For instance, if the editor were a text field, pressing ENTER within the text field could act as the signal to stop editing. In the case of the JCheckBox editor, selection could act as a signal to stop the editor. This disables the editor after each state change. Re-enabling the editor requires an extra selection of the node. If fireEditingStopped() isn't called, the tree data model isn't updated.

To stop editing after selection of the JCheckBox, attach an ItemListener to it.

```
ItemListener itemListener = new ItemListener() {
  public void itemStateChanged(ItemEvent itemEvent) {
    if (stopCellEditing()) {
      fireEditingStopped();
    }
  }
};
editor.addItemListener(itemListener);
```

The next method of the `CellEditor` interface we'll look at is `public boolean isCellEditable(EventObject event)`. The method returns a `boolean` to state whether the node at the source of the event is editable. In the case of our tree, a node is editable if it's a leaf node whose data is a `CheckBoxNode`. To find out if the event happens at a particular node, you need a reference to the tree where the editor is to be used. You can add this requirement to the constructor of the editor.

To find out which node is at a specific position during an event, you can ask the tree for the path of nodes to the event location. The path is returned as a `TreePath` object, which is examined again later in this chapter in the section "Class TreePath." The last component of the tree path is the specific node where the event happened. It is this node that you must check to determine if it's editable. If it is editable, the method returns `true`; if it isn't editable, `false` is returned. The node is editable if it's a leaf and if it contains `CheckBoxNode` data.

```
JTree tree;

public CheckBoxNodeEditor(JTree tree) {
  this.tree = tree;
}

public boolean isCellEditable(EventObject event) {
  boolean returnValue = false;
  if (event instanceof MouseEvent) {
    MouseEvent mouseEvent = (MouseEvent)event;
    TreePath path = tree.getPathForLocation(mouseEvent.getX(),
mouseEvent.getY());
    if (path != null) {
      Object node = path.getLastPathComponent();
      if ((node != null) && (node instanceof DefaultMutableTreeNode)) {
        DefaultMutableTreeNode treeNode = (DefaultMutableTreeNode)node;
        Object userObject = treeNode.getUserObject();
        returnValue = ((treeNode.isLeaf()) && (userObject instanceof
CheckBoxNode));
      }
```

```
      }
   }
   return returnValue;
}
```

The shouldSelectCell() method of the CellEditor interface allows you to decide whether or not a node is selectable. For the editor in this example, all cells can be selected. However, this method allows you to look at a specific node to see if it can be selected.

```
public boolean shouldSelectCell(EventObject event) {
   return true;
}
```

The last remaining method, getTreeCellEditorComponent(), is from the TreeCellEditor interface. Because we've subclassed CheckBoxNodeRenderer, we just need to get the renderer and use that as the editor. There are two minor changes besides just passing through all the arguments. Editors should always be selected and have the input focus. This simply forces two arguments to always be true. When the node is selected, the background is filled in. When focused, a border surrounds the editor when UIManager.get("Tree.drawsFocusBorderAroundIcon") reports true.

```
public Component getTreeCellEditorComponent(JTree tree, Object value,
      boolean selected, boolean expanded, boolean leaf, int row) {

   // editor always selected / focused
   return getTreeCellRendererComponent(tree, value, true, expanded, leaf, row,
true);
}
```

Finally, here is everything put together — the complete CheckBoxNodeEditor class source.

```
import javax.swing.*;
import javax.swing.event.*;
import javax.swing.tree.*;
import java.awt.*;
import java.awt.event.*;
import java.util.EventObject;

public class CheckBoxNodeEditor extends CheckBoxNodeRenderer implements
TreeCellEditor {
```

```
    EventListenerList listenerList = new EventListenerList();
    ChangeEvent changeEvent = null;

    JTree tree;

    public CheckBoxNodeEditor(JTree tree) {
      this.tree = tree;
    }

    public Object getCellEditorValue() {
      CheckBoxNode checkBoxNode = new CheckBoxNode(leafRenderer.getText(),

leafRenderer.isSelected());
      return checkBoxNode;
    }

    public void addCellEditorListener(CellEditorListener listener) {
      listenerList.add(CellEditorListener.class, listener);
    }

    public void removeCellEditorListener(CellEditorListener listener) {
      listenerList.remove(CellEditorListener.class, listener);
    }

    protected void fireEditingCanceled() {
      Object listeners[] = listenerList.getListenerList();
      for (int i = listeners.length-2; i>=0; i-=2) {
        if (listeners[i]==CellEditorListener.class) {
          // Lazily create the change event
          if (changeEvent == null) {
            changeEvent = new ChangeEvent(this);
          }
          ((CellEditorListener)listeners[i+1]).editingCanceled(changeEvent);
        }
      }
    }

    protected void fireEditingStopped() {
      Object listeners[] = listenerList.getListenerList();
      for (int i = listeners.length-2; i>=0; i-=2) {
        if (listeners[i]==CellEditorListener.class) {
          // Lazily create the change event
          if (changeEvent == null) {
```

```
          changeEvent = new ChangeEvent(this);
        }
        ((CellEditorListener)listeners[i+1]).editingStopped(changeEvent);
      }
    }
  }

  public void cancelCellEditing() {
    fireEditingCanceled();
  }

  public boolean stopCellEditing() {
    // validation if appropriate
    return true;
  }

  public boolean isCellEditable(EventObject event) {
    boolean returnValue = false;
    if (event instanceof MouseEvent) {
      MouseEvent mouseEvent = (MouseEvent)event;
      TreePath path = tree.getPathForLocation(mouseEvent.getX(),
mouseEvent.getY());
      if (path != null) {
        Object node = path.getLastPathComponent();
        if ((node != null) &&  (node instanceof DefaultMutableTreeNode)) {
          DefaultMutableTreeNode treeNode = (DefaultMutableTreeNode)node;
          Object userObject = treeNode.getUserObject();
          returnValue = ((treeNode.isLeaf()) && (userObject instanceof
CheckBoxNode));
        }
      }
    }
    return returnValue;
  }

  public boolean shouldSelectCell(EventObject event) {
    return true;
  }

  public Component getTreeCellEditorComponent(JTree tree, Object value,
      boolean selected, boolean expanded, boolean leaf, int row) {
```

```
  Component editor =
    getTreeCellRendererComponent(tree, value, true, expanded, leaf, row, true);

  // editor always selected / focused
  ItemListener itemListener = new ItemListener() {
    public void itemStateChanged(ItemEvent itemEvent) {
      if (stopCellEditing()) {
        fireEditingStopped();
      }
    }
  };
  if (editor instanceof JCheckBox) {
    ((JCheckBox)editor).addItemListener(itemListener);
  }

  return editor;
  }
}
```

> **NOTE** *Notice that there's no direct change of the data in the tree node. It's not the role of the editor to change the node. The editor only gets the new node value, returning it with getCellEditorValue().*

Creating the Test Program

The test program consists primarily of creating the CheckBoxNode elements. In addition to creating the tree data, the tree must have the renderer and editor associated with it and be made editable.

```
import javax.swing.*;
import javax.swing.tree.*;
import java.awt.*;
import java.util.Vector;

public class CheckBoxNodeTreeSample {
  public static void main(String args[]) {
    JFrame frame = new ExitableJFrame("CheckBox Tree");
```

```
    CheckBoxNode accessibilityOptions[] = {
      new CheckBoxNode("Move system caret with focus/selection changes", false),
      new CheckBoxNode("Always expand alt text for images", true)
    };
    CheckBoxNode browsingOptions[] = {
      new CheckBoxNode("Notify when downloads complete", true),
      new CheckBoxNode("Disable script debugging", true),
      new CheckBoxNode("Use AutoComplete", true),
      new CheckBoxNode("Browse in a new process", false)
    };
    Vector accessVector = new NamedVector("Accessibility", accessibilityOptions);
    Vector browseVector = new NamedVector("Browsing", browsingOptions);
    Object rootNodes[] = {accessVector, browseVector};
    Vector rootVector = new NamedVector("Root", rootNodes);
    JTree tree = new JTree(rootVector);

    CheckBoxNodeRenderer renderer = new CheckBoxNodeRenderer();
    tree.setCellRenderer(renderer);

    tree.setCellEditor(new CheckBoxNodeEditor(tree));
    tree.setEditable(true);

    JScrollPane scrollPane = new JScrollPane(tree);
    frame.getContentPane().add(scrollPane, BorderLayout.CENTER);
    frame.setSize(300, 150);
    frame.setVisible(true);
  }
}
```

Running the program and selecting a CheckBoxNode will enable the editor. After the editor is enabled, selecting the editor again causes the state of the node within the tree to change. The editor stays enabled until a different tree node is selected. See Figure 16-19 for an example of the editor in use.

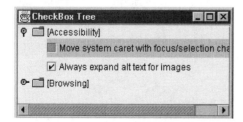

Figure 16-19: Our new CheckBoxNodeEditor in action

Working with the Nodes of the Tree   .

When you create a JTree, the type of objects at any spot in the tree can be any Object. There's no requirement that the nodes of the tree implement any interface or subclass any class. Nevertheless, the Project Swing component libraries provide a pair of interfaces and one class for working with tree nodes. These interfaces and the class are used by the default data model for the tree, DefaultTreeModel. However, the tree data model interface, TreeModel, permits any type of object to be a tree node.

The base interface for nodes is TreeNode, which defines a series of methods describing a read-only, parent-children aggregation relationship. Expanding on TreeNode is the MutableTreeNode interface, which allows you to connect nodes and store information at each node. The class that implements the two interfaces is the DefaultMutableTreeNode class. Besides implementing the methods of the two interfaces, the class provides a set of methods for traversing the tree and inquiring about the state of various nodes.

> **NOTE**   *The information that can be stored at each node is called the* user object.

Keep in mind that although these node objects are available, much work can be still performed without involving these interfaces and classes, as previously shown throughout this chapter. We'll now look at the two interfaces and single class as we explore the nodes of the tree.

Interface TreeNode

The TreeNode interface describes one possible definition for an individual part of a tree. It's used by one implementation of TreeModel, the DefaultTreeModel class, to store references to the hierarchical data that describes a tree. The interface allows you to find out which node is the parent to the current node, as well as get information about the set of child nodes. When the parent node is null, the node is the root of a tree.

```
public interface TreeNode {
  // Properties
  public boolean getAllowsChildren();
  public int getChildCount();
  public boolean isLeaf();
  public TreeNode getParent();
```

```
  // Other Methods
  public Enumeration children();
  public TreeNode getChildAt(int childIndex);
  public int getIndex(TreeNode node);
}
```

> **NOTE** *Normally, only nonleaf nodes allow children. However, security regulations may restrict nonleaf nodes from having children. Imagine a directory tree in which you don't have read access to a particular directory. Although the directory is a nonleaf node, it can't have child nodes because you don't have read access to find out what those children are.*

Interface `MutableTreeNode`

Although the `TreeNode` interface allows you to retrieve information about a hierarchy of tree nodes, it doesn't allow you to create the hierarchy. `TreeNode` just provides you access to a read-only tree hierarchy. On the other hand, the `MutableTreeNode` interface allows you to create the hierarchy and store information at a specific node within the tree.

```
public interface MutableTreeNode implements TreeNode {
  // Properties
  public void setParent(MutableTreeNode newParent);
  public void setUserObject(Object object);
  // Other Methods
  public void insert(MutableTreeNode child, int index);
  public void remove(MutableTreeNode node);
  public void remove(int index);
  public void removeFromParent();
}
```

When creating the hierarchy of tree nodes, you can either create nodes and add them to their parent, or you can create parent nodes and add children. To associate a node with a parent node, you set its parent with `setParent()`. By contrast, using `insert()` allows you to add children to a parent node. The arguments for the `insert()` method include an index argument. This index represents the position within the set of children to add the child node provided. The index is zero-based, so an index of zero will add the node as the first child of the tree.

Adding a node as the last child, instead of the first, requires you to ask the node with getChildCount() how many children it already has and then adding 1:

```
mutableTreeNode.insert(childMutableTreeNode, mutableTreeNode.getChildCount()+1);
```

> **WARNING** *At least for the DefaultMutableTreeNode class described next, setParent() sets a node to be the parent of a child node, even though it doesn't make the child node a child of the parent. In other words, don't call setParent() yourself; call insert() and it will set the parent accordingly.*

> **WARNING** *The insert() method doesn't allow a child node to be added if the child node is an ancestor to the parent. If that's attempted, an IllegalArgumentException will be thrown.*

Class *DefaultMutableTreeNode*

The DefaultMutableTreeNode class provides an implementation of the MutableTreeNode interface (which implements the TreeNode interface). When you're creating a tree from a Hashtable, an array, or a Vector constructor, JTree automatically creates the nodes as a set of type DefaultMutableTreeNode. If, on the other hand, you want to create the nodes yourself, you'd create one instance of type DefaultMutableTreeNode for every node in your tree.

Creating a *DefaultMutableTreeNode*

Three constructors are available for creating instances of DefaultMutableTreeNode. The information stored at every node is called the *user object*. When not specified by one of the constructors, this user object is null. In addition, you can specify whether a node is allowed to have children.

1.  ```
    public DefaultMutableTreeNode()
    DefaultMutableTreeNode node = new DefaultMutableTreeNode();
    ```

2.  ```
    public DefaultMutableTreeNode(Object userObject)
    DefaultMutableTreeNode node = new DefaultMutableTreeNode("Node");
    ```

3.  ```
    public DefaultMutableTreeNode(Object userObject)
    DefaultMutableTreeNode node = new DefaultMutableTreeNode("Node", false);
    ```
    ```

Building *DefaultMutableTreeNode* Hierarchies

Building a hierarchy of nodes of type DefaultMutableTreeNode requires creating an instance of type DefaultMutableTreeNode, creating nodes for its children, and then connecting them. Before using DefaultMutableTreeNode directly to create the hierarchy, let's first use our new NamedVector class to create a tree with four nodes: one root and three leaf nodes.

```
Vector vector = new NamedVector("Root", new String[]{"Mercury", "Venus",
"Mars"});
JTree tree = new JTree(vector);
```

When JTree gets a Vector as its constructor argument, it creates for the root node a DefaultMutableTreeNode and then creates one for each element in the vector, making each element node a child of the root node. The data for the root node unfortunately is not the "Root" you specify, but rather "root" and isn't shown.

If, instead, you wanted to use DefaultMutableTreeNode to manually create the nodes of a tree, or if you wanted to display the root node, the following shows that a few more lines would be necessary.

```
DefaultMutableTreeNode root = new DefaultMutableTreeNode("Root");
DefaultMutableTreeNode mercury = new DefaultMutableTreeNode("Mercury");
root.insert(mercury, 0);
DefaultMutableTreeNode venus = new DefaultMutableTreeNode("Venus");
root.insert(venus, 1);
DefaultMutableTreeNode mars = new DefaultMutableTreeNode("Mars");
root.insert(mars, 2);
JTree tree = new JTree(root);
```

Besides using the insert() method from MutableTreeNode to associate a child with a parent, DefaultMutableTreeNode has an add() method that automatically adds a child node at the end without providing an index.

```
DefaultMutableTreeNode root = new DefaultMutableTreeNode("Root");
DefaultMutableTreeNode mercury = new DefaultMutableTreeNode("Mercury");
root.add(mercury);
DefaultMutableTreeNode venus = new DefaultMutableTreeNode("Venus");
root.add(venus);
DefaultMutableTreeNode mars = new DefaultMutableTreeNode("Mars");
root.add(mars);
JTree tree = new JTree(root);
```

Both of the previous blocks of source create a tree like the one shown in Figure 16-20.

665

If you don't need a root node and want the same behavior as if you used NamedVector at the root of a tree, you could do the following, too.

```
String elements[] = {"Mercury", "Venus", "Mars"};
JTree tree = new JTree(elements);
```

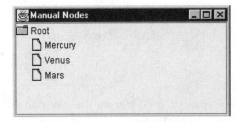

Figure 16-20: Using DefaultMutableTreeNode

DefaultMutableTreeNode Properties

As Table 16-5 shows, there are 22 properties of DefaultMutableTreeNode. Most of the properties are read-only, allowing you to find out information about the tree node's position and relationships. The userObject property contains the data specific to the node and that was provided to the DefaultMutableTreeNode when the node was created. The userObjectPath property contains an array of user objects, from the root (at index 0) to the current node (which could be the root).

PROPERTY NAME	DATA TYPE	ACCESS
allowsChildren	boolean	read-write
childCount	int	read-only
depth	int	read-only
firstChild	TreeNode	read-only
firstLeaf	DefaultMutableTreeNode	read-only
lastChild	TreeNode	read-only
lastLeaf	DefaultMutableTreeNode	read-only
leaf	boolean	read-only
leafCount	int	read-only
level	int	read-only
nextLeaf	DefaultMutableTreeNode	read-only
nextNode	DefaultMutableTreeNode	read-only
nextSibling	DefaultMutableTreeNode	read-only
parent	MutableTreeNode	read-write

(continued)

Table 16-5 (continued)

PROPERTY NAME	DATA TYPE	ACCESS
path	TreeNode[ ]	read-only
previousLeaf	DefaultMutableTreeNode	read-only
previousNode	DefaultMutableTreeNode	read-only
previousSibling	DefaultMutableTreeNode	read-only
root	boolean	read-only
siblingCount	int	read-only
userObject	Object	read-write
userObjectPath	Object[ ]	read-only

Table 16-5: DefaultMutableTreeNode properties

Querying Node Relationships

The DefaultMutableTreeNode class provides several ways to determine the relationship between two nodes. In addition, you can check to see if two nodes share a common parent.

Table 16-6 lists the various relationships that exist between two nodes. Each method returns a boolean value, indicating whether or not the relationship exists.

METHOD	DESCRIPTION
isNodeAncestor(TreeNode aNode)	Returns true if aNode is the current node or a parent of the current node; this recursively checks getParent() until aNode or null is found
isNodeChild(TreeNode aNode)	Returns true if the current node is the parent of aNode
isNodeDescendant(DefaultMutableTreeNode aNode)	Returns true if the current node is aNode or an ancestor of aNode
isNodeRelated(DefaultMutableTreeNode aNode)	Returns true if both the current node and aNode share the same root (are in the same tree)
isNodeSibling(TreeNode aNode)	Returns true if both nodes share the same parent

Table 16-6: Node relationship methods

If two nodes are related, you can ask for the root of the tree to find a shared ancestor. However, this ancestor might not be the closest ancestor within the tree. If a common node exists lower down in the tree, you can use the `public TreeNode getSharedAncestor(DefaultMutableTreeNode aNode)` method to find this closer ancestor. If none exists because the two nodes aren't in the same tree, `null` is returned.

> **NOTE** *The shared ancestor of a node and itself is the node itself.*

Traversing Trees

The `TreeNode` interface and `DefaultMutableTreeNode` class provide differing means of traveling to all the nodes below a specific node. Given a specific `TreeNode`, you can walk to each descendant node by going through the `children()` of each node, including the initial node. Given a specific `DefaultMutableTreeNode`, you can find all the descendants by following both `getNextNode()` and `getPreviousNode()` methods until no additional nodes are found. The following code demonstrates the use of the `children()` method of `TreeNode` to traverse an entire tree, given a starting node.

```
public void printDescendants(TreeNode root) {
  System.out.println(root);
  Enumeration children = root.children();
  if (children != null) {
    while(children.hasMoreElements()) {
      printDescendants((TreeNode)children.nextElement());
    }
  }
}
```

Although the `DefaultMutableTreeNode` implementation of `TreeNode` allows you to traverse a tree via the `getNextNode()` and `getPreviousNode()` methods, these methods are extremely inefficient and should be avoided. Instead, use one of the special methods of `DefaultMutableTreeNode` to produce one `Enumeration` of all of a node's children. Before looking at the specific methods, review Figure 16-21, which shows a simple tree to traverse.

Figure 16-21 will help you understand the four special methods of `DefaultMutableTreeNode`. These methods allow you to traverse a tree in any one of three ways, each `public` and returning an `Enumeration`:

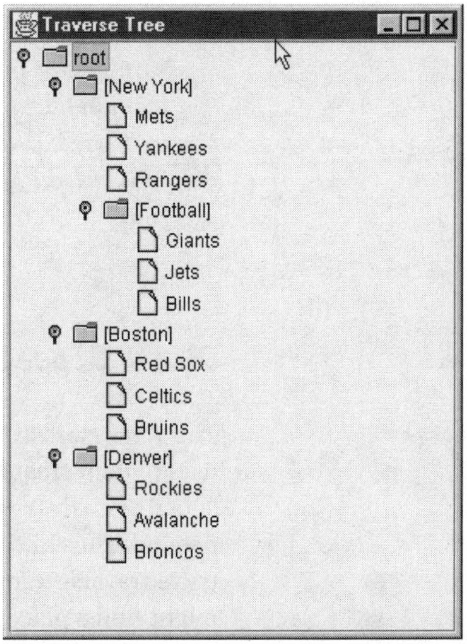

- preOrderEnumeration()—returns an Enumeration of nodes, like the printDescendants() method. The first node in the Enumeration is the node itself. The next node is that node's first child, then it's the first child of that first child, and so forth. Once a leaf node with no children is found, the next child of its parent is put in the Enumeration and its children are added to the list accordingly until no nodes are left. Starting at the root for the tree in Figure 16-21, this would result in an Enumeration of nodes in the following order: root, New York, Mets, Yankees, Rangers, Football, Giants, Jets, Bills, Boston, Red Sox, Celtics, Bruins, Denver, Rockies, Avalanche, Broncos.

- depthFirstEnumeration() and postOrderEnumeration()— returns an Enumeration that has practically the opposite behavior of preOrderEnumeration(). Instead of including the current node first and then adding the children, these methods add the children first and then add the current node to the Enumeration. For the tree in Figure 16-21, this results in an Enumeration of nodes in the following order: Mets, Yankees, Rangers, Giants, Jets, Bills, Football, New York, Red Sox, Celtics, Bruins, Boston, Rockies, Avalanche, Broncos, Denver, root.

Figure 16-21: Sample tree for traversal

- breadthFirstEnumeration()—returns an Enumeration of nodes added by level. For the tree in Figure 16-21, the Enumeration would be in the following order: root, New York, Boston, Denver, Mets, Yankees, Rangers, Football, Red Sox, Celtics, Bruins, Rockies, Avalanche, Broncos, Giants, Jets, Bills.

This leaves but one question: How do you get the starting node? Well, the first node could be selected as the result of a user action, or you can ask a tree's TreeModel for its root node. We'll explore TreeModel shortly, but the source to get the root node follows. Because TreeNode is only one possible type of object that can be stored in a tree, the getRoot() method of TreeModel returns an Object.

```
TreeModel model = tree.getModel();
Object rootObject = model.getRoot();
if ((rootObject != null) && (rootObject instanceof DefaultMutableTreeNode)) {
  DefaultMutableTreeNode root = (DefaultMutableTreeNode)rootObject;
  ...
}
```

> **NOTE** *I can think of only one reason why you'd want to create a replacement to the TreeNode interface to describe the basic requirements of a node in a JTree: If you want to use an Iterator from the new Java Collections API, instead of an Enumeration to return a list of children, you can create your own replacement to TreeNode. This isn't recommended, however.*

Class *JTree.DynamicUtilTreeNode*

The JTree class includes an inner class, JTree.DynamicUtilTreeNode, which the tree uses to help create the nodes for your trees. The DynamicUtilTreeNode is a DefaultMutableTreeNode subclass that doesn't create its child nodes until they're needed. The child nodes are needed when you either expand the parent node or try to traverse a tree. Although you normally wouldn't use this class directly, you might find a place for it. To demonstrate, the following example uses a Hashtable to create the nodes for a tree. Instead of having an invisible node at the root of the tree (with a userObject property setting of "root"), the root node will have a property of "Root".

```
DefaultMutableTreeNode root = new DefaultMutableTreeNode("Root");
Hashtable hashtable = new Hashtable();
hashtable.put ("One", args);
hashtable.put ("Two", new String[]{"Mercury", "Venus", "Mars"});
Hashtable innerHashtable = new Hashtable();
Properties props = System.getProperties();
innerHashtable.put (props, props);
innerHashtable.put ("Two", new String[]{"Mercury", "Venus", "Mars"});
hashtable.put ("Three", innerHashtable);
JTree.DynamicUtilTreeNode.createChildren(root, hashtable);
JTree tree = new JTree(root);
```

The code just listed creates a tree with the same nodes as shown in the TreeArraySample program in Figure 16-5. However, the nodes at the first level of the tree are in a different order. That's because the nodes are in a Hashtable in this example, instead of in a Vector as in the TreeArraySample. The first-level tree elements are added in the order returned by an Enumeration of Hashtable, instead of being in the order added to the Vector, as Figure 16-22 shows.

Dragging Tree Nodes

If you've ever tried to use drag and drop with `JTree` objects, you might have experienced some difficulty in getting all the pieces going. Let's look at an example that should help explain the pieces in their entirety. We'll create a tree from which we'll drag objects, and create a list in which we'll drop objects. The source will support any type of data object in a tree node. However, if a non-`String` user object is employed, a custom renderer is necessary. Figure 16-23 shows the final product.

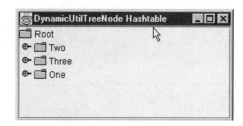

Figure 16-22: DynamicUtilTreeNode Hashtable tree sample

The first part of the example requires a `JTree` from which one can drag nodes. Objects that are the source of drag and drop need to implement the `public void dragGestureRecognized(DragGestureEvent dragGestureEvent)` method of the `DragGestureListener` interface; this signals the start of the dragging event. When the system determines that a drag gesture has started, you tell a `DragSource` that dragging has started and what object is being dragged.

Figure 16-23: Tree drag-and-drop example

```
import javax.swing.*;
import javax.swing.tree.*;
import java.awt.*;
import java.awt.dnd.*;
import java.io.IOException;

public class DraggableTree extends JTree implements DragGestureListener {
  DragSource dragSource = DragSource.getDefaultDragSource();

  final static DragSourceListener dragSourceListener = new
MyDragSourceListener();

  static class MyDragSourceListener implements DragSourceListener {
    public void dragDropEnd(DragSourceDropEvent DragSourceDropEvent) {
    }
    public void dragEnter(DragSourceDragEvent DragSourceDragEvent) {
    }
    public void dragExit(DragSourceEvent DragSourceEvent) {
    }
    public void dragOver(DragSourceDragEvent DragSourceDragEvent) {
    }
    public void dropActionChanged(DragSourceDragEvent DragSourceDragEvent) {
    }
  }
```

```
  public DraggableTree () {
    dragSource.createDefaultDragGestureRecognizer(this, DnDConstants.ACTION_COPY,
this);
  }

  public DraggableTree (TreeModel model) {
    super (model);
    dragSource.createDefaultDragGestureRecognizer(this, DnDConstants.ACTION_COPY,
this);
  }

  // DragGestureListener interface methods

  public void dragGestureRecognized(DragGestureEvent dragGestureEvent) {
    TreePath path = getSelectionPath();
    if (path == null) {
      // Nothing selected, nothing to drag
      System.out.println ("Nothing selected - beep");
      getToolkit().beep();
    } else {
      DefaultMutableTreeNode selection =
(DefaultMutableTreeNode)path.getLastPathComponent();
      TransferableTreeNode node = new TransferableTreeNode(selection);
      dragSource.startDrag(dragGestureEvent, DragSource.DefaultCopyDrop, node,
dragSourceListener);
    }
  }
}
```

The regular node of the tree is converted to a TransferableTreeNode for dragging. This class deals with converting the node of the tree to something that's draggable, depending on the data flavor desired. Because nodes of a tree may or may not be strings, you need to offer your own DataFlavor for the transfer to be able to support transferring the node's user object. Besides supporting the mapping of flavors to data objects, the class needs to implement the Transferable interface to be the object of a drag operation.

```
import javax.swing.tree.*;
import java.awt.dnd.*;
import java.awt.datatransfer.*;
import java.io.*;

public class TransferableTreeNode extends DefaultMutableTreeNode implements
Transferable {
```

```
  final static int TREE = 0;
  final static int STRING = 1;
  final static int PLAIN_TEXT = 2;

  final public static DataFlavor DEFAULT_MUTABLE_TREENODE_FLAVOR =
    new DataFlavor(DefaultMutableTreeNode.class, "Default Mutable Tree Node");

  static DataFlavor flavors[] = {DEFAULT_MUTABLE_TREENODE_FLAVOR,
DataFlavor.stringFlavor, DataFlavor.plainTextFlavor};

  private DefaultMutableTreeNode data;

  public TransferableTreeNode(DefaultMutableTreeNode data) {
    this.data = data;
  }

  public DataFlavor[] getTransferDataFlavors() {
   return flavors;
  }

  public Object getTransferData(DataFlavor flavor)
      throws UnsupportedFlavorException, IOException {
    Object returnObject;
    if (flavor.equals(flavors[TREE])) {
      Object userObject = data.getUserObject();
      if (userObject == null) {
        returnObject = data;
      } else {
        returnObject = userObject;
      }
    } else if (flavor.equals(flavors[STRING])) {
      Object userObject = data.getUserObject();
      if (userObject == null) {
        returnObject = data.toString();
      } else {
        returnObject = userObject.toString();
      }
    } else if (flavor.equals(flavors[PLAIN_TEXT])) {
      Object userObject = data.getUserObject();
      String string;
      if (userObject == null) {
        string = data.toString();
      } else {
        string = userObject.toString();
```

```
      }
      returnObject = new ByteArrayInputStream(string.getBytes("Unicode"));
    } else {
      throw new UnsupportedFlavorException(flavor);
    }
    return returnObject;
  }
  public boolean isDataFlavorSupported(DataFlavor flavor) {
    boolean returnValue = false;
    for (int i=0, n=flavors.length; i<n; i++) {
      if (flavor.equals(flavors[i])) {
        returnValue = true;
        break;
      }
    }
    return returnValue;
  }
}
```

The droppable object in this example is a JList. To be a drop site for a drag-and-drop operation, the site needs to implement the DropTargetListener interface. The notable method of this interface is public void drop (DropTargetDropEvent dropTargetDropEvent), called when an object has been dropped into the target site. This implementation of the method tries to find the richest data flavor for the object being dropped and then incorporates elements into the JList based on where in the list the drop happened. In addition to supporting the flavors from the DraggableTree, the target also supports DataFlavor.javaFileListFlavor for when a list of files is dropped onto it. When objects are dropped onto the list, they're added to a DefaultListModel.

```
import java.awt.*;
import java.awt.dnd.*;
import java.awt.datatransfer.*;
import javax.swing.*;
import java.io.*;
import java.util.*;
import java.util.List;

public class DroppableList extends JList implements DropTargetListener {

  DropTarget dropTarget;

  public DroppableList() {
    dropTarget = new DropTarget (this, this);
```

```
    setModel(new DefaultListModel());
}

public void dragEnter (DropTargetDragEvent dropTargetDragEvent) {
  dropTargetDragEvent.acceptDrag (DnDConstants.ACTION_COPY);
}

public void dragExit (DropTargetEvent dropTargetEvent) {
}

public void dragOver (DropTargetDragEvent dropTargetDragEvent) {
}

public void dropActionChanged (DropTargetDragEvent dropTargetDragEvent) {
}

public synchronized void drop (DropTargetDropEvent dropTargetDropEvent) {
  Point location = dropTargetDropEvent.getLocation();
  try {
   Transferable tr = dropTargetDropEvent.getTransferable();
    if (tr.isDataFlavorSupported(TransferableTreeNode.DEFAULT_MUTABLE_
  TREENODE_FLAVOR)) {
      dropTargetDropEvent.acceptDrop (DnDConstants.ACTION_COPY_OR_MOVE);
      Object userObject = tr.getTransferData(TransferableTreeNode.DEFAULT_
  MUTABLE_TREENODE_FLAVOR);
      addElement(location, userObject);
      dropTargetDropEvent.getDropTargetContext().dropComplete(true);
    } else if (tr.isDataFlavorSupported (DataFlavor.stringFlavor)) {
      dropTargetDropEvent.acceptDrop (DnDConstants.ACTION_COPY_OR_MOVE);
      String string = (String)tr.getTransferData (DataFlavor.stringFlavor);
      addElement(location, string);
      dropTargetDropEvent.getDropTargetContext().dropComplete(true);
    } else if (tr.isDataFlavorSupported (DataFlavor.plainTextFlavor)) {
      dropTargetDropEvent.acceptDrop (DnDConstants.ACTION_COPY_OR_MOVE);
      Object stream = tr.getTransferData(DataFlavor.plainTextFlavor);
      if (stream instanceof InputStream) {
        InputStreamReader isr = new InputStreamReader((InputStream)stream);
        BufferedReader reader = new BufferedReader(isr);
        String line;
        while ((line = reader.readLine()) != null) {
          addElement(location, line);
        }
        dropTargetDropEvent.getDropTargetContext().dropComplete(true);
```

```
          } else if (stream instanceof Reader) {
            BufferedReader reader = new BufferedReader((Reader)stream);
            String line;
            while ((line = reader.readLine()) != null) {
              addElement(location, line);
            }
            dropTargetDropEvent.getDropTargetContext().dropComplete(true);
          } else {
            System.err.println ("Unknown type: " + stream.getClass());
            dropTargetDropEvent.rejectDrop();
          }
        } else if (tr.isDataFlavorSupported (DataFlavor.javaFileListFlavor)) {
          dropTargetDropEvent.acceptDrop (DnDConstants.ACTION_COPY_OR_MOVE);
          List fileList = (List)tr.getTransferData(DataFlavor.javaFileListFlavor);
          Iterator iterator = fileList.iterator();
          while (iterator.hasNext()) {
            File file = (File)iterator.next();
            addElement(location, file.toURL());
          }
          dropTargetDropEvent.getDropTargetContext().dropComplete(true);
        } else {
          System.err.println ("Rejected");
          dropTargetDropEvent.rejectDrop();
        }
      } catch (IOException io) {
        io.printStackTrace();
        dropTargetDropEvent.rejectDrop();
      } catch (UnsupportedFlavorException ufe) {
        ufe.printStackTrace();
        dropTargetDropEvent.rejectDrop();
      }
    }
    private void addElement(Point location, Object element) {
      int index = locationToIndex(location);
      // If index not found, add at end, otherwise add one beyond position
      if (index == -1) {
        index = getModel().getSize();
      } else {
        index++;
      }
      ((DefaultListModel)getModel()).add(index, element);
    }
  }
```

The remaining part of the drag-and-drop example is a testing program. The example takes a DraggableTree and DroppableList and places them in a window within a JSplitPane. Running it produces Figure 16-23, shown earlier, with the initial list empty.

```java
import java.awt.*;
import javax.swing.*;

public class TreeTester {
  public static void main (String args[]) {
    JFrame f = new ExitableJFrame("Tree Dragging Tester");
    DraggableTree tree = new DraggableTree();
    JScrollPane leftPane = new JScrollPane(tree);
    DroppableList list = new DroppableList();
    JScrollPane rightPane = new JScrollPane(list);
    JSplitPane splitPane = new JSplitPane(JSplitPane.HORIZONTAL_SPLIT, leftPane,
rightPane);
    f.getContentPane().add (splitPane,  BorderLayout.CENTER);
    f.setSize (300, 200);
    f.setVisible (true);
  }
}
```

This program is meant to be only a small demonstration of the drag-and-drop capabilities within the Java 2 platform. This example won't work with JDK 1.1. Feel free to extend this example to support capabilities such as autoscrolling while dragging (simply implement the Autoscroll interface) or dropping onto a tree instead of onto a list.

Interface TreeModel

The TreeModel interface describes the basic data model structure for a JTree. It describes a parent-child aggregation relationship, which permits any object to be a parent or a child. There's one root to the tree, and all other nodes of the tree are descendants of this node. In addition to returning information about the different nodes, the model requires any implementers to manage a list of TreeModelListener objects so that the listeners can be notified when any nodes in the model have changed. The remaining method, valueForPathChanged(), is meant to provide the means of changing the contents of a node at a particular location.

```
public interface TreeModel {
  // Properties
  public Object getRoot();
  // Listeners
  public void addTreeModelListener(TreeModelListener l);
  public void removeTreeModelListener(TreeModelListener l);
  // Instance Methods
  public Object getChild(Object parent, int index);
  public int getChildCount(Object parent);
  public int getIndexOfChild(Object parent, Object child);
  public boolean isLeaf(Object node);
  public void valueForPathChanged(TreePath path, Object newValue);
}
```

Class *DefaultTreeModel*

The JTree automatically creates a DefaultTreeModel instance to store its data model. The DefaultTreeModel class provides an implementation of the TreeModel interface that uses TreeNode implementations at each node.

In addition to implementing the methods of the TreeModel interface, as well as managing a list of TreeModelListener objects, the DefaultTreeModel class adds several helpful methods, described next. The first pair of methods is for directly adding/removing nodes to or from a tree. The remaining methods are for notifying the data model when tree nodes are modified. If you don't insert/remove nodes into or from the model for a displayed tree with one of the first two methods, it's your responsibility to call a method from the second set.

- public void insertNodeInto(MutableTreeNode child, MutableParentNode parent, index int) — adds child node to parent's set of children at child position index (zero-based)

- public void removeNodeFromParent(MutableTreenode node) — causes node to be removed from tree

- public void nodeChanged(TreeNode node) — notifies model that a node has changed

- public void nodesChanged(TreeNode node, int childIndices[]) — notifies model that the child or children of a node have changed

- public void nodeStructureChanged(TreeNode node) — notifies model if node and children have changed

- `public void nodesWereInserted(TreeNode node, int childIndices[])` — notifies model that nodes were inserted as children of the tree node

- `public void nodesWereRemoved(TreeNode node, int childIndices[], Object removedChildren[])` — notifies model that child nodes were removed from tree and includes nodes as argument in method call

- `public void reload()` / `public void reload(TreeNode node)` — notifies model that there were complex changes made to the nodes and that the model should be reloaded from the root node down or from a specific node down

Interface *TreeModelListener/Class TreeModelEvent*

The `TreeModel` uses a `TreeModelListener` to report any changes to the model. When the `TreeModel` sends a `TreeModelEvent`, any registered listeners are notified. The interface includes notification methods for when nodes are inserted, removed, or changed, as well as one catchall method for when some or all of these operations are done simultaneously.

```
public interface TreeModelListener implements EventListener {
  public void treeNodesChanged(TreeModelEvent treeModelEvent);
  public void treeNodesInserted(TreeModelEvent treeModelEvent);
  public void treeNodesRemoved(TreeModelEvent treeModelEvent);
  public void treeStructureChanged(TreeModelEvent treeModelEvent);
}
```

Interface **TreeSelectionModel**

In addition to all trees' supporting a data model for storing nodes, a renderer for displaying nodes, and an editor for editing them, there's a data model called `TreeSelectionModel` for selective manipulation of tree elements. The `TreeSelectionModel` interface contains methods to describe the selected set of paths to the selected nodes. Each path is stored in a `TreePath`, which itself contains a path of tree nodes from the root object to a selected node. The `TreePath` class will be explored shortly.

The `TreeSelectionModel` interface that follows supports three modes of selection, with each mode specified by a class constant: `CONTIGUOUS_TREE_SELECTION`, `DISCONTIGUOUS_TREE_SELECTION`, and `SINGLE_TREE_SELECTION`. When the selection mode is `CONTIGUOUS_TREE_SELECTION`, only nodes situated next to each other can be selected simultaneously. The `DISCONTIGUOUS_TREE_SELECTION` mode means that there are no restrictions on simultaneous selection. With the remaining mode, `SINGLE_TREE_SELECTION`, only one node can be selected at a time.

> **NOTE** *The keys used to select multiple nodes are look-and-feel specific. Try using the CTRL-select or SHIFT-select keyboard combinations to choose multiple nodes.*

```java
public interface TreeSelectionModel {
  // Constants
  public final static int CONTIGUOUS_TREE_SELECTION;
  public final static int DISCONTIGUOUS_TREE_SELECTION;
  public final static int SINGLE_TREE_SELECTION;
  // Properties
  public TreePath getLeadSelectionPath();
  public int getLeadSelectionRow();
  public int getMaxSelectionRow();
  public int getMinSelectionRow();
  public RowMapper getRowMapper();
  public void setRowMapper(RowMapper newMapper);
  public int getSelectionCount();
  public boolean isSelectionEmpty();
  public int getSelectionMode();
  public void setSelectionMode(int mode);
  public TreePath getSelectionPath();
  public void setSelectionPath(TreePath path);
  public TreePath[] getSelectionPaths();
  public void setSelectionPaths(TreePath paths[]);
  public int[] getSelectionRows();
  // Listeners
  public void addPropertyChangeListener(PropertyChangeListener listener);
  public void removePropertyChangeListener(PropertyChangeListener listener);
  public void addTreeSelectionListener(TreeSelectionListener listener);
  public void removeTreeSelectionListener(TreeSelectionListener listener);
  // Other Methods
  public void addSelectionPath(TreePath path);
  public void addSelectionPaths(TreePath paths[]);
  public void clearSelection();
  public boolean isPathSelected(TreePath path);
  public boolean isRowSelected(int row);
  public void removeSelectionPath(TreePath path);
  public void removeSelectionPaths(TreePath paths[]);
  public void resetRowSelection();
}
```

Besides changing selection modes, the remaining methods allow you to monitor attributes of the selection path. Sometimes the methods work with row numbers and other times with TreePath objects. The selection model uses a RowMapper to map rows to paths for you. The abstract AbstractLayoutCache class provides a basic implementation of the RowMapper interface that's further specialized by the FixedHeightLayoutCache and VariableHeightLayoutCache classes. You should never have to access or modify the RowMapper or any of its implementations. To map rows to paths (or paths to rows), just ask a JTree.

Class *DefaultTreeSelectionModel*

The DefaultTreeSelectionModel class provides an implementation of the TreeSelectionModel interface that's initially in DISCONTIGUOUS_TREE_SELECTION mode and that supports all three selection modes. The class introduces none of its own methods; instead, it merely implements all the TreeSelectionModel interface methods, including methods for accessing the 11 properties listed in Table 16-7. In addition, DefaultTreeSelectionModel overrides the clone() and toString() methods of Object.

PROPERTY NAME	DATA TYPE	ACCESS
leadSelectionPath	TreePath	read-only
leadSelectionRow	int	read-only
maxSelectionRow	int	read-only
minSelectionRow	int	read-only
rowMapper	RowMapper	read-write
selectionCount	int	read-only
selectionEmpty	boolean	read-only
selectionMode	int	read-write
selectionPath	TreePath	read-write
selectionPaths	TreePath[]	read-write
selectionRows	int[]	read-only

Table 16-7: DefaultTreeSelectionModel properties

The primary reason to use the TreeSelectionModel is to change the selection mode of the model. For instance, the following two lines of source code change the model to single-selection mode:

```
TreeSelectionModel selectionModel = tree.getSelectionModel();
selectionModel.setSelectionMode(TreeSelectionModel.SINGLE_TREE_SELECTION);
```

If you're interested in finding out the selected path (or paths), you can ask the JTree directly. You don't have to get the selected path(s) from the model.

Interface *TreeSelectionListener/* Class *TreeSelectionEvent*

When the set of selected nodes within a tree changes, a TreeSelectionEvent is generated and any registered TreeSelectionListener objects of the TreeSelectionModel are notified. The TreeSelectionListener can be registered either with the JTree or directly with the TreeSelectionModel. The interface definition follows.

```
public interface TreeSelectionListener implements EventListener {
  public void valueChanged(TreeSelectionEvent treeSelectionEvent);
}
```

To demonstrate the use of the TreeSelectionListener, we'll provide yet another editor for when tree nodes are a check box. When using a TreeCellEditor, you'll note that an extra mouse selection is necessary to activate the editor. Instead of clicking the mouse, just selecting the node should change the state of the check box. For this to work, you can use a TreeSelectionListener. After changing the state of the node, you then need to clear the selection so that the next selection changes the state again. If you fail to clear the selection, trying to select the same node again generates no event because the node is already selected and the state can't change. Figure 16-24 shows the sample program in action.

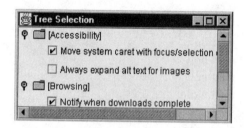

Figure 16-24: Sample using TreeSelectionListener to change state of check box nodes

The source for the program is listed next. In it, the TreeSelectionListener code is boldfaced. This specific listener says, in effect, that when a node is selected, get it. Then, if the node happens to be a CheckBoxNode, you change its state and notify the model of the change. After the state has been changed, clear the selection after all the other listeners have been notified.

```
import javax.swing.*;
import javax.swing.tree.*;
import javax.swing.event.*;
import java.awt.*;
import java.util.Vector;
```

```java
public class TreeSelectionSample {
  public static void main(String args[]) {
    String title = ("Tree Selection");
    JFrame frame = new ExitableJFrame(title);
    CheckBoxNode accessibilityOptions[] = {
      new CheckBoxNode("Move system caret with focus/selection changes", false),
      new CheckBoxNode("Always expand alt text for images", true)
    };
    CheckBoxNode browsingOptions[] = {
      new CheckBoxNode("Notify when downloads complete", true),
      new CheckBoxNode("Disable script debugging", true),
      new CheckBoxNode("Use AutoComplete", true),
      new CheckBoxNode("Browse in a new process", false)
    };
    Vector accessVector = new NamedVector("Accessibility", accessibilityOptions);
    Vector browseVector = new NamedVector("Browsing", browsingOptions);
    Object rootNodes[] = {accessVector, browseVector};
    Vector rootVector = new NamedVector("Root", rootNodes);
    JTree tree = new JTree(rootVector);

    CheckBoxNodeRenderer renderer = new CheckBoxNodeRenderer();
    tree.setCellRenderer(renderer);

    TreeSelectionModel selectionModel = tree.getSelectionModel();
    selectionModel.setSelectionMode(TreeSelectionModel.SINGLE_TREE_SELECTION);

    TreeSelectionListener treeSelectionListener = new TreeSelectionListener() {
      public void valueChanged(TreeSelectionEvent treeSelectionEvent) {
        final JTree treeSource = (JTree)treeSelectionEvent.getSource();
        TreePath path = treeSource.getSelectionPath();
        if (path != null) {
          DefaultMutableTreeNode node =
(DefaultMutableTreeNode)path.getLastPathComponent();
          Object userObject = node.getUserObject();
          if (userObject instanceof CheckBoxNode) {
            CheckBoxNode checkBoxNode = (CheckBoxNode)userObject;
            checkBoxNode.setSelected(!checkBoxNode.isSelected());
            DefaultTreeModel model = (DefaultTreeModel)treeSource.getModel();
            model.nodeChanged(node);
            Runnable runner = new Runnable() {
              public void run() {
                treeSource.clearSelection();
              }
```

```
            };
            SwingUtilities.invokeLater(runner);
          }
        }
      }
    };

    JScrollPane scrollPane = new JScrollPane(tree);
    frame.getContentPane().add(scrollPane, BorderLayout.CENTER);
    frame.setSize(300, 150);
    frame.setVisible(true);
  }
}
```

Class TreePath

The last major class to examine is TreePath. It has been used in many of the earlier examples in this chapter. It describes a read-only collection of nodes that map a path from the root node to another node, where the root could be the top of a subtree versus the root of the whole tree. Although two constructors exist to create TreePath objects, you'll normally deal with them only as the return value from a method. You can also create a new path by adding an element to an existing TreePath with public TreePath pathByAddingChild(Object child).

A TreePath can be thought of as an Object array, in which the first element of the array is the root of the tree and the last element is called the *last path component*. Normally, the elements of the array will be of type TreeNode. However, because TreeModel supports objects of any type, the path property of TreePath is defined to be an array of Object nodes. Table 16-8 lists this property and the remaining other three.

PROPERTY NAME	DATA TYPE	ACCESS
lastPathComponent	Object	read-only
parentPath	TreePath	read-only
path	Object[ ]	read-only
pathCount	int	read-only

Table 16-8: TreePath properties

To better understand TreePath, let's reuse the tree traversal sample tree from Figure 16-21, shown once more in Figure 16-25.

Using Figure 16-25 to visualize a tree starting from its root, the TreePath for the "Jets" node would be described by its properties as follows:

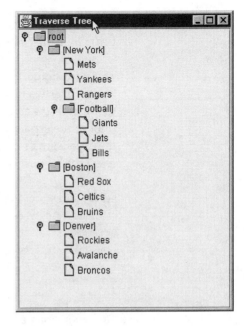

- lastPathComponent — a DefaultMutableTreeNode whose user object is "Jets"

- parentPath — a TreePath made up of the "root," "New York," and "Football" nodes

- path — an array of DefaultMutableTreeNode nodes whose user objects are "root," "New York," "Football," and "Jets"

- pathCount — 4

That's really all there is to the TreePath class. Just remember that you can't change an existing TreePath — you can only access its elements.

Figure 16-25: TreePath sample tree

Additional Expansion Events

Two listeners that can be registered with a JTree have yet to be discussed: a TreeExpansionListener and a TreeWillExpandListener.

Interface TreeExpansionListener/ Class TreeExpansionEvent

If you're interested in finding out when a tree node has been expanded or collapsed, you can register a TreeExpansionListener with a JTree. Any registered listener will be notified after the expansion or collapse of a parent node.

```
public interface TreeExpansionListener implements EventListener {
  public void treeCollapse(TreeExpansionEvent treeExpansionEvent);
  public void treeExpand(TreeExpansionEvent treeExpansionEvent);
}
```

Each of the methods has a TreeExpansionEvent as its argument. The TreeExpansionEvent class has a single method for getting the path to the expansion/ collapse node: public TreePath getPath().

Interface TreeWillExpandListener/ Class ExpandVetoException

The JTree supports the registration of a TreeWillExpandListener, whose definition follows. The two method signatures are similar to the TreeExpansionListener, and they can throw an ExpandVetoException. Any registered listener will be notified prior to the expansion or collapse of a parent node. If the listener doesn't want the expansion or collapse to happen, that listener can throw the exception to reject the request, stopping the node from opening or closing.

```
public interface TreeWillExpandListener implements EventListener {
  public void treeWillCollapse(TreeExpansionEvent treeExpansionEvent) throws
ExpandVetoException;
  public void treeWillExpand(TreeExpansionEvent treeExpansionEvent) throws
ExpandVetoException;
}
```

To demonstrate a TreeWillExpandListener, the following code won't permit either the "sports" node to be expanded in the default data model or the "colors" node to be collapsed.

```
TreeWillExpandListener treeWillExpandListener = new TreeWillExpandListener() {
  public void treeWillCollapse(TreeExpansionEvent treeExpansionEvent) throws
ExpandVetoException {
    TreePath path = treeExpansionEvent.getPath();
    DefaultMutableTreeNode node =
(DefaultMutableTreeNode)path.getLastPathComponent();
    String data = node.getUserObject().toString();
    if (data.equals("colors")) {
      throw new ExpandVetoException(treeExpansionEvent);
    }
  }
  public void treeWillExpand(TreeExpansionEvent treeExpansionEvent) throws
ExpandVetoException {
    TreePath path = treeExpansionEvent.getPath();
    DefaultMutableTreeNode node =
(DefaultMutableTreeNode)path.getLastPathComponent();
    String data = node.getUserObject().toString();
    if (data.equals("sports")) {
      throw new ExpandVetoException(treeExpansionEvent);
    }
  }
};
```

Don't forget to add the listener to a tree with a line of code similar to
`tree.addTreeWillExpandListener(treeWillExpandListener)`.

Summary

In this chapter, we explored the many classes related to the use of the `JTree`
component. We looked at tree node rendering with the `TreeCellRenderer` interface and the `DefaultTreeCellRenderer` implementation. We delved into tree
node rendering with the `TreeCellEditor` interface and the `DefaultCellEditor` and
`DefaultTreeCellEditor` implementations.

After reviewing how to display and edit a tree, we dealt with the `TreeNode`
interface, `MutableTreeNode` interface, and `DefaultMutableTreeNode` class for manually
creating tree objects. We explored the `TreeModel` interface and `DefaultTreeModel`
implementation for storing the data model of a tree, and the `TreeSelectionModel`
interface and `DefaultTreeSelectionModel` implementation for storing the selection model for a tree.

In addition, we looked at the many event-related classes for the various tree
classes, and the `TreePath` for describing node connection paths.

In Chapter 17, we'll explore the `javax.swing.table` package and its many classes
that can be used with the `JTable` component.

CHAPTER 17

Tables

CHAPTER 16 TOOK AN IN-DEPTH LOOK AT the Swing `JTree` component. In this chapter, we'll examine the many details of the `JTable` component. The component is the standard Swing component for displaying two-dimensional data in the form of a grid, as shown in Figure 17-1.

> **NOTE** *All the examples in this chapter will work fine without configuring your environment to display Japanese fonts. However, instead of seeing the ideographs, you will see characters such as question marks or boxes, depending upon your platform. In order to see the Kanji ideographs in the sample programs, you will need to be using the Japanese version of the* `font.properties` *file (*`font.properties.ja`*) and have the necessary Japanese fonts installed. In addition to the Windows NT installation CD, you can find the necessary Windows fonts at http://ftp.monash.edu.au/pub/nihongo/ ie3lpkja.exe. Solaris users must contact Sun to request the Asian outline fonts for Solaris environments. More on adding fonts to the Java runtime environment is at http://java.sun.com/products/jdk/1.2/docs/guide/internat/ fontprop.html.*

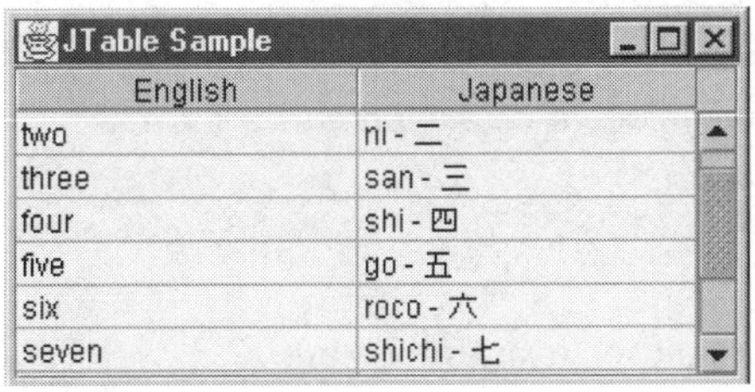

Figure 17-1: Sample JTable

Introducing Tables

Like the `JTree` component, the `JTable` component relies on numerous support classes for its inner workings. For the `JTable`, the support classes are found in the `javax.swing.table` package. The cells within the `JTable` can be selected by row, column, row and column, or individual cell. It's the responsibility of the current `ListSelectionModel` settings to control the selection within a table.

The display of the different cells within a table is the responsibility of the TableCellRenderer; the DefaultCellRenderer offers one such implementation of the TableCellRenderer interface in a JLabel subclass.

Managing the data stored in the cells is accomplished through an implementation of the TableModel interface. The AbstractTableModel provides the basics of an implementation of the interface without any data storage. By comparison, the DefaultTableModel encapsulates the TableModel interface and uses a vector of vectors for the data storage. You extend AbstractTableModel if you need a different type of storage than the kind supplied by the DefaultTableModel, for instance, if you already had the data in your own data structure.

The TableColumnModel interface and the DefaultTableColumnModel implementation of the interface manage the table's data as a series of columns. They work together with the TableColumn class to allow for greater flexibility in manipulating individual columns. For example, you can store columns of data in the TableModel in an order that's different than the display order within the JTable. The TableColumnModel manages a second ListSelectionModel to control table column selection.

At the top of every column is a column header. By default, the TableColumn class relies on the JTableHeader class to render a text column header. Nevertheless, you must embed the JTable in a scroll pane to see the default header.

Cells within a JTable can be editable. If a cell is editable, how the editing works depends on the TableCellEditor implementation, such as the DefaultCellEditor implementation. In addition, no classes exist to handle individual rows. Rows must be manipulated on a cell-by-cell basis.

Figure 17-2 shows these class interrelationships.

> **NOTE** *There are additional interrelationships among the elements used by the JTable component. These relationships will be explored later in this chapter with each specific interface and class.*

To visualize how the JTable elements all fit together, examine Figure 17-3.

Class JTable

We'll first look at the JTable class, which gives you a way to display data in tabular form.

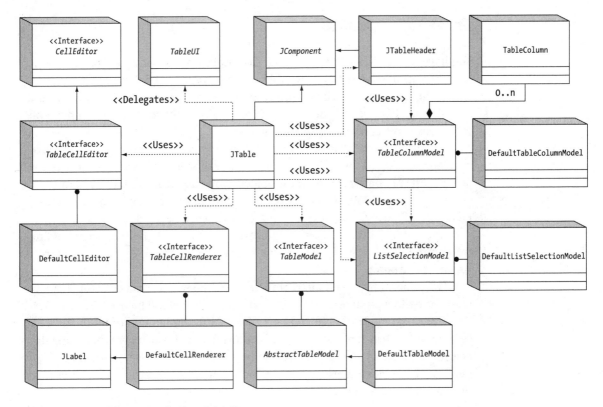

Figure 17-2: JTable UML relationship diagram

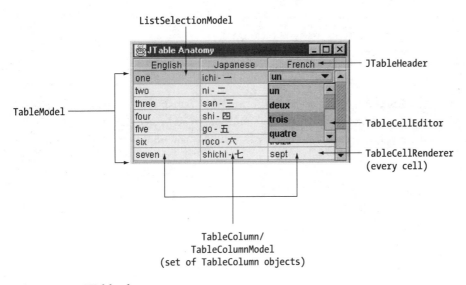

Figure 17-3: JTable elements

Creating a JTable

You have seven different ways at your disposal to create a JTable. The various constructors allow you to create tables from a number of data sources.

In the following list, the *no-arg* constructor creates a table with no rows and no columns. The second constructor takes two integers to create an empty table with a set number of rows and columns.

The next two constructors are useful when your tabular data is already in a specially structured form. For instance, if your data is already in the form of an array of arrays or a Vector of Vector objects, you can create a JTable without creating your own TableModel. A two-row-by-three-column table could be created from the array of {{"Row1-Column1", "Row1-Column2", "Row1-Column3"}, {"Row2-Column1", "Row2-Column2", "Row2-Column3"}}, with another array holding the column names. Similar data structures would be necessary for the vector-based constructor.

The remaining three constructors use JTable-specific data structures. If any one of the three arguments is missing, default settings will be used. For example, if you don't specify a TableColumnModel, the default implementation DefaultTableColumnModel is used and is auto-filled with a display order using the column order of the TableModel. When the selection model is missing, the ListSelectionModel will use multi-selection mode, which means that noncontiguous rows, but not columns, can be selected.

1. ```
   public JTable()
   JTable table = new JTable();
   ```

2. ```
   public JTable(int rows, int columns)
   JTable table = new JTable(2, 3);
   ```

> **NOTE** *Table components created from JTable constructors are editable, and not read-only. To change their contents in code, just call the public void setValueAt(Object value, int row, int column) method of JTable.*

3. ```
   public JTable(Object rowData[][], Object columnNames[])
   Object rowData[][] = {{"Row1-Column1", "Row1-Column2", "Row1-Column3"},
   {"Row2-Column1", "Row2-Column2", "Row2-Column3"}};
   Object columnNames[] = {"Column One", "Column Two", "Column Three"};
   JTable table = new JTable(rowData, columnNames);
   ```
   ```

4. ```
   public JTable(Vector rowData, Vector columnNames)
   Vector rowOne = new Vector();
   rowOne.addElement("Row1-Column1");
   rowOne.addElement("Row1-Column2");
   rowOne.addElement("Row1-Column3");
   Vector rowTwo = new Vector();
   rowTwo.addElement("Row2-Column1");
   rowTwo.addElement("Row2-Column2");
   rowTwo.addElement("Row2-Column3");
   Vector rowData = new Vector();
   rowData.addElement(rowOne);
   rowData.addElement(rowTwo);
   Vector columnNames = new Vector();
   columnNames.addElement("Column One");
   columnNames.addElement("Column Two");
   columnNames.addElement("Column Three");
   JTable table = new JTable(rowData, columnNames);
   ```

5. ```
   public JTable(TableModel model)
   TableModel model = new DefaultTableModel(rowData, columnNames);
   JTable table = new JTable(model);
   ```

6. ```
   public JTable(TableModel model, TableColumnModel columnModel)
   // Swaps column order
   TableColumnModel columnModel = new DefaultTableColumnModel();
   TableColumn firstColumn = new TableColumn(1);
   firstColumn.setHeaderValue(headers[1]);
   columnModel.addColumn(firstColumn);
   TableColumn secondColumn = new TableColumn(0);
   secondColumn.setHeaderValue(headers[0]);
   columnModel.addColumn(secondColumn);
   JTable table = new JTable(model, columnModel);
   ```

7. ```
   public JTable(TableModel model, TableColumnModel columnModel,
   ListSelectionModel selectionModel)
   // Set single selection mode
   ListSelectionModel selectionModel = new DefaultListSelectionModel();
   selectionModel.setSelectionMode(ListSelectionModel.SINGLE_SELECTION);
   JTable table = new JTable(model, columnModel, selectionModel);
   ```

Scrolling JTable Components

Like other components that may require more space than what's available, the JTable component implements the Scrollable interface and should be placed

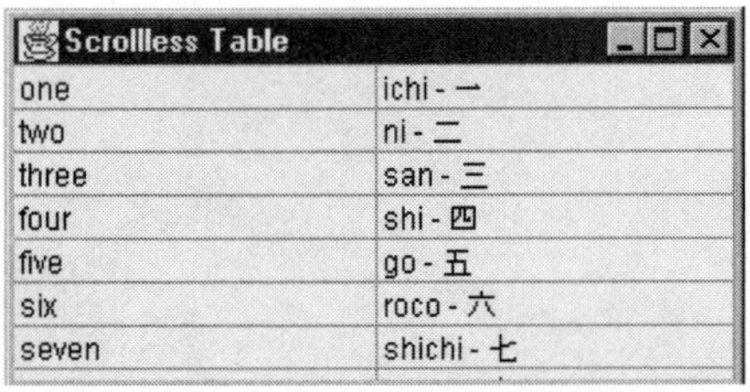

Figure 17-4: JTable without a JScrollPane

within a JScrollPane. Scrollbars will appear in a JScrollPane when a JTable is too big for the available screen real estate, and column header names will appear above each column. Figure 17-4 shows how the table in Figure 17-1 would appear if it weren't within a JScrollPane. Notice that neither column headers nor scrollbars appear. This means you can't determine the meaning of the data, nor can you scroll to the undisplayed rows.

Therefore, every table you create needs to be placed within a JScrollPane by using code similar to the following:

```
JTable table = new JTable(...);
JScrollPane scrollPane = new JScrollPane(table);
```

> **NOTE** *JTable contains a deprecated method:* public static JScrollPane createScrollPaneForTable(JTable table). *This method was used in JFC/Swing 1.0 to place a JTable within a JScrollPane and to automatically set its column headers. It proved useless (not designable) within GUI development environments such as VisualAge for Java and Visual Café and has since been replaced with the current behavior.*

Manually Positioning the JTable View

When a JTable within a JScrollPane is added to a window, the table will automatically appear with the table positioned so that the first row and column appear in the upper-left corner. If you ever need to return the position to the origin, you can set the viewport position back to the point (0, 0).

```
scrollPane.getViewport().setViewPosition(new Point(0,0));
```

For scrolling purposes, the block increment amount is the visible width/height of the viewport, depending on the direction of the scrollbar. The unit increment is 100 pixels for horizontal scrolling and the height of a single row for vertical scrolling. See Figure 17-5 for a visual representation of these increments.

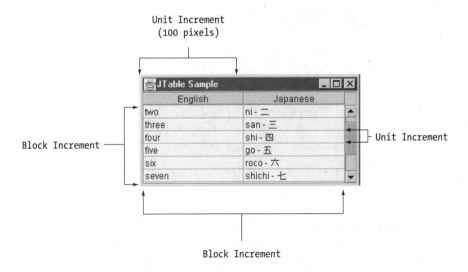

Figure 17-5: JTable scrolling increments

Removing Column Headers

As previously stated, placing a JTable within a JScrollPane automatically produces column header labels for the different column names. If you don't want column headers, such as in Figure 17-6, you can remove them one of many different ways.

The simplest way to remove the column headers is to provide empty strings as the column header names. With the third JTable constructor in the previous list of seven constructors, this would involve replacing the three column names with "", the empty string.

```
Object rowData[][] = {{"Row1-Column1", "Row1-Column2", "Row1-Column3"}, {"Row2-
Column1", "Row2-Column2", "Row2-Column3"}};
Object columnNames[] = {"", "", ""};
JTable table = new JTable(rowData, columnNames);
JScrollPane scrollPane = new JScrollPane(table);
```

Because this method of removing headers also removes the description of the different columns, you might want to use another way of hiding column headers. The simplest way is to just tell the JTable you don't want table headers:

```
table.setTableHeader(null);
```

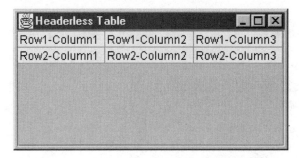

Figure 17-6: A JTable without column headers

Other ways exist to remove headers. They involve subclassing JTable and over-riding the protected method configureEnclosingScrollPane() or telling every TableColumn that its header value is empty. All of these are more complicated ways of performing the same task.

> **NOTE** *Calling scrollPane.setColumnHeaderView(null) doesn't work to clear out the column headers. Instead, it causes the JScrollPane to use the default column headers.*

JTable Properties

As Table 17-1 shows, the JTable has many properties. The 39 listed can be broken up into three logical groupings, plus one for miscellaneous properties. The three groupings are for display settings, selection settings, and auto resizing settings.

PROPERTY NAME	DATA TYPE	ACCESS
accessibleContext	AccessibleContext	read-only
autoCreateColumnsFromModel	boolean	read-write
autoResizeMode	int	read-write
cellEditor	TableCellEditor	read-write bound
cellSelectionEnabled	boolean	read-write
columnCount	int	read-only
columnModel	TableColumnModel	read-write bound
columnSelectionAllowed	boolean	read-write
editing	boolean	read-only
editingColumn	int	read-write

(continued)

Table 17-1 (continued)

PROPERTY NAME	DATA TYPE	ACCESS
editingRow	int	read-write
editorComponent	Component	read-only
gridColor	Color	read-write
intercellSpacing	Dimension	read-write
managingFocus	boolean	read-only
model	TableModel	read-write bound
preferredScrollableViewportSize	Dimension	read-write
rowCount	int	read-only
rowHeight	int	read-write
rowMargin	int	read-write
rowSelectionAllowed	boolean	read-write
scrollableTracksViewportHeight	boolean	read-only
scrollableTracksViewportWidth	boolean	read-only
selectedColumn	int	read-only
selectedColumnCount	int	read-only
selectedColumns	int[ ]	read-only
selectedRow	int	read-only
selectedRowCount	int	read-only
selectedRows	int[ ]	read-only
selectionBackground	Color	read-write bound
selectionForeground	Color	read-write bound
selectionMode	int	write-only
selectionModel	ListSelectionModel	read-write bound
showGrid	boolean	write-only
showHorizontalLines	boolean	read-write
showVerticalLines	boolean	read-write
tableHeader	JTableHeader	read-write
UI	TableUI	read-write
UIClassID	String	read-only

Table 17-1: JTable properties

Understanding Display Settings

The first subset of properties in Table 17-1 allows you to set various display options of the JTable. In addition to the inherited foreground and background properties from Component, you can change the selection foreground (selectionForeground) and background (selectionBackground) colors. You also control which (if any) gridlines appear (showGrid), as well as their color (gridColor). The remaining intercellSpacing property setting deals with the space between table cells.

Understanding Selection Modes

You can use any one of three different types of selection modes for a JTable. You can select table elements one row at a time, one column at a time, or one cell at a time. These three settings are controlled by the rowSelectionAllowed, columnSelectionAllowed, and cellSelectionEnabled properties. Initially, only row selection is allowed while the other two nodes are not. Because the default ListSelectionModel is in multi-select mode, you can select multiple rows at a time. If you don't like multi-select mode, you can change the selectionMode property of the JTable, causing the selection mode of the rows and columns of the JTable to change accordingly.

> **NOTE** *The ListSelectionModel class provides constants for the different selection modes. These are explored in the next section of this chapter.*

If you're ever interested in whether any of the rows or columns of the JTable are selected, you can inquire with one of the six additional properties of JTable: selectedColumnCount, selectedColumn, selectedColumns, selectedRowCount, selectedRow, and selectedRows.

Interface ListSelectionModel/Class DefaultListSelectionModel

The ListSelectionModel interface and DefaultListSelectionModel class were both covered with the JList component information in Chapter 13. They're used to describe the current set of rows and columns within the JTable component. They have three different settings, as shown in Table 17-2.

SELECTION MODES
MULTIPLE_INTERVAL_SELECTION (default)
SINGLE_INTERVAL_SELECTION
SINGLE_SELECTION

Table 17-2: JTable selection modes

The JTable has independent selection models for both rows and columns. The row selection model is stored with the selectionModel property of the JTable. The column selection model is stored with the TableColumnModel. Setting the selectionMode property of a JTable sets the selection mode for the two independent selection models of the JTable.

Once a selection mode has been set and a user interacts with the component, you can ask the selection model what happened, or, more precisely, what the user has selected. Table 17-3 lists the properties available to facilitate selection with the DefaultListSelectionModel.

PROPERTY NAME	DATA TYPE	ACCESS
anchorSelectionIndex	int	read-write
leadAnchorNotificationEnabled	boolean	read-write
leadSelectionIndex	int	read-write
maxSelectionIndex	int	read-only
minSelectionIndex	int	read-only
selectionEmpty	boolean	read-only
selectionModel	int	read-write
valueIsAdjusting	boolean	read-write

Table 17-3: DefaultListSelectionModel properties

If you're interested in knowing when a selection event happens, register a ListSelectionListener with the ListSelectionModel. The ListSelectionListener was demonstrated in Chapter 13 with the JList component.

> **TIP** *All table indices are zero-based. So, the first visual column is column 0 internally.*

Understanding Auto Resize Modes

The last subset of the JTable properties deals with the column resize behavior of the JTable. When the JTable is in a column or window that changes sizes, how does it react? Table 17-4 shows the five settings supported by a JTable.

MODES	DESCRIPTION
AUTO_RESIZE_ALL_COLUMNS	Adjusts all column widths proportionally
AUTO_RESIZE_LAST_COLUMN	Adjusts right-most column width only to give or take space as required by the column currently being altered; if no space is available within that column, then resizing will work with the previous column until a column with available space to consume is found
AUTO_RESIZE_NEXT_COLUMN	If you're reducing the width of a neighboring column, the neighboring column will grow to fill the unused space; if you're increasing the width of a column, the neighboring column will shrink
AUTO_RESIZE_OFF	Turns off user's ability to resize columns; can still be programatically resized
AUTO_RESIZE_SUBSEQUENT_COLUMNS (default)	Adjusts width by proportionally altering columns displayed to the right of the column being changed

Table 17-4: Auto resize mode constants

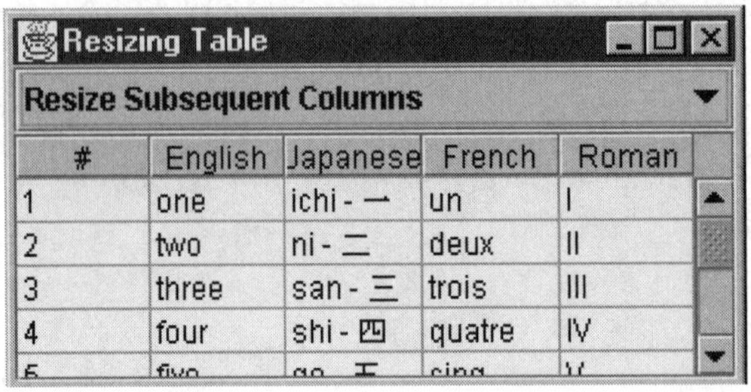

Figure 17-7: Demonstrating JTable resizing column modes

The following program demonstrates what effect each setting has when resizing table columns. Figure 17-7 shows the initial appearance of the program. Change the JComboBox and you change the column resize behavior.

```
import javax.swing.*;
import javax.swing.table.*;
import java.awt.*;
import java.awt.event.*;

public class ResizeTable {
  public static void main(String args[]) {

    Object rowData[][] = {
      {"1",  "one",   "ichi - \u4E00",   "un",     "I"},
      {"2",  "two",   "ni - \u4E8C",     "deux",   "II"},
      {"3",  "three", "san - \u4E09",    "trois",  "III"},
      {"4",  "four",  "shi - \u56DB",    "quatre", "IV"},
      {"5",  "five",  "go - \u4E94",     "cinq",   "V"},
      {"6",  "six",   "roco - \u516D",   "treiza", "VI"},
      {"7",  "seven", "shichi - \u4E03", "sept",   "VII"},
      {"8",  "eight", "hachi - \u516B",  "huit",   "VIII"},
      {"9",  "nine",  "kyu - \u4E5D",    "neur",   "IX"},
      {"10", "ten",   "ju - \u5341",     "dix",    "X"}
    };

    String columnNames[] = {"#", "English", "Japanese", "French", "Roman"};

    final JTable table = new JTable(rowData, columnNames);
    JScrollPane scrollPane = new JScrollPane(table);

    String modes[] = {"Resize All Columns", "Resize Last Column", "Resize Next
Column",
      "Resize Off", "Resize Subsequent Columns"};
    final int modeKey[] = {
      JTable.AUTO_RESIZE_ALL_COLUMNS,
      JTable.AUTO_RESIZE_LAST_COLUMN,
      JTable.AUTO_RESIZE_NEXT_COLUMN,
      JTable.AUTO_RESIZE_OFF,
      JTable.AUTO_RESIZE_SUBSEQUENT_COLUMNS};
    JComboBox resizeModeComboBox = new JComboBox(modes);
    int defaultMode = 4;
    table.setAutoResizeMode(modeKey[defaultMode]);
    resizeModeComboBox.setSelectedIndex(defaultMode);
    ItemListener itemListener = new ItemListener() {
      public void itemStateChanged(ItemEvent e) {
        JComboBox source = (JComboBox)e.getSource();
        int index = source.getSelectedIndex();
```

```
        table.setAutoResizeMode(modeKey[index]);
      }
    };
    resizeModeComboBox.addItemListener(itemListener);

    JFrame frame = new ExitableJFrame("Resizing Table");
    Container contentPane = frame.getContentPane();

    contentPane.add(resizeModeComboBox, BorderLayout.NORTH);
    contentPane.add(scrollPane, BorderLayout.CENTER);

    frame.setSize(300, 150);
    frame.setVisible(true);
  }
}
```

Rendering Table Cells

By default, the rendering of table data is done by a JLabel. Whatever value is stored in the table is rendered as a text string. The odd thing is that additional "default" renderers are installed for classes such as Date and Number subclasses, but they're not "enabled." I'll discuss how to enable these specialized renderers later in this chapter.

Interface TableCellRenderer/Class DefaultTableCellRenderer

The TableCellRenderer interface defines the single method necessary for that class to be a TableCellRenderer.

```
public interface TableCellRenderer {
  public Component getTableCellRendererComponent(JTable table, Object value,
boolean isSelected, boolean hasFocus, int row, int column);
}
```

By using information given to the getTableCellRendererComponent() method, proper renderer components can be created and sent on their way to display the appropriate content of the JTable. By "proper," I mean renderers that reflect the table cell state that you've decided to display, such as when you want to display selected cells differently than non-selected cells, or how you want the selected cell to be displayed when it has the input focus.

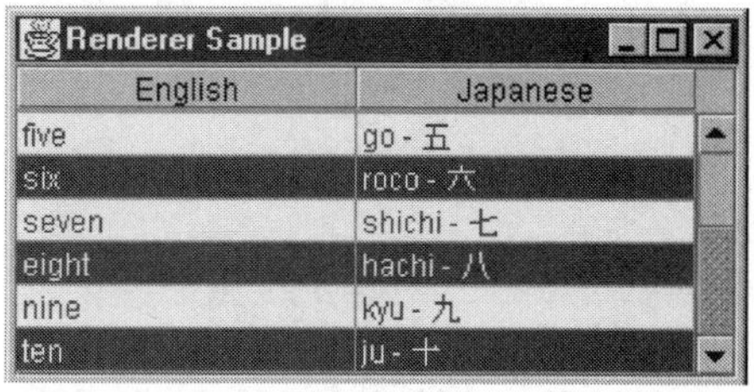

Figure 17-8: JTable with custom renderer

To see a simple demonstration of this, look at Figure 17-8, which shows a renderer that alternates colors based on which row the renderer is displayed within.

The source for this renderer follows:

```java
import java.awt.*;
import javax.swing.*;
import javax.swing.table.*;

public class EvenOddRenderer implements TableCellRenderer {

  public static final DefaultTableCellRenderer DEFAULT_RENDERER =
    new DefaultTableCellRenderer();

  public Component getTableCellRendererComponent(JTable table, Object value,
      boolean isSelected, boolean hasFocus, int row, int column) {
    Component renderer = DEFAULT_RENDERER.getTableCellRendererComponent(table, value,
      isSelected, hasFocus, row, column);
    Color foreground, background;
    if (isSelected) {
      foreground = Color.yellow;
      background = Color.green;
    } else {
      if (row % 2 == 0) {
        foreground = Color.blue;
        background = Color.white;
      } else {
        foreground = Color.white;
        background = Color.blue;
      }
    }
    renderer.setForeground(foreground);
    renderer.setBackground(background);
```

```
      return renderer;
    }
}
```

Renderers for tables can be installed for individual classes or for specific columns (there's more on columns later). To install the renderer as the default renderer for the JTable — in other words, for Object.class — use code similar to the following:

```
TableCellRenderer renderer = new EvenOddRenderer();
table.setDefaultRenderer(Object.class, renderer);
```

Once installed, the EvenOddRenderer will be used for any column whose class doesn't have a more specific renderer. It's the responsibility of the public Class getColumnClass() method of TableModel to return the class to be used as the renderer lookup for all the cells in a particular column. The DefaultTableModel returns Object.class for everything; therefore, EvenOddRenderer will be used by all table cells.

> **TIP** *Keep in mind that one renderer component is used for every cell of every column of a particular class. No individual renderer is created for each cell.*

The sample program that used the EvenOddRenderer to generate Figure 17-8 follows:

```
import javax.swing.*;
import javax.swing.table.*;
import java.awt.*;

public class RendererSample {
  public static void main(String args[]) {
    Object rows[][] = {
      {"one",   "ichi - \u4E00"},
      {"two",   "ni - \u4E8C"},
      {"three", "san - \u4E09"},
      {"four",  "shi - \u56DB"},
      {"five",  "go - \u4E94"},
      {"six",   "roco - \u516D"},
      {"seven", "shichi - \u4E03"},
      {"eight", "hachi - \u516B"},
      {"nine",  "kyu - \u4E5D"},
      {"ten",   "ju - \u5341"}
```

```
    };
    Object headers[] = {"English", "Japanese"};
    JFrame frame = new ExitableJFrame("Renderer Sample");
    JTable table = new JTable(rows, headers);
    TableCellRenderer renderer = new EvenOddRenderer();
    table.setDefaultRenderer(Object.class, renderer);
    JScrollPane scrollPane = new JScrollPane(table);
    frame.getContentPane().add(scrollPane, BorderLayout.CENTER);
    frame.setSize(300, 150);
    frame.setVisible(true);
  }
}
```

Using Tooltips

By default, your table cell renderers will display any tooltip text you've configured them to display. Unlike the JTree component, you don't have to manually
register the table with the ToolTipManager. If, however, your table doesn't display
tooltip text, the table will respond faster if you unregister the table with the
ToolTipManager by using code such as the following:

```
ToolTipManager.sharedInstance().unregisterComponent(aTable);
```

Handling JTable Events

There are no JTable events that you can register directly with the JTable. To find
out when something happens, you must register with one of the JTable model
classes: TableModel, TableColumnModel, or ListSelectionModel.

Customizing a JTable Look and Feel

Each installable Swing look and feel provides a different JTable appearance and
set of default UIResource value settings. Figure 17-9 shows the appearance of the
JTable component for the preinstalled set of look and feels: Motif, Windows,
Metal, and Macintosh. In all four cases, the third row is highlighted, where the
coloration shows the first column is being edited and the second isn't.

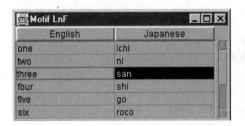

Motif

Windows

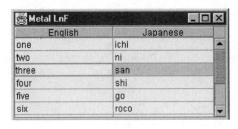

Metal

Macintosh

Figure 17-9: JTable under different look and feels

The available set of UIResource-related properties for a JTable is shown in Table 17-5. The JTable component has 11 different properties.

PROPERTY STRING	OBJECT TYPE
Table.background	Color
Table.focusCellBackground	Color
Table.focusCellForeground	Color
Table.focusCellHighlightBorder	Border
Table.font	Font
Table.foreground	Color
Table.gridColor	Color
Table.scrollPaneBorder	Border
Table.selectionBackground	Color
Table.selectionForeground	Color
TableUI	TableUI

Table 17-5: JTable UIResource elements

Interface TableModel

Now that we've looked at the basics of the JTable component, we can see how it manages its data elements. It does this with the help of classes that implement the TableModel interface.

The TableModel interface defines the framework needed by the JTable to acquire column headers and cell values, and modify those cell values when the table is editable. Its definition follows:

```
public interface TableModel {
  // Listeners
  public void addTableModelListener(TableModelListener l);
  public void removeTableModelListener(TableModelListener l);
  // Properties
  public int getColumnCount();
  public int getRowCount();
  // Other Methods
  public Class getColumnClass(int columnIndex);
  public String getColumnName(int columnIndex);
  public Object getValueAt(int rowIndex, int columnIndex);
  public boolean isCellEditable(int rowIndex, int columnIndex);
  public void setValueAt(Object vValue, int rowIndex, int columnIndex);
}
```

Class AbstractTableModel

The AbstractTableModel class provides the basic implementation of the TableModel interface. It manages the TableModelListener list and default implementations for several of the TableModel methods. When you subclass it, all you simply have to provide is the actual column and row count, and the specific values (getValueAt()) in the table model. Column names default to labels such as "A", "B", "C", ..., "Z", "AA", "BB", ..., and the data model is read-only unless isCellEditable() is overridden.

If you subclass AbstractTableModel and make the data model editable, it's your responsibility to call one of the fire*XXX*() methods of AbstractTableModel to ensure that any TableModelListener objects are notified when the data model changes:

```
public void fireTableCellUpdated(int row, int column);
public void fireTableChanged(TableModelEvent e);
public void fireTableDataChanged();
```

```
public void fireTableRowsDeleted(int firstRow, int lastRow);
public void fireTableRowsInserted(int firstRow, int lastRow);
public void fireTableRowsUpdated(int firstRow, int lastRow);
public void fireTableStructureChanged();
```

When you want to create a JTable, it's not uncommon to subclass AbstractTableModel in order to reuse an existing data structure. This data structure typically comes as the result of a Java Database Connectivity (JDBC) query, but there's no restriction requiring that to be the case. To demonstrate, the following anonymous class definition shows how you can treat an array as an AbstractTableModel.

```
TableModel model = new AbstractTableModel() {
  Object rowData[][] = {
    {"one",   "ichi"},
    {"two",   "ni"},
    {"three", "san"},
    {"four",  "shi"},
    {"five",  "go"},
    {"six",   "roco"},
    {"seven", "shichi"},
    {"eight", "hachi"},
    {"nine",  "kyu"},
    {"ten",   "ju"}
  };
  Object columnNames[] = {"English", "Japanese"};
  public String getColumnName(int column) {
    return columnNames[column].toString();
  }
  public int getRowCount() {
    return rowData.length;
  }
  public int getColumnCount() {
    return columnNames.length;
  }
  public Object getValueAt(int row, int col) {
    return rowData[row][col];
  }
};
JTable table = new JTable(model);
JScrollPane scrollPane = new JScrollPane(table);
```

Specifying Fixed JTable Columns

Now that you've seen the basics of how the TableModel and AbstractTableModel work, you can create a JTable with some fixed columns and some columns *not* fixed. To create columns that don't scroll, you need to place a second table in the row header view of the JScrollPane. Then when the user scrolls the table vertically, the two tables will remain in sync. The two tables then need to share their ListSelectionModel. That way, when a row in one table is selected, the row in the other table will automatically be selected. Figure 17-10 shows a table with one fixed column and four scrolling columns.

The source code used to generate Figure 17-10 follows.

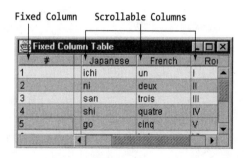

Figure 17-10: Fixed-column JTable

```java
import javax.swing.*;
import javax.swing.table.*;
import java.awt.*;

public class FixedTable {
  public static void main(String args[]) {
    final Object rowData[][] = {
      {"1",  "one",   "ichi",   "un",     "I"},
      {"2",  "two",   "ni",     "deux",   "II"},
      {"3",  "three", "san",    "trois",  "III"},
      {"4",  "four",  "shi",    "quatre", "IV"},
      {"5",  "five",  "go",     "cinq",   "V"},
      {"6",  "six",   "roco",   "treiza", "VI"},
      {"7",  "seven", "shichi", "sept",   "VII"},
      {"8",  "eight", "hachi",  "huit",   "VIII"},
      {"9",  "nine",  "kyu",    "neur",   "IX"},
      {"10", "ten",   "ju",     "dix",    "X"}
    };

    final String columnNames[] = {"#", "English", "Japanese", "French", "Roman"};

    TableModel fixedColumnModel = new AbstractTableModel() {
      public int getColumnCount() {
        return 1;
      }
      public String getColumnName(int column) {
        return columnNames[column];
      }
      public int getRowCount() {
```

```
          return rowData.length;
        }
        public Object getValueAt(int row, int column) {
          return rowData[row][column];
        }
      };

    TableModel mainModel = new AbstractTableModel() {
        public int getColumnCount() {
          return columnNames.length-1;
        }
        public String getColumnName(int column) {
          return columnNames[column+1];
        }
        public int getRowCount() {
          return rowData.length;
        }
        public Object getValueAt(int row, int column) {
          return rowData[row][column+1];
        }
      };

    JTable fixedTable = new JTable(fixedColumnModel);
    fixedTable.setAutoResizeMode(JTable.AUTO_RESIZE_OFF);
//    fixedTable.setSelectionMode(ListSelectionModel.SINGLE_SELECTION);

    JTable mainTable = new JTable(mainModel);
    mainTable.setAutoResizeMode(JTable.AUTO_RESIZE_OFF);
//    mainTable.setSelectionMode(ListSelectionModel.SINGLE_SELECTION);

    ListSelectionModel model = fixedTable.getSelectionModel();
    mainTable.setSelectionModel(model);

    JScrollPane scrollPane = new JScrollPane(mainTable);
    Dimension fixedSize = fixedTable.getPreferredSize();
    JViewport viewport = new JViewport();
    viewport.setView(fixedTable);
    viewport.setPreferredSize(fixedSize);
    viewport.setMaximumSize(fixedSize);
    scrollPane.setCorner(JScrollPane.UPPER_LEFT_CORNER,
  fixedTable.getTableHeader());
    scrollPane.setRowHeaderView(viewport);
```

```
JFrame frame = new ExitableJFrame("Fixed Column Table");

frame.getContentPane().add(scrollPane, BorderLayout.CENTER);
frame.setSize(300, 150);
frame.setVisible(true);
  }
}
```

Enabling the Default Table Cell Renderers

Earlier, I mentioned that the JTable provides default renderers for Date and Number classes. Let's look at the AbstractTableModel class and see how they're enabled.

The public Class getColumnClass(int column) method of TableModel returns the class type for a column in the data model. If the JTable class has a special renderer installed for that particular class, it will use it to display that class. By default, the AbstractTableModel (and DefaultTableModel) implementations of TableModel returns Object.class for everything. The AbstractTableModel class doesn't try to be smart about guessing what's in a column. However, if you know that a particular column of the data model will always be numbers, dates, or some other class, you can have the data model return that class type. This allows the JTable to try to be smart and use a better renderer.

To demonstrate, Table 17-6 shows the preinstalled renderers within the JTable. If you have a table full of numbers or just one column of numbers, you can override getColumnClass() to return Number.class for the appropriate columns; your numbers will be right-justified instead of left-justified. With dates, for instance, you'll get better-looking output.

CLASS	RENDERER	INFORMATION
Boolean	JCheckBox	centered
Date	JLabel	right-aligned uses DateFormat for output
ImageIcon	JLabel	centered
Number	JLabel	right-aligned uses NumberFormat for output
Object	JLabel	left-aligned

Table 17-6: Default JTable renderers

Figure 17-11 shows how a table might look before and after enabling the renderers.

You can choose to hardcode the class names for columns or have the getColumnClass() method be generic and just call getClass() on an element in the column. Adding the following code to an AbstractTableModel definition

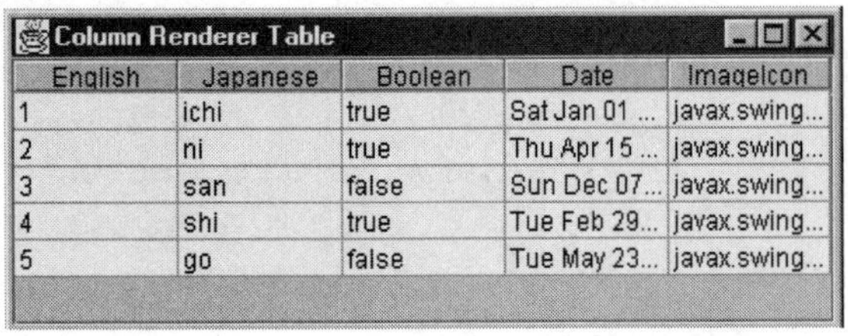

English	Japanese	Boolean	Date	ImageIcon
1	ichi	true	Sat Jan 01 ...	javax.swing...
2	ni	true	Thu Apr 15 ...	javax.swing...
3	san	false	Sun Dec 07...	javax.swing...
4	shi	true	Tue Feb 29...	javax.swing...
5	go	false	Tue May 23...	javax.swing...

Before

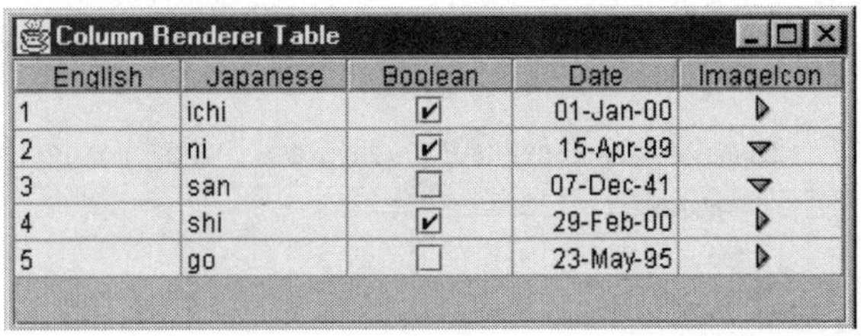

English	Japanese	Boolean	Date	ImageIcon
1	ichi	✔	01-Jan-00	▷
2	ni	✔	15-Apr-99	▽
3	san	☐	07-Dec-41	▽
4	shi	✔	29-Feb-00	▷
5	go	☐	23-May-95	▷

After

Figure 17-11: Before and after enabling the renderers

would allow the JTable to use its default renderers. This implementation assumes that all entries for a particular column are one class type.

```
public Class getColumnClass(int column) {
  return (getValueAt(0, column).getClass());
}
```

Class DefaultTableModel

The DefaultTableModel is a subclass of AbstractTableModel that provides its own Vector data structure for storage. Everything in the data model is stored within vectors internally, even when the data is initially part of an array. In other words, if you already have your data in an adequate data structure, don't use DefaultTableModel. Create an AbstractTableModel that just uses the structure instead of having a DefaultTableModel convert the structure for you.

Creating a DefaultTableModel

There are six constructors for DefaultTableModel. Four map directly to JTable constructors, whereas the remaining two allow you to create empty tables from a set of column headers with a fixed number of rows. Once you've created the DefaultTableModel, you pass it along to a JTable constructor to create the actual table and then place the table in a JScrollPane.

1. public DefaultTableModel()
   TableModel model = new DefaultTableModel()

2. public DefaultTableModel(int rows, int columns)
   TableModel model = new DefaultTableModel(2, 3)

3. ```
   public DefaultTableModel(Object rowData[][], Object columnNames[])
   Object rowData[][] = {{"Row1-Column1", "Row1-Column2", "Row1-Column3"},
   {"Row2-Column1", "Row2-Column2", "Row2-Column3"}};
   Object columnNames[] = {"Column One", "Column Two", "Column Three"};
   TableModel model = new DefaultTableModel(rowData, columnNames)
   ```

4. ```
   public DefaultTableModel(Vector rowData, Vector columnNames)
   Vector rowOne = new Vector();
   rowOne.addElement("Row1-Column1");
   rowOne.addElement("Row1-Column2");
   rowOne.addElement("Row1-Column3");
   Vector rowTwo = new Vector();
   rowTwo.addElement("Row2-Column1");
   rowTwo.addElement("Row2-Column2");
   rowTwo.addElement("Row2-Column3");
   Vector rowData = new Vector();
   rowData.addElement(rowOne);
   rowData.addElement(rowTwo);
   Vector columnNames = new Vector();
   columnNames.addElement("Column One");
   columnNames.addElement("Column Two");
   columnNames.addElement("Column Three");
   TableModel model = new DefaultTableModel(rowData, columnNames);
   ```

5. ```
   public DefaultTableModel(Object columnNames[], int rows)
   TableModel model = new DefaultTableModel(columnNames, 2)
   ```

6. ```
   public DefaultTableModel(Vector columnNames, int rows)
   TableModel model = new DefaultTableModel(columnNames, 2)
   ```

Filling a DefaultTableModel

If you choose to use a DefaultTableModel, you must fill it with data for your JTable to display anything. In addition to basic routines to fill the data structure, there are additional methods to remove data or replace the entire contents:

- Adding columns
  ```
  public void addColumn(Object columnName);
  public void addColumn(Object columnName, Vector columnData);
  public void addColumn(Object columnName, Object columnData[ ]);
  ```

- Adding rows

```
public void addRow(Object rowData[ ]);
public void addRow(Vector rowData);
```

- Inserting rows

```
public void insertRow(int row, Object rowData[ ]);
public void insertRow(int row, Vector rowData);
```

- Removing rows

```
public void removeRow( int row);
```

- Replacing contents

```
public void setDataVector(Object newData[ ][ ], Object columnNames[ ]);
public void setDataVector(Vector newData, Vector columnNames);
```

DefaultTableModel Properties

In addition to the rowCount and columnCount properties inherited from
AbstractTableModel, DefaultTableModel has three additional properties, as shown
in Table 17-7. The numRows property allows you to enlarge or shrink the table size
as you please. If you are growing the model, the additional rows remain empty.

PROPERTY NAME	DATA TYPE	ACCESS
columnCount	int	read-only
columnIdentifiers	Vector	writeOnly
dataVector	Vector	read-only
numRows	int	write-only
rowCount	int	read-only

Table 17-7: DefaultTableModel properties

Listening to JTable Events with a TableModelListener

If you want to dynamically update your table data, you can work with a
TableModelListener to find out when the data changes. The interface consists of
one method that tells you when the table data changes.

```
public interface TableModelListener extends EventListener {
  public void tableChanged(TableModelEvent e);
}
```

After the `TableModelListener` is notified, you can ask the `TableModelEvent` for the type of event that happened and the range of rows and columns affected. Table 17-8 shows the properties of the `TableModelEvent` you can inquire about.

PROPERTY NAME	DATA TYPE	ACCESS
column	int	read-only
firstRow	int	read-only
lastRow	int	read-only
type	int	read-only

Table 17-8: TableModelEvent properties

The event type can be one of three type constants of `TableModelEvent`, as listed in Table 17-9.

TYPES
INSERT
UPDATE
DELETE

Table 17-9: TableModelEvent type constants

If the `column` property setting for the `TableModelEvent` is `ALL_COLUMNS`, then all the columns in the data model are affected. If the `firstRow` property is `HEADER_ROW`, it means the table header changed.

Sorting JTable Elements

The `JTable` component doesn't come with built-in support for sorting. Nevertheless, this feature is frequently requested. Sorting doesn't require changing the data model, but it *does* require changing the view of the data model that the `JTable` has.

This type of change is described by the Decorator pattern, in which you maintain the same API to the data but add sorting capabilities to the view. Figure 17-12 illustrates what the general structure of the pattern.

The participants of the Decorator design pattern are the `Component`, `ConcreteComponent`, `Decorator`, and `ConcreteDecorator`(s) [A, B, C, ...]:

- `Component` — The component defines the service interface that will be decorated.

- `ConcreteComponent` — The concrete component is the object to be decorated.

- Decorator — The decorator is an abstract wrapper to a concrete component; it maintains the service interface.

- ConcreteDecorator — The concrete decorator objects extend the decorator by adding decorating responsibilities while maintaining the same programming interface. They redirect service requests to the concrete component referred to by their abstract superclass.

NOTE *The streams of the* java.io *package are examples of the Decorator pattern. The various filter streams add capabilities to the basic stream classes and maintain the same API for access.*

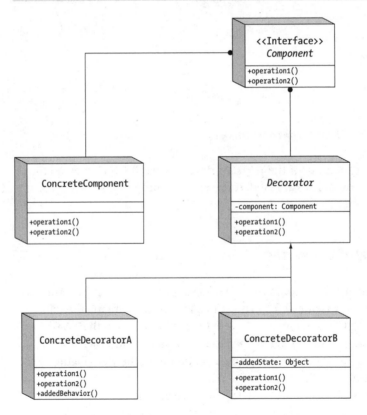

Figure 17-12: The Decorator pattern

In our particular case for table sorting, we have a simplified example with only the Component, ConcreteComponent, and Decorator, because there is only one concrete decorator. The Component is the TableModel interface, the ConcreteComponent is the actual model, and the Decorator is the sorted model.

In order to sort, you need to maintain a mapping of the real data to the sorted data, and from the user interface, you must allow the user to select a column header label to enable sorting of a particular column.

To use the sorting capabilities, you tell the TableSorter about your data model, decorate it, and create a JTable from your decorated model instead of the original. To enable the sorting by picking column header labels, you need to call the custom install() method of the TableHeaderSorter class shown in the following source code for the TableSorter class.

```
TableSorter sorter = new TableSorter(model);
JTable table = new JTable(sorter);
TableHeaderSorter.install(sorter, table);
```

> **NOTE** *I'll demonstrate the TableSorter in Chapter 18 and show how to sort a table of system properties.*

The main source code for the TableSorter class follows. It extends from the TableMap class, which follows the TableSorter class. The TableSorter class is where all the action is. The class does the sorting and notifying others that the data has changed.

```
import javax.swing.*;
import javax.swing.table.*;
import javax.swing.event.*;
import java.awt.event.*;
import java.util.*;

public class TableSorter extends TableMap implements TableModelListener {
  int indexes[] = new int[0];
  Vector sortingColumns = new Vector();
  boolean ascending = true;

  public TableSorter() {
  }

  public TableSorter(TableModel model) {
    setModel(model);
  }
```

```java
public void setModel(TableModel model) {
  super.setModel(model);
  reallocateIndexes();
  sortByColumn(0);
  fireTableDataChanged();
}

public int compareRowsByColumn(int row1, int row2, int column) {
  Class type = model.getColumnClass(column);
  TableModel data = model;

  // Check for nulls

  Object o1 = data.getValueAt(row1, column);
  Object o2 = data.getValueAt(row2, column);

  // If both values are null return 0
  if (o1 == null && o2 == null) {
    return 0;
  } else if (o1 == null) { // Define null less than everything.
    return -1;
  } else if (o2 == null) {
    return 1;
  }

  if (type.getSuperclass() == Number.class) {
    Number n1 = (Number)data.getValueAt(row1, column);
    double d1 = n1.doubleValue();
    Number n2 = (Number)data.getValueAt(row2, column);
    double d2 = n2.doubleValue();

    if (d1 < d2)
      return -1;
    else if (d1 > d2)
      return 1;
    else
      return 0;
  } else if (type == String.class) {
    String s1 = (String)data.getValueAt(row1, column);
    String s2 = (String)data.getValueAt(row2, column);
    int result = s1.compareTo(s2);

    if (result < 0)
      return -1;
```

```
        else if (result > 0)
          return 1;
        else
          return 0;
    } else if (type == java.util.Date.class) {
      Date d1 = (Date)data.getValueAt(row1, column);
      long n1 = d1.getTime();
      Date d2 = (Date)data.getValueAt(row2, column);
      long n2 = d2.getTime();

      if (n1 < n2)
        return -1;
      else if (n1 > n2)
        return 1;
      else
        return 0;
    } else if (type == Boolean.class) {
      Boolean bool1 = (Boolean)data.getValueAt(row1, column);
      boolean b1 = bool1.booleanValue();
      Boolean bool2 = (Boolean)data.getValueAt(row2, column);
      boolean b2 = bool2.booleanValue();

      if (b1 == b2)
        return 0;
      else if (b1) // Define false < true
        return 1;
      else
        return -1;
    } else {
      Object v1 = data.getValueAt(row1, column);
      String s1 = v1.toString();
      Object v2 = data.getValueAt(row2, column);
      String s2 = v2.toString();
      int result = s1.compareTo(s2);

      if (result < 0)
        return -1;
      else if (result > 0)
        return 1;
      else
        return 0;
    }
  }
}
```

```
public int compare(int row1, int row2) {
  for (int level=0, n=sortingColumns.size(); level < n; level++) {
    Integer column = (Integer)sortingColumns.elementAt(level);
    int result = compareRowsByColumn(row1, row2, column.intValue());
    if (result != 0) {
      return (ascending ? result : -result);
    }
  }
  return 0;
}

public void reallocateIndexes() {
  int rowCount = model.getRowCount();
  indexes = new int[rowCount];
  for (int row = 0; row < rowCount; row++) {
    indexes[row] = row;
  }
}

public void tableChanged(TableModelEvent tableModelEvent) {
  super.tableChanged(tableModelEvent);
  reallocateIndexes();
  sortByColumn(0);
  fireTableStructureChanged();
}

public void checkModel() {
  if (indexes.length != model.getRowCount()) {
    System.err.println("Sorter not informed of a change in model.");
  }
}

public void sort() {
  checkModel();
  shuttlesort((int[])indexes.clone(), indexes, 0, indexes.length);
  fireTableDataChanged();
}

public void shuttlesort(int from[], int to[], int low, int high) {
  if (high - low < 2) {
    return;
  }
  int middle = (low + high)/2;
```

```
    shuttlesort(to, from, low, middle);
    shuttlesort(to, from, middle, high);

    int p = low;
    int q = middle;

    for (int i = low; i < high; i++) {
      if (q >= high || (p < middle && compare(from[p], from[q]) <= 0)) {
        to[i] = from[p++];
      } else {
        to[i] = from[q++];
      }
    }
  }

  private void swap(int first, int second) {
    int temp       = indexes[first];
    indexes[first]  = indexes[second];
    indexes[second] = temp;
  }

  public Object getValueAt(int row, int column) {
    checkModel();
    return model.getValueAt(indexes[row], column);
  }

  public void setValueAt(Object aValue, int row, int column) {
    checkModel();
    model.setValueAt(aValue, indexes[row], column);
  }

  public void sortByColumn(int column) {
    sortByColumn(column, true);
  }

  public void sortByColumn(int column, boolean ascending) {
    this.ascending = ascending;
    sortingColumns.removeAllElements();
    sortingColumns.addElement(new Integer(column));
    sort();
    super.tableChanged(new TableModelEvent(this));
  }
}
```

> **NOTE** *The* TableSorter *borrows heavily from the* TableExample *that comes with the JFC/Swing release.*

The TableMap class serves as a proxy, passing along all calls to the appropriate TableModel class. It's the superclass of the TableSorter class shown previously.

```java
import javax.swing.table.*;
import javax.swing.event.*;

public class TableMap extends AbstractTableModel implements TableModelListener {

  TableModel model;

  public TableModel getModel() {
    return model;
  }

  public void setModel(TableModel model) {
    if (this.model != null) {
      this.model.removeTableModelListener(this);
    }
    this.model = model;
    if (this.model != null) {
      this.model.addTableModelListener(this);
    }
  }

  public Class getColumnClass(int column) {
    return model.getColumnClass(column);
  }

  public int getColumnCount() {
    return ((model == null) ? 0 : model.getColumnCount());
  }

  public String getColumnName(int column) {
    return model.getColumnName(column);
  }

  public int getRowCount() {
      return ((model == null) ? 0 : model.getRowCount());
  }
```

```
public Object getValueAt(int row, int column) {
  return model.getValueAt(row, column);
}

public void setValueAt(Object value, int row, int column) {
  model.setValueAt(value, row, column);
}

public boolean isCellEditable(int row, int column) {
  return model.isCellEditable(row, column);
}

public void tableChanged(TableModelEvent tableModelEvent) {
  fireTableChanged(tableModelEvent);
}
}
```

Installation of the sorting routines requires the registration of a MouseListener so that selection triggers the sorting process. Regular mouse clicks are ascending sorts; SHIFT-clicks are descending sorts.

```
import javax.swing.*;
import javax.swing.table.*;
import javax.swing.event.*;
import java.awt.event.*;
import java.util.*;

public class TableHeaderSorter extends MouseAdapter {

  private TableSorter sorter;
  private JTable table;

  private TableHeaderSorter() {
  }

  public static void install(TableSorter sorter, JTable table) {
    TableHeaderSorter tableHeaderSorter = new TableHeaderSorter();
    tableHeaderSorter.sorter = sorter;
    tableHeaderSorter.table  = table;
    JTableHeader tableHeader = table.getTableHeader();
    tableHeader.addMouseListener(tableHeaderSorter);
  }
```

```
    public void mouseClicked(MouseEvent mouseEvent) {
      TableColumnModel columnModel = table.getColumnModel();
      int viewColumn = columnModel.getColumnIndexAtX(mouseEvent.getX());
      int column = table.convertColumnIndexToModel(viewColumn);
      if (mouseEvent.getClickCount() == 1 && column != -1) {
        System.out.println("Sorting ...");
        int shiftPressed = (mouseEvent.getModifiers() & InputEvent.SHIFT_MASK);
        boolean ascending = (shiftPressed == 0);
        sorter.sortByColumn(column, ascending);
      }
    }
  }
}
```

Interface TableColumnModel

The TableColumnModel interface is one of those interfaces that lives in the background and usually doesn't require much attention. It basically manages the set of columns currently being displayed by a JTable. Unless triggered to do otherwise, when a JTable is created, the component builds a default column model from the data model, specifying that the display column order remain in the data model order.

When the autoCreateColumnsFromModel property of JTable is set (true) prior to setting the data model of the JTable, the TableColumnModel is automatically created. In addition, you can manually tell the JTable to create the default TableColumnModel if the current settings need to be reset. The public void createDefaultColumnsFromModel() method does the creation for you, assigning the new creation to the TableColumnModel of the JTable.

With all that automatically done for you, when would you need to look at the TableColumnModel? Usually, you'll look only when you don't like the defaults, or when you want to manually move things around. In addition to maintaining a set of TableColumn objects, the TableColumnModel manages a second ListSelectionModel which allows users to select columns from the table, as well as select rows.

Let's take a look at the interface definition before we get into the default implementation.

```
public interface TableColumnModel {
  // Listeners
  public void addColumnModelListener(TableColumnModelListener l);
  public void removeColumnModelListener(TableColumnModelListener l);
  // Properties
  public int getColumnCount();
  public int getColumnMargin();
```

```
    public void setColumnMargin(int newMargin);
    public Enumeration getColumns();
    public boolean getColumnSelectionAllowed();
    public void setColumnSelectionAllowed(boolean flag);
    public int getSelectedColumnCount();
    public int[ ] getSelectedColumns();
    public ListSelectionModel getSelectionModel();
    public void setSelectionModel(ListSelectionModel newModel);
    public int getTotalColumnWidth();
    // Other Methods
    public void addColumn(TableColumn aColumn);
    public TableColumn getColumn(int columnIndex);
    public int getColumnIndex(Object columnIdentifier);
    public int getColumnIndexAtX(int xPosition);
    public void moveColumn(int columnIndex, int newIndex);
    public void removeColumn(TableColumn column);
}
```

Class *DefaultTableColumnModel*

The DefaultTableColumnModel class defines the implementation of the TableColumnModel interface used by the system. It describes the general appearance of the TableColumn objects within the JTable by tracking margins, width, selection, and quantity. Table 17-10 shows the eight properties for accessing the DefaultTableColumnModel settings.

PROPERTY NAME	DATA TYPE	ACCESS
columnCount	int	read-only
columnMargin	int	read-write
columns	Enumeration	read-only
columnSelectionAllowed	boolean	read-write
selectedColumnCount	int	read-only
selectedColumns	int[ ]	read-only
selectionModel	ListSelectionModel	read-write
totalColumnWidth	int	read-only

Table 17-10: DefaultTableColumnModel properties

In addition to the class properties, you can add, remove, or move columns through the TableColumn class, which will be discussed shortly.

```
public void addColumn(TableColumn newColumn);
public void removeColumn(TableColumn oldColumn);
public void moveColumn(int currentIndex, int newIndex);
```

Listening to JTable Events with a TableColumnModelListener

One of the things you might want to do with a TableColumnModel is listen for TableColumnModelEvent objects with a TableColumnModelListener. The listener will be notified of any addition, removal, movement, or selection of columns, or changing of column margins, as shown by the listener interface definition. Do note that the different methods don't all receive TableColumnModelEvent objects when the event happens.

```
public interface TableColumnModelListener extends EventListener {
  public void columnAdded(TableColumnModelEvent e);
  public void columnMarginChanged(ChangeEvent e);
  public void columnMoved(TableColumnModelEvent e);
  public void columnRemoved(TableColumnModelEvent e);
  public void columnSelectionChanged(ListSelectionEvent e);
}
```

Because the listener definition identifies the event type, the TableColumnModelEvent definition only defines the range of columns affected by the change, as shown in Table 17-11.

PROPERTY NAME	DATA TYPE	ACCESS
fromIndex	int	read-only
toIndex	int	read-only

Table 17-11: TableColumnModelEvent properties

To see a demonstration of the TableColumnModelListener, you can attach a listener to one of your TableColumnModel objects:

```
TableColumnModel columnModel = table.getColumnModel();
columnModel.addColumnModelListener(...);
```

One such listener follows. It doesn't do much besides print a message. Nevertheless, you *can* use it to see when different events happen.

```
TableColumnModelListener tableColumnModelListener =
    new TableColumnModelListener() {
  public void columnAdded(TableColumnModelEvent e) {
    System.out.println("Added");
  }
  public void columnMarginChanged(ChangeEvent e) {
    System.out.println("Margin");
  }
  public void columnMoved(TableColumnModelEvent e) {
    System.out.println("Moved");
  }
  public void columnRemoved(TableColumnModelEvent e) {
    System.out.println("Removed");
  }
  public void columnSelectionChanged(ListSelectionEvent e) {
    System.out.println("Selected");
  }
};
```

Of course, you do have to create some code to elicit certain events. For instance, margins don't appear out of thin air. But you *can* add the same column multiple times to add more columns (or remove them). The following program tests out our new TableColumnModelListener.

```
import javax.swing.event.*;
import javax.swing.table.*;
import javax.swing.*;
import java.awt.*;

public class ColumnModelSample {
  public static void main(String args[]) {
    Object rows[][] = {
      {"one",   "ichi - \u4E00"},
      {"two",   "ni - \u4E8C"},
      {"three", "san - \u4E09"},
      {"four",  "shi - \u56DB"},
      {"five",  "go - \u4E94"},
      {"six",   "roco - \u516D"},
      {"seven", "shichi - \u4E03"},
      {"eight", "hachi - \u516B"},
      {"nine",  "kyu - \u4E5D"},
      {"ten",   "ju - \u5341"}
    };
```

```
        Object headers[] = {"English", "Japanese"};
        JFrame frame = new ExitableJFrame("Scrollless Table");
        JTable table = new JTable(rows, headers);

        TableColumnModelListener tableColumnModelListener =
            new TableColumnModelListener() {
          public void columnAdded(TableColumnModelEvent e) {
            System.out.println("Added");
          }
          public void columnMarginChanged(ChangeEvent e) {
            System.out.println("Margin");
          }
          public void columnMoved(TableColumnModelEvent e) {
            System.out.println("Moved");
          }
          public void columnRemoved(TableColumnModelEvent e) {
            System.out.println("Removed");
          }
          public void columnSelectionChanged(ListSelectionEvent e) {
            System.out.println("Selection Changed");
          }
        };

        TableColumnModel columnModel = table.getColumnModel();
        columnModel.addColumnModelListener(tableColumnModelListener);

        columnModel.setColumnMargin(12);

        TableColumn column = new TableColumn(1);
        columnModel.addColumn(column);

        frame.getContentPane().add(table, BorderLayout.CENTER);
        frame.setSize(300, 150);
        frame.setVisible(true);
      }
    }
```

Class TableColumn

The TableColumn class is another important class that lives behind the scenes. Swing tables consist of a group of columns which are made up of cells. Each of those columns is described by a TableColumn instance. Each instance of the TableColumn class stores the appropriate editor, renderer, name, and sizing information. TableColumn objects are then grouped together into a TableColumnModel to make up the current set of columns to be displayed by a JTable. One useful trick to remember is if you don't want a column to be displayed, remove its TableColumn from the TableColumnModel but leave it in the TableModel.

Creating a TableColumn

If you choose to create your TableColumn objects yourself, you can use any one of four constructors to create a TableColumn. They cascade by adding more constructor arguments. With no arguments, such as in the first constructor in the following list, you get an empty column with a default width (75 pixels), a default editor, and a default renderer. The modelIndex argument allows you to specify which column from the TableModel you'd like the TableColumn to display within the JTable. You can also specify a width, a renderer, or an editor if you don't like the defaults. You can also specify null for the renderer or editor if you like one default but not the other.

1. public TableColumn()
   ```
   TableColumn column = new TableColumn()
   ```

2. public TableColumn(int modelIndex)
   ```
   TableColumn column = new TableColumn(2)
   ```

> **TIP** *All column settings start at zero. Therefore, new TableColumn(2) uses column 3 from the TableModel.*

3. public TableColumn(int modelIndex, int width)
   ```
   TableColumn column = new TableColumn(2, 25)
   ```

4. public TableColumn(int modelIndex, int width, TableCellRenderer renderer, TableCellEditor editor)
   ```
   TableColumn column = new TableColumn(2, 25, aRenderer, aEditor)
   ```

TableColumn Properties

Table 17-12 lists the 11 properties of the TableColumn. These properties allow you to customize a column beyond the initial set of constructor arguments. Most of the time, everything is configured for you based on the TableModel. However, you can still customize individual columns through the TableColumn class.

PROPERTY NAME	DATA TYPE	ACCESS
cellEditor	TableCellEditor	read-write
cellRenderer	TableCellRenderer	read-write
headerRenderer	TableCellRenderer	read-write
headerValue	Object	read-write
identifier	Object	read-write
maxWidth	int	read-write
minWidth	int	read-write
modelIndex	int	read-write
preferredWidth	int	read-write
resizable	boolean	read-write
width	int	read-write

Table 17-12: TableColumn properties

NOTE   *If an identifier isn't specified, the headerValue setting is used instead.*

Icons in Column Headers

By default, the header renderer for a table displays text or HTML. Although you can get multiple lines of text and images with HTML, there may come a time when you want to display regular Icon objects within a header. To do this, you must change the header's renderer. The header renderer is just another TableCellRenderer.

So, if we were to create a renderer that treated the value data as a JLabel, instead of using the value to fill the JLabel or for that matter any JComponent, then the renderer would be a little more flexible for our needs. The following is one such renderer, which is used in the program that created Figure 17-13.

```
import java.awt.*;
import javax.swing.*;
import javax.swing.table.*;

public class JComponentTableCellRenderer implements TableCellRenderer {
  public Component getTableCellRendererComponent(JTable table, Object value,
```

```
                boolean isSelected, boolean hasFocus, int row, int column) {
        return (JComponent)value;
    }
}
```

Figure 17-13 shows how this renderer might appear with the DiamondIcon as the Icon. The source for the sample program follows.

```java
import javax.swing.*;
import javax.swing.border.*;
import javax.swing.table.*;
import java.awt.*;

public class LabelHeaderSample {
    public static void main(String args[]) {
        Object rows[][] = {
            {"one",   "ichi"},
            {"two",   "ni"},
            {"three", "san"},
            {"four",  "shi"},
            {"five",  "go"},
            {"six",   "roco"},
            {"seven", "shichi"},
            {"eight", "hachi"},
            {"nine",  "kyu"},
            {"ten",   "ju"}
        };
        String headers[] = {"English", "Japanese"};
        JFrame frame = new ExitableJFrame("Label Header");
        JTable table = new JTable(rows, headers);
        JScrollPane scrollPane = new JScrollPane(table);
```

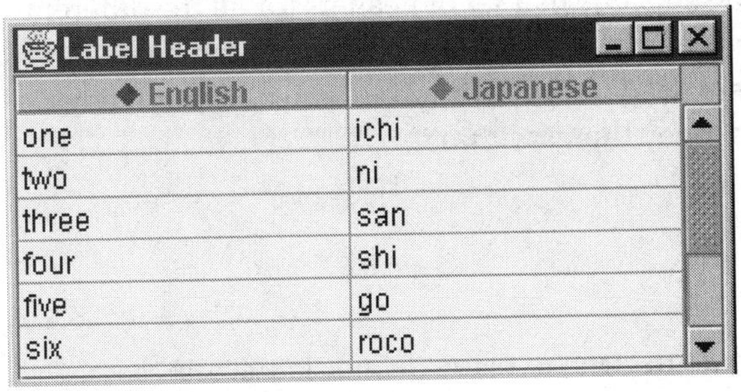

Figure 17-13: Icons in table headers

```
Icon redIcon = new DiamondIcon(Color.red);
Icon blueIcon = new DiamondIcon(Color.blue);

Border headerBorder = UIManager.getBorder("TableHeader.cellBorder");

JLabel blueLabel = new JLabel(headers[0], blueIcon, JLabel.CENTER);
blueLabel.setBorder(headerBorder);
JLabel redLabel = new JLabel(headers[1], redIcon, JLabel.CENTER);
redLabel.setBorder(headerBorder);

TableCellRenderer renderer = new JComponentTableCellRenderer();

TableColumnModel columnModel = table.getColumnModel();

TableColumn column0 = columnModel.getColumn(0);
TableColumn column1 = columnModel.getColumn(1);

column0.setHeaderRenderer(renderer);
column0.setHeaderValue(blueLabel);

column1.setHeaderRenderer(renderer);
column1.setHeaderValue(redLabel);

frame.getContentPane().add(scrollPane, BorderLayout.CENTER);
frame.setSize(300, 150);
frame.setVisible(true);
  }
}
```

Class JTableHeader

Each JTableHeader instance represents one of a set of headers for all the different columns. The set of JTableHeader objects is placed within the column header view of the JScrollPane. You rarely need to work with the JTableHeader directly. Nevertheless, you can configure many things within it.

Creating a JTableHeader

The JTableHeader has two constructors. One uses the default TableColumnModel, whereas the other is specified by the constructor.

1.  ```
    public JTableHeader()
    JComponent headerComponent = new JTableHeader()
    ```

2.  ```
    public JTableHeader(TableColumnModel columnModel)
    JComponent headerComponent = new JTableHeader(aColumnModel)
    ```

JTableHeader Properties

As Table 17-13 shows, JTableHeader has 11 different properties. These properties allow you to configure what the user can do with a particular column or how the column is shown. If your columns take an inordinate amount of time to draw, you might want to disable the updateTableInRealTime property (set to false). When true (the default setting), entire columns move around while the user drags a column header.

PROPERTY NAME	DATA TYPE	ACCESS
accessibleContext	AccessibleContext	read-only
columnModel	TableColumnModel	read-write
draggedColumn	TableColumn	read-write
draggedDistance	int	read-write
reorderingAllowed	boolean	read-write
resizingAllowed	boolean	read-write
resizingColumn	TableColumn	read-write
table	JTable	read-write
UI	TableHeaderUI	read-write
UIClassID	String	read-only
updateTableInRealTime	boolean	read-write

Table 17-13: JTableHeader properties

Using Tooltips

By default, if you set tooltip text for the table header, it's the same tooltip text for all columns headers. To specify a tooltip for a given column, you need to create or get the renderer, and then set the tooltip for the renderer. This is true for the individual cells, too.

Figure 17-14 shows how the results of this customization would appear. The source for the customization follows:

```
TableColumnModel columnModel = table.getColumnModel();
TableColumn englishColumn = columnModel.getColumn(0);
```

```
TableCellRenderer headerRenderer = englishColumn.getHeaderRenderer();
if (headerRenderer instanceof JComponent) {
  ((JComponent)headerRenderer).setToolTipText("Wave");
}
```

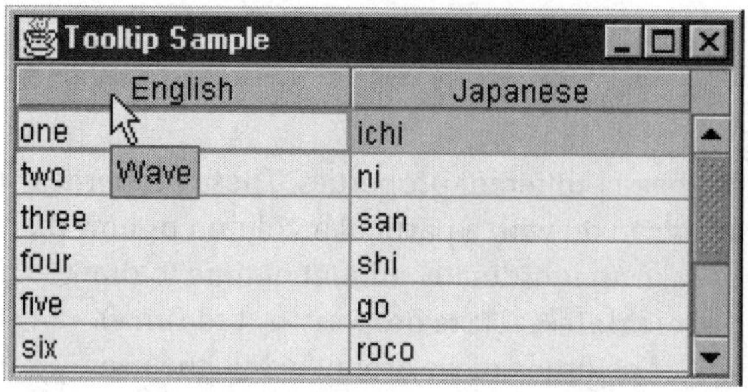

Figure 17-14: Header tooltips

Customizing JTableHeader Look and Feel

The available set of UIResource-related properties for a JTableHeader is shown in Table 17-14. The five settings control the color, font, and border for the header renderers.

PROPERTY STRING	OBJECT TYPE
TableHeader.background	Color
TableHeader.cellBorder	Border
TableHeader.font	Font
TableHeader.foreground	Color
TableHeaderUI	TableHeaderUI

Table 17-14: JTableHeader UIResource elements

NOTE *For an example of creating column headers spanning multiple columns, see the Java Programmer's Source Book at http://www.code-guru.com/java/Swing.*

Editing Table Cells

Editing JTable cells is nearly identical to editing JTree cells. In fact, the default table cell editor, DefaultCellEditor, implements both the TableCellEditor and TreeCellEditor interfaces, allowing you to use the same editor for both tables *and* trees.

Clicking on an editable cell will place the cell in edit mode. (The number of clicks depends on the type of editor.) In addition, the default editor for all cells is a JTextField. Although this works great for many data types, it's not always appropriate for many others. So, you should either not support editing of non-textual information or set up specialized editors for your JTable. With a JTable, you register an editor for a particular class type or column. Then, when the table runs across a cell of the appropriate type, the necessary editor is used. When no specialized editor is installed, the JTextField is used, even when it's inappropriate for the content!

Interface TableCellEditor/Class DefaultCellEditor

The TableCellEditor interface defines the single method necessary to get an editor cell for a JTable. The argument list for TableCellEditor is identical to the TableCellRenderer with the exception of the hasFocused argument. Because the cell is being edited, it's already known to have the input focus.

```
public interface TableCellEditor extends CellEditor {
  public Component getTableCellEditorComponent(JTable table, Object value,
boolean isSelected, int row, int column);
}
```

As described in Chapter 16, the DefaultCellEditor provides an implementation of the interface. It offers a JTextField as one editor, a JCheckBox for another, and a JComboBox for a third.

As Table 17-15 shows, in most cases the default editor is the JTextField. The editor offers the text representation of the data value for the initial editing value. You can then edit the contents. In most cases when you try to "save" the update, an Exception will be thrown as the JTextField tries to convert from a String back to the class derived from the original cell.

CLASS	EDITOR	INFORMATION
Boolean	JCheckBox	centered
Object	JTextField	left-aligned

Table 17-15: Default JTable editors

For instance, if you have a column of a `Color`, your `TableCellRenderer` can fill the cell or display a diamond icon. If you try to support editing the cell without installing a custom editor, you'll be prompted to fill in red, green, and blue (RGB) settings. However, the value can't be saved and you might see a series of exception error messages on your screen because the editor doesn't automatically convert the RGB value back into a `Color` value. The appearance of error messages depends on the data type of the data model. Figure 17-15 shows how the screen might appear after your attempting to "edit" several of the cells in the "Color" column. Basically, none of the edit operations succeeded.

Creating a Simple Cell Editor

To make life easier, you can provide a fixed set of color choices to the user. Then when a color is picked, you have the appropriate `Color` value to return to the table model. The `DefaultCellEditor` offers a `JComboBox` for just this situation in which each choice is the color. After configuring the `ListCellRenderer` for the `JComboBox` to display colors properly, you have a `TableCellEditor` for picking colors. Figure 17-16 shows how this might appear.

> **TIP** *Any time you can predefine all the choices, you can use the JComboBox as your editor through DefaultCellEditor.*

The following class represents the `TableCellRenderer` for the `Color` column of the previous example and the `ListCellRenderer` for the `JComboBox` `TableCellEditor`. Because of the many similarities of the two renderer components, their definitions are combined into one class.

```
import java.awt.*;
import javax.swing.*;
import javax.swing.table.*;
```

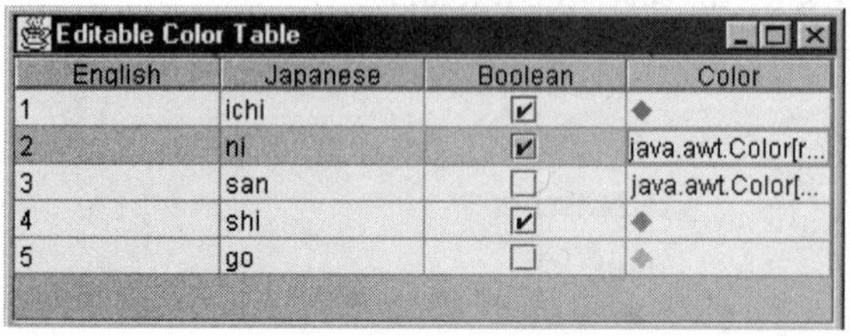

Figure 17-15: Faulty color editor

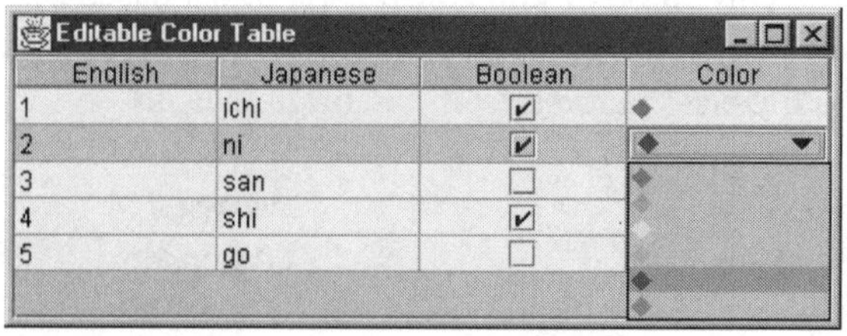

Figure 17-16: JComboBox color editor

```
public class ComboTableCellRenderer implements ListCellRenderer,
TableCellRenderer {
  DefaultListCellRenderer listRenderer = new DefaultListCellRenderer();
  DefaultTableCellRenderer tableRenderer = new DefaultTableCellRenderer();

  private void configureRenderer(JLabel renderer, Object value) {
    if ((value != null) && (value instanceof Color)) {
      renderer.setIcon(new DiamondIcon((Color)value));
      renderer.setText("");
    } else {
      renderer.setIcon(null);
      renderer.setText((String)value);
    }
  }

  public Component getListCellRendererComponent(JList list, Object value,
      int index, boolean isSelected, boolean cellHasFocus) {
    listRenderer =
(DefaultListCellRenderer)listRenderer.getListCellRendererComponent(
      list, value, index, isSelected, cellHasFocus);
    configureRenderer(listRenderer, value);
    return listRenderer;
  }

  public Component getTableCellRendererComponent(JTable table, Object value,
      boolean isSelected, boolean hasFocus, int row, int column) {
    tableRenderer =
(DefaultTableCellRenderer)tableRenderer.getTableCellRendererComponent(
      table, value, isSelected, hasFocus, row, column);
    configureRenderer(tableRenderer, value);
    return tableRenderer;
  }
}
```

To demonstrate the use of our new combined renderer and show a simple table cell editor, the following program creates a data model in which one of the columns is a Color. After installing the renderer twice and setting up the table cell editor, the table can be shown and the Color column can be edited.

```
import javax.swing.*;
import javax.swing.table.*;
import java.awt.*;
```

```
public class EditableColorColumn {

  public static void main(String args[]) {

    Color choices[] = {Color.red, Color.orange, Color.yellow, Color.green,
      Color.blue, Color.magenta};
    ComboTableCellRenderer renderer = new ComboTableCellRenderer();
    JComboBox comboBox = new JComboBox(choices);
    comboBox.setRenderer(renderer);
    TableCellEditor editor = new DefaultCellEditor(comboBox);

    JFrame frame = new ExitableJFrame("Editable Color Table");
    TableModel model = new ColorTableModel();
    JTable table = new JTable(model);

    TableColumn column = table.getColumnModel().getColumn(3);
    column.setCellRenderer(renderer);
    column.setCellEditor(editor);

    JScrollPane scrollPane = new JScrollPane(table);
    frame.getContentPane().add(scrollPane, BorderLayout.CENTER);
    frame.setSize(400, 150);
    frame.setVisible(true);
  }
}
```

The following is the table model used for this example and the next:

```
import java.awt.*;
import javax.swing.table.*;

public class ColorTableModel extends AbstractTableModel {

  Object rowData[][] = {
    {"1", "ichi", Boolean.TRUE, Color.red},
    {"2", "ni", Boolean.TRUE, Color.blue},
    {"3", "san", Boolean.FALSE, Color.green},
    {"4", "shi", Boolean.TRUE, Color.magenta},
    {"5", "go", Boolean.FALSE, Color.pink},
  };
  String columnNames[] = {"English", "Japanese", "Boolean", "Color"};
  public int getColumnCount() {
    return columnNames.length;
```

```
  }
  public String getColumnName(int column) {
    return columnNames[column];
  }
  public int getRowCount() {
    return rowData.length;
  }
  public Object getValueAt(int row, int column) {
    return rowData[row][column];
  }
  public Class getColumnClass(int column) {
    return (getValueAt(0, column).getClass());
  }
  public void setValueAt(Object value, int row, int column) {
    rowData[row][column]=value;
  }
  public boolean isCellEditable(int row, int column) {
    return (column != 0);
  }
}
```

Creating a Complex Cell Editor

Although the previous example demonstrates how to provide a fixed set of choices to the user in a combo box TableCellEditor, offering the JColorChooser as an option (at least in the case of colors) seems to be a better choice. When defining your own TableCellEditor, you must implement the single TableCellEditor method to get the appropriate component. You must also implement the seven methods of the CellEditor because they both manage and notify a list of CellEditorListener objects as well as control when a cell is editable.

Implementing the CellEditor interface involves many boilerplate implementations, such as one for maintaining and notifying the CellEditorListener list. Only the getCellEditorValue() method from the CellEditor methods requires customization for the editor. The JColorChooser pops up when the button that's used as the editor component is pressed.

```
import java.awt.*;
import java.util.*;
import java.awt.event.*;
import javax.swing.*;
import javax.swing.event.*;
import javax.swing.table.*;
```

```java
public class ColorChooserEditor extends JButton implements TableCellEditor {

  private static final int CLICK_START_COUNT = 2;

  protected EventListenerList listenerList = new EventListenerList();
  transient protected ChangeEvent changeEvent = null;

  Color savedColor;

  public ColorChooserEditor() {
    ActionListener actionListener = new ActionListener() {
      public void actionPerformed (ActionEvent actionEvent) {
        Color color = JColorChooser.showDialog(
          ColorChooserEditor.this, "Color Chooser", savedColor);
          ColorChooserEditor.this.changeColor(color);
      }
    };
    addActionListener(actionListener);
  }

  public void addCellEditorListener(CellEditorListener cellEditorListener) {
    listenerList.add(CellEditorListener.class, cellEditorListener);
  }
  public void removeCellEditorListener(CellEditorListener cellEditorListener) {
    listenerList.remove(CellEditorListener.class, cellEditorListener);
  }

  public void cancelCellEditing() {
    Object[] listeners = listenerList.getListenerList();
    for (int i=listeners.length-2; i>=0; i-=2) {
      if (listeners[i]==CellEditorListener.class) {
        if (changeEvent == null)
          changeEvent = new ChangeEvent(this);
        ((CellEditorListener)listeners[i+1]).editingCanceled(changeEvent);
      }
    }
  }

  public Object getCellEditorValue() {
    return savedColor;
  }

  public boolean isCellEditable(EventObject eventObject) {
```

```
    boolean editable = false;
    if (eventObject instanceof MouseEvent) {
      MouseEvent mouseEvent = (MouseEvent)eventObject;
      if (mouseEvent.getClickCount() >= CLICK_START_COUNT) {
        requestFocus();
        editable = true;
      }
    }
    return editable;
  }

  public boolean shouldSelectCell(EventObject eventObject) {
    boolean editable = false;
    if (isCellEditable(eventObject)) {
      MouseEvent mouseEvent = (MouseEvent)eventObject;
      if ((mouseEvent == null) || (mouseEvent.getClickCount() >=
CLICK_START_COUNT)) {
        requestFocus();
        editable = true;
      }
    }
    return editable;
  }

  public boolean stopCellEditing() {
    Object[] listeners = listenerList.getListenerList();
    for (int i=listeners.length-2; i>=0; i-=2) {
      if (listeners[i]==CellEditorListener.class) {
        if (changeEvent == null)
          changeEvent = new ChangeEvent(this);
        ((CellEditorListener)listeners[i+1]).editingStopped(changeEvent);
      }
    }
    return true;
  }

  private void changeColor(Color color) {
    if (color != null) {
      savedColor = color;
      setIcon(new DiamondIcon(color));
    }
  }
```

```
      public Component getTableCellEditorComponent (JTable table, Object value,
          boolean isSelected, int row, int column) {
        changeColor((Color)value);
        return this;
      }
    }
```

Figure 17-17 shows the `ColorChooserEditor` in action, with the associated table in the background.

A sample program using our new `ColorChooserEditor` follows. The example reuses the earlier `ColorTableModel` data model. Setting up the `ColorChooserEditor` simply involves setting the `TableCellEditor` for the appropriate column.

```
import java.awt.*;
import javax.swing.*;
import javax.swing.table.*;

public class ChooserTableSample {

  public static void main(String args[]) {

    JFrame frame = new ExitableJFrame("Editable Color Table");
    TableModel model = new ColorTableModel();
    JTable table = new JTable(model);
```

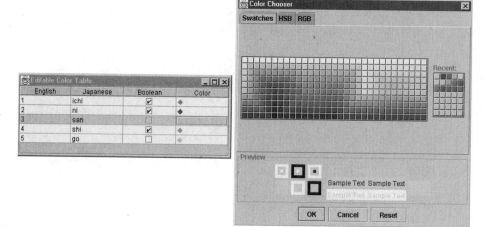

Figure 17-17: Pop-up color editor

```
TableColumn column = table.getColumnModel().getColumn(3);

ComboTableCellRenderer renderer = new ComboTableCellRenderer();
column.setCellRenderer(renderer);

TableCellEditor editor = new ColorChooserEditor();
column.setCellEditor(editor);

JScrollPane scrollPane = new JScrollPane(table);
frame.getContentPane().add(scrollPane, BorderLayout.CENTER);
frame.setSize(400, 150);
frame.setVisible(true);
    }
}
```

Summary

In this chapter, we explored the inner depths of the JTable component. We looked at customizing the TableModel, TableColumnModel, and ListSelectionModel for the JTable. We delved into both the abstract and concrete implementations of the different table models. In addition, we examined the inner elements of the various table models, such as the TableColumn and JTableHeader classes. We also looked into how to customize the display and editing of the JTable cells by providing a custom TableCellRenderer and TableCellEditor.

In the Chapter 18, we'll explore the pluggable look and feel architecture of the JFC/Swing component set.

CHAPTER 18

Understanding the Pluggable Look and Feel Architecture

IN CHAPTER 17, WE EXAMINED SWING'S `javax.swing.table` package and the JTable component. In this chapter, we'll take an in-depth look at the pluggable look and feel (PLAF) architecture that's available when you're working with the Swing component library.

All aspects of the Swing components are Java-based. Therefore, no native source code exists, such as there is with the AWT component set. If you don't like certain things the way they are, you can change them, and you often have many ways to do so.

The abstract `LookAndFeel` class is the root class for a specific look and feel. Each one of the installable look and feel classes, as they're described by the `UIManager.LookAndFeelInfo` class, must be a subclass of the `LookAndFeel` class. The `LookAndFeel` subclass describes the default appearance of Swing components for that look and feel.

The set of currently installed look and feel classes is provided by the `UIManager` class, which also manages the default display properties of all the components for a specific `LookAndFeel`. These display properties are managed within a special `UIDefaults` hash table. The display properties are either tagged with the empty `UIResource` interface or are UI delegates and therefore a subclass of the `ComponentUI` class. These properties can be stored as either `UIDefaults.LazyValue` objects or `UIDefaults.ActiveValue` objects, depending on their usage. Figure 18-1 helps you visualize the relationships among all these classes.

Class LookAndFeel

Implementations of the abstract `LookAndFeel` class describe how each of the Swing components will appear and how the user will interact with them. Each component's appearance is controlled by a UI delegate, which serves as both the view and the controller in the MVC architecture. Each of the predefined look and feel classes is contained within its own package, along with its associated UI delegate

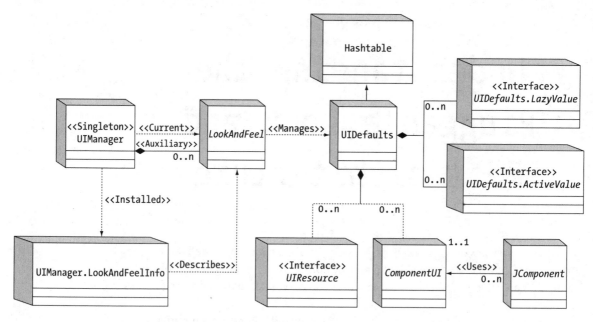

Figure 18-1: Pluggable look and feel key class diagram

classes. When configuring the current look and feel, you can use one of the pre-defined look and feel classes, or you can create your own. When you create your own look and feel, you can build on an existing look and feel, such as the BasicLookAndFeel class and its UI delegates, instead of creating all the UI delegates from scratch. Figure 18-2 shows the class hierarchy of the predefined look and feel classes.

Each of the look and feel classes has six properties, as shown in Table 18-1. These properties are all read-only and mostly describe the look and feel. The defaults property is slightly different, although. Once you get its UIDefaults value, you can then modify its state directly through its own methods. In addition, the UIDefaults for a LookAndFeel can be directly accessed and modified through the UIManager class.

PROPERTY NAME	DATA TYPE	ACCESS
defaults	UIDefaults	read-only
description	String	read-only
ID	String	read-only
name	String	read-only
nativeLookAndFeel	boolean	read-only
supportedLookAndFeel	boolean	read-only

Table 18-1: LookAndFeel properties

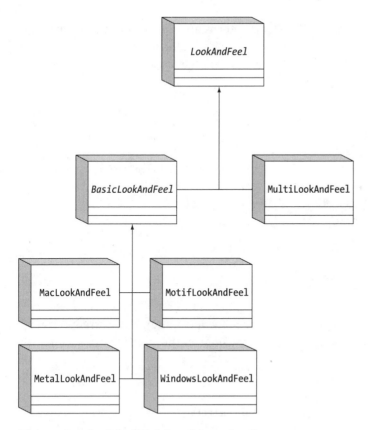

Figure 18-2: LookAndFeel class hierarchy diagram

The nativeLookAndFeel property enables you to determine if a particular look and feel implementation is the native look and feel for the user's operating system. For instance, the WindowsLookAndFeel is native to any system running one of the Microsoft Windows operating systems. The supportedLookAndFeel property tells you if a particular look and feel implementation can be used. With the WindowsLookAndFeel implementation, this particular look and feel class is only supported if the current operating system is Microsoft Windows. The MacLookAndFeel implementation is supported only on MacOS computers. The MotifLookAndFeel is another native look and feel class. It isn't locked to a particular operating system, nor is the MetalLookAndFeel.

Listing the Installed Look and Feel Classes

To discover which look and feel classes are installed in your current environment, ask the UIManager. The UIManager has a UIManager.LookAndFeelInfo[]

getInstalledLookAndFeels() method that returns an array of objects providing the textual name (public String getName()) and class name (public String getClassName()) for all the installed look and feel classes.

```
import javax.swing.*;

public class ListPlafs {
  public static void main (String args[]) {
    UIManager.LookAndFeelInfo plaf[] = UIManager.getInstalledLookAndFeels();
    for (int i=0, n=plaf.length; i<n; i++) {
      System.out.println("Name: " + plaf[i].getName());
      System.out.println("  Class name: " + plaf[i].getClassName());
    }
    System.exit(0);
  }
}
```

Running the program might generate the following output. Your current system configuration and/or changes to future versions of the Swing libraries could alter this result somewhat.

```
Name: Metal
  Class name: javax.swing.plaf.metal.MetalLookAndFeel
Name: CDE/Motif
  Class name: com.sun.java.swing.plaf.motif.MotifLookAndFeel
Name: Windows
  Class name: com.sun.java.swing.plaf.windows.WindowsLookAndFeel
```

Changing the Current Look and Feel

Once you know which look and feel classes are available on your system, you can have your program use any one of them. The UIManager has two overloaded setLookAndFeel() methods for changing the installed look and feel class:

- public static void setLookAndFeel(LookAndFeel newValue) throws UnsupportedLookAndFeelException

- public static void setLookAndFeel(String className) throws ClassNotFoundException, InstantiationException, IllegalAccessException, UnsupportedLookAndFeelException

Although the first version might seem to be the more logical choice, the second one is the more frequently used version. When you ask for the installed look and feel classes with `UIManager.getInstalledLookAndFeels()`, you get back the class names as strings, and not instances, of the objects. Because of the exceptions that can occur when changing the look and feel, you need to place the `setLookAndFeel()` call within a `try-catch` block. If you're changing the look and feel for an already created window, you need to tell the component to update its appearance with a call to the `public static void updateComponentTreeUI(Component rootComponent)` method of `SwingUtilities`. If the component hasn't been created yet, this isn't necessary.

The following source fragment demonstrates changing a look and feel:

```
try {
  UIManager.setLookAndFeel(finalLafClassName);
  SwingUtilities.updateComponentTreeUI(frame);
} catch (Exception exception) {
  JOptionPane.showMessageDialog (
    frame, "Can't change look and feel",
    "Invalid PLAF",
    JOptionPane.ERROR_MESSAGE);
}
```

Figure 18-3 illustrates the results of a demonstration program that can change the look and feel at runtime through either a `JComboBox` or `JButton` component. Frequently, you won't want to allow a user to change the look and feel; you may just want to set the look and feel at startup time.

Metal

Motif

Figure 18-3: Before and after changing the look and feel

The following is the complete example source code used to generate Figure 18-3.

```java
import java.awt.*;
import java.awt.event.*;
import javax.swing.*;
import javax.swing.plaf.*;

public class ChangeLook {

  public static void main (String args[]) {

    final JFrame frame = new ExitableJFrame("Change Look");

    ActionListener actionListener = new ActionListener() {
      public void actionPerformed(ActionEvent actionEvent) {
        Object source = actionEvent.getSource();
        String lafClassName = null;
        if (source instanceof JComboBox) {
          JComboBox comboBox = (JComboBox)source;
          lafClassName = (String)comboBox.getSelectedItem();
        } else if (source instanceof JButton) {
          lafClassName = actionEvent.getActionCommand();
        }
        if (lafClassName != null) {
          final String finalLafClassName = lafClassName;
          Runnable runnable = new Runnable() {
            public void run() {
              try {
                UIManager.setLookAndFeel(finalLafClassName);
                SwingUtilities.updateComponentTreeUI(frame);
              } catch (Exception exception) {
                JOptionPane.showMessageDialog (
                  frame, "Can't change look and feel",
                  "Invalid PLAF",
                  JOptionPane.ERROR_MESSAGE);
              }
            }
          };
          SwingUtilities.invokeLater(runnable);
        }
      }
    };

    UIManager.LookAndFeelInfo looks[] = UIManager.getInstalledLookAndFeels();
```

```
DefaultComboBoxModel model = new DefaultComboBoxModel();
JComboBox comboBox = new JComboBox(model);

JPanel panel = new JPanel();

for (int i=0, n=looks.length; i<n; i++) {
  JButton button = new JButton(looks[i].getName());
  model.addElement(looks[i].getClassName());
  button.setActionCommand(looks[i].getClassName());
  button.addActionListener(actionListener);
  panel.add(button);
}

comboBox.addActionListener(actionListener);

Container contentPane = frame.getContentPane();
contentPane.add(comboBox, BorderLayout.NORTH);
contentPane.add(panel, BorderLayout.SOUTH);
frame.setSize(350, 150);
frame.setVisible(true);
  }
}
```

> **NOTE** *Notice that the actual look and feel change is made in a call to SwingUtilities.invokeLater(). This is necessary because the handling of the current event must finish before you can change the look and feel.*

Besides programmatically changing the current look and feel, you can start up a program from the command line with a new look and feel. Just set the swing.defaultlaf system property to the look and feel class name. For instance, the following startup line would start the ChangeLook program, making the Motif look and feel the initial look and feel.

```
java -Dswing.defaultlaf=com.sun.java.swing.plaf.motif.MotifLookAndFeel ChangeLook
```

If you want a different default look and feel every time a program starts up, you can create a file, swing.properties, under the Java runtime directory (jre by default) with the appropriate setting. The swing.properties file needs to be in the lib directory of the Java runtime directory (jre/lib). For instance, the following line would cause the initial look and feel to be Motif all the time, unless programmatically changed or changed from the command line.

```
swing.defaultlaf=com.sun.java.swing.plaf.motif.MotifLookAndFeel
```

In addition to the `swing.defaultlaf` setting, the `swing.properties` file supports several other entries, as listed in Table 18-2. Each property allows you to override the default settings for the predefined look and feel setup. The auxiliary and multiplexing look and feels support accessibility, among other things. They will be discussed later in this chapter in the section "Using an Auxiliary Look and Feel."

PROPERTY NAME	DEFAULT VALUE WHEN UNSET
swing.defaultlaf	javax.swing.plaf.metal.MetalLookAndFeel
swing.auxiliarylaf	none
swing.plaf.multiplexinglaf	javax.swing.plaf.multi.MultiLookAndFeel
swing.installedlafs	Macintosh, Metal, Motif, Windows
swing.installedlafs.*.name	n/a
swing.installedlafs.*.class	n/a

Table 18-2: Swing properties file

> **TIP** *The* `swing.installedlafs` *and* `swing.auxiliarylaf` *property settings are comma-separated lists of installed look and feel classes.*

Customizing the Current Look and Feel

In Chapter 3, I discussed the Model-View-Controller architecture as well as how the Swing components combine the view and the controller into a UI delegate. Now, we'll delve into the UI delegate for the Swing components. Basically, if you don't like how a Swing component looks, you tell the `UIManager` to change it — and it will never again look the way it did.

Class UIManager

Whenever you need to create a Swing component, the `UIManager` class acts as a proxy to get information about the currently installed look and feel. That way, if you want to install a new look and feel, or change an existing one, you don't have to tell the Swing components directly — only the `UIManager`.

Each discussion of components in earlier chapters has been accompanied by a table of all the settings that can be changed through the UIManager. In addition, Appendix A of this book provides a combined alphabetical listing of all available settings. Once you know the property string for the setting you want to change, you call the public Object UIManager.put(Object key, Object value) method, which changes the property setting and returns the previous setting (if one existed). For instance, the following line changes the background to red for JButton components. After you put a new setting into the UIManager class lookup table, any components created in the future will use the new value, red.

```
UIManager.put("Button.background", Color.red);
```

Once you place new settings into the lookup table for the UIManager, the new settings will be used when you create a new Swing component. Old components aren't automatically updated; you must call their public void updateUI() method if you want them to be individually updated (or call updateComponentTreeUI() to update a whole window of components). If you're creating your own components, or are just curious about the current setting for one of the different component properties, you can ask the UIManager with one of the methods listed in Table 18-3.

METHOD NAME	RETURN TYPE
getObject(Object key)	Object
getBorder(Object key)	Border
getColor(Object key)	Color
getDimension(Object key)	Dimension
getFont(Object key)	Font
getIcon(Object key)	Icon
getInsets(Object key)	Insets
getInt(Object key)	int
getString(Object key)	String
getUI(JComponent component)	ComponentUI

Table 18-3: UIManager UIDefaults getter methods

In addition to the defaults property, which is used when you call the different put() and get() methods, the UIManager has seven class-level properties. These are listed in Table 18-4, one of which is listed with two different setter methods.

PROPERTY NAME	DATA TYPE	ACCESS
auxiliaryLookAndFeels	LookAndFeel[ ]	read-only
crossPlatformLookAnd FeelClassName	String	read-only
defaults	UIDefaults	read-only
installedLookAndFeels	UIManager.LookAndFeelInfo[ ]	read-write
lookAndFeel	LookAndFeel	read-write
lookAndFeel	String	write-only
lookAndFeelDefaults	UIDefaults	read-only
systemLookAndFeelClassName	String	read-only

Table 18-4: UIManager class properties

The systemLookAndFeelClassName property allows you to determine what the specific look and feel class name is for the user's operating system. The crossPlatformLookAndFeelClassName property enables you to find out what class name, by default, represents the cross-platform look and feel, javax.swing.plaf.metal.MetalLookAndFeel. Initially, the lookAndFeelDefaults property and the defaults property are equivalent. When you want to make changes to the look and feel, you make them in the defaults property. That way, the look and feel of a predefined look and feel doesn't change.

Class UIManager.LookAndFeelInfo

When you ask the UIManager for the list of installed look and feel classes, you're returned an array of UIManager.LookAndFeelInfo objects. From this array, you can find out the descriptive name of the look and feel (from the name property of the LookAndFeel implementation), as well as the class name for the implementation. As Table 18-5 shows, the two settings are read-only.

PROPERTY NAME	DATA TYPE	ACCESS
className	String	read-only
name	String	read-only

Table 18-5: UIManager.LookAndFeelInfo properties

Class UIDefaults

The LookAndFeel classes and the UIManager use a special UIDefaults hash table to manage the look-and-feel–dependent properties for the Swing components. The special behavior is that whenever a new setting is placed in the hash table with put(), a PropertyChangeEvent is generated and any registered PropertyChangeListener objects are notified. Many of the BasicLookAndFeel classes automatically register the UI delegate to be interested in property change events at the appropriate times.

If you need to change a number of properties at once, you can use the public void putDefaults(Object keyValueList[]) method, which causes only one notification event. With putDefaults(), the key-value entries alternate in a single-dimension array to cause buttons to have a default background color of pink and a foreground color of magenta:

```
Object newSettings[] = {"Button.background", Color.pink,
                        "Button.foreground", Color.magenta};
UIDefaults defaults = UIManager.getDefaults();
defaults.putDefaults(newSettings);
```

Because UIDefaults is a Hashtable subclass, you can find out all the installed settings by using an Enumeration to loop through all the keys or values. To simplify things a little, Figure 18-4 shows a program listing the properties sorted within a JTable.

Property String	Value
Button.background	javax.swing.plaf.ColorUIResour...
Button.border	javax.swing.plaf.BorderUIReso...
Button.disabledText	javax.swing.plaf.ColorUIResour...
Button.focus	javax.swing.plaf.ColorUIResour...
Button.font	javax.swing.plaf.FontUIResourc...
Button.foreground	javax.swing.plaf.ColorUIResour...
Button.margin	javax.swing.plaf.InsetsUIResou...
Button.select	javax.swing.plaf.ColorUIResour...
Button.textIconGap	4
Button.textShiftOffset	0
ButtonUI	javax.swing.plaf.metal.MetalButt...
CheckBox.background	javax.swing.plaf.ColorUIResour...
CheckBox.border	javax.swing.plaf.BorderUIReso...
CheckBox.disabledText	javax.swing.plaf.ColorUIResour...
CheckBox.focus	javax.swing.plaf.ColorUIResour...
CheckBox.font	javax.swing.plaf.FontUIResourc...
CheckBox.foreground	javax.swing.plaf.ColorUIResour...
CheckBox.icon	javax.swing.plaf.metal.MetalCh...
CheckBox.margin	javax.swing.plaf.InsetsUIResou...

Figure 18-4: Sample property lister display

NOTE   *Feel free to change the* UIDefaults *property lister program to support modification of property values.*

The source for the property listing program follows. It reuses several of the table sorting classes from Chapter 17.

```java
import javax.swing.*;
import javax.swing.table.*;
import java.awt.*;
import java.awt.event.*;
import java.util.*;

public class ListProperties {
  static class CustomTableModel extends AbstractTableModel {
    Vector keys = new Vector();
    Vector values = new Vector();
    private static final String columnNames[] = {"Property String", "Value"};

    public int getColumnCount() {
      return columnNames.length;
    }

    public String getColumnName(int column) {
      return columnNames[column];
    }

    public int getRowCount() {
      return keys.size();
    }

    public Object getValueAt(int row, int column) {
      Object returnValue = null;
      if (column == 0) {
        returnValue = keys.elementAt(row);
      } else if (column == 1) {
        returnValue = values.elementAt(row);

      }
      return returnValue;
    }
```

```java
  public synchronized void uiDefaultsUpdate(UIDefaults defaults) {
    Enumeration newKeys = defaults.keys();
    keys.removeAllElements();
    while (newKeys.hasMoreElements()) {
      keys.addElement(newKeys.nextElement());
    }

    Enumeration newValues = defaults.elements();
    values.removeAllElements();
    while (newValues.hasMoreElements()) {
      values.addElement(newValues.nextElement());
    }

    fireTableDataChanged();
  }
}

public static void main(String args[]) {
  final JFrame frame = new ExitableJFrame("List Properties");

  final CustomTableModel model = new CustomTableModel();
  model.uiDefaultsUpdate(UIManager.getDefaults());
  TableSorter sorter = new TableSorter(model);

  JTable table = new JTable(sorter);
  TableHeaderSorter.install(sorter, table);

  table.setAutoResizeMode(JTable.AUTO_RESIZE_ALL_COLUMNS);

  UIManager.LookAndFeelInfo looks[] = UIManager.getInstalledLookAndFeels();

  ActionListener actionListener = new ActionListener() {
    public void actionPerformed(ActionEvent actionEvent) {
      final String lafClassName = actionEvent.getActionCommand();
      Runnable runnable = new Runnable() {
        public void run() {
          try {
            UIManager.setLookAndFeel(lafClassName);
            SwingUtilities.updateComponentTreeUI(frame);
            model.uiDefaultUpdate(UIManager.getDefaults());
          } catch (Exception exception) {
            JOptionPane.showMessageDialog (
              frame, "Can't change look and feel",
              "Invalid PLAF",
```

```
            JOptionPane.ERROR_MESSAGE);
        }
      }
    };
    SwingUtilities.invokeLater(runnable);
  }
};

JToolBar toolbar = new JToolBar();
for (int i=0, n=looks.length; i<n; i++) {
  JButton button = new JButton(looks[i].getName());
  button.setActionCommand(looks[i].getClassName());
  button.addActionListener(actionListener);
  toolbar.add(button);
}

Container content = frame.getContentPane();
content.add(toolbar, BorderLayout.NORTH);
JScrollPane scrollPane = new JScrollPane(table);
content.add(scrollPane, BorderLayout.CENTER);
frame.setSize(400, 400);
frame.setVisible(true);
  }
}
```

> **TIP** *To reset a property to the default for the currently installed look and feel, set it to null. This will cause the component to get the original default from the look and feel.*

Interface UIResource

Every UIDefaults setting for the predefined look and feel classes uses a special marker interface, UIResource, that lets the UI delegate determine if a default value has been overridden. If you've changed a specific setting to a new value (for example, the "Button.background" setting to Color.pink), then the UIManager won't replace this setting when the installed look and feel changes. This is also true of a call to setBackground(Color.pink). Only when the value for a specific property implements the UIResource interface will the setting change when the look and feel changes.

The javax.swing.plaf package contains many classes that implement the UIResource interface. For example, the ColorUIResource class treats Color objects as UIResource elements. The following list contains all the predefined UIResource components available for customizing the installed look and feel.

- DefaultListCellRenderer.UIResource — DefaultListCellRenderer

- ScrollPaneLayout.UIResource — ScrollPaneLayout

- BorderUIResource.BorderUIResource.BevelBorderUIResource
  BorderUIResource.CompoundBorderUIResource
  BorderUIResource.EmptyBorderUIResource
  BorderUIResource.EtchedBorderUIResource
  BorderUIResource.LineBorderUIResource
  BorderUIResource.MatteBorderUIResource
  BorderUIResource.TitledBorderUIResource — Border

- ColorUIResource — Color

- DimensionUIResource — Dimension

- FontUIResource — Font

- IconUIResource — Icon

- InsetsUIResource — Insets

- DefaultTableCellRenderer.UIResource — DefaultTableCellRenderer

The following code demonstrates the use of the ColorUIResource class to set the button background to a value that *will* change when the installed look and feel changes:

```
Color background = new ColorUIResource(Color.pink);
UIManager.put("Button.background", background);
```

> **TIP** *Use of the specific UIResource implementation classes tends to be limited to those times when you're creating a custom look and feel.*

Class *UIDefaults.ActiveValue/UIDefault.LazyValue*

Besides implementing the UIResource interface, elements in the UIDefaults lookup table can be "lazy" or "active" if they implement one of the inner classes of UIDefaults: LazyValue or ActiveValue. Although a UIResource such as Color or Dimension isn't very resource intensive, a resource such as an Icon object is. When a Color or Dimension is placed in the UIDefaults table, the Color or Dimension is created and placed in the table. Whereas, with an Icon, and especially an ImageIcon, you don't want to create or load the icon class file until it's needed. For instance, you don't want to load the image file when an ImageIcon is loaded into the UIDefaults table. On the other hand, with something like a ListCellRenderer, you need to create a separate renderer for every JList component. Because you don't know how many renderers you'll need or which renderer will be installed, you can defer creation to a later time and get a unique version of the current renderer whenever you ask for one.

Now we'll look at the public Object makeIcon(Class baseClass, String imageFile) method of LookAndFeel. In order to handle the late loading of icon image files, the LookAndFeel class can automatically create a LazyValue class for loading an Icon. Because the image file won't be loaded until later, we need to provide the icon loader with the location of the icon image file (baseClass) and the file name (imageFile).

```
Object iconObject = LookAndFeel.makeIcon(this.getClass(), "World.gif");
UIManager.put("Tree.leafIcon", iconObject);
```

Next let's look at the UIDefaults.LazyValue definition and create a lazy version of the DiamondIcon.

```
public interface UIDefaults.LazyValue {
  public Object createValue(UIDefaults table);
}
```

In classes that implement the LazyValue interface, their constructors need to save any information that will be passed along to the real constructor, when the real constructor is asked, through the createValue() interface method. For the lazy diamond icon implementation that's about to be created, that state information consists of the color, selected state, and dimensions. Notice that in the following class definition, the LazyDiamondIcon class doesn't implement the Icon interface itself.

```
import java.awt.*;
import javax.swing.*;

public class LazyDiamondIcon implements UIDefaults.LazyValue {
```

```
    Color color;
    boolean selected;
    int width;
    int height;

    public LazyDiamondIcon(Color color, boolean selected, int width, int height) {
      this.color = color;
      this.selected = selected;
      this.width = width;
      this.height = height;
    }

    public Object createValue(UIDefaults defaults) {
      Icon icon = new DiamondIcon(color, selected, width, height);
      return icon;
    }
  }
}
```

To test the lazy diamond icon, you can associate an instance to the "Tree.openIcon" setting. Together with the previous change of the "Tree.leafIcon" setting to the World.gif icon, and using the default tree data model, the tree would look like Figure 18-5.

```
Object lazyDiamond = new LazyDiamondIcon(Color.green, true, 15, 15);
UIManager.put("Tree.openIcon", lazyDiamond);
```

The source code follows for the example that generated Figure 18-5 by using the two lazy values.

```
import java.awt.*;
import java.awt.event.*;
import javax.swing.*;
import javax.swing.plaf.*;

public class LazySample {

  public static void main (String args[]) {

    JFrame frame = new ExitableJFrame("Lazy Example");

    Object iconObject = LookAndFeel.makeIcon(LazySample.class, "World.gif");
    UIManager.put("Tree.leafIcon", iconObject);
```

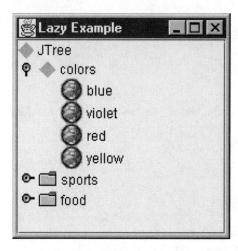

Figure 18-5: A tree created with "lazy" values

```
Object lazyDiamond = new LazyDiamondIcon(Color.green, true, 15, 15);
UIManager.put("Tree.openIcon", lazyDiamond);

JTree tree = new JTree();
JScrollPane scrollPane = new JScrollPane(tree);

Container contentPane = frame.getContentPane();
contentPane.add(scrollPane, BorderLayout.CENTER);
frame.setSize(200, 200);
frame.setVisible(true);
  }
}
```

NOTE *The DiamondIcon class was defined in Chapter 4.*

Unlike lazy values, active values act like instance-creation factories. Every time they're asked for a value with one of the get methods of UIManager, a new instance is created and returned. The interface method is the same as that for the UIDefault.LazyValue interface—only the interface name is different.

```
public interface UIDefaults.ActiveValue {
  public Object createValue(UIDefaults table);
}
```

To demonstrate, we'll create a factory that constructs JLabel components. The text of the label will function as a counter to show how many labels have been created. Whenever the createValue() is called, a new JLabel is created.

```java
import javax.swing.*;

public class ActiveLabel implements UIDefaults.ActiveValue {
  private int counter = 0;

  public Object createValue(UIDefaults defaults) {
    JLabel label = new JLabel(""+counter++);
    return label;
  }
}
```

To create the component, you need to install the ActiveLabel class with UIManager.put(). Once the class is installed, each call to get() the key out of the UIManager results in a new component being created. Figure 18-6 shows the component in use. Whenever the button is pressed, the UIManager.get() method is called and the component is added to the screen.

```java
UIManager.put(LABEL_FACTORY, new ActiveLabel());
...
JLabel label = (JLabel)UIManager.get(LABEL_FACTORY);
```

Figure 18-6: Using active values

The source code for the sample active program follows.

```java
import java.awt.*;
import java.awt.event.*;
import javax.swing.*;

public class ActiveSample {

  private static final String LABEL_FACTORY = "LabelFactory";

  public static void main (String args[]) {

    JFrame frame = new ExitableJFrame("Active Example");

    UIManager.put(LABEL_FACTORY, new ActiveLabel());

    final JPanel panel = new JPanel();

    JButton button = new JButton("Get");

    ActionListener actionListener = new ActionListener() {
      public void actionPerformed(ActionEvent actionEvent) {
        JLabel label = (JLabel)UIManager.get(LABEL_FACTORY);
        panel.add(label);
        panel.revalidate();
      }
    };
    button.addActionListener(actionListener);

    Container contentPane = frame.getContentPane();
    contentPane.add(panel, BorderLayout.CENTER);
    contentPane.add(button, BorderLayout.SOUTH);
    frame.setSize(200, 200);
    frame.setVisible(true);
  }
}
```

Using Client Properties

If changing all the UIResource properties known to the UIManager doesn't quite get the look and feel you desire, some of the UI delegate classes can provide their own customized capabilities that are hidden from API views. These customized capabilities are provided as "client properties" and are accessible from two JComponent methods: `public final Object getClientProperty(Object key)` and `public final void putClientProperty(Object key, Object value)`.

Client properties tend to be look-and-feel–specific attributes of a component that are meaningless for most look and feel implementations. Instead of subclassing the look and feel delegate to expose a property through a pair of getter/setter methods, the get/put client property methods provide access to a private instance-level lookup table to store a new property setting. In addition, as when making changes to the UIDefaults, modifying the client properties of a component notifies any registered property change listeners of the component.

Most of the specific client properties have already been discussed throughout this book with their respective components. Table 18-6 merely provides a single resource for finding all the configurable client properties. In the left-hand column, the text string for the property is listed first, followed by class variables to use in place of the text string. In most cases, these class variables aren't public, and therefore not usable, but they direct you to the class that does use the property. The right-hand column contains the class type to store with the property name. If the class type is a String, a list of valid values is provided, if appropriate.

PROPERTY NAME	CLASS TYPE / VALUES
"_KeyboardBindings" JComponent.KEYBOARD_BINDINGS_KEY	Hashtable
BasicButtonUI.class (not a String)	BasicButtonListener
"defeatSystemEventQueueCheck" used by SystemEventQueueUtilities, no key constant	null or anything
"html" BasicHTML.propertykey used by BasicLabelUI, BasicButtonUI, SwingUtilities, no key constant	View

"JComboBox.lightweightKeyboardNavigation"
 BasicComboBoxUI.LIGHTWEIGHT_
    KEYBOARD_NAVIGATION
 BasicComboPopup.LIGHTWEIGHT_
    KEYBOARD_NAVIGATION
	"Lightweight", "Heavyweight"

"JDesktopPane.dragMode" DefaultDesktopManager.DEFAULT_DRAG_MODE DefaultDesktopManager.FASTER_DRAG_MODE DefaultDesktopManager.OUTLINE_DRAG_MODE	null, "outline," "faster"
"EnableWindowBlit" JViewport.EnableWindowBlit	null or anything

(continued)

Table 18-6 (continued)

PROPERTY NAME	CLASS TYPE / VALUES
"JInternalFrame.isPalette" MetalInternalFrameUI.IS_PALETTE	Boolean
"JScrollBar.isFreeStanding" MacScrollBarUI.FREE_STANDING_PROP MetalScrollBarUI.FREE_STANDING_PROP	Boolean
"JSlider.isFilled" MacSliderUI.SLIDER_FILL MetalSliderUI.SLIDER_FILL	Boolean
"JToolBar.focusedCompIndex" BasicToolBarUI.FOCUSED_COMP_INDEX	Integer
"JToolBar.isRollover" MetalToolBarUI.IS_ROLLOVER	Boolean
"JTree.lineStyle" MetalTreeUI.LINE_STYLE	"Angled", "Horizontal", "None"
"labeledBy" JLabel.LABELED_BY_PROPERTY	JComponent
"layeredContainerLayer" JLayeredPane.LAYER_PROPERTY	Integer
"MacInternalFrame.isMax" MacDesktopManager.maxProp	Boolean
"MacInternalFrame.preIconSize" MacDesktopManager.preIconSizeProp	Dimension
"MacInternalFrame.prevSize" MacDesktopManager.prevSizeProp	Dimension
"nextFocus" JComponent.NEXT_FOCUS	Component
"paintActive" used by MetalIconFactory, no key constant	Boolean
"previousBounds" DefaultDesktopManager.PREVIOUS_ BOUNDS_PROPERTY	Rectangle
"ToolTipText" JComponent.TOOL_TIP_TEXT_KEY	String
"wasIconOnce" DefaultDesktopManager.HAS_BEEN_ ICONIFIED_PROPERTY	Boolean

Table 18-6: Swing's client properties

> **NOTE**   *Many of the properties in Table 18-6 are used internally by the specific component delegate implementations, and you'll never need to use them. Other properties, such as the drag mode for the desktop manager, seem to be means to add capabilities while keeping the API unaltered.*

To demonstrate the use of client properties, the following two lines change the "JToolBar.isRollover" attribute of a JToolBar to Boolean.TRUE. Other toolbars might not want this attribute set to Boolean.TRUE and would therefore leave that setting at Boolean.FALSE.

```
JToolBar toolbar = new JToolBar();
toolbar.putClientProperty("JToolBar.isRollover", Boolean.TRUE);
```

Creating a New UI Delegate

Sometimes, modifying a few of the UIResource elements of the Swing component isn't quite enough to get the appearance or behavior you desire. When this is the case, you need to create a new UI delegate for the component. Each Swing component has its own UI delegate for controlling the view and controller aspects of its MVC architecture.

Table 18-7 provides a listing of the Swing components, the abstract class that describes the UI delegate for each component, and the specific implementations for the predefined look and feels. For instance, calling the getUIClassID() method of a JToolBar will return the class ID string of "ToolBarUI" for its UI delegate. If you then ask the UIManager for the specific implementation of this UI delegate for the currently installed look and feel with a call to UIManager.get("ToolBarUI"), an implementation of the abstract ToolBarUI class is returned. Therefore, if you want to develop a custom look and feel for the JToolBar component, you must create an implementation of the abstract ToolBarUI class. Some components, like the JMenu, inherit these two settings directly from their parent class, in this case the JMenuItem.

SWING COMPONENT	CLASS ID	IMPLEMENTATION CLASS
JButton	ButtonUI	ButtonUI
JCheckBox	CheckBoxUI	ButtonUI
JCheckBoxMenuItem	CheckBoxMenuItemUI	MenuItemUI
JColorChooser	ColorChooserUI	ColorChooserUI
JComboBox	ComboBoxUI	ComboBoxUI
JComponent	n/a	ComponentUI

(continued)

Table 18-7 (continued)

SWING COMPONENT	CLASS ID	IMPLEMENTATION CLASS
JDesktopIcon	DesktopIconUI	DesktopIconUI
JDesktopPane	DesktopPaneUI	DesktopPaneUI
JEditorPane	EditorPaneUI	TextUI
JFileChooser	FileChooserUI	FileChooserUI
JInternalFrame	InternalFrameUI	InternalFrameUI
JLabel	LabelUI	LabelUI
JList	ListUI	ListUI
JMenuBar	MenuBarUI	MenuBarUI
JMenuItem	MenuItemUI	ButtonUI
JOptionPane	OptionPaneUI	OptionPaneUI
JPanel	PanelUI	PanelUI
JPasswordField	PasswordFieldUI	TextUI
JPopupMenu	PopupMenuUI	PopupMenuUI
JProgressBar	ProgressBarUI	ProgressBarUI
JRadioButton	RadioButtonUI	ButtonUI
JRadioButtonMenuItem	RadioButtonMenuItemUI	MenuItemUI
JScrollBar	ScrollBarUI	ScrollBarUI
JScrollPane	ScrollPaneUI	ScrollPaneUI
JSeparator	SeparatorUI	SeparatorUI
JSlider	SliderUI	SliderUI
JSplitPane	SplitPaneUI	SplitPaneUI
JTabbedPane	TabbedPaneUI	TabbedPaneUI
JTable	TableUI	TableUI
JTableHeader	TableHeaderUI	TableHeaderUI
JTextArea	TextAreaUI	TextUI
JTextField	TextFieldUI	TextUI
JTextPane	TextPaneUI	TextUI
JToggleButton	ToggleButtonUI	ButtonUI
JToolBar	ToolBarUI	ToolBarUI
JToolTip	ToolTipUI	ToolTipUI
JTree	TreeUI	TreeUI
JViewport	ViewportUI	ViewportUI

Table 18-7: Swing component delegates

NOTE Classes such as JWindow, JFrame, and JApplet are heavyweight components and therefore lack a UI delegate.

To demonstrate the creation of a new UI delegate, you can enhance the `ToolBarUI` for the Metal look and feel by extending the `MetalToolBarUI` class. The enhancements will cause the draggable toolbar frame to not be resizable and will allow you to customize the image icon on the draggable frame.

The draggable frame for the toolbar is created when the protected `JFrame` `createFloatingFrame(JToolBar toolbar)` method is called by the delegate. Because you don't need to do any customization *when* the frame is created — you only need to customize *what* is created — you just have to override the original implementation of the method. After creating the frame, you can make it not resizable by calling `setResizable(false)`. For the image icon associated with the frame, you can define your own property to store with the `UIManager` resource settings, `ToolBar.frameImageIcon`, and use that property to change the image icon with `public void setImageIcon(Image image)`. In addition to your directly using the property name, an available constant, `CustomToolBarUI.FRME_IMAGE_ICON`, can be used as the key to the `UIManager.put(key, value)` call.

```java
import javax.swing.*;
import javax.swing.plaf.metal.MetalToolBarUI;
import java.awt.*;
import java.awt.event.*;

public class CustomToolBarUI extends MetalToolBarUI {
  public final static String FRAME_IMAGEICON = "ToolBar.frameImageIcon";

  protected JFrame createFloatingFrame(JToolBar toolbar) {
    JFrame frame = new JFrame(toolbar.getName());
    frame.setResizable(false);
    Icon icon = UIManager.getIcon(FRAME_IMAGEICON);
    if (icon instanceof ImageIcon) {
      Image iconImage = ((ImageIcon)icon).getImage();
      frame.setIconImage(iconImage);
    }
    WindowListener windowListener = createFrameListener();
    frame.addWindowListener(windowListener);
    return frame;
  }
}
```

To use the new UI delegate, you need to create the class and associate it with the toolbar by using the `setUI()` method. Additionally, if you want to set the draggable frame image icon, you store the icon with the `UIManager` by using the `UIManager.put(CustomToolBarUI.FRAME_IMAGEICON, theImageIcon)`. Then, when you drag the toolbar outside the main window, it won't be resizable and may or may *not* have a different image icon.

```
ToolBarUI toolbarUI = new CustomToolBarUI();
Icon imageIcon = new ImageIcon("World.gif");
UIManager.put(CustomToolBarUI.FRAME_IMAGEICON, imageIcon);

JToolBar toolbar = new JToolBar();
toolbar.setUI(toolbarUI);
```

> **NOTE** *If the Icon you associate with the* CustomToolBarUI.FRAME_IMAGEICON *setting isn't an* ImageIcon, *an exception would be thrown at runtime.*

The changes made previously to the ToolBarSample program from Chapter 6 will result in the window shown in Figure 18-7 when the toolbar is dragged outside or above the main window. You really can't determine that it isn't resizable, but you *do* see the changed image icon of the frame.

The complete source for the example program follows:

```
import java.awt.*;
import java.awt.event.*;
import javax.swing.*;
import javax.swing.plaf.*;

public class ToolBarSample {

  private static final int COLOR_POSITION = 0;
  private static final int STRING_POSITION = 1;
  static Object buttonColors[][] = {
    {Color.red, "red"},
    {Color.blue, "blue"},
    {Color.green, "green"},
    {Color.black, "black"},
    null, // separator
    {Color.cyan, "cyan"}
  };
```

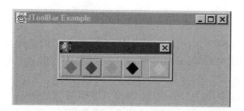

Figure 18-7: Using the new ToolBarUI

```
public static void main (String args[]) {

  ActionListener actionListener = new ActionListener() {
    public void actionPerformed (ActionEvent actionEvent) {
      System.out.println(actionEvent.getActionCommand());
    }
  };

  JFrame frame = new ExitableJFrame("JToolBar Example");

  ToolBarUI toolbarUI = new CustomToolBarUI();
  Icon imageIcon = new ImageIcon("World.gif");
  UIManager.put(CustomToolBarUI.FRAME_IMAGEICON, imageIcon);

  JToolBar toolbar = new JToolBar();
  toolbar.setUI(toolbarUI);
  toolbar.putClientProperty("JToolBar.isRollover", Boolean.TRUE);

  for (int i=0, n=buttonColors.length; i<n; i++) {
    Object color[] = buttonColors[i];
    if (color == null) {
      toolbar.addSeparator();
    } else {
      Icon icon = new DiamondIcon((Color)color[COLOR_POSITION], true, 20, 20);
      JButton button = new JButton(icon);
      button.setActionCommand((String)color[STRING_POSITION]);
      button.addActionListener(actionListener);
      toolbar.add(button);
    }
  }

  Container contentPane = frame.getContentPane();
  contentPane.add(toolbar, BorderLayout.NORTH);
  frame.setSize(350, 150);
  frame.setVisible(true);
  }
}
```

> **NOTE** *If you want to use the new UI delegate for all components, you can let the UIManager know about the delegate instead of manually calling setUI() after creating the component. In the example just listed, the source line would be UIManager.put("ToolBarUI", "CustomToolBarUI").*

The actual creation of the UI delegate is done somewhat indirectly, as shown by Figure 18-8. A call to the component constructor asks the UIManager for the UI delegate class. The UIManager maintains the list of delegates in its defaults property, a UIDefaults object. When the UIDefaults is queried for the delegate, it goes back to the component to ask which delegate is needed. After it finds the appropriate delegate implementation, the UIDefaults object tells the ComponentUI to create it, resulting in the actual UI delegate class being created. Once the UI delegate is created, it needs to be configured for the state of the specific model.

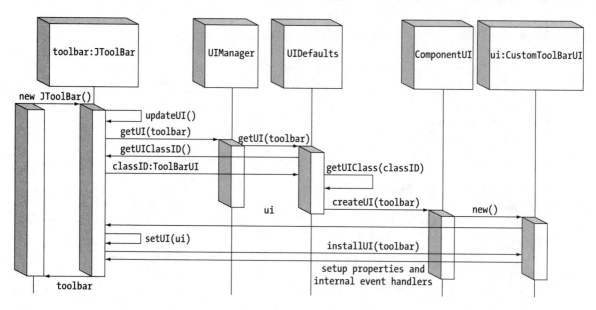

Figure 18-8: UI delegate creation sequence diagram

Creating a New Look and Feel

Most developers don't need to create completely new pluggable look and feels. Unless you were employed by a company that wanted you to customize everything to provide a unique experience, it usually isn't necessary to create a look and feel from scratch. Instead, what tends to happen is that you make minor modifications to an existing look and feel by providing some customized UI delegates. If you *do* want to create a new look and feel class, the only thing you have to do is create a subclass of the LookAndFeel class and you're done. You still have to provide the UI delegates, but whichever classes they are can now be more hidden from the Swing components.

Using the MacLookAndFeel on a Non-Macintosh

To demonstrate the creation of a new look and feel class, let's create a look and feel implementation that cancels out the platform requirement for the Mac UI delegate. By simply overriding the `public boolean isSupportedLookAndFeel()` method to return `true`, you effectively remove the platform requirement for the Mac look and feel class.

The following class definition shows how simple the creation of a new look and feel implementation can be.

```java
import javax.swing.UIDefaults;
import com.sun.java.swing.plaf.mac.MacLookAndFeel;
public class MyMac extends MacLookAndFeel {
  public String getID() {
    return "MyMac";
  }
  public String getName() {
    return "MyMac Look and Feel";
  }
  public String getDescription() {
    return "The MyMac Look and Feel";
  }
  public boolean isNativeLookAndFeel() {
    return false;
  }
  public boolean isSupportedLookAndFeel() {
    return true;
  }
}
```

If you want to run this Swing program on a non-Macintosh machine, you can get the look and feel to be the Mac look and feel. Just set your look and feel to be `MyMac` and make the look and feel class file available. With a JDK 1.1 environment, the class file only needs to be available in your CLASSPATH and will be started with the following command line:

```
java -Dswing.defaultlaf=MyMac ClassFile
```

With the Java 2 platform, look and feel classes must be loaded from a trusted source, and not CLASSPATH. Trusted locations can be specified from the command line by setting the -Xbootclasspath runtime command-line option. If they don't come from a trusted source, the look and feel class won't be loaded. Assuming the `MyMac` class definition is in the `C:\classes` directory, the fictitious `ClassFile` program will again come up with the Mac look and feel.

```
java -Xbootclasspath:c:\jdk1.2\jre\lib\rt.jar;c:\classes;c:\swing-1.1.1\mac.jar
  -Dswing.defaultlaf=MyMac ClassFile
```

> **NOTE** *You can make a similar change to the `WindowsLookAndFeel` class in order to use that look and feel on a non-Windows machine.*

For the Mac look-and-feel change to work properly, you need to provide the image files used for the icons of the look and feel from within the `icons` subdirectory of the `MyMac` directory structure. Table 18-8 lists those icons appropriate to the predefined look and feels. The `MyMac` look and feel needs all the Macintosh image files.

FILENAME	MACINTOSH	METAL	MOTIF	WINDOWS
Computer.gif	X			X
DesktopIcon.gif			X	
DetailsView.gif				X
Directory.gif	X			X
Error.gif	X	X	X	X
File.gif	X			X
FloppyDrive.gif	X			X
Folder.gif	X			
HardDrive.gif	X			X
HomeFolder.gif				X
Inform.gif	X	X	X	X
JavaCup.gif				X
ListView.gif				X
NewFolder.gif				X
Question.gif	X	X	X	X
RadioButtonDisabledOff.gif	X			
RadioButtonDisabledOn.gif	X			
RadioButtonEnabledOff.gif	X			
RadioButtonEnabledOn.gif	X			
RadioButtonPressedOff.gif	X			
RadioButtonPressedOn.gif	X			
ScrollDownArrow.gif			X	
ScrollDownArrowActive.gif			X	
ScrollKnobH.gif			X	

(continued)

Table 18-8 (continued)

FILENAME	MACINTOSH	METAL	MOTIF	WINDOWS
ScrollLeftArrow.gif			X	
ScrollLeftArrowActive.gif			X	
ScrollRightArrow.gif			X	
ScrollRightArrowActive.gif			X	
ScrollUpArrow.gif			X	
ScrollUpArrowActive.gif			X	
StandardBackground.gif			X	X
TrayBottom.gif			X	
TrayLeft.gif			X	
TrayRight.gif			X	
TrayTop.gif			X	
TreeClosed.gif	X		X	X
TreeCollapsed.gif	X			
TreeCollapsedPressed.gif	X			
TreeExpanded.gif	X			
TreeExpandedPressed.gif	X			
TreeIntermediate.gif	X			
TreeLeaf.gif	X			X
TreeLeafSelected.gif	X			
TreeNode.gif	X			
TreeOpen.gif	X		X	X
TreeSelected.gif	X			
TriangleClosed.gif	X			
TriangleClosedPressed.gif	X			
TriangleOpen.gif	X			
TriangleOpenPressed.gif	X			
TriangleTurned.gif	X			
UpFolder.gif				X
Warn.gif	X	X	X	X
WindowCloseEnabled.gif	X			
WindowClosePressed.gif	X			
WindowMinimizeEnabled.gif	X			
WindowMinimizePressed.gif	X			
WindowSizeEnabled.gif	X			
WindowZoomEnabled.gif	X			
WindowZoomPressed.gif	X			

Table 18-8: Look and feel image files

> **NOTE** *At the very least, the* `Error.gif,` *`Inform.gif,` `Question.gif,` and* `Warn.gif` *image files are needed by the* `JOptionPane` *component within all look and feels.*

If you don't want to sidestep the "native" requirement of the Macintosh look and feel, you can install individual UI delegates, such as the following, that use the Mac UI delegate for the `JButton` component:

```
UIManager.put("ButtonUI","com.sun.java.swing.plaf.mac.MacButtonUI").
```

Adding UI Delegates

Creating a new look and feel that has custom UI delegates involves creating a subclass of the `LookAndFeel` class. More likely, you'll create a subclass of `BasicLookAndFeel` or another of the predefined look and feel classes and then provide your custom delegates for some of the components. You can provide new implementations of *all* the delegates, but more likely you'll start off with one or two and build on that.

If you subclass the `BasicLookAndFeel` class, it has a `protected void initClassDefaults(UIDefaults table)` method to be overridden to install your custom UI delegates. Just put the delegates in the `UIDefaults` table for the look and feel, instead of in your program that wants to use the new delegate.

The following extension to the `MetalLookAndFeel` adds the previously defined `CustomToolBarUI` delegate as the `ToolBarUI` delegate for the look and feel. As more customized components are defined, you can add them in a similar way.

```
import javax.swing.UIDefaults;
import javax.swing.plaf.metal.MetalLookAndFeel;
public class MyMetal extends MetalLookAndFeel {
  public String getID() {
    return "MyMetal";
  }
  public String getName() {
    return "MyMetal Look and Feel";
  }
  public String getDescription() {
    return "The MyMetal Look and Feel";
  }
  public boolean isNativeLookAndFeel() {
    return false;
  }
```

```
public boolean isSupportedLookAndFeel() {
  return true;
}
protected void initClassDefaults(UIDefaults table) {
  super.initClassDefaults(table);
  table.put("ToolBarUI", "CustomToolBarUI");
}
}
```

> **NOTE** *When creating your own look and feel, be sure to copy or create icons for the* JOptionPane *pop-up windows. These icons should be named* Error.gif, Inform.gif, Question.gif *and* Warn.gif, *and they belong in the* icons *directory under the directory where the look and feel class file exists.*

Working with Metal Themes

The Metal look and feel class (javax.swing.plaf.metal.MetalLookAndFeel) provides the means to define *themes* to describe the default settings for the colors, fonts, and all the UIDefaults managed by the UIManager. By allowing users to change themes, they can get preferred coloration or font sizes with minimal work from the developer. By developing corporate themes, you can easily customize an interface without creating new look and feel classes or manually inserting new settings into current UIDefaults.

Class MetalTheme

Table 18-9 lists the 49 different properties that are available through the MetalTheme class. The various "primary" and "secondary" properties are abstract and must be implemented in a subclass. Of the remaining properties, the six whose names end with Font are also abstract and must be implemented by a subclass. Those six are as follows: controlTextFont, menuTextFont, subTextFont, systemTextFont, userTextFont, and windowTextFont. The remaining properties, by default, reuse one of the 11 primary/secondary values (or black and white) for their settings.

PROPERTY NAME	DATA TYPE	ACCESS
acceleratorForeground	ColorUIResource	read-only
acceleratorSelectedForeground	ColorUIResource	read-only
black	ColorUIResource	read-only

(continued)

Table 18-9 (continued)

PROPERTY NAME	DATA TYPE	ACCESS
control	ColorUIResource	read-only
controlDarkShadow	ColorUIResource	read-only
controlDisabled	ColorUIResource	read-only
controlHighlight	ColorUIResource	read-only
controlInfo	ColorUIResource	read-only
controlShadow	ColorUIResource	read-only
controlTextColor	ColorUIResource	read-only
controlTextFont	FontUIResource	read-only
desktopColor	ColorUIResource	read-only
focusColor	ColorUIResource	read-only
highlightedTextColor	ColorUIResource	read-only
inactiveControlTextColor	ColorUIResource	read-only
inactiveSystemTextColor	ColorUIResource	read-only
menuBackground	ColorUIResource	read-only
menuDisabledForeground	ColorUIResource	read-only
menuForeground	ColorUIResource	read-only
menuSelectedBackground	ColorUIResource	read-only
menuSelectedForeground	ColorUIResource	read-only
menuTextFont	FontUIResource	read-only
name	String	read-only
primary1	ColorUIResource	read-only
primary2	ColorUIResource	read-only
primary3	ColorUIResource	read-only
primaryControl	ColorUIResource	read-only
primaryControlDarkShadow	ColorUIResource	read-only
primaryControlHighlight	ColorUIResource	read-only
primaryControlInfo	ColorUIResource	read-only
primaryControlShadow	ColorUIResource	read-only
secondary1	ColorUIResource	read-only
secondary2	ColorUIResource	read-only
secondary3	ColorUIResource	read-only
separatorBackground	ColorUIResource	read-only
separatorForeground	ColorUIResource	read-only
subTextFont	FontUIResource	read-only
systemTextColor	ColorUIResource	read-only
systemTextFont	FontUIResource	read-only
textHighlightColor	ColorUIResource	read-only
userTextColor	ColorUIResource	read-only
userTextFont	FontUIResource	read-only

(continued)

Table 18-9 (continued)

PROPERTY NAME	DATA TYPE	ACCESS
white	ColorUIResource	read-only
windowBackground	ColorUIResource	read-only
windowTextFont	FontUIResource	read-only
windowTitleBackground	ColorUIResource	read-only
windowTitleForeground	ColorUIResource	read-only
windowTitleInactiveBackground	ColorUIResource	read-only
windowTitleInactiveForeground	ColorUIResource	read-only

Table 18-9: MetalTheme properties

DefaultMetalTheme

The DefaultMetalTheme class provides the only predefined theme. It calls itself the "Steel" theme and uses a blue-gray color scheme for the primary-secondary settings, respectively.

If you create your own theme, you'd probably subclass the DefaultMetalTheme, although that isn't absolutely necessary. Installation is done by setting the static currentTheme property of the MetalLookAndFeel class to your theme.

```
MetalTheme myTheme = new MyTheme();
MetalLookAndFeel.setCurrentTheme(myTheme);
```

Whereas most of the customizations of a MetalTheme are related to fonts and colors, the public void addCustomEntriesToTable(UIDefaults table) method allows you to override the default UIDefaults settings for the Metal look and feel. Therefore, not only do themes customize the fonts and colors of the Swing components, they can also customize any one of the many UIResource-related properties of the Swing components.

The following code demonstrates how to set two of the scrollbar settings for a specific theme. Remember to tag these settings with the UIResource interface when appropriate, and don't forget to initialize the table argument by your superclass implementation (eventually, this would be MetalTheme).

```
public void addCustomEntriesToTable(UIDefaults table) {
  super.addCustomEntriesToTable(table);

  ColorUIResource thumbColor = new ColorUIResource(Color.magenta);
  table.put("Scrollbar.thumb", thumbColor);
  table.put("ScrollBar.width", new Integer(25));
}
```

The Metalworks system demo provided by Sun comes with the examples for the Swing classes. It demonstrates the use of themes. One of the themes it defines reads the theme color settings from a property file. Instead of having to create a new class file every time you want to change the theme of your Swing application, you can read it from a file at runtime.

```
name=Funky
primary1=255,25,25
primary2=191,25,25
primary3=127,25,25
secondary1=25,25,255
secondary2=25,25,191
secondary3=25,25,127
white=0,0,0
black=255,255,255
```

Figure 18-9 shows the Funky theme just described used within the Metalworks demonstration program. Figure 18-9 also shows the Presentation theme it defines.

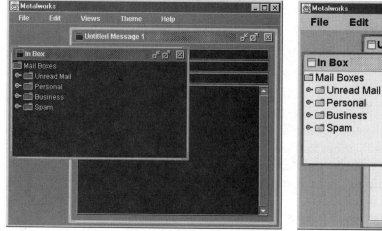

Funky

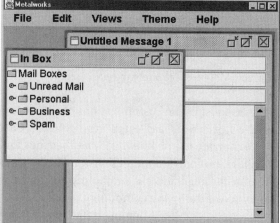

Presentation

Figure 18-9: Using Metal themes and the Metalworks demo

WARNING *There's a bug in the PropertiesMetalTheme class of the Metalworks demo program. Although the red, green, and blue values are meant to be specified in that order for each of the properties, the class accidentally swaps the blue and green elements.*

Using an Auxiliary Look and Feel

Swing provides for multiple look and feel classes to be active at any one time through the MultiLookAndFeel, or as specified by the swing.plaf.multiplexinglaf property in the swing.properties file. When multiple look and feels are installed, only one look and feel will be visual and paint the screen. The remaining versions are called auxiliary look and feels and tend to be associated with accessibility options, such as for screen readers. Another possible auxiliary look and feel is that of a logger, which records those components that are interacted with in a log file.

Auxiliary look and feel classes are registered with the runtime environment by configuring the swing.auxiliarylaf property within the swing.properties file. If multiple classes are specified, the entries need to be separated by commas. In addition to your using the properties file, you can install a look and feel within a program by calling the public static void addAuxiliaryLookAndFeel(LookAndFeel lookAndFeel) method of UIManager. Once installed, the multiplexing look and feel class automatically creates and manages UI delegates for all the installed look and feel classes.

To find out which auxiliary look and feel classes are installed, you can ask the UIManager through its public static LookAndFeel[ ] getAuxiliaryLookAndFeels() method. This returns an array of the actual LookAndFeel objects, versus the UIManager.LookAndFeelInfo array you get back from the getInstalledLookAndFeels() method.

NOTE *Nothing stops multiple look and feel classes from rendering to the screen for the same component. It's the responsibility of the auxiliary look and feel creator to take care not to compete with the primary look and feel when rendering to the screen.*

Summary

In this chapter, we explored the pluggable look and feel architecture of the Swing components. Because all aspects of the Swing components are written in the Java language, if you don't like an aspect of a component, you can simply change it. And changing it is what this chapter showed you how to do.

First, we learned how to query for the preinstalled `LookAndFeel` classes and how to change our current look and feel. Next, we learned how to customize the current look and feel by modifying its `UIDefaults` through the `UIManager`. We saw how these default settings can implement the `UIResource` interface so that the settings change when the look and feel class changes. In addition, we saw how these resources can implement the `UIDefaults.ActiveValue` and `UIDefaults.LazyValue` interfaces for better utilization of resources. Moreover, we saw how client properties are hidden from the API view but are also available for customizing the look and feel of a component.

To customize the look and feel of various components, we explored creating new UI delegates as well as new look and feel classes, some of which could be nonvisual or auxiliary. The Metal look and feel also contains a specialized behavior through its use of themes, which was also explored.

In Chapter 19, we'll look at the Swing undo framework, which is used for designing undoable and redoable operations.

CHAPTER 19

Becoming Undone

IN CHAPTER 18, YOU DISCOVERED HOW TO customize your Swing-based applications by examining the pluggable look and feel architecture support that's available. In this chapter, you'll examine the undo framework provided with the Java Foundation Classes release as part of the Swing packages.

The JFC 1.1 release from Sun includes a facility for supporting undo operations within your applications. It allows you to support undoable and redoable operations that change the state of your data. Although the framework is part of the Swing release, it's usable within your own applications. Usage of the classes in this framework isn't limited to component-based applications — the changed data can be for adding undo capabilties to applications of your own creation.

> **NOTE** *Although technically part of the JFC/Project Swing release as an element in the javax.swing.undo package, the undo facility actually belongs in the java.util package. Unfortunately, this would make it unusable within JDK 1.1, because Swing text packages use this undo facility. Because Sun couldn't alter the Core API set under JDK 1.1, you'll find the undo support as part of the JFC/Swing component release, and it is therefore usable under both the JDK 1.1 and the Java 2 platforms.*

Working with the Undo Framework

Found in the javax.swing.undo package, the undo framework includes five classes, two interfaces, and two exceptions. To support the undo framework, a related interface and event are included in the javax.swing.event package. At the root of it all is the UndoableEdit interface. The interface forms the basis for encapsulating operations that can be undone or redone using the Command design pattern.

The root implementation class of the undoable command is the AbstractUndoableEdit class. Don't let the class name fool you, though — it isn't truly abstract. The children of the root command are the CompoundEdit and StateEdit command classes. The CompoundEdit class allows you to combine multiple undoable operations, in which some of the undoable operations could be StateEdit objects that store state changes. The Swing text components create DefaultDocumentEvent commands when their contents change. The command is a subclass of CompoundEdit as well as an inner class of AbstractDocument. An additional encapsulated command is the UndoManager, which is a subclass of CompoundEdit. The UndoManager manages the edit operations on an editable object by serving as an UndoableEditListener and responding to the creation of each UndoableEditEvent. When an UndoableEdit can't be undone, a CannotUndoException is thrown. In addition, when an UndoableEdit can't be redone, a CannotRedoException is thrown. If you want to create objects that support undoable and redoable operations, the objects need to implement the StateEditable interface, and they can use the UndoableEditSupport class to help manage the list of UndoableEdit objects. Figure 19-1 shows the interrelationships of these classes found in the javax.swing.undo and javax.swing.event packages.

Using the Undo Framework with Swing Text Components

Before going into the details of the individual pieces of the undo framework, I'll demonstrate how to use the framework with the Swing text components. (If this is all you need, you won't have to understand how the rest works.) The Swing text components already support the necessary undo and redo capabilities; you merely have to manage them with an UndoManager and tell the manager when to undo/redo something. The example program will look like Figure 19-2, with one JTextArea having two buttons on a toolbar for undoing and redoing a text operation.

To enable the JTextArea shown in Figure 19-2 to support undoable operations, you must attach an UndoManager as an UndoableEditListener to the Document of the component. First you create the manager, and then you attach it.

```
UndoManager manager = new UndoManager();
textArea.getDocument().addUndoableEditListener(manager);
```

Once the manager is attached to the document of the JTextArea, it will monitor all changes to the contents of the text area. Because each of the Swing text components has a Document data model, you can associate an UndoManager with each of the components.

After attaching the manager to the text component, you must provide some means to tell the manager to undo/redo an operation. Normally this would be done through a menu selection or a toolbar button selection. In Figure 19-2, this is done with the help of a JToolBar, with one button for each command. For the "Undo" button, you want the manager to undo an operation. Therefore, the ActionListener for the button should call the public void undo() method of the UndoManager. The "Redo" button's ActionListener should call the manager's public void redo() method. The undo() and redo() methods each throw a different exception that must be dealt with.

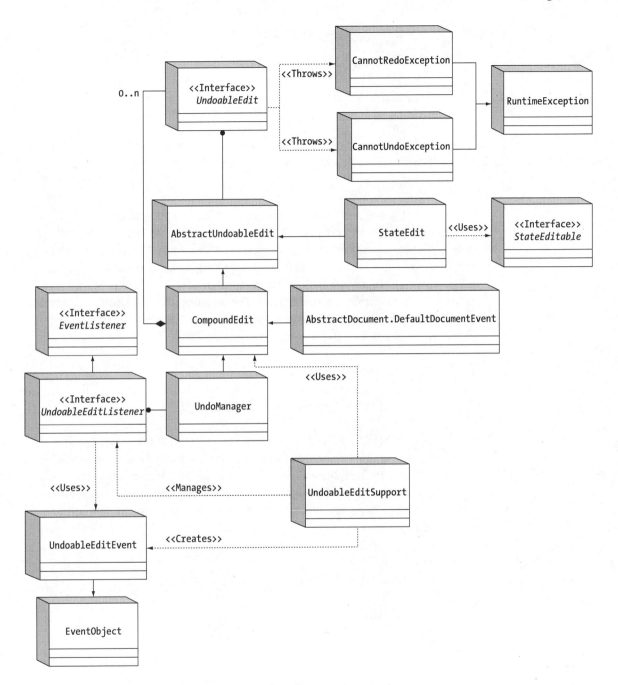

Figure 19-1: Undo framework UML relationship diagram

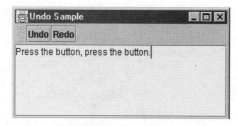

Figure 19-2: Undo Swing usage demonstration

Because the functionality necessary for the undo and redo buttons is the same for all managers, I created a helper UndoManagerHelper class to create Action objects for you. These objects can be used by a JMenuBar, a JToolBar, or anything else that can respond to ActionListener for dealing with the undo and redo operations. You need to ask the helper class for each Action and then associate that Action with the appropriate component. For instance, the following three lines of source code will take a previously created UndoManager and add the necessary undo/redo buttons for a JToolBar.

```
JToolBar toolbar = new JToolBar();
toolbar.add(UndoManagerHelper.getUndoAction(manager));
toolbar.add(UndoManagerHelper.getRedoAction(manager));
```

Using the undo facility with the Swing text components is that easy. The actual UndoManagerHelper class definition follows. If you don't like the default labels shown in Figure 19-2, additional methods are available that support customization. In addition, if an exception is thrown during the undo/redo operation, a warning message pops up. The warning message and pop-up window title are also customizable.

```
import javax.swing.*;
import javax.swing.undo.*;
import java.awt.*;
import java.awt.event.*;

public class UndoManagerHelper {

  public static Action getUndoAction(UndoManager manager, String label) {
    return new UndoAction(manager, label);
  }
  public static Action getUndoAction(UndoManager manager) {
    return new UndoAction(manager, "Undo");
  }
```

```
public static Action getRedoAction(UndoManager manager, String label) {
  return new RedoAction(manager, label);
}
public static Action getRedoAction(UndoManager manager) {
  return new RedoAction(manager, "Redo");
}

private abstract static class UndoRedoAction extends AbstractAction {
  UndoManager undoManager = new UndoManager();
  String errorMessage = "Cannot undo";
  String errorTitle = "Undo Problem";
  protected UndoRedoAction(UndoManager manager, String name) {
    super(name);
    undoManager = manager;
  }
  public void setErrorMessage(String newValue) {
    errorMessage = newValue;
  }
  public void setErrorTitle(String newValue) {
    errorTitle = newValue;
  }
  protected void showMessage(Object source) {
    if (source instanceof Component) {
      JOptionPane.showMessageDialog((Component)source, errorMessage,
errorTitle, JOptionPane.WARNING_MESSAGE);
    } else {
      System.err.println(errorMessage);
    }
  }
}

public static class UndoAction extends UndoRedoAction {
  public UndoAction(UndoManager manager, String name) {
    super(manager, name);
    setErrorMessage("Cannot undo");
    setErrorTitle("Undo Problem");
  }
  public void actionPerformed(ActionEvent actionEvent) {
    try {
      undoManager.undo();
    } catch (CannotUndoException cannotUndoException) {
      showMessage(actionEvent.getSource());
    }
```

```
      }
    }

    public static class RedoAction extends UndoRedoAction {
      String errorMessage = "Cannot redo";
      String errorTitle = "Redo Problem";
      public RedoAction(UndoManager manager, String name) {
        super(manager, name);
        setErrorMessage("Cannot redo");
        setErrorTitle("Redo Problem");
      }
      public void actionPerformed(ActionEvent actionEvent) {
        try {
          undoManager.redo();
        } catch (CannotRedoException cannotRedoException) {
          showMessage(actionEvent.getSource());
        }
      }
    }

  }
```

NOTE *One thing you can do to improve these helper actions is to have them enabled only when the particular operation is available.*

The complete source for the example shown in Figure 19-2 is listed next. With the help of the new UndoManagerHelper class, the most difficult part of using the undo framework with the Swing text components has been greatly simplified.

```
import javax.swing.*;
import javax.swing.undo.*;
import java.awt.*;

public class UndoSample {
  public static void main(String args[]) {
    JFrame frame = new ExitableJFrame("Undo Sample");
    JTextArea textArea = new JTextArea();
    JScrollPane scrollPane = new JScrollPane(textArea);
```

```
UndoManager manager = new UndoManager();
textArea.getDocument().addUndoableEditListener(manager);

JToolBar toolbar = new JToolBar();
toolbar.add(UndoManagerHelper.getUndoAction(manager));
toolbar.add(UndoManagerHelper.getRedoAction(manager));

Container content = frame.getContentPane();
content.add(toolbar, BorderLayout.NORTH);
content.add(scrollPane, BorderLayout.CENTER);
frame.setSize(300, 150);
frame.setVisible(true);
  }
}
```

If you plan to use the undo framework with only the Swing text components, you can skip reading the rest of the chapter. On the other hand, if you want to use the framework with other components, or even in a noncomponent setting, you'll want to read the remaining sections, which describe the inner workings of the framework in detail.

The Command Design Pattern

The undo facility of the javax.swing.undo package utilizes the Command design pattern. Before looking at the specifics of the individual undo framework interfaces and classes, let's step back to review the pattern. Figure 19-3 shows the structure of the pattern as it relates to the specific classes of the framework and the Swing text components. If you were using the framework outside the Swing text components, the Document element would be replaced with your client application and/or receiver.

The participants of the Command design pattern are the Command, Concrete Command, Client, Invoker, and Receiver.

- Command—The UndoableEdit interface defines the interface for executing the undo/redo operations.

- Concrete Command—Instances of the AbstractUndoableEdit class, or more specifically its subclasses, implement the necessary Command interface. They bind the commands to the receiver (Document) to modify its contents.

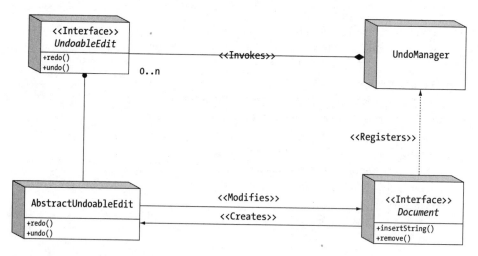

Figure 19-3: The command pattern

- Client — In the case of the Swing text components, the Document does the creation of the actual AbstractUndoableEdit subclass, by default an AbstractDocument.DefaultDocumentEvent.

- Invoker — The UndoManager serves as the Invoker of the UndoableEdit command. Normally, someone else tells the Invoker when to do the invoking. However, it's the Invoker who notifies the specific UndoableEdit instance when to undo/redo the command.

- Receiver — The Document is the receiver of the command from the actual AbstractUndoableEdit subclass. It knows how to process the request.

When working outside the Swing text component, you'll need to create your own UndoableEdit interface to act as the Concrete Command for the pattern. Instead of implementing the interface directly, you merely need to subclass the AbstractUndoableEdit class to encapsulate the specific information about your command.

The design pattern is quite powerful. No matter which command class you're using within the pattern, you can set up capabilities, such as macros for tasks along the lines of automated testing, because the Invoker can sequence the commands at its leisure.

Interface UndoableEdit

We've seen the undo framework in action with the Swing text components and reviewed the Command design pattern. Let's now look at the individual pieces of the framework that are involved. The first such piece is the UndoableEdit interface, whose definition is shown next.

```java
public interface UndoableEdit {
  // Properties
  public String getPresentationName();
  public String getRedoPresentationName();
  public boolean isSignificant();
  public String getUndoPresentationName();
  // Other Methods
  public boolean addEdit(UndoableEdit anEdit);
  public boolean canRedo();
  public boolean canUndo();
  public void die();
  public void redo() throws CannotRedoException;
  public boolean replaceEdit(UndoableEdit anEdit);
  public void undo() throws CannotUndoException;
}
```

This interface defines the operations that can be done to an object that should support undo and redo capabilities. In addition to describing the supported operations, the interface implicitly defines the three states that an undoable operation can be in, as shown in Figure 19-4.

The flow between states goes as follows:

- When an UndoableEdit command is first created, the operation is in the Undoable state.

  - The purpose of the die() method is to release resources for an UndoableEdit before the "garbage collector" decides to clean things up and place the command in the Done state.

  - Calling the undo() method either throws a CannotUndoException or causes the command to be undone and the state to change to Redoable.

  - Calling the redo() method either throws a CannotRedoException or causes the command to be done again and the state to stay at Undoable.

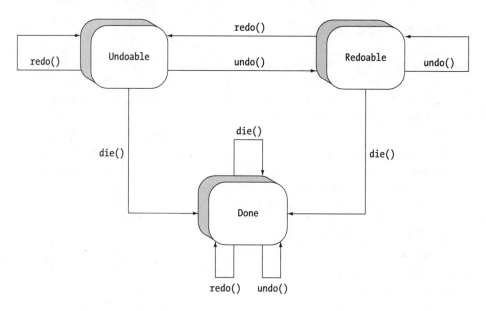

Figure 19-4: The UndoableEdit state chart

- When the operation is in the Redoable state, the command has already been undone.

  - Calling the die() method releases any resources and places the command in the Done state.

  - Calling the undo() method either throws a CannotUndoException or causes the command to be undone again and the state to stay at Redoable.

  - Calling the redo() method either throws a CannotRedoException or causes the command to be redone, returning the state to the Undoable state.

- When the operation is in the Done state, calling undo(), redo(), or die() leaves the operation in that state.

Some state changes aren't commonplace; however, all state changes are supported. The specifics are left to the Command that you're using. For instance, Microsoft Word allows you to continuously repeat the last command if the capabilities make sense—such as when formatting a paragraph or just typing a phrase.

Class *AbstractUndoableEdit*

The AbstractUndoableEdit class provides a default implementation for all the methods of the UndoableEdit interface. Although you might guess from the name that the class is abstract, it isn't. However, you tend to work with subclasses of the class anyway, and never with a direct instance of this class.

By default, AbstractUndoableEdit commands are *significant*. What significance you place on the significant property depends on your usage of the command. In addition, the class restricts repetition of undoable state changes. Unless overridden by a subclass, exceptions are thrown if you try to redo something in the Undoable state or undo something in the Redoable state.

The class doesn't support adding or replacing UndoableEdit operations. Further, it provides default presentation names for the undoPresentationName and redoPresentationName properties ("Undo" and "Redo" respectively), but gives none for the presentationName property. Subclasses should provide at least a presentation name to provide something more meaningful than the default settings.

> **NOTE** *A source code note implies that the Undo and Redo presentation names will be translated into foreign languages in a future release.*

Class *CompoundEdit*

The CompoundEdit class allows you to combine multiple undoable operations into a single operation. For instance, you may want to combine all the keystrokes for typing a whole word into a single CompoundEdit command. This would allow you to continuously redo the typing of a whole word in multiple places. Without combining the separate keystrokes, redoing the last command would only redo the last single keystroke.

The CompoundEdit class uses a read-only inProgress property to report whether the command is still being combined. Initially the property is true. When in progress, additional commands can be added to the compound command with addEdit(UndoableEdit anEdit). To mark the end of a set of commands, you'd call the end() method. Only after you combine all the commands can they be undone or redone. Figure 19-5 illustrates this.

With a CompoundEdit, if you undo() the edit, all added commands are undone. This is the same with redo(): All commands in the set are redone.

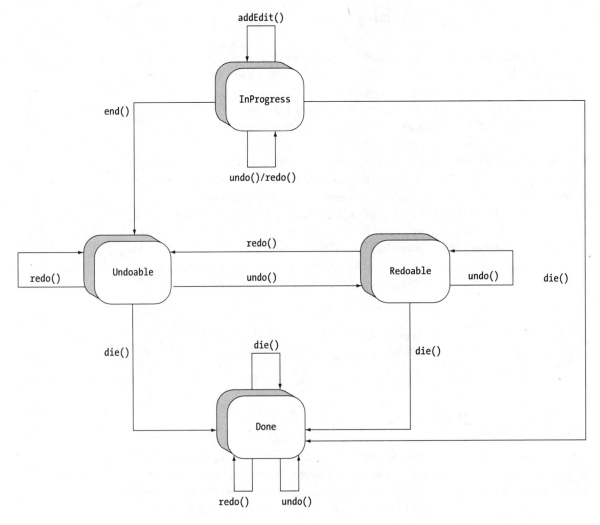

Figure 19-5: The CompoundEdit state chart

Class UndoManager

The UndoManager class is a specific subclass of CompoundEdit that tracks the history of edit commands, potentially for an entire application. The number of undoable commands the manager can track is defined by a configurable limit property whose initial value is 100.

When isInProgress() reports true, the UndoManager acts somewhat like a backward CompoundEdit, in which individual edits can be undone and redone. Once end() has been called, the UndoManager acts like a CompoundEdit, but without the ability to undo or redo individual edit commands. In addition, the

UndoManager has one more available state — Undoable or Redoable — for when the manager has undone at least one command, can still undo more, but can also redo the undone command(s).

Besides being able to directly add editable operations with addEdit(), the manager also serves as an UndoableEditListener. When the UndoableEditEvent happens, the listener adds the event's UndoableEdit command to the manager with addEdit(). In addition, you can clear out the edit queue with public void discardAllEdits(). After the manager receives the end() method, the sequence goes back to looking like Figure 19-5, leaving the bottom three states (Undoable, Redoable, and Done) shown in the chart.

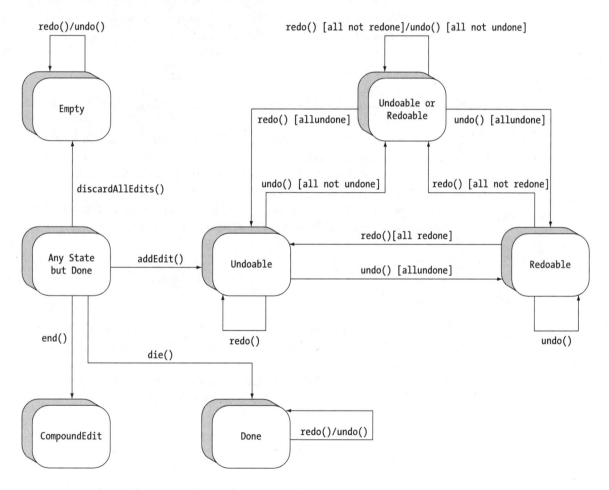

Figure 19-6: The UndoManager state chart

Keep in mind that certain undo() and redo() calls can throw exceptions. In addition, when you ask the UndoManager to undo or redo an edit command, the request undoes (or redoes) all commands up to the last significant one.

The transformation of the UndoManager into a CompoundEdit might seem confusing to some users: This transformation allows you to have a secondary UndoManager for certain suboperations that, once completed, become a single CompoundEdit to be passed along to the primary UndoManager.

> **NOTE** *Some developers might find it useful to extend the* UndoManager *to expose the* UndoableEdit *list that it is managing. Then they can display the presentation names of the various edit commands. Fortunately — or unfortunately — by default these aren't exposed.*

InterfaceUndoableEditListener and Class UndoableEditEvent

The UndoManager implements the UndoableEditListener interface so that it can be notified when undoable operations happen. The listener, whose definition is shown in this section, uses an UndoableEditEvent to tell interested objects when a command that can be undone has happened. Of all the classes in the Swing-related packages, only the AbstractDocument class (as defined in the Document interface) comes with built-in support to add these listeners.

```
public interface UndoableEditListener implements EventListener {
  public void undoableEditHappened(UndoableEditEvent undoableEditEvent);
}
```

When creating your own classes that support undoable operations, you'll need to maintain your own list of listeners with the help of the UndoableEditSupport class, described next.

The UndoableEditEvent class includes one property, edit, that returns the UndoableEdit object for the event: public UndoableEdit getEdit().

Class UndoableEditSupport

The UndoableEditSupport class is similar to the JavaBeans classes PropertyChangeSupport and VetoableChangeSupport. All three of these classes manage a list of a specific type of listener. In the case of the UndoableEditSupport class, that type of listener is the UndoableEditListener. You add listeners with

`public void addUndoableListener(UndoableEditListener listener)` and remove
them with `public void removeUndoableListener(UndoableEditListener listener)`.

When you want to notify listeners that an `UndoableEdit` operation has
happened, you call the `public void postEdit(UndoableEdit anEdit)` method,
which creates an `UndoableEditEvent` and calls the `undoableEditHappened()` method
of each listener.

> **NOTE** *The class also includes support for combining multiple undoable
> edit commands into a* `CompoundEdit` *with the* `public void beginUpdate()`
> *and* `public void endUpdate()` *methods.*

The basic framework for the class usage follows. Normally, you tie the undoable
event to some other operation. In this example, it's tied to the moment an
`ActionEvent` happens, and therefore any registered `ActionListener` objects need
to be notified.

```java
import javax.swing.undo.*;
import javax.swing.event.*;
import java.awt.event.*;
import java.awt.*;

public class AnUndoableComponent {
  UndoableEditSupport undoableEditSupport = new UndoableEditSupport(this);
  ActionListener actionListenerList = null;

  public void addActionListener(ActionListener actionListener) {
    actionListenerList = AWTEventMulticaster.add(actionListener,
actionListenerList);
  }

  public void removeActionListener(ActionListener actionListener) {
    actionListenerList = AWTEventMulticaster.remove(actionListener,
actionListenerList);
  }

  public void addUndoableEditListener(UndoableEditListener undoableEditListener)
{
    undoableEditSupport.addUndoableEditListener(undoableEditListener);
  }

  public void removeUndoableEditListener(UndoableEditListener
```

```
undoableEditListener) {
    undoableEditSupport.removeUndoableEditListener(undoableEditListener);
}

protected void fireActionPerformed(ActionEvent actionEvent) {
    actionListenerList.actionPerformed(actionEvent);
    // Need to create your custom type of undoable operation
    undoableEditSupport.postEdit(new AbstractUndoableEdit());
}
}
```

A Complete Undoable Program Example

Now that you've seen the main classes for the Swing undo framework, let's put together a complete example, defining our own undoable class. The undoable class will be a drawing panel in which each mouse click defines a point that will be drawn in a polygon. The screens in Figure 19-7 show the drawable panel in action, before and after an undo operation.

The main program looks practically identical to the earlier example of supporting undo and redo operations in a Swing text component listed in the section "Using the Undo Framework with Swing Text Components." You need to simply create an UndoManager to manage the undoable operations and associate it to the undoable object. The usage of the undo framework works the same here, except that the undoable object is the yet-to-be-created UndoableDrawingPanel class that's coming up shortly.

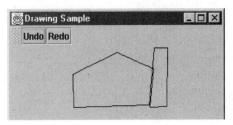
Before undo

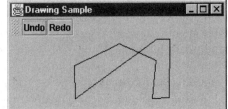
After undo

Figure 19-7: The undoable drawing panel at work

```
import javax.swing.*;
import javax.swing.undo.*;
import java.awt.*;
```

```
public class UndoDrawing {
  public static void main(String args[]) {
    JFrame frame = new ExitableJFrame("Drawing Sample");

    UndoableDrawingPanel drawingPanel = new UndoableDrawingPanel();

    UndoManager manager = new UndoManager();
    drawingPanel.addUndoableEditListener(manager);

    JToolBar toolbar = new JToolBar();
    toolbar.add(UndoManagerHelper.getUndoAction(manager));
    toolbar.add(UndoManagerHelper.getRedoAction(manager));

    Container content = frame.getContentPane();
    content.add(toolbar, BorderLayout.NORTH);
    content.add(drawingPanel, BorderLayout.CENTER);
    frame.setSize(300, 150);
    frame.setVisible(true);
  }
}
```

The `UndoableDrawingPanel` class is a component that draws a polygon within itself based on a set of points within the polygon. New points are added to the polygon whenever the mouse is released. If you don't want the component to support undoable operations, you wouldn't need to do anything beyond collecting points for the drawing panel.

For the panel to support undoable operations, it has to do two things. First, it must maintain a list of `UndoableEditListener` objects. This can be easily done with the help of the `UndoableEditSupport` class, as shown in the section "UndoableEditSupport Class" earlier in this chapter. The second task involves creating an `UndoableEdit` object, prior to any state changes, and posting it to the registered listeners. Because the state of the drawing panel is the polygon, this property must be exposed in the drawing class.

Because the `UndoableEdit` implementation class `UndoableDrawEdit` is yet to be defined, I'm supplying the following definition for the `UndoableDrawingPanel` class. Nothing in the class is particularly complicated. The important thing to remember when defining an undoable class is that the undoable event must be created *before* the state of the component changes.

```
import javax.swing.*;
import javax.swing.event.*;
import javax.swing.undo.*;
import java.awt.*;
import java.awt.event.*;
```

```
public class UndoableDrawingPanel extends JPanel {
  UndoableEditSupport undoableEditSupport = new UndoableEditSupport(this);
  Polygon polygon = new Polygon();

  public UndoableDrawingPanel() {
    MouseListener mouseListener = new MouseAdapter() {
      public void mouseReleased(MouseEvent mouseEvent) {
        undoableEditSupport.postEdit(new
UndoableDrawEdit(UndoableDrawingPanel.this));
        polygon.addPoint(mouseEvent.getX(), mouseEvent.getY());
        repaint();
      }
    };
    addMouseListener(mouseListener);
  }

  public void addUndoableEditListener(UndoableEditListener undoableEditListener)
{
    undoableEditSupport.addUndoableEditListener(undoableEditListener);
  }

  public void removeUndoableEditListener(UndoableEditListener
undoableEditListener) {
    undoableEditSupport.removeUndoableEditListener(undoableEditListener);
  }

  public void setPolygon(Polygon newValue) {
    polygon = newValue;
    repaint();
  }

  public Polygon getPolygon() {
    Polygon returnValue;
    if (polygon.npoints == 0) {
      returnValue = new Polygon();
    } else {
      returnValue = new Polygon(polygon.xpoints, polygon.ypoints,
polygon.npoints);
    }
    return returnValue;
  }
```

```
  protected void paintComponent(Graphics g) {
    super.paintComponent(g);
    g.drawPolygon(polygon);
  }
}
```

When defining the custom implementation of the UndoableEdit interface, you can choose to implement the complete interface or you can subclass the AbstractUndoableEdit class and override any appropriate methods. More typically, you'll just subclass AbstractUndoableEdit. The minimum methods to override are undo() and redo(), although you'll probably also choose to override getPresentationName() to give a better name to the undoable operation.

Because the Command design pattern has the Concrete Command (that is, the UndoableEdit implementation) invoke the operation, the constructor must save any information necessary to make the operation undoable. In the case of the drawing panel, you need to save a reference to the panel and its current polygon. Then, when the operation is asked to undo itself, the original polygon can be restored. To support redoing the undo operation, the undo() method must also save the new polygon, otherwise the redo() operation wouldn't know how to change things back. It may sound like quite a bit of work, but it really isn't. The complete class definition for the UndoableEdit implementation follows.

```
import javax.swing.undo.*;
import java.awt.*;

public class UndoableDrawEdit extends AbstractUndoableEdit {
  UndoableDrawingPanel panel;
  Polygon polygon, savedPolygon;

  public UndoableDrawEdit(UndoableDrawingPanel panel) {
    this.panel = panel;
    polygon = panel.getPolygon();
  }

  public String getPresentationName() {
    return "Polygon of size " + polygon.npoints;
  }

  public void redo() throws CannotRedoException {
    super.redo();
    if (savedPolygon == null) {
      // Should never get here, as super() doesn't permit redoing
      throw new CannotRedoException();
```

```
    } else {
      panel.setPolygon(savedPolygon);
      savedPolygon = null;
    }
  }

  public void undo() throws CannotUndoException {
    super.undo();
    savedPolygon = panel.getPolygon();
    panel.setPolygon(polygon);
  }
}
```

And that's it! The last two classes make the first UndoDrawing example class work. When creating your own undoable classes, you will need to subclass a nonundoable class and then add the necessary support to make it undoable. In addition, you need to define an UndoableEdit implementation to support your specific class.

Using the StateEditable Interface and StateEdit Class

In the previous example, it was the responsibility of your custom UndoableEdit implementation to maintain the before-and-after state of the undoable object. The Swing undo framework also supports the ability of an object outside the undoable edit implementation to manage the state. When using an outside object for state management, it isn't necessary to implement the UndoableEdit interface yourself. Instead, you can use the StateEdit class as the UndoableEdit implementation. The StateEdit class then relies on a class to implement the StateEditable interface to manage the before-and-after storage of the state of an undoable object (within a Hashtable).

We'll explore using the StateEditable interface with a StateEdit instance by rewriting the UndoableDrawingPanel example. The StateEditable interface consists of two methods and a meaningless string constant. An object that supports the undoing of its operations stores its state with the storeState(Hashtable) method. This is all the information about the state of the object that can change. Then, restoring the state of the object is done in the restoreState(Hashtable) method.

```
public interface StateEditable {
  public final static String RCSID;
  public void restoreState(Hashtable state);
  public void storeState(Hashtable state);

}
```

Using this interface with the updated, undoable drawing panel involves implementing the interface and storing/getting the polygon shown in Figure 19-7. That's because the polygon is the only state information we care about undoing. The appropriate source code follows. When writing the restoreState() method, keep in mind one thing: The Hashtable that the restoreState() method returns contains only key-value pairs that changed. It's possible that the get() method of the Hashtable returns null for something that you explicitly put() in the hash table. Therefore, you're required to add an if-null check after getting any state information from the hash table.

```
public class UndoableDrawingPanel2 extends JPanel implements StateEditable {
...
private static String POLYGON_KEY = "Polygon";
public void storeState(Hashtable state) {
  state.put(POLYGON_KEY, getPolygon());
}

public void restoreState(Hashtable state) {
  Polygon polygon = (Polygon)state.get(POLYGON_KEY);
  if (polygon != null) {
    setPolygon(polygon);
  }
}
```

After you've implemented the StateEditable interface, you can use the StateEdit class as the UndoableEdit implementation. Where the previous UndoableDrawingPanel example created a custom UndoableDrawEdit, the new class creates a StateEdit instance. The StateEdit constructor accepts a StateEditable object that you're going to change, and an optional presentation name. After creating the StateEdit object, modify the StateEditable object and then tell the StateEdit to end() the modifications to the StateEditable object. When the StateEdit object is told that the modifications have ended, it compares the before-and-after states of the state editable object and removes any key-value pairs that didn't change from the hash table. You can then post the UndoableEdit to the list of UndoableEditListener objects through the list maintained by the UndoableEditSupport class.

```
StateEdit stateEdit = new StateEdit(UndoableDrawingPanel2.this);
// Change state of UndoableDrawingPanel2
polygon.addPoint(mouseEvent.getX(), mouseEvent.getY());
// Done changing state
stateEdit.end();
undoableEditSupport.postEdit(stateEdit);
```

After it's posted, the UndoManager manages the StateEdit instance of UndoableEdit, just like any other undoable edit object. The UndoManager can then request the StateEdit object to tell its StateEditable object to restore its previous state. This holds for any other UndoableEdit object. Therefore, no other source code needs to change.

The following reworking (again, with changes shown in bold) of the UndoableDrawingPanel example, listed earlier in this chapter under "A Complete Undoable Program Example," uses the StateEditable/StateEdit combination. The essential parts that use the new interface are boldfaced in the class definition that follows. The test program from that earlier section of the chapter is included as the main() method to keep everything together. With the exception of the class name change for the drawing panel, the test program didn't change and will still result in what you see in Figure 19-7.

```
import javax.swing.*;
import javax.swing.event.*;
import javax.swing.undo.*;
import java.awt.*;
import java.awt.event.*;
import java.util.Hashtable;

public class UndoableDrawingPanel2 extends JPanel implements StateEditable {
  private static String POLYGON_KEY = "Polygon";
  UndoableEditSupport undoableEditSupport = new UndoableEditSupport(this);
  Polygon polygon = new Polygon();

  public UndoableDrawingPanel2() {
    MouseListener mouseListener = new MouseAdapter() {
      public void mouseReleased(MouseEvent mouseEvent) {
        StateEdit stateEdit = new StateEdit(UndoableDrawingPanel2.this);
        polygon.addPoint(mouseEvent.getX(), mouseEvent.getY());
        stateEdit.end();
        undoableEditSupport.postEdit(stateEdit);
        repaint();
      }
    };
    addMouseListener(mouseListener);
  }
```

```java
    public void addUndoableEditListener(UndoableEditListener undoableEditListener)
{
        undoableEditSupport.addUndoableEditListener(undoableEditListener);
    }

    public void removeUndoableEditListener(UndoableEditListener
undoableEditListener) {
        undoableEditSupport.removeUndoableEditListener(undoableEditListener);
    }

    public void storeState(Hashtable state) {
        state.put(POLYGON_KEY, getPolygon());
    }

    public void restoreState(Hashtable state) {
        Polygon polygon = (Polygon)state.get(POLYGON_KEY);
        if (polygon != null) {
            setPolygon(polygon);
        }
    }

    public void setPolygon(Polygon newValue) {
        polygon = newValue;
        repaint();
    }

    public Polygon getPolygon() {
        Polygon returnValue;
        if (polygon.npoints == 0) {
            returnValue = new Polygon();
        } else {
            returnValue = new Polygon(polygon.xpoints, polygon.ypoints,
polygon.npoints);
        }
        return returnValue;
    }

    protected void paintComponent(Graphics g) {
        super.paintComponent(g);
        g.drawPolygon(polygon);
    }

    public static void main(String args[]) {
        JFrame frame = new ExitableJFrame("Drawing Sample2");
```

```
        UndoableDrawingPanel2 drawingPanel = new UndoableDrawingPanel2();

        UndoManager manager = new UndoManager();
        drawingPanel.addUndoableEditListener(manager);

        JToolBar toolbar = new JToolBar();
        toolbar.add(UndoManagerHelper.getUndoAction(manager));
        toolbar.add(UndoManagerHelper.getRedoAction(manager));

        Container content = frame.getContentPane();
        content.add(toolbar, BorderLayout.NORTH);
        content.add(drawingPanel, BorderLayout.CENTER);
        frame.setSize(300, 150);
        frame.setVisible(true);
    }
}
```

Summary

This chapter took both a short and a long look at the undo framework found in
the javax.swing.undo package with support from javax.swing.event. You saw how
the framework support arrives already built into the Swing text components. In
addition, you learned how to build support into your own classes. With the interfaces and classes found in the undo framework, you can make any editable
component support both undo and redo capabilities.

This chapter is followed by Appendix A, where you'll find a complete listing
of all the settable properties of the UIManager, enabling you to customize a look
and feel without having to go to the trouble of creating a new one.

UI Manager Properties

THROUGHOUT THIS BOOK YOU'LL FIND TABLES that list the property names and data types for all the UIResource elements of specific Swing components. Although these tables serve to list all the information about a specific component, I figured it would be handy to also group all the information about property names in one place.

With that in mind, Table A-1 provides a complete list of properties used by the predefined look and feel classes — Motif, Macintosh, Metal, and Windows — provided with the Swing 1.1.1 release. The table indicates with an "X" which of the four look and feel classes uses a particular property.

To change the default setting for any one of these properties, you need to notify the UIManager by storing a new setting in the lookup table of the UIManager. For instance, to change the default text for the "Yes" button on a JOptionPane, you'd replace the "OptionPane.yesButtonText" property with the new setting UIManager.put("OptionPane.yesButtonText", "Si");. Then, any component created after the setting change will get the new value: "Si". If you want a *displayed* component to get the new setting, you must call its updateUI() method.

When you change the current look and feel, any custom settings you install may be lost. If the class of the property value setting implements the UIResource interface (an empty marker interface such as Serializable), then the setting will be replaced by the default setting of the look and feel. For example, the first setting that follows would be saved when the look and feel changes; the second would not.

UIManager.put("OptionPane.background", Color.red);

versus

UIManager.put("OptionPane.background", new ColorUIResource(Color.red));

If the property value setting does not implement the UIResource interface, then the property setting is retained when the look and feel changes.

> **WARNING**   *A word of caution about the information in Table A-1: The specific set of available properties changes with each JFC/Project Swing release. This table reflects the current settings for release 1.1.1. Some properties may not be in earlier versions, and others may have been replaced in later versions. The changes tend to be minor, but they do exist. For a resource that lists the specific properties available with each release, see the Swing PLAF Differences list at http://www.gargoylesoftware.com/ papers/plafdiff.html from Gargoyle Software.*

PROPERTY STRING	OBJECT TYPE	MOTIF	MACINTOSH	METAL	WINDOWS
activeCaption	Color	X	X	X	X
activeCaptionBorder	Color	X	X	X	X
activeCaptionText	Color	X	X	X	X
Button.background	Color	X	X	X	X
Button.border	Border	X	X	X	X
Button.dashedRectGapHeight	Integer				X
Button.dashedRectGapWidth	Integer				X
Button.dashedRectGapX	Integer				X
Button.dashedRectGapY	Integer				X
Button.disabledText	Color		X	X	
Button.focus	Color			X	X
Button.font	Font	X	X	X	X
Button.foreground	Color	X	X	X	X
Button.margin	Insets	X	X	X	X
Button.select	Color	X	X	X	
Button.selectText	Color		X		
Button.textIconGap	Integer	X	X	X	X
Button.textShiftOffset	Integer	X	X	X	X
ButtonUI	String	X	X	X	X
CheckBox.background	Color	X	X	X	X
CheckBox.border	Border	X	X	X	X
CheckBox.darkShadow	Color				X
CheckBox.disabledText	Color		X	X	
CheckBox.focus	Color	X		X	X
CheckBox.font	Font	X	X	X	X
CheckBox.foreground	Color	X	X	X	X
CheckBox.highlight	Color				X
CheckBox.icon	Icon	X	X	X	X
CheckBox.margin	Insets	X	X	X	X
Checkbox.select	Color			X	

(continued)

Table A-1 (continued)

PROPERTY STRING	OBJECT TYPE	MOTIF	MACINTOSH	METAL	WINDOWS
CheckBox.shadow	Color				X
CheckBox.textIconGap	Integer	X	X	X	X
CheckBox.textShiftOffset	Integer	X	X	X	X
CheckBoxMenuItem.acceleratorFont	Font	X	X	X	X
CheckBoxMenuItem.acceleratorForeground	Color	X	X	X	X
CheckBoxMenuItem.acceleratorSelectionForeground	Color	X	X	X	X
CheckBoxMenuItem.arrowIcon	Icon	X	X	X	X
CheckBoxMenuItem.background	Color	X	X	X	X
CheckBoxMenuItem.border	Border	X	X	X	X
CheckBoxMenuItem.borderPainted	Boolean	X	X	X	X
CheckBoxMenuItem.checkIcon	Icon	X	X	X	X
CheckBoxMenuItem.disabledForeground	Color		X	X	
CheckBoxMenuItem.font	Font	X	X	X	X
CheckBoxMenuItem.foreground	Color	X	X	X	X
CheckBoxMenuItem.margin	Insets	X	X	X	X
CheckBoxMenuItem.selectionBackground	Color	X	X	X	X
CheckBoxMenuItem.selectionForeground	Color	X	X	X	X
CheckBoxMenuItemUI	String	X	X	X	X
CheckBoxUI	String	X	X	X	X
ColorChooser.background	Color	X	X	X	X
ColorChooser.cancelText	String	X	X	X	X
ColorChooser.font	Font	X	X	X	X
ColorChooser.foreground	Color	X	X	X	X
ColorChooser.hsbBlueText	String	X	X	X	X
ColorChooser.hsbBrightnessText	String	X	X	X	X
ColorChooser.hsbGreenText	String	X	X	X	X
ColorChooser.hsbHueText	String	X	X	X	X
ColorChooser.hsbNameText	String	X	X	X	X
ColorChooser.hsbRedText	String	X	X	X	X
ColorChooser.hsbSaturationText	String	X	X	X	X
ColorChooser.okText	String	X	X	X	X
ColorChooser.previewText	String	X	X	X	X
ColorChooser.resetText	String	X	X	X	X
ColorChooser.rgbBlueMnemonic	Integer	X	X	X	X
ColorChooser.rgbBlueText	String	X	X	X	X
ColorChooser.rgbGreenMnemonic	Integer	X	X	X	X
ColorChooser.rgbGreenText	String	X	X	X	X
ColorChooser.rgbNameText	String	X	X	X	X
ColorChooser.rgbRedMnemonic	Integer	X	X	X	X

(continued)

Table A-1 (continued)

PROPERTY STRING	OBJECT TYPE	MOTIF	MACINTOSH	METAL	WINDOWS
ColorChooser.rgbRedText	String	X	X	X	X
ColorChooser.swatchesDefaultRecentColor	Color	X	X	X	X
ColorChooser.swatchesNameText	String	X	X	X	X
ColorChooser.swatchesRecentSwatchSize	Dimension	X	X	X	X
ColorChooser.swatchesRecentText	String	X	X	X	X
ColorChooser.swatchesSwatchSize	Dimension	X	X	X	X
ColorChooserUI	String	X	X	X	X
ComboBox.background	Color	X	X	X	X
ComboBox.border	Border	X			X
ComboBox.control	Color	X			
ComboBox.controlForeground	Color	X			
ComboBox.disabledBackground	Color	X	X	X	X
ComboBox.disabledForeground	Color	X	X	X	X
ComboBox.font	Font	X	X	X	X
ComboBox.foreground	Color	X	X	X	X
ComboBox.listBackground	Color		X	X	
ComboBox.listForeground	Color		X	X	
ComboBox.selectionBackground	Color	X	X	X	X
ComboBox.selectionForeground	Color	X	X	X	X
ComboBoxUI	String	X	X	X	X
control	Color	X	X	X	X
controlDkShadow	Color	X	X	X	X
controlHighlight	Color	X	X	X	X
controlLightShadow	Color	X			
controlLtHighlight	Color	X	X	X	X
controlShadow	Color	X	X	X	X
controlText	Color	X	X	X	X
desktop	Color	X	X	X	X
Desktop.background	Color	X	X	X	X
DesktopIcon.background	Color			X	
DesktopIcon.border	Border		X	X	X
DesktopIcon.font	Font			X	
DesktopIcon.foreground	Color			X	
DesktopIcon.icon	Icon	X			
DesktopIconUI	String	X	X	X	X
DesktopPaneUI	String	X	X	X	X
DirectoryPaneUI	String	X			
EditorPane.background	Color	X	X	X	X
EditorPane.border	Border	X	X	X	X

(continued)

Table A-1 (continued)

PROPERTY STRING	OBJECT TYPE	MOTIF	MACINTOSH	METAL	WINDOWS
EditorPane.caretBlinkRate	Integer	X	X	X	X
EditorPane.caretForeground	Color	X	X	X	X
EditorPane.font	Font	X	X	X	X
EditorPane.foreground	Color	X	X	X	X
EditorPane.inactiveForeground	Color	X	X	X	X
EditorPane.keyBindings	KeyBinding[ ]	X	X	X	X
EditorPane.margin	Insets	X	X	X	X
EditorPane.selectionBackground	Color	X	X	X	X
EditorPane.selectionForeground	Color	X	X	X	X
EditorPaneUI	String	X	X	X	X
FileChooser.acceptAllFileFilterText	String	X	X	X	X
FileChooser.cancelButtonMnemonic	Integer	X	X	X	X
FileChooser.cancelButtonText	String	X	X	X	X
FileChooser.cancelButtonToolTipText	String	X	X	X	X
FileChooser.detailsViewButtonAccessibleName	String			X	X
FileChooser.detailsViewButtonToolTipText	String			X	X
FileChooser.detailsViewIcon	Icon	X	X	X	X
FileChooser.directoryDescriptionText	String	X	X	X	X
FileChooser.enterFileNameLabelMnemonic	Integer	X			
FileChooser.enterFileNameLabelText	String	X			
FileChooser.fileDescriptionText	String	X	X	X	X
FileChooser.fileNameLabelMnemonic	Integer			X	X
FileChooser.fileNameLabelText	String			X	X
FileChooser.filesLabelMnemonic	Integer	X			
FileChooser.filesLabelText	String	X			
FileChooser.filesOfTypeLabelMnemonic	Integer			X	X
FileChooser.filesOfTypeLabelText	String			X	X
FileChooser.filterLabelMnemonic ·	Integer	X			
FileChooser.filterLabelText	String	X			
FileChooser.foldersLabelMnemonic	Integer	X			
FileChooser.foldersLabelText	String	X			
FileChooser.helpButtonMnemonic	Integer	X	X	X	X
FileChooser.helpButtonText	String	X	X	X	X
FileChooser.helpButtonToolTipText	String	X	X	X	X
FileChooser.homeFolderAccessibleName	String			X	X
FileChooser.homeFolderIcon	Icon	X	X	X	X
FileChooser.homeFolderToolTipText	String			X	X
FileChooser.listViewButtonAccessibleName	String			X	X
FileChooser.listViewButtonToolTipText	String			X	X

(continued)

Table A-1 (continued)

PROPERTY STRING	OBJECT TYPE	MOTIF	MACINTOSH	METAL	WINDOWS
FileChooser.listViewIcon	Icon	X	X	X	X
FileChooser.lookInLabelMnemonic	Integer			X	X
FileChooser.lookInLabelText	String			X	X
FileChooser.newFolderAccessibleName	String			X	X
FileChooser.newFolderErrorSeparator	String	X	X	X	X
FileChooser.newFolderErrorText	String	X	X	X	X
FileChooser.newFolderIcon	Icon	X	X	X	X
FileChooser.newFolderToolTipText	String			X	X
FileChooser.openButtonMnemonic	Integer	X	X	X	X
FileChooser.openButtonText	String	X	X	X	X
FileChooser.openButtonToolTipText	String	X	X	X	X
FileChooser.pathLabelMnemonic	Integer	X			
FileChooser.pathLabelText	String	X			
FileChooser.saveButtonMnemonic	Integer	X	X	X	X
FileChooser.saveButtonText	String	X	X	X	X
FileChooser.saveButtonToolTipText	String	X	X	X	X
FileChooser.updateButtonMnemonic	Integer	X	X	X	X
FileChooser.updateButtonText	String	X	X	X	X
FileChooser.updateButtonToolTipText	String	X	X	X	X
FileChooser.upFolderAccessibleName	String			X	X
FileChooser.upFolderIcon	Icon	X	X	X	X
FileChooser.upFolderToolTipText	String			X	X
FileChooserUI	String	X	X	X	X
FileView.computerIcon	Icon	X	X	X	X
FileView.directoryIcon	Icon	X	X	X	X
FileView.fileIcon	Icon	X	X	X	X
FileView.floppyDriveIcon	Icon	X	X	X	X
FileView.hardDriveIcon	Icon	X	X	X	X
FocusManagerClassName	String	X	X	X	X
inactiveCaption	Color	X	X	X	X
inactiveCaptionBorder	Color	X	X	X	X
inactiveCaptionText	Color	X	X	X	X
info	Color	X	X	X	X
infoText	Color	X	X	X	X
InternalFrame.activeTitleBackground	Color	X	X	X	X
InternalFrame.activeTitleForeground	Color	X	X	X	X
InternalFrame.border	Border	X	X	X	X
InternalFrame.closeIcon	Icon	X	X	X	X
InternalFrame.closePressed	Icon		X		

(continued)

Table A-1 (continued)

PROPERTY STRING	OBJECT TYPE	MOTIF	MACINTOSH	METAL	WINDOWS
InternalFrame.font	Font		X	X	
InternalFrame.icon	Icon	X		X	X
InternalFrame.iconifyIcon	Icon	X	X	X	X
InternalFrame.iconifyPressed	Icon		X		
InternalFrame.iconizeIcon	Icon			X	
InternalFrame.inactiveTitleBackground	Color	X	X	X	X
InternalFrame.inactiveTitleForeground	Color	X	X	X	X
InternalFrame.maximizeIcon	Icon	X	X	X	X
InternalFrame.maximizePressed	Icon		X		
InternalFrame.minimizeIcon	Icon	X	X	X	X
InternalFrame.minimizeIconBackground	Color				X
InternalFrame.paletteBorder	Border			X	
InternalFrame.paletteCloseIcon	Icon			X	
InternalFrame.paletteTitleHeight	Integer			X	
InternalFrame.titleFont	Font	X	X	X	X
InternalFrame.windowShadeBorder	Border		X		
InternalFrameUI	String	X	X	X	X
Label.background	Color	X	X	X	X
Label.disabledForeground	Color	X	X	X	X
Label.disabledShadow	Color	X	X	X	X
Label.font	Font	X	X	X	X
Label.foreground	Color	X	X	X	X
LabelUI	String	X	X	X	X
List.background	Color	X	X	X	X
List.border	Border	X	X	X	X
List.cellRenderer	ListCellRender	X	X	X	X
List.focusCellHighlightBorder	Border	X	X	X	X
List.font	Font	X	X	X	X
List.foreground	Color	X	X	X	X
List.selectionBackground	Color	X	X	X	X
List.selectionForeground	Color	X	X	X	X
ListUI	String	X	X	X	X
menu	Color	X	X	X	X
Menu.acceleratorFont	Font	X	X	X	X
Menu.acceleratorForeground	Color	X	X	X	X
Menu.acceleratorPressedForeground	Color		X		
Menu.acceleratorSelectionForeground	Color	X	X	X	X
Menu.arrowIcon	Icon	X	X	X	X
Menu.background	Color	X	X	X	X

(continued)

Table A-1 (continued)

PROPERTY STRING	OBJECT TYPE	MOTIF	MACINTOSH	METAL	WINDOWS
Menu.border	Border	X	X	X	X
Menu.borderPainted	Boolean	X	X	X	X
Menu.checkIcon	Icon	X	X	X	X
Menu.consumesTabs	Boolean	X	X	X	X
Menu.disabledForeground	Color		X	X	
Menu.font	Font	X	X	X	X
Menu.foreground	Color	X	X	X	X
Menu.margin	Insets	X	X	X	X
Menu.selectionBackground	Color	X	X	X	X
Menu.selectionForeground	Color	X	X	X	X
MenuBar.background	Color	X	X	X	X
MenuBar.border	Border	X	X	X	X
MenuBar.font	Font	X	X	X	X
MenuBar.foreground	Color	X	X	X	X
MenuBarUI	String	X	X	X	X
MenuItem.acceleratorDelimiter	String	X	X	X	X
MenuItem.acceleratorFont	Font	X	X	X	X
MenuItem.acceleratorForeground	Color	X	X	X	X
MenuItem.acceleratorSelectionForeground	Color	X	X	X	X
MenuItem.arrowIcon	Icon	X	X	X	X
MenuItem.background	Color	X	X	X	X
MenuItem.border	Border	X	X	X	X
MenuItem.borderPainted	Boolean	X	X	X	X
MenuItem.checkIcon	Icon	X	X	X	X
MenuItem.disabledForeground	Color		X	X	
MenuItem.font	Font	X	X	X	X
MenuItem.foreground	Color	X	X	X	X
MenuItem.margin	Insets	X	X	X	X
MenuItem.selectionBackground	Color	X	X	X	X
MenuItem.selectionForeground	Color	X	X	X	X
MenuItemUI	String	X	X	X	X
menuPressedItemB	Color				X
menuPressedItemF	Color				X
menuText	Color	X	X	X	X
MenuUI	String	X	X	X	X
OptionPane.background	Color	X	X	X	X
OptionPane.border	Border	X	X	X	X
OptionPane.buttonAreaBorder	Border	X	X	X	X
OptionPane.cancelButtonText	String	X	X	X	X

(continued)

Table A-1 (continued)

PROPERTY STRING	OBJECT TYPE	MOTIF	MACINTOSH	METAL	WINDOWS
OptionPane.errorIcon	Icon	X	X	X	X
OptionPane.font	Font	X	X	X	X
OptionPane.foreground	Color	X	X	X	X
OptionPane.informationIcon	Icon	X	X	X	X
OptionPane.messageAreaBorder	Border	X	X	X	X
OptionPane.messageForeground	Color	X	X	X	X
OptionPane.minimumSize	Dimension	X	X	X	X
OptionPane.noButtonText	String	X	X	X	X
OptionPane.okButtonText	String	X	X	X	X
OptionPane.questionIcon	Icon	X	X	X	X
OptionPane.warningIcon	Icon	X	X	X	X
OptionPane.yesButtonText	String	X	X	X	X
OptionPaneUI	String	X	X	X	X
Panel.background	Color	X	X	X	X
Panel.font	Font	X	X	X	X
Panel.foreground	Color	X	X	X	X
PanelUI	String	X	X	X	X
PasswordField.background	Color	X	X	X	X
PasswordField.border	Border	X	X	X	X
PasswordField.caretBlinkRate	Integer	X	X	X	X
PasswordField.caretForeground	Color	X	X	X	X
PasswordField.font	Font	X	X	X	X
PasswordField.foreground	Color	X	X	X	X
PasswordField.inactiveForeground	Color	X	X	X	X
PasswordField.keyBindings	KeyBinding[ ]	X	X	X	X
PasswordField.margin	Insets	X	X	X	X
PasswordField.selectionBackground	Color	X	X	X	X
PasswordField.selectionForeground	Color	X	X	X	X
PasswordFieldUI	String	X	X	X	X
PopupMenu.background	Color	X	X	X	X
PopupMenu.border	Border	X	X	X	X
PopupMenu.font	Font	X	X	X	X
PopupMenu.foreground	Color	X	X	X	X
PopupMenuSeparatorUI	String	X	X	X	X
PopupMenuUI	String	X	X	X	X
ProgressBar.background	Color	X	X	X	X
ProgressBar.backgroundHighlight	Color			X	
ProgressBar.border	Border	X	X	X	X
ProgressBar.cellLength	Integer	X	X	X	X

(continued)

Table A-1 (continued)

PROPERTY STRING	OBJECT TYPE	MOTIF	MACINTOSH	METAL	WINDOWS
ProgressBar.cellSpacing	Integer	X	X	X	X
ProgressBar.font	Font	X	X	X	X
ProgressBar.foreground	Color	X	X	X	X
ProgressBar.foregroundHighlight	Color			X	
ProgressBar.selectionBackground	Color	X	X	X	X
ProgressBar.selectionForeground	Color	X	X	X	X
ProgressBarUI	String	X	X	X	X
RadioButton.background	Color	X	X	X	X
RadioButton.border	Border	X	X	X	X
RadioButton.darkShadow	Color				X
RadioButton.disabledOff	Icon		X		
RadioButton.disabledOn	Icon		X		
RadioButton.disabledText	Color		X	X	
RadioButton.focus	Color	X		X	X
RadioButton.font	Font	X	X	X	X
RadioButton.foreground	Color	X	X	X	X
RadioButton.highlight	Color				X
RadioButton.icon	Icon	X	X	X	X
RadioButton.margin	Insets	X	X	X	X
RadioButton.off	Icon		X		
RadioButton.on	Icon		X		
RadioButton.pressedOff	Icon		X		
RadioButton.pressedOn	Icon		X		
RadioButton.select	Color			X	
RadioButton.shadow	Color				X
RadioButton.textIconGap	Integer	X	X	X	X
RadioButton.textShiftOffset	Integer	X	X	X	X
RadioButtonMenuItem.acceleratorFont	Font	X	X	X	X
RadioButtonMenuItem.acceleratorForeground	Color	X	X	X	X
RadioButtonMenuItem. acceleratorSelectionForeground	Color	X	X	X	X
RadioButtonMenuItem.arrowIcon	Icon	X	X	X	X
RadioButtonMenuItem.background	Color	X	X	X	X
RadioButtonMenuItem.border	Border	X	X	X	X
RadioButtonMenuItem.borderPainted	Boolean	X	X	X	X
RadioButtonMenuItem.checkIcon	Icon	X	X	X	X
RadioButtonMenuItem.disabledForeground	Color		X	X	
RadioButtonMenuItem.font	Font	X	X	X	X
RadioButtonMenuItem.foreground	Color	X	X	X	X

(continued)

Table A-1 (continued)

PROPERTY STRING	OBJECT TYPE	MOTIF	MACINTOSH	METAL	WINDOWS
RadioButtonMenuItem.margin	Insets	X	X	X	X
RadioButtonMenuItem.selectionBackground	Color	X	X	X	X
RadioButtonMenuItem.selectionForeground	Color	X	X	X	X
RadioButtonMenuItemUI	String	X	X	X	X
RadioButtonUI	String	X	X	X	X
scrollbar	Color	X	X	X	X
ScrollBar.arrowBackground	Color		X		
ScrollBar.arrowColor	Color		X		
ScrollBar.arrowHighlight	Color		X		
ScrollBar.arrowShadow	Color		X		
ScrollBar.background	Color	X	X	X	X
ScrollBar.border	Border	X	X	X	
ScrollBar.darkShadow	Color			X	
ScrollBar.foreground	Color	X	X	X	X
ScrollBar.highlight	Color			X	
ScrollBar.maximumThumbSize	Dimension	X	X	X	X
ScrollBar.minimumThumbSize	Dimension	X	X	X	X
ScrollBar.pressedArrowBackground	Color		X		
ScrollBar.pressedArrowHighlight	Color		X		
ScrollBar.pressedArrowShadow	Color		X		
ScrollBar.pressedThumb	Color		X		
ScrollBar.pressedThumbDarkShadow	Color		X		
ScrollBar.pressedThumbHighlight	Color		X		
ScrollBar.pressedThumbLightHighlight	Color		X		
ScrollBar.pressedThumbShadow	Color		X		
ScrollBar.shadow	Color			X	
ScrollBar.thumb	Color	X	X	X	X
ScrollBar.thumbDarkShadow	Color	X	X	X	X
ScrollBar.thumbHighlight	Color	X	X	X	X
ScrollBar.thumbLightHighlight	Color		X		
ScrollBar.thumbLightShadow	Color	X	X	X	X
ScrollBar.thumbShadow	Color		X	X	
ScrollBar.track	Color	X	X	X	X
ScrollBar.trackDarkShadow	Color		X		
ScrollBar.trackHighlight	Color	X	X	X	X
ScrollBar.trackLightHighlight	Color		X		
ScrollBar.trackShadow	Color		X		
ScrollBar.width	Integer		X	X	
ScrollBarUI	String	X	X	X	X

(continued)

Table A-1 (continued)

PROPERTY STRING	OBJECT TYPE	MOTIF	MACINTOSH	METAL	WINDOWS
ScrollPane.background	Color	X	X	X	X
ScrollPane.border	Border		X	X	X
ScrollPane.font	Font	X	X	X	X
ScrollPane.foreground	Color	X	X	X	X
ScrollPane.viewportBorder	Border	X			
ScrollPaneUI	String	X	X	X	X
Separator.background	Color	X	X	X	X
Separator.foreground	Color	X	X	X	X
Separator.highlight	Color	X	X	X	X
Separator.shadow	Color	X	X	X	X
SeparatorUI	String	X	X	X	X
Slider.background	Color	X	X	X	X
Slider.border	Border	X			
Slider.darkShadow	Color		X	X	
Slider.focus	Color	X	X	X	X
Slider.focusInsets	Insets	X	X	X	X
Slider.foreground	Color	X	X	X	X
Slider.highlight	Color	X	X	X	X
Slider.horizontalThumbIcon	Icon		X	X	
Slider.majorTickLength	Integer		X	X	
Slider.minorTickLength	Integer		X		
Slider.shadow	Color	X	X	X	X
Slider.thumb	Color		X	X	
Slider.trackWidth	Integer		X	X	
Slider.verticalThumbIcon	Icon		X	X	
SliderUI	String	X	X	X	X
SplitPane.activeThumb	Color	X			
SplitPane.background	Color	X	X	X	X
SplitPane.border	Border	X	X	X	X
SplitPane.dividerSize	Integer	X	X	X	X
SplitPane.highlight	Color	X	X	X	
SplitPane.shadow	Color	X	X	X	X
SplitPaneUI	String	X	X	X	X
StandardDialogUI	String	X	X	X	X
TabbedPane.background	Color	X	X	X	X
TabbedPane.contentBorderInsets	Insets	X	X	X	X
TabbedPane.darkShadow	Color	X	X	X	X
TabbedPane.focus	Color	X	X	X	X
TabbedPane.font	Font	X	X	X	X

(continued)

Table A-1 (continued)

PROPERTY STRING	OBJECT TYPE	MOTIF	MACINTOSH	METAL	WINDOWS
TabbedPane.foreground	Color	X	X	X	X
TabbedPane.highlight	Color	X	X	X	X
TabbedPane.lightHighlight	Color	X	X	X	X
TabbedPane.nonSelected	Color		X	X	
TabbedPane.selected	Color			X	
TabbedPane.selectedTabPadInsets	Insets	X	X	X	X
TabbedPane.selectHighlight	Color			X	
TabbedPane.shadow	Color	X	X	X	X
TabbedPane.tabAreaBackground	Color			X	
TabbedPane.tabAreaInsets	Insets	X	X	X	X
TabbedPane.tabInsets	Insets	X	X	X	X
TabbedPane.tabRunOverlay	Integer	X	X	X	X
TabbedPane.textIconGap	Integer	X	X	X	X
TabbedPane.unselectedTabBackground	Color	X			
TabbedPane.unselectedTabForeground	Color	X			
TabbedPane.unselectedTabHighlight	Color	X			
TabbedPane.unselectedTabShadow	Color	X			
TabbedPaneUI	String	X	X	X	X
Table.background	Color	X	X	X	X
Table.focusCellBackground	Color	X	X	X	X
Table.focusCellForeground	Color	X	X	X	X
Table.focusCellHighlightBorder	Border	X	X	X	X
Table.font	Font	X	X	X	X
Table.foreground	Color	X	X	X	X
Table.gridColor	Color	X	X	X	X
Table.scrollPaneBorder	Border		X	X	X
Table.selectionBackground	Color	X	X	X	X
Table.selectionForeground	Color	X	X	X	X
TableHeader.background	Color	X	X	X	X
TableHeader.cellBorder	Border	X	X	X	X
TableHeader.font	Font	X	X	X	X
TableHeader.foreground	Color	X	X	X	X
TableHeaderUI	String	X	X	X	X
TableUI	String	X	X	X	X
text	Color	X	X	X	X
TextArea.background	Color	X	X	X	X
TextArea.border	Border	X	X	X	X
TextArea.caretBlinkRate	Integer	X	X	X	X
TextArea.caretForeground	Color	X	X	X	X

(continued)

Table A-1 (continued)

PROPERTY STRING	OBJECT TYPE	MOTIF	MACINTOSH	METAL	WINDOWS
TextArea.font	Font	X	X	X	X
TextArea.foreground	Color	X	X	X	X
TextArea.inactiveForeground	Color	X	X	X	X
TextArea.keyBindings	KeyBinding[ ]	X	X	X	X
TextArea.margin	Insets	X	X	X	X
TextArea.selectionBackground	Color	X	X	X	X
TextArea.selectionForeground	Color	X	X	X	X
TextAreaUI	String	X	X	X	X
TextField.background	Color	X	X	X	X
TextField.border	Border	X	X	X	X
TextField.caretBlinkRate	Integer	X	X	X	X
TextField.caretForeground	Color	X	X	X	X
TextField.font	Font	X	X	X	X
TextField.foreground	Color	X	X	X	X
TextField.inactiveForeground	Color	X	X	X	X
TextField.keyBindings	KeyBinding[ ]	X	X	X	X
TextField.margin	Insets	X	X	X	X
TextField.selectionBackground	Color	X	X	X	X
TextField.selectionForeground	Color	X	X	X	X
TextFieldUI	String	X	X	X	X
textHighlight	Color	X	X	X	X
textHighlightText	Color	X	X	X	X
textInactiveText	Color	X	X	X	X
TextPane.background	Color	X	X	X	X
TextPane.border	Border	X	X	X	X
TextPane.caretBlinkRate	Integer	X	X	X	X
TextPane.caretForeground	Color	X	X	X	X
TextPane.font	Font	X	X	X	X
TextPane.foreground	Color	X	X	X	X
TextPane.inactiveForeground	Color	X	X	X	X
TextPane.keyBindings	KeyBinding[ ]	X	X	X	X
TextPane.margin	Insets	X	X	X	X
TextPane.selectionBackground	Color	X	X	X	X
TextPane.selectionForeground	Color	X	X	X	X
TextPaneUI	String	X	X	X	X
textText	Color	X	X	X	X
TitledBorder.border	Border	X	X	X	X
TitledBorder.font	Font	X	X	X	X
TitledBorder.titleColor	Color	X	X	X	X

(continued)

Table A-1 (continued)

PROPERTY STRING	OBJECT TYPE	MOTIF	MACINTOSH	METAL	WINDOWS
ToggleButton.background	Color	X	X	X	X
ToggleButton.border	Border	X	X	X	X
ToggleButton.disabledBackground	Color		X	X	
ToggleButton.disabledSelectedBackground	Color		X	X	
ToggleButton.disabledSelectedText	Color		X	X	
ToggleButton.disabledText	Color		X	X	
ToggleButton.focus	Color	X		X	X
ToggleButton.font	Font	X	X	X	X
ToggleButton.foreground	Color	X	X	X	X
ToggleButton.margin	Insets	X	X	X	X
ToggleButton.select	Color	X	X	X	
ToggleButton.text	Color		X	X	
ToggleButton.textIconGap	Integer	X	X	X	X
ToggleButton.textShiftOffset	Integer	X	X	X	X
ToggleButtonUI	String	X	X	X	X
ToolBar.background	Color	X	X	X	X
ToolBar.border	Border	X	X	X	X
ToolBar.dockingBackground	Color	X	X	X	X
ToolBar.dockingForeground	Color	X	X	X	X
ToolBar.floatingBackground	Color	X	X	X	X
ToolBar.floatingForeground	Color	X	X	X	X
ToolBar.font	Font	X	X	X	X
ToolBar.foreground	Color	X	X	X	X
ToolBar.separatorSize	Dimension	X	X	X	X
ToolBarSeparatorUI	String	X	X	X	X
ToolBarUI	String	X	X	X	X
ToolTip.background	Color	X	X	X	X
ToolTip.border	Border	X	X	X	X
ToolTip.font	Font	X	X	X	X
ToolTip.foreground	Color	X	X	X	X
ToolTipUI	String	X	X	X	X
Tree.background	Color	X	X	X	X
Tree.changeSelectionWithFocus	Boolean	X	X	X	X
Tree.closedIcon	Icon	X	X	X	X
Tree.collapsedIcon	Icon	X	X	X	X
Tree.darkCollapsedIcon	Icon		X		
Tree.darkExpandedIcon	Icon		X		
Tree.drawsFocusBorderAroundIcon	Boolean	X	X	X	X
Tree.editorBorder	Border	X	X	X	X
Tree.editorBorderSelectionColor	Color	X			

Table A-1 (continued)

PROPERTY STRING	OBJECT TYPE	MOTIF	MACINTOSH	METAL	WINDOWS
Tree.expandedIcon	Icon	X	X	X	X
Tree.font	Font	X	X	X	X
Tree.foreground	Color	X	X	X	X
Tree.hash	Color	X	X	X	X
Tree.iconBackground	Color	X			
Tree.iconForeground	Color	X			
Tree.iconHighlight	Color	X			
Tree.iconShadow	Color	X			
Tree.leafIcon	Icon	X	X	X	X
Tree.leftChildIndent	Integer	X	X	X	X
Tree.line	Color			X	
Tree.openIcon	Icon	X	X	X	X
Tree.rightChildIndent	Integer	X	X	X	X
Tree.rowHeight	Integer	X	X	X	X
Tree.scrollsOnExpand	Boolean	X	X	X	X
Tree.selectionBackground	Color	X	X	X	X
Tree.selectionBorderColor	Color	X	X	X	X
Tree.selectionForeground	Color	X	X	X	X
Tree.textBackground	Color	X	X	X	X
Tree.textForeground	Color	X	X	X	X
TreeUI	String	X	X	X	X
Viewport.background	Color	X	X	X	X
Viewport.font	Font	X	X	X	X
Viewport.foreground	Color	X	X	X	X
ViewportUI	String	X	X	X	X
window	Color	X	X	X	X
windowBorder	Color	X	X	X	X
windowText	Color	X	X	X	X

Table A-1: UIResource Elements for the predefined look and feels

APPENDIX B

About the CD-ROM

THE COMPANION CD-ROM FOR *John Zukowski's Definitive Guide to Swing for Java 2*
is a hybrid that is readable on Windows 95, 98, and NT 3.5 or later, and UNIX
operating systems. This appendix tells you what you'll find on the CD and a little
bit about how to use it.

Loading the CD Contents

After you insert the CD-ROM into the appropriate drive, nothing will happen.
You must manually copy the contents from the CD-ROM to your local hard drive.
The copying can be done with Explorer, File Manager, or from the command line.

With Explorer/File Manager, just drag the contents of the Zukowski_code
directory from the CD-ROM to wherever you wish to install it. The command
examples that appear later in this appendix were written under the assumption
that you've copied the CD contents to the root level on your local PC hard drive
or under your home directory on UNIX.

From the command line on a PC, enter a command similar to the following,
depending upon which is your CD-ROM drive and where you wish to install the
contents:

```
xcopy /s d:\Zukowski_code c:\Zukowski_code
```

Be sure to answer "D" for directory when xcopy asks if the destination is a file or
directory.

To use the contents of the CD, you must have a system that is capable of
running the Java 2 platform, sometimes referred to as JDK 1.2. For about 95 per-
cent of the examples, you can get by with a JDK 1.1 runtime environment.
However, with the JDK 1.1 environment, you will come across some examples
that will not work without modification.

The actual recommended system requirements are dependent on the Java
platform you are using. Review the requirements that came with the Java
Development Kit you are using.

What's on the CD?

The CD-ROM contains all the source code and compiled class files from the programming examples in the book, along with some pictures of my dog and various other image files used in the examples. The files are grouped by chapter number and will be found in subdirectories of the individual chapter directories.

You can copy the whole directory tree to your hard disk or load an individual source code file into your favorite editor or Java IDE from the CD and start working with it. As described in the following section, you will need to have a directory containing certain utility classes in your CLASSPATH or store a Jar file in the jre\lib\ext directory.

All of the source examples use the default package. If you decide to reuse anything, feel free to recompile the classes into a package structure appropriate to your development environment. In order to give you maximum flexibility, I didn't want to force a package structure into the examples based on the chapter in which a class was defined.

Some Tips on Using the CD

What I'm about to say is *very important* and addresses the single biggest thing that Java product users complain about: In order to use the examples found in this book, you *must* add the zukowski-swing.jar file found on the CD-ROM to your CLASSPATH. This is because you need to tell Java about certain utilities classes that many of the example programs use. Assuming you've copied the Zukowski_code directory tree from the CD-ROM to the root-level of your local hard drive, the appropriate CLASSPATH settings are noted in the following two sections of this appendix.

> **NOTE**   *UNIX users should use similar CLASSPATH settings that include the appropriate directory names for their UNIX platform. **Remember:** In UNIX, a : (a colon) rather than a ; (a semicolon) is used as the separator character for the CLASSPATH on Windows platforms.*

For the Java 2 Platform

You'll need to use a command similar to the following under Windows, with the exact setting dependent on where you place the copy of the JAR file:

```
set CLASSPATH=c:\Zukowski_code\zukowski-swing.jar;.
```

> **TIP** *For the Java 2 platform, you can take advantage of the Java Extensions Framework and just copy the zukowski-swing.jar file to the jre\lib\ext directory under your JDK installation directory. If you do this, you will not need to alter your CLASSPATH.*

You'll need to use a command similar to the following under UNIX, with the exact setting dependent on where you place a copy of the JAR file and what login shell you use:

```
setenv CLASSPATH /home/username/Zukowski_code/zukowski-swing.jar:.
```

or possibly

```
CLASSPATH = /home/username/Zukowski_code/zukowski-swing.jar:.
export CLASSPATH
```

For the Java 1.1 Platform

Although this book covers Swing for the Java 2 platform, most of the examples in this book should work with the latest version of Swing for JDK 1.1. Using the code for JDK 1.1 with Swing installed requires a slightly longer CLASSPATH setting, and you may need to change the directory to the one specific to the "point" release of the JDK you are using and/or the JFC Swing release. Here's an example of what you can use:

```
set CLASSPATH=c:\jdk1.2.2\lib\classes.zip;c:\swing-
1.1.1\swingall.jar;c:\Zukowski_code\zukowski-swing.jar;.
```

If you would like to preserve the old CLASSPATH settings and just append the zukowski-swing.jar file, you can enter the following, assuming you've placed the JAR file in the designated directory tree:

```
set CLASSPATH=%CLASSPATH%;c:\Zukowski_code\zukowski-swing.jar
```

Places to Go for More Information

Although the CD-ROM doesn't include a Java Development Kit or a JFC 1.1 with a Swing 1.1 release, you can get the latest releases from the Web fairly easily.

(Because point releases, including betas, do seem to be appearing frequently, this option seemed like the best choice for a book on Swing.)

For a list of Java Development Kits for different platforms, see the list I maintain at http://java.about.com/msub2.htm. A fast kit for Windows platforms is available from IBM; it's called the *IBM Developer Kit and Runtime Environment for Windows, Java Technology Edition*. For the latest JFC with Swing release, visit http://java.sun.com/products/jfc, although an early access version may be available at the Java Developer Connection at http://developer.java.sun.com/developer/earlyAccess/jfc/.

> **NOTE:** *To the best of my knowledge, the examples in this book do not contain any code that is affected by the Y2K boundary. However, I cannot guarantee that user code written using these examples will be free of defects that may cause Y2K problems. The Java runtime itself is Y2K compliant as of JDK 1.1.6. For more information on the Y2K compliance of Sun's Java technology products, see http://www.sun.com/y2000/cpl.html.*

If You Have Any CD Problems

For technical support on using the CD, please send an e-mail message to **support@apress.com**. Your e-mail should include the nature of your problem or question, what system you are running Swing on, what JDK and Swing versions you are using, and the setting for your CLASSPATH. Finally, please be sure to tell us the best way to contact you.

Index

D

G

J

L

M

Q

R

U

Apress™
License Agreement (Single-User Products)

THIS IS A LEGAL AGREEMENT BETWEEN YOU, THE END USER, AND APRESS. BY OPENING THE SEALED DISK PACKAGE, YOU ARE AGREEING TO BE BOUND BY THE TERMS OF THIS AGREEMENT. IF YOU DO NOT AGREE TO THE TERMS OF THIS AGREEMENT, PROMPTLY RETURN THE UNOPENED DISK PACKAGE AND THE ACCOMPANYING ITEMS (INCLUDING WRITTEN MATERIALS AND BINDERS AND OTHER CONTAINERS) TO THE PLACE YOU OBTAINED THEM FOR A FULL REFUND.

APRESS SOFTWARE LICENSE

1. GRANT OF LICENSE. APress grants you the right to use one copy of this enclosed APress software program (the "SOFTWARE") on a single terminal connected to a single computer (i.e., with a single CPU). You may not network the SOFTWARE or otherwise use it on more than one computer or computer terminal at the same time.

2. COPYRIGHT. The SOFTWARE copyright is owned by APress or its suppliers and is protected by United States copyright laws and international treaty provisions. Therefore, you must treat the SOFTWARE like any other copyrighted material (e.g., a book or musical recording) except that you may either (a) make one copy of the SOFTWARE solely for backup or archival purposes, or (b) transfer the SOFTWARE to a single hard disk, provided you keep the original solely for backup or archival purposes. You may not copy the written material accompanying the SOFTWARE.

3. OTHER RESTRICTIONS. You may not rent or lease the SOFTWARE, but you may transfer the SOFTWARE and accompanying written materials on a permanent basis provided you retain no copies and the recipient agrees to the terms of this Agreement. You may not reverse engineer, decompile, or disassemble the SOFTWARE. If SOFTWARE is an update, any transfer must include the update and all prior versions.

4. DUAL MEDIA SOFTWARE. If the SOFTWARE package contains both 3.5" and 5.25" disks, then you may use only the disks appropriate for your single-user computer. You may not use the other disks on another computer or loan, rent, lease, or transfer them to another user except as part of the permanent transfer (as provided above) of all SOFTWARE and written materials.

LIMITED WARRANTY

LIMITED WARRANTY. APress warrants that the SOFTWARE will perform substantially in accordance with the accompanying written material for a period of 90 days from the receipt. Any implied warranties on the SOFTWARE are limited to 90 days. Some states do not allow limitations on duration of an implied warranty, so the above limitation may not apply to you.

CUTOMER REMEDIES. APress's entire liability and your exclusive remedy shall be, at APress's option, either (a) return of the price paid or (b) repair or replacement of the SOFTWARE that does not meet APress's Limited Warranty and which is returned to APress with a copy of your receipt. This limited warranty is void if failure of the SOFTWARE has resulted from accident, abuse, or misapplication. Any replacement SOFTWARE will be warranted for the remainder of the original warranty period or 30 days, whichever is longer. These remedies are not available outside of the United States of America.

NO OTHER WARRANTIES. APress disclaims all other warranties, either express or implied, including but not limited to implied warranties of merchantability and fitness for a particular purpose, with respect to the SOFTWARE and the accompanying written materials. This limited warranty gives you specific rights. You may have others, which vary from state to state.

NO LIABILITIES FOR CONSEQUENTIAL DAMAGES. In no event shall APress or its suppliers be liable for any damages whatsoever (including, without limitation, damages from loss of business profits, business interruption, loss of business information, or other pecuniary loss) arising out of the use or inability to use this APress product, even if APress has been advised of the possibility of such damages. Because some states do not allow the exclusion or limitation of liability for consequential or incidental damages, the above limitation may not apply to you.

U.S. GOVERNMENT RESTRICTED RIGHTS

The SOFTWARE and documentation are provided with RESTRICTED RIGHTS. Use, duplication, or disclosure by the Government is subject to restriction as set forth in subparagraph (c)(1)(ii) of The Rights in Technical Data and Computer Software clause at 52.227-7013. Contractor/manufacturer is APress, 6400 Hollis Street, Suite 9, Emeryville, CA 94608.

This Agreement is governed by the laws of the State of California.

Should you have any questions concerning this Agreement, or if you wish to contact APress for any reason, please write to APress, 6400 Hollis Street, Suite 9, Emeryville, CA 94608.

Learning Resources
Centre